Wellington

XVIII JUNI MDCCCXV

Wellington

The Road
to the Lion's Mound

1769–1815

DANIEL RES

CITADELLE

First published in the Czech language 2018
This fully revised and updated edition was published 24th May 2020

CITADELLE, Amerigo s.r.o.
Distribution of the English-language edition:
York Publishing Services Ltd., York, UK

ISBN 978-80-907311-2-7

CONTENTS

LIST OF ILLUSTRATIONS

16. Sir David Baird GCB, KC Colonel of the 24ᵗʰ Regiment, 1811 (mezzotint) by Henry Raeburn (1756–1823) (after), © National Army Museum, London / Bridgeman Images.
17. Memorial erected to General Sir Ralph Abercromby and fallen British soldiers in the Alexandria (Chatby) Military and War Memorial Cemetery, Egypt. Photo © Mark Thomas Jones.
18. Robert Stewart, Viscount Castlereagh, 1817 (oil on canvas), by Sir Thomas Lawrence, Royal Collection Trust © Her Majesty Queen Elizabeth II, 2020 / Bridgeman Images.
19. Guerrier Ecossais, Gravée par N. Bertrand, © Author's Collection.
    The Army and Navy representing the only conversation between the Great Commanders, Wellington (1769–1852) and Nelson (1758–1805) c. 1890 (chromolitho.), English School, (19ᵗʰ century) , © National Army Museum, London / Bridgeman Images.
20. Catherine Pakenham, Duchess of Wellington, English School, 19ᵗʰ century, © Stratfield Saye Preservation Trust.
21. Lord Douro and Lord Charles Wellesley as small children by Henry Edridge, © Stratfield Saye Preservation Trust.
22. Bombardment of Copenhagen, 1807, Napoleonic Wars, Denmark, Danish School, 19ᵗʰ century, © G. Dagli Orti / De Agostini Picture Library / Bridgeman Images.
23. The 95ᵗʰ Rifles; Battle of the Pyrenees, 1813, 1900 (w/c on paper) by Richard Simkin, © National Army Museum, London / Bridgeman Images.
24. A Baker rifle, commonly used by the British Rifle Brigade, © Wikimedia Commons, online at: https://upload.wikimedia.org/wikipedia/commons/3/32/Baker_rifle.png.
25. Portrait of Jean-Andoche Junot, Duke of Abrantes (Bussy-le-Grand, 1771 – Montbard, 1813),
26. © Musee de la Ville de Paris, Musee Carnavalet, Paris, France / G. Dagli Orti /De Agostini Picture Library / Bridgeman Images.
27. The 20ᵗʰ Light Dragoons at the Battle of Vimeiro, 21st August 1808 by Richard Simkin, © John Spink Fine Watercolours, London / Bridgeman Images.
28. The Convention of Cintra, a Portuguese gambol for the amusement of John Bull © The British Museum.
29. Lieut. Gen. Sir John Moore K.B, Pub. by Richard Evans, engr. Romney, illustration from 'An Historical Account of the Battle of Waterloo' by William Mudford, 1816 © Author's Collection.
30. William Carr Beresford, Viscount Beresford by Sir William Beechey, oil on canvas, 1814–1815, NPG 6094, © National Portrait Gallery, London.
31. Jean-de-Dieu Soult (1769–1851) Duke of Dalmatia, 1856 (oil on canvas) by Louis Henri de Rudder, © Château de Versailles, France / Bridgeman Images.
32. Battle of Talavera, Illustrator: William Heath; Stadler, J.C London, 1819, © British Library Board. All Rights Reserved / Bridgeman Images.
33. William Wellesley-Pole, 3rd Earl of Mornington, by John Hoppner, © Stratfield Saye Preservation Trust.
34. Lord Hill, coloured engraving by Shepperson, © Author's Collection.
35. Lieut. General Lord Hill K.B., Pub. by Richard Evans, engr. Romney, illustration from 'An Historical Account of the Battle of Waterloo' by William Mudford, 1816 © Author's Collection.

36. The Archduke Charles rallying his Troops at the Battle of Aspern 1809, Henry Colburn delin. A. Warren Sculp. Published by J. Stradford, London, 11th August 1810, © Author's Collection.
37. Killing no Murder, or a New Ministerial way of settling the affairs of the Nation!, 1809 by Isaac Robert Cruikshank, (colour etching) © Private Collection / Bridgeman Images.
38. Colquhoun Grant by George Jones, pencil, 1815–1820, NPG 5261 © National Portrait Gallery, London.
39. View of the hilly terrain to the north of Lisbon, which forms "natural walls" not far from the town of Torres Vedras, Photo © Daniel Res.
40. Today's view of the originally Moorish castle that embodied redoubt no. 27 in the first of Wellington's defensive Lines of Torres Vedras complex, Photo © Daniel Res.
41 and 42. The inner spaces of the Saint Vincent fortress, Photo © Daniel Res.
43 and 44. The preserved military road near Fort Alqueidão, close to the city of Sobral, Photo © Daniel Res.
45. Wellington's headquarters in Pero Negro, Photo © Daniel Res.
46. Fort Saint Julian, around which the third defensive line of the Torres Vedras complex was built, Photo © Daniel Res.
47. Battles of the British Army, Busaco, the Bivouac before the Battle. Illustration for The Illustrated London News, 11 April 1896, engraving after R. Caton Woodville, © Author's Collection.
48. Battles of the British Army, Busaco, General Craufurd's Word of Command, "43rd and 52nd, charge!" Illustration for The Illustrated London News, 11 April 1896, engraving after R. Caton Woodville, © Author's Collection.
49. View from the position of Wellington's forces spread across the Busaco Ridge toward the position of Masséna's army, Photo © Daniel Res.
50. Portrait of Andre Masséna, Duke of Rivoli (1756–1817), Prince of Essling, Marechal of Empire Painting by Edme Adolphe Fontaine (1814–1878) 19th century Sun. 2.15 × 1.4 m Versailles, musee du Chateau, Photo © Photo Josse / Bridgeman Images.
51. Memorial to honour the fallen soldiers in the Battle of Busaco, Photo © Daniel Res.
52. View of the hilly landscape around the town of Sobral, near which Marshal Masséna first laid eyes upon Wellington's Lines of Torres Vedras, Photo © Daniel Res.
53. Remains of Fort Alqueidão, built near the town of Sobral, through which passed the first defensive lines of the Torres Vedras complex, Photo © Daniel Res.
54. Frederick, Count of Schaumburg-Lippe-Buckeburg, 1759 (oil on canvas) by Johann Georg Ziesenis, © Belvoir Castle, Leicestershire / Bridgeman Images.
55. Francis Rawdon, Marquis of Hastings (Earl of Moira), engraved by G. Parker, after painting by M.A. Shee, © Author's Collection.
56. Building of the former Town Hall in the Portuguese city of Santarem, Photo © Daniel Res.
57. Close-up of a Portuguese man on the tiling inside the former Santarem Town Hall, Photo © Daniel Res.
58. A view of the siege and storming of Ciudad Rodrigo in Spain on 19th January 1812, (engraving), Unknown Artist, (19th century), © National Army Museum, London / Bridgeman Images.

59. General Robert Craufurd (1764–1812) (litho.), English School, (19th century), Photo © Ken Welch Private Collection / Bridgeman Images.
60. The Devil's Own, 1812, 1908 (w/c on paper), by Richard Caton Woodville, © National Army Museum, London / Bridgeman Images.
61. Lieut. Gen. Picton, Sheppereson Del., S.G. Walker, Published by Brightly and Childs, 1815, © Author's Collection.
62. Auguste Frederic Louis Viesse de Marmont (1774–1852), Duke of Ragusa and Marshal of France by Paulin Jean Baptiste Guerin (oil on canvas), © Versailles, Château De Versailles / G. Dagli Orti /De Agostini Picture Library / Bridgeman Images.
63. His Royal Highness, The Prince Regent of Great Britain, Pub. by Richard Evans, Engr. by Romney, illustration from 'An Historical Account of the Battle of Waterloo' by William Mudford, London 1816, © Author's Collection.
64. Wellington's dispatch from 30th June 1812 informing the British Government about the successful conquering of the fortresses in Salamanca. © Author's Collection.
65. Sir George Scovell, by William Salter, oil on canvas, 1834–1840, NPG 3752, © National Portrait Gallery, London.
66. Battles of the British Army, Salamanca. Illustration for The Illustrated London News, 12 October 1895, engraving after Richard Caton Woodville, © Look and Learn / Illustrated Papers Collection / Bridgeman Images.
67. General, The Hon. Sir E. M. Pakenham, painted posthumously by Martin Cregan. © Tullynally Estate.
68. Major General John Alexander Dunlop Agnew Wallace (c. 1775–1857) 1835 (oil on canvas), by Herbert Sidney, © National Army Museum, London / Bridgeman Images.
69. Salamanca, 21st July 1812, from 'The Victories of the Duke of Wellington', engraved by T. Fielding, pub. 1819 (coloured engraving), after Richard Westall, © The Stapleton Collection / Bridgeman Images.
70. Field Marshal Lord Fitzroy James Henry Somerset, 1st Baron Raglan G.C.B., 1821 (oil on paper on canvas) by Jan Willem Pieneman, © Historic England / Bridgeman Images.
71. General the Hon. Sir Galbraith Lowry Cole, GCB, 1809 (oil on canvas), by Domenico Pellegrini, © National Trust Photographic Library / Bridgeman Images.
72. The Duke of Wellington's dressing case with silver and ivory fittings, © Apsley House, The Wellington Museum, London / Bridgeman Images.
73. The Duke of Wellington's Sword (metal and leather), © Apsley House, The Wellington Museum, London / Bridgeman Images.
74. Battle of Vitoria, 21st June 1813, © Lebrecht History / Bridgeman Images.
75. Louis XVIII, Roi de France et de Navarre, A Paris chez l'Auteur, © Author's Collection.
76. Portrait of Italian singer Giuseppina Grassini (1773–1850) in the role of Zaire in Voltaire's play of the same name by Marie Elisabeth Louise Vigee Le Brun, Rouen, musee des Beaux Arts, Photo © Photo Josse / Bridgeman Images.
77. Clemens Lothar Wenzel, Prince Metternich, 1815 (oil on canvas) by Sir Thomas Lawrence, Royal Collection Trust © Her Majesty Queen Elizabeth II, 2020 / Bridgeman Images.

78. The Congress of Vienna, Sitting of the Plenipotentiaries of the Eight Powers who signed the Treaty of Paris in 1815, engraved by Edmond Morin, © Author's Collection.

79. George (Gebhart) Leberecht Blucher, Prince de Wagstaedt, dessiré d'aprés nature par Melle de Noireterre, 1814, © Author's Collection.

80. Summoned to Waterloo, Brussels, 1815, c. 1898 (colour litho.), after Robert Alexander Hillingford, © National Army Museum, London / Bridgeman Images.

81. Equestrian Portrait of Napoleon I, 1810 (oil on canvas) by Joseph Cahbord, © Museo Napoleonico, Rome, / Bridgeman Images.

82. The Duke of Wellington by Thomas Lawrence, © Mark Fiennes Archive / Bridgeman Images.

83. The Death of Frederick William, Duke of Brunswick-Wolfenbüttel at the Battle of Quatre Bras, 1815, c. 1836 (oil on canvas), by Johann Friedrich Matthai, Royal Collection Trust © Her Majesty Queen Elizabeth II, 2020 / Bridgeman Images.

84. Henry Paget, 2nd Earl of Uxbridge and 1st Marquess of Anglesey, c. 1809–14 (oil on canvas), Royal Collection Trust © Her Majesty Queen Elizabeth II, 2020 / Bridgeman Images.

85. Portraits of the General Officers, from 'An Historical Account of the Battle of Waterloo', published by M. Colburn, 1817 (coloured aquatint), English School, (19th century) , © National Army Museum, London / Bridgeman Images.

86. Closing the Gates at Hougoumont by Robert Gibb, oil on canvas, 1903, © National War Museum of Scotland / Bridgeman Images.

87. Scotland For Ever! 1881 (oil on canvas), by Lady Elizabeth Butler, © Leeds Museums and Galleries (Leeds Art Gallery) U.K. / Bridgeman Images.

88. A new memorial at Hougoumont, Photo © Daniel Res.

89. Present view of Château Hougoumont, Photo © Daniel Res.

90. A dried-out but surprisingly well-preserved tree with clearly visible bullet holes located just several feet from Hougoumont, Photo © Daniel Res.

91. Today's view from the top of the Lion's Mound to La Haye Sainte Farm, Photo © Daniel Res.

92. Portraits of various Allied Generals and Monarchs who had a considerable share in Napoleon's final defeat in the Coalition Wars. Engraving Pub. by R. Bowyer, London 1815. © Author's Collection.

93. Francois I, Empereur d' Autriches, Roi de Hungrie et Boheme, A Paris chez l'Auteur, © Author's Collection.

94. Charles-Luis, Archiduc d' Autriche, Notreterre del 1814, Velyn Sculp., A Paris chez l'Auteur, © Author's Collection.

95. The Black Brunswicker, 1860 (oil on canvas) by John Everett Millais, © Lady Lever Art Gallery, National Museums Liverpool / Bridgeman Images.

96. Portrait of Frederick William, Duke of Brunswick-Wolfenbuettel, 1809, by Johann Christian August Schwartz, © DHM / Bridgeman Images.

97. Conte Giuseppe Venceslao Radetzky, Ex Libris, © Author's Collection.

98. Charles Schwarzenberg, Duc de Krumau, A Paris chez l'Auteur, © Author's Collection.

LIST OF MAPS

1) Map of Central South India showing the routes taken by the armies of General Harris and General Stuart, February – May 1799, Map by John Amrytage (John Fawkes), © John Armytage

2) Storming of the Seringapatam, 4th May 1799, Map by John Amrytage (John Fawkes), © John Armytage

3) Battle of Assaye, 23rd September 1803, Map by John Amrytage (John Fawkes), © John Armytage

4) Wellington's Battles and Sieges in India 1799–1803, Map by Marek Jodas, © Marek Jodas

5) Battle of Vimeiro, 21st August 1808, Map by John Armytage (John Fawkes), © John Armytage

6) Battle of Oporto (The Crossing of Douro), 12th May 1809, Map by John Amrytage (John Fawkes), © John Armytage

7) Battle of Talavera, French Attack 28th July, Map by John Armytage (John Fawkes), © John Armytage

8) The Lines of Torres Vedras, Map by Simão Luz Soriano, *História da Guerra Civil* (Lisbon 1874), © Wikimedia Commons, online in: https://upload.wikimedia. org/wikipedia/commons/e/ef/Mapa_linhas_de_torres_vedras.png

9) Battle of Busaco, 27th September 1810, Map by John Armytage (John Fawkes), © John Armytage

10) Battle of Fuentes de Oñoro, 3rd – 5th May 1811, Map by John Armytage (John Fawkes), © John Armytage

11) Storming of Ciudad Rodrigo, 19th January 1812, Map by John Armytage (John Fawkes), © John Armytage

12) Storming of Badajoz, 6th April 1812, Map by John Armytage (John Fawkes), © John Armytage

13) Battle of Salamanca, 22nd July 1812, Map by John Armytage (John Fawkes), © John Armytage

14) Attack on Burgos, 19th September – 25th October 1812, Map by John Armytage (John Fawkes), © John Armytage

15) Retreat from Burgos – Autumn 1812, Map by John Armytage (John Fawkes), © John Armytage

16) Battle of Vitoria 21st June 1813, Map by John Armytage (John Fawkes), © John Armytage

17) Wellington's Battles and Sieges in the Peninsular War 1808–1814

18) Waterloo Campaign, 15th – 18th June 1815, Map built upon Wikimedia Commons, CC BY-SA 3.0, © Wikimedia Commons, online in: https://en.wikipedia.org/wiki/Waterloo_campaign#/media/File:Waterloo_Campaign_map-alt3.svg

19) Battle of Quatre Bras, 16th June 1815, Map by John Armytage (John Fawkes), © John Armytage

20) Battle of Waterloo, 18th June 1815 at 11 a.m., Map by John Armytage (John Fawkes), © John Armytage

21) Battle of Waterloo, 18th June 1815 at 4 p.m., Ney's great cavalry attack, Map by John Armytage (John Fawkes), © John Armytage

22) Battle of Waterloo, 18th June 1815 at 7 p.m., The Attack of the Guard, Map by John Armytage (John Fawkes), © John Armytage

PREFACE

Don't be too certain of learning the past from the lips of the present.
Beware of the most honest broker. Remember that what you are told is really
threefold: shaped by the teller, reshaped by the listener, concealed from both by
the dead man of the tale.

The Real Life of Sebastian Knight – Vladimir Nabokov

Arthur Wellesley, 1ˢᵗ Duke of Wellington (1769–1852) is one of the most prominent figures not only in British, but also world history. Despite this fact, the study of his persona has been somewhat surprisingly neglected both in the Czech Republic and the majority of Continental Europe. Wellington became one of the most distinguished generals of all time and never experienced the bitterness of defeat on the battlefield. He managed seamlessly to follow up his military career with a rich path in politics, during which he was twice named Prime Minister. Therefore, at the end of his life, he supported Queen Victoria, who prized the Duke not only as an honourable man who was boundlessly devoted to the Crown, but also as a friend and invaluable advisor. Wellington quite rightfully wrote himself into the annals of world history with his victory at the Battle of Waterloo, where in 1815 together with Prussian General Blücher he defeated the French Emperor Napoleon, bringing his impressive military career to a definitive end. Thanks to this fact, in the words of Russian Tsar Alexander I, he became the 'conqueror of the world's conqueror', which after many victorious battles on the Iberian Peninsula definitively secured his position as a world hero and a notable "celebrity" of his time. For the majority of the inhabitants of the Old Continent, it was clearly more important that, thanks to the allied victory at Waterloo, peace finally reigned in Europe after more than twenty years of conflict and bloodshed.

But why should a Czech historian write a book on the Duke of Wellington, about whom so many interesting works have been written by scores of excellent scholars of history from throughout the Anglosphere?

It is my true hope that my "outsider's" point of view on the Anglo-Saxon world and of Wellington's life will provide a new conveyance and fresh look at the Duke's persona by offering new sources originally written in Czech and German (as today's Czech Republic in Wellington's time was a part of the Austrian Empire as the Kingdom of Bohemia), new and original ideas, and finally a Central European context, which will perhaps provide a new angle on the Duke's long life and deeds.

I have always been interested primarily in European history in a global context, and in terms of the history of individual countries, Great Britain has become the focal point of this interest. Nonetheless, as a Czech I first encountered the figure of Arthur Wellesley, 1st Duke of Wellington (1769–1852) when at the age of thirteen, I laid eyes upon the first historical novel in Bernard Cornwell's multivolume *Sharpe Series*, in which Wellington is described in detail, after which I enthusiastically read the whole series of novels throughout my adolescent years.

Moreover, over the course of time my interest in the Duke of Wellington began to take on a more serious dimension. In 2014, I began to study history at the Faculty of Arts at Charles University in Prague, and set off the following summer on a trip to Great Britain. During my educational journey around the British Isles, I planned a visit to Wellington's country residence, Stratfield Saye House, as one of my main destinations, as I wanted to see with my own eyes the place that was so closely linked to the man who had made such an impression on me in my childhood and adolescence. The guide's intriguing narration there, together with the authentic and intimate atmosphere of the residence, which today belongs to Wellington's descendants – who with great care keep the residence in the same condition as during Arthur Wellesley's life, giving one the impression that the "Great Duke", as he is called there, was still alive in Stratfield – strengthened my interest in the study of Wellington's persona.

Over the course of this trip, I also bought *Wellington: The Iron Duke*, my first academic biography of Arthur Wellesley written by British historian Richard Holmes. After reading it, I made the definitive decision to write my university bachelor's thesis on Wellington. Over the course of writing my thesis, Professor Martin Kovář served as a great mentor to me, and his forthcoming approach and measured advice was invaluable, especially in the initial phases. Nonetheless, I had absolutely no idea at the time that this topic would gradually engulf me to such a degree that a whole book would be written, and that during its preparation I would visit many more sites connected to Wellington, read countless letters, memoirs, and academic publications of the time and make numerous additional visits to Stratfield Saye. After the defence of my bachelor's thesis, I thus decided to continue on in my work and develop it into a book, which took roughly one year of intensive work, whereupon the book was published in Czech. Shortly before the Czech publication, I attempted to contact Bernard Cornwell, who had *de facto* led me to my interest in Wellington and the Napoleonic Wars in his novels. To my great delight, Bernard Cornwell did in fact reply, congratulating me on my efforts, which – on my path to the English version that you are now holding in your hands – brought me more great encouragement, a fact for which I am extremely grateful to Mr Cornwell. Mark Thomas Jones also played a wholly crucial role in my decision to publish the book in English. I met Mark during one of my summer holidays in England whilst visiting Great Malvern Priory, Malvern, Worcestershire, where I told him of my work hitherto. During our conversation, he was the first to suggest the idea of me having my book translated into English. Subsequently, he provided his advice on the individual chapters with unceasing energy throughout the whole period and far beyond the scope of the mere correctness of the English translation. He also gave me advice on additions to the English version and original elements of Wellington's life that I might focus on in my further research to make the book as beneficial to its readers as possible and prevent the final version from repeating the now rather tired and familiar quotes and facts from Wellington's life. I am indebted to Mark for his time, guidance, suggestions and encouragement. After various adjustments, the final version of this book was coincidentally completed in the summer of 2019, the 250th anniversary year of Wellington's birth.

In British historiography, Wellington's remarkable path in life is often divided into his military career, during which the Duke's life is described from his birth to his victory at Waterloo over Napoleon, and his political career, in which individual authors deal with Wellington's fate after 1815 until his death in 1852. I have also selected this two-part model and in the first volume of the book I focus on Wellington's life from his birth in Ireland to the drama of the Battle of Waterloo. I am now in the process of working on a second volume devoted to Wellington's political career. The two most well-known and in my opinion best biographies on Wellington, which served as the primary source of information for my book, are also two-part works that follow this aforementioned "traditional division" of Wellington's life. The first of these two biographies is the long-unequalled biography by Elizabeth Longford, which was published in the early 1970s. The author presents the Duke's military career in the first volume entitled *Wellington: The Years of the Sword* and his political career in the following work entitled *Wellington: Pillar of State*. The author of the second and even more exhaustive two-part biography with many opinions and sources, which was published seven years ago, is Professor Rory Muir, who divided his extensive work on Wellington into the following two volumes: *Wellington: The Path to Victory, 1769–1814* and *Wellington: Waterloo and the Fortunes of Peace 1814–1852* (for more on sources and literature, see the Bibliography). While writing this publication, I naturally drew primarily from the first volumes of these two excellent biographies; at the same time, however, I attempted to create a wholly new and unique viewpoint of Wellington's personality and the aforementioned additions using a "Central European perspective". For instance, I have focused on Wellington's attitude towards the wounded and also about his Intelligence Service, about which outstanding works have been written in the last two decades. Despite this fact, this element seemed to me to be somewhat absent from Wellington's biographies written hitherto in the direct context of Wellington's campaigns and plans. In addition, I was strongly surprised by a fact that I stumbled upon during my study of the well-known discussions between Wellington and his friend John Wilson Croker. In one passage of these discussions, which were taken down by Croker, Wellington quite clearly points to Archduke Charles as having been the best commander of the Napoleonic War (the first man to defeat Napoleon in the field Battle of Aspern-Essling in 1809), which certainly sheds new light on the widespread claim that he acknowledged Napoleon as the best general. According to Croker, Wellington said that '[Arhchduke Charles] knows more about it [warfare] than all of us put together...than Buonaparte or any of us. We are none of us worthy to fasten the latchets of his shoes...' Subsequently, Wellington quite correctly noted that the ingenious abilities of Archduke Charles had been taking a toll on his already poor health: 'but his mind or his health has, they tell me, a very peculiar defect...'[1] Archduke Charles was a Habsburg, specifically the younger brother of Austrian Emperor Francis I. As a result of centuries of consanuinity and royal inbreeding, the

Habsburg Royal House gradually began to degenerate and therefore had increasing and unavoidable health problems that included the Habsburg Jaw, a form of mandibular prognathism, gastrointestinal problems and in some instances mental retardation.

I personally consider the seventh chapter together with the final supplementary chapter to be the greatest contribution made by this book. In the seventh chapter, I focus in detail on what is, in my opinion, the still greatly neglected system of fortifications built roughly thirty kilometres from Lisbon, called the Lines of Torres Vedras, in the context of the Napoleonic Wars. As my interest in the Lines of Torres Vedras gradually grew, I took a trip to Portugal during the course of writing this book in order to see this undertaking, which was truly monumental for its time, with my own eyes: I must say that Wellington's skilful use of the topography and the size of various fortifications, which today are still quite intact, give off an astounding impression. As is my assertion, the whole defensive system held crucial importance for Wellington's victory in the Peninsular War and is some of the best proof of his unique organizational skills. In my opinion, the importance of the Lines of Torres Vedras was summarized quite succinctly by former Portuguese President Aníbal Cavaco Silva in his speech given during the 200th anniversary of their construction directly in the town of Torres Vedras, through which pass the lines of the fortifications, of which there were ultimately one hundred and fifty two: 'Here the tide of the Peninsular War was turned. It was the beginning of the end of the Napoleonic adventure that had put Europe at the mercy of sword and shot.'[2] In the seventh chapter, I thus attempt to provide an answer to the question of what inspired Wellington to construct the Lines of Torres Vedras. I place Wellington's defence of Portugal over the course of the Peninsular War in the context of the defence of Portugal led by Count William of Schaumburg-Lippe (1724–1777) during the Seven Years' War (1756–1763). The remarkable similarities between Wellington and Lippe's actions in Portugal immediately caught my attention. It is for this reason that I posit that Wellington may have built his plans on the defence of Portugal on the memoirs of the Count of Schaumburg-Lippe. I compare both campaigns and search for concurrences between them while presenting and analysing sources from the time.

In the supplementary chapter, using the context of Wellington in the Peninsular War, I then introduce a new point of view, i.e. from the angle of the Habsburg Monarchy (the Austrian Empire from 1804) with a narrower focus on events in the Czech lands in the era of the Napoleonic Wars. For instance, this chapter deals with the fascinating story of the Duke of Brunswick's Black Legion, which was formed in the Czech town of Náchod and from there fought their way to Wellington's forces in Portugal in 1809. It has been proved fairly recently that at least forty nine soldiers of this corps, including one officer, came from the territory of today's Czech Republic, twelve of which exclusively spoke Czech at the beginning of their campaign.* Here we encounter Wellington's correspondence with a member of the Bohemian nobility, Marshal Karl Philipp of Schwarzenberg, who led the allied troops to victory over Napoleon at Leipzig. Another interesting figure and Czech nobleman with whom the reader will become acquainted in this chapter is Schwarzenberg's Chief-of-General Staff, Joseph Radetzky von Radetz, whose name for many is more strongly linked to the revolution of 1848, during which Radetzky held the territories of the Habsburg Monarchy in Italy as Field Marshal for Austria, than to the Napoleonic Wars.

At the same time, I will attempt in this biography to provide readers with a closer look at Wellington not only from the position of commander (which would limit the text to a didactic and often tedious descriptive list of individual battles), but as a human being with various contradictions, numerous doubts about himself, life dreams, hopes, disappointments, pros and cons. For example, I present Arthur Wellesley as a passionate reader and skilful rider, for whom horsemanship – in addition to being a practical skill – was a good form of entertainment and active relaxation. Furthermore, I depict Wellington as a capable organizer and hard-working person who did, however, have frequent and serious problems while delegating even the simplest of tasks to his inferiors, thanks to which at least a portion of the social spectrum today would easily have labelled him a "workaholic". In terms of his private life, I analyse in detail the rocky and contradiction-filled story of Wellington's marriage with Catherine Pakenham, which was compared by contemporary authors to the story of Odysseus and Penelope and at the same time, for better or for worse, is highly telling of the Duke's personality. I have reached the conclusion that during his life

---

* Czech historian Karel Sáček has carried out remarkable work in his investigation of the soldiers from the ranks of the Black Legion from today's Czech Republic and has studied the topic now for 17 years.

Wellington underwent stages of development from a 'dreamy, idle and shy lad' to an often lovelorn and unrestrained youth, and finally to a man of principle with strong personal convictions and values.

Despite all the single-mindedness and reserve that were an indisputable part of Wellington's complicated character and which he used as a general and politician of global importance, I perceive him ultimately as a man teeming with a keen-edged sense of humour, who often felt crushed by the horrors of war, which he saw primarily as his duty but at the same time certainly did not bring him any pleasure. This fact is best attested by the following sentence, which is often attributed to Wellington, which he allegedly spoke shortly after the Battle of Waterloo: 'I always say that next to a battle lost, the greatest misery is a battle gained.'[3] Even if we were to cast doubt on the authenticity of these words, which are often cited by historians, I can say with a clear conscience that similar emotional declarations are far from scarce in Wellington's life. For this reason, I would like for the sake of illustration to cite a hitherto little-known letter (located today in the Třeboň State Archive, Czech Rep.) which Wellington wrote only days after the Battle of Waterloo to a member of the Bohemian nobility and General of the Allied Forces, Austrian Field Marshal Karl I Philipp, Prince of Schwarzenberg:

> My dear Prince, thank you for your letter from the 21st [of June], which I received this evening. Our battle on the 18th [of June] was one of the most important and, as you yourself know, was absolute. God has hitherto been well-disposed to me and I shall not want to ever fight again, for I am crushed by the loss of my long-time friends and acquaintances. My partner in war and ally [Marshall Blücher] is enjoying good health, although he is still somewhat plagued by the results of the fall from his horse, which they killed under him in the battle [of Ligny]. With highest regards, Wellington.[4]

During his rich military career, the Duke of Wellington took part in several dozen battles and smaller-scale skirmishes, the vast majority of which he experienced in the position of commander-in-chief. He was never defeated as supreme commander in a field battle, a fact which we can claim with absolute certainty about few other individuals in history. Nonetheless, Wellington felt that providing a faithful description of the battle would have been almost futile. In the Duke's opinion, each participant in combat experienced the battle from his own subjective point of view and, for this reason, presenting an objective interpretation of the whole battle remained simply impossible. In a letter addressed to Lady Salisbury in 1850, Wellington remembered the words he spoke to Scottish novelist Sir Walter Scott after the author informed Wellington that he would like to write a book on the Battle of Talavera: 'It would be as easy to write the account of a ball as of a Battle! Who was the Partner of Who? Who footed to each other? Who danced down all the couples?'[5]

In the pages of this book, I logically describe several battles in succession and attempt to present them in the most rounded manner possible; however, if we leave the issue of the interpretation of sources aside, I wholly agree with the Duke of Wellington that being completely objective is simply not possible, as all of us have been shaped from a young age by the circumstances around us, thanks to which we acknowledge various life values which, whether we like it or not, are reflected in our everyday behaviour. The "pitfalls" of each historian and at the same time each reader are summarized concisely by novelist Vladimir Nabokov, who is also quoted at the beginning of this preface:

> Don't be too certain of learning the past from the lips of the present. Beware of the most honest broker. Remember that what you are told is really threefold: shaped by the teller, reshaped by the listener, concealed from both by the dead man of the tale.[6]

Therefore, I consider the private letters written by Wellington and his contemporaries to be the "most objective" source. For example, contrary to official memoirs, these letters were not written with the intention of being made public. If I am to ask myself honestly, after my study of history at university and the countless hours spent preparing this book, what sense there is in writing and reading about history, the following and basically simple answer comes to my mind: It is said that we cannot change the past, but we can learn from it and attempt to become better people. And, at the end of the day, we read history simply because we enjoy doing so.

PROLOGUE

'Our Atty'

When Sir Thomas Lawrence, court painter of the Prince-Regent, the future King George IV, painted Arthur Wellesley, 1st Duke of Wellington shortly after his victory over Napoleon at Waterloo, he left us with the most famous of Wellington's portraits. In the portrait, Wellington is portrayed in full strength and at the height of his military career. He is of slim build, depicted from the waist up with arms crossed, and dressed in a red British field marshal's uniform with golden epaulettes and a white cravat. The Duke, with his angular aristocratic face, which is lined with short brown hair and dominated by his famous Roman-like aquiline nose, stares out of the painting with a serious, pensive look in his blue-grey eyes. It is a gaze of determination and experience – the look of a soldier and commander, and of a forty-seven-year-old man who had already experienced countless battles in which he had seen many a friend and enemy perish (See Image XIV).

During his long and eventful life of eighty-three years, Wellington earned a series of characteristic nicknames. Due to his prominently bent nose, ordinary soldiers often called him 'Old Hookey' or 'Nosey' for amusement as is typical of the British sense of humour, but also referred to him with deep respect and devotion as 'Our Atty', which was short for Arthur.[7]

Due to his elegant style of dress and thorough care for his outward appearance, he was known most often among the officers as 'Beau', a nickname that was synonymous with that fellow Old Etonian, dandy and arbiter of men's fashion in Regency England – George Bryan 'Beau' Brummell. The Duke was a fastidious man, who was accustomed to shaving twice a day, which was rather unusual for the time, and always appeared in public meticulously kempt. Such a soigné individual possibly provides clues to a person whose attention to detail was not just a matter of personal appearance, but of an approach to life and its many and varied challenges.

The second nickname officers used to describe him was *Peer*. This "compliment" was given to him after he was promoted in rank to the Viscount of Wellington after his victory over the French in the Battle of Talavera in 1809. The Portuguese most often called him 'Douro, Douro!', a somewhat odd nickname that he received after his unforgettable crossing of the Portuguese River Douro, which took French Marshal Masséna wholly by surprise and was crucial in liberating Portugal from the French Army. The Spanish, who were also the Duke's allies alongside the Portuguese against Napoleonic France in the Peninsular War, commonly called him 'Águila' (Spanish for Eagle). In addition to the prominence of the Duke's nose, this nickname came about thanks to his strenuous efforts to oversee everything (including the actions of his allies) personally and attentively with his "eagle eye".[8]

In an effort to characterize Wellington as faithfully as possible as a commander, one soldier (who was unfortunately not identified) wrote the following about him after the Battle of Waterloo:

> What has especially gained him the love of his men is, that he is in the highest degree just, that he exercises the most assiduous care for the supply of the army, and that he personally examines whether the soldier has any grounds for complaints which admit of remedy: and he has gained the confidence of the soldiers because he acts without passion, because he spares the men when the result would not be answerable to the sacrifice required to obtain it, and never does out of vanity any thing* which the soldier must pay for with his blood, because he chooses his position with the greatest care, so that victory may be certain when he gives the signal for battle.[9]

---

*   The direct quotations in this book have been cited verbatim and may thus contain spelling errors and language variations of the time.

CHAPTER ONE

'A Dreamy, Idle and Shy Lad'

The origin of the distinguished Wellesleys in Britain goes back almost eight hundred years. Almost continually until today, the family has engaged in politics and has often played a prominent role in the service and governing of the country. Today, the head of the family is Charles Wellesley, the 9th Duke of Wellington, who interestingly is married to Princess Antonia of Prussia, a great-granddaughter of Kaiser Wilhelm II of Germany. Like his illustrious ancestor, the current Duke of Wellington was also educated at Eton College and sits in the House of Lords.

The name Wellesley first appears in a medieval document dated to the second half of the 12th century. The document is located in Wells Cathedral in the charming town of Wells in the county of Somerset in South West England.[10] There is still some conjecture as to the precise origin of the historic Wellesleys, although it can reasonably be assumed that the Wellesleys were originally Normans who came to England among the ranks of William the Conqueror's soldiers or belonged to the original Anglo-Saxons who supported William's claim to the English throne. Whatever their origin, they clearly stood on the winning side, as after William's victory at Hastings over Anglo-Saxon King Harold in 1066, they received properties near the town of Wells (roughly 200km west of London), where today the hamlet of Wellesley Farm can still be found.[11] In addition, one of the oldest versions of the family name "Welles-Leighs"* evokes a link with the town of Wells itself, which may have been connected to the family much earlier and, in the author's opinion, gives proof of the Anglo-Saxon origins of the Wellesley family. Subsequently, Arthur's predecessors left England in 1171 for Ireland along with the military expedition of King Henry II, the second husband of one of the most prominent women of the Middle Ages, Eleanor of Aquitaine and father of the famous crusader Richard the Lionheart. During the expedition, there is proof that Sir Wellesley was Henry's Standard Bearer. The Wellesley Family gradually took root in Ireland, amassed properties there, and was rewarded for its service to the king with prominent positions in the Royal Court. A list of the most prominent medieval predecessors of the Duke of Wellington would not be complete without mentioning Sir William Wellesley, who in the second half of the 14th century took part in sessions of Parliament. William became the royal administrator of Irish Kildare and Carbury Castle and the Sheriff (i.e. the executor of royal power in a given region) of County Kildare. In addition, he was greatly honoured by the English Monarch Richard II, who endowed him with a life-long income of twenty pounds per annum, which he used to buy properties several dozen miles northwest of Dublin in County Meath, Ireland. Over the centuries, these properties became the basis of the family's fortune. Several generations later, the Wellesleys found themselves at odds with the Monarch. In the first half of the 17th century, King Charles I had the property of the present head of the family, Valerian Wellesley, confiscated as Valerian's conscience prevented him from abandoning his Catholic faith and converting to Protestantism. The new face of Protestant Christianity, i.e. the Church of England, was instituted in England and Ireland in 1534 by Henry VIII for dynastic and opportunistic reasons (i.e. the need to divorce and marry again with a view to begetting a male heir and to gain funds by confiscating the property of the Catholic Church). In addition to appointing himself as the head of this newly-established church, Henry

---

** This version is used by Jane Wellesley in her publication *Wellington: A Journey Through My Family* (London 2009), p. 14. Wellesley does not, however, delve deeper into the similarity between the name Welles-Leighs and the town of Wells where the first written source mentioning the family name is archived. Thus, this presents an opportunity for further research, perhaps by linguists, although the similarity between the two names may only be coincidental.

VIII was also known for his appreciable appetite and six consecutive wives, two of which ended up on the executioner's block. Nonetheless by the Seventeenth Century, after the English Civil War (1642–1651) and the subsequent short-lived rule of Lord Protector Oliver Cromwell, Gerald Wellesley, son of Garret Valerian, regained the family estates with the help of a request addressed to King Charles II. Contrary to his father, Gerald Wellesley did not greatly emphasize his conscience in the request, stating that he had personally always been merely an "innocent Protestant". This evidently achieved the desired results, as by doing so he gained all his lands back from the Crown. After Charles II returned his family estates, he immediately changed his name to Wesley, which was a far more commonly used variation of the name that drew much less attention in such an uncertain time.[12] Over the course of the Duke of Wellington's life, the family name was changed back to its original spelling "Wellesley" due to their growing prestige, as the family began to feel the need to stand out from the crowd in which the "innocent Protestant" Gerald had so dearly wished to be a member.

From the time the Wellesleys settled in Ireland in the 12th century, the family married only among the narrow circle of the other Anglo-Norman families near them and by doing so set themselves apart from the original Irish inhabitants. In terms of Arthur Wellesley's lineage, the Colley Family clearly played one of the most important roles. As the "innocent Protestant" Gerald remained without a male heir, the Wellesleys (now officially the Wesleys) were threatened by an interruption in their lineage. Therefore, Gerald decided to adopt his cousin Richard Colley – grandfather of the future Duke of Wellington – as his heir. Thanks to almost six hundred years of repeated intermarrying, the Anglo-Norman families in Ireland were linked in such a way that the Colleys had Wellesley blood in their veins thanks to their predecessors. Thanks to this fact, Richard Colley was an ideal candidate for Gerald as an adopted heir.[13] In order to inherit the Wesleys' estate, however, Colley had to promise to accept their family name, thus becoming Richard Wesley in place of Richard Colley. This new-found Wesley invested the family's mutual properties into family estates in County Meath, in which the primary Wesley residence, Dangan Castle, was located. In the areas surrounding the castle, he had beautiful gardens and a picturesque lake created, complete with boats and islands. In addition, he did not hesitate to invest rather large sums into the modernization of the castle itself in order to meet the needs of an 18th century nobleman after its renovation. Wholly in line with the spirit of the times, when society was fascinated with antiquity, Richard had numerous sculptures of ancient gods commissioned for the castle's gardens. These sculptures included Bacchus, god of unbridled revelry, or Apollo, god of the sun, all dominated by a monumental group of sculptures depicting the abduction of Persephone were prominently situated in the main courtyard in front of the house. In the immediate surroundings of the residence, there were also several ceremonial cannons from which salvos were fired in honour of any member of the family celebrating a birthday. In addition to renovating Dangan, Richard also managed to rise in the ranks of British aristocracy, as he was elevated to the title of Baron Mornington in 1746.* Hobbies of Wellington's grandfather Richard Wesley (formerly Colley) primarily included music, which would soon prove to be hereditary in the family. Richard himself was an enthusiastic violinist and, according to the testimony of his contemporaries, possessed quite a skill at playing the instrument. Thanks to this fancy, Richard met celebrated composer George Frideric Handel in the early 1740s as he took part in organizing a concert for him in Dublin. He even managed to convince Handel to visit him at Dangan, where Handel played a small organ concert for the Wesley Family and their friends from the surrounding areas. It is worth remembering that Handel's oratorio *Messiah* had been given its premier in Dublin in 1742.

When Richard Wesley died in 1758, all property passed to his only son and heir Garret Wesley. Handel's undoubtedly impressive concert, which Garret witnessed at the age of seven at Dangan, may have inspired him to choose the path of composer as well. Garret, father to Arthur, future Duke of Wellington, showed an uncommon skill for music from a young age. His favourite activity as a child was listening to his father Richard play the violin. Thanks to this, Garret himself was already able to play the instrument skilfully by the age of five and began to compose his own work by the age of nine. It thus came as no surprise when, in adulthood, he was named music professor at Trinity College and soon became

---

* Since the early modern period, British nobility has been divided into higher nobility (*peerage*) and lower nobility (*the landed gentry*). Peers are addressed *Lord* and their titles are arranged in the following ascending order: Baron, Viscount, Earl, Marquess, and Duke. Members of the gentry are addressed *Sir* and hold titles of either knights or baronets.

an acknowledged musician and composer. Some of his works are still played at classical music performances in Britain today. Furthermore, he managed much like his father to heighten the family's prestige by rising in the ranks of British nobility from Baron to Earl Mornington.[14] Despite this fact, he does not seem to have been highly active in politics, and therefore it is not wholly clear as to the merits that earned Garret the title of Earl. The following might provide at least a partial explanation: As he led quite an active social life in Dublin, which he preferred over administering Dangan in the countryside, he had made many useful contacts in the Irish capital that may have helped him in gaining the title of Earl. Another common answer to this question is that Garret's music had caught the attention of none other than British Monarch George III himself, who as an inveterate patron of the arts and sciences rewarded him with the title of Earl for his activity as a composer.[15]

At the age of twenty three, Garret married Anne Hill, the sixteen-year-old daughter of Arthur Hill, a banker and the future Viscount of Dungannon. Over the course of the thirty years of their marriage, nine children were born, seven of whom survived to adulthood. Almost immediately after their wedding in 1760, the oldest son Richard, heir to the family estate and his father's title of Earl, was born. The next son Arthur, who died in childhood, came after Richard. The third son in line was William, later known as Wellesley-Pole, as he was adopted by the Pole family, similarly to his ancestor Richard Colley, who was adopted years before into the Wesley family. After William came a son Francis and a daughter Anna. Francis, however, did not live past his childhood. Finally, in 1769, Arthur Wesley, future Duke of Wellington, came into the world. It is truly remarkable that three of his greatest military opponents were born in the same year as he: Marshal Soult and Marshal Ney, whom the Duke successfully defeated during the Peninsular War in Portugal and Spain, and primarily Napoleon Bonaparte, Arthur's most famous antagonist with whom he clashed at Waterloo, were all born in 1769.[16]

Shortly after Arthur, Gerald Valerian was born. He later won recognition through his career in the Church. The abundant line of descendants of the Wesleys was completed by their daughter Mary and their youngest, Henry. Thus, two daughters and five sons lived to adulthood, making the future Duke of Wellington the middle child.[17] Immediately after Wellington's life began, we are confronted with the mystery of when and where in 1769 he was actually born. Wellington himself always celebrated his birthday on 1ˢᵗ May, which is the most commonly listed date of his birth. The record of his baptism from St Peter's Anglican Church in Dublin, however, is dated 30ᵗʰ April, and in local papers called *Exshaw's Gentleman's Magazine*, we can also find the date of Arthur's birth listed as 29ᵗʰ April. It is rather improbable for both records to be incorrect, which places Wellington's birthday before 1ˢᵗ May 1769.[18] In Wellington's time, early baptisms took place directly after birth more or less exclusively in cases in which the new-born seemed sickly or was in danger of dying. Therefore, Arthur Wesley is most likely to have been born at the end of April if he had been an ailing child and was thus given an expeditious baptism; conversely, he would have been born at the beginning of April or even during March if he seemed to be a healthy infant. In the latter case, the family would wait for the arrival of members of the extended family or other prominent figures who came as a godfather to the baptism, which thus took place several weeks after the birth of the child.*

The question of where Wellington was born has proven to be a far greater mystery. Possibilities of the Duke's birthplace naturally include Dangan Castle, the family home in Dublin, and many others, including a story of his premature birth in a carriage on the way to the Irish capital or on the deck of a ship during his mother's journey to Ireland from England. The next potential candidate for the site of Wellington's birth is the small town of Trim, located roughly thirty miles northwest of Dublin. Local contemporary historian Thomas Murray documented an amazing total of nine sites directly in Trim or its immediate surroundings that are said to be the place where the Duke of Wellington first came into the world. To complicate matters still further, Wellington at an advanced age personally cited another Irish town, Athy, as his birthplace.[19] Although the matter is unclear, in the light of the record of baptism in St Peter's Church in Dublin it is possible to assert that Arthur was born in the family home in Dublin at 6 Merrion Street**, which Wellington's mother,

---

* Christopher Bell, *The Birth of Arthur Wesley*, online article in: https://www.waterlooassociation. org.uk/2019/03/29/the-birth-of-arthur-wesley/
In his biography on Wellington written in the 19th century, for example, George Gleig cites the Duke's birthdate as 3ʳᵈ April 1769; however, he cites the source of this information rather unconvincingly as *'an old Dublin newspaper'*.

** Today the Wellesleys' Dublin home (the so-called Mornington House) can most likely be found in 26 Upper Merrion Street as a part of the Merrion Hotel.

Lady Mornington, also pointed out as the place where he came into the world. On the other hand, Christopher Bell from *The Waterloo Association* recently claimed that if Wellington had been a healthy child, he could easily have been born in Trim, where his parents also owned the so-called Mornington House, or at Dangan. In this case, he would have been born at the beginning of April or even earlier, after which he may have been transported to Dublin for baptism at the end of April. I personally tend towards this theory and agree that it may explain the contradictions in various testimonies of Wellington's birth.*

It is clear, however, that Arthur was brought up on the Dangan family estate until he was seven, and these years were likely to have been happy ones. The beautiful gardens surrounding the estate were surely well-suited for childhood games and the nearby church school in the town of Trim, which Arthur attended as a boy, provided the ideal conditions for starting school. The old stone building of Arthur's former school in Trim was known as "Talbot's Castle". It is a rather curious fact that the name of the building in which Wellington – who dedicated the majority of his military career in battle against the French – spent much of his time as a boy was taken from John Talbot, 1st Earl of Shrewsbury, a soldier from the 15th century who earned the nickname 'The Scourge of France' on the pages of Shakespeare's historical play Henry VI thanks to his successful operations on England's side in the Hundred Years' War. To his father's unconcealed delight, Arthur Wesley also inherited the family's musical talent, providing him (to a certain degree) with heightened attention. However, on Lady Mornington's initiative the whole family soon moved to London. In taking this step, Arthur's ambitious mother wanted to ensure that the boys would rid themselves of their Irish accent, a fact that could have otherwise disadvantaged them in terms of their careers in later life. In London, Arthur attended Brown's Seminary, later known as Oxford House Academy, in King's Road, Chelsea, and was certainly not an

---

*   Bell, *The Birth of Arthur Wesley*, online article in: https://www.waterlooassociation.org.
     uk/2019/03/29/the-birth-of-arthur-wesley/. In this excellent article, Christopher Bell
     summarizes in great detail the issues surrounding Wellington's birth. For instance, he cites the
     interesting fact that historian John Murray held an interview with the then 100-year-old Mrs
     Rose Daly, whose family had lived in Trim for generations. During the interview, Mrs Daly
     informed him that her grandmother had been personally present as a nurse in Trim during
     Wellington's birth.

exemplary student. In addition, since childhood he had suffered regularly from bouts of illness and was generally of poor health. Instead of spending his free time taking part in the frenzied ball games on the school pitch of Brown's Seminary, he preferred to observe the players from the shade of a large tree, calling out loudly when he saw one of them cheating.[20]

While Arthur dealt with his problems at school, all of Britain was shaken by the report in 1781 of Lord Cornwallis' capitulation to the American rebels at Yorktown, which for the British sovereign George III spelled the definitive loss of his North American colonies. Twelve-year-old Arthur, however, was struck by a wholly different event – the sudden death of his forty-six-year-old father, Lord Mornington. Thus, quite suddenly the oldest of the Wesley boys, Richard, became the head of the family at the young age of twenty one. He was forced to interrupt his promising studies at Oxford, which he had only just begun, and help his mother care for his younger brothers and sisters. One of his first decisions was to ensure that his siblings received a good education, sending young Arthur to Eton College that same year. Richard himself had made a good name for the family at Eton as an exceptional student and was primarily talented in the area of classical languages (Latin and Greek). Arthur, unfortunately, seemed considerably less promising. The only subject in which he seemed relatively successful was mathematics, which in light of the number of subjects taught was naturally unsatisfactory. Arthur felt uncomfortable in the exceptionally distinguished society of Eton, which included the sons of three dukes, several marquesses, and many other earls, and thus lived in his own world. He often wandered around the school's gardens, entertaining himself by climbing trees or jumping over ditches. Years later, the Duke admitted to a friend from battle that he had felt very lonely at school, a fact that his friend noted in the following: 'for he walked generally alone... and seldom took part either in the cricket matches or the boat-races which were then, as they are now, in great vogue among Etonians.'[21] The fact that he did not get along well with his classmates as an outsider from Ireland did not, however, mean that he was unable to fend for himself. When necessary, Arthur did not shy away from conflict. For example, after one of the numerous arguments that took place at the time between Arthur and his classmate, Bobus Smith, the whole affair turned into a brawl.[22] Bobus himself recalled the incident years later with humour: 'I had a fight and he beat me soundly... I was the Duke of Wellington's first victory.'[23] On holiday, which Arthur spent in the countryside in Northern Wales with his maternal grandmother, Lady Dungannon, he fared considerably worse after he picked a fight with the son of a local blacksmith. The boy quickly overpowered him, a fact which paradoxically served to win over the otherwise lonely Arthur, as it resulted in the boys becoming friends. With thunderous laughter over a glass of spirits, the blacksmith's son was fond of boasting in his old age of having 'beaten the man who beat Napoleon.'[24]

In addition to his poor marks in school, Wellington's studies at Eton are inherently linked to the famous quote on the victory at Waterloo: 'The battle of Waterloo was won on the playing fields of Eton.' Nonetheless, it is highly possible that this sentence, which is one of the more famous quotes associated to Wellington, was paradoxically never spoken by the Duke himself. The quote was published in the unauthorized work of a popular publisher and member of the French Parliament, Count Montalembert, several years after the Duke's death.* This may have been a loose paraphrasing on Montalembert's part of the words that Wellington spoke with laughter after visiting Eton in 1818, this time as the famous victor of Waterloo. There he reminisced on the childhood games with which he passed the time in the school's gardens: 'I really believe I owe my spirit of enterprise to the tricks I used to play in the garden [of Eton].'[25]

Nonetheless, it remains a fact that the Duke did not fare well as a student. He was a problematic pupil and did not enjoy his studies. The harshly authoritative approach of the masters, which also included corporal punishment, evoked in him a resistance and reluctance to study rather than the necessary motivation to do so. Similar to Wellington, almost one century later, another son of the nobility would be subjected to this strict system of British aristocratic education. In his studies, this child felt just as absolutely alone as the Duke, and considered the time to be the worst years of his life. In adulthood, he went so far as to

---

*   Muir, *Wellington: The Path to Victory*, p. 8. Andrew Roberts, one of several historians who supports the authenticity of the quote (Andrew Roberts, *Wellington and Napoleon* (London 2003), p. 5.), nonetheless points to the fact that by the "playing fields of Eton" the Duke may have meant the area of a nearby mill where the pupils of Eton would go to fight in order to settle their matters.

state that: 'In all the twelve years I was at school no one ever succeeded in making me write a Latin verse …'[26] This boy's name was Winston Churchill, and despite his failures at school, in his case Harrow School, Eton's arch-rival, he went on to become, much like Arthur Wesley, Commander-in-Chief and Prime Minister of Britain. Thus, poor marks clearly did not mean a lack of intelligence. Both Wellington and Churchill's whole lives were marked by the belief in doing things based on one's own convictions. They required every affair to carry meaning and, perhaps thanks to this trait, they both were able to achieve such remarkable things.

Soon after, despite his initial resistance to learning, Wellington became a passionate reader, and had already read by the age of twenty the works of authors such as philosopher John Locke. Literature in general remained one of his great hobbies until the end of his life. He did not lose all love for Eton either and, thanks to Wellington's decision, both his sons also attended his alma mater. During his lifetime, he often regretted not having completed a university education, although such was the esteem in which Wellington was held in later life that he was appointed Chancellor of Oxford University, a position that he held from 1834 until 1852, a fact which he was rightfully proud of.

After three years of study at Eton, which seemed to be a constant annoyance to the young Wellington, Arthur left school (either for poor marks or a lack of family finances) and travelled with his mother to Brussels. There, as a sixteen-year-old youth, he received private tuition from a local lawyer, Luis Goubert. At the time Arthur was a resident there, Brussels and all of Belgium was called the Austrian Netherlands and was under the rule of Habsburg ruler Joseph II (the son of Empress Maria Theresa), an enlightened monarch who was Holy Roman Emperor as well as King of Bohemia and Hungary.

It seems the young Arthur Wesley held his new tutor, Mr Goubert in high regard. Years later, when Brussels was quite literally flooded with allied troops at the end of the Napoleonic Wars, threatening to disturb the populace, Wellington (now as Field Marshal of the British Army) had a special guard deployed outside Goubert's home to prevent any overzealous soldiers from committing foul acts to him or his family.[27] Wellington himself remembered the whole event in the following:

As I rode into Brussels the day after the battle of Waterloo [today the capital of Belgium is roughly 19 miles from the site of the famous battle], I passed the old house, and recognized it, and pulling up, ascertained that the old man [Luis Goubert] was still alive. I sent for him and recalling myself to his recollection, shook hands with him, and assured him that for old acquaintance' sake he should be protected from all molestation.[28]

Nothing, however, pointed to the fact that Arthur's attitude toward learning would change in any great way. A classmate from his studies in Brussels, John Armytage, said the following about him years later: 'Arthur Wesley was extremely fond of music and played well upon the fiddle, but he never gained indication of any other species of talent.'[29] In Brussels, Lady Mornington (Arthur's mother) appreciated her son's positive traits such as his constant good humour and honesty, but his attitude towards education truly began to bother her. She expressed these concerns in a letter to a female friend in the following manner: 'I vow to God, I don't know what I shall do with my awkward son Arthur. He's food for powder and nothing more.' [30] At the time, the future duke was not overly excited about the prospect of a career in the army, but he acquiesced to his mother's wishes. Soon he was signed up to a French military school – the Royal Academy of Equitation located within the Château de Pignerolle situated to the east of the town of Angers in the Loire Valley. This military academy had more than two hundred years of tradition and the most famous of its graduates included those such as George Villiers, 1st Duke of Buckingham, a famous character who featured in Alexandre Dumas' *The Three Musketeers*. Extensive stables with a spacious riding-hall formed an indelible part of the massive, white-plaster buildings of the Academy. In addition to equitation, which was the most important field of instruction at Angers, pupils learned fencing, marksmanship, mathematics, and languages. These were all skills that were essential to any good officer of the time. Dance lessons were also an integral part of a cadet's education at the Academy. Dance was taught twice a day at Angers, as it was assumed that every true gentleman in the 18th century should know how to dance in at least a tolerable manner. Balls and dances served as an opportunity to establish social contacts and enable the distinguished gentlemen to meet young noblewomen.

Most importantly, however, Arthur suddenly began to excel in this new environment. He improved his already decent knowledge of French, which would remain the foreign language that the Duke spoke best throughout his life. Because at the end of the 18th century French had more or less replaced Latin in the royal courts of Europe as the international language of diplomacy, knowledge of the language proved to be essential for young noblemen.[31] Primarily, however, Arthur was slowly becoming an excellent rider and it was likely at the Academy in Angers that his affinity for horses and riding in general developed. Furthermore, this formative time spent on the Continent fostered in Arthur an appreciation of many of the finer things in French culture and sowed the seeds for him being a lifelong Francophile in many respects.

The fact that Wellington felt at home in the saddle also proved essential in his later career as a commander, during which he always preferred a personal style of command. On his campaigns, during which he was constantly in motion as if in the style of a medieval ruler, he always strove to communicate in person with his allies, observe the manoeuvres of his enemy, reconnoitre the landscape, and issue orders on the organization of the army. In situations of battle, he would give words of encouragement to his men from the saddle in the most critical of moments when the lines of battle threatened to be breached. When it was necessary during war, he did not hesitate to saddle up his horse – even in the middle of the night – to see personally to a given matter. One of his officers from the Peninsular War wrote the following of the Duke: 'He was like a centaur, seeming part of his horse, and he slept as soundly in his saddle as if in his bed.'[32] Throughout Arthur's whole life, horse-riding was also a means of physical fitness and respite.

The director of the military academy in Angers, the motto of which was *Grace and Valour*, was Marcel Avril de Pignerolle, a devoted royalist and adherent to the so-called *ancien régime*. Simply put, the values of the "old regime" were based on the conservative conviction that only the ruler and higher nobility should take part in the leadership of the state. The director naturally instilled these values in his pupils, including Arthur Wesley. During the French Revolution, de Pignerolle was arrested in 1793 and unfortunately murdered for these same convictions.[33] In the years to come, this fact surely influenced Wellington's strongly critical stance on the Revolution and its ideals. As for the students of the Academy, it was quite common that a score of Englishmen and other foreigners studied alongside the French (including young Wellington, a total of 334 cadets were registered in his class at the academy). To Arthur's great pleasure, he found that two cadets from Ireland were among the ranks of his class-mates – a Mr Walsh and Mr Wingfield. Arthur immediately befriended them, creating a strong trio known by the nickname of *'groupe des lords'*.[34] Instruction took place in a relatively friendly atmosphere, and from time to time the cadets were even invited to Director Pignerolle and his wife's home to dinner or invited to join the local nobility at events. These so-cial gatherings were meant to teach the cadets good manners and the behaviour of proper gentleman. The Duke of Wellington keenly recalled the dinners with Duchess de Sabran, whose maternal approach in those years took the place of the somewhat unhappy relationship with his own mother. Later, he humorously recalled feasts with Louis-Hercule, Duke de Brissac, who was known for brazenly piling upon his plate the juiciest morsels of food first and only after serving his guests – a "truly stellar example" for the young gentlemen-to-be. To the Duke's dismay, how-ever, even this passionate gourmand did not escape being murdered by Revolutionaries during the 9th September Massacres of 1792.

Evenings in the company of Madame Pignerolle were also certain-ly held in a congenial atmosphere, as she often played cards with the cadets, confiscating the winnings when the stakes became too high in the effort to prevent the cadets from succumbing to gambling. Another favourite pastime of the *'groupe des lords'* – although it should be men-tioned in respect of the Academy's motto that it was neither a graceful nor valiant game – involved dropping coins on the heads of passers-by from the windows of the Academy. The only thing that partially marred Arthur's time at Angers was his continuously poor health, which often led to his absence from class. In times of illness, his terrier Vick kept him company, and refused to leave his side whilst in the grounds of the Academy.[35]

One evening when Pignerolle was hosting two noblemen from Britain at the Academy, the men asked whether he had any especially promis-ing pupils from England. The director, with no promising boys from England in his class, did have one from Ireland, and replied: 'one Irish lad of great promise, of the name Wesley.'[36] Thus the director seems to be the first person to have spotted the potential in the future Duke. When in his old age Wellington replied to questions regarding his childhood, he described himself as 'a dreamy, idle and shy lad'[37] However, thanks to Pignerolle's positive influence, this was certainly no longer the case once Arthur graduated from the Academy in Angers. This formative time not only shaped Arthur, but also furnished him with valuable insights into the French psyche as well as a better understanding of some of the martial values of the French Officer Class.

Youth in Ireland: Gambling, Laughable Loves, and Kitty Pakenham

I t was November 1787 when eighteen-year-old Arthur Wesley, replete with expectations, returned from Angers to England. The first of his family to greet him was his mother, Lady Mornington, who could not believe her eyes at the deep transformation that had taken place in her son during a period of less than two years. In place of the idle and clumsy adolescent dreamer a handsome, charismatic young man now stood before her as if by the stroke of a magic wand. With a sarcasm that was typical of her, however, she greeted him with the following words: 'do believe there is my ugly boy Arthur.'[38] This, however, was a part of her style of upbringing: she wanted to raise the strongest possible character in her boys and her scathing humour and certain degree of severity evidently served this purpose better than exaggerated praise and pampering. However, as a price for this attitude, her relationships with all her sons throughout her life remained rather cold. Despite her mask of indifference, however, she was wholly dazzled by Arthur's appearance and manner. For perhaps the first time, she

felt rightfully proud of Arthur when, in a letter addressed to two aristocratic Anglo-Irish women who were known as the Ladies of Llangollen and
played a prominent role at the time in the halls of the British aristocracy
and with whom she planned to acquaint herself, she wrote:

> There are so many little things to settle for Arthur who is just got into the ar-
> my and is to go to Ireland in the capacity of aid-de-camp to Lord Buckingham
> and must be set out a little for that, in short I must do everything for him and
> when you see him you will think him worthy of it.[39]

The Ladies of Llangollen were Lady Eleanor Butler and Sarah Ponsonby,
who had fled their families in order to escape forced marriages. By shar-
ing the expenses, they had bought *Plas Newydd*, a house not far from the
town of Llangollen in North Wales, where they lived together. Among
the elite of British Society, their act was considered highly romantic,
and thus the ladies suddenly became famous as their independence was
celebrated and also condemned by some from their aristocratic milieu.
When Arthur, accompanied by his grandmother Lady Dungannon (who
lived close to Llangollen) visited them at the beginning of 1788, the ladies
seemed to be quite charmed by his appearance, much like Arthur's mother. Lady Butler even noted in her diary that he was 'A charming young
man. Handsome, fashioned, tall and elegant.'[40]

Regardless of this "miraculous transformation", it was now necessary
for Arthur to find his position and begin his career in the adult world.
Over the course of Arthur's studies, the oldest of the Wesley brothers
Richard, now 2nd Earl of Mornington, fully proved his potential after first
entering the Irish House of Commons and Irish House of Lords and then
entering the British House of Commons as Member of Parliament for
Bere Alston. It is important to note that some parliamentary seats were
easily "bought", as were votes, and the 18th and the early 19th century were
synonymous in British political circles with Rotten or Pocket Boroughs
of which Bere Alston in Devon was later deemed one. That said, Richard
had evidently decided upon the career of politician and, along with his
growing prestige, felt a keen sense of duty as the head of the family to
care for his siblings. In doing so, he did not hesitate to use his widen-
ing network of contacts and influence to ensure that those he held dear
benefitted accordingly. However, the fact that the Wesley family did not

exactly abound with money proved to be a barrier for Richard in his efforts to provide all members of his family with the best possible standing. This was due to the fact that Richard and Arthur's grandfather had spent large portions of the family estate on renovating Dangan. As Richard's growing political career was naturally quite expensive in terms of the costs of representation, as a consequence the family's finances suffered further. In order for Richard, who now lived in London, to ensure careers for his four brothers, he was inevitably forced to sell the family home, Mornington House in Dublin and Dangan Castle, the idyllic place of Arthur's childhood. In addition, the boys' maternal grandmother, Lady Dungannon, with whom Arthur so fondly spent his holidays during his study at Eton, nearly ended up in debtor's prison due to her lavish lifestyle and expenses – a problem which, to his dismay, he was also forced to deal with.[41] Despite these difficulties, Richard managed to gain a seat for William in the Irish Parliament in the position of Member of Parliament for Trim. As for his other brothers, Gerald and Henry were still studying at Eton, where they fared considerably better (this time to Richard's delight) than Arthur had in the past. As was mentioned above and contrary to the scanty hopes his family had placed in him, Arthur now emerged in a wholly new light after his return from the military academy in Angers. Richard now began eagerly to establish both a military and political career for Arthur. Richard's scheme was prudent, as he expected time would tell which field Arthur would excel in and which one would thus be a greater benefit to the family. Suddenly, in Richard's eyes (just like in his mother's), Arthur was no longer a clumsy boy with no future.

Arthur was first given the lowest officer's rank of Ensign in the British Army in the 73rd Highland Regiment of Foot. Soon, however, Richard managed to move him up to the 76th Regiment, this time as a lieutenant. Because this regiment was soon to be deployed in the East Indies*, however, Richard was once again quick to use his influence, ensuring Arthur a quick change of deployment to the 41st Regiment of Foot.[42] It is my assertion that this event gives proof of the fact that, at the given moment, Arthur planned to use his brother's influence primarily for a political career and a military career was initially only a secondary matter. In the

---

* In more simple terms, the colonies in the area of the East Indies made up of the territory of today's India and a part of the Middle East. To the British, the West Indies meant the areas of today's Caribbean and America.

meantime, Richard managed to arrange a relatively prestigious position for Arthur as an aide-de-camp to George Nugent-Temple-Grenville, 1ˢᵗ Marquess of Buckingham, Lord Lieutenant of Ireland. Lady Mornington (Arthur's mother), who was beside herself with joy at the news, wrote to the Ladies of Llangollen: 'He is wonderfully lucky, in six months he has got two steps in the army and appointed aide-de-camp to Lord Buckingham which is ten shillings a day.'[43]

Thus, by a twist of fate, Arthur's initial career became linked to the land of his birth. He began to work as aide-de-camp to the Lord Lieutenant of Ireland in 1788 and a year later he received authorization to take up his first role in the position of politician. Due to favourable conditions at the time, his brother William was preparing to take a step up in his career by running for the British House of Commons in Westminster in order to take a seat next to Richard. Arthur was now to fill the seat freed by William in the Irish Parliament as Member of Parliament for Trim. For these reasons, just before elections in the town in 1789 the future Duke of Wellington gave his very first political speech there during his pre-election campaign.[44] The speech dealt with awarding the so-called right of Freeman of the Corporation, which among other privileges included the right to vote and be elected to the Irish Parliament, to a prominent leader of the Irish nationalist move-ment Henry Grattan. Arthur argued that the single reason that this right was to be granted to Grattan was the fact that he was without a shadow of a doubt a highly respected figure – but, if all people were to gain this title based on respect, Ireland would soon be brimming with "Freemen" (or free citizens of the town's community). He argued that this would set a danger-ous precedent. Thanks to his speech, Grattan was not granted the right of freeman and Arthur subsequently won the elections to the Irish Parliament in 1790, where he regularly sat as the Member of Parliament for Trim.[45]

In the winter of this year, 7ᵗʰ December 1790 to be precise, Arthur Wesley was also initiated into a Freemasonic Lodge at Trim. By join-ing the Freemasons, he was following a family tradition. Arthur's father Garret had been the Grand Master of the Grand Lodge of Ireland, and his brother Richard (who most likely led Arthur to the Freemasons) had managed to do the same eight years prior to Arthur's entrance into the group. There is evidence that Arthur Wesley paid membership fees in the Freemasonic Lodge at Trim for five years. However, considering the fact that his brother Richard reached the rank of Grand Master for the whole of Ireland after only two years, it seems somewhat surprising that Arthur did not pass the first level even after five, it is evident that he paid little attention to the study of freemasonry. The only more significant proof of his participation in the Lodge at Trim is Arthur Wesley's purchase of an English Lottery Ticket on 16th February 1795 from the Lodge treasurer*, which gives proof of a wholly different fancy to which the young Wellington devoted much more of his attention to other matters than he did to becoming a Freemason. After Wellington had become a celebrated individual, the Freemasons of Dublin, to where the Lodge at Trim was moved in 1836, wished to name their new Lodge after Wellington; however, it was a proposition which he clearly refused, replying to Mr Carleton, Secretary of the Masonic Lodge in Dublin that:

[the Duke] perfectly recollects he was admitted to the lowest grade of Free Masonry in a Lodge which was fixed at Trim, in the County of Meath. He has never since attended a Lodge of Free Masons. He cannot say that he knows anything of the Art. His consent to give this Lodge his Name would be a ridiculous assumption of the reputation of being attached to free Masonry; in addition to being a misrepresentation, The Duke of Wellington hopes, therefore, that Mr Carleton will excuse the Duke for declining to comply with his suggestion...[46]

In addition to politics, Arthur also had time for entertainment and all the distractions and possible vices of youth during his years spent in Ireland. He was not a prudish or exaggeratedly ambitious young man, nor was he extremely "unrestrained" as his youth often tends to be sensationally portrayed

---

*   Yasha Beresiner, *Wellington: Soldier, Politician and Initiated Freemason*, online article in: http://www.freemasons-freemasonry.com/beresiner13.html
Perhaps the most famous but in my opinion rather ridiculous claim concerning Wellington's masonic connection is the following "conspiracy theory", according to which in 1815, Wellington, along with a group of French Freemasons, rescued Marshal Ney, "one of his masonic brothers", from execution, subsequently aiding him to flee to America, where Ney allegedly lived out the rest of his life in peace and died several decades later. In reality, of course, Ney was mercilessly executed in Paris on 7th December 1815. Nonetheless, a remarkable record on this topic exists by Bohemian chronicler and mayor of the Czech village of Milčice near Prague, František Vavák (1741–1816), which I happened to stumble upon while researching the context. Vavák wrote the following note: '*On 7th December (18–15), Marshal Ney, due to his terrible betrayal, was sentenced to death and shot according to Parisian law. However, he was shot only with mercury, and using this front was able to easily flee the country, as the whole matter had been arranged with his friends by bribery.*' Quoted in: František Vavák: *Paměti Františka Vaváka, Kniha VI–VII (1810–1816)*, (Praha 2009), p. 407. This record is clear proof that the legend of Ney's rescue must have spread throughout Europe shortly after the whole incident, as evidenced by the fact that the news managed to reach the chronicles of a Czech-speaking author in a small village in the Austrian Empire.

in literature. Together with Wesley, the Marquess of Buckingham had a to-tal of eighteen aides-de-camp, all of which were roughly Arthur's age. One of Irish Deputies, Sir Jonah Barrington, remembered that Arthur Wesley 'was then ruddy-faced and juvenile in appearance, and popular enough among the young men of his age and station.'[47] In terms of lifestyle, there is no reason to assume that Arthur differed in any significant way from his contemporaries. Lady Buckingham called the young men the "awkward squad", as they did not make the best impression on her after being nom-inated to their positions. Shortly after Arthur's arrival to Ireland in 1788, a celebration of the hundredth anniversary of the Glorious Revolution* took place. After toasting throughout the morning to all things possible – from the anniversary of the Glorious Revolution and King George's health to the winner of that day's horse races – it was thus no surprise that once the gentlemen arrived to dinner with Lady Buckingham and the other la-dies, the whole affair ended in an indecorous manner, as the Marquess of Buckingham could hardly stand up, the butler was muttering incompre-hensibly, and the aides-de-camp were in quite a similar state.[48]

In addition to alcohol, gambling was a great temptation for young noblemen at the end of the 18th century in Europe. It had become a fash-ionable affair, not infrequently transforming into an addiction, and often brought both the distinguished and undistinguished to destitution. In his now-classic novel *The Memoirs of Barry Lyndon Esq.*, English writer William Makepeace Thackeray (1811–1863) immortalized the period's obsession with gambling. Barry, the protagonist of Thackeray's pica-resque novel is a shabby-genteel Irish nobleman whose story plays out in the mid-18th century as he repeatedly escapes dire financial situations throughout his life by playing games of chance, invariably in card games. The parties that Barry attends, held by a fictitious noble couple from Dublin, are described by Thackeray with a certain degree of poetic license and quite succinctly illustrated the environment of the time when young Wellington worked as aide-de-camp to the Irish Lord Lieutenant in the following:

---

* The 'Glorious' or 'Bloodless' Revolution (1688 – 1689) marked the overthrow of King James II (House of Stuart) by the British aristocracy, who held concerns about James' son Catholic and heir, James Francis Edward, and the accession of William III with Mary II of England to the English throne.

After dinner, you may be sure that cards were not wanting, and that the company who played did not play for love merely. To these parties persons of all sorts would come: young bloods from the regiments garrisoned in Dublin, young clerks from the Castle, horse-riding, wine-tippling, watchmen-beating men of fashion about town, such as existed in Dublin in that day more than in any other city with which I am acquainted in Europe. [49]

By all accounts, the young Arthur Wesley was no exception and was a relatively passionate gambler who like the central character in *Barry Lyndon* enjoyed indulging in cards. Just like today, the great enchantment of cards was in their promise of easy and relatively quick winnings. In addition, Arthur had always had a taste for fashion and invested rather large amounts of money in clothing. Purchasing books and building his own library also became a hobby on which Arthur did not hesitate to spend even larger amounts of money than on clothing, a fact that was less usual in light of his age and financial situation.[50] Generally speaking, Arthur as aide-de-camp to the Lord Lieutenant led a relatively costly lifestyle despite the fact that, as the middle son of the noble family, he barely possessed any of his own personal funds. At the time, gambling was a socially acceptable opportunity for a gentleman to "earn a few extra shillings" and should not be judged completely by today's standards. Contrary to some of his other "headstrong" contemporaries, Arthur began to manifest a discretion in gambling that would later play a role in his life, as he never allowed himself to sink into unpayable debts. On the contrary, he managed surprisingly to improve his financial situation quite considerably by winning the sum of 150 guineas* from 'Buck' Whaley. He bet that Arthur could not walk the six-mile route from Dublin's periphery of Cornelscourt to the middle of Leeson Street, located in the centre of town, in under one hour. Arthur Wesley managed it in fifty five minutes and thus claimed his winnings.[51] Despite the extra earnings, he was too often forced to borrow money in his younger days. Years later in a discussion with a friend, Wellington recalled with displeasure the period when he lived partially on credit, saying the following about debts: 'It [debt] makes a slave of a man. I have often known what it was to be in want of money, but I never got helplessly into debt.' [52]

---

* One gold guinea was equal to 21 shillings. One hundred and fifty guineas was thus roughly a year's salary for an aide-de-camp of the Lord Lieutenant.

Two gentlemen, John Cradock and William Fremantle, were two of Arthur's best friends from the "awkward squad" of young aides-de-camp. Among other passions, all three young men were connected by their considerable affection for the fairer sex. In this aides-de-camp trio, Cradock clearly held the greatest reputation of "local Casanova" and – thanks to his prodigious love life – soon became known in Dublin's noble society as 'The Town Bull of Dublin' and 'Beau Cradock'. Arthur and his friends had sufficient opportunity to make acquaintances in their positions as aides-de-camp to the Lord Lieutenant during frequent Sunday picnics and balls or at banquets organized by the local aristocracy and the town's dignitaries, social occasions of quality and status which many ladies were eager to attend.[53] One of the officers serving in Arthur's regiment at the time described young Wellington's behaviour when he served as aide-de-camp in Dublin in the following manner: 'social in his habits… but never given to excess…his personal appearance and manners were extremely neat and elegant.'[54] The wife of Cradock's half-brother wrote the following in regard to Arthur's social life during the period: 'He was extremely good humoured, and the object of much attention from the female part of what was called 'very gay society'.'[55] By all accounts, Arthur was popular with women, but in Cradock's words fell in love for the first time in a more serious manner with one Mrs Stretford: 'Now more in love with Mrs. Stretford than I can describe, all his minor loves before are quite forgot.'[56] Falling so intensely in love fits the character of a timid and romantic young man rather than that of a seasoned philanderer. Nonetheless, Arthur may have had a certain Don Juan reputation in Dublin in his twenties (it was not by chance that he was a friend of the 'Town Bull' Cradock), as a certain Mr Butler refused to rent out a suite of rooms to Arthur in his home. This was allegedly because Butler's wife and daughter lived on the ground floor and the man was not willing to risk an affair between them and the young aide-de-camp Wesley. Contrary to this, Butler had previously rented out rooms to aide-de-camp and Arthur's friend William Fremantle without problem, a fact that is relatively telling.[57]

Another affair of Arthur's took place one sunny afternoon when the beautiful Lady Aldborough – the mistress of the Lord Lieutenant of Ireland himself (the Marquess Buckingham's tenure ended in 1789 and he was replaced by John Fane, 10th Earl of Westmorland) whose relationship with the Lord Lieutenant was an open secret – graced Arthur by offering him a ride in her carriage to a picnic taking place on the outskirts of Dublin. Flattered,

Arthur accepted the offer, however Lady Aldborough ejected him from the carriage halfway to the picnic, arguing that his company had struck her as "dull". What actually took place in the carriage, however, is likely forever to remain a mystery.[58] The next event relating to Arthur's adolescent loves – this one being much less flattering – took place in Dublin in 1790. Together with Fremantle, they were fined ten pounds each for an "imbroglio" in which they attempted to forcefully enter the home of a Dublin lady, Mrs Anna Sweetenham (most likely in a considerable state of intoxication), who refused to open the door. The exact reason they were trying to enter the home is unknown, but it is highly likely that she had an involvement with one of the men. The relatively mild punishment in the form of a rather minor fine (although £10 was a considerable sum for most people in Ireland in those days) for the two "trouble-makers" is proof of the fact that the whole situation seemed more comic to the court than tragic. Nonetheless, in 1792, after his previous and often Kundera-like "laughable loves", Arthur began in all seriousness to court a young lady named Kitty Pakenham* (the daughter of Edward Pakenham, Baron Longford, who was a wealthy pioneer of new revolutionary technologies in agriculture), with whom he began to fall deeply in love. Kitty, who was twenty years old at the time and three years younger than Arthur, was a charming, petite, slim, brown-haired girl with gentle features, fair skin, and grey-brown eyes. Maria Edgeworth, a distant relative of the Pakenhams and later a famous Anglo-Irish author of works including *Castle Rackrent* (1800) and *Belinda* (1801) became one of her best friends. Both of the young ladies were fond of the world surrounding Dublin's elite in which their beauty was highly desired. Kitty, known as 'Lady Longford's Lilly' because of her fair skin, had a whole score of admirers and suitors in Dublin.[59]

The Pakenham Family lived at Pakenham Hall (now known as Tullynally Castle), an aristocratic estate located roughly sixty miles west of Dublin and approximately thirty miles from Dangan Castle, the Wellesleys' former family estate. Lord Longford naturally also owned a home directly in Dublin. It is thus highly probable that Arthur had already met Kitty prior to 1792, but their relationship now took on a serious air, as Kitty was certainly not indifferent to Arthur's feelings. Years later, she claimed to have fallen in love with Arthur literally "at first sight". The young aide-de-camp Wesley, who since 1791 was captain of the 58th Regiment of Foot,

* Full name Catherine Dorothea Sarah Pakenham.

began to pay regular visits not only to Pakenham Hall, but to the Dublin home of Kitty's father, where the young couple would often meet. The picturesque surroundings of Lough Derravaragh, located several dozen miles west of Dublin, offered some of the most romantic places for their mutual appointments. Kitty's Uncle Thomas Pakenham, a captain in the Royal Navy, lived nearby and willingly housed the couple on visits. A passion for music and literature were the primary interests that the enamoured couple shared. Kitty was well-read, wrote poetry and, as a deeply devout person who took her Christian duties very seriously. All of these traits, including her appearance, must have made a strong impression on Arthur, as meeting her had a significant influence on his life in the years to come. The smitten Arthur therefore came forward with his intention to marry her. He subsequently asked Edward Pakenham for his daughter's hand in marriage, as he was the one who had the final word on the matter. Kitty's father refused Arthur, but evidently intimated to him rather affably during their conversation that a mere infantry captain (albeit an aide-de-camp to the Irish Lord Lieutenant) and a middle son without money or title was not a sufficiently good "catch", implying that Arthur should work hard on bettering himself. In doing so, Pakenham at least gave Arthur a certain hope that, if he could attain a better standing in the future and gain a certain amount of property, the marriage could perhaps take place.[60] After the conversation with Lord Longford, Arthur bid farewell to his youthful amusements and began to devote himself feverishly to his career. He ceased to attend card games and, in their place, borrowed a considerable sum of money from his brother Richard with which he bought the rank of major and soon after of Lieutenant-Colonel in the 33rd Regiment of Foot. He also stopped playing the violin, which in his new direction in life was only costing him precious time, and allegedly threw the instrument into the fire in a fit of rage.* In terms of his military career, he requested combat deployment together with several companies of the 33rd Regiment that were to be deployed as auxiliary corps to the West Indies despite all the risks of various tropical diseases that were one of the threats of the local conditions there. As the second-highest ranking officer of the regiment, however, he did not receive permission from the army to deploy with so

---

* Longford, p. 34. However, it seems more probable that Arthur Wesley gave or sold his violin to a friend. See: Joan Wilson, *A Soldier's Wife, Wellington's Marriage* (London 1987), p. 14.

few of the regiment's companies. This later proved to be a great stroke of good fortune for Arthur as the majority of the men in these units ended up dying of yellow fever whilst stationed in the Caribbean. [61]

Contrary to former times, he became uncommonly active in speaking in the Irish Parliament (evidently, he still had not decided whether he wanted to be a soldier or a politician) in the effort to make new influential acquaintances and a good name for himself. It should be added here that his appearances as a speaker were average; according to first-hand accounts, the young Arthur Wesley at first glance did not seem especially talented in politics or rhetoric.[62] Arthur's rather unsuccessful efforts in this area were summarized quite succinctly by Irish deputy Sir Jonah Barrington, a first-hand witness of Arthur's speeches, when he said the following about the young Wesley:

> He occasionally spoke in Parliament, but not successfully, and never on important subjects, and evinced no promise of that unparalleled celebrity and splendour which he has since reached...[63]

Nonetheless, in 1794 Arthur summoned up his courage and took off on horseback toward Pakenham Hall to ask the family for his bride-elect's hand in marriage. Because Edward Pakenham was now dead, Arthur was forced to make his request to the new Lord Longford, Kitty's brother Thomas, who was only twenty years old at the time. Despite Arthur's efforts throughout the two years prior, Thomas point blank refused Arthur's request, which was one of the greatest humiliations of his life and was compounded by the fact that it came from a young man five years his junior. In the Pakenhams' view (which was primarily the view of Kitty's mother, Lady Longford), Kitty clearly had a claim to a better groom than a twenty-five-year-old lieutenant-colonel with a significant lack of assets and prospects. Kitty's brother Ned, for instance, had already attained the rank of major at the age of seventeen.

Arthur understood why he had been refused two years earlier by Kitty's father. He began to take his life more seriously, attempting to carve out a place for himself among the British aristocracy – a place that he would claim, as was evidently his fantasy, alongside Kitty Pakenham. He believed that, through diligence, he would achieve his goal. From that point on, he began to concentrate more and more on his military career, a fact that would soon dash his hopes. Much like a lovelorn youth who is unrequited by the one he loves and joins the army, Arthur began to spend an increasing amount of time training his men in the barracks of the 33rd Regiment.

Over the course of 1794, the 33rd Regiment received their expected call to war. Arthur's regiment was to join the British corps under the command of Francis Rawdon, Earl of Moira, and immediately depart for the front in Flanders (today's Belgium).[64] There he was to engage in battle against the armies of Revolutionary France, with which Britain had already been at war for over a year.* Just before embarking and his subsequent departure to battle, Arthur penned Kitty the following lines:

> As Lord Longford's determination is founded upon prudential motives and may be changed should my situation be altered before I return to Ireland, I hope you will believe that should anything occur which may induce you and him to change your minds, my mind will remain the same. In the meantime with the best wishes for your happiness believe me, Your most attached and obedient servant, A. Wesley [65]

Judging by this letter, young Arthur was desperate. It is my assertion that he had invested all hopes in the idea that he might distinguish himself in war, gaining a higher rank and perhaps a coveted noble title of his own (In Britain primogeniture prevailed, and it was always the eldest son who inherited the noble title from his father. In Arthur's case, the eldest son Richard inherited the title of Earl of Mornington. The other sons were left to fight their way toward a title more or less on their own or seek opportunities for preferment in the Army or the Church.). His determination to stand up to the armies of Revolutionary France may also have been given added impetus by the tragic news of the execution of Arthur's much-liked director from Angers, Marcel Avril de Pignerolle, who as a loyal supporter of King Louis XVI fell victim to the French Revolution in December 1793. This was perhaps the first time in Arthur's life that he experienced a more significant existential crisis and began to ask questions regarding his purpose in life. Thus, just like many young men have done before and after him, he set off to seek out his riches and glory in war, the cruelty of which he could not yet fathom.

---

*   According to some of Wellington's biographers, including Elizabeth Longford, the young Wellington addressed his first request for Kitty's hand in marriage to her brother Thomas in the spring of 1793 (at the time when Kitty's father was already dead). Thus, it happened roughly one year later than historian Rory Muir cites.

Soldier or Politician?
The British Army
and Initial Combat
Experience in Flanders

W hen Lady Mornington, Arthur Wesley's mother, once declared that her son would only be "food for powder", she was
likely pointing out the disconsolate position of the soldier in
British society at the end of the eighteenth century and the sinking popularity of the military in the eyes of the public. Britain had established
a regular army in 1661 following the Restoration of the Stuart monarch,
Charles II. In light of the absence of a police force, the English Army
– aside from waging war – was put in charge of the suppression of rebellions and maintaining order, a fact which certainly did not add to its
popularity. For instance, during riots in Edinburgh in 1736, the captain
of the local company ordered a military intervention in order to disperse
the rebelling mob that was threatening to enter the town hall. Three
civilians were killed in the gunfire, and the captain was condemned to

death by the jury of a civil court. In the light of the circumstances, he was eventually given a royal pardon, but the reckless mob nonetheless fought their way into his cell, taking justice into their own hands and lynching the pitiable Captain John Porteous.[66] Many other such cases have been documented. An English constitutional lawyer named Dicey, who was familiar with the legal order of the time, perhaps most succinctly summarized the precarious position of the British soldier of the 18th century in the following words:

> The position of a soldier may be, both in theory and in practice, a difficult one. He may, as it has been well said, be liable to be shot by a Court-Martial if he disobeys an order, and to be hanged by a judge and jury if he obeys it.[67]

Beginning in the 18th century, however, it should be mentioned that the British Army was basking in the reflected glory of the celebrated commander John Churchill, First Duke of Marlborough, who achieved many notable victories in the War of the Spanish Succession (1701–1714) against the France of Louis XIV (sometimes called the Sun King). Britain was unambiguously victorious in the Seven Years' War (1756–1763), when it engaged primarily in battles in America and India – its primary opponent and historically traditional enemy once again being France. The valiant leadership and death of General James Wolfe in the Battle of the Plains of Abraham* (1759) enabled the British to gain considerable territory in Canada during the Seven Years' War and made Wolfe into a national hero. General Robert Clive's victory two years earlier over Siraj ud-Daulah, the Nawab of Bengal, and his French support troops at the Battle of Plassey (1757) in India, ensured British domination in that part of the world and strengthened the position of the East India Company; naturally, the British public applauded these victories enthusiastically.[68] In addition, Britain's victory in the Seven Years' War strengthened its position as the leading naval power and set it on a trajectory to become a colonial superpower. However, as the famous Old Testament proverb goes, "pride goeth before destruction", and during the following War of American Independence (1776–1781),

---

* Also known as the Battle of Quebec.

which many British initially saw as one of just many rebellions (the suppression of which was a part of the everyday work of their soldiers), the American colonists' victory proved to be a complete humiliation for the British Army. Unimaginative and reactionary British commanders proved wholly unable to react to the skilful manoeuvres of American Commander George Washington and his generals. The war was a costly setback that underscored the fact that the British Army would require reforms. Unfortunately for Britain, however, these reforms only finally took place once pressure came from the Napoleonic Wars with France and after a considerable contribution was made by the Duke of Wellington.[69]

The common soldiers who made up the regular British Army were drafted exclusively by their voluntary decision, which was wholly unique in Europe at the time. Many of these volunteers, however, did not in fact have much choice in the matter. Those who were escaping from the law often let themselves be "voluntarily" drafted into the military. Among them were burglars, poachers, procurers, rapists, and other criminal elements. Thus, in many cases, judges offered them the choice of either the military or the gallows. It is therefore no surprise that they enlisted "willingly" in such great numbers.[70] The next group of military "volunteers" entered the army out of hunger (Interestingly, to this very day the British Army still actively recruits from parts of the country that are especially economically and socially deprived.). These men were often paupers who for various reasons could not earn their own living. Nonetheless, a large proportion of soldiers was still traditionally acquired by the eloquence, enticement, and promises of recruiting officers, who often purchased alcohol for their potential recruits. Every newly enlisted recruit also received the so-called "King's shilling" on the spot. The heartstrings of patriotism were also naturally plucked, but promises of undying glory, women, and fabulous wealth remained the primary allure. Thus, *"Women, Wealth, and Glory!"* was the slogan used around Britain by recruiting officers.[71] The reality of a soldier's everyday life was of course diametrically different.

The draft system of British ranks and the situation at the end of the 18th century is described by many authors, including historian Michael Howard, who very accurately writes about Wellington and the British Army in his essay:

The ranks were still made up of long-serving volunteers who had said good-bye virtually for ever to civil life. They were tempted in by the immediate lure of bounty money, and once in they endured appalling hardships, not so much on active service – which must at times have come as a blessed relief – as in disease-ridden tropical garrisons where they might languish for twenty years or more, and in the foetid squalor of overcrowded barracks at home. Drink was their only solace and escape, and discipline could be enforced only by plentiful application of the lash. Service under such conditions – and they were the normal conditions of the eighteen century – attracted only the desperate. The Army was regarded as a midden fit only for outcasts...[72]

With some exceptions, officers of the British Army primarily hailed from the ranks of the aristocracy and gained their individual positions based on contacts, nepotism and money. Therefore, it was wholly routine that an officer's rank was bought and sold just as any other commodity. Due to this fact the army was rife with corruption, which created a clientelist system, while individual military abilities and talent were invariably a secondary consideration. Promotions from the rank and file of the army to the status of even the lowest rank of officer rarely took place.[73] A practical example of the business of "rank trafficking" in the British Army was mentioned in the previous chapter concerning Arthur Wesley who, in his efforts to gain the favour of Kitty's father, quickly became a lieutenant-colonel from a mere captain by taking advantage of the money and influence of his brother, a deputy in parliament. Thanks to this fact, he commanded a whole battalion (of roughly 800 men) at the age of twenty five without ever having seen battle, even from afar. If we are to return to the example of "Ned" Pakenham, Kitty's brother (who was meant to serve as a role-model to Arthur), we find that he bought the rank of major when he was only seventeen years old, becoming the *de facto* deputy of a battalion commander at such a young age. In the moments they were faced with true combat, it was therefore no surprise that these inexperienced youths would sometimes lose their nerve. If these situations were not remedied by one of the considerably more experienced lower ranking officers or sergeants, they could end in absolute catastrophe. In his monumental and hitherto unmatched thirty-volume work on the British Army, Sir John William Fortescue described the corps of officers in the beginning of the 18th century quite succinctly:

The commanders of the new army who had been juggled into seniority by the Government and the army-brokers, were not fit to command a company, much less a brigade. Some of them were boys of twenty-one who knew nothing of their simplest duties. Though they went cheerfully into action, they looked upon the whole campaign as an elaborate picnic. [74]

Military historian Michael Howard added:

There was some professional improvement as the war [with Revolutionary and later Napoleonic France] proceeded, but for the majority of officers the regiment was an agreeable club, a uniformed extension of Bucks' or Boodles' [London gentlemen's clubs, where alcohol was abundant, smoking was permitted, and men engaged heavily in gambling], and a campaign was equally an extension of the fox hunting with which they normally passed winter.[75]

Technically speaking, the British Army had barely changed over the course of the 18th century. The infantry, cavalry, and artillery made up the three main types of ground troops, while the system of fortifications of the time had remained for over one hundred years in the style of Sébastien de Vauban (1633–1707), a famous military engineer of French monarch Louis XIV. For clarification, the Vauban style of constructing fortifications refers to fortifications of a star-shaped character, often accompanied by smaller outlying redoubts. In the Czech lands, a typical example of this type of military site is the old fortification town of Josefov.* Due to the pressure of aggression on the part of revolutionary France and later Emperor Napoleon, however, great changes in military tactics and technology took place during Wellington's lifetime.[76] The primary weapon of the foot-soldier in the 18th century was a flintlock musket, which gradually replaced the already antiquated matchlock muskets. Specifically, from the 1730s onwards the British Army exclusively used the Brown Bess musket, which in its era was evidently the most proficient mass-produced weapon of its kind in the world. In various versions, it remained in use

---

* In the former Habsburg Monarchy, three typical examples of this type of military site are still preserved: the old fortification town of Josefov (Bohemia), the Terezín fortress (Bohemia), and the Leopoldov fortress (Slovakia). Terezín (or Therezienstatd) was used during WWII as a concentration camp while Leopoldov was a notorious prison during the communist era in Czechoslovakia (1948-1989) that housed political prisoners who protested against the Comunist regime.

until the time of the Indian Mutiny (1857).[77] Perhaps the most convincing proof of how popular the weapon was can be found in the fact that, in terms of British military historiography, the whole epoch is sometimes referred to as the Age of Brown Bess. In addition to this legendary weapon, another essential element of the British infantryman's equipment was the famous red coat. From a British perspective, we can also speak of this period (i.e. the 18th and 19th centuries) as the Era of the Redcoats. In order for the infantryman to load his Brown Bess in battle, he first had to tear open a paper cartridge full of powder with his teeth, pour a portion of the powder into the pan of the flintlock that was located just above the hammer of the weapon, then close the pan to keep the powder in place. The remaining powder from the cartridge had to be poured into the weapon's barrel. A bullet was then added atop the powder, while the remainder of the paper was used as padding to keep the bullet in place. Now the musket's hammer, which was fitted with a piece of flint, could finally be cocked, allowing the musket to be fired. After the trigger was pulled, the flintlock would strike the pan, igniting the gunpowder. This spark then ignited the powder charge that was poured down the barrel and the gun would fire. After intense training, a soldier was able to repeat this almost machine-like and rather complicated process three to four times per minute. Over time, the British infantry thus built up a reputation of being the best in the world in loading and firing thanks to their strict discipline.[78]

Nonetheless, the strength of this weapon was not as threatening as it may have seemed at first glance. From a modern perspective, the gun's greatest shortcoming was its abysmal record for accuracy. An expert on firearms of the time, British General George Hanger, summarized the musket in the Age of Brown Bess thus:

> A soldier's musket, if not exceedingly ill bored and very crooked, as many are, will strike the figure of man at 80 yards, it may even at a hundred, but a soldier must be very unfortunate indeed who shall be wounded by a common musket at 150 yards, provided his antagonist aims at him, and, as to firing at a man at 200 yards with a common musket, you may just as well fire at the moon and have the same hopes of hitting your object. [79]

The musket was deadliest in battle at a distance of 50 to 60 yards. However, allowing the enemy to come this close was truly a challenge of nerves for the soldiers involved. In order for a general victory to be scored, it was essential for soldiers to be led by a good commander who could accurately estimate the best moment to give the order to fire. Nonetheless, an experiment at the time carried out by the Prussian Army showed that up to forty percent of soldiers would still miss their mark at the "ideal distance" of fifty yards.[80] In addition, another unfavourable element of the weapon was that it could completely fail to fire, as the process of firing the musket included many interdependent variables. Faults included worn barrels and flints or insufficient ignition of the powder in the pan. The weather was naturally also a factor that could make using the musket more difficult. Heavy rain and high wind could render the musket nearly impossible to fire.

In regard to the organization of the British infantry, the basic combat unit was the battalion, which was most often made up of five hundred to eight hundred men. During military campaigns, which often took place far away from the regiment's home barracks in Britain, the number of soldiers naturally often decreased significantly due to the fallen, injured, and ill. The smallest number of men with which a battalion could still effectively operate was roughly three hundred soldiers. Each regiment was commonly made up of two battalions; it was common, however, that only one was sent into combat while the other (reserve) battalion stayed in Britain, where it drafted and trained newcomers and fulfilled its important function of policing. Men from its ranks were also naturally sent to replenish those of the battalion that were at war. Each regiment was then allotted an ordinal number. For instance, when referring to the fighting 33rd Regiment in which the young Wellington served, we are referring only to the first battalion of the 33rd Regiment.[81] The whole battalion was always commanded by a lieutenant-colonel who was represented by two majors. Each battalion was made up of eight companies, each of which was led by one captain, who – similarly to the lieutenant-colonel – had two subordinate officers, a lieutenant and an ensign. The number of privates of one company ranged from thirty to one hundred soldiers. The officers of a company also had several sergeants and corporals at their disposal, the numbers of which always depended on the size of the individual company. In large-scale battles, individual battalions were joined to form brigades and divisions: a brigade was made up of three battalions (roughly two thousand men) and, similarly, a division was made up of three brigades (approximately six thousand men). Both brigades and divisions were commanded by a general; only the commander-in-chief of the army stood above the division generals in the hierarchy of the British Army.[82]

In battle throughout the whole 18th century, battalions mostly fought using linear tactics divided into three lines, one behind the other. The basic formation for movement during field campaigns was a "route column" in which the individual men stood in ordered lines four to six men wide, while the length of the column depended on the size of the battalion. If the infantry battalion came into direct contact with the enemy cavalry and depending on the severity of the situation, it could create a defensive square formation most commonly known as an "infantry square" or "carré". The efficiency of the infantry square's defence against cavalry attack stemmed from the first line of soldiers, who formed the square by assuming a kneeling position, fixing the butt of their muskets into the ground with their bayonets pointing upward. This line of glaring bayonets, which basically functioned like spears, would suddenly "bristle" against attacking enemy cavalry. This also allowed the other soldiers to fire comfortably over the heads of the first line of these "lancers". The officers of the battalion were located at the centre of the square from where they organised defence and gave their men individual orders.[83]

The next crucial element of armies of the time – the cavalry – was traditionally divided into light and heavy cavalry in the British Army. To be more exact, it was divided into light and heavy dragoons. In addition, the British were unique in the fact that, contrary to the majority of the armies of major European powers at the time, they did not use "cuirassiers". As direct descendants of the armour-clad medieval knights, these soldiers still wore an iron cuirass (which now covered only the chest) and thanks to this were commonly considered to be the heaviest type of cavalry in the 18th century. The British heavy cavalry thus differed from the light cavalry not in its use of cuirasses, but in larger breeds of horses and heavier types of weapons. In terms of weapons, the British heavy cavalry used long cavalry backswords with a straight blade. In battle, the heavy cavalry served most often to strike definitive blows, which were led at full gallop on the enemy's weakened lines. An equally important task of the heavy cavalry was naturally the pursuit of a defeated enemy. In contrast, the light cavalry used smaller but sturdier breeds of horses and was therefore

used primarily for reconnaissance in the surrounding terrain and collecting supplies. Contrary to heavy backswords, the light dragoons wielded
curved cavalry sabres in battle.[84] In terms of organization, the cavalry
was most often organized into units called squadrons. Each regiment was
made up of four squadrons while the overall number of cavalry regiments
– just like infantry battalions – was ideally around eight hundred men. In
the midst of war, however, the British cavalry regiments usually consisted
of five to six hundred cavaliers, who as primary groupings commonly
formed half-squadrons of roughly one hundred riders, which proved over
time to be the most effectively-commanded battle grouping in the heat
of war.[85]

The last of the primary elements of armies in the era of the Napoleonic
Wars was the artillery. At the end of the 18th century, the artillery was divided up according to weight of the artillery shell that the given cannon
could fire. Smaller six or twelve-pound cannons (i.e. firing projectiles
of six to twelve pounds) were attached to limbers (a two-wheeled cart
which supports an artillery piece during transportation) and, because
they were not extremely heavy, they could be manoeuvred about the field
during battle. This field artillery was also called cavalry artillery, as it was
most often carted around the battlefield by three or four pairs of horses.
The Swedes were the first to use mobile field cannons in this way during
the Thirty Years' War (1618–48). Until then, heavy cannons had been
transported with great effort prior to battle to the most suitable positions according to a commander's judgment and were fired throughout
the battle without a chance to react to the manoeuvres of the enemy.
Heavier static artillery – for example twenty-four or thirty-two pound
cannons – were used in the 18th century almost exclusively for sieges on
cities and fortresses. After these heavier-calibre cannons were transported
with great effort to artillery batteries that had been previously dug by
military engineers (often known as sappers), their main task was to create
breaches in fortifications before the following infantry assault was led on
the given town or fortress.[86] In the period of the Napoleonic Wars, three
primary types of projectiles were used in cannons. The oldest and most
common type of shell was the classic cannon ball, which was designated for firing at long distances. For field artillery, its effective range was
roughly 800 yards. On the open battlefield, however, so-called "canister
shot" was unrivalled in terms of its devastating effect. Simply speaking,

canister was a small tin container filled with musket balls that tore open as soon as it was fired, striking the ranks of the enemy with a deadly hail of projectiles. With this fearsome cartridge, cannons could be transformed into massive "early-modern" shotguns. Due to its terrifying power, correct use of canister shot could easily tip the scales of victory in favour of one side or the other. Its indisputable weak point, however, remained its limited range, as canister was effective at a maximum distance of 400 yards. The third type of artillery munitions was the spherical case, which in principle was a hollow metal cannonball that, similar to canister, was filled with musket balls. However, contrary to canister shot, the explosion of this shell was timed according to the length of its fuse, which was located directly in the centre of the grenade. This allowed spherical shells to explode directly above the heads of the advancing enemy or directly in their ranks, also yielding devastating effects. The inventor of this terrifying ammunition was a lieutenant of the British Royal Artillery Henry Shrapnel (whose surname is now synonymous for the fragments of exploding grenades and shells) and only the British had possession of it for some time, a fact which naturally provided the British Army with a considerable advantage.[87]

Above is thus a general overview of the makeup of the British Army at the time when Arthur Wesley, already a lieutenant-colonel and commander of the 33rd Regiment, embarked in mid-summer 1794 in the Irish port town of Cork together with his soldiers, sailing for the Belgian port of Ostend. From there they would soon join the ranks of the First Coalition in the battle against Revolutionary France. Since April 1792, France had been at war with Austria (i.e. the Habsburg Monarchy – the term Austria can be used correctly from 1804 on, when the Austrian Archduke and King of Bohemia and Hungary Francis II had himself crowned Francis I, Emperor of Austria – for the sake of simplification, the term Austria will be used in contexts before 1804 as well) after it attacked Flanders (the area of today's Belgium that at the time belonged to the territories of the Habsburg Monarch Francis II as the Austrian Netherlands).

The National Legislative Assembly, which momentarily stood at the head of Revolutionary France (which despite that fact was still officially a monarchy under the rule of Louis XVI), called for an immediate war, as its newly elected deputies planned to use their armies to export the new revolutionary ideas – symbolized by the three famous words: *Liberté*, *Egalité*, *Fraternité* – to all of Europe. At the same time, they believed that, similarly to France, absolutist monarchies would be overthrown in other states around Europe. In addition, even King Louis XVI himself was in favour of war, as he hoped that, in the event that European powers were successful in defeating his country, the forces of Revolution would be weakened and discredited and his power would be returned to him by foreign rulers, chiefly by Francis II, the Holy Roman Emperor, whose aunt was Louis XVI's wife Marie Antoinette.

As a reaction to French aggression against Francis II (against whom France – in the naïve hope that the Princes of the Holy Roman Empire would not fight against it – declared war, but did so against him "only" as the King of Bohemia and Hungary and not the Emperor of the Holy Roman Empire), Prussia also declared war on France based on a recent prior treaty of alliance with Austria. After doing so, Prussia sent its army to help the Austrians in Belgium under the command of Charles William Ferdinand, Duke of Brunswick. France, which now dearly needed to mobilize its large-scale army against the growing superiority of the enemy's armies, was in a state of panic. The French revolutionary government quickly and publicly declared its propaganda slogan of *"La patrie en danger"* (The Country in Danger), by which it meant to call to the army as many people as it could from the ranks of the citizenry. This ostentatious and populist call to arms did indeed attract scores of spirited volunteers from the same ranks that witnessed the beginning of the French Revolution, which is traditionally considered to have started on 14th July 1789 when the Bastille fortress and prison in Paris fell. These volunteers came from a newly constructed and (theoretically) absolutely equal civil society that firmly believed in the revolutionary ideas that it promoted. In addition, on 20th September 1792 the French Revolutionary Army of General Charles François Dumouriez pulled off a stunning and surprise victory over the Prussians led by the Duke of Brunswick at Valmy, leading to a definitive overthrow of Louis XVI's constitutional monarchy in Paris the next day and subsequently replacing it with a republic. A few weeks later on 6th November, much to the delight of the Parisians, the French Revolutionary Army also managed to defeat the Austrians led by Duke Albert of Saxe-Teschen, the governor of the Austrian Netherlands, at Jemappes.[88] After this defeat, Austrian troops nonetheless continued to defend their territory; however, Prussian forces gradually began to withdraw from Flanders as a result of their defeat at the Battle of Valmy, yet another French victory in which Dumouriez had been instrumental, this time ably assisted by General François Christophe Kellerman.

In this situation, which was not developing particularly well for the members of the first Anti-French Coalition, Britain officially entered the war with revolutionary France in February 1793. Great Britain, similarly to the majority of Europe, was shocked by the execution of French ruler Louis XVI, which took place on 21st January of this epochal year (1793)*. Shortly after in March, it seemed that the tables were turning again in favour of the allies of the first Anti-French Coalition and that the whole revolution would soon be over. France, including Dumouriez, had suffered a crushing defeat by the Austrians at Neerwinden, where, among other elements, regiments drafted from Bohemian territory played a decisive role in the Austrian victory, sparking the deepest crisis hitherto in the French revolutionary regime.[89] It is also of interest to note that two young officers from the community of Bohemian nobility had also fought in the ranks of the Habsburg Imperial Army in Flanders: Karl Philipp, Prince of Schwarzenberg, future commander-in-chief of the Sixth Anti-Napoleonic Coalition and victor of the famous 'Battle of the Nations' at Leipzig, and his future Chief-of-General Staff Joseph Radetzky von Radetz. Nonetheless, it is not highly improbable that they encountered young Arthur Wesley in Flanders (Austrian Netherlands).

The immediate fears of enemy troops marching on Paris after the French defeat at Neerwinden significantly helped spark the June coup in the French National Convention (as a legal authority, the National Legislative Assembly was substituted by the Convention – a *de facto* elected chamber of deputies – as a result of elections in June 1792), after which the infamous Reign of Terror took place in France under the direction of Maximilien Robespierre, who led the rather ironically named Committee of Public Safety that was responsible for the increasingly dictatorial rule and a climate of fear and denunciation across France. Under pressure by the Committee, the famous Decree on General Military Conscription (in French *Levée en masse*) on 23rd August 1793, which mandatorily called all fighting-fit men aged eighteen to twenty-five to arms. The decree followed on in the footsteps of the previous proclamation of the *"La patrie*

---

*   The famous French author Victor Hugo selected this "most tumultuous" year of the French
      Revolution as the theme for his very last novel, which he laconically titled *Ninety-Three*.

en danger" and was primarily based on the idea that, in addition to the insufficient size of the French professional army (whose loyalty to the new regime was doubtful at best), the ordinary citizens should arm themselves against the powerful enemies surrounding France. For the first time in human history, this new republican government ordered a general mobilization to take place, by which France acquired an army of almost one million men practically overnight. The change in establishment and generally to social order in revolutionary France led to a significant transformation of the corps of officers within the massive and newly created French Army. While before 1789 almost ninety percent of officers were of noble origin, by 1794 only three percent had remained at their posts thanks to the Revolution – the noblemen, who had by vast majority stood in opposition to the revolution, either ended up en masse on the guillotine or went into exile. Free officer positions thus presented an opportunity for civilians or soldiers from the lower ranks of the former Royal Army based on their talent and abilities, not on background, money or contacts. This initially represented a certain advantage for the French in comparison to the system of class and patronage upon which the officer corps functioned in other armies. Consider the following: before the Revolution in 1789, out of Napoleon's twenty six future field marshals, three were only privates (Jourdan, Oudinot, Bernadotte) and four sergeants (Ney, Soult, Lefebvre, Augereau), while Marshal Victor-Perrin was only a member of a military band in the ranks of the former Royal Army. Nonetheless, within a few years a clientelist system would also be created in the French Army.[90]

In the meantime, Britain sent an army corps of 40,000 men to the battlefield in Flanders made up of units from Britain and soldiers from Hanover, which was also ruled by British sovereign George III. Prince Frederick August, Duke of York, the second-born son of the British monarch, took personal command of the corps. With his expeditionary army, the Duke of York laid siege to the Port of Dunkirk in September 1793; the whole campaign, however, proved to be one great catastrophe since its very onset. Due to the significant increase in French forces gained by mass mobilization and poor cooperation with the Royal Navy, his expeditionary corps soon found itself in danger of being surrounded. Therefore, the Duke immediately gave orders to retreat, which in and of itself was certainly not a poor decision. However, due to the woeful leadership of the British officer corps, which lacked almost all signs of authority, a wave of panic spread through the British troops like an epidemic, and the Duke of York proved to be insufficiently authoritative in preventing this from happening. Thus, instead of an organized retreat, the whole action was transformed into an unseemly and chaotic rush to safety. In addition to their honour, the British also left behind thirty siege cannons, three hundred barrels of gunpowder, and a sizeable quantity of precious food supplies in Dunkirk for the French to claim.

The British Army was naturally ridiculed by the public and the morning papers abounded with disparaging caricatures of the Duke of York. As a result of these events, Frederick August gained something of a reputation as a man who preferred various amusements such as wild drinking and female company over action during his campaign. In his defence, however, it should be added that these criticisms were not wholly warranted; the Duke of York was certainly not lacking in courage and enthusiasm, but his natural authority and commanding talent did leave something to be desired. Nonetheless, he would later prove himself to be a skilled administrator and a successful reformer of the British Army, and Wellington himself even praised him for some of his later reforms.[91]

In the middle of July 1794, in this miserable situation for the British, an auxiliary corps disembarked in the Belgian port of Ostend under the command of Francis Rawdon, Earl of Moira. Among the corps' ranks was Arthur Wesley and his 33rd Regiment. Moira and his men were to attempt to turn the war in Flanders in the favour of the Anti-French Coalition, and its first task was to defend Ostend from the advancing French. Because the French units of Marshal Jean-Baptiste Jourdan had in the meantime secured a decisive victory over the Austrians (who were allies of Britain) at the Battle of Fleurus, they were now suddenly advancing on Moira's troops in vastly superior numbers. For this reason, Moira's whole corps therefore received immediate orders to leave the small Belgian port town to its own fate and move to Antwerp, where the main British forces commanded by the Duke of York were now located. The main portion of Moira's corps marched to the Duke of York's units along dry land while the majority of supplies, injured or sick men, and all valuables in Ostend were to be evacuated by sea aboard British vessels. Together with several other units, Wesley's regiment was tasked with covering the whole operation, and for this purpose Moira went so far as to allow the young

Lieutenant-Colonel Wesley to command the whole brigade. The British managed to embark in time without difficulty and at this juncture a battle with the superior French forces did not take place. It is my assertion that this trust on Moira's behalf is proof of the fact that he saw in Arthur Wesley an organizationally skilled regimental commander and a reliable, highly principled soldier. In addition, both Moira and Wesley were of Anglo-Irish stock, a factor that might also have played its part. After the successful evacuation from Ostend, Moira's corps – including Wesley's 33rd Regiment, which arrived by boat – joined the main British Army of the Duke of York just outside of Antwerp. Nonetheless, before the end of July 1794 the defeated Austrians withdrew definitively from Flanders (Austrian Netherlands) as a result of the debacle at Fleurus and sought to continue the fight in the Rhineland and Northern Italy. This left Britain completely alone in Flanders, and the position of the Duke of York's forces therefore became extremely precarious.

Partially due to these circumstances, Arthur Wesley soon found himself for the first time in his life in the centre of real battle. Similar to what happened at Ostend, his 33rd Regiment received orders in the ranks of the British rear-guard led by Sir Ralph Abercromby to cover the retreat of the main British forces (now the whole army of the Duke of York) that were camped near the small Belgian town of Boxtel from French domination.[92] This time, however, while covering the British retreat his regiment was attacked by French cavalry, which pursued the British units that had been defeated in the battle previously and were now fleeing. Arthur first ordered the 33rd to form a line, allowing the enemy to come within the ideal 50-yard distance for musket fire, and subsequently gave the order to fire. The 33rd Regiment repeated this process several times under the command of the young Lieutenant-Colonel Wesley, whereupon the attacking Frenchmen willingly drew back from the hail of bullets. As a result, the French chose not to interfere in any other attempts by the British to retreat from Boxtel. During the skirmish, Arthur Wesley clearly experienced the considerable firepower of a well-trained British infantry battalion first-hand as it had managed to spread out properly in a line against the enemy. This would prove to be a valuable lesson for him in the future. It is worth noting that the young Wellington did not order his battalion to assume a safer square formation (carré) against the cavalry, which would have limited their firepower. Instead, he opted for a line formation that allowed for the highest number of soldiers' muskets to fire as possible – this decision in view of the situation was undoubtedly the correct one and was one that would pay off many times in the future.

One of the British officers in combat at Boxtel described the whole event in the following manner:

> Fortunately the Thirty-Third regiment was formed in the rear, and opening to allow (the fugitives) to pass, wheeled up, and initially throwing a few cool and well-directed volleys into the enemy's squadrons obliged him to decamp precipitately, enabling Abercromby to retire without further molestation.[93]

Wellington's first experience with battle at Boxtel was recorded by one of his first Victorian biographers in the following (in regard to the time the work was created, however, it should be noted that the record is somewhat exaggerated):

> The French hussars advanced to charge, and, for a minute, the situation of the embarrassed [British] troops was most alarming. Perceiving the disorder, Colonel Wellesley [correctly Lieutenant-Colonel Wesley at that time] deployed 33d into line, immediately in rear of the household troops. Opening his centre files, he permitted the broken cavalry to retire, and then closing up his ranks again, occupied the road, and held the enemy in check. The French advanced with their usual confidence, and the 33d, reserving their fire, coolly until the regiment received their colonel's [correctly Lieutenant-Colonel's] order, and delivered a close and searching volley, that fell with murderous effect into the crowded ranks of the Republicans, and their rapid and well-directed fusillade completed the enemy's repulse.[94]

For their exemplary behaviour in battle, the 33rd and its Lieutenant-Colonel Wesley subsequently received justified commendation from the Duke of York himself, which was conveyed to Wesley and his regiment personally by Sir Abercromby: 'The Duke of York's thanks and his to the Thirty-Third for their good conduct on the 15th [September 1794]'.[95] However, this commendation did not bring Arthur any glory or improvement in rank and, frankly speaking, may at most have served to warm his heart.[96] Nonetheless, "warmth" of any kind would soon be welcomed by the British, as the cruel winter was now approaching. Meanwhile, Arthur

Wesley was becoming increasingly frustrated with the whole campaign, which seemed to have morphed into one of constant British retreat.

Wesley and his regiment soon followed the whole British Army, which in December 1794 retreated past the Waal River, where the British attempted to hold their defensive line throughout the winter, waiting passively to see what step the enemy would take next and going on seemingly pointless manoeuvres that often took place in the middle of the night. In a letter addressed to his cousin, Sir Chichester Fortescue, Arthur Wesley described the quandary of the British command mentioned above, but also did not neglect to make note of the interesting and almost compassionate relationship between the soldiers of both camps, as they struggled with the harsh winter weather in the merciless field conditions on both sides of the river:

> At present the French keep us in a perpetual state of alarm, we turn out once, sometimes twice, every night, the officers and men are harassed to death, and if we are not relieved, I believe there will be very few of the latter remaining shortly. I have not had my clothes off my back for a long time, and generally spend the greatest part of the night upon the bank of the river... [Waal] Although the French annoy us much at night they are very entertaining during the daytime, they are perpetually chattering with our officers and soldiers, and dance the carmagnol* upon the opposite bank whenever we desire them, but occasionally the spectators on our side are interrupted in the middle of the dance by a canon-ball from theirs.[97]

The continuing failures of the British campaign in Flanders and the absolute ineffectiveness of the high command naturally gave rise to sarcastic comments and ridicule in Britain at the expense of the Duke of York. The following spiteful rhyme referring to the fruitless retreats and manoeuvres of the British commander soon spread like wildfire through the streets of London: 'The noble Duke of York. He had ten thousand men, He marched them up to the top of the hill, And he marched them down again.'[98] Although the Duke of York was the son of the British

---

* This is the both the name of the song and the vigorous dance that accompanied the melody of *La Carmagnole*. The origin of the song is traced to 1792, although its authors are unknown. The song enjoyed significant popularity among revolutionaries and was often played while forcing the French nobility and clergy to dance to it as an act of humiliation.

King, mounting criticism and pressure in the months prior to December 1794 culminated in his position as Commander-in-Chief in Flanders being withdrawn. The British government, led by Prime Minister William Pitt the Younger, intended to replace him with the Prussian commander and experienced soldier Charles William Ferdinand, Duke of Brunswick despite his recent defeat at Valmy. In light of the state and position of the British Army, the Duke of Brunswick politely refused this "highly favourable offer". The Duke of York was succeeded by the seasoned British Lieutenant-General William Harcourt; to the great dismay of the British Crown, however, the situation on the battlefield continued to be one of seemingly endless and exhausting retreats.

Later, Wellington would blame not only the British Commander-in-Chief for the failures of the Duke of York's campaign in Flanders, he also uncompromisingly and collectively blamed all the highest commanding officers, whose ineffectuality exasperated him. Reflecting on events, he commended the behaviour of the common soldiers during this infamous British campaign, when years later he told one of his friends, Lord Ellesmere, that: 'The [British] infantry regiments were as good in proper hands as they are now [in 1837] but the system was wretched.'[99] To put this into context, Wellington commended the common soldiers of the regular Spanish Army in a similar manner for their bravery during the battles he was to experience several years later on the Iberian Peninsula. Generally speaking, due to his perfectionist nature he often could not stand the Spanish officers and their constant postponement of affairs, which was accompanied by the notorious 'mañana' (although this certainly was not the case in all situations; for example, Wellington thought highly of the Spanish General Pedro Caro, Marquis of la Romana, or General Miguel Ricardo de Álava, with whom he maintained a warm, friendly relationship until his death). Furthermore, he often blamed Spanish officers for being haughty and indifferent and not earning the respect of their men. He emphasized the fact that the corps of officers – similar to that of the British Army of the time – was made up of inexperienced commanders installed in their positions via patronage, as Wellington did not hesitate to point out in his old age to one of his friends at the time, Lord Stanhope: 'That happens from want of confidence in their officers. And how should they [Spanish troops] have any? Their officers had seen no service and knew nothing.'[100] This comment is strikingly reminiscent of Wellington's following comment about the British command during the campaign in Flanders from 1793 to 1795, and it is very probable that the Spanish officer corps during his later battles on the Iberian Peninsula in many ways strongly reminded him of it:

> I was on the Waal [in Flanders], I think, from October to January, and during all that time I only saw once one general from [British] headquarters... We had letters from England, and I declare that those letters told us more of what was passing at headquarters than we learnt from the headquarters themselves... The real reasons why I succeeded in my own campaigns is because I was always on the spot – I saw everything and did everything for myself.[101]

In my opinion, the aforementioned at least points to the fact that, contrary to his officers, Wellington did not look at his common soldiers in a condescending manner. He always strove to judge the behaviour of all members of the army in a rational way, according to the situation, and on a case-to-case basis if possible.

Wesley's negative opinion of the high command during the campaign of 1793 to 1795 was further supported by another event during which he caught sight of a British general drinking port wine with the other officers in the command headquarters when an Austrian messenger arrived with an urgent despatch directly from the camp of the Austrian command headquarters. The British general accepted the despatch, but did not open it. Instead of troubling himself with the message, he proclaimed calmly that the affair would surely wait until tomorrow, pouring himself another glass of wine. Understandably, Wesley was aghast at such irresponsible behaviour:[102]

> I have seen a packet handed in from the Austrian headquarters, and thrown aside unopened, with a remark, that will keep till tomorrow morning. It has always been a marvel to me how any one of us [in the British Army] escaped.[103]

As a result of the utter ineffectuality of the British command in terms of how they led subsequent military operations against the French, the degree of disorganization and uncertainty grew. Arthur Wesley, however, saw an even greater problem that pointed to the inability of the British generals at the time – the wholly inadequate provision of supplies. Due to irregular and miserably organized deliveries, the British were not receiving even the most basic of their needs in sufficient quantity. They suffered from a desperate lack of muskets, clothing, and – worst of all – food. Once the worst of the freezing temperatures in January 1795 had set in, the men languished and died in miserable conditions by the hundreds from hypothermia, illness, and malnutrition. Arthur Wesley himself, who had never enjoyed robust health over the course of his life hitherto, became gravely ill in the winter months of 1795 and suffered from high fevers. Two hundred men in his battalion had already succumbed to the conditions of the field. For comparison, only one of Wesley's soldiers had been killed and only seven others suffered injuries in the fight against the French. Furthermore, poor supplies drove the miserable British soldiers to looting, a fact which antagonized and alienated the local population, which conversely welcomed the French as liberators and helped them along their way. The growing desperation that loomed over the British troops during the campaign was succinctly noted by an officer of the British Army at the time:

> Despised by our enemies [the French], without discipline, confidence or exertion among ourselves, hated and more dreaded than the enemy, even by the well-disposed inhabitants of the country [Flanders/Austrian Netherlands] every disgrace and misfortune is to be expected.[104]

Realizing how important it was to have the local population on one's side in the land where the field expedition took place proved to be a crucial experience for Arthur Wesley in the years to come, and would be one he would draw on later as commander. [105]

At the beginning of January, there is proof that Arthur Wesley saw combat once again with his 33rd Regiment during a series of British retreats as he defended General Dundas' wing at the village of Meteren against French revolutionary troops. Wesley's actions at Meteren were described by another of his early Victorian biographers, journalist J. H. Stocqueler, who as an observer took part for instance in the First Anglo-Afghan War:

> Upon a subsequent occasion at Meteren…Lieutenant-Colonel Wellesley did good service in forcing a confident body of Republican troops to abandon an attack upon the position of Generals Dundas and Dalwick. Occupying Meteren with a wing of the 33rd, two field-pieces, and a squadron of Hussars, Colonel Wellesley was obliged by superior numbers to fall back upon the British lines, losing his cannon in the retrogression. Reinforced by the other wing of his regiment, he, in turn, became the assailant, regained the guns, and repulsed the enemy: then falling back upon the post of Geldermalsen, he maintained himself with the 42nd and 78th Highlanders, and the 33rd, until the French retired after repeated efforts to dislodge him.[106]

Ill, free from all illusions of war, and wholly frustrated by the dilettantism of the commanding officers, Arthur Wesley made a request to the high command in January 1795 that he be granted permission to return to Britain. The request was at first refused by the command, but in February (most likely due to the fact that, in the eyes of high command the situation in Flanders was utterly hopeless for the British troops) it was accepted, leaving Arthur Wesley to return to Ireland as a "mere" lieutenant-colonel. Shortly afterwards, he was followed by the whole British Army, which had retreated all the way to Bremen, where they were evacuated by the Royal Navy, marking the definitive withdrawal from Flanders for the defeated British troops.[107] A British officer that took part in this tragic and final retreat described the misery, illness, and death that reigned in the British camp:

> Far as the eye could reach over the whitened plain were scattered gun-limbers, wagons full of baggage, of stores, of sick men… Beside them lay the horses, dead, around them scores and hundreds of soldiers, dead, here a straggler who had staggered onto the bivouac and dropped to sleep in the arms of the frost, there a group of British and Germans [Hanoverian soldiers in the service of the British Crown] around an empty rum-cask…one and all stark, frozen, dead.[108]

During this catastrophic campaign, Arthur Wesley must have surely realized the fragility of human life at war. Death lurked everywhere – not only in the form of enemy bullets but in the horrific field conditions and for want of food. Thanks to this experience, Wellington in his later campaigns therefore placed a considerable emphasis on the importance of supplies. Years later, he noted the following about Flanders: 'I learnt what one ought not to do, and that is always something.'[109] Furthermore he once remarked: 'I learned more by seeing our own faults, and the defects of our system in the campaign of Holland [Flanders campaign], than anywhere else.'[110]

Despite all his hopes, the war did not bestow any luck upon Arthur Wesley. He gained neither riches nor glory, and thus would not win the woman of his heart. With a salary of only five hundred pounds per year and the post of Irish deputy in Trim, which he had held before his departure to war and had now taken up again, he was forced to live again partially on credit. It seemed that, for the moment, he had sobered up from his military ambitions and placed all his energy in his political career after his return to Ireland. Firstly, he applied to the post of Secretary at War under the government of the new Lord Lieutenant of Ireland John Jeffreys Pratt, 1st Marquess Camden, which would have tripled his income and at the same time represented a considerable rise in social standing. Nonetheless, there was great interest in this position and, under pressure from the competition of more influential and well-connected candidates, Arthur eventually withdrew voluntarily from the race. The second office that he strove vehemently to secure was the post of Surveyor-General to the Ordnance. The Master-General of Ordnance (of which Surveyor-General to the Ordnance was *de facto* a deputy) was in charge of administration dealing with the organization of artillery regiments, administrating fortresses in Ireland, maintaining order in the country (which was handled usually by the second, non-combat battalions), and the country's defence in the event of attack.[111] As fate would have it, however, the candidacy also proved to be an unfortunate choice for the young Arthur Wesley, as the post was held by Kitty's uncle, Sir Thomas Pakenham, who was serving in the Royal Navy and was the same man who had hosted the young enamoured couple during Arthur's visits to his home on the banks of the picturesque Lough Derravaragh. Once Arthur Wesley learned of this connection, he naturally withdrew his request, but to his great regret he was not able to forestall the offence it had caused the Pakenhams. Despite all appeals made by Arthur's older brother Richard, Lord Mornington, to the new Lord Lieutenant of Ireland, in whose services Wesley had again taken up his old role as aide-de-camp, no significant political function in the government could be found that would spell a rise in his social status. Nonetheless, Wesley travelled to London around that time, evidently to visit his brother Richard.

It was at this time that the prominent painter of the era, John Hoppner (who was contending for the favour of the British court and aristocracy with just one other brilliant British portrait painter, Thomas Lawrence), created the first preserved painting of the roughly twenty-six-year-old Arthur Wesley, the future Duke of Wellington (See Image III).[112] We can see the handsome young man in Hoppner's painting portrayed with full cheeks, a keen gaze, and (evidently on the painter's initiative) gently pursed lips, as society of the time considered a wide mouth and fleshy lips to be a sign of plebeian origin. In comparison to Wellington's later portraits, the vast majority of which were painted by Sir Thomas Lawrence, Arthur Wesley is depicted here in his lieutenant-colonel "red coat" of the 33rd Regiment and painted with longer, powdered hair in keeping with contemporary military fashion (this was evidently a wig, which Wellington later refused to wear). During this time, John Hoppner was commissioned to paint the majority of the Wesley family's members as well. In a discussion with his brother Arthur, which took place more than forty years later, Richard said the following in regard to Hoppner's portrait of the young Wellington: 'It is remarkable, much the best which exists of you, the likeness is perfect and conveys the true expression of your countenance.'[113]

After two years of futile attempts at gaining a prestigious political function, Arthur Wesley definitively gave up and subsequently decided to return to the army. At the head of his 33rd Regiment, he received an offer from the British government to be deployed to the territory of the British colonies in the Caribbean in the ranks of an army that was thirty thousand men strong and led by Wesley's former superior, Sir Abercromby, under whom he first experienced war first-hand at Boxtel. Although service in this part of the world was not overly alluring due to the high mortality rate caused by tropical diseases and lead poisoning resulting from the use of lead water pipes, Wesley, with no alternative on the horizon, decided to accept the offer. After all, he had himself endeavoured before to gain service in this part of the world in the effort to be quickly deployed while striving to make an impression on Kitty's father. After he informed Lord Camden of his decision and requested Lord Camden not to expect him for the position of aide-de-camp in the following year, the Irish Lord Lieutenant sent him the following reply in a friendly tone but nonetheless clearly indicated that Wesley could not expect a promotion any time soon if he remained in Ireland.

> I am very sorry that we are likely to lose you next winter, at the same time I cannot but approve of your determination to accompany your Regt to the West Indies [i.e. the colonies in the Caribbean and South America] as I am convinced a profession once embraced should not be given up. I shall be very glad if I can make some arrangement satisfactory to you against you come back, but if a vacancy should happen, in the Revenue Board, I fear the Speaker's [i.e. Speaker of the Irish Parliament] son must have the first.[114]

Despite his choice, fate fancied his presence elsewhere, and Arthur Wesley sailed toward the West Indies aboard the British flotilla in November 1795 but was forced back to Portsmouth in Southern England after several days due to a strong storm. When the flotilla attempted once again to sail out to the open sea following repairs to storm damage, it was forced to seek shelter a second time in the ports of Southern England due to bad weather. Thus, the whole mission was postponed indefinitely, allowing Arthur Wesley to wait out the rest of the winter of 1795–1796 in relative comfort on land. In addition, the British Government soon decided to react to French General Napoleon Bonaparte's campaign in Egypt, which posed a potential threat to the lucrative British trading enclaves in India* Based on a decision by the government, British positions in East India (today's India) were to be reinforced due to this new threat. This led Wesley and his 33rd Regiment to be redeployed to the Indian subcontinent. This event would soon prove to be one of the most crucial events in Wellington's life. Living conditions in India were certainly far more favourable than in the Caribbean; that said, many Europeans who visited India succumbed to the climate and myriad tropical diseases. Perhaps more importantly, however, a number of local rulers hostile to the British and usually paid off by the French persisted on the Indian Peninsula despite previous British victories there. It was now crucial to defeat these

---

* If Napoleon were to conquer Mameluk-ruled Egypt (i.e. almost all of today's Northern Africa), he would acquire a route via which he could attack India (i.e. through today's Iraq, Iran, Afghanistan, and Pakistan – a route which, coincidentally, was also taken by Alexander the Great). The British, who dominated India, were naturally threatened by such an advance.

leaders in order to secure the survival of the British enclaves in India. This was an extraordinary opportunity for Arthur Wesley to prove his abilities.[115] Furthermore, a potential career in India could offer a path to considerable riches. For example, men such as General Robert Clive, the Victor of the Battle of Plassey who defeated Suraj-ud-Daulah, the Nawab of Bengal who had been supported by the French in 1773, or the first British Governor-General Warren Hastings, had made fabulous fortunes there in the past whilst serving the Crown. It is therefore my assertion that, after his catastrophic campaign in Flanders, Arthur Wesley believed he should try at all costs to gain high command in order to be, as he said himself, 'always on the spot and to do everything himself'. He most likely believed that, in command, he would finally be capable of achieving a glorious victory for himself and for Britain.

CHAPTER FOUR

India: 'Citoyen Tipu' and the Battle of Assaye

During the spring of 1796 the 33rd Regiment sailed once again for the British East Indies to the port of Calcutta, Bengal on the lower Ganges delta in the east of the Indian Peninsula. For the time being, however, its commander Arthur Wesley, a newly appointed Colonel, remained in Britain. In line with his nature, which was now beginning to show clear signs of the perfectionism that Wellington would be so famous for in the future, he began to duly prepare for his stay in the east. He resigned from both his post as Irish deputy and aide-de-camp to the Lord Lieutenant of Ireland, whereupon he withdrew a considerable sum of money, the amount of fifty pounds, which he planned to spend on books that would accompany him to India.[116]

Because the receipt of this remarkable purchase has been preserved, the analysis of Wellington's library is a relatively straightforward affair. The receipt contains a total of forty one book titles and one sturdy sea chest intended to serve as a mobile library. Many of the titles consisted of multiple volumes. For instance, the complete works of Jonathan Swift (seen on the receipt as one item), which the young colonel was evidently taking on board for entertainment, was made up of twenty four volumes. The choice of Swift, the eminent cleric, essayist, political pamphleteer and satirist is in many ways an unsurprising choice as like Wellington he was also Anglo-Irish and a staunch Anglican. The books that he had already bought should also be noted. All in all, he took approximately two hundred books with him to India. Much of the library was practical in nature including histories, languages, and the life and culture of the Indian Continent. Wesley's travel library contained grammar books on Arabic, Bengali, and Persian, a number of publications devoted to previous military campaigns that had taken place on Indian soil, including the recently published *Memoirs of the Life of the Right Hon. Warren Hastings*, the renowned General Governor of the British colonies in India.[117] Other titles in Wesley's Indian travel library that are certainly of interest include Caesar's *Commentaries on the Gallic War*, which Wellington – similar to Napoleon – saw to be a timeless work in terms of the history of war, Plutarch's *Parallel Lives*, and the famous treatise by Scottish economist and philosopher Adam Smith, *The Wealth of Nations*, in which the author promotes the advantages of free trade, coining the term "the invisible hand of the market".[118] This thorough preparation for his stay in India was impressive to say the least. British officers usually passed the time on the lengthy voyage to Calcutta by drinking, gaming and gambling, and saw the trip as extremely tiresome. Arthur, however, had taken a whole carry-on library with him, which was naturally not only designated for the voyage itself, but for the time in general that he was to spend away from home.

Naturally, military practice is a completely different affair than military theory. However, it is my assertion that Wellington's well-documented and detailed theoretical preparation played a significant role in his later military and political success and became one of the stable traits of his character. The habit of preparing properly for everything that awaited him and, if possible, thinking out his plans in detail proved to be an advantage throughout the rest of his career and one that helped him vanquish many an adversary. The quest for knowledge and self-improvement marked Wellington out as something of an autodidact.

The troops reached Calcutta after an arduous journey in the middle of February 1797. Captain Elers of the 12th Regiment of Foot, who travelled with his regiment to India together with Wesley's 33rd Regiment, left us in his memoirs from the period of this voyage with a unique letter on the appearance and behaviour of the twenty-seven-year-old Arthur:

> In height he was about 5 feet, 7 inches, with a long, pale face, remarkably large aquiline nose, a clear blue eye and the blackest beard I ever saw. He was remarkably clean in his person, and I have known him shave twice in one day, which I believe was his constant practice....He spoke at this time remarkably quickly, with, I think, a very, very slight lisp.[119]

At the time of Wesley's arrival, the British presence in India had grown out of the trading initiatives and influence of the East India Company and was divided into three so-called "Presidencies", Bengal, with the port of Calcutta in the northwest, Madras in the south, and Bombay in the west of the Indian Subcontinent. Each British Presidency had its own government headed by a governor and an independent army, while all the Presidencies were administratively subject to the Governor-General in Calcutta, who held *de facto* supreme power over the British enclaves in India. Bengal, where Arthur disembarked, was clearly the richest of all Presidencies, and trade there was booming; Bombay, on the other hand, was the oldest British trading station in India and had yet to be fully developed. The other most significant states in India included the Maratha Confederation, Kingdom of Hyderabad and the Kingdom of Mysore. The Maratha Empire was a united, free grouping of rulers, many of whom had long been at constant war with one another, a fact that over time had considerably weakened the empire. Hyderabad, located roughly in the centre of the Indian Peninsula, now remained the only remnant of the once glorious Mughal Empire, and its ruler Nizam Ali Khan (Asaf Jah II) had now reached a venerable age and had no interest in creating tension.[120]

At the time, the last "big player" on the Indian scene and most hostile toward the British was Tipu Sultan, ruler of the Kingdom of Mysore, located in southern India. The Sultan was a stocky, obstinate man of small stature who had led an unsuccessful war with the British from 1790 to 1792 and was ultimately defeated by the British General of the time, Governor-General Lord Cornwallis.* Cornwallis used a more defensive

---

* Lord Charles Cornwallis was also the Commander-in-Chief of the British Army in the American Revolutionary War and thus carried his share of the blame for losing the British colonies in America. In 1781 he signed the famous British capitulation at Yorktown.

strategy of battle and, once he had the opportunity to launch an offensive on the Mysorean Sultan, was forced to end his campaign before the gates of Tipu's capital of Seringapatam, thus failing to conquer it. In addition, Tipu now maintained contact with the French, who quite willingly sent their officers to Mysore in order to train the Sultan's army – all with the aim of disserving the British. It is worth noting that the *Arthashtra,* an ancient Indian treatise on statecraft (originally written in Sanskrit), is believed to have been the first to express the ideas featured in the proverb: 'the enemy of my enemies is my friend'. As a further sign of cordial ties between the French and the Mysore, French diplomats later began to call Tipu himself 'Citoyen Tipu'*, putting the proverbial "crown" on the whole alliance.[121]

Shortly after his arrival in Calcutta, Arthur and his 33rd Regiment reported to Governor-General of British India John Shore. Lord Cornwallis, who had held the position of Governor-General before Shore, provided Arthur with a letter of recommendation for the occasion, in which he wrote that Colonel Wesley is 'a sensible man and a good officer'.[122] In a letter to a friend, Shore's son later wrote that his father seemed to be quite thrilled by the new Colonel of the 33rd Regiment and allegedly said of Arthur Wesley that he was much impressed by his 'union of strong sense and boyish playfulness which he had never seen exemplified in any other individual'.[123] One of Arthur's first steps after landing in Calcutta was to issue a special order of rules for his regiment during their deployment in India, which quite succinctly illustrates the extent of power that a colonel of the British Army had over the men of his regiment at the end of the 18th century. Arthur's order included numerous hygienic measures; one that stands out among them, for instance, is the requirement for his men to wash their feet twice a day. These rules evidently served to help keep his regiment in good health. The mandatory requirement for regular marksmanship exercises and marches were meant to help keep the soldiers fit and in good condition. The order for the mandatory attendance of all his soldiers at Sunday services is also intriguing, primarily while considering the issue of Arthur's relationship to religion.[124] Furthermore, Arthur Wesley's order strictly banned all members of his regiment from gambling. His order also dealt with the issue of the social

---

*   French for 'Citizen'.

lives of his British soldiers in terms of their relations with local women rather benevolently:

> The Soldiers are not to bring into Barracks any Common Prostitute, if they do the Sergeant must turn them out and confine the man, however if any man wishes to keep a native woman and obtains his Captain's permission to do so, there is no objection to her being in the Barracks, and the Officer will be cautious not to give permission to any but well-behaved man.[125]

Despite the fact that gambling – contrary to having social relations with local women – was strictly forbidden, Sir Amos Norcott, one of the captains of the 33rd Regiment, was anything but "well-behaved" in this respect, as he gambled his way into a considerable debt that amounted to almost 600 pounds. Norcott seriously considered selling his rank of captain and withdrawing from the army, as it seemed to be the only way for him to solve the precarious situation in which he found himself. Nevertheless, Colonel Wesley valued Norcott as a good officer and soldier to such a degree that he decided to pay his debt out of his own funds. Norcott, however, was forced to swear upon his honour that he would never gamble again – a promise which he humbly kept.

In Calcutta, Arthur soon became a regular participant in the famous and lively parties held by William Hickey, a local British lawyer and renowned *bon vivant* whose extensive memoirs are a valuable source of information on the everyday lives of the British in India. Hickey, who was hosting a St. Patrick's Day celebration (17th March 1797), requested Wesley – the only native Irishman present – to give an introductory speech before the first toast, a matter which in Hickey's words he performed 'with peculiar credit to himself'.[126] Hickey's parties often lasted until the early hours of the morning (and the St. Patrick's Day celebration was certainly no exception) and he evidently revelled in them, calling his guests, usually consisting of the British community serving in Madras, the "jovial society". In return, Hickey often received invitations to parties held by the 33rd Regiment, which in his eyes certainly did not fall short of his own soirées in terms of entertainment and the consumption of alcohol. During one of these events, the officers of the 33rd Regiment, including Colonel Wesley, allegedly made twenty two toasts (a number that, naturally, may have been exaggerated) before allowing the guests to drink at the tempo at which they pleased: 'The next day I was incapable of leaving my bed, from an excruciating headache, which I did not get rid of for eight-and-forty hours, indeed, a more severe debauch I never was engaged in in any part of the world,'[127], Hickey recalled of the whole event. During the regular "social gatherings" of the time, Hickey pointed out that Arthur was a "proficient drinker".[128] The fact that Arthur managed to "hold his share" in Hickey's eyes during these often "demanding" social events was most likely thanks to his previous experience with the frequent Dublin parties that he attended in the role of aide-de-camp to the Lord Lieutenant of Ireland.

However, Colonel Wesley's time in Calcutta was cut short as his regiment soon received orders to board a ship and join the planned attack against the Port of Manila in the Spanish-controlled Philippines, as Spain – as an ally of France – was at war with Britain at the time. As it had happened several times previously in Arthur's life, however, the mission was suddenly recalled and the 33rd Regiment returned to Calcutta. Nonetheless, during the voyage to Manila, the Regiment and its colonel Arthur Wesley were witness to a rather unusual and tragic incident. Shortly before the mission to Manila, the 33rd Regiment were assigned a new military chaplain, a respected Mr Blunt, who was Hickey's protégé and was personally recommended by him to Arthur. However, one day during the voyage, Mr Blunt appeared on deck 'abominably drunk', after which he shed his clothes and began running about, naked as the day he was born, among the soldiers and sailors from one end of the deck to the other. During his whole drunken episode he:

> exposed himself to both soldiers and sailors, running out of his cabin stark naked into the midst of them, talking all sorts of bawdy and ribaldry, and singing scraps of the most blackguard and indecent songs, so as to render himself a common laughing stock.

The day after this excess, the captain of the ship called upon Mr Blunt, who justifiably was not spared of the captain's harsh words. This was something the captain would soon regret, however, as the poor parson began to be psychologically intimidated by nearly the whole crew. In light of the situation, Mr Blunt suffered a complete mental breakdown. He locked himself in his cabin and refused to come out. The officers, who began gradually to realize the gravity of the situation, consequently attempted to convince him to serve Holy Communion while attempting in various ways to cheer him up. As the commander of the whole regiment, Arthur Wesley himself then attempted to comfort Mr Blunt by saying that: 'no one would think the worse of him for the little irregularities committed in a moment of forgetfulness: ... the most correct and cautious men were liable to be led astray by convivial society, and no blame ought to attach to a cursory debauch.' Despite all persuasion, Mr Blunt remained unwilling to abandon his cabin and ten days later he was found dead, as he had allegedly 'fretted himself to death'.[129]

After his return to Calcutta, Arthur Wesley was not satisfied by continuing to spend his free time at Mr Hickey's parties and with the other officers. He decided instead to write up an economic treatise on the state of trade in the British Presidency of Bengal (evidently influenced by Adam Smith's revolutionary publication *The Wealth of Nations*), in which, for instance, he analysed the sugar trade or the effect of the rainy seasons on Indian agriculture, something that certainly did not fit the standard activities of a typical colonel of the time. As nothing arose that might require Arthur's immediate presence in Calcutta, he took a private trip at the beginning of 1798 to Madras in order to acquaint himself firsthand with the atmosphere and conditions in another British Presidency and gain a better notion of the overall British position in India. Arthur Wesley spent two whole months in Madras. He returned from his excursion to Calcutta at the beginning of May on board the *HMS Endeavour*, as it was the most convenient connection by sea between the two British presidencies. The Captain of the *Endeavour*, Mr Eastwick, began to take a liking to Arthur during his voyage. He later recalled their acquaintance in the following words:

When I became acquainted with [Colonel Wesley] he was a very spare man, (as indeed he remained ever afterwards), most conversable and sociable, and without more pride than he ought to have. His behaviour towards ladies was exceedingly courteous... One day I happened to show him a miniature of my wife, and his first exclamation was: 'Surely she is not so handsome as this!' His living was plain, and he drank but sparingly, and this at a time when hard drinking was considered fashionable. His wants were very few, and it is amazing what little sleep he required. Whenever I was on deck, late at night or early in the morning (and in those days I never slept more than two or three hours at a stretch), I always seemed to find him pacing the quarterdeck. There was one relaxation of which he was very fond, and that was a game of high whist, which he, the two Messrs Simpson... [two other passengers on the Endeavour. It is not clear whether they were related or this was a mere coincidence of names]" and myself played regularly every evening.[130]

In mid-May 1798, Arthur received momentous news after his return from Madras. His eldest brother Richard Wesley had been nominated to the position of Governor-General of British India. Arthur's youngest brother Henry had also travelled to Calcutta together with Richard as the Governor's aide-de-camp. Furthermore, upon being nominated to the position of Governor-General, Richard decided to change the family surname from the present "Wesley" to the older, original version "Wellesley". He made the decision in order to create a stronger distinction for his family after the rise in their prestige. Some historians have posited that the name change might also have been made to distance the family from the low church Methodist associations that were synonymous with the surname Wesley. This change became a reality after he was given the office of Governor-General (i.e. for reasons that were exactly the opposite of those that led his forefather Gerald to change the name), as "Wesley" was a far more commonly used variation of the name in Britain. A change of this character after the rise in a family's status was common practice in Britain and was therefore nothing out of the ordinary.

The newly formed "Welleslian Triumvirate" now clearly aimed to join forces in order to acquire fabulous riches and a good name in India while strengthening the British position there. War seemed to be the easiest path for the Wellesley brothers to achieve these goals. The most glaringly obvious local enemy (and one who truly posed a threat to Britain) was none other than 'Citoyen Tipu'. Richard was naturally the brother most teeming with ambition, and he intended to declare war on Tipu as soon as possible. It is interesting to note that Arthur (now Wellesley), who had now been in India for longer than Richard and had a better knowledge of the local conditions, at first dissuaded his brother from declaring war and by doing so showed a great deal of providence. The Governor of Madras, Lord Edward Clive (son of the famous Robert Clive, the aforementioned victor of the Battle of Plassey) also took a strong stance against war with

Tipu and was a man whom Arthur did not wish to antagonize – Arthur was apprehensive of Clive's influential contacts in London, which could easily lead to Richard's withdrawal. In light of the new circumstances, Arthur soon left Calcutta after meeting with his brothers and sailed with the 33rd Regiment in August 1798 to Madras. Here, as Richard's mediator, he intended to convince Lord Clive of the necessity of war against Tipu.[131]

The Mysorean Sultan's growing hostility toward the British and continually more open negotiations with the French made Arthur's attempts at persuasion much easier. Tipu, known as the 'Tiger of Mysore' (Tipu means Tiger in Arabic), loathed the British with a vengeance. In addition to his undoubted courage in battle, the forty-eight-year-old Sultan had also gained notoriety for himself over the course of his life primarily by his cruelty. He kept a group of his own real tigers, to which he would throw various prisoners, and had other captives tortured by his *jettis*, a group of unusually strong men selected specifically for such a horrific task. Proof of Tipu's sadistic tendencies are best portrayed by the fact that his favourite "toy" was a wooden sculpture, which was made a yard and a half long in the shape of a tiger feeding upon a British soldier. As if this was not enough, the bowels of this morbid device were complete with a relatively complex mechanism that, once wound up, would simulate the sounds of human moans, bringing pleasure to its owner.* Furthermore, 'Citoyen Tipu' evidently planned to drive the British out of India with the help of French troops that would come to his aid from Egypt and together he and the French would share the spoils. At the beginning of August 1798, however, British Admiral Horatio Nelson inflicted a crushing defeat over the French Navy in the three-day Battle of the Nile, also known as the Battle of Aboukir Bay, (1st–3rd August 1798), significantly complicating the situation for Tipu's French allies in Egypt. General Bonaparte had defeated the Mamelukes in the Battle of the Pyramids (also known as the Battle of Embabeh) over the course of July in his Egyptian campaign, but soon failed to conquer Acre, definitively halting his advance. In addition to the capable commander of the city, who was nicknamed 'Al-Jazzar' (English for 'The Butcher' – a fact which tells much about his character),

---

* Today Tipu's morbid device can be seen in the collections of the Victoria and Albert Museum in London.

Admiral of the British Royal Navy Sir Sidney Smith, who often remains overlooked and in the shadow of Admiral Nelson, took a leading role in defeating Napoleon before the gates of Acre. As Acre was a port town, Sir Sidney Smith managed to supply the town with ease by sea and simultaneously had his ships and gunboats bombard Napoleon's soldiers. He also personally aided in the defence of the town directly from its walls.* Therefore, the only real aid that the French subsequently provided to Tipu was one mere troop of French soldiers (approximately one hundred men) who sailed from the French colony on the Island of Mauritius.[132]

In the light of this change in circumstances and after some brief hesitation, Edward Clive gave the go ahead for war against Mysore, leaving nothing to prevent an attack on Tipu's kingdom. Governor-General Richard Wellesley therefore did not hesitate and gave the order on 3rd February 1799 for the immediate launch of a campaign on the Mysorean capital of Seringapatam. Two independent British armies were sent toward Tipu's royal seat, whereupon they intended to join forces before the gates of the city and consequently conquer it, quickly putting an end to the whole war. Ideally, Tipu Sultan was to be captured dead or alive. The first British Army of roughly 20,000 men, the ranks of which included Arthur Wellesley, was commanded by General Harris, who marched on Seringapatam from the west from neighbouring Madras. The second British Army of 10,000 men under the command of General Stuart marched toward the heart of Tipu's kingdom from Bombay and planned to attack him from the northeast.[133] Europeans made up only a third of this British Army, as the majority of British troops consisted of so-called "sepoys" (or also "sipahis") – native recruits in the service of the British Army. Concerning Tipu's forces, the Sultan's army possessed approximately 30,000 men, which meant that the strength of the warring sides was in principle equal.[134]

---

* The beautiful historical city of Acre, which is located in what is now Israel and in Medieval times was the last and longest-resisting bastion of the Crusaders in the Holy Land, now stopped Napoleon as well, as he suffered his first defeat there. During this campaign, Napoleon had already massacred about 4,000 defenders of Jaffa after their surrender. Acre formally belonged under the rule of the Ottoman Empire, but in reality, it was run by a local ruler, Ahmed Pasha, nicknamed 'Al-Jazzar'. After what happened to the garrison in nearby Jaffa after surrendering to Napoleon, it is no surprise that Pasha refused to capitulate under any circumstances. Nonetheless, without the vital help of Sir Sidney Smith, the town would have most likely fallen and Napoleon would have been able to continue on in his advance. The Siege took place from 20th March to 21st May 1799.

Initially, Arthur's role in the campaign was unclear, as two older and more experienced colonels were given preference over him in the general staff of General Harris' Madras Army. Nevertheless, one of them, Arthur's good friend Colonel Ashton, suffered a fatal wound in a duel shortly before the campaign. Arthur thus took Ashton's place in Harris' staff. Before Ashton died, however, he left Arthur Wellesley his favourite white horse, a stallion named Diomed, which – being an Arabian thoroughbred of high value – clearly evoked the envy of many officers. In the meantime, Richard had scored a significant political victory in his campaign preparations by winning over the support of the Nizam of Hyderabad, as his ally against Tipu. Subsequently, Richard arranged for Arthur to be named official adviser and thus became *de facto* commander of the army corps that the Nizam sent to aid the British.

This nomination, which on Richard's part was an evident act of patronage to Arthur, who was merely a colonel, logically created far more enemies than Ashton's gift of Diomed did. Namely, it antagonized the experienced General David Baird, who was twenty years Arthur's senior and the commander of Harris' brigades who was vying for the position of Commander of the Nizam's forces.[135] This hot-blooded Scotsman had fought in the previous war against Tipu in the ranks of Lord Cornwallis' troops and was taken captive. He survived only thanks to luck, his naturally robust health, and his high rank. General Baird spent four long years in Tipu's dungeons under Seringapatam in horrific conditions, chained to his cellmate, with a bullet lodged in his shoulder. It is thus understandable that he took the campaign personally. Proof of Baird's robust and sanguine character is perhaps best evidenced in a story (albeit certainly exaggerated) of his mother's reaction after receiving the news of her son's abysmal situation in Tipu's prison, when – without grief for her son – she proclaimed: 'Lord pity the man that is chained to our Davie!'[136]

Arthur's primary task, which was given to him by General Harris, who could say only good things of Arthur, was to care for the provision of supplies for the whole army. The British would have to march two hundred and fifty miles along poor, unsurfaced roads from Madras to Seringapatam and, based on this fact, Arthur ensured that the army would have a staggering 100,000 mules to carry supplies. He also spread the word to traders and bazaar owners far and wide that the British would need quality goods throughout their journey and were willing to pay handsomely for them. Thus, crowds of Indian traders "pursued" the British in caravans along their whole journey. One British officer who took part in the campaign described the event with the following words:

> The market of General Harris's army equals in extent, and in the variety of articles exposed for sale, that of a populous city. The followers of an army are so numerous, that on a moderate calculation they may be considered to exceed the number of fighting men in the proportion of five to one. The appearance of our army on the march from a neighbouring hill is truly surprising. It may be compared with the emigration of the Israelites from Egypt...[137]

Thanks to the measures that Arthur put in place, the British soldiers had a sufficient amount of all they needed throughout the whole campaign, which was in marked contrast to the parlous situation that the British armies faced during their deployment in Flanders, a horrific experience for Arthur which he strove not to repeat by using his personal influence in organizing all necessities.[138]

The first serious clash between General Harris' Army and Tipu's soldiers took place only 30 miles from Seringapatam in the village of Mallavelly. Roughly 3,000 of the Sultan's men occupied the ridge west of the village, blocking the path to Tipu's capital city. Therefore, on Harris' orders Arthur Wellesley set off with six battalions of the Nizam's men and his 33rd Regiment into battle against the Mysorean positions in order to drive out Tipu's men from their positions and open the road to Seringapatam.[139] The Mysorean infantry took the initiative in a fairly surprising (albeit not highly tactical) attack on Arthur's advancing units while the Mysorean cavalry engaged General Baird's brigade. However, several British salvos that Arthur skilfully ordered from the saddle of Diomed soon broke down the attackers and forced them into a chaotic retreat to safety. Thus, the path to Seringapatam was again clear. In addition to this unquestionable victory, a despatch had arrived at Harris' staff in the meantime on the victory of the Bombay Army of British General Stuart, which had defeated the Mysorean Army led by Tipu himself at Sedaseer. Shaken, the Sultan and the remainder of his soldiers retreated definitively behind the walls of Seringapatam. Harris' troops, along with Arthur Wellesley, arrived to the Mysorean capital without serious incident on 5th April 1799.[140] Nonetheless, Seringapatam possessed an optimal defensive position, a fact which saved Tipu's hide in previous years during Lord Cornwallis' siege and was one that he was now relying on. His capital city of roughly 150,000 inhabitants spread out over an island in the middle of the Kaveri (Cavery) River. The distributary channels of the river provided him with a natural defence in addition to the city's walls. With the exception of Tipu's soldiers, time acted as the greatest enemy to the British Army as the river basin could be crossed relatively easily in the spring, but always burst its banks with the arrival of summer monsoons, turning the city into an impregnable water fortress. The British thus needed to conquer Seringapatam by roughly the end of May when the first monsoon rains usually began to fall. On the other hand, the city walls, which reached up to thirty feet in height, did not represent a significant barrier to British cannons. The city walls included several smaller redoubts housing the defender's cannons and three fortified gates around which the fortification walls had been strengthened, but they certainly were not the modern European star-shaped ("Vauban -type") fortifications jutting out along the whole perimeter of the bastion. In order for Harris to take Seringapatam as quickly as possible, he planned to concentrate all fire of the British siege cannons on one single spot in the city's fortifications: he intended for his units to bombard the western side of the city from the south bank of the Kaveri while Stuart's army fired upon the same spot from the north bank of the river. Once a sufficient rupture in the out-dated walls was created, the British would immediately launch an assault on the city. Digging work for the siege artillery batteries was postponed until the arrival of Stuart's Bombay Army, which according to reports from Harris' reconnaissance units was to arrive at the town any moment.[141]

In the meantime, however, Tipu's last outlying defensive positions located in the village of Sultanpettah southeast of the city needed to be destroyed. Several irregularly positioned houses that made up the village were located in a small woodland called Sultanpettah Tope, which provided ideal cover for Tipu's men during a potential attack. In addition, a relatively wide irrigation canal ran in front of the village and woodland, which the British first had to cross in their attack and which provided the Mysoreans with another useful natural defence. After his previous success at Mallavelly, Arthur Wellesley himself was tasked with taking the woodland and village. For this purpose, Harris sent him on with his

33rd Regiment, this time accompanied by only two battalions of Madras sepoys.[142] To support Wellesley's attack, Lieutenant-Colonel Robert Shawe and his 12th Regiment were ordered to take the area north of the woodland in order to hold back any reinforcements that Tipu might send from the city to the village.[143]

When Colonel Wellesley received orders to attack, night had already begun to fall on Seringapatam. During his advance through the woodland, Arthur was likely to have been ill-at-ease, as keeping his men together in the darkness was understandably a much more difficult task than in broad daylight. The soldiers, aligned in a route column with their bayonets fixed, had not been ordered to load their muskets in order to avoid an accidental shot revealing their whereabouts during the night offensive. However, Tipu's soldiers were sooner or later sure to hear their advance in the silence of the evening. In the poor terrain, the British first managed seamlessly to cross the irrigation channel; once they found themselves on the other side, however, they were greeted with a hail of salvos from Mysorean muskets in the woodland and houses of the village. Under this intense enemy fire, confusion began steadily to grow within the British ranks. Nonetheless, several of the infuriated front British lines quickly thrust forward on Arthur's orders into the woodland, where the British subsequently waged a bloody man-to-man bayonet battle, where each man was essentially left up to his own devices. Meanwhile, the battlefield had been shrouded in the Stygian dark of an Indian night, and the men could not see even a step ahead of them. Thus, the British units began increasingly to break up as a result of futile attacks on the silhouettes of Tipu's soldiers that flashed before them. Arthur became increasingly aware that he would not be able to regain control of his men in the forest in the dark. This backdrop of utter confusion was accompanied by the deafening salvos of the Sultan's rocketeers. These Indian rockets, to a certain degree more reminiscent of today's modern fireworks than military technology, did not have an overly destructive effect, but certainly had a strongly negative impact on the psyche of the British soldiers thanks to the deafening sound they emitted. Therefore, in the midst of this chaos, Arthur decided to travel back in the middle of the night for the five companies that he had left as reserves before the attack. In the darkness, however, he evidently passed by them, causing the British attack to fail completely.[144] According to eyewitnesses, a breathless Wellesley finally rushed into Harris' command station around midnight, reporting to the general that: 'He [Wellesley] had not carried the Tope'.[145] During this failed attack, a young lieutenant Fitzgerald was killed, while forty others suffered lighter or more serious injuries. Twelve British soldiers were taken captive, where a dreadful fate awaited them in the hands of Tipu's fearsome *jettis*. Colonel Wellesley himself was hit in the knee during the clash, but as it was from a bullet that had ricocheted, he was luckily only lightly bruised. The following day and with considerably greater power, Arthur took Sultanpettah Tope without incident.[146]

Vigorous discussions are still held to this day on the topic of the Battle of Sultanpettah Tope. The author of this book is personally inclined toward the interpretation that, from a strictly military perspective, it was a relatively insignificant event. General Harris did not blame Wellington in any way for the failure and wrote the following in his diary regarding the relatively inconsequential losses: 'Altogether, circumstances considered, we got off very well.'[147] Heightened interest in the whole event likely arose later due to Wellington's prestige. Therefore, in various publications a certain Colonel Richard Bayly is often quoted. In Bayly's memoirs of the night, Arthur, in tears, allegedly cried out hysterically: 'My God, I'm ruined for ever! What shall I do?'* It is surely possible that, as a result of his momentary failure, Arthur Wellesley lost his nerve and commented on the whole attack with a score of expletives; however, in light of the fact that the battle was not one of crucial importance and merely a skirmish in the Indian forest, Bayly's narrative does seem somewhat exaggerated. In addition, the veracity of Bayly's memoirs has recently been refuted quite convincingly by historian Rory Muir, who clearly proves that Bayly met Wellington for the first time in person in 1803, four years after the event. After a time, Bayly himself admitted to the fact that he took this specific report of Wellington's alleged panicked behaviour after the attack of Sultanpettah Tope from another officer whose name he was "unfortunately" unable to recall. In addition, the memoirs themselves were published toward the end of Arthur's life when Wellington was a famous figure. Bayly evidently hoped that by using sensational stories of this sort he would gain a considerable amount of wealth.[148] It is also my

---

* Richard Bayly, *Diary of Colonel Bayly, 12th Regiment, 1796–1830* (London 1896), p. 88. Although the term "diary" is used in the title of the publication, proof exists that it was written several decades after the events described.

assertion that Wellesley's character equally refutes any sort of hysterical self-pity. Therefore, considering Wellington's behaviour over the course of his whole life, this reaction cited by Bayly seems to be wholly out of character and irrelevant. Nonetheless, the fact remains that the Battle of Sultanpettah Tope was a clear defeat for Wellesley and a harsh lesson in terms of his poorly prepared nocturnal attack. As a result of the whole operation, Arthur wrote the following lines in a letter addressed to his brother Richard, in which he clearly shouldered any blame:

> My dear Mornington [Richard's title],... On the night of the 5th [of April 1799] we made an attack upon the enemy's outposts, which, at least on my side, was not quite so successful as could have been wished. The fact was that the night was very dark, that the enemy expected us, and were strongly posted in an almost impenetrable jungle. We lost an officer killed and others and some men wounded (of the 33rd), and at last, as I could not find out the post which it was desirable I should occupy, I was obliged to desist from the attack, the enemy also having retired from the post. In the morning they re-occupied it, and I attacked it again at daylight, and carried it with ease and little loss... I got a slight touch on the knee, from which I have felt no inconvenience, on the night of the 5th, and I have come to a determination, when in my power, never to suffer an attack to be made by night upon an enemy who is prepared and strongly posted, and whose posts have not been reconnoitred by daylight.[149]

Ten days after the incident in Sultanpettah Tope, the Bombay Army of General Stuart arrived as expected at Seringapatam and took its position on the north bank of the Kaveri River. Immediately after the arrival of this second army, the British dug out siege artillery batteries and began to bombard the western walls of the city according to Harris' plan. On 3rd May 1799, the artillerymen were successful in breaching the walls sufficiently, whereupon it was possible to launch a general attack on the town the following day. The assault was planned for one o'clock in the afternoon, which Harris assumed would be a relatively surprising time to carry out the whole operation, what with the sun and the fact that Indians normally rested during the heat of the day. Two British brigades were tasked with carrying out the primary attack. The first brigade attacked from Stuart's camp from the north and the second from Harris'

MAP OF CENTRAL SOUTH INDIA SHOWING THE ROUTES TAKEN BY THE ARMIES OF GENERAL HARRIS AND GENERAL STUART
February – May 1799

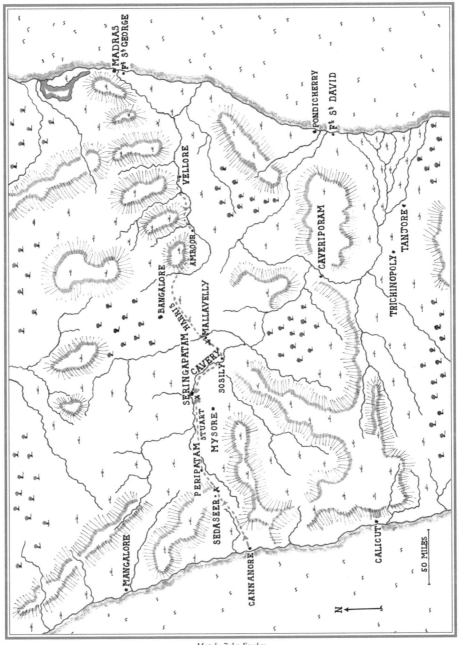

—— *Map by John Fawkes* ——

camp from the south. Directly in front of the western walls, both brigades planned to unite in one compact unit of soldiers charging with their bayonets through the breach in the wall, crushing the Mysorean defenders. This time, the honour of taking command of the whole operation was given to General Baird.[150] This natural-born Scottish warrior was as brave as a lion (as Wellington himself would later say of him) and was certainly in his rightful place as the commander of the attack. In addition, he had old scores to settle with Tipu. Thus, waving a sabre over his head in a hail of the defenders' bullets, he fearlessly drove his men through the breach in the wall with the following words: 'Now, my brave fellows, follow me, and prove yourselves worthy of the name of British soldiers!'[151] The defence of Tipu's men soon collapsed under Baird's determined, unceasing pressure, whereupon the victorious British soldiers soon furiously charged into the city. It was Tipu Sultan's own personal and brave decision to take part in the defence of the city in the area known as the Water Gate on the north side of the city's fortifications, where he was struck in the temple by a British bullet during the battle and died on the spot. Arthur Wellesley only finally entered the fray as the commander of the third reserve brigade at the moment the battle had been more or less won.

Therefore, Wellesley's chief task was to prevent the British soldiers of both brigades from plundering the city, as they had worked themselves into a militant rage during the bloody battle. He managed to protect the local population, which was to come under British rule, at the unfortunate price of the lives of four British soldiers, who were hanged as an exemplary punishment to other possible wrongdoers. Arthur personally checked Tipu's pulse, after which he was officially proclaimed dead.[152] It is highly probable that Wellesley's successful intervention, which spared many civilian lives in the Mysorean capital, partially played a role in the decision to name him Governor of Seringapatam.

Naturally, commander of the victorious attack General Baird was incandescent with rage, as he had seated himself in the Sultan's palace, expecting that his nomination to the post of Governor after his courageous actions in conquering the city would be a mere formality. In Baird's understandably biased view, Arthur Wellesley – the "favoured brat" and "the General-Governor's little brother" – had now stolen his deserved professional promotion from him for the second time in quick succession.

It should be noted that Arthur Wellesley was indeed the most suitable candidate for the post in light of all its requirements. He knew at least the basics of the local Indian dialects, but perhaps the most important factor that played in his favour was his considerable popularity among the Indians, as he always showed them respect and treated them equally, something that could certainly not be said of many of the British and, coincidentally, especially not of General Baird. Furthermore, the inhabitants of Seringapatam saw Arthur as an honourable man who had prevented British soldiers from ransacking their properties and violating their womenfolk. In a discussion with John Wilson Croker, Wellington spoke of the whole affair in the following manner:

> I never inquired the reason for his [Baird's] appointment, or of Baird's being laid aside. There were many other candidates [for Governor Seringapatam] besides Baird and myself, all senior to me, some to Baird. But I must say that I was the fit person to be selected. I had commanded the Nizam's army during the campaign, and had given universal satisfaction. I was liked by the natives... Baird was a gallant, hard-headed, lion-hearted officer, but he had no talent, no tact; had strong prejudices against the natives, and he was peculiarly disqualified from his manners, habits &c., and it was supposed his temper, for the management of them...[153]

The overall spoils gained from conquering Seringapatam amounted to roughly one million pounds, making Arthur's personal share a hefty 4,000 pounds, finally allowing him to become more or less financially independent after years of insecurity. As the initiator responsible for the whole operation, Richard was named a marquess for his successful campaign, but only in the Peerage of Ireland, a post which he disdainfully labelled as being merely a "double-gilt potato".[154] Despite this fact, he was exceedingly satisfied with the result of the campaign, as British territory in India almost doubled after Mysore was captured.[155] Arthur's commander in the victorious war with Tipu, General Harris, whom the British crown had also handsomely rewarded, was now preparing to return home to England. For this reason, Arthur did not hesitate to make use of the opportunity of his departure to send him the following wishes for the future, accompanied by thanks for his prior cooperation: 'I shall never forget the many marks of favour and kindness I have received from you, for which I again return my thanks. Whenever you go, I shall always be glad to hear of your happiness, of your success, there is no doubt.'[156]

By conquering Seringapatam, Arthur earned a rather large sum of money for the first time in his life, after which he immediately wrote to his brother Richard with the intention of paying off the old debt for Richard's purchase of his Lieutenant-Colonelcy:

> My share of the prize-money [for taking Seringapatam], amounting in jewels to about 3000 pagodas and in money to 7000 [about £4000], will enable me to pay the money which you advanced to purchase my Lieutenant-Colonelcy... I will put it into 8 per cent loan, and will send you the securities with a statement of the account as accurately made out as possible from my memory.[157]

Nonetheless, Richard, who was financially rather well off at the moment, generously refused Arthur's honest proposal and did not accept the money from his brother, who, compared to him, was still not in the best financial situation. For the majority of his first year in the office of Governor of Seringapatam, Arthur Wellesley was nonetheless occupied by an unpleasant affair. A certain Dhoondiah Waugh – a former mercenary of Tipu and a man of highly dubious character whom the Sultan himself after some time threw into prison – had escaped during the chaos surrounding the British siege of Seringapatam and was now putting together the remainder of Tipu's soldiers and other various criminal elements willing to stand against the new British rule of Mysore. After escaping, Dhoondiah had somewhat curiously declared himself Mysorean King and ordered to be called the 'King of the Two Worlds' (meaning of Earth and the Heavens, evidently for its religious overtones). By the end of 1799, his "dubious" army had been defeated (not surprisingly) by the British under the command of General Harris; Dhoondiah, however, managed to escape and continued to spark turmoil around the whole kingdom. Lord Clive, the Governor of Madras now called upon Arthur Wellesley to capture the 'King of the Two Worlds' with these explicit instructions: 'You are to pursue Dhoondiah Waugh wherever you may find him, and hang him on the first tree.'[158]

In order to track down Dhoondiah, Arthur Wellesley gathered together seven infantry battalions (roughly 5,500 men) and five cavalry regiments (roughly 1,300 cavalrymen) at the beginning of June 1800 and

STORMING OF SERINGAPATAM
4ᵗʰ May 1799

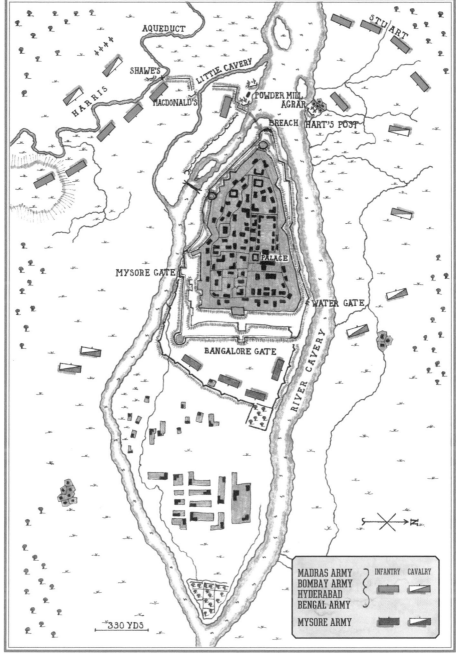

AQUEDUCT

STUART

SHAWE'S

LITTLE CAVERY

HARRIS

MACDONALD'S

POWDER MILL
AGRAR

BREACH   HART'S POST

MYSORE GATE

PALACE

WATER GATE

BANGALORE GATE

RIVER CAVERY

MADRAS ARMY	INFANTRY	CAVALRY
BOMBAY ARMY		
HYDERABAD		
BENGAL ARMY		
MYSORE ARMY		

330 YDS

N

— *Map by John Fawkes* —

took command of the subsequent manhunt. Over the summer of 1800 he pursued Dhoondiah intensely across nearly every corner of Mysore, whereupon he managed at the end of July to catch and disperse at least a portion of Dhoondiah's army.[159] After a series of defeats, the undisciplined army of the 'King of the Two Worlds' was struck by a wave of desertion; Dhoondiah himself and the most loyal of his followers, however, continued to elude Arthur. Wellesley therefore began to succumb to a bout of pessimism, proof of which can be seen in two letters that he wrote over the course of August to Lieutenant-General Close, whom he had known since his time in the campaign against Seringapatam. In the first letter, Wellesley writes: 'The war will literally have no object nor no end, if we are to follow a single man with a few horsemen to the end of the world.' The second, written nine days later, reads: 'It is clear I shall never catch him.'[160] This was evidently only a temporary stroke of melancholy, as Arthur Wellesley continued to doggedly pursue Dhoondiah, which ended a month later in success after Arthur finally pinpointed the 'King of the Two Worlds', who had surrounded himself with his newly recruited army of roughly 6,000 "soldiers".

At this time, Arthur Wellesley possessed only four cavalry regiments (roughly 1,000 men), as he had advanced in front of the remainder of his units in order to pursue Dhoondiah. Because Dhoondiah's army was made up of various criminals and rogues rather than trained soldiers, Wellesley gave the order for an immediate cavalry attack, which he personally commanded. A British officer who was a direct participant in the attack described the subsequent events that took place in quick succession:

> Col. Wellesley with that alacrity and determination which he has shewn on all occasions gave immediate orders to charge...the 19th [Light Dragoons] & 1st Regiment (Native cavalry) charged their front, while the 25th [Light Dragoons] & 2nd [Native cavalry] followed as a reserve. The regular manner in which our Cavalry moved down soon threw them into confusion, & Dhoondiah falling in the first onset they fled in all directions. We pursued the largest Body for about four miles...[161]

Proof of the doubtful abilities of Dhoondiah's "soldiers" can also be seen in the fact that Wellesley's men lost only one soldier during the attack, while sixteen men from their ranks were counted as injured after the battle. Arthur's forces slaughtered between three and four thousand enemies including the 'King of the Two Worlds' himself.[162] After the battle, the British were surprised to find Dhoondiah's young and terror-stricken son, Salabut Khan, in Dhoondiah's caravan. Arthur treated his son like a true gentleman – he took the boy into his care, travelling with him back to Seringapatam. The moment he left India, he gave Salabut full access to sufficient funds for him to finish his necessary education.

Thanks to his successful apprehension of Dhoondiah, Arthur Wellesley's nomination to the position of Governor of Seringapatam over time proved to be the right choice. Immediately after assuming the post of governor, he had the damages caused by the siege on the city repaired and had a public announcement made that British soldiers in the city's garrison were to behave in the same manner toward Indian civilians as they would to the British, naturally sparking another rise in his popularity among the local populace. The fact that he was exceptionally popular among the Indians can be seen quite clearly in retrospect in the uncommonly heartfelt thanks that were sent to him by the inhabitants of Seringapatam on the occasion of the completion of his function in the office of Mysorean Governor.[163] Ironically, the greatest problem Wellesley faced during his period in office was corruption and theft on the part of the British officers, several of whom he was forced to court-martial. These officers often stole brazenly from military stores in order to make money by selling the stolen goods on the black market. During these trials, Wellington further enhanced his reputation as an honest, upright and incorruptible man. For example, Arthur Wellesley penned the following words about the dishonest practice of some British officers to his brother Richard, Lord Mornington: 'I should be ashamed of doing any of the dirty things that I am told are done in some of the Commands...'[164] The following anecdote is linked to this period of time: once during Governor Arthur Wellesley's time in his Mysorean office, a certain raja offered him a bribe of 50,000 pounds if he disclosed confidential information on negotiations with the other Maratha rajas. Arthur reacted to the offer by saying: "Can you keep a secret?" he asked the Indian. "Yes!" the raja blurted out eagerly, expecting to be told the confidential information. "So can I", came Wellesley's chilly answer, naturally putting a quick end to the negotiations.[165]

Despite his significant successes and rising prestige, Arthur still yearned for high command of his "own military campaign" and, in 1801, Richard ultimately helped him to do so. Arthur was to lead a campaign against the French island of Mauritius. The campaign, however, was shifted to Egypt, as it seemed necessary to drive out the remainder of the French forces who remained there, albeit in significantly reduced numbers, since Napoleon's invasion in 1796. In light of the fact that the Egyptian campaign required a much more extensive military operation than the expedition to Mauritius and Arthur was still only a colonel, Richard ultimately passed high command to another more competent individual in terms of rank and length of his duty in the army (i.e. his seniority), despite the fact that he had explicitly promised it to Arthur regardless of the scale of the whole operation. As fate often appears to have a sense of humour, the man who was now given command was none other than the Scottish-born General Sir David Baird. The news that he would be given the post of commander-in-chief of the campaign now being prepared in place of Arthur Wellesley naturally bestowed upon Baird a sweet feeling of satisfaction and no doubt a degree of *schadenfreude* at the thought of Arthur Wellesley's reaction, as this decision did indeed leave Arthur overcome by a wave of bitter disappointment.[166] Therefore, Richard wrote to his brother the following lines in an attempt to explain his decision: 'You must know that I could not employ you in the chief command of so large a force as is now to proceed to Egypt without violating every rule of the service.'[167] Despite Richard's explanation for his change of heart, which he clearly did for justifiable and sensible reasons, contrary to the promise he gave, Arthur continued to feel aggrieved and saw Richard's behaviour as a clear betrayal:

> I was at the top of the tree in this country, the governments of Fort St George [the head of the British government in Madras] and Bombay, which I had served, placed unlimited confidence in me... But this supersession has ruined my prospects, founded on any service that I may have rendered.[168]

Arthur complained of Richard's actions in a letter to Henry, the youngest of the brothers. Colonel Wellesley was therefore to take part in the campaign "only" as the commander of a regiment or brigade. This fact deeply offended him – all the more so as Baird was to be his commander.

Arthur, however, fell severely ill before the campaign even began. He suffered from high fevers, followed by the skin disease called "the Malabar itch", an affliction caused by parasites. In order to be cured, he was forced undergo unpleasant baths in a solution of nitric acid.[169] Due to the illness and loss of command, he even considered leaving India. However, General Baird, who was informed of his miserable state, set off to see Arthur in person in order to support him in his difficult time, an act which demonstrated considerable magnanimity and thought. He even convinced Arthur to follow him to Egypt as his second-in-command once he had recuperated. In a conversation between Baird and the seriously ill Arthur Wellesley that took place over the patient's bed, a definitive reconciliation must have taken place between the two soldiers that soon seemed to grow into friendship. Arthur later acknowledged Baird's gentlemanly actions in the following: 'The General [Baird] behaved to me as well as a man could.'[170] The rivalry between these two erstwhile rivals thus came to an end. For a time, it seemed as if Arthur's "Malabar itch" appeared to be cured, however, the high fever returned, and he was eventually unable to take part in the expedition to Egypt. In an ironic twist of fate, General Baird did not ultimately receive high command either, as General Sir Ralph Abercromby (Arthur's former commanding officer during the Flanders campaign) was nominated at the last minute to the position of commander of the whole operation. Nonetheless, the Egyptian Campaign ended quite successfully for the British, as they defeated the French in 1801 at Alexandria, definitively ending France's attempt to rule Egypt.[171] However, the loss of Sir Abercromby, who was struck by a musket-ball in the thigh on 21st March at the Battle of Alexandria and died a week later of gangrene, took some of the gloss off the British victory. The memorial erected to General Sir Ralph Abercromby and the British fallen still stands in Alexandria (Chatby) Military and War Memorial Cemetery, and the said monument features the following inscription: *To The Memory of General Sir Ralph Abercromby KBC and the Officers and Men Who Fell At The Battle of Alexandria March 21 1801.* Historians would do well to learn a salutary lesson from this inscription as some might have taken it literally and have assumed that Abercromby had died the same day.[172]

Meanwhile, Arthur Wellesley had regained his health and once again resumed the duties of Governor of Seringapatam with vigour. According to his contemporaries, Arthur's illness had made him more solemn and, despite his still rather young age, the first of several grey hairs had begun to appear. Captain George Elers, who served at the time with Wellesley as a member of the garrison in Seringapatam, wrote the following of the everyday life of the British in the city at the time:

> We used to get up early in the morning and attend the garrison parade, and Colonel Wellesley used, of course, to be saluted by the Guards as they marched off. His dress at this time consisted of a long coat, the uniform of the 33rd Regiment, a cocked hat, white pantaloons, Hessian boots and spurs, and a large sabre, the handle solid silver, and the mounting of the scabbard of the same metal, but all gilt. He never wore powder, though it was at that time the regulation to do so. His hair was cropped close. I have heard him say he was convinced the wearing of hair powder was very prejudicial to health as impending the perspiration...[173]

In Elers' letter, it is certainly of interest to note that Arthur refused his obligation to wear a wig, which had to be powdered and was doubtlessly quite uncomfortable to wear in the hot Indian climate. This event finely illustrates the fact that, although throughout his life Wellington strictly adhered to his duty, he did not hesitate to violate a certain measure if it seemed illogical to him. According to Elers, after Arthur recuperated, he regained both his strength and good temper, upon which he began to eat more healthily and drank less alcohol after his experience of being ill:

> Colonel Wellesley kept a plain but good table. He had a very good appetite, and his favourite dish was a roast saddle of mutton and salad...He was very abstemious with wine, drank four or five glasses with people at dinner, and about a pint of claret after. He was very even in his temper, laughing and joking with those he liked, speaking in his quick way, and dwelling particularly upon the few (at that time) situations he had been placed in before the enemy, the arrangements he had made, and their fortunate results, all of which were applauded by his staff, who had shared in the glory and the peril.[174]

Calling five glasses of wine a small amount of alcohol might surely seem strange to today's readers. It should however be taken into consideration that, as was described previously in Arthur's experiences in Dublin and the parties he attended in the company of Mr Hickey, alcohol was consumed in considerably larger amounts than it is now, as acquiring good drinking water was often highly problematic, especially in the colonies. Drinking alcohol was also fashionable among the aristocracy of the time. However, wine and beer were made to be significantly weaker, i.e. with a considerably lower alcohol content than today. For instance, the daily allowance of beer for one sailor in the Royal Navy on Admiral Nelson's legendary flagship, the *HMS Victory*, was one whole gallon (i.e. eight pints) per day. In the event that beer ran out on board the ship, the sailors were not forced to go dry; on the contrary, they were allotted alcohol according to the formula of one gallon of beer = one pint of wine or one half pint of rum. [175] At the time, Arthur Wellesley himself shared his new formula (which is perhaps still quite relevant to a person living in today's age) for strong health and a satisfied life with his brother Henry in a letter:

> I know but one receipt for good health in this country, and that is to live moderately, to drink little or no wine, to use exercise, to keep the mind employed, and, if possible, to keep in good humour with the world. The last is the most difficult, for, as you have often observed, there is scarcely a good tempered man in India.[176]

Also contrary to Winston Churchill, who can barely be pictured without the characteristic cigar in his mouth, Arthur Wellesley never succumbed to smoking tobacco in the form of a pipe or cigar. Wellington most likely only smoked once in his life. This took place much later in life and in the company of the Prince Regent, later British King George IV, who made Arthur an "offer he couldn't refuse" in the form of a cigar. After a few puffs, however, Wellington – who at the time was the most famous British commander and hero – capitulated and left his cigar unfinished – surely to the great amusement of the Prince Regent, who on the contrary was well known for his Bohemian lifestyle and was quite accustomed to smoking.[177]

During the time that Wellesley spent as Governor of Seringapatam, Arthur was kept company (just as in his adolescence) by a terrier named Jack who accompanied him on occasional hunts. In Elers' words, Jack was 'a very great pet and favourite of Colonel Wellesley's.'[178] Captain

Elers goes on to reminiscence about how, in addition to hunting, he would also play billiards with Colonel Wellesley. Hunting and billiards games aside, there is proof that Arthur Wellesley also had an affair with a young English beauty named Isabella Frees. Because Wellesley was unmarried, there would have been nothing wrong with the whole relationship; Mrs Frees, on the contrary, was married, and her husband was British officer Captain John Frees who administered the military stockrooms in Seringapatam. Nonetheless, the captain silently tolerated the relationship between his wife and the Governor, whereupon Mrs Frees gave birth to a healthy baby boy at the beginning of July 1802, the father of whom with all probability was Arthur Wellesley, who willingly took on the role of the boy's godfather. Further proof that he was the father can be seen in the fact that the boy was named Arthur. When he was sent several years later from India to study in England, where the boy was to be cared for by his aunt, who unfortunately died suddenly shortly after, Arthur Wellesley provided him with a room in his own home and financed his studies from his own funds. Furthermore, he continued to support the young man Arthur Frees in his following career.[179]

In terms of the events on the global political scene, the French had ejected the Austrians from the ranks of the Anti-French Coalition in 1800 during the War of the Second Coalition after two quick successive victories at Marengo (Napoleon himself triumphed here, managing to reverse a battle that the French had very nearly lost) and Hohenlinden, forcing the Austrians to sign the Treaty of Lunéville at the beginning of February 1801. Once Austria was out of the game, Britain remained alone in the war against France. After nine years of constant battle with the French, which played out on battlefields and seas throughout the world, Britain also signed the Treaty of Amiens in March 1802. For this reason, William Pitt the Younger, who was decidedly in favour of the continuation of the conflict, resigned from his post as British Prime Minister. Pitt was replaced soon after in the post of Prime Minister by Sir Henry Addington, who had helped negotiate the treaty with the French. Arthur Wellesley, who meanwhile had been promoted to the recently available office of major-general, had serious concerns about signing a treaty with the French and the fall of Pitt's government. He assessed the whole situation with the words:

If... Mr. Pitt is no longer in office, I fear that our country is in but a bad way at this moment. It is impossible that any party formed of the remnants of his administration can have strength, or indeed abilities, to keep down the factions in England and at the same time to carry on the war in the manner in which it ought to be carried on, and thus, after a nine years' struggle, we shall be ruined by our own folly.[180]

Despite the ground-breaking news of peace, a considerable danger began to loom over the British in India, as a civil war broke out with new intensity between the rajas of Maratha, who ruled nearly all the northern area of the Indian Subcontinent, giving rise to a strong and victorious coalition of anti-British rajas. Specifically, this concerned the allied group of rajas of the Jaswant Rao Holkar, Bhonsle Raja of Berar, and Daulat Rao Sindhia, the last of whom possessed the largest army and therefore the greatest influence. These rajas first fought amongst themselves for power over the Maratha Confederacy. Holkar first defeated Sindhia and removed Maratha's Peshwa Baji Rao II from his post. The office of Peshwa based at Poona was a position equivalent to the Prime Minister of Maratha and was the post of the true ruler of the confederation, as the King of the Marathas at the time remained only a powerless puppet. However, ruined Baji Rao II made his way to British territory and signed a peace treaty with them at Bassein, a small, charming town on the coast near Bombay. According to this treaty, Baji Rao II became a "protected prince" of the British Governor-General. This was a strong argument for Holkar, Sindhia and Raja of Berar to forget their old grievances and unite in one strong coalition against the British. In addition, in May 1803 Britain was again in a state of war with France, which was willingly providing open support to these three rajas (as it had done similarly with Tipu in the past) regardless of the Treaty of Amiens, which thus had little chance of lasting. In addition to the French support of the rajas, the primary pretext for renewing the military conflict between the British and the French was the dispute over the strategic Mediterranean island of Malta, which the British refused to leave after receiving explicit French orders to do so. Similarly, the French refused the British Crown's request to withdraw their troops from the Netherlands and Switzerland. Therefore, as a result of these events, Britain also officially declared war on the insurgent Maratha rajas at the beginning of August 1803, in which

Wellesley – as a recently promoted major-general, finally received the high command that he had struggled for so dearly.[181]

The extensive territory controlled by the Maratha Confederacy was located in the north of India and took up nearly all the space between the British presidencies of Bombay and Bengal. Arthur Wellesley set off for battle as Commander-in-Chief with 15,000 men and attempted to force the Marathas into a single decisive battle, after which it would be possible to subdue the rebellious rajas and sign a treaty with them that would be advantageous to Britain.[182] Because the main intentions of the British were merely to "pacify" the Marathas, restore Baji Rao II to the position of Peshwa, and make the Maratha Confederacy a British ally again, Arthur Wellesley gave the following general orders to the whole army a day before his troops crossed the borders of the Maratha Empire:

> The troops will enter the Maratha territory tomorrow morning, but they are not to consider it as an enemy's country. The strictest order and discipline must be observed, and everything that is required from the country must be paid for. Major-Gen. Wellesley will certainly punish any person who may be found guilty of a breach of this order.[183]

Firstly, in comparison to the way armies of the time often acted, such controlled and considerate behaviour toward the civilian population was exceedingly humane. Secondly, such orders were meant to work in the favour of the British in the time to come, as Arthur's troops would not be in danger of revenge on the part of the civilian population in the form of raids that harried the French troops during the war on the Iberian Peninsula. In addition, there were many Indians in the British Army serving as sepoys, and they undoubtedly appreciated this peaceable treatment of their fellow countrymen. The conscientious manner in which the British allegedly followed this order during the campaign was described by one of Wellesley's officers with a typical British sense of humour: 'The respect paid to persons and property is as great as if we had an English jury to decide on all our acts.'[184]

As Arthur partially feared, the Marathas and their army continued to retreat, luring the British farther and farther into the centre of their extensive territory. After several weeks of exhausting pursuit of the Maratha Army, Arthur finally received hopeful news on 21st September from his scouts, who reportedly spotted at least a portion of the primary Maratha Army at the town of Bhorkardan located only thirty miles north of the present position of the British troops. After brief deliberation, Arthur divided his army into two halves in order to speed up his advance through the rugged, hilly terrain that divided him from the assumed Maratha position, as a smaller army was naturally able to navigate in the difficult terrain much more quickly. Arthur's decision to divide his army was also partially influenced by fears that the Marathas would again slip past him, as there were two access roads that led to their position and, due to the fact that each part of the divided British Army was advancing on Bhorkardan over one of them, the British now successfully blocked both. After dividing his army, Wellesley entrusted half of his troops to Colonel Stevenson, leaving himself in command of the remaining units. According to his plan of operations, both halves would ideally re-join under his command on 24th September in close proximity to Bhorkardan and immediately commence their long-yearned-for and decisive battle with the Marathas.

Nonetheless, Wellesley's scouts quite surprisingly spotted not only a portion of the enemy's army, but the whole Maratha Army of roughly 50,000 soldiers in the early hours of 23rd September in a wholly different location than Bhorkardan. The Marathas were located only six miles away from the position of Wellesley's half of the army near the village of Assaye. The Maratha Army held a very strong defensive position, as it was protected both from the north and south by mighty rivers. The River Kaitna provided the front of the Maratha Army with defence while their rear was covered by the River Juah together with the village of Assaye. Arthur Wellesley thus found himself in quite a dilemma. He considered waiting for Stevenson, who could manage to draw in with his second half of the British Army the next day and risk the Marathas' withdrawal again, or immediately attack the seven-fold stronger army, as he momentarily had only 7,000 soldiers due to the division of his troops – a step which would be highly risky. Wellesley's units had only twenty cannons compared to the hundred that the Marathas possessed. In addition, thanks to their own scouts the Maratha commanders were convinced of the fact that the British were close by, although they did not yet know their plans.[185] Nonetheless, Major-General Wellesley made a quick decision. He called upon his officers and ordered for the men to prepare for an immediate attack. He would later justify his actions in a letter addressed to his good friend, the newly named Governor of Madras, Sir Thomas Munro, in the following:

> When I found their whole army, and contemplated their position, of course I considered whether I should attack immediately, or should delay till the following morning. I determined upon the immediate attack, because I saw clearly, that, if I attempted to return to my camp at Naulniah [the village in which Arthur's caravan and supplies were located], I should have been followed thither by the whole of the enemy's cavalry, and I might have suffered some loss; instead of attacking, I might have been attacked there in the morning, and, at all events, I should have found it very difficult to secure my baggage, as I did, in any place so near the enemy's camp, in which they should know it was: I therefore determined upon the attack immediately.[186]

Wellesley's plan, in which the element of surprise played a great role, faced one fundamental challenge from its very onset. The Maratha Army, the ranks of which personally included Sindhia and the Raja of Berar, were holding their positions on the opposite bank of the River Kaitna, which Wellesley would first have to cross. As it was clear to him that a head-on frontal attack of the Marathas' line that led over the enemy-controlled ford would equal sheer suicide, he sought to find another more remote crossing east of the Marathas' position. By doing so, he planned to cross the Kaitna as quickly as possible and attack the Marathas unexpectedly at their flank from the left wing. However, his Indian scouts repeatedly reported to him that no other crossing existed across the Kaitna at this given spot. Arthur Wellesley, who did not take "no" for an answer, saddled Diomed and set off to look for the crossing himself. Through his telescope, he soon noticed two villages on opposing banks of the River Kaitna that were strikingly close to one another, east of the Marathas' position.[187] It immediately struck Wellesley that the two villages were not built that way by chance, and therefore logically inferred that the much-desired crossing would be there. 'I immediately said to myself that men could not have built two villages so close to one another on opposite sides of a stream without some habitual means of communication, either by boats or a ford – most probably by the latter.'[188]

Thus, he sent a staff officer without delay to the villages, where he found the assumed ford linking both villages. Subsequently, under Wellesley's command, the combat-ready British troops quickly set off toward the crossing. During their march, however, they were soon spotted by the Maratha Army, which took Arthur by surprise with their dexterity, as they managed to perform a wholly disciplined and speedy ninety-degree shift to the east with the organizational skill of any of the best-trained European armies. Thanks to this manoeuvre, the Maratha units stood in line, prepared and facing the British, who were still crossing the newly discovered ford over the Kaitna. The Marathas were commanded by an experienced German soldier, Anthony Pohlmann, who had been hired by the Maratha raja Daulat Sindhia. In addition, Pohlmann had several French officers at his disposal and, unfortunately for the British, they had done fine work in training the Maratha troops. The Maratha artillerymen also managed this complex manoeuvre and the British, who were still crossing the Kaitna, suddenly stood facing all of Pohlmann's one hundred cannons, which began to fire mercilessly upon them, slowly heightening British losses. One cannonball even flew only a yard past Arthur himself as he was crossing the river and tore off the head of his aide-de-camp. Once the British finally crossed the Kaitna under constant enemy fire, they lined up hastily under Wellesley's supervision into two infantry lines, followed by a third made up of the cavalry under Lieutenant-Colonel Maxwell's command.[189]

The British lines, which were naturally much shorter in length than those of the Marathas, attacked toward the centre and right wing of the Marathas. As Wellesley did not intend to wait longer due to the withering fire of enemy cannons, he took charge of the centre and left wing of the British line and launched an immediate attack. Arthur gave Colonel Orrok command of the right wing, which had evidently not been spread out to its fullest extent. Arthur gave clear orders to Orrok to avoid the village of Assaye on the Maratha's left wing where Pohlmann's units seemed to have a strong position that was additionally defended by the homes in the village. Under Wellesley's command, the advancing British soon reached the firing range of the Maratha artillerymen's devastating canister shots, which began to cause more appalling losses among the British ranks as Wellesley's whole line staggered in its forward advance. Several British sepoys from the Madras regiments that were deployed at Arthur's centre even began to throw away their muskets and flee. At that moment, Major-General Wellesley was again forced to intervene. He brought his centre and left wing back into file while personally leading his men in a renewed attack through the hail of deadly canister shots.[190] Lieutenant-Colonel Colin Campbell from the 78th Highlanders Regiment wrote home in a letter that the faltering British lines at this critical moment 'moved forward rapidly' thanks to Arthur's immediate measures.[191] The British soon reached the Marathas' cannons in the centre of the field and on the left wing, mercilessly slaying the cannoneers and continuing determinedly in their attack on the Maratha infantry that was now located beyond the newly captured cannon. The Scottish 78th Highlanders (of which Lieutenant-Colonel Campbell was a member) were especially determined in the following British attack against the Maratha infantry. Enraged by the prior attack and driven forward by their bagpipers, they quite literally charged over Pohlmann's infantry that was holding its position behind the artillery. Thanks to this charge, the infantry completely collapsed, making a chaotic flee for safety.[192]

Despite the success of Wellesley's units fighting at the centre and left wing, the British right wing had found itself in serious trouble. Despite Arthur's explicit orders, Colonel Orrok had led the right wing too close to the village of Assaye, where both of his regiments were decimated by fearful canister fire.* As soon as the Maratha cavalry noticed Orrok's predicament, they took advantage of the situation and charged straight-away at his disorganized regiments. At that moment, Lieutenant-Colonel Patrick Maxwell, commander of the British cavalry, took the initiative and reacted promptly by immediately charging with his 19th Regiment of light dragoons to face off with the Maratha cavalry. After a short battle, Maxwell managed to force the enemy cavalry to retreat, saving the remainder of Wellesley's right wing and also preventing the British Army from impending encirclement from the north.[193]

---

*   *'When the enemy changed their position, they threw their left to Assaye, in which village they had some infantry, and it was surrounded by cannon. As soon as I saw that, I directed the officer commanding the picquets [Colonel Orrok] to keep out of shot from that village, instead of that, he led directly upon it.'*
A letter from Arthur Wellesley to the Governor of Madras Thomas Munro, Nov. 1st, 1803, quoted in: John Bradshaw, *Sir Thomas Munro and the British Settlement of Madras Presidency* (Oxford 1894), p. 126.

BATTLE OF ASSAYE
23rd September 1803

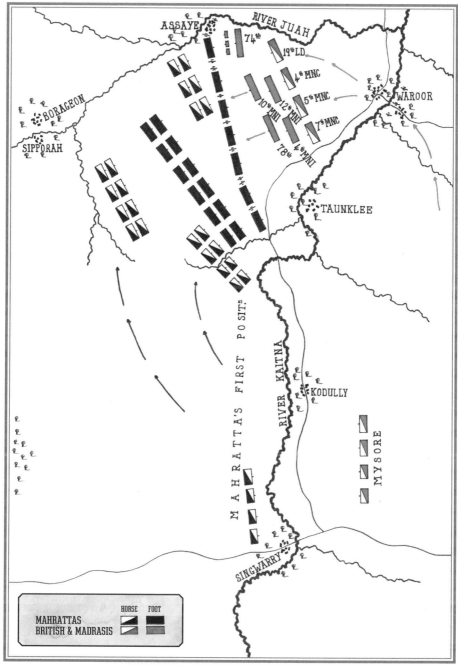

ASSAYE

RIVER JUAH

74th

19th LD

4th MNC

5th MNC

7th MNC

10th MNI

12th MNI

18th

MNI

WAROOR

BORAGEON

SIPPORAH

TAUNKLEE

MAHRATTA'S FIRST POSITN.

RIVER KAITNA

KODULLY

MYSORE

SINGWARRY

	HORSE	FOOT
MAHRATTAS		
BRITISH & MADRASIS		

— *Map by John Fawkes* —

On the opposite side of the battlefield, Wellesley had in the meantime ceased to pursue Pohlmann's fleeing infantry and was leading an attack on the remaining artillerymen on the former left wing of the Maratha line in the village of Assaye (from the British Army's point of view, this was the right wing that had been led into battle by Colonel Orrok), where Lieutenant-Colonel Maxwell was attempting to remedy the situation with his cavalry. During this attack, Wellesley's second horse was killed beneath him, putting Arthur in immediate and mortal danger for the second time that day. Diomed had fallen under him prior to this as he was run through by an enemy pike during a frontal attack against Pohlmann's infantry at the Marathas' centre and right wing.* Nonetheless, British units – now on the ground – saw to their general, quickly coming to his aid with all possible urgency. Soon after, the whole Maratha artillery position (including cannon located in the village of Assaye) was decisively conquered.[194] Desperate, Pohlmann continued in an attempt to organize the remainder of his fleeing infantry and cavalry west of Assaye for a final stand; however, this chaotic endeavour was disrupted by Maxwell, who again readily attacked with his cavalry. To Wellesley's chagrin, however, Patrick Maxwell was shot and killed during the final attack of his considerably exhausted cavalry. Nonetheless, the whole disrupted Maratha Army began to flee confusedly in all directions, leading to a decisive British victory.[195] In a letter to his father written immediately after the battle and in reaction to Arthur's brave actions, Lieutenant-Colonel Colin Campbell wrote the following:

> The General was in the thick of the action the whole time, and had a horse killed under him. No man could have shown a better example to the troops than he did. I never saw a man so cool and collected as he was the whole time...[196]

Similarly in a letter home, one of Wellesley's aides-de-camp Mountstuart Elphinstone wrote of Arthur's inspiring actions during the battle:

> The General will doubtless get great credit for this, I am sure he deserves it. It is nothing to say of him that he exposed himself on all occasions, and behaved with perfect indifference in the hottest fire...in the most anxious and

---

*   To Arthur's great delight, Diomed survived his injuries and fully recuperated within half a year.

important moments he gave his orders as coolly and as clearly as if he had been inspecting a corps, or manoeuvring at a review.[197]

The Governor of Madras Sir Thomas Munro also gave many words of praise concerning the victory at Assaye, but objected to how risky and perhaps even imprudent Wellesley's actions were; he did, however, write the following lines about the battle to Arthur:

> I have seen several accounts of your late glorious victory over the combined armies of Sindhia and the Berár man...I can, however see dimly through the smoke of the Maráthá guns... that a gallanter action has not been fought for many years in any part of the world. When not only the disparity of numbers, but also of real military force, is considered, it is beyond all comparison a more brilliant and arduous exploit than that of Aboukir [the naval battle in which Nelson defeated the French Flotilla – today better known as the Battle of the Nile].[198]

The Battle of Assaye was without a doubt a great victory, but one for which the British nonetheless paid a heavy price. British losses amounted to a total of 1,584 dead, wounded, or missing, which made up more than one fifth of all of Wellesley's deployed troops. Losses on the Maratha side reached up to 6,000 dead and wounded. It should be noted that, under the pressure of defeat, many Maratha soldiers deserted, and a handful of Maratha soldiers even plundered their own caravans. Out of all the British units, the 74th Regiment of Foot fighting on Orrok's right wing suffered the heaviest losses, as a mere 75 of its 498 men emerged from the battle without injury.[199] Several days after the battle, Arthur Wellesley himself wrote to one of his friends at the time, Captain John Malcolm:

> Their infantry is the best I have ever seen in India, excepting our own, and they and their equipments far surpass Tippoo's. I assure you that their [the Marathas'] fire was so heavy that I much doubted at one time whether I should be able to prevail upon our troops to advance, and all agree that the battle was the fiercest that has ever been seen in India. Our troops behaved admirably, the sepoys astonished me.[200]

Although Arthur was evidently dissatisfied with Orrok's fatal error on the right wing, he praised his bravery in a letter to Sir Thomas Munro:

> I do not wish to cast any reflection upon the officer who led the picquets [Colonel Orrok]. I lament the consequences of his mistake, but I must acknowledge that it was not possible for a man to lead a body into a hotter fire than he did the picquets on that day at Assaye.[201]

The brutality of the clashes at Assaye and the treacherous path to Wellington's first great victory in a field battle is evidenced in a conversation that took place at the time when Wellington's military career was already at its end, during which British Ambassador George Chad asked Arthur what, from a military perspective, was his most brilliant victory. The Duke answered the question (in a rather surprising manner in light of his rich military career) in one word: 'Assaye.'[202]

Although physically and mentally exhausted, it was clear that Arthur Wellesley was rightfully proud of his men after their victory at Assaye. Nonetheless he felt considerable regret for the incurred losses of his 'remarkable troops'. He spent the night immediately after the battle at a farm nearby directly among the wounded British soldiers (according to eyewitnesses, he spent the night not far from a seriously wounded officer) and certainly did not sleep soundly. Years later, he wrote of this unpleasant evening:

> Strange impressions come now and then after a battle, and such came to me after the battle of Assaye in India. I slept in a farm yard, and whenever I awaked, it struck me that I had lost all my friends, so many had I lost in that battle. Again and again, as often as I awaked, did it disturb me. In the morning I inquired anxiously after one and another, nor was I convinced that they were living till I saw them.[203]

Several days later, before the British withdrew, Arthur personally visited the injured and made sure they had a sufficient amount of all necessary items. He also provided them with a continuous supply of wine at his own expense. However, in terms of the injured, who he wished to secure and care for as best he could, he faced problems from his British ally, the Nizam of Hyderabad, who refused to house them in one of his fortresses and provide them with safety from a potential enemy raid. Wellesley, however, was not willing to back down from his duties and risk leaving his wounded men in an unprotected place: 'The Nizam's servants are behaving ill, and I cannot get a place of security for my wounded soldiers,'[204] Arthur wrote in irritation in reaction to Nizam's dismissive behaviour. Ultimately, after a series of negotiations, he managed to provide his injured with satisfactory conditions in the Adjuntee Fortress, even though he was disturbed by the fact that the fortress was located too close to the enemy borders, as he wrote in a letter to Colonel Merrick Shawe:

> I have just returned from seeing my wounded men, they are tolerably comfortable, and I hope safe in the fort [Adjuntee], but I wish they were in a greater distance from the frontier...[205]

Exactly one month after the Battle of Assaye, Wellesley visited his wounded in Adjuntee and was clearly pleased, as he wrote to the commander of the Bombay Army, General Stuart: 'I have the pleasure to inform you that the wounded officers and men are doing remarkably well. Some of the former, and many of the latter, have returned to their duty.'[206] Nonetheless, before the next campaign against the Marathas, Arthur – moved by the losses suffered – told his second-in-command Colonel Stevenson: 'I acknowledge that I should not like to see again such a loss as I sustained on the 23rd September [the day of the Battle of Assaye], even if attended by such a gain.'[207]

In my opinion, the Battle of Assaye, similarly to Wellesley's whole military career in India, shows that Wellington should by no means be labelled merely a "defensive general" as is sometimes the case in popular culture and some literature. During all of Wellington's military campaigns in India, he was each time in the role of the attacking side and – with the exception of the incident in Sultanpettah Tope – he was always clearly victorious. For instance, in reference to their offensive strategy in the Maratha Campaign, Arthur wrote Colonel Stevenson the following lines in a letter: 'Dash at the first fellows that make their appearance, and the campaign will be our own...A long defensive war would ruin us.'[208] These words, penned by Wellesley himself, surely point to a commander who was a far cry from a "defensive general". At Assaye, he almost certainly used his sabre – albeit as Commander-in-Chief – in face-to-face battle with the enemy, which was wholly uncommon among high commanders of the time. With his prompt behaviour, bravery, and willingness to set a personal example to his wavering troops, unhesitant to put his life at stake, he succeeded in scoring an exceedingly important victory for Britain at the Battle of Assaye. The aforementioned lines of Wellesley's correspondence clearly show how much he appreciated his men, friends, and human life in general. Despite his tough demeanour, he would display this trait throughout his rich and varied military career, during which he was often wholly disgusted with the horrors of war. In spite of his clear sensitivity, he managed to maintain a cool head and make clear decisions in the heat of battle as if in a "trance", sometimes becoming overpowered by his emotions only after the battle was long since won.

In November 1803, Arthur defeated the demoralized Marathas, who were low on men, at Argaon (also known as the Battle of Argaum), from which he emerged with incomparably lower losses than at Assaye with only 46 dead. Before the end of 1803, he conquered the Maratha mountain fortress of Gawilghur, the fall of which caused the Marathas to sign a final capitulation, marking the victorious end of the whole war for Britain. For his victory on the battlefield, Arthur Wellesley received the award of Knight Grand Cross of the Order of the Bath. Later, as a reminder of the old roguery of their youth, this order of knighthood was pinned on Arthur Wellesley in his sleep by his long-time friend, the 'Town Bull of Dublin' John Cradock, who also happened to sail to India in search of good fortune and wealth.

In addition to his royal honour, Arthur Wellesley fetched himself a considerable estate in the form of a reward for his campaign in the amount of 42,000 pounds, making him into a relatively affluent man. Arthur Wellesley therefore came to the conclusion that it was high time to return home. Cradock, who upon his arrival was happy to have a good friend in a relatively influential position in India, naturally attempted to dissuade Arthur from returning to England. Nonetheless, Arthur told Cradock his honest reasons for his decision to depart, which he would change under no condition:

WELLINGTON'S BATTLES
AND SIEGES IN INDIA 1799-1803

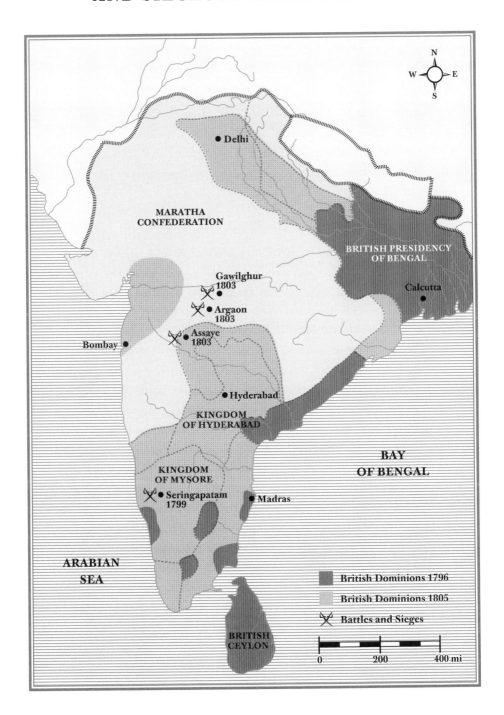

You think about my staying in India like a man who has just come out, and I like one who has been here for seven years involved in perpetual troubles. I acknowledge that I am anxious to a degree which I cannot express to see my friends again, and even if I was certain that I should not be employed in England at all, there is no situation in India which would induce me to stay here. I am not rich in comparison with other people, but very much so in comparison with my former poverty, and quite sufficiently so for my own wants & desires. I got a great deal of prize money in the last war, which with what I got before, and a sum of money which the Court of Directors gave me for a service rendered to them in this country, and the accumulation of interest upon those sums, have rendered me independent of all office or employment. [209]

Arthur Wellesley set off for the lengthy trip to Britain on 10th March 1805 on board the *HMS Trident*. Coincidentally, he stopped for a whole month during the voyage on the island of St. Helena, the same place where Napoleon Bonaparte would spend the final years of his life. In addition, in June 1805 Richard Wellesley was recalled from his position as Governor-General and he also decided to return to Britain.[210] Arthur Wellesley had certainly learned much from India. He became an experienced organizer in the field of supplying an army while proving his ability to provide his troops with all necessary supplies, even during military campaigns led over long distances into the depths of enemy territory and over exacting terrain. He also proved himself to be a skilled strategist and commander who refused to succumb to fear during battle and showed his capability to react promptly to immediate developments. Carrying out his function as the Governor of Seringapatam also taught Arthur Wellesley an important lesson in the political theatre as he was forced to resolve various sensitive issues including tackling corruption, negotiating with the local rajas, and hosting prominent figures that came to Seringapatam from Britain. He also fully developed his talent there in maintaining friendly ties with the local population. In 1816, several months after the Battle of Waterloo, Arthur was later asked by one of the British generals, who praised Arthur for his uncommon activity on the day of the victorious battle, how it was possible that he had managed to ride tirelessly to and fro under enemy fire across the whole battlefield. Wellington replied: 'Ah, that is all India.'[211]

As Arthur Wellesley neared the shores of Britain after almost nine years spent in India, he clearly and justifiably felt that he had succeeded. In addition to his money and being made a Knight Grand Cross of the Order of the Bath, he may have also taken pleasure during the long voyage in the heartfelt salutations that he had received from the citizens of Seringapatam:

> May you long continue to dispense to us that full stream of security and happiness, which we first received with wonder... and, when greater affairs shall call you from us, may the God of all castes and all nations deign to hear with favour our humble and constant prayers for your health, your glory, and your happiness.[212]

'My Die is Cast.'
From India to the Tumult
of the Peninsular War

Sir Arthur Wellesley caught sight of the English coastline from aboard the frigate *HMS Trident* after nine long years spent in India. He was now a thirty-six-year-old Major-General and, as of 1804, a Knight of the Most Honourable Order of the Bath. Arthur finally came ashore on 10th September 1805 and a mere two days later, he was at the British Army Headquarters in Horse Guards in Central London where he was called upon by Lord Castlereagh, the Secretary of State for War and the Colonies.*

While Arthur Wellesley was in India, Britain had been completely alone in its war with Napoleonic France since 18th May 1803. Little over a week later (26th May) the French invaded and occupied Hanover, a territory of which the British Monarch, George III was the Prince-Elector.

---

* Guedalla, p. 121. For the sake of simplification, I will use only "War Minister" or "Minister for War" further in the text in place of the official name of the post, which was "Minister of State for War and the Colonies".

After the British declared war on France, Napoleon began to gather an immense army near Boulogne in Northern France in preparation to invade Britain, giving the army the optimistic title of the 'Army of England' (at the time, armies were often named after the area in which they were formed or in which they were meant to subsequently operate). In March 1804, with ever-growing confidence, yet fearful of supposed conspiracies, Napoleon gave orders for French dragoons to cross the River Rhine and make for Etthenheim in Baden to capture Louis Antoine de Bourbon, Duke of Enghien, a *prince du sang* of the House of Condé, a cadet branch of the Royal House of Bourbon. The Duke of Enghien was accused of treasonable activity against the French Republic, arraigned before what amounted to little more than a kangaroo court, tried, sentenced to death and shot in the dried moat of Château de Vincennes to the east of Paris. The European royal courts (similarly to Louis XVI's execution nine years prior) were outraged by this act and the Russian Tsar Alexander I himself labelled the Duke's execution a murder. In addition, Napoleon, who had declared himself First Consul for life and by doing so definitively gained unlimited power over France, had all British civilians on the continent arrested after the renewal of hostilities with Britain. This included diplomats, which at the time was viewed as an egregious violation of international law. Napoleon became First Consul of France after the Military Coup of the 18th Brumaire when he managed on a lone vessel to evade the British Navy that was patrolling the Mediterranean Sea, arriving safely from Egypt to Paris and not hesitating to leave the rest of the French Army in North Africa to their own fate.

Thanks to these events, after three years out of office William Pitt the Younger became British Prime Minister in May 1804, this time replacing Henry Addington. By 2nd December 1804, Napoleon had himself nominated Emperor in Paris, placing the crown on his own head in the presence of Pope Pius VII. By doing so, he embittered not only many anointed figures around Europe, but also many of his hitherto supporters on the "old continent", for example the famous composer Ludwig van Beethoven, who until then had still looked upon Napoleon as the bearer of idealistic revolutionary ideals. Through this coronation ceremony, the new French Emperor had "revealed his cards" to the eyes of all Europe and by many was viewed as little more than a power-hungry usurper. During

May 1805, the insatiable Napoleon declared himself King of Italy and annexed the newly-founded Ligurian Republic as an additional French satellite. This was the proverbial "last straw" for European monarchs, and during August 1805 British Prime Minister William Pitt the Younger finally managed to form (the now Third) Anti-French Alliance. All factors pointed to the British Army soon being deployed on the continent once again along with allied armies. This time Austria, led by Emperor Francis II, and Russia, ruled by Tsar Alexander I, would fight alongside the British against France.[213]

While shortly after his arrival from India Arthur Wellesley waited in the vestibule of Horse Guards for a meeting with Lord Castlereagh the Minister for War, he met a one-armed man who he immediately recognized from many paintings and newspaper portraits. This man, dressed in a dark-blue uniform of the Royal Navy, was none other than the illustrious Admiral Horatio Nelson, the hero of the Battle of the Nile.[214]

Wellesley enthusiastically struck up a conversation with Nelson but was initially disappointed by the naval hero's disposition. Nelson at the time was going through a difficult period, as British society had been scandalized by his relationship with Emma, Lady Hamilton, the wife of Sir William Hamilton, the former British Ambassador to the Kingdom of Naples. Nelson apparently behaved toward Arthur Wellesley with seeming disinterest for this reason and quite willingly made his disdain for the whole world evident, a fact which Wellington recalled years later in the following: 'He entered at once into conversation with me, if I can call it conversation, for it was almost all on his side, and all about himself, and , really, in a style so vain and silly as to surprise and almost disgust me.'[215]

After a short time, Nelson interrupted his monologue and left the room for a moment. When he came back, his behaviour suddenly and dramatically changed. He had evidently learned from someone that the tall, sun-tanned gentleman without a wig was not just another inexperienced "whippersnapper in an officer's uniform" who had never seen battle and had nothing better to do than target the Admiral and his personal life as the majority of society had begun to do, but a veteran of Assaye, Major-General Arthur Wellesley.[216] As if a completely different person now stood before Arthur, Nelson, now "transformed", began asking with interest about his experience in India and discussing various military and political affairs: 'That surprised me equally and more agreeably than the first part of our interview had done, in fact, he talked like an officer and a statesman...I don't know that I ever had a conversation that interested me more.'[217] as Wellington later shared his feelings with a friend. It is certainly a remarkable coincidence that the day following this discussion, the Admiral boarded the Royal Navy's flagship *HMS Victory* and set off with a fleet that was made up of 27 ships of the line to confront the combined Franco-Spanish fleet of some 33 vessels off Cape Trafalgar. In the Battle of Trafalgar* on 21st October 1805, Nelson and his forces inflicted a decisive defeat on the Franco-Spanish fleet led by French Admiral Villeneuve, thus ending Napoleon's hopes of invading Britain. Nelson paid for this magnificent victory with his life and it is interesting to note that Wellington was one of the last people to speak to Nelson before he set off to do battle and to enter the annals of history.

The situation in which Britain found itself in 1804 and 1805 is strikingly reminiscent of the situation in 1940 when Hitler's Army was preparing to invade England. The English Channel – just as for the French one hundred and thirty-five years earlier – formed the final barrier before invasion. The Second World War of course differed from this situation in that the primary British defences were formed by the air force, not the navy. With some degree of exaggeration in terms of its strategic significance, we could even compare the Battle of Trafalgar to the Battle of Britain, as victory in both battles was crucial for Britain in that it caused the aggressors to rethink and change tack. The connection between the period in which Britain faced the threat of Napoleon's invasion and the danger of occupation by Adolf Hitler's *Wehrmacht* was noted by British Prime Minister Winston Churchill in his speech given a day after the successful evacuation of more than 330,000 British soldiers from the French port of Dunkirk back to Britain on 4th June 1940:

> When Napoleon lay at Boulogne for a year [in 1804] with his flat-bottomed boats and his Grand Army [Grande Armée] he was told by someone: 'There are bitter weeds in England.'...In the days of Napoleon the same wind which would have carried his transports across the Channel might have driven away

---

* Cape Trafalgar, where the battle took place, is located on the Southwest coast of Spain.

the blockading fleet. There was always the chance, and it is that chance which excited and befooled the imagination of many Continental tyrants...I have, myself, full confidence that if all do their duty, if nothing is neglected, and if the best arrangements are made, as they are being made, we shall prove ourselves once again able to defend our Island home, to ride out the storm of war, and to outlive the menace of tyranny, if necessary for years, if necessary alone.[218]

Nonetheless, on 20th October 1805 on the continent, i.e. only one day before the naval Battle of Trafalgar, Napoleon quite conclusively defeated the Austrian Army of Marshal Mack at Ulm and conquered Vienna several days later. This terrifying news arrived to England on 2nd December (coincidentally the anniversary of Napoleon's coronation as Emperor) and deeply unsettled the whole country, as Britain still knew nothing of Nelson's victory at Trafalgar. Naturally, the figure most strongly affected was Prime Minister William Pitt the Younger, the driving force behind the Third Coalition. However, only four days later the news of Nelson's great victory over the Franco-Spanish fleet arrived in Britain, transporting the country from a period of anxiety and trepidation into one of exuberant celebration. Almost overnight, the Prime Minister went from a criticized figure to a celebrated hero. The whole nation and Parliament now lionized Pitt and gave him their heartfelt thanks.[219] The Prime Minister's speech in respect of these ovations became one of the most famous in British history: 'I return you many thanks for the honour you have done me, but Europe is not to be saved by any single man. England has saved herself by her exertions, and will, as I trust, save Europe by her example.'[220]

It was at this time that Arthur Wellesley made a significant impression on the Prime Minister, who was surely aware of the fact that he would need capable generals in the renewed war with France. William Pitt repeatedly invited him on hunting trips, after which he wrote the following complimentary words about Arthur Wellesley: 'I never met any military officer with whom it was so satisfactory to converse.'[221] Wellesley's character impressed Pitt for its honesty and ability to make brief and clear judgements on the matter being discussed. In addition, the fact that Arthur was always able to state his unequivocal opinion on a given issue immediately also appealed to him. This was certainly a pleasant change of pace from the ambiguous talk of politicians with whom the Prime Minister was forced to lead his daily communications. Pitt wrote the following of Arthur Wellesley:

> He never made a difficulty, or hid his ignorance in vague generalities. If I put a question to him, he answered it distinctly, if I wanted an explanation, he gave it clearly, if I desired an opinion I got from him one supported by reasons that were always sound.[222]

Nonetheless, not everyone held Arthur Wellesley in such high regard as William Pitt. At the time, Wellesley's victory at Assaye was celebrated with due enthusiasm, but it had taken place a whole eighteen months earlier. Since then, the headlines of British newspapers began to be filled primarily with Napoleon's looming invasion of Britain and subsequently with Nelson's naval triumph, which averted this imminent danger. Therefore, after his return from India, Arthur seemed more like yesterday's hero. In addition, his adversaries claimed that victories in the colonies did not carry the same weight as those won on European battlefields.[223] Arthur Wellesley's most influential critics at the time were Prince Frederick, Duke of York (Wellesley's former commander at the time of the unfortunate campaign to Flanders in 1794 and 1795) and even King George III himself. Despite this fact and most likely thanks to an intervention by William Pitt, Arthur Wellesley was given command of an infantry brigade setting off for Prussia at the beginning of December. The brigade was to disembark there and, along with other British troops, support the allied armies of the Third Coalition, in which Britain intended to incorporate the Prussians along with Austria and Russia. Nonetheless, the wheels of fortune can be fickle, and in the meantime another unexpected event took place on the continent. On 2nd December 1805, Napoleon had emerged the undisputed victor from the Battle of Austerlitz in Moravia, where he crushed the Austro-Russian Army and thus the Third Coalition. Arthur Wellesley's mission to Prussia was thus naturally recalled, as there was no sense in leading an operation due to the destruction of the Austro-Russian forces. After the time of triumph, this sudden defeat of Britain's allies also took a serious toll on William Pitt's health. At the beginning of the new year, the health of the Prime Minister (Arthur's supporter), which had been troublesome all his life, worsened to such an extent that he died, possibly from a peptic ulcer, on 23rd January 1806 at the age of 46. Shortly before his death, Pitt allegedly claimed with more than a degree of resignation that, thanks to the unstable political situation caused by the speedy territorial changes due to Bonaparte's constant expansion, a map of Europe would be completely useless to everyone for the next ten years to come.[224]

Now lacking more prominent connections, Arthur Wellesley was now nominated as a mere commander of just one brigade guarding Hastings on the South Coast of England, where he was officially ordered to face any possible French landings, of which there was of course little risk after the events of Trafalgar. In all reality, it was a relatively insignificant position. When a friend asked Wellington years later how he felt militarily about being given such a "ridiculous post" of commander of a garrison in England after having commanded an army of many thousands as Commander-in-Chief in India, winning glory and the laurels of victory, Wellington merely replied:

> I am nimmukwallah as we say in the East, that is, I have eaten of the King's salt, and, therefore, I conceive it to be my duty to serve with unhesitating zeal and cheerfulness, when and whenever the King or his Government may think proper to employ me.[225]

Nonetheless, in addition to his unexciting military service in Hastings, Arthur – the "nimmukwallah" – began again to engage in the domestic political scene as he managed to win as a Tory* in parliamentary elections in Westminster as a candidate for the South England coastal town of Rye. During his appearances in Parliament as an MP, Arthur primarily defended the policy that his brother Richard had practiced while in the post of Governor-General of India – the importance of the Maratha War, of which there were still many critics among members of Parliament despite the clear British victory there. In spite of the various differences that existed between Arthur and Richard in India, Arthur made his loyalty clear to his brother through his actions in Parliament, showing all that the Wellesley Family stood together immovably.[226]

---

* In British politics at the time, the Tories were a predecessor of today's Conservative Party. In opposition were the Whigs, a party that over the years gave rise to the Liberal Party.

In addition, Arthur was also dealing with an important personal matter. Although it may seem nearly unbelievable, over the course of almost nine years that he spent in India, the still-unmarried Kitty Pakenham had waited faithfully for Arthur Wellesley (much like Penelope waited for her Odysseus in Homer's famous epic) in Ireland. During this long period of mutual separation, Arthur had kept a certain degree of contact with Kitty despite his earlier marriage proposal having been rebuffed by her family. Whilst overseas the couple only exchanged occasional correspondence through mediators. Moreover, this mutual communication was complicated by the fact that post between India and Ireland could take up to nine months to arrive by sea. At the beginning of 1801, Arthur was first given news of Kitty from Dublin by Colonel William Beresford, whom Arthur had known for years from his previous role of aide-de-camp to the Lord Lieutenant of Ireland, in the following and at least encouraging lines: 'I know not if Miss Pakenham is an object to you or not – she looks as well as ever.'[227]

At the time, Mrs Olivia Sparrow, a family friend of the Pakenhams (and especially of Kitty herself) sent a letter to Arthur in India regarding his relationship with Kitty. Mrs Sparrow had a brother in Calcutta and thus willingly took the role of mediator between Kitty and Arthur Wellesley. Although Olivia's letter to Arthur has unfortunately been lost, Arthur Wellesley's very telling reply to it from August 1801 is fortunately preserved:

> You may recollect a disappointment that I met with about 8 years ago [i.e. Arthur's refusal by Kitty's brother Thomas in 1794], in an object in which I was most interested. Notwithstanding my good fortune, and the perpetual activity of the life which I have led, the disappointment, the object of it, and all the circumstances are fresh upon my mind, as if they had passed only yesterday... I wish to shew you that the merit of your friend [Kitty] is still felt... When you see your friend do me the favour to remember me to her in the kindest manner.[228]

Taking this letter into consideration, it is wholly evident that Arthur Wellesley still regarded Kitty with considerable fondness.

Kitty, who had meanwhile ceased to hold any hopes of seeing Arthur again, accepted an offer to marry Mr Lowry Cole. Therefore, at this critical

1. Dangan Castle, County Meath, Ireland. The idyllic place of Arthur Wesley's (the future Duke of Wellington's) childhood, where he was raised until his family moved to London in 1776. Dangan is also considered to be one of Wellington's possible birthplaces.

2. Arthur Wesley's father, Garret Wesley, 1st Earl of Mornington died unexpectedly when Arthur Wesley was just twelve years old. Thus, Arthur's oldest brother, twenty-one-year-old Richard, was forced to care for the whole family as the "new head of the household".

3. Arthur Wesley's mother, Anne Hill,
Countess of Mornington.

4. Catherine 'Kitty' Pakenham
on a drawing by John Slater, 1811.

5. A recruiting sergeant alluring new recruits into the British Army.
During the Napoleonic Wars, becoming a member of the British Army was done on a voluntary basis.
Therefore, in addition to enticing words and grand promises, recruiting officers often used alcohol
as a means of acquiring new recruits.

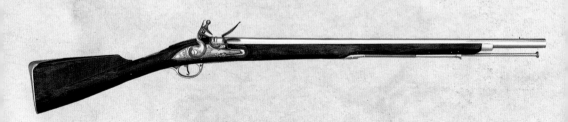

6. A 'Brown Bess' musket. The primary and now legendary weapon of the British Infantry,
used throughout the whole Napoleonic era.

FATIGUES OF THE CAMPAIGN IN FLANDERS.

7. Caricature made by James Gillray called *Fatigues of the Campaign in Flanders*. Published in Britain in May 1793, it sharply criticizes the Commander-in-Chief, the Duke of York and his generals during the Campaign against Revolutionary France in Flanders (or the Austrian Netherlands). James Gillray was the son of a soldier and had set off for the Austrian Netherlands before creating the drawing. What he saw – similarly to the young Arthur Wesley – deeply incensed him.

8. Prince Frederick, Duke of York, the second son of the British King George III. He was the Commander-in-Chief of the British forces in Flanders, under whose command Arthur Wesley served as Lieutenant-Colonel of the 33rd Regiment.

9. Richard Wellesley, 2nd Earl of Mornington, the oldest brother of Arthur Wellesley, painted as Governor General of India by Robert Hume in 1803.

10. Wellington's youngest brother Henry Wellesley, who travelled to India with the oldest of the Wellesley brothers, Richard (who had just recently been appointed Governor General) as his aide-de-camp.

11. Tipu Sultan, ruler of the Kingdom of Mysore in southern India, dubbed the 'Tiger of Mysore', was well known for his bravery as well as his cruelty. His French allies at the time also referred to him as 'Citoyen Tipu'.

12. Tipu Sultan's favourite toy. The Mysorean Sultan hated the British with all his heart, and therefore commissioned the creation of this rather morbid machine, which was carved from wood into the likeness of a tiger devouring a British soldier. Inside it is a complex mechanism that simulates human groans when played. Today "Tipu's toy" may be viewed in the Victoria and Albert Museum, London.

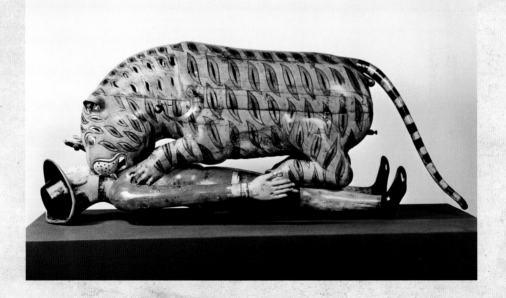

13. The storming of Seringapatam by the British Army.
The attack on Tipu's capital was led by Major-General David Baird on 4th May 1799.

14. Finding of the body of Tipu Sultan. Arthur Wellesley is said to have checked
Tipu's pulse personally and claimed him for dead.

15. Major-General Arthur Wellesley leading his men on a charge against the Mysorean troops in the Battle of Assaye in India on 21st September 1803 on the back of the seriously wounded Arab charger Diomed.

16. Major-General David Baird, Wellington's rival and later friend from his campaigns in India, posing heroically with his horse. Baird spent four long years in Tipu's dungeons under Seringapatam in horrific conditions, chained to his cellmate with a bullet lodged in his shoulder. It is thus understandable that he saw the campaign in 1799 as a sort of "personal revenge". Baird was a Scotsman well known for his temperamental nature and personal bravery in combat. After receiving the news of her son's abysmal situation in Tipu's prison, his mother is claimed to have said: "Lord pity the man that is chained to our Davie!"

17. Memorial erected to General Sir Ralph Abercromby and fallen British soldiers in the Alexandria (Chatby) Military and War Memorial Cemetery, Egypt.

18. Robert Steward, Lord Castlereagh,
Wellington's long-time friend and colleague,
who successively held the positions of British
Minister of War and Minister of Foreign Affairs.

19. A Scottish Highlander –
engraving made from the painting
by A. Laby, a painter from the circle
of Emperor Napoleon's court
painter Jacques-Louis David.

20. A coloured lithograph from the end of the 19ᵗʰ century called *The Army and Navy*,
representing the only discussion between these two great commanders,
the Duke of Wellington of the Army, and Admiral Nelson of the Navy. Behind them are visible symbols
of their most famous victories at Waterloo and Trafalgar.

21. Arthur Wellesley's wife, Kitty Pakenham, as the duchess of Wellington, on a painting by an unknown artist. Kitty was not overly fond of being depicted and thus few portraits of her exist.

22. Wellington's sons, Arthur Richard and Charles as infants. Wellington placed this picture on the lid of his dressing case, which he used on the Iberian Peninsula to remind him of home and family.

23. The Bombardment of Copenhagen in September 1807.
General Arthur Wellesley, who negotiated the Danish capitulation along with two other high-ranking officers, did not agree with the bombardment of the city despite its indisputable efficiency, as civilians were likely to suffer the most, a fact he considered to be unethical.

24. Soldiers of the 95th Rifles in combat, equipped with their Baker rifles.
In comparison to loading a musket, these rifles took twice as long to load,
but their effective range was roughly four times farther than that of a musket. The British Riflemen
belonged to the elite of the light infantry units of their time.

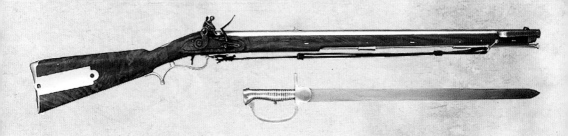

25. A Baker rifle, commonly used by the British Rifle Brigade.

26. French General Jean-Andoche Junot, commander of the first French invasion of Portugal in 1807–1808.

27. The attack of the 20th Light Dragoons at the Battle of Vimeiro, Portugal.

THE CONVENTION of CINTRA, a Portuguese Gambol for the Amusement of IOHN BULL.

LIEUT: GEN! SIR JOHN MOORE, K.B.

28. A political cartoon sharply criticising the Convention of Cintra, which that was circulated in the British press and named *Convention of Cintra. A Portuguese Gambol for the Amusement of John Bull.* John Bull, the fictitious figure sitting in the bottom right frame of the cartoon, is meant to depict a typical Englishman. The couplet from the fifth frame of the cartoon says: 'This is the *Convention* that Nobody owns, that saved old Junot's Baggage and Bones, altho' Sir Arthur (whose Valour and skill) began so well and ended so ill, had beat the French who took the Gold that lay in the city of Lisbon.'

29. Lieutenant-General Sir John Moore, Commander-in-Chief of the British Army at the Battle of Corunna, which took place 16th January 1809.

30. British General and Field Marshal of the Portuguese Army, Lord William Beresford. In 1809–1810, he intensively trained the Portuguese troops after properly armed at the expense of the British Government.

31. French Marshal Nicolas Jean Soult. He particularly distinguished himself in the Battle of Austerlitz in 1805, where he led Napoleon's troops in a decisive attack. Wellington and Soult fought against one another for the first time in the Battle of Oporto in 1809.

32. The Battle of Talavera
(27–28 July 1809).
We can see Arthur Wellesley giving
orders in the centre of the etching.

33. William Wellesley-Pole, later 3rd Earl
of Mornington, was Wellington's older brother
and frequent correspondent. William
was adopted at a young age by the Pole Family
and thus changed his name
from Wellesley to Wellesley-Pole.

34. and **35.** General Rowland Hill, commonly known among his soldiers as 'Daddy' Hill for his genial attitude toward the men and his everlasting optimism. During the Peninsular War, Hill was one of Wellington's most reliable generals. Finally, in the Battle of Waterloo, Wellington trusted him with the command of one of his army corps.

LIEUT GENERAL LORD HILL, K.B.

36. Archduke Charles, Commander-in-Chief personally leading the Austrian Army's counterattack against the French in the Battle of Wagram 1809.

37. The memorable duel between Minister for War Lord Castlereagh and Foreign Minister Lord Canning that took place on 21st September 1809 in Putney Heat Park. British society was greatly shocked by this duel between government officials, a fact which the Whigs used to their advantage, nearly bringing about the fall of the Tory Government.

Colonel Grant
on the
2 M Genl Staff in
the Peninsula
Waterloo

38. Major Colquhoun Grant, who was much liked by the Spanish people and dubbed 'Granto Bueno', was the "best of the best" of Wellington's so-called exploring officers. He spoke excellent Spanish, French and Portuguese. Throughout the whole Peninsular War, he worked behind enemy lines and provided Wellington with invaluable information. Toward the end of the war, he even operated in Paris, the heart of Napoleon's Empire. The story of this "James Bond" of the Peninsular War itself could certainly fill a whole novel.

39. View of the hilly terrain to the north of Lisbon, which forms "natural walls" not far from the town of Torres Vedras, through which passed the first defensive line of Wellington's Lines of Torres Vedras fortification system.

40. Today's view of the originally Moorish castle that embodied redoubt no. 27 in the first of Wellington's defensive Lines of Torres Vedras complex.

41. and **42.** The inner spaces of the Saint Vincent fortress.

43. and **44.** The preserved military road near Fort Alqueidão, close to the city of Sobral, which was constructed in order to better supply the individual fortresses that formed the Lines of Torres Vedras.

45. Wellington's headquarters in the small village of Pero Negro, located in close proximity to the first defensive lines of the Torres Vedras fortification system.

46. Fort Saint Julian, around which the third defensive line of the Torres Vedras complex was built. In the event that Masséna's army surmounted the first two lines, Wellington's army would board ships in the adjacent harbour and be evacuated to Britain. Today there is a picturesque beach on the same site.

47. Wellington (right centre) sits with members of his staff by the fire in the evening before the Battle of Busaco. The scene is somewhat romanticised, as Wellington forbade fires in his camp before battle in order to prevent the enemy from knowing his army's exact position and numbers.

48. Major-General Robert Craufurd,
giving the order to charge against Marshal Ney's columns in the Battle of Busaco.

49. View from the position of Wellington's forces spread across the Busaco Ridge toward
the position of Masséna's army.

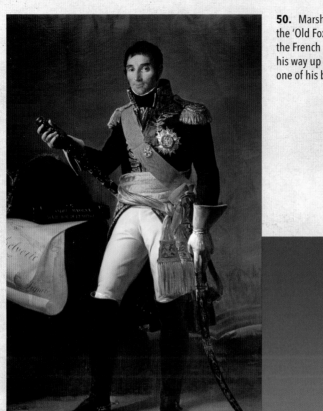

50. Marshall André Masséna, nicknamed the 'Old Fox', was just a common private before the French Revolution. Nonetheless, he worked his way up the ranks and Napoleon valued him as one of his best and most capable field marshals.

51. Memorial to honour the fallen soldiers in the Battle of Busaco, which is placed directly on the steep Ridge of Busaco along which Wellington deployed his army in a remarkably strong defensive position.

52. View of the hilly landscape around the town of Sobral, near which Marshal Masséna first laid eyes upon Wellington's Lines of Torres Vedras.

53. Remains of Fort Alqueidão, built near the town of Sobral, through which passed the first defensive lines of the Torres Vedras complex.

54. Count William of Schaumburg-Lippe (1724–1777). Commander-in-Chief of the British expeditionary forces that defended Portugal during the Seven Years' War against the Franco-Spanish invasion in 1762. There are many obvious similarities between his defence of Portugal and the one led by Wellington. It is possible that Wellington planned parts of his defence of Portugal based on La Lippe's work *Mémoire de la Campagne de Portugal de 1762*.

55. Francis Rawdon-Hastings, Earl of Moira, was Wellington's commander in Flanders and later mentioned the impact that the Count of Schaumburg-Lippe's plans may have had on Wellington in his defence of Portugal.

56. Building of the former Town Hall in the Portuguese city of Santarém – in all probability, Wellington spent a few nights here, as did Marshal Masséna during his retreat from the Lines of Torres Vedras. Today there is a municipal museum on the same site.

57. Close-up of a Portuguese man on the tiling inside the former Santarem Town Hall. The character's face was chipped off by Masséna's soldiers, who were venting their frustration during the humiliating retreat from the Lines of Torres Vedras.

moment, Olivia did not hesitate to intervene and show her Arthur's let-ter from India, after which Kitty summoned up the courage thanks to Arthur's repeated interest in her to refuse Cole using the influence of the Sparrow Family despite her mother and brother's wishes. Nonetheless, it is likely that Kitty did not tell her family the true reason that she turned the kind and admittedly handsome Mr Cole away. As she noted openly in a letter from May 1802 to Olivia, she evidently feared that her family would perhaps again refuse Arthur (who at the time was thousands of miles away and was still not famous for his victory at Assaye, which took place in 1803) as a potential husband:

> Olivia, you know my heart, at least I believe you do, as well as I know it myself. You know how sincerely I am interested in his happiness and can imagine what gratitude I feel (indeed much more than can be expressed) for his kind remembrance. My dearest Olivia, you know I can send no message: a kind word from me he might think binding to him and make him think himself obliged to renew a pursuit which perhaps he might not then wish or my family (at least some of them) take kindly.[229]

This letter is clearly the best evidence of Kitty's good-hearted character and her lasting affection for Arthur. Nonetheless, the pressure on the part of her family to marry Lowry Cole combined with uncertainty concern-ing Arthur's return took a serious toll on her health, when she suddenly and unexpectedly suffered a nervous breakdown. After Arthur's return to Britain, she felt considerably better, but the earlier nervous tension had inevitably left lasting effects on her behaviour. Olivia Sparrow, who still remained Kitty's ardent intermediary, contacted Arthur just a week after his return from India in a letter that has also now been lost. However, we can again gain a relatively reasonable image of the whole affair based on Arthur's reply to Olivia's letter dated 24th September 1805. It is evident in the letter that Olivia Sparrow had reprimanded Arthur for not mak-ing immediate contact with the miserable Kitty after his return. Arthur Wellesley, however, had more pressing matters – only two days after his arrival from India he was called upon to report immediately to Lord Castlereagh at the War Department due to the on-going war with France. Understandably, he did not let Kitty know of his return via Olivia, as he had justifiable concerns that he would not be allowed to enjoy his homecoming for long. In his own defence Arthur penned the following to Olivia:

> All I can say is that if I could count myself capable of neglecting such a woman [Kitty], I would endeavour to think of her no more… What is to become of your friend [Kitty] in the winter? Does she remain in Ireland? … I am very apprehensive that after having come from India for one purpose only, I shall not accomplish it. I think it is not improbable that if troops under orders for embarkation should be sent to the Continent, I shall be ordered to go with them and possibly never see you or her again.[230]

As we now know, Arthur's mission on the continent was soon cancelled due to Bonaparte's victory at Austerlitz (2nd December 1805) and the dissolution of the Third Coalition, allowing him to remain in Britain and continue on in his courtship of Kitty Pakenham. Arthur's statement that he had returned from India 'for one purpose only', by which he evidently meant his renewed efforts to marry Kitty, is perhaps evidence that, at least at the given moment, Arthur Wellesley was thinking much more romantically than he was later willing to admit. If we remember the following words that Arthur penned to Mr Cradock shortly before his departure from India: 'I acknowledge that I am anxious to a degree which I cannot express to see my friends again, and even if I were certain that I should not be employed in England at all, there is no situation in India which would induce me to stay here.'[231], we may assume that Kitty Pakennham in all probability held a prominent place amongst these "friends" in Arthur's future plans. Although Olivia once again faithfully handed over Arthur's letter from early September 1805 to Kitty, Arthur's words evidently did not completely relieve her of uncertainty in terms of Arthur's intentions to marry her, as she wrote to Olivia in reaction to Arthur's last letter.

> What can I say, I can know nothing of his mind but what you have told me you assure me he still regards me he has authorized you to renew the proposition he made some years ago but my Olivia I have in vain sought in his letter for one word expressive of a wish that the proposition should be accepted of.[232]

However, Kitty did not need to doubt for long about Arthur Wellesley's intentions, as she subsequently received Arthur's official request for her hand in marriage, which she immediately and joyfully accepted with understandable emotion. Her proverbial "I do" to Arthur's request also contained the following words:

> I should be the most undeserving of beings were I capable of feeling less than gratitude in return for the steadiness of your attachment... To express what I feel at this moment would be quite impossible. I will therefore only say that I am conscious of a degree of happiness of which till now I had no idea.[233]

However, Kitty feared that she had changed after such a long period of mutual separation, and thus she asked Arthur with modest urgency for the two to meet before the wedding:

> It is indeed my earnest wish to see you... I do not think it fair to engage you before you are quite positively certain that I am indeed the very woman you would choose for a companion a friend for life. In so many years I may be much more changed than I am myself conscious of. If when we have met you can tell me...[234]

In this letter, Kitty again expressed her good nature and the integrity of her thoughts. At the same time, however, we can observe a sign of her inner uncertainty. Nonetheless, Arthur Wellesley remained single-minded and uncompromisingly persisted in his decision to marry Kitty despite their long period of separation and wrote to her that for this reason he saw no need for a meeting before the wedding. His decision seems difficult to understand. Why did he refuse to see Kitty before the marriage after so many years of separation? It is true that he had given Kitty his word that the wedding would take place. If he were now to refuse, he would place Kitty in a highly precarious situation, as it is highly likely that he had learned from Olivia the circumstances under which Kitty had refused Mr Cole's earlier proposal. Arthur surely loved her very much (at least in his youth), but over the long years spent in India he had perhaps idealized this love for her into a more platonic notion. It should also be mentioned that Arthur's bruised male ego from years past may have also played a significant role in his decision, as he was ignominiously refused as Kitty's suitor and now intended to demonstrate to the Pakenhams his importance. All this, however, is pure speculation that can just as easily be disputed. Why Arthur refused to see Kitty before the wedding will thus forever remain a mystery. However, the clear fact remains Arthur Wellesley soon received a letter from Kitty's mother and brother Thomas, in which they both gladly gave their blessings for the marriage in light of Arthur's sound financial situation, his knighthood, and the certain fame that he had gained in India. As thanks, Arthur Wellesley also quickly wrote to Olivia Sparrow for her efforts in the role of the intermediary. 'Now my dearest friend, you may wish me joy for I am the happiest man in the world.'[235]

The wedding between Sir Arthur Wellesley, Knight of the Order of the Bath, and Catherine (Kitty) Pakenham took place according to Arthur's wishes without delay on 10th April 1806 at the Pakenham Hall estate in Ireland. The ceremony took place symbolically in the same place where Arthur was refused by his bride's brother Thomas twelve years earlier and marked ten years since he had embarked for India. Throughout this whole time, the thirty-six-year-old groom had not once seen his thirty-three-year-old bride in person.[236]

The vast majority of biographies on Wellington (from Elizabeth Longford to the works of Christopher Hibbert and Richard Holmes) quote the following words that the slightly shocked Arthur was said to have whispered to his brother Gerald, who acted as minister during the marriage, in reaction to Kitty's transformed appearance after seeing her for the first time after years on the day of the wedding: 'She has grown ugly, by Jove!' However, this story is first documented in sources fifty years later in the diary of Lady Francis Shelley.[237] After having analysed the Duke's correspondence, it is my personal assertion that it was highly unlikely (but not impossible) that Wellington, as a highborn Anglican, would have whispered "By Jove!" in the priest's ear. Nonetheless, in the sources that were studied for this publication Wellington regularly used the characteristic interjection "By God!". It is, however, my assertion that the story is quite probably another myth of Wellingtoniana.

The romantic story of the relationship between Arthur Wellesley and Kitty Pakenham, in which love triumphs over all obstacles and long separation as it does in Homer's Odyssey (a book that was also a favourite among the society of the time) soon became highly popular in Britain. Kitty was even invited to the Royal Court, where Queen Charlotte (wife of King George III) personally asked her about the circumstances of her amorous story.

I am happy to see you at my Court, so bright an example of Constancy.' [the Queen told Kitty] 'But did you really never write one letter to Sir Arthur Wellesley during his long absence? 'No, never, Madam.' 'And did you never think of him?' 'Yes, Madam, very often.'[238]

Despite this fact, the sad truth remains that the marriage was an unhappy one from the very beginning. During their long years of separation, both Arthur and Kitty had changed. Arthur Wellesley had become an ambitious man who had gone through harsh lessons in life, seen hellish battle at Assaye, and earned social and political admiration. After his return home, he seemed to be fully focused on his career and expected a supportive wife at his side to give him the necessary support in his times of insecurity, whereas Kitty, who had gone through a difficult period culminating in a nervous breakdown, hoped more for a peaceful family life in the Irish countryside and began to feel ill-at-ease in society. In addition, over the course of the long separation, Arthur (contrary to Kitty) had not remained faithful. Before his departure and after his return from India, he had visited the infamous London courtesan Harriette Wilson. He was evidently not faithful to Kitty even while in India, where in all probability he fathered an illegitimate son, Arthur Frees. At the time, however, extramarital affairs (especially among men) were viewed as a relatively common occurrence. Marriage was basically an agreed contract on the part of the families involved, and passionate love was not expected in the spouses' relationship.[239] However, the clear fact remains that, throughout his whole life, Wellington was keen to surround himself with personable, independent, and intelligent women whose company he enjoyed. His favourites included figures such as Lady Frances Shelley, the Italian contralto Giuseppina Grassini (Napoleon's former lover), the Russian Princess Catherine Bagration, and, in his more senior years, Harriet Arbuthnot. However, at no time in his life did he allow any of his relationships to be scandalized and the majority of these alleged affairs remain unconfirmed. In addition, Arthur never divorced Kitty, which was far from impossible in Britain at the time; we can perhaps claim that, at least at the end of their married lives, they began once again to find mutual understanding.

Despite the rather tepid relationships between the newlyweds, less than a year after the wedding on 3rd February 1807, Kitty gave birth to Arthur's son and heir Arthur Richard. As this was Kitty's first child at the age of thirty four, the absolutely seamless birth was just short of a miracle at the beginning of the 19th century.[240] After the wedding, Arthur and Kitty purchased a home in London at 11 Harley Street. Coincidentally, the London neighbourhood in which the Wellesleys settled served as a refuge for many French emigrants who did not approve of the French revolution and Napoleon's government that had risen from it in France. Arthur Wellesley subsequently received an offer to purchase a considerably larger residence that was but a short distance from their house in Harley Street; however, after serious deliberation Arthur chose to refuse the offer for financial reasons. It seems that after the years spent outside Britain, Arthur was somewhat surprised at the extremely high costs of living in London, a fact he did not hesitate to share in a letter to his friend Mr Malcolm in India in order to prepare him for the change in affairs after his return. Nonetheless, Arthur soon received a lucrative job offer for the position of Chief Secretary to the Lord Lieutenant of Ireland, Charles Lennox, the 4th Duke of Richmond. He decided to accept the position of Chief Secretary, leading him to return to Dublin, the city of his birth.

Ireland's citizens, the majority of whom were Roman Catholics, wished for either a measure of, or full independence from Britain. As a direct consequence of agitation in this regard, a tense atmosphere had loomed over the country for several years. As an obstinate Tory, Arthur Wellesley was naturally in favour of preserving the *status quo* and that meant a continuation of the union between Ireland and Britain, which was created by the Acts of Union during Pitt's government in 1801. At the same time, in terms of Irish nationalism he defended a policy of openness and providing the highest level of autonomy. However, the moment the Irish stood up against the Crown and demanded full independence, in Arthur's opinion there would be no other choice but to crush the uprising by force.[241] According to historian Elizabeth Longford, this period also gave rise to another of Wellington's most commonly popularized witticisms (this time not a myth), when his Irish origin was discussed critically at a social event. In reply, Wellington spoke the following words: 'Because a man is born in a stable that does not make him a horse.'[242]

Arthur, Kitty and young Arthur Richard moved to Dublin; the whole family now lived in a comfortable residence designated for the Chief Secretary for Ireland in Dublin's Phoenix Park. In addition, it is likely that Kitty felt much more at ease in Ireland than in cosmopolitan London society, which teemed with all the new fashion trends and products of all kinds but also with intense social scrutiny, gossip and scandal. Because the new post led Arthur Wellesley and his family back to Ireland, he found himself travelling often, primarily to London, where he took part in sessions of the British Parliament, as the Irish Parliament had been dissolved on 31st December 1800 by the Acts of Union. Thus, care for their new household in Phoenix Park fell on Kitty Pakenham's shoulders, a duty which, however, was expected from a wife at the time as her natural obligation. The less than six-month-old Arthur Richard fell ill with the measles, which the worried Kitty immediately informed Arthur of in London as he was taking part in sessions of the Parliament there. Despite the fact that measles – especially in such a small child – was not something to be completely dismissed, Arthur wrote to his wife from London in an effort to support and reassure her as much as possible: 'I have no apprehensions for the Meazles being convinced that it is a mild disorder, & one that has no bad consequences, if the Patient is well taken care of as it is going off.'[243] Fortunately, Arthur was not mistaken and to his delight his small son recovered within a few days. In addition, in the middle of the summer of 1807 it became clear that Kitty was again pregnant, after which she brought a second baby boy into the world on 16th January 1808. The proud father and mother named him Charles.*

Nonetheless, the first disagreements between Arthur and Kitty slowly began to surface. Years later, Wellington (now with some degree of retrospection) called these disputes with his wife 'domestic annoyances'. For example, during one of Arthur's trips to London, Kitty sacked the family gardener in the early summer of 1807, as one of Kitty's servants, who had fallen in love with the gardener, had taken her own life due to his unrequited love. Arthur did not agree with this step, and did not hesitate

---

*   Although Arthur Richard, who subsequently became the 2nd Duke of Wellington, remained childless, Charles' sons Arthur and Henry went on to become the 3rd and 4th Dukes of Wellington respectively. Thus, Charles' line, to which the present 9th Duke of Wellington belongs (coincidentally also named Charles Wellesley), proved to be the most prominent. See: Jane Wellesley, *A Journey Through My Family*, pp. 174–175.

to share this with Kitty in a letter: 'Let the Gardener be taken back. It is evident that he had nothing to say to the death of the woman...it would not be very charitable to dismiss him from my Service: and I shall certainly not dismiss him.'[244]

Another dispute between Arthur and Kitty in the summer of 1807 dealt with shared finances. More exactly, it concerned an unpaid bill for a bricklayer for work that he had carried out on their home in Phoenix Park. The bricklayer, who had evidently not received payment from Kitty, now approached Arthur in search of payment. He in turn penned Kitty the following mild reprimand because of the matter: 'I enclose a letter from a Bricklayer. I thought you had paid him. Let me know whether you have or not.'[245] The problem most likely arose from the simple fact that Kitty had not asked Arthur in time for money for the household. However, Kitty succumbed to a mild hysteria over the whole affair, which is evidenced in the following words from Arthur in a letter from the end of July 1807:

My dearest Kitty,... I am much concerned that you should have thought of concealing from me any want of money which you might have experienced. I don't understand now how this want occurred [the unpaid bill to the bricklayer], or why it was concealed, & the less there is said or written upon the subject the better, for I acknowledge that the conclusion I draw from your conduct upon the occasion is that you must be mad, or you must consider me to be a Brute, & most particularly fond & avaricious of money. Once for all you require no permission to talk to me upon any subject you please, all that I request is that a piece of work may not be made about trifles...& that you may not go into tears because I don't think them deserving of an uncommon degree of attention.[246]

While Arthur dealt with these 'domestic annoyances', the political situation on the continent had once again seriously deteriorated, as after Austerlitz Napoleon continued to strengthen his hold on German territory. Under the rule of King Frederick William III, Prussia strove at all costs to avoid war, a fact which inevitably subordinated them more and more perceptibly to Napoleon's influence. Prussia first accepted the suggested exchange of Kłodzko County for Hanover, which as the ancestral home of British Monarch George III, who was a Hanoverian, was a highly sensitive territory to Britain. Prussia then signed an agreement in Paris on closing Prussian ports for British vessels. A short while later, Prussia annexed Hanover and thus none of the European powers were surprised when on 11th May 1806 Britain declared war on Prussia.

Events on the continent continued to deteriorate rapidly. On 12th July 1806, Napoleon Bonaparte established the Confederation of the Rhine on the territory of the Holy Roman Empire, bringing a *de facto* end to the Holy Roman Empire after more than eight hundred years. Due to these events, the hitherto Emperor of the Holy Roman Empire Francis II abdicated on 6th August 1806, causing the Holy Roman Empire to be definitively abolished *de jure*. In addition, Francis II had already reacted to Bonaparte's coronation as French Emperor in December 1804 and his deteriorating power in the Holy Roman Empire in anticipation of the Empire's possible collapse when he had himself declared Austrian Emperor Francis I on 11th August 1804. From this point on, the terms Austria and Austrians (hitherto referred to as Habsburgs or Imperial soldiers) should be used. Napoleon's newly established Confederation of the Rhine was made up of sixteen German states (also called duchies or principalities – these domains were artificially created from the former territory of the Holy Roman Empire to fit Bonaparte's needs), which received official independence. In reality however, they were merely protectorates under Napoleon's sway. Clear proof of this can be seen in the fact that one of the requirements of the members of the Confederation of the Rhine was to provide 60,000 soldiers for Napoleon's future campaigns. In addition, the French Army soon began to operate regularly on the right bank of the Rhine, permanently occupying the fortresses of Verden and Essen in territory of what is today's Germany. These steps taken by Napoleon along with Prussia's growing humiliation finally lead Prussia's monarch Frederick William III in September 1806 to join the ranks of the newly formed Fourth Anti-French Coalition alongside Britain, Russia, Sweden, and Saxony.

However, shortly after its entrance into the Fourth Coalition, the Prussians were crushingly defeated twice in one day on 14th October 1806 in the Battles of Jena and Auerstedt, which were decisive for the whole campaign. Three days later, the French defeated Prussia's reserve army at Halle and continued to take the Prussian capital city of Berlin before the end of October. Prussia fell so quickly that the Russian troops that were coming to its aid had no time to engage actively in battle. On 21st November 1806 in Berlin, the triumphant Napoleon declared his famous Continental Blockade on Britain (which dominated at sea and in the colonies), which forbade Continental states from importing British goods. Everything that came from England was to be either confiscated or destroyed. Napoleon subsequently defeated the Russians on 14th June 1807 in Eastern Prussian Friedland, leading Russian Tsar Alexander I to sign the Treaty of Tilsit on 7th July. The Tsar was forced to acknowledge the newly established Duchy of Warsaw and the Confederation of the Rhine, and agree to uphold the Continental Blockade, and renounce his ambitions for power in the Balkans. Two days later, an official treaty was signed with Prussia, an event that was catastrophic for Frederick William III. Prussia lost more than half of its territory and over five million subjects. The following new states were formed from this portion of former Prussian territory: The Duchy of Warsaw (in today's Poland) and the Kingdom of Westphalia (in today's Germany), the throne of which was given to Napoleon's youngest brother, Jérôme Bonaparte.[247]

In 1807 the threat of a French invasion of the British Isles returned. Napoleon planned to absorb the Dano-Norwegian Navy,* making an invasion of Britain once again viable, as the Dano-Norwegian Fleet together with that of Portugal was the last force that could compete against the British Navy. George Canning, British Foreign Secretary** called upon Denmark to give up its naval fleet voluntarily under "British protection". The Danes, who hoped to maintain neutrality (although justifiably influenced by their fear of Napoleon), ultimately refused the offer, leading the British government to take their navy by force. For this reason, in July 1807 a military expedition was sent from Britain under the command of General Lord Cathcart, whose task it was to conquer Copenhagen and take the Dano-Norwegian Fleet that was at anchor there. Arthur Wellesley, who would have known that William Cathcart had been Commander-in-Chief in Ireland from 1803–1805, saw the whole operation as a chance to further his career and clearly

---

* The Kingdoms of Denmark and Norway were in a union that lasted 434 years until it ended in 1814.

** The function of Foreign Minister at the time carried the official title of Secretary of State for Foreign Affairs.

intended to take part. He first received permission to leave Ireland from the Lord Lieutenant the Duke of Richmond and then convinced War Minister Lord Castlereagh to give him command of a British division selected for the Copenhagen Expedition. During the operation, Arthur Wellesley once again encountered the famous General Baird, as Baird had also taken command of a British division destined for Denmark. The British disembarked near Copenhagen in mid-August and immediately laid siege to the Danish capital. Wellesley quickly distinguished himself in battle as he and his division crushed the Danish units heading for Copenhagen in attempts to lift the siege. General Wellesley managed to surprise the ill-prepared Danes in an abrupt attack near the small seaport of Køge southwest of Copenhagen, where he scored an effortless and convincing victory.[248] In terms of the losses incurred by the Danes during their defeat, Arthur Wellesley wrote the following lines:

> The loss of the enemy has been very great, many have fallen, and there are nearly 60 officers and 1100 men prisoners. In their flight they have thrown away their arms and clothing, and many stands of the former have fallen into our hands. I believe that we have taken 10 pieces of cannon...[249]

The relatively seamless course of battle was also confirmed by Richard Howard, who fought in the ranks of the 95th (Rifle) Regiment of Foot (commonly called the 95th Rifles) under Arthur Wellesley's command:

> We gave three cheers and charged them ourselves, with three companies of the 92nd and two troops of light horse. We drove them all out of the town [Køge] with great loss on the enemy's side. We pursued them for two or three miles into the country.[250]

Nonetheless, as was the case in the period of the Napoleonic Wars, which still showed signs of gentlemanly behaviour between warring sides, Wellesley released all sixty Danish officers on parole. This meant that although the men could return home freely, they were not allowed to raise their weapons against the British for an agreed period of time. In some cases, officers who were given parole were not freed, but their weapons were returned to them and they were treated gentlemanly – almost as if they were guests – under the condition that they promised not to attempt an escape until they were exchanged for a captured British officer.*

After their defeat at Køge, the Danes had no time to make any other significant attempt at liberating Copenhagen, as on 2nd September 1807 the Royal Navy under the command of Admiral James Gambier bombarded the city for three days with heavy mortar fire including some 300 Congreve Rockets**, resulting in fires and widespread destruction and the deaths of 195 civilians and a further 768 casualties.*** As a result of the bombardment, Copenhagen capitulated within five days and thus the Dano-Norwegian Fleet fell into British hands. Arthur Wellesley, who was entrusted by General Lord Cathcart with negotiating the Danish capitulation along with two other high-ranking officers, did not however agree with the bombardment of the city despite its indisputable efficiency (although he was later blamed for ill-advisedly risking the lives of his men while taking the city walls thanks to a poorly prepared assault), as civilians were likely to suffer the most, a fact he considered to be unethical. He appreciated how bravely his men had fared at Køge, but at the same time he was frustrated by his soldiers' repeated acts of theft and their disrespectful behaviour toward the local populace. Specifically, Arthur Wellesley complained that the British were 'very unpopular' amongst the locals living in proximity to Copenhagen. In a letter penned to the commander of the whole operation, General Lord Cathcart, he added that he was 'so fully convinced that soldiers guilty of marauding are unfit for any service, that he [Wellesley] is determined to put a stop to their disgraceful practices.'251 Lieutenant-General John Coffin, who was in charge of military supply throughout the mission, expressed similar thoughts regarding the unsuitable behaviour of the British troops throughout the campaign as well in the following lines written to a friend: 'The outrages

---

*   One of the best examples of medieval knightly behaviour and freeing captives on parole, a tradition which was followed in releasing officers during the Napoleonic Wars, is without a doubt the case of the capture of French King John II (or John the Good) during the Hundred Years' War between England and France at the Battle of Poitiers in 1356. Edward of Woodstock, Commander-in-Chief of the victorious English at Poitiers, known more commonly by his nickname "the Black Prince", released the defeated French King, whom he had captured during battle, on parole on the condition that the French paid an agreed ransom within a given time for their captured ruler. When the French King failed to gather the money in time, John II gave himself up once again voluntarily to captivity in the Tower of London.

**   A military rocket designed by the inventor and rocket artillery pioneer Sir William Congreve and modelled on the Mysorean rockets that had been used against the British in India.

***   A total of 2,000 mortars were fired upon the city.

committed by our troops [during the Copenhagen campaign] were worthy of a band of Cossacks [evidently a reference to the Russian light cavalry].'[252] However, British officers managed to return a large portion of the stolen property back to its original owners among the Danish populace. One of the largest scandals (although one with a "happy ending") was caused by Wellesley's 95th Rifles, who "accidentally robbed" a Danish princess who at the time was staying at her residence in the countryside away from the capital. The incident took place during the pursuit of the defeated Danish soldiers fleeing from Køge; among other stolen objects from the princess' possessions, a silver plate was of the highest value. Fortunately, the officers of the 95th Rifles virtuously reported the stolen items and all spoils, including the valuable silver plate, were handed over to Major-General Wellesley, who made a personal apology to the princess, returning all of her possessions with the words: 'I cannot sufficiently express my concern at the occurrence of this event... I now send those articles and entreat your Highness to pardon...'[253] Before taking Copenhagen, General Baird was slightly injured in one of the evidently few skirmishes with Danish troops that took place in the immediate surroundings of the besieged city. Arthur Wellesley expressed his thoughts on the matter in a letter penned to General Lord Cathcart in the following: 'I am sorry to hear that General Baird is wounded, but I hope that his wound will not be attended by any bad consequences.'[254] Fortunately for Baird, the injury healed well and the general quickly recovered.

Overall, the Copenhagen Expedition of 1807 (sometimes known as the Second Battle of Copenhagen) was a clear success, as British losses amounted to less than 300 dead and wounded out of 18,000 deployed soldiers.[255] Despite this fact (and perhaps because of the simplicity of the story), the Copenhagen Expedition did not enjoy much popularity in British society. Lady Henrietta Ponsonby, the sister of the famous fashion icon and one of the first women engaged in high politics in Britain, Georgiana Cavendish, Duchess of Devonshire*, wrote of the dominant sentiment concerning the Danish campaign: 'The Mob do not seem to value it as they ought, considering what it saves us from.' [256]

In my opinion, the Battle of Køge is further proof that Wellington was far from being merely a defensive general. It is important to note

---

* The story of Georgiana Cavendish was portrayed in the film *The Duchess* (2008) starring Keira Knightley as Lady Georgiana.

that the British and Danish forces were not evenly matched, as the latter were largely made up of a militia and had half the number of cavalry of the British. To date, academic literature about the period has paid relatively little attention to the battle. In Arthur Wellesley's view, the battle was a successful and surprising attack on an enemy position that led to a speedy victory. Proof that General Lord Cathcart appreciated Arthur Wellesley's communication skills can be seen in the fact that he named Major-General Wellesley as one of the three officers to negotiate Danish capitulation. In addition to the military actions, one other significant event concerning Arthur Wellesley took place during the campaign in Copenhagen. One of the British Generals taking part in the expedition, Major-General Thomas Grosvenor is believed to have taken his favourite mare with him, who soon proved to be in foal and therefore had to be sent back to England. There the mare bore a young colt, which was given the name Copenhagen after the destination of the campaign. The stallion was later bought by Colonel Charles Wood, who sold Arthur Wellesley the horse whilst serving as a cavalry officer in Spain. The chestnut stallion became Wellington's favourite horse, and he subsequently rode him at the Battle of Waterloo. Today, Copenhagen's final resting place is in the grounds of Stratfield Saye House, the Hampshire home of the Dukes of Wellington since 1817.[257]

After the successful expedition to Copenhagen, Arthur once again began to focus wholly on his military career, a fact which can be seen in his letter to the Foreign Minister Lord Canning, in which he noted after his return from Denmark: 'I shall be happy to aid the government in any manner they please, and am ready to set out for any part of the world at a moment's notice.'[258] Canning saw absolutely no reason to disoblige Arthur Wellesley's request. Together with Francisco de Miranda, an advocate of Venezuelan nationalism living in exile in London, Canning decided to send Arthur Wellesley as Commander-in-Chief of the next British expeditionary army, whose mission was to fight against the Spanish in their South American colony of the Captaincy General of Venezuela. During this military mission to South America, Arthur Wellesley was to be given 9,000 men; he received high command primarily thanks to his promotion to Lieutenant-General in April 1808, once again ranking him somewhat higher in the hierarchy of the British Army.[259] At the same time, however, the situation on the Continent was dramatically transforming. In reaction to the British capture of the Dano-Norwegian fleet, Napoleon ordered General Jean-Andoche Junot to attack Portugal in order to gain immediate control of the Portuguese Navy, which was the absolute last opportunity for Napoleon to fulfil his plan of invading Britain. An additional and valid reason for the French Emperor to carry out an immediate attack on Portugal was the refusal on the part of the Portuguese government in maintaining the Continental Blockade,* a fact which clearly placed Portugal on the side of Britain, its long-time ally.** Spain, as Napoleon's ally, provided Junot's troops arriving from France free passage. On 30th November 1807, Lisbon fell into the hands of the French Army without significant resistance while the Portuguese Royal Family managed to escape at the last minute by sea to Brazil with the help of Dom João VI (John VI of Portugal), who ruled in Portugal as prince-regent in place of his mentally ill mother Queen Maria I. Although the French succeeded in taking Lisbon in a remarkable fourteen days, the Portuguese Navy had managed in the nick of time to sail to Britain for safety, a fact that was a considerable blow for Napoleon. Although the French appeared to speedily conquer Portugal and initially its citizens seemed to be relatively open to French revolutionary ideals, the French soon incited a wave of resistance due to their cruel behaviour towards the populace. Directly after the occupation of Lisbon, the French General Junot, who Napoleon had appointed Governor of Portugal, issued the following lofty statement in which he referred to the whole French invasion as a mission aimed at liberating the Portuguese people:

---

*　As well as the historic alliance between England and Portugal, there was extensive trade between the two countries thanks in part to the likes of The Methuen Treaty (1703), a military and commercial treaty signed during the Spanish Wars of Succession.

**　In the mediaeval period, the important Treaty of Windsor (1386) was signed between the Kingdoms of England and Portugal. The Treaty supported mutual trade and also guaranteed military support. It was thus a counterbalance to the alliance between France and the Crown of Castile (later Spain). The signing of the Treaty of Windsor was preceded by the Battle of Aljubarrota (1385), in which England supported John I of Portugal with an army against the Crown of Castile, which aspired to conquer Portugal. Thanks to the Portuguese-English victory at Aljubarrota, Portugal survived as an independent state. From this period, the alliance has continued until today with noble marriages and various treaties. British Prime Minister Winston Churchill called this alliance between England and Portugal one that was *'without parallel in world history.'* See Ben Trowbridge, *History's Unparalleled Alliance: the Anglo-Portuguese Treaty of Windsor, 9th May 1386*, online article in: https://history.blog.gov.uk/2016/05/09/historys-unparalleled-alliance-the-anglo-portuguese-treaty-of-windsor-9th-may-1386/

People of Lisbon, live quietly in your houses. Do not fear my army or myself, it is only our enemies and wrongdoers who should frighten us. The Great Napoleon, my master, has sent me to protect you. I will protect you.[260]

It did not take long for the Portuguese to notice and feel the impact of the French occupation, from the replacement of the Portuguese flag with the French tricolour on the historic landmark of *Castelo de São Jorge* that overlooks Lisbon to the curtailing of the rights and freedoms of the Portuguese people. Gradually, Junot issued a decree banning the possession of weapons followed by the official dissolution of the Portuguese Army. Junot's seizure of power definitively culminated in the dispersal of the Portuguese Government accompanied by the demand of payment in the amount of forty million cazadors to French coffers by the end of February 1808 at the latest. In lieu of this, Junot did not hesitate to issue an order for all gold and silver to be gathered from Portuguese churches. A massive anti-French uprising soon broke out. Oporto, Portugal's second largest city became the centre of a Portuguese insurgency and declared its independence from French rule under the direction of the Bishop of Oporto, António José de Castro. France despatched additional troops (supposedly to bolster its situation in Portugal), but en route they crossed into Spain on 16th February 1808 and to all intents and purposes became an army of occupation. The French occupation of cities such as Barcelona, Pamplona and San Sebastián was greatly resented, with many Spaniards directing their ire towards the Spanish Monarch in general, and the Prime Minister Manuel de Godoy in particular. King Charles IV of Spain and his *valido* (favourite) de Godoy were blamed for the Treaty of Fontainebleau (27th October 1807), the provisions of which had permitted the French to enter Spain in order to attack neighbouring Portugal. Little over a month later the Mutiny of Aranjuez took place, with the mutineers demanding that the Spanish Monarch dismiss the unpopular de Godoy. Two days later King Charles IV was forced to abdicate in favour of his son Ferdinand (Ferdinand VII), who was believed to be of the opinion that Spain should enter into an alliance with Britain. Napoleon, seeking to pre-empt any possible trouble from the Spanish Royal House of Bourbon and under the false pretence of resolving the conflict, inveigled Charles and Ferdinand to travel to Bayonne in the southwest corner of France. The two Spanish Bourbons were fearful of Napoleon's power and thought it diplomatic to accept the invitation, although because of recent events and a degree of acrimony between Charles and Ferdinand they travelled separately. Charles duly informed Napoleon that he had only renounced the Spanish throne under duress and thus the abdication in Ferdinand's favour was legally null and void. Napoleon's mind was made up – he would decide Spain's destiny. Ferdinand was sent a letter informing him that Napoleon had decided that the best thing for Spain would be the replacement of the Bourbon Dynasty by a French prince. Charles "surprisingly" abdicated again in favour of Napoleon's brother Joseph Bonaparte, who thus officially became the new Spanish Monarch. Ferdinand finally yielded to pressure from Napoleon and abdicated his right to the Spanish throne.* This "abdication farce" evidently fooled no one, but it did provide a semblance of legitimacy to the government of Joseph Bonaparte. Thus, Spain became another satellite of France over the course of 1808. The Abdications of Bayonne presaged what across the Hispanic world has become known as the Spanish War of Independence (1808–1814), a conflict that overlapped with the Peninsular War.

In Spain, hostility towards the French grew by the day and erupted into violence in Madrid on the 2nd May 1808, an event known as the *Dos de Mayo Uprising*. The French forces under the command of Marshal Joachim Murat brutally suppressed the uprising and exacted a fearful vengeance over the coming days, immortalized on canvas by the Spanish artist Francisco Goya in his painting *The Third of May 1808*. Riots broke out elsewhere in Spain, very similar to what had happened in Portugal, and as a consequence representatives of both the Portuguese and Spanish anti-French opposition were dispatched to London to seek British military aid against French occupation. The British Government reacted positively to their request by deciding to send a British auxiliary expedition army to Portugal, from where it would be able to continue into Spain, assuming of course it could liberate Portugal from the French.[261]

Arthur Wellesley's troops were to be used for this planned operation, as his troops intended for Venezuela were already in a state of campaign readiness and ready for immediate embarkation. Thus, instead of Venezuela, Wellesley's destination was now Portugal, as the Spanish enemy had also paradoxically become a new ally against Napoleon. This

---

*   Napoleon, concerned that Ferdinand might become a rallying point for anti-French opposition, had him taken to Château de Valençay where he was kept under house arrest for six years.

naturally changed nothing of the fact that Arthur Wellesley was to return to war once again without delay.[262] Nonetheless, it was clear to Wellesley and the British Government that British troops under Wellesley's command on the Iberian Peninsula would literally need every single available ally. One of the most significant of these allies was Spanish commander Pedro Caro, Marquis of la Romana. Napoleon, who was aware of the potential danger that pro-British General la Romana might pose to him in the future thanks to his sympathies, had the foresight to remove him shortly before placing his brother Joseph on the Spanish throne. At the time, la Romana commanded 14,000 Spanish soldiers loyal to Ferdinand VII that could now significantly aid Wellesley in his mission on the Iberian Peninsula. Because the Spanish had been official allies of Napoleon before the "abdication farce" in favour of King Joseph, the French Emperor, who was now at the zenith of his power in Europe, managed to order the relocation of la Romana and his troops to the Danish Islands in the Northern Sea under the obvious pretence that la Romana's men were to help the French guard the coast from violations of the continental blockade aimed against trade with Britain. It must have been wholly clear to Napoleon that la Romana intended more to aid the British in this "forbidden" trade than thwart it, but it was a small price to pay in the French Emperor's strategic plans to remove la Romana from the Spanish scene. As we have already seen, however, the Spanish uprising against Joseph Bonaparte broke out with great intensity and without help from la Romana. Therefore, Napoleon immediately sent Marshal Bernadotte to the Danish Islands to force la Romana and his men to swear loyalty to his brother Joseph as the new Spanish ruler. La Romana was an honourable man and Napoleon hoped that his move would easily knock la Romana out of the game. Moreover, if the Spaniard ultimately refused to swear loyalty to Joseph, Napoleon would have him taken prisoner unceremoniously on the isolated Danish Islands – a scheme the French Emperor evidently cooked up, amused by his slyness, over a glass of select champagne. Opposed to this, however, were the British Government headed by Minister for War Castlereagh and of course Lieutenant-General Wellesley, as the British certainly did not intend to lose la Romana and his men in the fight against Bonaparte. Therefore, the British Government planned immediately to carry out a sudden rescue operation aimed at transporting la Romana and his army back to Spain where he could fight along with Wellesley against the French. If la Romana's evacuation was to be successful, it was of course crucial to inform the Spanish General of the plan for his rescue and acquaint him with it in detail. La Romana and his men were located on the third largest island of today's Funen (Fyn) in Denmark and four British agents who had attempted to reach them were exposed during their efforts and consequently executed mercilessly. Thus, a fifth agent emerged – a courageous Scottish clergyman, Father Robertson. This intrepid monk had served for many years in the Dominican Church in the city of Regensburg in Bavaria and thus spoke German almost like a native. Therefore, the British Government decided to put its faith in Father Robertson's excellent German. Father Robertson was to impersonate a German cigar merchant travelling to the port city of Bremen on business. Once he reached Bremen, the local clergymen would help him with transport to the Island of Funen to contact la Romana. At the end of May 1808, Lieutenant-General Wellesley met with Robertson in person before finally selecting him for the mission: "Tell me, Mr Robertson, are you a man of courage?" Wellesley roundly addressed the monk. The father laconically and quite courageously replied: "Try me. Sir Arthur." Wellington was pleased by this direct and bold reply just as much as he was with Father Robertson himself, replying to the man of God with a touch of humour: "That's what we mean to do."[263] Thus it was decided, upon which the Government gave the mission the go-ahead after Sir Arthur's recommendation of Robertson was made. As a "German expert on cigars" and equipped with forged documents allowing him to travel across Napoleonic Europe, Robertson set off courageously for Bremen. Initially everything went exceedingly smoothly. Robertson, who must have possessed a good deal of the "actor's talent", seamlessly reached the port of Bremen, successfully established contact with the local clergymen there, and safely reached the Island of Funnen, where he stealthily met with la Romana under the pretence of selling first-class cigars to the Spanish soldiers. During their meeting, he informed the Spaniard where and when he was to organize his men for the British evacuation. In the next phase of the plan, however, a significant crack appeared in Robertson's scheme for the mission. Robertson did not have a well-thought-out plan for contacting the British Navy that was to evacuate him, and was caught by a regiment of the Danish Army after he began to wave a coloured handkerchief on the coast of Funen at a British frigate that was passing by in an attempt to gain attention, a scene reminiscent of the not-so-subtle improvisations of the famous film agent Johnny English. The Danes logically arrested him on the spot on suspicion of espionage. Nonetheless, he managed to convince the Danes that he was "merely" attempting to sell cigars for profit to the British as he had done successfully with the Spaniards. The Danes, who were appeased by the fact that he had admitted to his misdemeanour (as his attempt to trade with the British was in violation of the continental blockade), let him go free on the condition that he would "walk the straight and narrow" with his business. If he had fallen into the hands of a French patrol, he may not have had as much luck. After his release, Robertson was successful in sending a message to Admiral Keats and with his help organized la Romana's evacuation by the Royal Navy. Before the French and their commander Marshal Bernadotte realized what was happening, the British had managed successfully to evacuate a whole 9,000 of the 14,000 Spanish soldiers including General la Romana (which was the most important achievement in order for the mission to be considered successful), taking him to Spain where la Romana immediately began to fight the French. Despite the failure to evacuate the other 5,000 Spaniards, the mission was still a great British triumph, all primarily thanks to the one 'man of courage': the Scotsman Father Robertson.[264]

As Arthur Wellesley was briefing his friend and successor to the post of Chief Secretary for Ireland John Wilson Croker shortly before his departure to Portugal on his previous activities in the position, he fell silent for a moment during the conversation. In the pause that ensued, Croker asked him what he was thinking about, to which Arthur Wellesley replied:

> To say the truth, I am thinking of the French that I am going to fight. I have not seen them since the campaign in Flanders, when they were capital soldiers, and a dozen years of victory under Bonaparte must have made them better still. They have, besides, it seems, a new system of strategy which has out-manoeuvred and overwhelmed all the armies of Europe. Tis enough to make one thoughtful, but no matter: my die is cast, they may overwhelm me, but I don't think they will out-manoeuvre me. First, because I am not afraid of them as everyone else seems to be, and secondly, because, if what I hear of their system of manoeuvres is true, I think it a false one against steady troops.[265]

This 'new system of strategy', which had scored one victory after another for the French as they pitted themselves against those European states that opposed them following the regicide of Louis XVI. The French needed to mobilize the greatest army they could in the shortest amount of time, which was made possible by the patriotic fervour of its citizens and a modernizing approach and more egalitarian form of government. In France, the Committee of Public Safety declared the populist slogan: *"La Patrie en danger!"*, leading to general military duty for all men between the ages of eighteen and twenty-five, ultimately allowing the French to build an army of up to one million men. Thus, not only had a political revolution taken place in France, but a military revolution as well – mass conscription gave rise to the necessity to create new fighting tactics in the French Army. Since the end of the Thirty Years' War, European battlefields were almost exclusively dominated by linear tactics based on deploying the army into lines forming three rows. However, the creation and preservation of this formation in the form of combat lines was relatively demanding in terms of training, as the primary power of a line stemmed from regular and coordinated fire in salvos. French generals suddenly had control of extremely large numbers of men, many of whom were insufficiently trained recruits. New French tactics, which Napoleon built upon and developed, attempted to adapt to these circumstances and make use of them to the best of their ability.[266]

In terms of France's innovative military tactics, so-called *voltigeurs** – a wholly new type of light-infantry fighting force – were deployed first against enemy lines. *Voltigeurs* advanced in a scattered skirmish line against the enemy's line. They generally fought most in pairs and as they simply fired at will, they did not need a great amount of training for this style of battle. Such a novel approach was designed to weaken the enemy's line with its irregular fire while remaining small, scattered targets for the mass fire of the enemy's lines. Americans Revolutionaries were the first to use light infantry with great success against the British during in the American Revolutionary War (1776–1783), first inspiring the French and consequently the rest of Europe.[267]

After the *voltigeurs'* attack, the next novelty in the French Army was deployed – an attack led in a formation of a deep route column advancing

*   French for 'vaulters'.

against the thin enemy line. The width of the French column with the force of one battalion (ideally 800 men) was made up of roughly forty to eighty men with a depth of nine to twelve rows. In addition, French battalions were often merged into one massive column that contained up to eighty or more rows, while the width of the column could be adjusted at will according to the number of men forming it. This massive formation of soldiers thus appeared daunting and conveyed menace. In addition, leading an attack in a column – similarly to the skirmish line – was less demanding in terms of training in comparison to advancement and battle in an extended line. An additional and indisputable advantage of the column was a sort of crowd psychology effect that had a positive effect on inexperienced recruits. Although the first lines of the column could panic under enemy fire, the rushing crowd of men in the back rows pushed them forward by the sheer mass of their marching bodies, making it basically impossible to flee. In simple terms, a column in battle could be compared to a massive battering ram of men.[268] This "living" battering ram rushed against the lines of other European armies that stood three or (at a maximum) four rows deep and was often victorious thanks to its fearful appearance alone. In addition, this mass form of attack was supported by the beating of drums and a military band playing *La Marseillaise**, the lyrics of which tore at the foundations of the "old regime", which was based on the power of the Monarch, so perfectly that Napoleon himself had the song banned after having himself crowned Emperor. *La Marseillaise* was therefore later substituted for cries of *"Vive l'Empereur"* during French column attacks. Nonetheless, French generals often disobeyed the ban on the song due to its stirring psychological effect on the troops, allowing *La Marseillaise* to continue to be played during attacks.

Despite these facts, French columns had an Achilles' heel, namely their limited firing power. Only the first two lines could fire, which in an ideal situation meant only one hundred and fifty muskets. It was upon exploiting this weakness that Arthur Wellesley intended to base his plan, which would ultimately lead to victory over the French. When confronting French troops, he planned to spread out his battalions into only

---

*   La Marseillaise was composed by a general duty soldier of the Revolutionary Army. The following excerpt from the song precisely illustrated the new concept of society and the beginning of a new era of nationalism: *'Arise children of the fatherland, the day of glory has arrived, against us tyranny's bloody standard is raised! To arms, citizens! March! March! Let impure blood water our furrows!'*

two rows instead of the classic three, which did not allow for the back row to fire. By doing so, he would maximize British firepower, as both lines would be able to fire continually, leaving no British musket unused. Thus, the horrific fire of all eight hundred barrels of the British battalion would be concentrated on the French column. As an admirer of Julius Caesar and the legendary General Hannibal of antiquity, Wellesley also intended to take maximum advantage of the terrain. Ideally, he planned to deploy his two-row line on the peak of a ridge, forcing the French column to advance uphill, which would slow their advance as much as possible and provide British muskets with the longest possible time to fire. In the case of more intense enemy artillery fire, the British could withdraw behind the ridge, which would provide them with natural cover from the French artillerymen. This method of battle was soon to enter into military history as the "reverse slope tactic". British units were able to fire three to four shots per minute and Arthur Wellesley believed that even a massive French column could not withstand such firepower. At the same time, however, he must have been well aware of the fact that persevering in the line only two rows deep would require strong morale and a high degree of courage from his men.[269] It is my assertion that it was exactly this strategy that Arthur Wellesley had in mind when he told John Wilson Croker that the French would not withstand troops that were determined to doggedly hold their positions. Also, based on his discussion with Croker ('They may overwhelm me, but I don't think they will out-manoeuvre me.'), I believe Arthur Wellesley must have been plagued by the following question: Will the British manage to stand their ground when face to face with a ferocious column while deployed in a line narrowed to two rows, fire only at the final moment? He was soon to learn the answer.

The British intervention army sailed under Arthur Wellesley's command to Portuguese shores in mid-July 1808. Wellesley now had 14,000 men at his disposal to liberate Portugal, as his original army destined for the Venezuelan expedition was expanded to include the five-hundred-man corps of General Brent Spencer, who also became Wellesley's second-in-command for his position of Commander-in-chief. Like Arthur Wellesley, Spencer was Anglo-Irish and had a wealth of military experience, including having served with General Sir Ralph Abercrombie's army during the Egyptian Campaign (1801) and the Copenhagen Campaign of 1807. Prior to Arthur's departure, Lady Eleanor Butler, one of the popular Ladies of Llangollen, gave him a Catholic prayer book in Spanish before he embarked for the Iberian Peninsula with which he quickly began to learn Spanish over the course of the voyage. According to reports that he had at his disposal, roughly 15,000 men headed by General Junot were waiting to confront the British troops on Portuguese soil.[270]

Several days later (1ˢᵗ August 1808), Wellesley and his whole army disembarked in the village of Figueira da Foz near the estuary of the Mondego River located near the Portuguese university town of Coimbra roughly one hundred and twenty miles north of Lisbon. A young Mr Murchison, then a sixteen-year-old warrant officer of the 36ᵗʰ Regiment of Foot serving under Wellesley, later in life beautifully described Arthur Wellesley's arrival in Portugal:

> It was a fine calm hot day, with little or no surf on the sterile and uninhabited shore, with its wide beach and hillocks of blown sand...Perhaps I am the only person now [in 1854] living, who saw the future Wellington place for the first time his foot on Lusitania...[i.e. Portugal – Lusitania was the Roman province that once stretched over Portuguese territory] He certainly was not twenty paces from me, and the cheerful confident expression on his countenance at that moment has ever remained impressed on my mind.[271]

On the day following the British landing, Arthur Wellesley immediately issued an official declaration to the Portuguese people:

> People of Portugal: the time is arrived to rescue your country, and restore the government of your lawful Prince... The glorious struggle in which you are engaged is for all that is dear to man, the protection of your wives and children, the restoration of your lawful prince, the independence, nay, the very existence of your kingdom, and for the preservation of your holy religion, objects like these can only be obtained by distinguished examples of fortitude and constancy.[272]

The reaction of the vast majority of Portuguese was highly enthusiastic and the British were welcomed as liberators. This fact was strengthened by the rapidly growing cruelty of the French, who brazenly seized food and anything else they so desired, "living off the land". French barbarity to the Portuguese came to be embodied by the infamous massacre that took place in Évora following the French victory against a combined Portuguese-Spanish force at the Battle of Évora (29th July 1808). The brutal slaughter of innocent men, women and children authorized by the French General Louis Henry Loison, nicknamed 'Maneta' (One-Handed), continues to echo down the years in Portugal. Growing hatred among the Portuguese toward their French conquerors was succinctly summarized in a poem from an anonymous Portuguese author:

> That scoundrel Junot Came to protect us! Came, but it was to rob us.
> And steal our silver. Junot and the Bloody One-Handed Say that Portugal is theirs.
> To the devil with them. And worse for him who send them. Even the sea is in turmoil.
> And even the fleets of ships. More nations are joining us, Going to war against France.[273]

In addition, Arthur Wellesley issued to his troops the same orders that had proved effective in India stating that British soldiers were to pay honourably for all items, as Portuguese citizens were British allies in the war against France and friends to His Highness King George, a code of behaviour that was in stark contrast to that of the French soldiers.[274] The method of living off the land at the time was standard practice for European armies and Arthur Wellesley's order was therefore refreshingly novel when compared with what was customary. However, it unfortunately had to be enforced often via flogging British soldiers while rather heavily burdening British coffers. Over time this peaceful policy towards the local population would redeem itself many times over.

Shortly after issuing this proclamation to the Portuguese people, Arthur received an urgent dispatch from Lord Castlereagh in which he was notified of the fact that the Government in London had decided to send another 15,000 British troops to Portugal. In view of the growing importance of the campaign, it was the opinion of senior army officials and Horse Guards that a person of more senior years was required to lead the campaign. Sir Hew Whitefoord Dalrymple, acting Governor of Gibraltar, was named the new Commander-in-Chief of the whole operation. Sir Harry Burrard, who was already on his way to Portugal, was chosen as Dalrymple's second-in-command. However, the fact that London had allowed Arthur Wellesley in a dispatch to continue on at will in his planned advance on Lisbon remained good news for him.[275] Arthur, who had been withdrawn from command once already while in India in favour of General Baird, reacted (contrary to the former situation) relatively calmly and resolutely to this sudden loss of command in a letter he penned to his friend and former superior from the times he held the post of Chief Secretary for Ireland, the Duke of Richmond: 'I hope that I shall have beat Junot before any of them [i.e. Dalrymple and Burrard] shall arrive, and then they will do as they please with me.'[276]

Thus, Wellesley immediately marched all British forces toward Lisbon. During this advance, one thousand five hundred men from the ranks of the Portuguese Army, which had been disbanded by the French, spontaneously joined the British soldiers, swelling the number of Arthur's troops closer to 16,000. The first clash of the conflict with the French, now known historically as the Peninsular War, took place on 14th August 1808 near a windmill close to the ancient town of Óbidos, complete with its preserved medieval walls. Although the event was merely a skirmish between light infantry units in which the 95th Rifles defeated the French *voltigeurs*, the clash would become a symbol for the dominance of British light infantry regiments over the French throughout the whole course of the Napoleonic Wars.[277]

The first British light infantry regiment was created as a reaction to the success of French *voltigeurs* in the Revolutionary Wars and their method of skirmish-line battle in 1797. Contrary to the typical British redcoats, the "British Riflemen" or "Rifle Corps" – as these light infantry regiments were officially called – wore dark-green uniforms in order to be better camouflaged in their surroundings much like today's soldiers. The primary difference on the British side, which ultimately proved to be an advantage against the French light infantry, was the weapon they used. In place of the classic smoothbore musket, the British Riflemen used the so-called "Baker rifle" with a grooved barrel from gunsmith Ezekiel Baker. Thanks to the rifled bore, the bullet was given rotation in the barrel and thus its effective range in comparison to the musket was considerably enhanced. In addition to its extended striking distance, the rifle was also a much more accurate weapon than the classic musket. At a distance of two hundred yards, the British Riflemen rarely missed their target and at three hundred yards at least one out of five marksmen would reliably hit their targets. On the downside, the rifle's significant disadvantage was its slow loading process, as a rifleman could manage only one to two shots per minute in comparison with the three to four shots fired by a musketeer.[278] Nonetheless, one rifleman under Arthur Wellesley's command in Portugal was convinced by the fact that the rifle was a much more advantageous weapon for light infantry soldiers despite the fact that it took longer to load when he claimed the following: 'In ninety-five cases out of a hundred, two rifle shots shall cause more death and destruction than three or four discharges from a musket.'[279]

Although he was a great innovator of military tactics, Napoleon seemed to some surprisingly and strongly distrustful of novelties in military technology. Therefore, he forbade his light infantry to be equipped with rifles due to their slower loading process. In addition, when given permission by their officers the British Riflemen were not forced to keep a fixed formation and could freely use any available cover and the terrain to fire at the enemy either kneeling or lying down. Such a flexible approach provided great accuracy and protection. A manual created in 1803, especially for light infantry riflemen units, reads:

> Vigilance, activity, and intelligence, are particularly requisite... [the light infantrymen] should know how to take advantage of every circumstance of ground which can enable him to harass and annoy the enemy, without exposing himself... In some situations they must conceal themselves by stooping, in others they must kneel, or lie flat upon the ground... To fire seldom and always with effect should be their chief study... Noise and smoke is not sufficient to stop the advance of soldiers accustomed to war: they are to be checked only by seeing their comrades fall.[280]

Therefore, it would not be an exaggeration to claim that these riflemen were one of the first corps of special forces in the world. The most important factor for Arthur Wellesley was to possess units of these riflemen that were able to fend off attacks by the French *voltigeurs* while preventing them from disrupting Wellesley's standard infantry. Thus the 95th Rifles are one of the most famous corps in the British Army. In popular culture, for example, these riflemen units have been immortalized in the historical novels of the famous British author Bernard Cornwell, who set some

of his novels during this campaign, with Richard Sharpe – the protagonist in these historical novels – serving amongst the British riflemen
fighting under Arthur Wellesley's command in the Peninsular War. The
Sharpe novels were later made into a British television series in which
Sean Bean (also known for characters such as Boromir in *Lord of the Rings*
or Eddard Stark in *Game of Thrones*) played Richard Sharpe.

After the skirmish at Óbidos, French troops under the command
of General Henry Françis Delaborde attempted to thwart the British
advance toward Lisbon near the town of Roliça. To do so, however,
Delaborde had only 4,000 men at his disposal. As was expected, Arthur
Wellesley managed fairly easily to force Delaborde's army to retreat after a short skirmish thanks to his superior numbers.[281] After the battle,
Delaborde retreated throughout the whole course of the following night;
Wellesley, however, refrained from a night pursuit of the defeated enemy
as he evidently still had the unfortunate experience of the night skirmish
in the Indian village of Sultanpettah in his memory: 'The French retreated, all night of the action, by the new road. I wish we had pursued them,
but feel every confidence in Sir. A. W. [Arthur Wellesley]'[282] wrote one of
Wellesley's officers of the situation after the battle. Although the Battle
of Roliça (17th August 1808) was not seen as a significant British victory
(in light of the disparities in numbers) as the French had retreated in
an organized fashion and without any greater losses, it was still a clear
success thanks to which Wellesley could continue on immediately in his
advance on Lisbon.

Over the course of the next few days, Arthur Wellesley's men
neared the village of Vimeiro situated roughly thirty-five miles from the
Portuguese capital. According to plan, Arthur's troops were to be joined
with the first reinforcements there arriving from Britain. Together with
the new regiments, Sir Harry Burrard, the first of Wellesley's two new-
ly-nominated superior generals, was expected to arrive. In the meantime,
Wellesley received an urgent message from British scouts with information concerning the position of General Junot, who was marching at
the head of French forces straight toward Wellesley in order to prevent
Lisbon from falling into British hands. According to the scouts, Junot's
army was not far away, although the information regarding the number
of Junot's men that was presented to Wellesley seemed rather contradictory. In reality, after joining the defeated General Delaborde, the French

Marshal's army amounted to a mere 13,000 men and 23 cannons. In addition, Junot had no hope of reinforcements in the days to come, as French forces in Spain were fully engaged with pacifying the country. At the time, Arthur Wellesley had 17,000 soldiers and 17 field cannons. As he expected a possible clash with Junot's army, he deployed his units in an advantageous defensive position on a ridge before the village of Vimeiro, as this ridge was excellently suited to his "reverse slope tactic".[283] In addition, if Junot did not attack his position, Lieutenant-General Wellesley evidently intended to take the initiative and carry out his own attack on the French the following day. Wellesley was likely to have been aware that time was against Junot regarding the imminent arrival of British reinforcements that were nearing Portugal. Therefore, it was highly likely that the French would be the first to attack his position on the ridge. Wellesley was convinced that Junot would thrust forward boldly in an attack. The vanity of the French may have played its own role in Arthur's deliberations, as Napoleon and his marshals had grown accustomed to scoring victories regularly throughout Continental Europe over recent years, often despite seemingly disadvantageous conditions.

Nonetheless, Sir Harry Burrard's vessel arrived on Portuguese shores near Vimeiro, officially making him the new Commander-in-Chief of British forces in Portugal. As soon as Arthur Wellesley learned of Burrard's arrival, he immediately set off for the coast to visit Sir Harry on his boat to brief him in person of the present situation. Sir Burrard, who intended to spend the following night on his boat, gave Arthur Wellesley clear orders to return to his army and take no further action until Burrard arrived. Thus, Wellesley returned to his camp at Vimeiro with mixed feelings, as command was to be taken from him definitively the following day. To his chagrin, he saw he would fail to defeat Junot, who was evidently lying in wait. However, in the morning hours of 21st August 1808, Junot suddenly aligned his men and led a surprising attack in full force on the British positions. As Sir Burrard was still on his vessel, where he was unsuspectingly preparing for breakfast, and there was no time to waste, Arthur Wellesley took the full burden of command in the following battle.[284]

Junot launched an attack with two brigades which he sent to take the northern section of the ridge where the British were located. By so doing, he was attempting an outflanking manoeuvre as the British were deployed only in the southern section of the ridge before the village of Vimeiro. After outflanking the British, Junot evidently intended for his troops to attack Wellesley's left wing along the ridge of the summit while at the same time giving the order to his main troops to launch a coordinated frontal attack on the British position. However, Arthur Wellesley noticed this manoeuvre in time and managed to line the north of the ridge with his troops before the arrival of the French, who upon observing the British there decided to abandon their efforts. After the failed attempt at outflanking, Junot immediately sent two massive columns under the command of General Thomierès against the primary British position on the south of the ridge. The French launched an attack with several corps of *voltigeurs*, who were easily driven back by the British light infantry regiments (the 95th Rifles and the 60th (Rifle) Regiment), who skilfully covered themselves in the terrain, making use of the longer firing range of their rifles.[285] The riflemen caused considerable losses to the French, as one of the commanding officers leading the attack of Junot's *voltigeurs* at Vimeiro noted:

> I was sent out to skirmish against some of those in green – grasshoppers [the common French nickname for British riflemen]... they were behind every bush and stone, and soon made sad havoc among my men, killing all the officers of my company, and wounding myself without being able to do them any injury. This nearly drove me to distraction.[286]

After Junot's rather unsuccessful commencement of battle, Thomierès' columns, which were forty men wide and eighty lines deep (i.e. a total of roughly 6,500 men in the attack), were ordered to use brute force in breaking through the British lines. Under the roar of drums and periodic cries of "*Vive l' Empereur!*", these two masses of soldiers slowly moved forward, inexorably closing in on the British position and hoping to make short work of the thin enemy line as they had done many times before. From a bird's eye view, the scene would have been reminiscent of two massive bricks (i.e. the French columns) closing in on a taught rope (the British line).

However, once the breathless French, who were forced to advance up a steep hill against British lines, neared the summit of the ridge, an event took place that proved to be a characteristic of most of the battles of the

Peninsular War. Each column was soon greeted by a prepared British battalion extended into two lines according to Wellesley's orders to allow all eight hundred muskets to be capable of firing simultaneously. The moment the French came within a distance of fifty-five yards, the first deafening British salvo was fired, followed by additional salvos at intervals of roughly fifteen seconds. The French soldiers, who until then had often defeated the majority of their enemies merely thanks to the fearsome appearance of their columns, now found themselves in a grave situation. General Thomierès quickly realized something must be done, as the advance of his soldiers had been halted almost completely due to the devastating British fire. Thomieres thus attempted to take the initiative by also spreading his men out in a line in order to confront the British with the full firepower of their own French muskets. It was, however, too late. During the attempt to deploy into a line, the French began to flee in desperation for safety under the perpetual British fire, a situation which neither Thomierès nor his officers were able to prevent. At this very moment, the desperate nature of the French became apparent as the British light infantry's Riflemen returned to action and soon began mercilessly shooting the fleeing French until they were out of range of their fatally accurate "Baker rifles".[287]

The battle continued in an almost identical scenario across the whole length of the British-occupied ridge. The French columns of Junot's brigades were forced to flee again and again by the British troops' machine-like fire. As was his custom, Arthur Wellesley continuously travelled on horseback behind his lines, carefully surveying the ebb and flow of the battle. In one of his memoirs, Private Harris from the 95th Rifles recalled one of Wellesley's numerous "passages" behind the British lines:

> We were generally enveloped in smoke and fire, and sometimes unable to distinguish or make remarks upon what was going on around, whilst we blazed away at our opponents, but occasionally we found time to make our comments upon the game we were playing. Two or three fellows near me were observing what was going on just in the rear, and I heard one man remark, 'Here comes Sir Arthur and his staff', upon which I also looked back and caught sight of him...[288]

Another description of Wellesley's unceasing activity during the Battle of Vimeiro was recorded by a warrant officer of the 36th British Regiment of Foot Mr Murchison, who was carrying the colours of his Regiment into battle. Arthur Wellesley intended to stop the victorious advance of the 36th Regiment at his left wing, which had driven the French in this zone far back down the ridge to the neighbouring hamlet of Ventosa. Wellesley most likely feared that his men would travel too far in their pursuit of the enemy, which could thus expose them to a counterattack by the French cavalry:

> Sir Arthur Wellesley overtook us after a smart gallop. He had witnessed from a distance our steady and successful charge, and our capture of the guns, and he now saw how we were thrusting the French out of this hamlet [Ventosa]. Through the sound of the musketry, and in the midst of much confusion, I heard a shrill voice calling out: 'Where are the colours of the 36th?' and I turned round (my brother Ensign, poor Peter Bone, having just been knocked down), and looking up in Sir Arthur's bright and confident face, said, 'Here they are sir!' Then he [Arthur Wellesley] shouted, 'Very well done my boys: Halt, halt – quite enough!'[289]

Murchison proudly recalled. General Junot, who was slowly beginning to realize that he was losing the battle, sent two of his remaining elite grenadier battalions (under the command of General Kellerman) that he had been keeping for an emergency situation to attack as a final attempt at tipping the scales in France's favour. These battalions actually managed to break through a point in Wellesley's line and enter the narrow streets of Vimeiro, where a merciless man-to-man battle took place between the British and the French. Moments later, however, Kellerman's brigade found itself surrounded by British battalions, which had drawn down from the other areas of the ridge and – despite the bravery of its men – had no chance to succeed.[290] This final attack made by the French was also soon thwarted. It was at this moment that Junot's defeat proved irreversible, whereupon Arthur Wellesley issued an order for a cavalry attack by the 20th Regiment of Light Dragoons. Accompanied by exuberant cheers from Wellesley's staff, the Regiment dashed at the French, who were now fleeing in every direction. Sergeant Landsheit from the 20th Regiment of Light Dragoons, who took part directly in the cavalry attack, described what then took place in his memoirs:

'Now, Twentieth! Now!' shouted Sir Arthur, while his staff clapped their hands and gave us a cheer, the sound of which was still in our ears, when we put our horses to their speed.[291]

The British cavalry, absorbed by their seeming victory, soon however lost all restraint and continued on in their attack all the way to Junot's camp. There, as a consequence of their presumptuousness, they were ruthlessly crushed by the French cavalry, whose superiority was more than six-fold, as they had not hitherto had the chance to engage effectively in battle. The Light Dragoons of the 20th Regiment paid for their imprudence with the lives of a quarter of their men. Their failed operation ultimately remained the only blot on Arthur Wellesley's otherwise dazzling record of victory that day. In all, British-Portuguese losses at Vimeiro amounted to roughly seven hundred men in comparison to two thousand fallen or injured Frenchmen. The British had also taken the majority of Junot's cannons as spoils of war.[292] Also, despite driving back the pursuing British cavalry, the French now found themselves in absolute disarray and were retreating uncontrollably in all directions. The decision to pursue Junot, however, was wholly up to Harry Burrard, who had hurried to the battlefield as soon as he learned about the ongoing clash. Arthur, who clearly had a better overview of the present situation, did not hesitate to address him immediately with the following recommendation:

> Sir Harry, now is your chance. The French are completely beaten, we have a large body of troops that have not yet been in action. Let us move on Torres Vedras. You take the force here straight forward, I will bring round the left with the troops already there. We shall be in Lisbon in three days.[293]

The evidently careful Sir Burrard was nonetheless fully aware of the fact that Sir Hew Dalrymple, Acting Governor of Gibraltar, who was to replace him in the position of commander, was now nearing Vimeiro. Thus, ordered the victorious British troops to return to their camp at Vimeiro. From a purely military perspective, this decision proved to be wholly incomprehensible. However, it should be noted that in Burrard's defence, the fear of making a fatal error moments before the arrival of his superior perhaps played a role and is understandable from a human perspective. The following morning, Sir Hew Dalrymple arrived at Vimeiro.

Arthur Wellesley again attempted to convince his new commander to set out immediately after Junot's forces, as there may still have been time for a pursuit. Sir Hew Dalrymple answered Wellesley's advice by stating that he wished to talk first to Sir Burrard, avoiding a definite decision. To his disappointment, Lieutenant-General Wellesley received an order to remain in the camp at Vimeiro after a short discussion between the two new British commanders.[294] It should be noted that the newly arriving generals were not sufficiently oriented in terms of their present situation, which partially excuses their circumspection. Nonetheless, it is my assertion that, due to their unfamiliarity with the situation, they should have relied on Arthur Wellesley's judgment, as he had been in Portugal for almost a month, during which time he managed to score two victories in battle.

Surprisingly, the French ultimately influenced the new British command's next step against the enemy. The demoralized Junot, who realized his situation was hopeless in the light of his incurred losses and the additional British reinforcements that continued to disembark, offered the British an immediate ceasefire the following day, which Dalrymple happily accepted without continuing to pursue Junot. The specific conditions of the armistice were negotiated with Sir Hew Dalrymple by Junot's deputy, General François Kellerman directly in the village of Vimeiro in the presence of Arthur Wellesley and General Burrard. As soon as Dalrymple signed the peace treaty with Kellerman, the French General – in anticipation that the agreement would not be "embraced with open arms" by the British – cleverly suggested that the victor of the Battle of Vimeiro Arthur Wellesley be the one to sign the armistice for the British. Dalrymple did not hesitate to order Arthur to do so, and General Sir Harry Burrard, the last of the British generals, also attached his signature to the treaty. The armistice was then reformulated into a peace convention, which was signed at the Palace of Queluz on 30th August 1808 by Sir Hew Dalrymple and General Junot as the Convention of Cintra – according to the town where Dalrymple had set up his command headquarters after the battle. In the Convention, Dalrymple quite incomprehensibly offered Junot highly advantageous peace terms which still cause incredulity to this day. Based on the Convention, the Royal Navy would transport all Junot's French troops, their equipment (including all 23 cannons) to France. In addition, the French were permitted to keep all of the spoils of war they had managed to collect in Portugal hitherto. Such spoils are believed to have included Portuguese royal treasure including its Palace's art collection. The Convention of Cintra naturally invoked a wave of outrage in Britain and today is viewed as one of the most ignominious moments in history concerning British generals.[295]

The then twenty-four-year-old Henry John Temple, 3rd Viscount Palmerston, who was to become one of the most prominent Prime Ministers of Victorian Britain, wrote the following words about the Convention of Cintra to his sister in a letter that perfectly encapsulates the prevailing sentiment in Britain at the time: 'What a pretty business this Portuguese Expedition has turned out! I think Dalrymple's capitulation by far the most disgraceful to the British army of any that were ever signed.'[296] The Emperor Napoleon himself thanked Junot for the unbelievable conditions under which he negotiated his "capitulation", but on the contrary made it wholly clear to him his displeasure at the fact that Junot had let himself be defeated suddenly by the presumptuous British after years of French victories on the continent – one which he considered to be his after the Royal Navy had marred his plans in the sea – as Junot's defeat quite seriously disrupted the myth of French invincibility in field battles of the years past:

> You have done nothing that is dishonourable. You have brought me back my soldiers, my standards, and my guns. I had hoped, however, that you would do better. You secured the convention, not so much by your foresight as by your courage, and the English are right in blaming the general who signed it. ... Before the end of the year, I intend myself to place you once more at Lisbon.[297]

Napoleon wrote to his general. The British press did not spare its criticism of the Convention either, when one of the many caricatures parodying the circumstances in which the peace accord was ratified, appeared alongside a rhyme that admitted the merits of Arthur Wellesley but condemned the overall conditions of the treaty.

> This is the Convention that Nobody owns,
> that saved old Junot Baggage and Bones,
> altho Sir Arthur (whose Valour and skill began so well but ended so ill,)
> had beaten the French who took the Gold that lay in the City of Lisbon.[298]

The great poet Lord Byron himself even commented critically on the affair in his famous narrative poem *Childe Harold's Pilgrimage*:

> And ever since that martial synod met,
> Britannia sickens, Cintra! at thy name;
> And folks in office at the mention fret,
> And fain would blush, if blush they could, for shame.[299]

Arthur Wellesley, who had "begun so well", was immensely disappointed in the behaviour of his two senior officers, as he wrote to the Minister for War Lord Castlereagh the second day after the disgraceful armistice was signed (23rd August 1808):

> Although my name is affixed to this instrument, I beg that you will not believe that I negotiated it, that I approve of it, or that I had any hand in wording it... I should prefer to go home to staying here. However, if you wish me to stay, I will, and I only beg that you will not blame me, if things do not go on as you and your friends in London wish they should.[300]

On the following day (24th August), Arthur sent a letter written in an even more frank and confessional tone to his brother William:

> I wish that I was away from this Army. Things will not flourish as we are situated and organized [i.e. under Dalrymple and Burrard's command] ... There is no more confidence in me on the part of the Chiefs than if I had been unsuccessful... [They] ask my opinion about everything and never act according to it... is this the confidence in the opinion of a Man who has conducted the Service successfully to the present moment, which is to make him responsible to his friends in the Govt. for events which will occur here?... It is quite ridiculous...[301]

Thus, there is not a shadow of a doubt that Arthur Wellesley disagreed with the Convention from the very beginning. Despite winning at Vimeiro and saving Lisbon from the French, Dalrymple, Burrard, and Wellesley, whose signatures were attached to the Convention of Cintra, were all recalled from Portugal and summoned to appear before a military tribunal. The trial took place in November 1808 and was headed by Sir

BATTLE OF VIMEIRO
21ˢᵗ August 1808

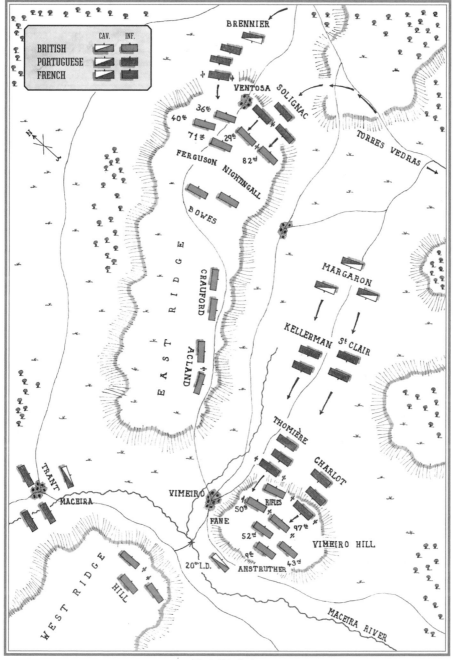

BRENNIER

BRITISH
PORTUGUESE
FRENCH

CAV. INF.

VENTOSA SOLIGNAC

TORRES VEDRAS

36ᵗʰ
40ᵗʰ
71ˢᵗ 29ᵗʰ
82ᵈ

FERGUSON NIGHTINGALL

BOWES

MARGARON

EAST RIDGE

CRAUFORD

ACLAND

KELLERMAN Sᵗ CLAIR

THOMIÈRE

CHARLOT

TRANT

MACEIRA

VIMEIRO

THOMIÈRE

RIFLES

FANE

50ˢ

52ᵈ 97ᵗʰ

VIMEIRO HILL

20ᵗʰ L.D.

ANSTRUTHER

9ᵗʰ 43ᵈ

WEST RIDGE HILL

MACEIRA RIVER

—— *Map by John Fawkes* ——

David Dundas. According to eye witnesses, a sharp exchange of views took place between Wellesley and Dalrymple, as Arthur from the very start claimed that he had signed the Convention only upon the orders of his Commander-in-Chief, which for him was the end of the whole affair. Simply speaking, Arthur Wellesley based his defence on the argument that he was only following orders:

> I was not the negotiator, and could not be, and was not so considered, the Commander of the Forces [Darlymple] being present in the room, deciding upon all points, and taking part in all discussions. If indeed the Commander of the Forces had given me instructions to negotiate this instrument, and I had then negotiated and signed it, I might have been responsible for its contents, or at all events for the manner in which it was drawn up, but as it is, my signature is a mere form,[302]

he said before the Court. In addition, he pointed out the fact that he had suggested to both generals after the victory at Vimeiro to immediately pursue Junot, which each general subsequently and quite incomprehensibly refused. According to witnesses, Harry Burrard seemed apathetic and kept himself in the background (such behaviour was characteristic for Sir Harry even during the expedition itself). The three were officially released by the Court but Hew Dalrymple – as Commander-in-Chief and evidently the main initiator of Cintra – was subsequently withdrawn from his post as Acting-Governor of Gibraltar. Aside from their damaged reputations, Wellesley and Burrard were released without punishment. After being exonerated by the Court, Arthur Wellesley, as the undisputed engineer of the British victory at Roliça and Vimeiro, received at least partial satisfaction in the form of official, public thanks from the British Parliament for his service to the Crown.[303] As for Dalrymple and Burrard, they were quietly removed from command and never served in prominent positions again.

Over time the British public's interest in the Convention of Cintra gradually waned, as it was now fully occupied with the new events taking place on the Iberian Peninsula. Under the leadership of the new commander Lieutenant-General Sir John Moore (who Arthur Wellesley saw at the time as the most competent British officer), British troops had launched an offensive, crossing the Portuguese border and entering

Spain. There, however, Moore was confronted by a new French offensive, one in which Napoleon himself was the driving force. The French Emperor, alarmed by the defeats at Roliça and Vimeiro and followed by the loss of Lisbon, quickly marched in person with his army to the Iberian Peninsula in order to remedy the situation. Moore decided on a tactical retreat with a view to evacuating the British forces by sea via the Galician port of Corunna in Northern Spain. Napoleon ordered Marshal Jean de Dieu Soult to intercept the British and ensure that they were unable to make their escape. Doggedly pursued by the French, with both armies suffering privations due to the winter conditions, the British finally made it through to Corunna, only to have Soult arrive before the embarkation had been completed. Battle ensured on 16th January 1809, one in which the British were engaged in an action aimed at enabling them to complete their retreat. The fighting was fierce, and whilst precious time was indeed bought, the bulk of the British Army managed to escape. This, however, came at a price, one that included the French occupying Corunna and its vicinity, the loss of a sizable amount of military stores and leaving their Spanish allies at the mercy of Napoleon's forces. Of the Battle of Corunna, the British sought to claim a tactical victory, whilst the French claimed a strategic one. As for Moore, he was struck by a cannon shot in the left shoulder and mortally wounded.[304] Another British commanding officer and Wellesley's old acquaintance General Baird was also seriously wounded, losing his left arm in battle. Until then, Arthur had corresponded with his now good friend Baird throughout the whole expedition from Britain, during which the Scottish General kept him informed of all events. Baird, who was of a robust character by nature, survived the injury, recovered, and was subsequently given a pension. In addition, he received the well-earned title of Baronet from King George.* The British Army, which had lost its commander, had to be quickly evacuated from Spain by the Royal Navy in order to avoid capture.[305] However, the British remained in Portugal, a fact which Napoleon did not intend to tolerate.

---

* After recovering from his injury in the Battle of Corunna, General David Baird never fought again. Several years later, he was named Mayor of Kinsale in the south of Ireland. In 1828, Baird returned to the land of his origin, where he gained the post of Governor of Fort George on the eastern coast of Scotland. He passed away peacefully a year later at the age of 71.

In reaction to these events, Arthur Wellesley sent the Minister for War Lord Castlereagh the now famous *Memorandum on the Defence of Portugal* on 7th March 1809, in which he delivered a statement to the British that the mere 30,000 British soldiers in cooperation with the local population, partisans, and the remainder of the Portuguese Army were capable of defending Portugal against enemy forces that had at least a three-fold superiority (i.e. around one hundred thousand Frenchmen).[306] Based on this memorandum and in light of Sir John Moore's death and the injury of General Baird, the government suggested nominating Arthur Wellesley as Commander-in-Chief in Portugal. Even King George III was now favourably disposed towards Arthur, as he had been impressed by the Memorandum that he provided him with his enthusiastic support. This seemed rather surprising, as the British Monarch had hitherto viewed Arthur Wellesley rather negatively. In addition, Wellesley – contrary to the other commanders – was one of the few to have recently scored a series of victories for Britain, leading the King to change his opinion of Arthur. Moreover, at this time King George's son Frederick, Duke of York was no longer Commander-in-Chief of the British Army due to a scandal involving his current mistress, a certain Mary Anne Clarke, who was believed to be selling army commissions with the full knowledge of the Duke of York. Thus, partially thanks to 'favourable' circumstances, in April 1809 Arthur Wellesley was officially nominated Commander-in-Chief of British Forces on the Iberian Peninsula and now began to prepare for the second time in his life to sail for Portugal. Contrary to the previous Portuguese Expedition, however, there was no danger of him being replaced in the position of Commander-in-Chief during the campaign. To his undisguised relief, however, Arthur Wellesley was not yet fated to clash with Napoleon. The French Emperor had abandoned the Iberian Peninsula in 1809 and left command in Spain to his marshals, as he received an alarming report informing him that Austria was mobilizing and planned again to declare war on France alongside Britain by attacking the French in Central Europe.*

---

*   Gordon Corrigan, *Wellington: A Military Life*, (London and New York 2001), pp. 124–125.
     On 10th April 1809 Napoleon noted: *'Intercepted dispatches addressed to M. de Metternich* (at this
     time Austrian ambassador in Paris), *and his demand for passports, show clearly enough that Austria
     is on the point of beginning hostilities, if she has not already done so...'*, quoted in: R. M. Johnston,
     Philip Haythornthwaite (eds.), *In the Words of Napoleon* (London 2002), p. 216.

The Viscount of Wellington: Crossing the Douro and the Battle of Talavera

As the spring of 1809 neard, Arthur Wellesley found himself immersed in preparations for the upcoming Portuguese Campaign. Before his departure for war, Arthur went to the Lord Lieutenant of Ireland, the Duke of Richmond, to put in a good word for the Ladies of Llangollen as long-time friends of the Wellesley Family, asking for the Ladies to be awarded a pension of fifty pounds per year. Just before he embarked for the shores of Portugal, he also had to deal with another 'domestic annoyance' with his wife Kitty. Her younger brother Henry Pakenham had fallen into debt due to gambling and, after continuous pleading, had managed to convince his sister to lend him a considerable sum of money that Arthur had given Kitty before his departure to run the household. Poor Kitty subsequently had no way to pay her own dues, whereupon one of the businessmen whom Kitty owed money began to press Arthur to pay the sum. Arthur naturally had his hands full at that time with preparing his troops and, when told by the irritated businessman what had happened, he was incandescent with rage. One argument for this anger was that a similar dispute had already clearly taken place among the couple due to the unpaid bricklayer and now the situation had been repeated under even more unpleasant circumstances. The whole event unfortunately had a woeful effect on the final days that Arthur spent with his family before his departure.[307]

Based on his memorandum, General Wellesley was given an army of thirty thousand men with which, after making the necessary preparations, he embarked and sailed on 14th April 1809, making for Lisbon. His primary task was clear: defend Portugal from the next expected French invasion. During the evening of the first day at sea, the British fleet was caught in a violent storm. The situation throughout the night deteriorated to such a degree that the captain of Arthur's vessel sent the General's aide-de-camp to inform Wellesley to put his boots on and come up to the deck, where there would be the greatest chances of survival in case of a shipwreck. Nonetheless, Wellesley informed his aide-de-camp to tell the captain that he would be able to swim better without his boots on and intended to stay exactly where he was. Ultimately, they managed to weather the storm without damage and Arthur Wellesley – boots or no boots – was fortunately not forced to take to the water.

After several more days of smooth sailing, Arthur Wellesley disembarked at Lisbon without mishap with his whole army on 22nd April 1809. Major Edward Cocks, who had served under Wellesley's command during the Peninsular War in the ranks of the 16th Light Dragoon Regiment, reacted to the news confirming Arthur's high command in Portugal in a letter to his father in the following words, which perhaps best illustrate the considerable trust the men had in their new commander – the popular victor of Assaye and Vimeiro: 'Sir Arthur Wellesley has taken the command of the army and inspired fresh spirit into every breast.'[308] Arthur was also enthusiastically greeted in the streets of Lisbon by the Portuguese, who well remembered that it was he who had rescued Lisbon from Junot the year before. However, the French were still faring quite successfully on the Iberian Peninsula, as the French Marshal Nicolas Soult, who had in the meantime entered Portuguese territory with his army of twenty-three thousand men, brutally taking Oporto with the loss of only 80 men whilst the city's defenders and civilian population were forced to the quayside and slaughtered. Precise figures are hard to come by, but estimates vary from 4,000 to 20,000 – little wonder then that hatred of the French grew ever more intense.

Soult had worked his way up to the position of French Marshal quite literally "from scratch". Before the French Revolution, he had held the position of a mere private and thus took skilful advantage of the "breaking down of social barriers" (which until the Revolution were mostly based on the medieval social hierarchy of the three estates*) in the French Army that was made possible by the Revolution and the demise of the *ancien régime*. He distinguished himself at the Battle of Austerlitz in which he led a decisive attack with Napoleon's forces. Despite Soult's successful advance, however, Lisbon still remained outside the French Army's reach. Arthur Wellesley left a portion of his units in the Portuguese capital under the command of his Division General John Randoll Mackenzie, who was tasked with defending the city in the case of a failure on Wellesley's part, whilst he ventured north as quickly as possible with an army of twenty-thousand men in order to deal with Marshal Soult. Wellesley first intended to liberate Oporto, driving out the French from Portugal for the second time in two years. Only if Arthur Wellesley was successful in defeating Soult and by so doing gaining a rear position would he be able to contemplate a subsequent campaign into Spain, where the remainder of the Spanish Army was holding out against superior French forces in the fight for a free Spain under the rule of King Ferdinand VII.

As a result of the recent taking of Oporto, there were several hundred injured men among Marshal Soult's troops and he thus left his army in the city for the time being to allow his men to regain their strength. The port city of Oporto, where the French were now located, stretches along the northern bank of the great River Douro, which provided Soult's men with the perfect defence. In order for Wellesley and his troops to attack him, they would first have to cross this mighty river. Soult ordered all the bridges and other vessels that would otherwise allow Wellesley's divisions to cross the river to be destroyed. Once these tasks seemed to have been completed, the French Marshal had the impression of relative safety – he assumed that the British had no chance of crossing the Douro.[309] However, the princes of Maratha had been similarly sure of their advantageous position on the bank of the River Kaitna near the

---

* The estates of the realm: 1) clergy (the First Estate) 2) nobles (the Second Estate) 3) peasants and bourgeoisie (the Third Estate).

village of Assaye years before. Thanks to his extraordinary persistence, Arthur Wellesley had managed to cross the Kaitna and it seemed now that he would manage to repeat the achievement.

Wellesley and his army were situated on the north bank of the Douro at Villa Nova de Gaia. The British commander based himself at a Convent of Serra do Pilar, from where he hoped to gain some idea of the nature of the French position. Colonel John Waters and General Murray were sent to reconnoitre the area with a view to scouting for vessels to cross the Douro. As luck would have it, they received intelligence that at Avintes a submerged ferry was under repairs. Colonel Waters, a fluent Portuguese speaker, persuaded local villagers to allow the British forces to avail themselves of the ferry. Once assembled, General Murray took two battalions and two squadrons across the river and headed back downstream to the north bank to Oporto. Waters found a barber, an escapee from Oporto, with a skiff who he persuaded to row him across the Douro to the south bank, along with the Prior of Amarante serving as a guide and several local peasants.[310] This crossing resulted in another vital discovery, which was immediately reported to Wellesley. A Portuguese farmer knew of the whereabouts of four hidden cargo vessels used for the transportation of wine. He now proudly unveiled this "treasure trove" to the British: the boats were each able to accommodate up to thirty British soldiers per crossing. As soon as Wellesley had the vessels safely transferred to his camp, he created a plan for the taking of Oporto. At the edge of the city was the Bishop's Seminary and this appeared not to have been occupied by the French. Wellesley hoped that the first British units to cross the river would fortify the Seminary before the unsuspecting French could get their bearings, providing cover for 600 British Infantry to be ferried across the river.[311]

The moment Arthur was informed by his commanding officers that everything was in place to cross the river, on 12th May 1809 at roughly half past ten in the morning he issued a simple order: "Well! Let the men begin to cross!"[312] Initially, everything from a British standpoint seemed to go exceedingly smoothly and the French appeared absolutely stunned. The first British units crossed the river without any problem whatsoever and in a similar fashion occupied the building of the Bishop's Seminary, which was meant to serve as a bridgehead for Wellesley's men. Once the French guards finally came to their senses, they immediately sent a messenger to Marshal Soult to inform him of Wellesley's surprising attack. Soult, however, initially refused in any way to believe the alarming report claiming that units of British "redcoats" had suddenly appeared on the north bank of the Douro as if "out of thin air".[313] He allegedly turned to the messenger with the following words: "Bah! It's a party of red-coated Swiss who've been down to bathe."*

Once Marshal Soult realized that these truly were Wellesley's soldiers and not a group of off-duty Swiss troops enjoying a bath, he immediately had a whole brigade mobilized in a frantic attempt to remedy his initial hesitation. He then gave orders for three battalions of the 17th Léger to mount an assault on the Seminary. The building, however, was now full of British soldiers who rained down devastating musket and rifle fire on their enemy from a position of relative safety. This allowed them to repulse Soult's men easily while the number of British soldiers on the north bank of the river continued to be reinforced as more and more were ferried across. Therefore, the French Marshal soon saw that the situation was desperate and, aware that there were additional French troops in Spain, decided to order a tactical retreat from the city in at least a relatively organized fashion. The moment the last fleeing French were repelled from Oporto by British soldiers, thousands of jubilant Portuguese flooded the streets with cries of "*Viva los Inglesos!*" and "*Viva Grand Britania!*"[314], enthusiastically welcoming the British soldiers as their liberators. The whole scene was described quite vividly by a member of the 3rd British Foot Guards Regiment who personally took part in the final phase of battle:

> We pursued the fugitives through the town, but they would not stop for us… We went through the town amidst shouts of 'Viva', a shower of roses, and a hail of handkerchiefs. Even the nuns protruded their heads through the railings of the convent to welcome our arrival.[315]

In addition, Marshal Soult was forced to leave the whole French supply caravan in Oporto, which included seventy cannons and 1,500 injured French. The overall losses that Soult's men suffered in the fight for the

---

* Longford, op. cit., p. 181. Under the name "Helvetic Republic", Switzerland was one of Napoleon's satellites; Swiss soldiers, who coincidentally also wore red coats like the British, served as auxiliary corps in Soult's army.

city amounted to 4,000 men. In comparison, the British lost only five hundred soldiers, thus giving Arthur Wellesley his next dazzling victory, one which gave also lent him one of his many future nicknames. After the Battle of Oporto, the Portuguese nicknamed him 'Douro, Douro!', which was chanted by Portuguese units anytime and anywhere Wellesley appeared before them after defeating Soult in his unexpected crossing of the River Douro.[316]

After liberating Oporto, Arthur Wellesley planned to march his army into Spain. Wellesley soon began to run out of finances as his army paid the local population honestly for all supplies in contrast to the French, who lived off plundering the countries in which they were deployed. For Wellesley to realize his campaign to Spain, he desperately needed additional funds from the British government, which had promised him the sum of 400,000 pounds, but to date had only given him roughly one quarter of the money. Thankfully these financial woes were solved quickly by a member of perhaps the most famous family of bankers in history, Nathaniel Meyer Rothschild, who founded the London House of Rothschild in 1803–1804. Proof of the significance of the Rothschilds' finances is most evident in the fact that Nathaniel Rothschild later provided the British Government with a loan of eleven million pounds for one single year of campaigning during for the Peninsular War. According to one of the most famous stories in British history, his brother James, disguised as a woman, personally smuggled in the necessary funds in gold from the Rothschild Banking House over half of France to Wellington's camp on the Iberian Peninsula in the spirit of the old proverb "The darkest place is under the candlestick". Once these financial problems were resolved thanks to the significant contribution made by the Rothschilds, the British Government gave Arthur Wellesley permission to launch his campaign into Spain.[317]

Arthur set off for the Spanish border with nearly his whole army (roughly 25,000 men), leaving only a few British battalions in Lisbon under the command of General William Beresford (Arthur's aforementioned and long-time acquaintance with whom he exchanged letters during his stay in India concerning Kitty Pakenham), who was charged with the challenging task by the British Government of training and transforming a decidedly disorganized Portuguese Army into an efficient fighting force to face French units alongside the British.

BATTLE OF OPORTO
(THE CROSSING OF DOURO),
12st May 1809

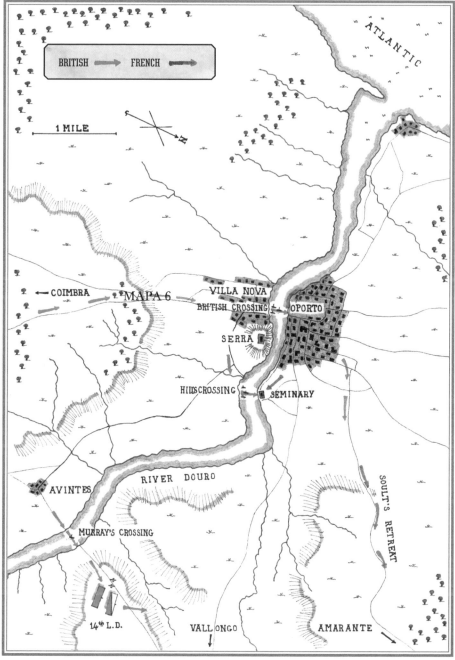

BRITISH → FRENCH →

1 MILE

N

ATLANTIC

COIMBRA →

MAPA 6

VILLA NOVA

BRITISH CROSSING

OPORTO

SERRA

HILLSCROSSING

SEMINARY

SOULT'S RETREAT

AVINTES

RIVER DOURO

MURRAY'S CROSSING

14th L.D.

VALLONGO

AMARANTE

— *Map by John Fawkes* —

It is important to appreciate the context of what had been happening in Portugal in earlier years, especially the impact of a natural disaster that laid the country low. On 1ˢᵗ November 1755 the Kingdom of Portugal's capital was struck by a massive earthquake that caused fires and triggered a tsunami. Lisbon and much of its surrounding area was devastated; historians estimate that 85% of all buildings were destroyed and at least a quarter of the city's population killed in the Great Lisbon Earthquake. It is no wonder then that the country was left in a parlous situation, such that funds for the armed forces were in short supply for many years to come.[318]

Nonetheless, Beresford, who was named Field Marshal of Portugal by the Portuguese Government, was now backed with British money with which he could acquire the necessary equipment for the Portuguese soldiers. Over the course of the following months, for example, Beresford received 30,000 brand-new dark-blue military uniforms from Britain for Portuguese troops.* The Portuguese light infantry (called *caçadores*) were then equipped by the British with brown coats and, primarily, the same deadly Baker rifles held by the British Riflemen.[319] In initially taking up the task of creating a highly professional army out of the Portuguese, Beresford possessed the necessary enthusiasm to carry it out when he had the following declaration addressed to the Portuguese Army published in Lisbon shortly after being nominated to his post:

> I am convinced of the military disposition and talents of the Portuguese, for whom any training and standardisation serves to demonstrate that they are today what they always were, if not the best, then certainly equal to the bravest and most intrepid in Europe.[320]

This statement of praise was naturally intended to motivate the Portuguese before undergoing the intense training that awaited them. Despite his commendatory attitude, however, Beresford intended from the very start to maintain the strict discipline he was accustomed to in the British Army in accordance with the official orders for the Portuguese soldiers that he issued in quick succession:

---

* Throughout the whole war, British factories produced a staggering 190,000 uniforms for Portugal's soldiers.

All deserters, without exception, will be shot... English Provost Marshal has been ordered to punish Portuguese Soldiers in the same way as English Soldiers when they are found separated from their Corps, or looting, and in the case of the latter, to hang them.[321]

read Beresford's merciless orders. In the meantime, after crossing the border into Spain Arthur Wellesley planned in conjunction with the Spanish allied forces of General Gregoria Garćia de la Cuesta to defeat another Napoleonic Marshal, Claude Victor-Perrin. However, the fact that the second French Army of Marshal Horace Sébastiani was located not far from Victor-Perrin's troops represented a considerable danger for Wellesley and Cuesta. If the French armies managed to join forces in time, French forces would equal those of the allied forces. However, if the French marshals could be prevented from joining forces and Sébastiani was kept out of the game for a time, Wellesley and Cuesta would have a superiority of 52,000 troops over Victor-Perrin's 20,000 French. Alone, Victor-Perrin could not have the slightest chance of avoiding certain destruction. Wellesley planned to meet personally with General Cuesta as soon as possible in order to assess the situation and agree on the best possible strategy to isolate and crush Victor-Perrin.

From the very beginning of the allied campaign, however, nothing seemed to go well between Arthur Wellesley and General Cuesta. The meeting between the two generals took place in the small village of Miravete near the Portuguese-Spanish border, where the advisory meeting of allies was planned for the late afternoon. Wellesley's guide unfortunately lost his way, causing Arthur Wellesley to arrive at the meeting in the middle of the night, a fact which certainly did not make an ideal first impression on Cuesta. In addition, the sixty-eight-year-old Spaniard had failing health and he expected soon to lose his position as General of the Spanish Army and being pensioned off. Thus, Cuesta was certainly not brimming with enthusiasm to cooperate with Wellesley.[322] Historian Philip Guedalla does not spare his words of criticism concerning Cuesta, characterizing the Spanish General thusly: 'Composed in equal parts of pride and failing health, [Cuesta] was the embodiment of Spain in its very worst, – old, proud, incompetent, and ailing...'[323]

Although cooperation between Wellesley and Cuesta initially seemed quite problematic due to their mutual antipathy, the generals managed to agree on a promising strategy after lengthy negotiations: Cuesta's subordinate General Francisco Javier Venegas received orders to engage Sébastiani with a portion of the Spanish Army while Cuesta and Wellesley decided to set out immediately on a swift march toward Victor-Perrin and attack him with the remaining forces as soon as possible. For the time being, the plan worked wonderfully and beyond expectation. On 22nd July 1809, the allied Anglo-Spanish Army under Wellesley and Cuesta's command succeeded in cornering Victor-Perrin with their unexpectedly swift movements. The Frenchman soon saw that there was no escape from the enemy and decided to take up an advantageous defensive position on the River Alberche. This was exactly what the allies had calculated was likely to happen. On the following day (23rd July 1809), Wellesley and Cuesta ordered a coordinated attack on Victor-Perrin's positions. The British planned to attack from the north while Cuesta's units would take the French by surprise according to plan from the west. Before sunrise and quite long in advance, Wellesley's disciplined divisions stood at their positions; however, there was still no sign of the Spanish to the west in Arthur's telescope. After the burning summer sun rose above the horizon, Wellesley definitively lost his temper and rode off to find out personally "what the devil was going on" in the Spanish camp. When he finally stormed into the Spanish camp at full gallop, drenched in perspiration, he found out that instead of preparing for battle, the Spanish were taking a *"siesta"*, whereupon he was told that the soldiers were still too exhausted from the arduous route marches over the previous days. At that moment, Wellesley's anger knew no bounds; he was, however, powerless to do anything about the obstinate Spanish commanded by Cuesta.[324] As if this were not enough, Sébastiani had since ousted Venegas and was now dangerously close to the allied forces with his army. Victor-Perrin was soon informed of this fact and slipped quite literally through allied hands in the night, allowing both French Armies to unite successfully. Finally, the newly-named King of Spain and officially the head "commander" of French troops on the Iberian Peninsula, none other than Napoleon's elder brother Joseph Bonaparte, had in the meantime managed to arrive in Madrid with a view to joining forces with Sébastiani and Victor-Perrin together with Marshal Jourdan's troops. It was soon evident that the French had skilfully created a formidable army ready to crush the Anglo-Spanish forces in one decisive battle.

Although Arthur Wellesley and Cuesta had lost their initial advantage over the French (which was primarily the fault of the Spanish General), they now steadily marched on to face them side by side, knowing they shared a mutual goal. After several days of unfruitful manoeuvres against one another, both warring sides found themselves on the western bank of the River Tagus near the town of Talavera de la Reyna. The positioning of Wellesley and Cuesta's soldiers was as follows: the right allied wing, situated in the south, was made up of Spanish units and relied on the town of Talavera, which stretched along the bank of the River Tagus and provided the Spanish there a natural defence from the south. The centre with the left wing of the Allied Army was occupied by Wellesley's British divisions marching to the north toward a small hill called Medellín, which provided the allied left wing – similarly to the River Tagus from the south – with an ideal defence from the north. The French spread out in parallel to face the allied positions. Both armies were divided by the small stream Portina, which was quite easy to cross and did not present a significant barrier. In terms of the power of both armies, neither side possessed a significant advantage, as both enemy camps had roughly 50,000 men prepared for battle.[325]

As battle became increasingly imminent, Arthur Wellesley rode as fast as he could to the La Torres farmstead nearby, which in addition to its farm buildings included a small stone tower that offered a good view of the French positions. As soon as Arthur reached the settlement on horseback, he left his horse in the hands of the several aides-de-camp that had accompanied him and climbed to the top of the tower in order to get a detailed view of the present position of the French troops. While analysing the French position and searching for possible weaknesses, Wellesley was taken by surprise. Several enemy light infantry reconnaissance divisions had managed to close in on La Torres unobserved, attacking Wellesley and his small company from behind. The surprised Arthur was saved by the quick thinking of his aides-de-camp, who did not panic and waited for their commander to climb down from the tower and jump on the horse they had prepared for him. The British company galloped off at lightning speed toward their camp, accompanied by a hail of bullets fired from French muskets only several dozen feet away that flew just over their heads. Miraculously, no one was injured: 'If the French had been cool, they might have taken us all.'[326] Arthur recalled the tense situation.

In history and at present, however, the word "if" carries little weight. Darkness soon descended over Talavera and Arthur Wellesley, in place of an inglorious end with a bullet in his back, hurried to the north of the British lines to Medellín Hill, against which the French launched a surprise attack despite it being night.[327]

Fortunately for the British, the defence of Medellín was led by one of Wellesley's most reliable generals Rowland Hill, knows among the soldiers as 'Daddy' Hill for his genial attitude toward the men and his everlasting optimism. Thanks to his skilful command, British units managed to hold their ground, although it had been a close-run thing. To be on the safe side, after his arrival to Medellín Arthur Wellesley spent the night wrapped in his coat under the clear sky. On the following day, 28th July 1809, Josef Bonaparte launched a full-force attack. However, the French columns – traditionally accompanied by the fearsome roll of drums and cries of *"Vive l'Empereur"* – were gradually cut down once more by the mechanical fire of the thin two-row line of redcoats. At one certain moment, the battle was going so promisingly for Anglo-Spanish forces that Major-General John Sherbrooke's British division, located roughly at the centre of the allied lines, decided to fix bayonets and pursue one of the broken French columns. However, Sherbrooke's men were taken by surprise by French reserves and the pursuers soon became the pursued. Due to Sherbrooke's attack and quite unfortunately for the allies, a dangerous breach opened in their lines toward which the French quickly directed the massive attack of their columns.

Instantly, Arthur Wellesley realized that this could be a decisive moment for the whole battle. He immediately brought a fresh division of General John Randoll Mackenzie's redcoats to this critical point on the battlefield. The British closed this gap in their lines at the last possible moment, quickly leading to a merciless man-to-man skirmish in which sabres and bayonets came to the fore in place of musket fire. On the British side, brave combatants General Mackenzie and Colonel Charles Donnellan, whose 48th Regiment was the first on the site of the most brutal clashes, both fell in battle. Donnellan, who as an old-fashioned officer was the only man in Wellesley's Army still to wear a tricorne hat (at the time already a relic of the past in terms of the British Army's uniform), passed on command of the 48th Regiment with ceremonial decorum to his second-in-command after being shot by a French musket bullet, ordering him to continue on firmly in the attack against the advancing French: 'Major Middlemore, you will have the honour of leading the 48th to the charge.'[328] Major George Middlemore naturally accepted this honour and fared excellently. Together with the other battalions of Mackenzie's division, the British held their positions and forced the French to retreat at this section of their line.

In the meantime, the Spanish were faring equally well in the south of the battlefield despite the fact that the beginning of the battle started off on the wrong foot, as a portion of the Spanish units were startled by fire from their own light infantry, which was located several dozen yards in front of the primary Spanish forces, causing them to flee. At this moment, however, General Cuesta remedied the situation by sending the fleeing units back to their positions. In the following clash with the "real" enemy (i.e. French columns), the Spanish – who in their advantageous position were supported by the town of Talavera from the south – held wonderfully as they repulsed all French attempts at breaking their lines.[329] By the evening, several more French attacks followed by allied counterattacks took place. However, no side managed to overcome or break their opponent. The French ultimately cleared their positions, leaving behind them twenty valuable cannons for their opponents to claim. Major Edward Cocks, serving in the 16th Light Dragoon Regiment, wrote a letter home to his father in England on both the bravery of General Mackenzie and the dauntlessness of Arthur Wellesley, who as Commander-in-Chief once again seemed to have been everywhere he was needed on the battlefield:

> My favourite horse was wounded under me but is likely to do well. The gallant General Mackenzie, the man who did more than anyone towards our victory, is killed... Everybody deeply regrets Mackenzie. Sir Arthur's staff suffered, he was the whole time in the most critical part of the action.[330]

Arthur Wellesley had escaped death at Talavera by only a whisker. Toward the end of battle, he was struck in the shoulder with a bullet. As the projectile had ricocheted, however, he emerged (similarly to his time in India) without serious injury. This bullet, however, was not the only one: Arthur, exhausted from battle, took off his elegant coat in his tent in order to rest. While doing so, he saw he would immediately need a new one, as there was a finger-wide hole in the coat made by another bullet. Somewhat shaken, he described the whole situation in detail to the Charles Lennox 4ᵗʰ Duke of Richmond in a letter:

> You will see the account of the great battle we fought yesterday. Our loss is terribly great. Your nephew is safe. His horse was shot under him on the 27ᵗʰ [July]. Almost all my Staff are either hit or have lost their horses, and how I have escaped unhurt I cannot tell. I was hit in the shoulder at the end of the action, but not hurt, and my coat shot through.[331]

The Battle of Talavera was the bloodiest and clearly largest battle that British soldiers had engaged in since the famous battles between the Duke of Marlborough and France's Sun King, Louis XIV during the War of the Spanish Succession roughly a century earlier. Among the battles of the Peninsular War, Talavera was a clear and important victory for Arthur Wellesley, but was one that came at a high price compared to the dazzling achievements of Vimeiro or Oporto. French casualties totalled 7,268 men killed, captured or wounded, while British casualities amounted to 5,363 men killed, captured or wounded, a quarter of British forces fighting at Talavera and a whole sixth of all British soldiers deployed on the Iberian Peninsula.[332] In the light of their overall superiority in size, these losses were a considerably smaller problem for the French than for the British, as the overall number of French forces deployed south of the Pyrenees was now roughly 250,000 men (the British Army had less than 30,000 men on the Pyrenean Front).[333] Simply speaking, the British could not afford any more such losses in the present situation. Despite this fact, the battle was still a considerable success for Wellesley and for this the British Crown awarded him the title of Viscount of Wellington of Talavera*, allowing him to take a considerable step up the ladder of British aristocracy and so became Lord Wellington in place of his knighthood.

Due to Arthur's absence, the small merchant town of Wellington located in Somerset County in the south of England to which Arthur's new title of Viscount was related was chosen by his brother William.

---

* Adding the name of the battlefield onto an aristocratic title gained for the given battle was a common practice in Britain. For example, Horatio Nelson was named Baron of Burnham Thorpe (a village in Norfolk, where Nelson was born) and of the Nile (for his victory in the Battle of the Nile).

BATTLE OF TALAVERA
French Attack 28ᵗʰ July 1809

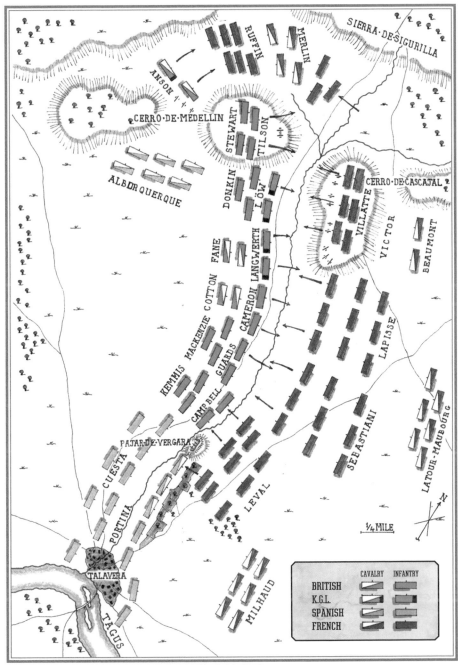

SIERRA·DE·SIGURILLA

RUFFIN

MERLIN

ANSON

CERRO·DE·MEDELLIN

STEWART

TILSON

CERRO·DE·CASCAJAL

DONKIN

LÖW

VILLATTE

VICTOR

BEAUMONT

ALBURQUERQUE

FANE

CAMERON LANGWERTH

LAPISSE

KEMMIS MACKENZIE COTTON

GUARDS

CAMPBELL

SEBASTIANI

PAJAR·DE·VERGARA

CUESTA

LEVAL

LATOUR·MAUBOURG

PORTINA

¼ MILE

N

TALAVERA

MILHAUD

TAGUS

	CAVALRY	INFANTRY
BRITISH		
K.G.L.		
SPANISH		
FRENCH		

—— *Map by John Fawkes* ——

The choice appealed to Arthur, and as soon as he learned of it in a letter from William, he did not hesitate to commend his brother warmly for the decision. Thus, from this point on, Arthur Wellesley primarily used the signature of Lord Wellington. As thanks from the Spanish Government for his victory at Talavera, Wellesley received six exemplary Andalusian stallions and, more importantly, high command of the Spanish troops. Despite this great honour and acknowledgment of his skills as commander, this nomination was somewhat bittersweet for Arthur, as it came only after the battle was fought. If he had received command of Spanish forces earlier, he may have been able to trap Marshal Victor-Perrin.[334]

Shortly after the Battle of Talavera, Italian painter Domenico Pellegrini painted a portrait of the new Viscount of Wellington, placing the single and glorifying word *"Invicto"* ("Unconquerable") before Arthur's name, which was inscribed at the bottom section of the painting. Nonetheless, the evidently delighted and good-humoured Wellington, who clearly admired the painting, intended to poke a bit of fun at the somewhat exaggerated and pompous *"Invicto"* by quickly scrawling the following words under the inscription: "Don't halloo till you are out of the wood" (See Image VII).[335]

In a letter addressed to one of his friends still living in India from the period of his Indian campaign in which he, among other affairs, inquired about the young Salabut (Dhoondiah's son, whom Wellington paid to be educated), Wellington wrote the following lines in a slightly less humorous manner on the Battle of Talavera:

We have had hard work [On the Iberian Peninsula], and shall have still harder, but I don't despair. I have an unanimous army, I agree well with all the authorities in Portugal and Spain, and I believe I have the good wishes of the whole world. The battle of Talavera was the hardest fought of modern times. The fire at Assye [Assaye] was heavier while it lasted, but the battle of Talavera lasted for two days and a night... P.S. Pray how does Salabut Khan get on? Though he did call me a ... [expletive intentionally omitted in the printed dispatch] because I would not allow him to eat pork, I cannot avoid being anxious about him.[336]

All of Britain seemed to be quite thrilled at Arthur Wellesley's victory, as his proud brother William Wellesley-Pole informed him:

Your action of Talavera has delighted and astonished the whole community... you would be gratified if you could see how People exult in your military glory, and how proud the nation is of possessing such a general.[337]

Wellington was congratulated from afar by the British Government and many other Tory deputies and as a celebration of the victorious battle, the long and apologist poem by J. W. Croker, simply entitled *The Battle of Talavera*, was written. Although Croker was Arthur's friend and his poem was highly popular judging by its sales (the poem saw eight publications), Wellesley later noted the following after reading the poem with a touch of irony: 'I did not think a battle could be turned into anything so entertaining.'[338] Nonetheless, there were many critical voices in the lobbies of British society, naturally among the Whigs, who formed the opposition at the moment in Parliament. These "croakers"*, as Wellington would later often call them, claimed that in light of the massive French advantage on the battlefield the whole war on the Iberian Peninsula was doomed to fail and would inevitably end (as many other British attempts at creating an Anti-Napoleonic front on the continent) in a disgraceful retreat and the subsequent rescue of the miserable British troops by the praised Royal Navy.[339] One of the leading Whigs of the time, Earl Charles Grey (who even served as Prime Minister in the 1830s and whose name may remind us of the world-famous Earl Grey tea) was convinced – as many other "croakers" were – of the inexorable failure of Wellington's military campaign and publicly stated the following rather piercing words after Talavera: 'I am convinced that in six weeks' time, there will not remain a single British soldier in the Peninsula except as a prisoner.' [340]

Wellington's next hard-hitting critic after the Battle of Talavera insisted that the war was costing too many lives and chiefly was unjustifiably expensive. According to the Whigs' catastrophic scenarios, the continually growing costs of war could soon lead Britain to national bankruptcy. Some "croakers" even accused Wellesley of deciding to fight at Talavera for purely opportunistic reasons in order to gain a title and disdainfully resented his advancement within the British aristocracy.[341]

---

* This term is described in detail in Elizabeth Longford's biography of Wellington. She explains that the term "croaking" was used in English at the turn of the 18th to 19th century to signify an incessant "grumbling" or defeatism. See Longford, p. 215.

In the meantime, on the opposite side of Europe the anticipated war between Austria and France broke out in the spring of 1809. The Austrians, encouraged by Wellesley's achievements on the Iberian Peninsula and British finances, thus entered into the Fifth Anti-French Coalition alongside Britain. The Austrians managed relatively quickly to build a new army, which was primarily thanks to the Imperial patent on the creation of a militia from the common folk who, thanks to the plundering they suffered after Austerlitz, held strongly hostile sentiments toward the French. By mobilizing its masses, Austria partially replicated France's sudden creation of a massive army based on a conscription system in the years of the French Revolution. In addition, the Commander-in-Chief of Austrian troops, Archduke Charles, Duke of Teschen had been the first one to defeat the "undefeatable" Napoleon on a field battle at Aspern-Essling, which took place from 22nd to 23rd May 1809, causing a great sensation for a time in Europe. Fighting took place mainly on the northern bank of the Danube River near the villages of Aspern and Essling, where Napoleon gradually attempted to transport his army from the southern bank of the powerful river with the help of pontoon bridges. However, Archduke Charles ultimately defended the northern bank. This was largely due to the fact that he managed in the afternoon hours of the next day to break through Napoleon's pontoon bridge with the help of burning rafts which his men sent down the Danube.[342]

In regard to Wellington's opinion of Archduke Charles' commanding capabilities, the following and extremely interesting discussion that Wellington enthusiastically led with his friend John Croker in the 1820s is very telling:

[Croker]: He [Wellington] quoted the Archduke Charles's book, and I asked whether the Archduke was really a great officer? [Wellington]: "A great officer? Why, he knows more about it than all of us put together."[Croker]: "What than Buonaparte… or yourself? [Wellington]: "Aye! Than Buonaparte or any of us. We are none of us worthy to fasten the latchets of his shoes, if I am to judge from his book and his plans of campaign. But his mind or his health has, they tell me, a very peculiar defect. He is admirable for five or six hours, and whatever can be done in that time will be done perfectly, but after that he falls into a kind of epileptic stupor, does not know what he is about, has no opinion of his own, and does whatever the man at his elbow tells him.[343]

It is my assertion that this discussion is especially interesting for two reasons: firstly because Wellington puts the rather widely accepted claim that he considered Napoleon to be the best commander of his time into a slightly different light (although at the same time he admits that Charles' state of health significantly reduced his overall qualities as a commander), and secondly in terms of the analysis of Wellington's reading habits. Croker does not unfortunately tell us specifically what book Wellington was so fondly quoting. In my opinion, it must have been one of the two of the following publication's by the Archduke which had been translated from German (which Wellington did not speak) to French at the time of Wellington's discussion with Croker: *Campagne de 1799 en Allemagne et en Suisse* (*Geschichte des Feldzugs von 1799 in Deutschland und in der Schweiz*) and *Principes de la stratégie, développés par la relation de la campagne de 1796 en Allemagne* (*Grundsätze der Strategie erläutert durch die Darstellung des Feldzugs 1796*).

In addition, both of these works were evidently the most popular of all that the Archduke had written, as nearly thirty editions of each book had been produced by the end of the 19th century. The former publication deals with the description of the Archduke's military campaigns in the War of the Second Coalition against Revolutionary France. Personally, and based on Croker's record, however, I believe that Wellington was most probably referring to the latter-mentioned publication by the Archduke, as it is of a much more theoretical character and deals with the principles of war in a general context. Charles partially illustrates these principles in his campaign in 1796, which took place during the War of the First Coalition on the territory of today's Germany, where Charles achieved several important victories over the French. The Archduke begins the first chapter of the book with a simple but succinct claim:

> Strategy is a military science. It is the origin of a specific plan according to which subsequent and specific military measures are realized. It is the fundamental, characteristic skill of a High Commander. Tactics are then a military art. They tell us exactly how to proceed in an individual situation according to a given strategic concept and are an essential skill of each commanding officer.[344]

Nonetheless, Napoleon managed to defeat Archduke Charles just a few weeks later in another exceptionally bloody two-day battle, which took place from 5th to 6th July 1809 at Wagram, where Napoleon this time managed successfully to cross the Danube. Despite his failing health, Archduke Charles was not only an excellent military theoretician, but also a brave man who, similarly to Wellington, often set a personal example to his soldiers. For example, on the first day of the Battle of Wagram he personally led Vincent's Dragoons in a counterattack against Napoleon's forces with great success. In the Austrian Army, regiments were traditionally named after their owner, who was usually a specific general or a prominent nobleman. Vincent's Dragoons were formerly named Latour's and had distinguished themselves in previous Coalition Wars with France.

Nonetheless, General Latour had died not long before and the regiment was placed in the ownership of General Vincent. For this reason, together with its general the regiment lost its name, with which it had won renown throughout all of Europe, a fact which naturally took a toll on the morale of all the troops. After Vincent's Dragoons were forced to retreat several times in the attempt to support Charles' failing centre during the first day of the Battle of Wagram, the Archduke decided personally to take command and skilfully play on the chord of their former glory, as French soldier Marcelin Marbot, who served under Napoleon at Wagram, wrote in his memoirs:

> Vincent's Dragoons, it is clear that you are no longer Latour's Dragoons! [Archduke Charles yelled in the direction of the retreating Vincent's Dragoons] Humiliated by the warrantable rebuke, the regiment replied: "Yes, yes we still are!" – "Good, then!" called the Archduke and drew his sword proudly. "If you want to prove that you deserve your former glory, follow me!" And despite the bullet injury, he charged at the French! Vincent's regiment set off just behind him with indescribable enthusiasm. His attack was fearful and Oudinot's [the French general leading the attack on Charles' centre] grenadiers retreated with great losses. The Archduke's brief speech so roused the Dragoons that they first stopped Oudinot's grenadiers and then charged Lamarque's division and gained back two thousand captured troops and five colours of the regiment that this division had so recently captured from the Austrians! The Archduke Charles congratulated the Dragoons with

the words: "From now on you will take pride in the name Vincent, which you have made just as famous as that of Latour!"[345]

The next day, however, Archduke Charles was forced to retreat from Wagram, upon which he decided to move to Znaim (Znojmo) in the southeast of today's Czech Republic, where he rose once again to face Napoleon. Nonetheless, after another two days of heavy fighting, an armistice was signed at Znaim, which for Austria culminated in the signing of another humiliating treaty in the Schönbrunn Palace in Vienna in October 1809. As a result, the glory of the victory at Aspern-Essling was wholly overshadowed and Austria was once again eliminated from the conflict.[346] Ultimately, the humbled Austrians lost almost 40,000 square miles of their territory (Galicia, Carinthia, Carniola, Salzburg, and part of today's Croatia) together with three and a half million citizens. To top off this humiliation, Emperor Francis' Austrian Army was not allowed according to the Treaty of Schönbrunn to exceed 150,000 men. The only thing that may have at least partially consoled the Austrians (in addition to the first ever defeat of Napoleon in a field in the annals of history) was the fact that the French had lost approximately 10,000 more men than their opponent in their recent battles with the Austrian Empire, much thanks to the commanding prowess of Archduke Charles.*

Minister for War, Lord Castlereagh was aware of the fact that Britain would be alone in the war with France after Austria's defeat, and the whole brunt of the conflict would thus likely shift to Spain and Portugal; he did however put his unwavering trust in Arthur Wellesley's abilities:

> We have a devil of a task before us in the Peninsula now that Austria is disposed of – If any man alive can carry us through it Wellesley will, and whatever may be the issue – I am Confident he will personally rise with its difficulties.[347]

Lord Canning, the Secretary of State for Foreign Affairs, also expressed himself in a similar manner on the recent victory at Talavera in the following words (which were perhaps even more flattering than those of

---

* The Austrians had lost roughly 46,000 men and the French 56,000 men in all the battles of 1809. See: Zdeněk Šašinka, *Bitva u Znojma: k otázce péče o raněné a pohřbívání v období napoleonských válek* in: Historický obzor, 2010, 21(1/2), pp. 27–35.

Lord Castlereagh) in his written instructions to the newly nominated British Ambassador to Portugal:

> In Wellesley... you will find everything that you can wish – frankness – temper – honesty – quickness – comprehensiveness – and military Ability – not only eminent beyond any other military commander that could be chosen – but perhaps possessed by him alone, of all our Commanders, in a degree that qualifies for great undertakings [i.e. leading the war in Portugal].[348]

However, Arthur Wellesley himself felt rather uneasy to say the least from the recent reports of Austria's absolute defeat as he mentions in a letter addressed at the time to George Berkeley, Vice-Admiral of the Royal Navy: 'I hope that the defeat of the Austrians has not been so decisive as the French accounts would make it.'[349] Unfortunately for him and Britain, Wellington would soon learn that the French were not overly exaggerating when it came to their crushing victory over the Austrians.

A dramatic situation took place soon later on the British political scene as Lord Portland's government fell over the course of September. Coincidentally, Minister for War Lord Castlereagh and Foreign Minister Lord Canning, who so highly praised Arthur Wellesley after Talavera and were his greatest supporters in government were the same men who took the lion's share of responsibility for the fall of the government. In addition to the failure of Austria, to which Britain paid out over one million pounds in subsidies, an unfortunate military expedition planned by the two aforementioned ministers that targeted the island of Walcheren and aimed to conquer the port of Antwerp also significantly contributed to the fall of the government. Poor organization and inept command resulted in a shambolic and extremely costly failure (in terms of both finances and troops) by British forces, who were surrounded by French forces and subsequently forced to retreat, resulting in over 4,000 British dead, the majority of whom fell to illness* without ever firing their muskets. The whole Walcheren Campaign thus strongly reminded the British of the bitter campaign in Flanders in 1793–1795, of which Wellington and others were highly critical.

---

*   Malaria was the most common affliction among British troops. See: Richard Aldington, *Wellington* (London, Toronto 1946), p. 136, p. 142.

The proverbial "icing on the cake" and simultaneously the most distinct symbol of the government crisis was the duel that took place between Minister for War Lord Castlereagh and Lord Canning. The duel took place on 21st September 1809 in Putney Heat Park on the outskirts of London. The challenger was Lord Castlereagh, who accused Lord Canning of duplicitous behaviour and efforts to lay all blame for the "Walcheren fiasco". During the duel, Canning shot off the button of Castlereagh's coat lapel while the aggrieved Minister for War also shot his rival, lightly injuring him in the thigh. Although both ministers emerged from the duel without any permanent injury to their health, British society was greatly shocked by the duel between government officials, a fact which the Whigs used to their advantage, ostentatiously condemning the whole affair with spiteful glee as barbaric and objectionable.[350] Thanks in part to Arthur Wellesley's success at Talavera, however, power still remained in the hands of the Tories despite the various negative opinions, a fact which represented a certain silver lining amongst the criticisms of the Tory cabinet. However, the ruling party was not likely to survive another failure. Lord Spencer Percival took control of the new government while the office of the Minister for War, which was surely the most relevant post to the newly named Lord Wellington, as the Minister for War was *de facto* his direct superior, was taken by Robert Jenkinson, Lord Liverpool after Lord Castlereagh.[351]

Arthur Wellesley naturally followed the news on the domestic political situation in Britain with considerable interest. Contrary to his greatest rival, Emperor Napoleon, who reported to none other than himself, Arthur was to a great degree dependent on the British Government. For this reason, he was forced to maintain good ties with the Government throughout the whole course of his military service and be something of a politician himself. Arthur Wellesley's requests addressed to the British Government included regular and repeated requests for finances, supplies, and men. Nonetheless, Wellington had had relatively smooth relations with the British ministers hitherto (he was even good friends with Lord Castlereagh) and it seemed that the new Minister for War held Arthur in high regard and would attempt to do his utmost for him in the Government:

> I think I may be, perhaps, of more use to you in your command in Portugal than any other person who could be placed in the same situation. Let me

know your wants and your wishes... and I will do my best for you, though I cannot promise I shall always succeed... I regret Castlereagh and all he has suffered.[352]

wrote Lord Liverpool to Arthur Wellesley soon after his nomination. However, the most positive consequence of the fall of the government for Arthur was indubitably his oldest brother Richard Wellesley's nomination to the post of Foreign Minister.[353] Despite this fact, Wellington criticized the political squabbling and the general partisan politics in a letter addressed to his other brother William Wellesley-Pole:

> I never felt any inclination to dive deeply in party Politics, I may be wrong but the conviction in my mind is that all the misfortunes of the present reign, the loss of America, the success of the French revolution etc., are to be attributed in a great degree to the Spirit of Party in England, & the feeling I have for a decided party politician is rather that of contempt than any other. I am very certain that his wishes & efforts for his party very frequently prevent him from doing that which is best for the Country, & induce him to take up the cause of foreign powers against Britain, because the cause of Britain is managed by his party opponents.[354]

Over two hundred years later, many contemporary political representatives – who often do injustice to the issues being discussed and to the general interest of the state – would do well to take these sentiments to heart while engaging in the political fray, especially around issues such as Brexit. Although the government crisis seemed vanquished for the time being, problems were quite likely in store for Arthur, as Napoleon decided to send in the region of 140,000 more soldiers immediately to the Iberian Peninsula after defeating the Austrians. These soldiers had but one goal: conquering Portugal and ultimately driving Wellington's presumptuous British troops into the sea. In the beginning, the French Emperor planned to take command of his army personally, but because he planned soon to marry Austrian Princess Marie Louise from the venerable and Royal House of Habsburg (the forty-year-old Napoleon planned the new marriage shortly after his divorce from his first wife, French noblewoman Joséphine de Beauharnais, with whom he had had a childless marriage), which was intended to place the proverbial crown on Austria's humiliation and at the same time provide Bonaparte with a legitimate heir with noble blood for his Empire, he ultimately left command up to one of his most trusted marshals, André Masséna. During the Revolutionary Wars, Masséna managed to gain an excellent reputation as a commander and held the telling nickname of the 'Old Fox'. In addition, Napoleon retrospectively called Masséna (and Marshal Suchet) the most capable of all his marshals, which was naturally not a statement of little significance from a commander of Napoleon's experience and renown.

Over the course of time, however, one third of the 140,000 men that Masséna had at is his disposal were forced to guard supply routes, as Spanish and Portuguese guerrillas began to make matters increasingly difficult for the French supply lines. In addition, since the beginning of the Peninsular War the French had managed to escalate hostilities with the ordinary Portuguese and Spanish people largely due to their haughty behaviour and frequent acts of cruelty. Wellington personally was disgusted by the French's behaviour toward civilians. For example, upon observing Marshal Soult's retreat through the Portuguese countryside, he provided the following damning image:

> Their soldiers [the French] have plundered and murdered the peasantry at their pleasure, and I have seen many persons hanging, in the trees by the sides of the road, executed for no reason that I could learn, excepting that they have not been friendly to the French invasion and usurpation of the government of their country, and the route of their column, on their retreat, could be traced by the smoke of the villages to which they set fire.[355]

Arthur Wellesley noted at the time, expressing his open disgust. The French, however, would come to pay dearly for this brutality and recklessness. In Portugal in 1808, Portuguese farmer Jacinto Correia was executed at the orders of the hated French General Loison, alias 'Maneta', for killing two of his soldiers who were attempting to rob the farmer unscrupulously. During the short trial, the verdict of which was already clear to all, Correia spoke the legendary sentence that would serve as a battle cry to hundreds of Portuguese partisans while attacking French supply divisions: *"So Todos Fossem como eu, ne mun Frances ficava vivo!"* ("If all were like me, not a single Frenchman would remain alive!")[356] When Arthur Wellesley pursued Marshal Soult to the Spanish border after defeating him at Oporto, he noted that, in addition to the many murdered Portuguese and burnt villages, Soult's path of retreat was 'strewed with the carcases of horses and mules, and of French soldiers who were put to death by the peasantry...'[357]

The anti-French guerrilla movement in Spain was perhaps even more merciless and famous than that of Portugal. The Spanish guerrillas fought what they called *Guerra a Cuchillo* – literally "war to the knife", i.e. one of cruelty, ambushes, bloodthirstiness, assassinations, torture, and revenge.[358] Over the course of time in the Peninsular War, dozens of self-appointed "people's commanders" who hated the French with all their heart and soul began to operate throughout the whole Spanish Kingdom. The most famous Spanish guerrilla fighter was most likely the farmer Juan Martín Diéz, more known for his nickname 'El Empecinado' ('The Undaunted' or 'The Unstoppable'), whose name justifiably struck fear into the hearts of the French. With only twelve men, 'El Empecinado' operated in the forests roughly halfway between Madrid and Burgos, where he assaulted and captured French soldiers, subsequently killing them in the most brutal of manners – by stoning them, boiling them in oil, or burying them in the earth in remote areas up to their necks, where he would let his detested captives die of thirst. Guerrilla tactics were used not only by small groups like those of 'El Empecinado' – for example in Navara Province in the northwest of Spain, a people's commander gathered eight hundred men in the Pyrenees and persistently assaulted the French with his small-scale army.[359]

In addition to the help of Portuguese and Spanish partisan freedom-fighters, Wellington's Intelligence Service also proved absolutely vital. This service was to a large degree based on cooperation with the guerrillas and was unmatched in history as an organization in terms of its gradually developing structure. However, as author Terry Crowdy very concisely states in his book *The Enemy Within: A History of Spies, Spymasters and Espionage*, it should be noted that Wellington's Intelligence Service as the forerunner of MI6 (Britain's Secret Intelligence Service) was still in an "embryonic stage" despite its indisputable qualities at the time.[360] In 1803, a special division called the Depot of Military Knowledge was founded under the jurisdiction of the Secretary-at-War. This division's primary task was to create a narrowly focused scientific library primarily containing the most precise and up-to-date maps of all the states of the time, which in comparison to today's Google Maps and other various scientific conveniences was a rather costly affair. In addition, it strove to collect the most current information on the present political situation in the world. Nonetheless, when Wellington landed in Lisbon in 1809, the maps he possessed were not of the highest quality despite all the efforts of the division mentioned above. Despite the initial lack of good-quality maps, the issue that perhaps plagued Wellington the most was not the fact that his maps failed to show various rural Portuguese and Spanish villages; instead, his greatest worry was the absolute lack of accurate information on the number and location of French soldiers. For this reason, Arthur Wellesley began to build his own "Field Intelligence Service" very soon after his second landing in Portugal. This service reported directly to him and was to be his "second eyes and ears".[361] The core of Wellington's organization was formed by so-called "exploring officers" who throughout the course of the Peninsular War perfected their activities and regularly provided their commander with invaluable information. Wellington placed the same high demands on these men as were placed on their famous British spy-film successors such as James Bond or Johnny English (depending on whom you prefer). Firstly, they had to be accomplished riders with an excellent sense of orientation in the terrain, thanks to which these exploring officers were able to evade Napoleon's patrols. For their task, they received from Wellington only the quickest and most tenacious horses. Furthermore, it was crucial that they spoke the necessary languages perfectly: for Wellington's needs, these were primarily French, Portuguese, and Spanish, which would allow them to communicate easily with the local populace. Like true "agents", they often managed with a bit of resourcefulness to fool their French enemies. The final and key requirement of these men (perhaps somewhat surprisingly to some) was sufficient artistic talent, as perhaps the most important part of their work stemmed from the ability to precisely and quickly record the exact positions and equipment of the enemy's army. In addition, thanks to their drawing skills, these soldiers created the hitherto insufficient and immensely important detailed maps that Arthur Wellesley used for the elaborate planning of his campaigns. Together with these crucial traits, the soldiers were required to fulfil the last and most fundamental criterion, which was Wellington's absolute trust in their character, honest behaviour, and secrecy in the event that they were captured by the enemy.

Being an exploring officer was naturally a highly dangerous position and many of these brave men never lived to see the end of the war despite the fact that the vast majority of them wore military uniforms on their missions so that, in the event of capture, they would be treated as soldiers and not automatically shot on site for espionage. The most famous and evidently "best of the best" of Wellington's exploring officers was 29-year-old Major Colquhoun Grant.* This courageous soldier spent the year of 1798 in French captivity and therefore spoke French perfectly. He also spoke Portuguese very skilfully, but his greatest skill was Spanish, which he spoke like a native. Grant had even mastered the language in its various dialects. Wellington's friend George Robert Gleig, who served under Arthur Wellesley during the Peninsular campaign as an ensign and after the war became a priest and writer, said about Grant that he:

> possessed the talent of acquiring languages to a marvellous degree. He spoke Spanish, Portuguese, and French with a facility and correctness to which Englishmen rarely attain, and with the use of the language he put on the manner and well-nigh the appearance of Spaniard, Portuguese, or Frenchman, as the case might be... He had emissaries everywhere, in all towns and villages in or about which French troops were quartered, and if common rumour might be trusted, some even at the head-quarters of the French armies themselves.[362]

Grant loved Spain and Spanish culture and the Spaniards took a similar liking to him. This naturally gave him a huge advantage in his dangerous, solitary missions well behind the French lines. The Spaniards aided Grant using all possible means and called him 'Granto Bueno', which speaks for itself in terms of his popularity. Wellington's head of the Medical Department Dr James McGrigor, who was Grant's brother-in-law (Grant had married his sister), wrote of his relative:

> Colquhoun Grant had a singular talent, not only for the acquisition of languages, but of the different dialects of languages. He was a proficient in those of all the provinces of Spain, was intimately acquainted with all their customs, their songs, their music, and with all their habits and prejudices. He

---

* Major Grant is generally considered to have been the inspiration for the character of Major Michael Hogan in Bernard Cornwell's Sharpe series.

was moreover an enthusiastic admirer of the Spanish character, was well read in all their popular works, and he danced even their national dances most admirably.[363]

Grant was thus the ideal man for Wellington as an exploring officer: he was almost constantly behind enemy lines, drawing maps and charting the numbers of enemy positions while the civilian population helped him hide and provided him with supplementary information. It is no surprise that on one occasion Wellington declared the following about potentially losing Grant: '... the loss of a brigade could scarcely have been more felt by me...' and also 'The information coming from Grant, I know it is correct, and is most valuable.'[364] French Colonel Marcelin Marbot recalled that during the Peninsular War:

one very dark night an Englishman, dressed in officer's uniform, got into a small boat on the left bank [of the River Tagus] a little above Punhete [today's Constancia in Portugal], landed in silence, passed through the French outposts, and at daybreak walked boldly towards our workshops, examining everything at his ease as if he had belonged to the staff of our army...[365]

We do not know with complete certainty whether at this moment Marbot was referring specifically to Grant or a different exploring officer; it is however clear that this was at least a "trip" done in Grant's style and this audacious Englishman was very probably 'Granto Bueno'.

Another important intelligence officer that belonged to the very first of Wellington's exploring officers during the Peninsular War was Sir Andrew Leith-Hay, a relative of General James Leith, who commanded Wellington's 5th Division. At the beginning of the Peninsular War, Sir Andrew primarily followed the situation in Northern Spain. On one occasion, his contacts amongst the Spanish guerrillas took him all the way to Madrid, from where he continued to weave his way through Spain, mapping French positions for several days in order to submit his valuable report to Wellington. In the challenging terrain and behind enemy lines, he managed to travel an incredible 900 miles in only fifteen days.[366]

The third outstanding exploring officer whom Wellington was especially fond of also from a personal perspective was Major Edward Cocks (who also served in the 16th Light Dragoons and was already quoted above). Wellington highly valued his sense of duty, intelligence and bravery. He considered him to be one of the most talented officers in the whole army and, in the light of his young age, saw great promise in him for the British Army. A priceless fact for us, however, is that Cocks' detailed diary has been preserved. Cocks used the diary as an aid during his work as exploring officer, and thanks to it today we can gain detailed insight into the everyday life of these brave men. For an illustration, below are excerpts in chronological order from Cocks' notes over the course of five consecutive days:

> [Day 1] Today's account state Victor [Marshal Claude Victor-Perrin], with upwards of 20 000 men as being in full march for Almoden Roque.
>
> [Day 2] Having bought a horse of Roche I set out, accompanied by two dragoons of Fernando VII [this was either a Spanish regiment named after King Ferdinand VII, or Cocks was simply referring to two Spanish dragoons], in order to reconnoitre the movements of the French on the left.
>
> [Day 3] Majeza: 4 leagues, 4 and half hours. Brig-Gen D. Francisco Capons commanded here. He had about 2,000 infantry. Cabezasubias: 2 leagues, 3 hours. A small but comfortable village. I procured only wheat here for my horses...
>
> [Day 4] Abrazatortas: 2 leagues, 3 hours... The Venta [a village called Venta Nuova] lies a little to the left...
>
> [Day 5] I was anxious to cross the route of the enemy and forward my intelligence to Lord Wellington...[367]

Over the course of the Peninsular War, another wholly indispensable man to Wellington was Sir George Scovell, who reported to the Intelligence Service but dealt with tasks that were rather different than those of the classic exploring officers. If you have ever heard of Alan Turing, who deciphered the famous German 'Enigma Code' whilst working at Bletchley Park during the Second World War, we might claim somewhat hyperbolically that Scovell gradually became to Wellington what Turing became to Churchill – i.e. his primary decipherer. However, contrary to Turing, Scovell gained this position more by way of chance. This cavalry officer came from humble beginnings and, similarly to Grant, displayed a truly exceptional talent for languages from a young age. While still at school, he had mastered Ancient Greek, Latin and French. During the Peninsular War, Wellington put him in charge of a rather bizarre group made up of Portuguese and Spanish soldiers and some French deserters (mainly from so called Sisters Republic in Holland, Switzerland and Italy), who were known as "Army Guides", as they were assumed at least theoretically to know the local landscape. In addition to the command of a group of Army Guides, Scovell was also placed in charge of all army communications as a member of Wellington's staff.

During their regular clashes with the French, local fighters leading the guerrilla war often captured French messengers carrying correspondence not only among individual French armies on the Iberian Peninsula but often also between Napoleon's marshals and the Emperor himself. Although French messengers made efforts to hide the dispatches properly, they would naturally reveal their hiding places while subjected to torture. In addition, Wellington began to pay princely sums to the guerrilla troops for intercepted dispatches, a fact which of course strongly boosted the partisans' patriotic determination. There is proof that at least two hundred French messengers were killed during the Peninsular War. *"Los guerrilleros"* thus regularly delivered a great deal of French documents, which often betrayed the highly detailed military intentions of Bonaparte's marshals. Therefore, French messengers began to be accompanied by increasingly powerful military escorts for there to be at least some hope for the message to be delivered. This in no way discouraged many of the guerrilla chiefs, who in many cases continued to strike success in capturing French envoys. The French soon began to encrypt their documents with special codes so they would at least be unreadable to Wellington if their messengers were caught. It was clear to Arthur Wellesley that this new problem would need to be solved. In the light of his significant disadvantage in terms of the number of French troops on the Iberian Peninsula, the most accurate information possible on the intentions of the enemy was of utmost importance. Wellington, however, did not want to send the encrypted letters to Britain, where the government could assign them to university professors for decoding. He feared (and not unjustifiably so) that the French had many spies in Britain, who would inevitably find out the code had been cracked by the professors. Thus, almost all the officers of Wellington's staff took turns trying to crack the code until it was Scovell's turn, he being a mere Captain at the time. To Wellington's great pleasure and relief, he managed to crack the French code in only a matter of days.[368] As we know, languages were Scovell's passion, and he employed the book *Cryptographia, or The Art of Decyphering* by David Arnold Conradus to help decipher the French code. This book contained the basic precepts for correctly deciphering secret codes in various languages including French. Thanks to Conradus' work, Scovell managed with relative ease to make sense of the code used by Napoleon's Army, which contained only 50 numbers.[369]

Wellington's main spy in Spain was Reverend Dr Patrick Curtis, Professor of Natural History and Astronomy at the University in Salamanca. Within the church, this 72-year-old Irishman had an elabo-rate network of spies throughout all of Spain, and collected all possible information on the French at Salamanca and, either via the British explor-ing officers or his own contacts, skilfully sent reports off to Wellington.[370]

The French soldiers already present on the Iberian Peninsula were thus continually occupied with insurgents scattered throughout Spain – this included the remaining units of the regular Spanish Army. The port town of Cádiz, where the elected junta had taken control over the coun-try, became the centre of Spanish resistance for its position at a highly inaccessible point on the southwest cape of Spain and its ability to be supplied by the sea. The town continued successfully to ward off the French despite the fact that it was plagued almost constantly by sieges of French troops. Nonetheless, despite all these problems roughly 80,000 French soldiers were free to be ordered under Masséna's command. Arthur Wellesley was thus in danger of soon facing an almost three-fold advantage. Therefore, he decided to withdraw to his defensive position (which was, as I assert, carefully planned) in Portugal, the order for which he issued at the end of August 1809.[371]

The Lines of Torres Vedras and the Defence of Portugal – in the Footsteps of William of Schaumburg-Lippe

T he approaching autumn of 1809 came upon Arthur Wellesley and his British army during their infamous retreat toward Lisbon. The oppressive atmosphere looming over the retreating troops was only strengthened by increasing difficulties in supplying provisions. Despite this fact, Wellington unflinchingly stuck to the order that his soldiers were to purchase everything honestly from their Spanish and Portuguese allies. Even when his men had sufficient funds (which often was not the case), there was often nothing to buy, as few provisions were left to be purchased in the "militarily exhausted" valley of the Guadiana River. Thus, some of Wellesley's regiments quickly found themselves on the verge of starvation and the morale of his men began to drop as quickly as the temperatures outside. With the approaching autumn sleet, various diseases began to spread at an alarming pace among the miserable British. This poor condition of health plagued Commander-in-Chief Lord Wellington as well, as he admitted to the British Ambassador in Lisbon John Villiers on 20th September: 'I have not been well for above a month, and have still hanging upon me a low fever which I cannot shake off.'[372]

The sickness and misery of the British units culminated in the beginning of December 1809, when nearly a third of the soldiers in Wellesley's thirty-thousand-man army were placed out of service on the sick list. It is therefore no surprise that, due to these circumstances, the so-called "croaking" and criticism of the whole campaign began to spread swiftly not only among the Whig Members of Parliament in Britain, but also throughout all ranks among Wellington's own men deployed in the Iberian Peninsula. Many of Wellington's soldiers now held grave fears of ultimately being driven ignominiously back into the sea, leaving the sacrificed lives of their comrades and all their successes hitherto in vain.[373] For Wellington, this was likely one of the most arduous periods in his whole lengthy military career.

The gravity of the situation in the British ranks can be seen, among other things, in the fact that General Rowland 'Daddy' Hill, a hardened commander who was liked by all, wrote the following pessimistic words home:

> I am confident we can do no good by remaining [on the Peninsula]. The Spanish and Portuguese Cause in my mind is hopeless, they will do nothing for themselves, and we can do no more than we have done. It appears to me that a storm is brewing and it behoves us to keep a good look out to take care of ourselves.[374]

Even more unsparing than 'Daddy' Hill in his commentary on the current state of affairs on the Iberian Peninsula was Captain William Warre, aide-de-camp to General William Beresford. In his letter home, Captain Warre also pointed out the link between the Pyrenean western front and British foreign policy on one hand and the eastern front opened by the Austrians against the French with the support of the British government on the other. The Austrians, who were the only ally with of greater significance to Britain in the anti-Napoleonic Fifth Coalition, were soon defeated and forced into suing for peace:

There never was such folly as sending an army into Spain again... We are very low in spirits at the bad accounts from Austria. A peace in that country will decide the fate of these most undoubtedly. [Evidently referring to the Napoleonic Wars in general] We may prolong the war and sacrifice many lives, but I am convinced it will be to no purpose...[375]

It should be mentioned that, in light of the situation on the Iberian Peninsula and reports of Napoleon's further triumphs, the complaints and pessimistic mood among the British soldiers was certainly not un-justified. Even General Moore, who was acknowledged throughout the British Army for his commanding skills and fell less than a year prior at the Battle of Corunna had proclaimed that Portugal, to which Wellington was now retreating, would be undefendable against the French. Arthur Wellesley, who held Moore in high esteem, nonetheless refused to agree with this point from the very beginning and was now naturally discon-certed by the "system of croaking" (as he himself called it) in his army, as he wrote to General Beresford: 'The croaking which already prevails in the Army and particularly about headquarters, is disgraceful to us as a nation and does infinite mischief to the cause.'[376]

The gradual success of General Beresford in training Portuguese units brought at least a partial boost in British morale. Slowly but surely, results began to show, as the British general had been intensively train-ing the Portuguese for almost a year, specifically since February 1809. Beresford was first successful in considerably rejuvenating the Portuguese officer corps despite significant resistance on the part of the Portuguese, whereupon he increased the salaries of all Portuguese troops, rapidly re-ducing the numbers of deserters. The remainder of the training involved serious toil and regular drill under the command of British officers and sergeants that was similar to the exercises of the British infantry at their barracks back in Britain. Over the course of several months and thanks to Beresford's remarkable efforts, an army of 25,000 men was created and fully equipped, primarily at the expense of the British. This was no doubt a significant success. Portuguese troops were now almost equal to British forces and could thus play a considerable role in defending their nation.[377]

How the hastily trained and equipped Portuguese would fare in battle, however, remained a sensitive issue. Critics of the Portuguese Army, convinced that the Portuguese could not be relied on despite

Beresford's efforts, included men such as Major-General Charles Stewart (half-brother of Lord Castlereagh):

> The question is then reduced to Portugal. After all that W. [Wellington] has said on the defence of it, I am sure if he has means he will fight it to the last. He may make a long stand, but it must be with the British troops alone, for whatever Beresford may say, be satisfied his Portuguese army are as little to be trusted as our Spanish friends.[378]

As if this were not enough, Perceval's new government, which began more frequently to ask Arthur's opinion on the prospects of British engagement on the Iberian Peninsula, gradually began to pose problems for Wellington. Despite assumptions, even Wellington's brother Richard, who held the influential position of Foreign Minister, was not making the situation in Government any easier on Arthur. On the contrary, in the company of the members of the Tory government, Richard soon found himself in complete isolation due to a scandalous affair with courtesan Sally Douglas. The scandal took on epic proportions in Britain when Richard decided to publicly move Sally – or 'Mol' as she was called – into the Wellesley's London residence at Apsley House, which stood not far from Buckingham Palace.* For political reasons, the other ministers kept their distance from Richard. Arthur was naturally enraged by his brother's foolishness and, with a considerable amount of sarcasm, wrote the following home to another Wellesley brother, William Wellesley-Pole, with whom he was especially close at the time:

> I wish that Wellesley [Richard] was castrated, or that he would like other people attend to his business and perform too. It is lamentable to see talents and character and advantages such as he possesses thrown away upon whoring.[379]

Arthur Wellesley was thus forced to bear the full burden of ensuring essential communication with the Government and reassuring it that Portugal was able to be defended against the French. Despite all the difficulties the British were presently experiencing on the Pyrenean front, Wellesley

---

* Longford, p. 214. Under the weight of societal pressure, Richard moved Sally Douglas out of Apsley House but continued to pay her an allowance of 4,500 pounds annually. Nonetheless, his reputation was permanently marred.

wrote the following to Robert Jenkinson, the 2nd Earl of Liverpool, the Secretary of State for War and the Colonies in mid-November 1809 in two letters sent in quick succession:

> The enemy [the French] will find it difficult, if not impossible, to obtain possession of Portugal...I should not act fairly by the government if I did not tell them my real opinion, which is, that they will betray the honour and interest of the country if they not continue their efforts in the Peninsula, which, in my opinion, are by no means hopeless.[380]

Wellington's declaration was enough for the War Minister and the whole of Perceval's government to promise him aid in the form of additional provisions, finances, and reinforcements. Thus, for the time being the Pyrenean front remained intact.

Wellesley had a very good reason to make the statement that "the enemy will find it difficult, if not impossible, to obtain possession of Portugal", as in mid-November, when he wrote the previous lines to Lord Liverpool, his secret plan to destroy the French – led by the 'Old Fox' Masséna – was already in full swing. The British Government and the vast majority of British troops, however, lacked even the slightest inkling of this plan, as the attempt to keep it in complete secrecy was a condition for its success. It was an undertaking that at the time was unprecedented: a massive system of fortifications beginning approximately thirty two miles (i.e. roughly two days of marching) north of Lisbon called the Lines of Torres Vedras.

From the beginning of October 1809, Wellington personally and almost incessantly mapped the mountainous terrain north of Lisbon over the full breadth of the small peninsula between the Atlantic and the River Tagus where, at its southern edge, the Portuguese capital is located. Wellington attentively observed the terrain, spoke with the local inhabitants, and assiduously recorded all his findings. Arthur's head military engineer Colonel Richard Fletcher accompanied him. 'I know that his Lordship [Wellington] and the Col. [Fletcher] have been riding all over the country [between the Atlantic and the Tagus] for 30 miles round and have nearly knocked up Fletcher's stud...'[381], wrote one of Wellington's military engineers, Lieutenant Jones, in a letter home. These efforts culminated in the final order to build the system of Torres Vedras fortifications, which Wellington delivered to Fletcher in detailed written form on 20th October 1809. As a basis for the specific location of the fortress, Wellington possessed older maps created by French military engineer Vincent and Portuguese Major Neves Costa. Construction began in full at the beginning of November. After it was completed, the Torres Vedras fortification system comprised of three primary defensive lines of multiple fortresses. Ultimately, an impressive total of 152 fortresses were built. After completion, these small star-shaped fortresses, or redoubts, which were often mutually linked by a network of trenches and defensive mounds, possessed 524 cannons and exposed the enemy to crossfire at many points along its defensive lines. The Lines of Torres Vedras were ultimately capable of housing approximately 35,000 men.[382]

The effectiveness of this network of fortifications, however, was primarily in the location of its individual and smaller fortresses (redoubts), which were placed on the small peaks of the mountain range and made maximum use of the hilly terrain north of Lisbon that the chain of redoubts copied. In areas where the slopes were not sufficiently steep, they were artificially heightened, allowing the naturally hilly terrain to be transformed into a sort of massive natural rampart. The slopes of the hills, which contained the fortification network at their peaks, were completely deforested, stripping potential attackers of any possible cover in their attempts to surmount the lines. This would have exposed them to merciless fire until the last possible moment. Each redoubt was protected by a 15-foot deep and 10-foot wide trench, at the bottom of which were placed singed, pointed wooden stakes. Defenders dug so-called *"trous-de-loup"* ("wolf traps") in various places just in front of the small forts. These traps consisted of pits dug roughly three yards deep, covered on top with brush and lightly covered with earth. A sharpened stake at the bottom awaited any poor unfortunate wretch who fell into the trap.

On the reverse side of the hilly terrain, which was hidden from the eyes of potential attackers, tens of miles of military roads were built. This enabled not only the transport of cannons, howitzers, and mortars to their positions in the small forts; the roads also made it possible to conveniently deliver supplies to the personnel of each redoubt. In order to perfect the effectiveness of the defensive system, Wellington then had all the possible areas located in front of the lines flooded, damming various rivulets that flowed down from the hills. [383]

THE LINES OF TORRES VEDRAS
1810–1811

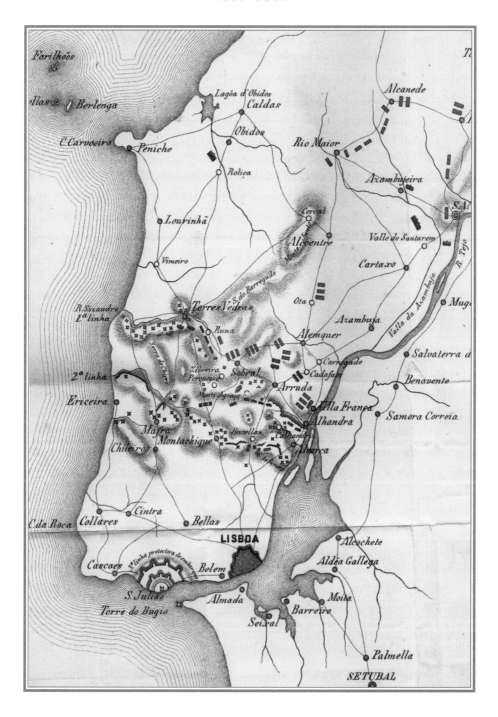

The first and longest line of the fortification system stretched a distance of some 32 miles south from the Atlantic across the towns of Torres Vedras and Sobral and on to the Tagus. It was made up of 70 fortifications equipped with 319 cannons. Above the town of Torres Vedras, which lent its name to the whole system of fortifications, loomed a medieval Moorish castle. Thanks to the undertakings of Wellington's military engineers, the castle was fully used for the defensive lines and was rebuilt into redoubt (fortress) number 27. The second line was located seven miles closer towards Lisbon and had 69 fortresses and 215 cannons spread out between the ocean and the Tagus over a "mere" 22 miles. According to Wellington's plans, the second defensive line would halt Masséna definitively. The strategic significance of the Lines of Torres Vedras was strengthened by the way they were positioned, as the first two lines of fortifications blocked all paths leading to Lisbon, providing the city with a perfect defence. The final line was then built at a length of two miles around the San Julian harbour fortress and was intended to provide the British with a sufficient amount of time to board their ships and evacuate in a worst-case scenario.* Lisbon was thus defended from the north by the Lines of Torres Vedras; the Atlantic provided natural cover for the city from the south and west while the Tagus, lined with British sloops-of-war, provided protection from the east.

In addition, the whole defensive system of fortifications possessed a highly sophisticated system of communication. Ten massive semaphore lines were placed at carefully selected redoubts (mostly those built on the highest points) along the whole length of the Lines. A "semaphore line", which is now a relatively obscure term, was basically a simple mechanism made up of a large wooden column with a transverse arm that was attached to the top of the column, forming a right angle. Several anchored ropes, one next to the other, led from the arm of the semaphore to the ground with balls attached to them. Soldiers operating the semaphore could then move the balls up and down the whole length of the ropes; the position of an individual ball represented a certain code that could be translated into words. In simpler terms, the whole device at first glance would probably be reminiscent of a giant abacus. The principle of the whole system, including the coded combinations, was taken from the British Royal Navy, the ships

---

*   Thompson, p. 50. The third line in the area of the port of San Julian was made up
of 13 fortresses with 94 cannons.

of which communicated with one another on a similar basis but used flags instead of balls. The semaphore stations were also equipped with special telescopes that helped operators receive messages from the neighbouring semaphore that was miles away. They would then pass the message on until it reached its final destination. Messages could only be sent during daylight hours. In cases of poor weather, transferring messages was nearly impossible. Nonetheless, the idea to build a semaphore line on the Lines of Torres Vedras was one of Wellesley's many ingenious moves, as it further bolstered the defensive capabilities of the whole fortification system. The semaphore lines placed on the Lines of Torres Vedras made it possible to relay messages directly from Wellesley's command station, which he had set up on a spacious manor in the small village of Pero Negro, stretching almost three miles toward Lisbon beyond the first chain of forts, in only seven minutes to all parts of the Lines.[384]

Five to ten thousand workers from the ranks of Portugal's civilian population, joined by several militia divisions, gradually took up work on constructing the Lines.[385] Wellington divided up the whole system of fortifications into several sections, entrusting the work on each section to one (usually British) military engineer. At the beginning of January 1810, military engineer Captain Mulcaster informed his friend Captain Burgoyne of the progress of work:

> My intrenchments are getting on, but not so rapidly as I had hoped, for I have met with large proportion of rock and hard gravel... I wish you could see my intrenchments. Unlucky dogs that ever have to attack them![386]

For Wellington, the effort to keep everything in the utmost secrecy was the most important element. This, however, seemed nearly impossible in regard to the extent of the size of the undertaking.

At the beginning of 1810, the condition of Wellington's units began to improve and the sick list was not nearly as long as it had been before. Thanks to a shorter supply route in Portugal, problems with provisions subsided. In addition, Arthur Wellesley received promised reinforcements from England, after which the number of British troops in his army grew to 35,000. Together with these new regiments, Wellington was also sent new and high-ranking officers from the British command in Horse Guards. They included men such as General Thomas Picton and Colonel

Lowry Cole (who was coincidentally the man who unsuccessfully courted Kitty Pakenham at the time of Wellesley's stay in India; despite this
affair, however, he got on well with Wellington), who were time-proved
and experienced soldiers who were a considerable asset to any regiment.
Nonetheless, the list of newly arriving officers also included men of ill
repute who had made their way to Wellington merely by means of patronage. Perhaps the worst example of these "nepotistic" officers was
embodied in General William Erskine, "a drunkard and a dissolute who
was nearly blind and likely to have been mentally unhinged." Erskine
had been sent home from Spain as "indisposed" the year before and
was now returning to the Pyrenean Front after proper "recuperation".
Colonel Landers, who similarly to Erskine had also been suspended of
his service, also spelled disaster for Wellington. Wellesley wrote of his
new "reinforcements" in the following message: 'Really when I reflect
upon the characters and attainments of some of the General officers of
this army... I tremble... I only hope that when the enemy reads the list
of their names he trembles as I do.'[387] In order to keep at least Landers
out of action, Wellington named him "perpetual President of General
Courts-Martial".[388]

Despite these minor inconveniences, Wellington now had a long-awaited reason to be optimistic, as his army had completely recovered and was
now being well fed. In April 1810, he even wrote: 'The Army is more efficient than it has ever been yet.'[389] Other than a few doubters, the British
troops held an unwavering faith in their hitherto undefeated commander. New arrival General Thomas Picton wrote the following about the
atmosphere among the troops in a letter home: 'Lord W. [Wellington]
is a great favourite with everyone, high and low...'[390] Captain John Cars
expressed a similar sentiment about Arthur around the same time: 'He is
a good soldier and very much beloved by the army.'[391]

From Wellington's perspective, the British had recovered at the eleventh hour, as Marshal Masséna withdrew into Spain with his army in
May of 1810 and, according to Bonaparte's orders, immediately began
to prepare all that was necessary to attack Portugal. Surprisingly, he still
had no inkling of the Lines of Torres Vedras. Thus, in Masséna's eyes,
the greatest barrier in advancing on Lisbon was the feared fort city of
Almeida and its massive ramparts, which were located on Portugal's border and which the French marshal now planned to attack. Now, at the

end of August, French artillery batteries were prepared to fire in front of Almeida and began to bombard the town.

Partly due to a rather incredible accident, the French were able to celebrate victory almost immediately – Almeida, which was expected by all to withstand its invaders for at least a number weeks, fell in one day. This was due to the fact that one of the initial shots fired by French siege cannons struck the munitions depot in the centre of the town. A massive explosion ensued, causing immense human and material losses. The commander of the fortress did not take long to appreciate the gravity of the situation and decided upon unconditional surrender. This event, which took place at the beginning of his campaign, left Masséna euphoric – it seemed that luck was on his side.[392]

The speedy surrender of Almeida, which aroused great pride and delight among the French, sparked a similar amount of sheer terror among the ranks of the Portuguese. Naturally, Wellington was also unpleasantly surprised. After the fall of Almeida, Masséna proceeded without delay to march on Lisbon; this time, however, a more difficult advance was in store for him, as Arthur Wellesley quickly began to implement the second crucial element of his plan (after the construction of the Lines of Torres Vedras) to defend Portugal – a scorched earth policy with one goal in mind: to starve the French completely. The whole Portuguese civilian population was thus to flee to safety behind the Lines of Torres Vedras. On Wellington's orders, tens of thousands of terrified Portuguese travelled from all corners of the country, carrying only their most necessary and valuable possessions toward Lisbon to find refuge from the French behind Wellington's lines in the town and its closest surroundings. Food, carriages, and everything else that could have been of use to Masséna's men in their advance and could not be carried away was simply destroyed by the Portuguese at Wellington's orders, turning the majority of the kingdom into a wasteland.[393]

There was another thorn in Masséna's side during the course of his advance into Portuguese territory – the *"Ordenanza"*, which Wellington strongly supported. This term refers to traditional Portuguese common law, the roots of which reach back to the Middle Ages. Under Ordenanza, the sovereign could call the common population to arms in cases of direct endangerment. When Ordenanza was declared, each village in Portugal was forced to call up a certain number of men. These common soldiers operated to a certain degree like the partisans in Spain and basically led a wholly independent and parallel guerrilla war against the French in Portugal.* Thanks to the declaration of Ordenanza, the ranks of irregular Portuguese guerrilla troops who had fought hitherto against the French significantly increased. These soldiers are often even listed collectively under the name Ordenanza.

Masséna already began to have trouble in supplying his grand army during the Siege of Almeida, which was largely destroyed after the explosion. Thus, out of his 80,000 men, he was able to advance with "only" a force of 65,000 soldiers against Arthur Wellesley's "Leopards" (the French used this term for the British soldiers, as it referred to the three golden leopards in red on the English coat of arms).[394] André Masséna probably believed that this number, which was almost double the amount of British soldiers, would be more than enough to secure victory.

Nonetheless, the French were forced to move through the difficult mountainous terrain of the Portuguese province of Lower Beira, where some of the mountain peaks reached up to two thousand meters above sea level and the quality of the paths in the period of the Napoleonic Wars was poor to say the least. In addition, Masséna made the wholly incomprehensible decision to pass through one of the most difficult mountains trails in his advance on Lisbon. It is true that the French marshal possessed only grossly insufficient maps and he had possibly hoped that this less densely occupied area would not be so thoroughly stripped of foodstuffs and afflicted by the scorched earth policy.[395] Whatever Masséna's reason was for the decision, this time it was Arthur Wellesley who was euphoric, as the French were now losing all the extra time they had gained with their lightning-quick victory in Almeida. After Wellington learned of the direction of Masséna's advance, he immediately and delightedly remarked: 'There are certainly many bad roads in Portugal, but the enemy has taken decidedly the worst in the whole kingdom.'[396] In addition, the French were unable to find a sufficient amount of food, even in the surrounding areas of the "worst path", which was beginning to make

---

* Oman, *A History of the Peninsular War, vol. III*, pp. 181–182. Despite Wellington's repeated requests, Masséna did not want to acknowledge the status of Ordenanza fighters as regular soldiers and had them executed mercilessly. It should be added here that Ordenanza fighters in turn attacked the French throughout Portugal in ambush style attacks and killed them with extreme brutality similarly to the partisans in Spain. In addition, they did not wear uniforms and there was hardly any discipline among their ranks.

Masséna somewhat uneasy: 'All our marches are across desert, not a soul to be seen anywhere, everything abandoned... We cannot find a guide anywhere.'[397] wrote the French marshal of his campaign.

On the other hand, it should be noted that the scorched earth policy had not been carried out by the Portuguese as thoroughly as Wellington would have wished. The French remained in a tolerable condition, as they were able to find various provisions that the Portuguese, contrary to orders, had not destroyed but only hidden from sight. Thanks to this fact, the voices of the defeatists and "croakers" who declared the war to be lost continued to be heard among Wellington's men, although they remained a minority throughout. Before definitively retreating past the Lines of Torres Vedras, Arthur Wellesley decided to offer Masséna a battle, but only on the condition that it would take place in the location he chose himself. It is my assumption that the main reason Wellington decided to face the French was the desire to test the Portuguese Army in battle, as Napoleon, Masséna, and – frankly speaking – even the British officers did not consider it to be a true fighting force that could significantly influence the course of the war.

Despite this fact, Wellington trusted General Beresford, who was wholly satisfied with the Portuguese at the end of the summer of 1810, and gradually incorporated all twenty five thousand Portuguese soldiers into the British Army. In Wellington's divisions, Portuguese regiments were most commonly mixed with British ones so that the inexperienced Portuguese would be side by side with the seasoned British soldiers, something which seemed to be an eminently sensible solution. In making this decision, Wellington immediately gained an army of roughly fifty thousand men, which he deployed in a line on the peak of the almost 10-mile-long Busaco mountain ridge* that stretched from the north southwards between the convent building where Wellington set up his command, and the Mondego River; the main road to Lisbon ran near the convent, which was located at the northernmost end of the ridge. This steep ridge, reaching 549 meters above sea level at its peak, provided Wellington with an extremely strong position. Many British officers even refused to believe that Masséna would be so brave or foolhardy as to attack such a firmly held position.[398]

*   Spellings of the mountains also include "Bussaco" or "Serra do Buçaco", which is the original Portuguese term. The spelling "Busaco" used in this text is taken from academic Anglo-Saxon literature (Works by R. Muir, E. Longford and others).

The French marshal, however, was certainly no coward; moreover, he needed the battle. Before daybreak on 27th September 1810, he gave the order to attack. According to Masséna's plan, fourteen thousand men led by General Reynier began a direct attack on the centre of Wellington's line. This mass of attackers was divided into two massive columns under the command of Generals Heudelet and Merle. Their primary task was to defeat Wellington's troops at the centre of the ridge and then continue on over its peak north toward the Carmelite Convent of the Holy Cross at Busaco, where they would attack the left wing of the British-Portuguese line. Masséna's deputy commander Marshal Ney was then to support the French attack on the left wing with a whole other division that Ney was to lead into battle along the main road to Lisbon and thus surround the British on the left wing.

From the beginning, the French were unsuccessful in carrying out Masséna's plan, as Heudelet's line happened directly upon Picton's British-Portuguese 3rd division after a long and exhausting climb and were quickly and brutally repelled. In the meantime, Merle's units, which were deployed roughly one mile north, were doing considerably better, as Wellington's men were unable to effectively cover the whole ten-mile area. The first troops of Merle's light infantry successfully closed in on the unoccupied gap between the lines of the British-Portuguese Army. At that moment, however, the ferocious Irishmen of the 88th Regiment of Foot – better known as the Connaught Rangers – charged the French along with three additional British-Portuguese regiments. Despite the fact that they were met by eleven of Merle's regiments containing many seasoned veterans from Marengo and Austerlitz, who felt this was their chance to grant Masséna his victory, the commander of the Connaught Rangers, Colonel Wallace, did not waste time. He immediately ordered a bayonet attack on the French before they could even reach the summit of the hill.[399] Before the attack, Wallace turned to his men with the following words: 'When I bring you face to face with those French rascals, drive them down the hill – don't give the false touch, but push home to the muzzle!'[400] The Connaught Rangers, shouting "*Faugh a Ballagh! Faugh a Ballagh!* (Clear the way!)" at the top of their lungs in their native Gaelic charged the surprised Frenchmen who, although superior in number, realized the ferocity of the attack and began to flee after only a brief clash.[401] Arthur Wellesley, who rode past and witnessed the whole event, congratulated the commander of the Connaught Rangers on his success: 'Upon my honour, Wallace, I never witnessed more gallant charge than that just now made by your regiment.' [402] The French then made their third and final attempt to conquer Wellington's centre but were repelled again, this time by General Leith's division, which Wellington had left hidden on the opposite side of the ridge. Wellington then gave the following order to General Hill, whose division, which had hitherto held its position on the British right flank on the southern part of the ridge, also shifted to the centre of Wellington's line: 'If they attempt this point again, Hill, you will give them a volley and charge bayonets, but don't let your people follow them too far down the hill.'[403]

In the meantime, Marshal Ney, who was evidently reacting to the cloud of smoke at the centre of the ridge, set out along the main road, whereupon his lines clashed with General Craufurd's Light Division on the left wing of Wellington's position near the convent. The Light Division (as its name implies) was primarily made up of light infantry regiments that included the legendary riflemen of the 95th Regiment in green coats, who inflicted notable casualties on Ney's men throughout their climb thanks to the long striking distance of their weapons. The moment Ney's shaken regiments finally approached the peak of the ridge, they met a fate similar to that of Merle's troops, as Craufurd ordered the majority of his division to attack immediately with bayonets: 'Now!... Revenge the death of Sir John Moore! Charge! Charge! Huzza!'[404] Craufurd gave the order in a booming voice. After a heated head-to-head clash with the Light Division, Ney's men wavered, finally retreating after suffering heavy losses. Together with Craufurd's Light Division, the 19th Infantry Regiment of Cascais especially distinguished itself in the merciless battle against Ney's soldiers that took place in the close surroundings of the Busaco convent. In addition to its own the regimental colours, this regiment carried another noteworthy item into battle at Busaco: their traditional protector, Saint Anthony of Padua, in the form of a statue. Saint Anthony lived as a Franciscan monk at the turn of the 12th and 13th century and devoted a significant portion of his life to preaching in Italy. He was, however, originally Portuguese and hailed from Lisbon. The Cascais Regiment, which had possessed the sculpture as a sort of "battle talisman" for over one hundred years, therefore believed that its men would be protected from defeat and thus came to name the sculpture

Saint Anthony the Warrior (St. Antonio Milítar). At a certain point in the battle, the 19th Regiment was stripped of its sculpture, which was then held "captive" by the French. The enraged soldiers of the Cascais Regiment then charged forth alongside the British with renewed intensity against the French, attempting to wrestle back their sculpture of Saint Anthony at any cost. In the end, this quest proved successful.[405]

In light of the overwhelming losses that Ney suffered in warding off the enemy, the French did not have the determination to attack Wellington's positions again. The French Colonel Marcelin Marbot described the situation at the end of the battle: 'Wellington was reviewing his troops who were saluting him with their hurrahs, while the French at the foot of the mountain were in gloomy silence...'[406] The French left nearly 4,500 fallen men on the Busaco Ridge, whereas Wellington lost only 1,252. One remarkable fact that is worthy of note symbolizes the role that the Portuguese units played in Wellesley's victory – of the number of the fallen listed above, both the Portuguese and British suffered the exact same number of losses, i.e. 626 apiece.[407]

Wellington's actions in the Battle of Busaco were very concisely summarized by an officer of the King's German Legion (from the Hanover units that served under Wellington during the Peninsular War), Lieutenant August Schaumann in his memoirs:

As usual ... Lord Wellington showed extraordinary discretion, calm, forethought, and self-composure. He gave orders in a resonant, firm voice. They were short and clear. There is not a single whit in him of that glaring pompousness that the commander of an army often parades, surrounded by his shining gold-draped staff. He wears neither an overly extravagant hat nor gold-embroidered galloons; no decorations or distinctions – he wears a simple, two-horned hat, a white neckcloth, grey jacket, and a light sabre that swings at his side.[408]

In the end, the Portuguese units held their ground at Busaco stupendously, as Schaumann also points out in his memoirs:

The Portuguese fought with great courage, which confirmed the excellent work of Marshal Beresford, who had trained them. In their performance, they also reciprocated Lord Wellington's masterful military strategy, as it

BATTLE OF BUSACO
27ᵗʰ September 1810

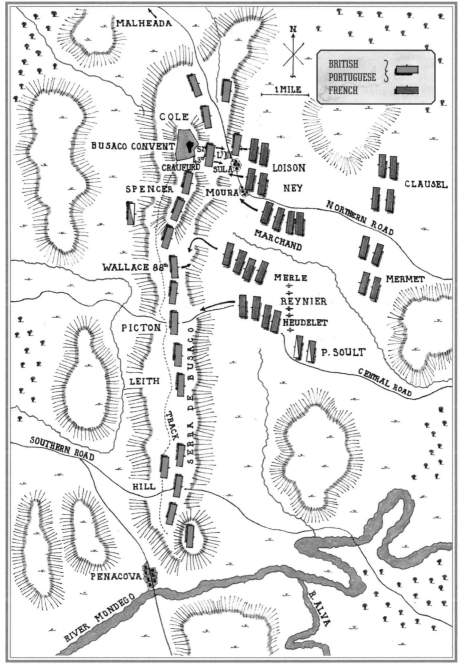

— *Map by John Fawkes* —

was he who ordered their regiments to be mixed with the British and brought them to an advantageous position from which they could demonstrate their determination and get a taste for combat in a large battle. They acted just as gallantly as the British units and fought so staunchly that the French thought they must have been British soldiers in Portuguese uniform.[409]

Arthur Wellesley himself also mentioned the performance of the Portuguese units after the battle in a personal message to War Secretary Lord Liverpool:

It [the Battle of Busaco] has brought the Portuguese levies into action with the enemy for the first time... They have proved that the trouble which has been taken with them has not been thrown away, and that they are worthy of contending in the same ranks with British troops.[410]

From Wellington's perspective, the letter was most likely intended as an effort to silence at least partially the Whigs and all the other "croakers" who had made derogatory remarks about the martial abilities of the Portuguese troops. After his experience with the response of the British public to the victorious Battle of Talavera, Wellington had insight and was well aware of the fact that he would not be able to completely silence the critics of the campaign on the Iberian Peninsula, as he wrote in a letter to his brother William: 'The croakers about useless battles will attack me again on that of Busaco, notwithstanding that our loss was really trifling.'[411]

Despite his critics at home, Wellington was praised by at least one enemy abroad for his gallantry after the recent battle: After the Battle of Busaco, French Colonel Marcelin Marbot commended Wellington's noble behaviour towards French General Simon, whom Wellington's soldiers found seriously wounded on the ridge after the battle:

Wellington treated him [General Simon] with much kindness, and as soon as he was fit to be moved, sent him as a prisoner of war to England. Later on he was allowed to return to France, but his horrible wound did not permit him to serve again.[412]

Nonetheless, the defeat at Busaco was far from meaning that Masséna's army had been destroyed. He still possessed 60,000 combat-ready

Frenchmen determined to secure a definitive victory for Napoleon and avenge their fallen comrades at Busaco. The second day after the battle, Masséna withdrew, as he had decided to circumvent Wellington's strong defensive position by an outflanking manoeuvre from the north, continuing his advance on Lisbon and crushing the British there under more favourable conditions. The unsuspecting French, however, were in for an unpleasant surprise in the form of the Lines of Torres Vedras.

Wellington withdrew behind the lines on 8th October 1810, coincidentally on the same day that torrential autumn rains began to fall on Portugal. At the time, Masséna began to get wind of the first vague rumours that Lord Wellington had taken up a defensive position behind "the lines". This news, however, did not seem out of the ordinary to either Masséna or the other French generals at the time, as the term "lines" had been used in military jargon for centuries in the sense of deploying an army in a linear formation, much like Wellington's men had done previously on the Busaco Ridge. It could also be a term for a situation in which one or more armies controlled a certain space, for instance holding a line on a river. This at least provides a partial explanation of why a structure of such mass proportions managed to elude the French. Just as Wellington had planned and hoped, the French, although it may seem wholly unbelievable, had no idea of the construction of the lines for a whole year and were to learn of them at the very last moment. Masséna could not have imagined in his wildest dreams that he would be up against such a spectacular series of fortifications.

Marshal Masséna first laid eyes upon the Lines of Torres Vedras on 14th October 1810 not far from the town of Sobral, near which one of the largest of all the redoubts was located – the Alqueidão fortress*. The fortress was equipped with 24 cannons and a regiment of 1,600 men. Masséna naturally went into a furious rage; in various forms of vituperation, he cursed all collaborators from the ranks of the Portuguese and Spanish one by one – the so-called *"afrancesados"* that had marched along

---

*   Today Alqueidão is clearly the most preserved fortress of the whole Lines of Torres Vedras and is surely worth a visit. In addition, an observation point was built here in 2010, offering unique views of the positions from which Masséna's troops approached. The second fortress that no visitor on the trail of the Lines of Torres Vedras should miss is Fort St. Vincent, located directly in the town of Torres Vedras opposite the medieval castle there, which was used to guard the surrounding valley. Fort St. Vincent was reconstructed during Salazar's regime and restored nearly to its original state.

with his army – and primarily the officers of his own Intelligence Service, none of whom had been capable of informing him of the fortifications in time.[413] The personnel deployed in the fortresses and trenches that made up the Lines of Torres Vedras were largely made up of Portuguese civilians from the ranks of the citizen soldiery, who were accompanied by 9,000 Spaniards led by General Romana. These were troops who had been evacuated from the Island of Funnen due to the ultimate bravery of Father Robertson. Only 2,500 men from the ranks of the British soldiers were moved into the fortresses. Nearly the whole British-Portuguese field army thus remained behind the lines at Wellington's full disposal, ready to attack the French in the event that they should overcome the Lines of Torres Vedras at any given point.[414] From the back of his horse, Marshal Masséna subjected the lines to detailed analysis. He then sent Marshal Ney, his second-in-command, the following evaluation of the situation:

> The enemy is dug in up to the teeth. He has three lines of works that cover Lisbon. If we seized the front line of redoubts, he would throw himself into the second line… I have already visited the line three times to the right and left and I see great works bristling with canons… I do not believe this is the moment to attack the enemy. A check would destroy all our hopes and would overthrow the state of things, so we will indulge in temporising.[415]

Masséna, however, could not wait forever, as the scorched earth policy – although not carried out perfectly – had begun to take its toll on the French. The autumn rains, ever-present mud and damp, together with the drop in night-time temperatures and insufficient supplies, had become Masséna's greatest enemies for the time being. The thought of retreating across all of Portugal in such dismal conditions with the British-Portuguese army at their heels represented an alternative for the French that was no less grim than remaining in their camp. With undisguised delight, Wellington wrote home to his brother William about Masséna's position:

> My opinion is that the French are in a scrape… I have no idea what French will, or rather what they can do. I think it is certain that they can do us no mischief, and they will lose the greatest part of their army if they attack us. They will starve if they stay much longer, and they will experience great difficulty in their retreat.[416]

Despite this fact, Masséna remained camped in front of the Lines of Torres Vedras for more than a month. The situation became more and more difficult by the day and, in mid-November, he ordered the inevitable retreat. However, when a British officer reported to Wellington that the French Army had gone, the Commander-in Chief, who was busy shaving, didn't seem at all surprised, as he simply answered: 'Ay, I thought they meant to be off.'[417]Masséna's retreat from the Lines of Torres Vedras took place in two stages – at first Masséna pulled back to Santarém, staying there until March 1811 until he was again forced by starvation to continue in his retreat back to Spain. The French reached the Spanish border by the beginning of April 1811 after an arduous and exhausting march, during which almost 25,000 men were lost due to hunger, illness, and numerous ambushes by Ordenanza and guerrilla troops.[418]

Once the plan of the Lines of Torres Vedras was declassified, Wellington became a true hero in Britain. For the moment, even the croakers, who had criticized the engagement of British units on the Iberian Peninsula for so long, seemed to have been silenced. Wellington's overwhelming success was difficult for them to stomach, but in most cases they were able to acknowledge that they had been wrong and praised Wellington. Even Charles Grey, one of the leading figures of the Whigs, requested an opportunity to speak in the House of Commons. He stood up and said these complimentary words about Wellington:

> By the most patient perseverance under unfavourable circumstances, and at the moment of action by the most skilful combination of force and the most determined courage, a great success has been achieved.[419]

Arthur Wellesley, praised on all sides, naturally radiated good spirits as he enjoyed his deserved ovations after months of criticism and constant tension. It seemed that France and its Emperor could ultimately be defeated. In order for victory to be conceivable, however, it would be necessary to drive the French out of Spain, a fact that Wellington was of course well aware of.

Ever since I became interested in Wellington's military career, the Lines of Torres Vedras have fascinated me. Therefore, naturally, I took a journey to Portugal to see this fascinating construction project with my own eyes, and I must say I was not disappointed. Wellington's remarkable use of the topography, the remains of military roads and fortifications – mainly the preserved Fort of Alqueidão – truly left a lasting impression on me. In the words of military engineer Captain Mulcaster, I would not have wished to be among the 'unlucky dogs' who were ordered to attack the Lines of Torres Vedras. In my opinion, this massive system of fortifications and its fearsome and almost unsettlingly preconceived system of trenches and bunkers, which was widely put to use during World War I, is the most remarkable enterprise of Wellington's impressive military career. It is even more remarkable in light of the fact that Wellesley was able to keep the whole structure a secret from the French until the final moment and by doing so scored a definitive victory over Masséna, forcing him to retreat. This allowed Lord Wellington to come out of what at first glance looked like a losing position and take the offensive.

Although this was one of the defining moments of the Peninsular and Napoleonic Wars, scholars have paid insufficient attention to the construction and role of the Lines of Torres Vedras. Military historian Mark S. Thompson pointed to this fact relatively recently in his work *Wellington's Engineers: Military Engineering in the Peninsular War 1808–1814* when he wrote the following:

> Most people interested in the Peninsular War will have heard of the Lines of Torres Vedras, but probably not much more. Even modern works on the Peninsular War have treated it very lightly... It is understandable that there is less interest in this part of the war as it does not involve any battles and the Lines were never assaulted. However, the Lines of Torres Vedras were every bit as important to Wellington as his victories on the field of battle.[420]

Where did Wellington find the inspiration for a construction as massive as the Lines, which were historically unprecedented at the time, and how thoroughly in advance had he planned it all? In the following pages, I attempt to provide answers to these questions.

From the very beginning of his military career, Arthur Wellesley strongly proved himself as a commander who put an enormous emphasis on military theory and the most thorough study of available information on the country in which his upcoming campaign was to take place. As was described above, this trait was best documented in Wellington's engagement in British India thanks to preserved accounts of purchases made for his

Indian library and the many testimonies of his contemporaries. If we are to recall the publications that Wellesley acquired in this period, he also studied previous military conflicts that had taken place in India, the geography of the Indian subcontinent, and local languages and dialects. Another account of purchases from the period before his departure to India proves that his library at the time also included a publication on the colonies in the British West Indies entitled *History Civil and Ecclesiastical, of the British Colonies in the West Indies*. He evidently purchased the book when his regiment was meant to depart to that part of the world after receiving initial orders.[421]

If we take these facts into consideration, it seems most probable that Arthur Wellesley prepared for his campaign on the Iberian Peninsula just as thoroughly as he prepared himself for his stay in India and the military campaign there. He was a strictly methodical and diligent individual; a clear plan of advancement with a detailed and premeditated strategy became a firm trait of his overall character. In addition, reading books on various topics remained one of Wellington's favourite pastimes and, especially in later years, took up a considerable amount of his free time. For historians, however, analysing Wellesley's preparations for the Peninsular War is somewhat more difficult. Written sources in this respect are much sparser and no accounts of book purchases have survived or have been mapped as was the case with his campaign in India.

In addition, before the first Portuguese campaign, which ended with a brilliant victory at Vimeiro (21st August 1808) and was followed by the infamous Convention of Cintra (signed on 30th August 1808), Wellesley simply did not have a sufficient amount of time for detailed theoretical preparation. The goal of his mission was changed at the last moment when Portugal replaced Venezuela as the new destination of Wellesley's expedition. For comparison, before sailing to India, Wellesley had several months to accumulate and study the necessary materials; before the Portuguese campaign he had only three weeks, which he evidently spent controlling and preparing his army and hastily studying Portuguese geography.

Nonetheless, it is my assertion that in respect to the second campaign to Portugal, Wellesley prepared just as thoroughly as he had before departing to India. He could have begun to entertain the idea of his possible return to the Portuguese Front by November 1808, i.e. just after the court session held on the signing of the Convention of Cintra ended. Arthur Wellesley most likely saw a return to the Portuguese theatre as an opportunity to clear his name definitively, which did in fact take place after his subsequent victories. First and foremost, I would like to introduce here a hypothesis that points to the fact that the work entitled *Mémoire de la Campagne de Portugal de 1762* served as a crucial document for Wellington's plans for the defence of Portugal, perhaps also for the construction of the Lines of Torres Vedras, and also for the completion of his famous *Memorandum on the defence of Portugal*. The author of the fairly brief *Mémoire de la Campagne de Portugal de 1762* (the whole manuscript is roughly 67 pages long) was William, Count of Schaumburg-Lippe, or simply Count La Lippe, (1724–1777), who was commander of the British-Portuguese Army in the period of the Seven Years' War, during which time he defended Portugal against the Spanish-French Army in 1762. Schaumburg-Lippe's memoirs are devoted to the defence of Portugal during this campaign and were evidently first published in 1770.* Count La Lippe wrote his work in French, which at the time had replaced Latin as the language of scholars and diplomats, and French – as was mentioned above – was the foreign language that Arthur Wellesley knew best of all, and thus reading in this language did not pose a significant barrier to him.

When I first became acquainted via academic literature dealing with the Seven Years' War with Count La Lippe's defence of Portugal, which he was tasked with by the British government in 1762, I was immediately drawn to the uncanny similarity between La Lippe's military campaign and that of Wellington's, which had taken place in Portugal merely fifty years later. This remarkable conjuncture between both campaigns led me to a more detailed analysis of Schaumburg-Lippe's military career and the idea that Wellington may well have used Count La Lippe's still relatively fresh experiences in planning his own defence of Portugal. Therefore, I would like to return to the period of the Seven Years' War (1756–1763) several decades earlier before continuing on in the description of Arthur Wellesley's fate and the circumstances under which Wellington may have first come in contact with La Lippe's memoirs. During the Seven Years' War, William of Schaumburg-Lippe was faced with the same task as Arthur Wellesley in 1809 – to defend Portugal with the British expeditionary army against a considerably larger army. Let us now acquaint ourselves at least in brief with the Count of Schaumburg-Lippe and his campaign in Portugal.

---

* The original print with this date is located in the British Library, London.

Count William was born in London in 1724, the eldest son of Adolf Wolfgang, Count of Schaumburg-Lippe, and Margareta, Countess of Oyhuasen, the illegitimate daughter of British King George I. As George's grandson, albeit an illegitimate one, William held close ties with the British royal court. In addition, the county of Schaumburg-Lippe stretched along a border with Hanover, the electorate of which was coincidentally also the British Monarch and William's grandfather George I.* William took the throne of the county of Schaumburg-Lippe after the death of his father in 1748. He gained his first military experience in the War of the Austrian Succession, during which he took part in the famous Battle of Dettingen in 1743, fighting against the French on the side of the British-Austrian Pragmatic Army** defending the interests of Maria Theresa and her claim to take the throne of the Habsburg Monarchy. During the Seven Years' War, he took part in battles again on the side of the British, when both his kinship ties and the significant financial debt his small county had incurred with Hanover brought him into a military alliance with Britain and Prussia.[422] Over the course of the Seven Years' War, Count William La Lippe first served on the territory of the Holy Roman Empire in the British-Hanover Army under the command of Duke Ferdinand of Brunswick. Among these troops, he took part again in clashes against the French. He first distinguished himself as an artillery commander in 1759 in the Battle of Minden in which Ferdinand of Brunswick's troops defeated French troops under the command of Marshal Contades.[423] During the following two offensives led by Ferdinand of Brunswick that took place in 1760 and 1761, William was now tasked as an experienced artillery general with besieging the strategically important fortresses of Wessel and Kassel. Due to a lack of men and cannons, he was not able to capture these fortresses, but he did gain valuable experience in building artillery batteries.

In the meantime, the French managed to sign a treaty of alliance with the hitherto neutral Spanish King Charles III. Thanks to this, Britain found

---

* With Napoleon's declaration of the Confederation of the Rhine, the county of Schaumburg-Lippe was abolished in 1806.

** The Allied Army was known as the Pragmatic Army because it supported the so-called Pragmatic Sanction of 1713, based upon which Habsburg Emperor Charles VI named his eldest daughter Maria Theresa as his heir and subsequently sovereign of the Habsburg Empire despite the fact that a woman was not allowed to ascend the throne in the time of pragmatic sanctions. After the death of Emperor Charles, however, many states refused to acknowledge the pragmatic sanction, resulting in the *War of the Austrian Succession* (1740–1748).

itself in January 1762 at war with Spain, as it was now a new ally of France. The so-called *"Pacte de Famille"* (a newly established alliance between France and Spain between the Kings of Bourbon, specifically Charles III in Spain and Louis XV in France) attempted to bring Portugal to its side against Britain. In addition, the wife of the King of Portugal Joseph I was a Spanish princess who also came from the House of Bourbon; Portugal, however, did not hesitate to refuse this offer to create an anti-British alliance with France and Spain, as it had already signed a treaty of alliance and trade with Britain. One of the conditions that France and Spain imposed on Portugal was its immediate declaration of war on Britain.

As a reaction to Portugal's refusal to join the *"Pacte de Famille"*, the Franco-Spanish Army of 22,000 men under the command of the Marquis of Sarria crossed the Portuguese border at the end of April 1762 in an attempt to overpower the stubborn Portuguese. In turn, Portugal declared war simultaneously on France and Spain on 5th May. However, a massive and unexpected wave of resistance arose on the part of the common population against Sarria's troops. The common people were called to arms by Joseph I under the law of Ordenanza just as in 1810 during Marshal Masséna's invasion described above.

When, after several days, the vanguard of Sarria's men of a force of roughly 5,000 soldiers closed in on the harbour city of Oporto, they were forced into a shameful retreat by Portuguese Ordenanza units made up mostly of peasants, the ranks of which even included women armed with muskets. The surprisingly strong resistance of the people and the remarkable bravery of the country's subjects was soon accompanied with supply problems that managed to force Sarria to retreat back to Spain at the beginning of May without engaging in one single larger-scale battle with the Portuguese. It seemed wholly clear, however, that the *"Pacte de Famille"* troops would return, this time in much larger numbers.[424]

Meanwhile, a British expedition of roughly 7,000 men under the command of then seventy-year-old Baron Tyrawley sailed in to help Portugal, just as Arthur Wellesley would do less than fifty years later. After arriving by ship, the elderly baron suffered a fright when he laid his eyes upon the miserable state of the Portuguese Army. Not only were the Portuguese soldiers not receiving munitions and other necessary equipment (for instance only a third of the soldiers had uniforms), the fact that the Portuguese were mostly incapable of carrying out even the most basic military manoeuvres was even worse. Furthermore, the majority of Portuguese border fortresses were in a dilapidated condition. Tyrawley was so disconcerted by the situation of the Portuguese Army that he resigned from the position of Commander-in-Chief of the Anglo-Portuguese forces shortly after his arrival to the country. In his place and partially thanks to his numerous contacts in the British court, the aforementioned Count William of Schaumburg-Lippe, veteran of Dettingen and Minden, was called upon without delay.[425]

Shortly after arrival, Joseph I named William Field Marshal of the Portuguese Army in the hopes that he would defend the country in such a dire situation. The Portuguese troops that Count La Lippe was about to take over were roughly 40,000 men strong on paper; in reality, however, he received only 9,000 combat-ready Portuguese. Despite these inadequacies, he wasted no time and almost immediately began to train the Portuguese units. From the start, he battled with illiteracy among his officers, poor discipline, and frequent desertion. In order to improve the morale of the Portuguese officers, he ordered an increase in their food rations and personally began to see to the payment of their regular wages, which until then were often several months in arrears. His (in the best sense of the term) upstanding German military drill and inexhaustible energy seemed decidedly odd to the Portuguese and their tranquil southern temperament. On the other hand, the integrity and enthusiasm of the new commander together with intense military training gave them a new sense of purpose and motivation. The state of the Portuguese Army thus slowly began to improve.[426] The primary motivational element during this intense training, which fostered the willingness of the Portuguese to cooperate in full with Count William La Lippe, was embodied in the French-Spanish "enemy at the gates". Wellington also ran into similar problems, as the Portuguese Army had seen a strong decline since Count Schaumburg-Lippe's time. Despite this fact, Count William's previous success in training the Portuguese may have been the stimulus for Wellington to order General Beresford to begin to quickly reform the Portuguese Army and integrate them into the ranks of the British troops just as William La Lippe had done.

A change in commander-in-chief had not only taken place on the Anglo-Portuguese side, but in the Franco-Spanish camp as well. The Marquis of Sarria, who was withdrawn due to his shortcomings, was replaced by a somewhat more experienced general – the Spanish grand don

WELLINGTON

Pedro Pablo Abarca de Bolea, Count of Aranda, whose grandiose lineage stretched far back to medieval Aragonese nobility. In addition to changing generals, the restructured Franco-Spanish Army also strongly increased in number and now possessed an army of 42,000 men. In August of 1762, the army crossed the Portuguese border for a second time and marched on Lisbon under Aranda's command. William La Lippe's hastily organized British-Portuguese Army of roughly 15,000 men, which was up against an army almost three times that number, set out to stop them. Naturally, few had any great hopes for his success in defending Portugal. After weighing up his realistic military options, he decided upon a purely defensive tactic in the coming war. The tactic was based primarily on the principle of "partisan war" (guerre de chicane), as he did not wish to wage a large-scale field battle against the enemy due to their numerical superiority.[427] He was also surely well aware of the success and ferocity of the Portuguese peasants in defending Oporto and thus planned to fully integrate this "third situation" into his plans. He focused primarily on evasive manoeuvres, small-scale skirmishes, and ambush attacks, which were ideal for use in the natural conditions of Portugal. Count La Lippe strove to make the most of every ford, ridge, and mountain pass. He often transformed these natural barriers into small outlying positions. He also had many dilapidated fortresses that dated back to medieval times renovated and manned with at least small units. These small fortresses served as bases for this partisan-style war. La Lippe carried out one of the most successful examples of such an attack at the end of August 1762 when his men ventured all the way into Spanish territory. In the town of Valencia de Alcantara, they caught Aranda's non-combatant forces wholly by surprise and took as many as two hundred Spanish soldiers and one general hostage.[428]

The Count of Aranda was forced to advance toward Lisbon across the difficult terrain of Lower Beira just as Marshal Masséna would do decades later. At this moment, William of Schaumburg-Lippe ordered a scorched earth policy to be carried out, the same method Wellington would choose as described above. The Count of Schaumburg-Lippe, who began to use a scorched earth policy against the enemy in 1762, wrote the following in his memoirs:

> Lower Beira could not offer the enemy any food, wagons, or villagers willing to help during the campaign through the country. The Count of Santiago

[one of the Portuguese commanding officers] received the following orders: see to it that everything disappear from the province that could be eaten or helpful to the enemy in their march.[429]

For this reason, the starving Franco-Spanish Army was exceptionally cruel toward the local population in efforts to force them to provide at least some supplies. There was, however, simply no food left in the province.[430] The Portuguese people's resistance, which sought retribution, also began to increase its operations. During the night, Aranda's men suddenly began to disappear and were often found hanged on the trees lining the muddy paths. The advance through the mountainous areas of Portugal gradually became a nightmare for Aranda's units. In addition, torrential rains came at the end of October and beginning of November, transforming the already poor paths into muddy swamp (let us note here that Wellington also planned his retreat behind the Lines of Torres Vedras in the month of October). Growing desertion, loss of life due to illness, strengthening partisan attacks, and the occasional ambush by soldiers of La Lippe's army accompanied by the absolute lack of food forced the Count of Aranda to order a dishonourable retreat back to Spain. The Count of Schaumburg-Lippe described the situation of the Franco-Spanish Army in the following words:

> From all of this, anyone can conjure an image of the enemy's humiliation. As they were forced into inactivity, they were decimated by the lack of food, desertion, and illnesses. Their horses died for lack of fodder and suffered injuries caused by the appalling condition of the roads. The matter was as such – the enemy quickly realized that he is far from conquering Portugal and his further attempts would lead to the absolute destruction of his army.[431]

It is thus possible to assert that these events, as described by Count of Schaumburg-Lippe in his memoir, may have partially inspired Arthur Wellesley to use a scorched earth policy, as Masséna's fate did not differ greatly from the result of Aranda's campaign.

La Lippe's victory culminated in the fact that the former command of Aranda's army fell into hands of his men in the town of Castelo Branco, where troops captured several thousand sick and injured Frenchmen and Spaniards. Aranda had left these men behind in the hopes that the better-supplied enemy would manage to take better care of them. The scathing losses of the Franco-Spanish Army suffered during the invasion of Portugal in 1762 are cited to be roughly 20,000–25,000 men (if we look back to Masséna's losses, we can yet again observe a similarity), with most of Aranda's men dying of illness and malnutrition.[432] In comparison, Count William La Lippe's losses were estimated to be merely 1,200 men, of which the total of the fallen British amounted to only 828 soldiers.[433] The difference between casualties between the warring sides is thus bewildering – in my opinion, this may have also intrigued Wellington, who, due to his position, could not afford to lose a great number of men.

Subsequently, at Aranda's request an armistice was signed on 24th November 1762 in Fontainebleau between Britain and Portugal on one side and France and Spain on the other, finally putting a definitive end to the conflict on the Pyrenean Front of the Seven Years' War in a victory for William La Lippe. Despite expectations, the Count of Schaumburg-Lippe was thus truly successful in defending Portugal through his non-traditional partisan concept of warfare, skilful use of geographical conditions, and scorched earth policy. In light of the victory of La Lippe's army over an enemy roughly triple the size, this remarkable achievement is often dubbed the "Fantastic War" in contemporary academic literature. Thanks to his triumphant victory and preservation of Portugal, Count William received 80,000 gold moidares as reward from King Joseph I of Portugal along with eight miniature gold and silver field cannons. In addition, he was asked in the name of the King, who was highly satisfied with him, to stay on for a time in Portugal and continue in the already successfully initiated reforms of the Portuguese Army.

William of Schaumburg-Lippe agreed and continued to train the victory-emboldened Portuguese. Together with his commander, a considerable number of British officers also remained in Portugal, seeing the offer as a suitable opportunity to improve their portfolios and thus glad to help La Lippe's in his efforts. The Count of Schaumburg-Lippe also received a reward from the British sovereign, who awarded him with the lifelong title of Marshal of the British Army, which was also a remarkable distinction. When William returned to the county of Schaumburg-Lippe in 1764, adorned with the laurels of a glorious commander, his renown had spread all over Europe thanks to his remarkable victory in Portugal.[434]

Count William continued to devote himself primarily to literary activity focused on military theory and the administration of his county, where he founded one of the first military academies on the territory of the Holy Roman Empire (roughly in today's Germany). Soon after its foundation, his academy gained substantial popularity, as the count himself taught there in person. William of Schaumburg-Lippe became an enlightened figure in the proper sense of the term and his ideas were in many ways revolutionary. He promoted the idea that the cause of the majority of wars was recklessness and greed and waging war was intrinsically immoral. According to William, the only justifiable war was a defensive one. He believed that if defensive technologies could be improved in warfare (primarily fortifications and artillery), the enemy would be put at such a disadvantage that even smaller states would be capable of effectively defending themselves against insatiable superpowers. In turn, this would ultimately result in general stability and peace (in my opinion, La Lippe's reputation in the field of waging defensive warfare could have been an additional reason for Wellington to pay special attention to William's memoirs in planning his own defence of Portugal). Count William of Schaumburg-Lippe died in 1777,[435] a time when Arthur Wellesley – who was to "walk in William's footsteps" and with a great degree of likelihood study his military memoirs – was a boy of eight.

The fact that Arthur Wellesley was in possession of Schaumburg Lippe's memoirs over the course of the Peninsular War is briefly mentioned by historian Phillip Guadalla in his biography of Wellington published in the 1930s. In his publication, Guadalla refers to a dispatch containing a list of literature that was sent to Wellington over the course of 1810. This preserved dispatch note proves that the *Memoirs of William of Schaumburg-Lippe* were delivered to Arthur Wellesley on 5th April 1810.[436] Nonetheless, it is my personal assumption that Wellesley may have already studied La Lippe's memoirs in 1809 during his preparations to return to the Iberian Peninsula and relied on them to a considerable degree in writing his famous *Memorandum for the Defence of Portugal*. La Lippe's memoirs may thus have "travelled" to Wellington over the course of the Peninsular War as an already verified and useful source of information to be reviewed from time to time. Let us now take a look at Wellesley's *Memorandum for the Defence of Portugal* in greater detail.

In this memorandum, which was crucial in terms of his military career and led him to be charged with the chief command over British forces in Portugal, Arthur Wellesley stated: 'I have always been of opinion that Portugal might be defended, whatever might be the result of the contest in Spain...'[437] He continues in the memorandum to write that, in his opinion, it would be sufficient in the future to deploy a British army of 20,000 men in Portugal while taking into consideration that it would surely take some time before the combat capability of the regular Portuguese Army was renewed. Therefore, Wellesley continues on in the memorandum with the statement that it seems essential in the meantime to deploy at least 30,000 British troops in Portugal: 'The British force employed in Portugal should, in this view of the question, not be less than 30 000 men, of which number 4000 or 5000 should be cavalry.'[438] In terms of the enemy's numbers that would be needed to conquer Portugal, he goes on to claim: 'My opinion was, that even if Spain should have been conquered, the French would not have been able to overrun Portugal with a smaller force than 100 000 men.'[439] Arthur Wellesley is *de facto* claiming that the British would certainly be capable of withstanding roughly three times the number of enemy troops in Portugal.

If we recall William's campaign, the Count of Schaumburg-Lippe stood with an army of 15,000 men against 42,000 hostile soldiers, meaning he was forced to face an enemy roughly three times greater than his own in number. This striking similarity in the proportions of these numbers (among other facts) during the Count of Schaumburg-Lippe's campaign with those of Wellington's campaign may, in my opinion, be proof of the fact that La Lippe's memoirs served as an important basis for his memorandum. Proof of the fact that some individuals in British society in the times of the Napoleonic Wars were well aware of the link between the Count of Schaumburg-Lippe's campaign during the Seven Years' War and Wellington's campaign in 1810 and the fact that Wellington may have read Count La Lippe's memoirs earlier than 5th April 1810 can be found in two letters that are described below.

The author of the first letter, Lord Francis Rawdon, Earl of Moira (1754–1826), who happened to be Arthur Wellesley's commander in the years of his first military campaign in Flanders (1794–5), wrote the following lines in a letter sent on 16th February 1810 (i.e. a month and a half before the date on the dispatch confirming that Schaumburg-Lippe's memoirs cited by Guedalla had been delivered to Wellington) addressed to Colonel John McMahon:

Ld. Wellington is acting upon the plans of Comte la Lippe [William, Count of Schaumburg-Lippe]... Demonstration will be made along the Douro. Ld. Wellington's attention will be drawn to prevent the passage of the enemy there.[440]

These "plans" of the Count of Lippe may have pointed to William's memoirs. The author of the second contemporaneous letter, which puts Wellington's campaign into the context of William of Schaumburg-Lippe's actions, was Lord Hugh Percy, 2nd Duke of Northumberland (1742–1817). In a letter dated 5th March 1810 (i.e. exactly a month before proof that La Lippe's memoirs were delivered), also addressed to John McMahon, he wrote the following:

I find that Ld. Wellington has totally disregarded the plan which the Count La Lippe gave in and left for the defence of Portugal, and has struck out an entire new plan of his own. Those parts which La Lippe looked upon as the tenderest parts of the frontiers, and to be more particularly attendet to, his Lordship [Wellington] has left totally open, without so much as a single British soldier... The old Roman adage of Finis Coronat opus [the end crowns the work], is a very true one. Count La Lippe saved Portugal and frustrated all the joint attempts of the French and Spanish armies that attacked him... I wish with all my heart Lord Wellington may show himself as good General and save Portugal this second time.[441]

The Duke of Northumberland is pointing to the fact that Wellington had deviated from the Count of Lippe's plan, which on the other hand is perhaps proof of the fact that Wellington had until then drawn inspiration from it and the connection between both campaigns to a certain degree resonated with some among British military and political circles. Wellington was naturally not copying Count William La Lippe's plan to the letter, as the period and military tactics had moved on considerably over the course of 50 years; nonetheless, it is my opinion that Wellington drew upon much of La Lippe's strategy as he – exactly like William of Schaumburg-Lippe – transformed Portugal into an impregnable fortress.

In terms of this sudden "disregard" for Lippe's plan and "striking out" one of his own, Wellington truly did leave the Portuguese fortresses abandoned and in ill repair, as his construction and military engineers had begun to build the massive series of wholly new fortresses to create the defensives Lines of Torres Vedras in November 1809. This was where Wellington's genius and innovation showed. Northumberland, however, could not have known this, as Arthur Wellesley, as was mentioned several times before, kept this massive structure a total secret. As regards William's second primary weapon used in the defence of Portugal, i.e. scorched earth policy, Wellington proceeded in a wholly identical manner and, as we know now, 'saved Portugal this second time' in line with Northumeberland's wish. If we are to return only to the indisputable facts in order to provide a general summary while fully taking into consideration the narrative value of the letters mentioned above by Lords Moira and Northumberland dated 16th February and 5th March, 1810, we should hold firm to the fact that there is proof that Schaumburg-Lippe's memoirs were delivered into Wellington's hands on 5th April 1810, i.e. roughly six months after he issued the order to build the Lines of Torres Vedras. Even this fact, however, does not absolutely guarantee that Wellington truly read the memoirs. I am, however, personally convinced to a considerable degree that, thanks to so many striking similarities between the two campaigns, Wellington's personal traits, and the aforementioned written evidence (i.e. letters by Rawdon and Northumberland), Wellington studied William of La Lippe's memoirs with the greatest probability in the winter of 1808, just after proceedings were completed on the justification of the Convention of Cintra, or at least before the construction of the defensive Lines of Torres Vedras (October 1809). Count La Lippe's memoirs served as a seminal work that Wellington employed in his plans to defend Portugal and may have inspired him to build the fortification system of Torres Vedras.

The next strong impulse that in my opinion may have led Wellington to the idea of building the Lines of Torres Vedras and which therefore should not be overlooked may have been the network of Portuguese mills built centuries before in close proximity to the area north of Lisbon and elsewhere due to the favourable wind conditions on the ridges of the hills. When I first closed in on the Lines of Torres Vedras by car, I mistakenly took the ruins of these various mills to be the remainders of Wellington's redoubts that made up the Lines of Torres Vedras. In addition to being a careful strategist, Arthur Wellesley was mainly a man of action who placed an emphasis on common sense both in war and his private life. If we recall his first great triumph in the Battle of Assaye, which he won thanks to the discovery of a new crossing over the Kaitna River, Wellington told his friend J. W. Croker that he detected the ford using common sense:

> I fought and won the battle of Assaye, the bloodiest, for the numbers, that I ever saw, and this was all from having the common sense, to guess that men did not build villages on opposite sides of a stream without some means of communication between them.[442]

Therefore, it is my assertion that these old windmills located in significant number on the ridges of the hills close to Lisbon may have given the impression in the eyes of an experienced soldier of strategically placed potential redoubts, which may have attracted Wellington's attention and given rise to the idea of building a complex defence system on the ridges for an emergency situation* and to permanently ensure the presence of British troops in Portugal. On the pages of Wellington's dispatches, we can immediately find several examples proving these old windmills played a truly significant role as fortification elements in the construction of the Lines of Torres Vedras. We find the specific role of the old mills for example in Wellington's memorandum from 13th October 1810, in which he issued the following order instructing his troops on how to act if Masséna's men were to attack the first defensive line in the area between Zibreira and Sobral:

> When the army shall be ordered to occupy the position of Zibreira... Lieut. General Sir Brent Spencer's division, with its right at the two windmills between Zibreira, and the redoubts of Sobral [a small town located in the centre of the first line of fortresses], will occupy a line extending to an old mill on the right of Zibreira, and thence to another old mill on the left of the church of Zibreira, bringing their left to the ravine. This line extends about 1000 yards.[443]

In the event that another area of the Lines of Torres Vedras (near S. Jago dos Velhos) was attacked, Wellington wrote the following lines to General Craufurd in the beginning of October, in which the windmills also play a defensive role:

---

*   The Count of Schaumburg-Lippe also fortified small redoubts from which he led a partisan war.

My intention in bringing up a brigade to S. Jago dos Velhos was, not to limit the space which I wished you to attend to, but to have a body of troops in readiness to throw in upon the ground about Trancoso, and extending from No. 8 [a redoubt] to the mills (marked A in your plan), in case the enemy should make a push at the valley of Calhandriz.[444]

Finally, in the event of attack of another segment of the Lines, Wellington instructed General 'Daddy' Hill on the following:

Major Gen... W. Lumley will examine all the roads leading from his cantonments to the redoubt No.8, and to the windmill about 800 yards on the right of that redoubt, in the rear of the Quinta de Belhaco, to the Quinta de Belhaco by those windmills, as well as by Transoco, to the redoubt No. 9., and the ground extending from the right of No. 9, to the point on which Brig. Gen. Craufurd will have the battery constructed...[445]

Whatever it was that brought Wellington to the idea and subsequent realization of the construction of the Lines of Torres Vedras, I agree with the former president of Portugal, Mr Aníbal Cavaco Silva, who declared the following in a speech given in 2009 in honour of the 200th anniversary of the construction of the Lines:

Here [at the Lines of Torres Vedras] the tide of the Peninsular War was turned. It was the beginning of the end of the Napoleonic adventure that had put Europe at the mercy of sword and shot. The retreat would come to a final halt at Waterloo five years later.[446]

Construction of the Lines of Torres Vedras cost the British Government a total of 100,000 pounds.[447] This fact is described in the following anecdote, which points out the often underestimated position of the Lines in the history of the Napoleonic Wars: it is said that the sum paid for the construction of the Lines of Torres Vedras was indisputably one of the most profitable investments in military history, and the creator of this investment "bull's eye" was naturally none other than Arthur Wellesley, the future Duke of Wellington.

The Gates to Spain: Ciudad Rodrigo and Badajoz

Masséna's defeat before the Lines of Torres Vedras marked the definitive end of an episode known today in Portuguese history as the Third French Invasion. The First Invasion is considered to be the occupation of Lisbon by General Junot in 1808 and the second the taking of Oporto by Marshal Soult one year later. Nonetheless, all three invasions had one thing in common: Arthur Wellesley was ultimately the reason for France's failure every time. He had defeated Junot at Vimeiro and Soult at Oporto, while Masséna was halted by Wellington's defensive Lines of Torres Vedras in accordance with the proverb that "good and bad things come in threes".

Once Wellington had defeated Masséna at Busaco and subsequently forced him into an excruciating retreat from the Lines of Torres Vedras, he slowly began to ponder his next mission to Spain, as he intended once again to attempt to liberate the country. During the French retreat from Portugal, Wellington and his troops observed Masséna and his army, who suffered more and more as the days went on. During his march, Masséna set up camp for a time in the Portuguese town of Santarém, awaiting reinforcements from Spain which, however, never arrived. Over the course of their short stay in Santarém, the frustrated Frenchmen managed to destroy the typical Portuguese blue-and-white tile decorations on the local town hall occupied by Masséna and his staff in quite a striking manner. The French chipped away the tiles from the faces or at least eyes of all the Portuguese depicted on the painted tile scenes – motifs from Portuguese history or everyday life – that decorated the walls of the town hall's interior.[448] At the beginning of March, the starving French troops abandoned Santarém and continued on toward the Spanish-Portuguese border, which they crossed in April 1811. Wellington also subsequently passed through Santarém with his army, and it is highly probably that he also spent the night in the town hall, the same place where Marshal had stayed two days earlier.[449] Unfortunately for the citizens of Santarém, who for various reasons had refused to abandon their homes and retreat to safety behind the Lines of Torres Vedras, the brutality of the starving French troops manifested itself not only in wanton vandalism of Santarém's town hall. Wellington and his soldiers were met with a gruesome scene upon entering the town.

> Mothers were hung up with the children by their sides, and fires lighted below them. Men and children, half-murdered, thrown upon the burning embers of the houses they [French] had set on fire. In short murder and desolation mark their [French] track in letters that ought never to be forgotten by the Portuguese for generations to come.[450]

British officer Robert Ballard Long recalled the atrocities committed by the French in attempts to exact food from the remainder of the town's population. The cruelty which Masséna's depleted forces (who left behind their own men who were either too injured or exhausted to march on) continued to inflict on the civilians who had not fled to safety behind the Lines of Torres Vedras in their desperate retreat to Spain was described by one Thomas Pococke, member of the 71st Glasgow Regiment, Highland Light Infantry:

> We could not advance 100 yards without seeing dead soldiers of the enemy stretched upon the road, or at a little distance from it, who had lain down to die, unable to proceed through hunger and fatigue. We could not pity them, miserable as they were. Their retreat resembled more that of famished wolves

than men. Murder and devastation marked their way, every house was a sep-ulchre, a cabin of horrors! Our soldiers used to wonder why the Frenchmen were not swept by heaven from the earth, when they witnessed their cruelties. In a small town called Safrea, I saw twelve dead bodies lying in one house upon the floor! Every house contained traces of their wanton barbarity...[451]

During the final phase of Masséna's retreat, one smaller-scale skir-mish took place between the French's rear-guard and British troops near the small town of Redinha, an encounter which was of no strategic signif-icance but one in which Arthur Wellesley played quite a remarkable role. At Redinha, Wellesley was closely monitoring the retreating French with his handheld telescope, whereupon he was spotted and suddenly became the target of enemy artillery fire. However, as a man who was accustomed to placing his life in the hands of fate during great battles, Wellesley did not seem to take much notice. Lieutenant Schaumann, evidently fascinat-ed by the event, recorded the whole occurrence in his memoirs:

I cannot refrain from describing an incident witnessed to-day by my cous-in Gustav, proving how coolheaded Lord Wellington was. Gustav, with twenty-four hussars of the regiment, was ordered to act as escort to Lord Wellington when the latter went to reconnoitre the enemy's position. His lordship rode right into the zone of the French battery fire, and jumping from his horse, examined the position with a telescope. The French battery concentrated its fire on this point, and their shells fell incessantly about the Commander-in-Chief and the detachment of hussars. But Lord Wellington did not allow himself to be perturbed by this, and remained dismounted about a quarter of an hour...The detachment [in which his cousin Gustav was deployed] lost several horses as the result of the enemy fire.[452]

Subsequently, Arthur Wellesley officially thanked his troops for their 'excellent conduct' while pursuing Masséna toward the Portuguese-Spanish border. He also called upon three selected regiments, which in previous days had distinguished themselves in several skirmishes with the retreating French, each to nominate one of their sergeants to be advanced in rank.[453] Several days later, he issued a declaration to the citizens of Portugal who had gathered behind the Lines of Torres Vedras in which he informed them that they could now return safely to their homes:

The Portuguese nation are informed that the cruel enemy who had invaded
Portugal, and devastated their country, have been obliged to evacuate it,
after suffering great losses, and have retired... The inhabitants of the country
are therefore at liberty to return to their occupations.[454]

After Masséna's defeat, Wellington found himself full of enthusiasm and
excitement. After months of immeasurable struggle, constant tension, and
stress, his plan for the Lines of Torres Vedras had finally borne fruit. Thanks
to Beresford's intensive training, the Portuguese troops fared excellently at
Busaco and Wellesley could now count on them in his future campaigns.

We have given the French a handsome dressing, and I think they will not say
again that we are not a manoeuvring army. We may not manoeuvre so beautifully as they do, but I do not desire better sport than to meet one of their
columns en masse, with our lines.[455]

When it seemed that Portugal had once again been successfully defended,
British Minister for War Robert Jenkinson, Lord Liverpool, congratulated Wellesley on his excellent accomplishments and sought to ascertain
the next steps he intended to take:

I congratulate you most sincerely upon the successful conclusion of all your
operations, as far as relates to the defence of Portugal. The event has most
fully confirmed all your predictions, and the eyes of the world are now completely open to the wisdom of the system upon which you have been acting.
I shall be most anxious to learn your future views...[456]

Wellington replied to Liverpool in a wholly open manner, stating that
the basis for his next advance would be maintaining control of Portugal
– thus, in a worst case scenario, Arthur Wellesley would always have the
option to retreat behind the Lines of Torres Vedras:

Depend upon it that Portugal should be the foundation of all your operations in the Peninsula, of whatever nature they may be, upon which point
I have never altered my opinion. If they are to be offensive, and Spain is to
be the theatre of them, your commanders must be in a situation to be entirely
independent of all Spanish authorities, by which means alone they will be

enabled to draw some resources from the country, and some assistance from the Spanish armies,[457]

Wellington wrote to Liverpool. At the beginning of 1811, information began to reach Arthur Wellesley via messages from Lord Liverpool (and others) of the growing tensions between Napoleon and the Russian Tsar Alexander I. The core of the disputes was the so-called Continental Blockade against Britain, by which Napoleon (speaking in simple terms) banned Russians and the rest of Continental Europe from trading with the British, an order that the Russians gradually began to violate. In terms of Russo-French relations, more fuel was added to the proverbial fire by Russia's non-committal attitude concerning Napoleon's offer to marry the Tsar's sister Anna Pavlovna, who after Bonaparte's divorce with Empress Joséphine was the second most suitable candidate on Bonaparte's list of potential wives next to Austrian Princess Marie Louise, whom Napoleon ultimately married. Thus, Wellington wrote the following lines home to one of his friends:

> If there is a war in the north [between Russia and France] I think we shall make Boney's situation in Spain this year [1811] not a bed of roses, if there is not a war in the north this year, it is impossible that his fraudulent and disgusting tyranny can be endured much longer, and if Great Britain can only hold out I think we shall yet bring the affairs of the Peninsula to a satisfactory termination.[458]

However, before marching into Spanish territory, Arthur Wellesley – who to his own great satisfaction was finally taking the offensive – first and foremost needed to conquer two crucial fortified Spanish cities: Ciudad Rodrigo in the north and Badajoz in the south-west about ten miles from the Spanish-Portuguese border, which guarded the two primary routes between Portugal and Spain and were for the time being in French hands. In order to take the cities as swiftly as possible, Wellington decided to divide his forces. He assigned a portion of his army (20,000 men*) to General Beresford, entrusting him with the siege of Badajoz, which

---

* British regiments made up roughly half of Beresford's forces; the remaining portion of his army was made up of Portuguese.

controlled the primary southern route into Spain. He set off personally with the remaining units (also accompanied now by new arrivals from the British 7th Division) north to deal with Ciudad Rodrigo.[459] Nonetheless, Wellington faced one more formidable barrier in the north of Portugal – the Almeida Fortress, the fortifications of which Masséna had managed to repair. The local garrison there was the last French enclave in Portugal. Before Wellington could attack Ciudad Rodrigo, it was first necessary to take Almeida. Wellington's troops began their siege of the fortress on 14th April 1811. Although his troops soon closed off the areas immediately surrounding Almeida, they were not able to take the stronghold by direct attack, as they lacked the heavy siege cannons that were needed to create breaches in the massive, newly rebuilt walls of the fortress. Thus, Wellington had no other choice but to attempt to starve Almeida's poorly supplied garrison. Marshal Masséna did not hesitate to use this situation to his advantage, granting a fortnight of recuperation to his army, which had suffered immensely during its recent and horrific retreat and was now finally well-supplied in a camp near the Spanish city of Salamanca. Masséna then immediately remobilized his troops and hurried at once to attack Wellington's position in the effort to free Almeida from its siege, clear his name, and avenge the injuries he had suffered hitherto.[460]

Arthur Wellesley left the several thousand men that were crucial in blockading Almeida and, with the remainder of the Anglo-Portuguese Army of roughly 38,000 troops, set off to face Masséna's oncoming troops. The French Marshal managed with remarkable speed to gather 48,000 combat-ready troops and therefore held a considerable numerical advantage. Wellington, however, would ultimately make the choice for the location of the upcoming battle. Like so many times before, he and his men took an advantageous position at the peak of a ridge, which this time was located directly on the Portuguese-Spanish border roughly 12 miles east of the Almeida Fortress. On Wellington's left flank in the valley under the ridge was the village of Fuentes de Oñoro, which Arthur Wellesley immediately occupied using several Scottish Highlander regiments. It was here on 3rd May 1811 that Masséna attacked. As a result, brutal skirmishes soon broke out in the winding streets of the relatively extensive village that lasted almost the whole day. By evening, the French had clearly been repelled, but the remaining British troops holding the village were on the verge of exhaustion. Both armies spent the next day manoeuvring, after which both sides put up white flags signifying a ceasefire in order to remove their wounded from the streets of Fuentes de Oñoro. The next day, the French renewed their attack in full force.[461]

Contrary to the highly advantageous position that Wellington held at Busaco, his location at Fuentes de Oñoro had one major weakness. South of where Wellington's troops were deployed on the elevated ridge over Fuentes de Oñoro was a deforested and flat landscape covered only sparsely with bushes, which provided Masséna with the ideal opportunity to perform an outflanking manoeuvre. Wellington, who justifiably feared such a scenario, immediately ordered his British 7th Division to the area. There, they took over a space on the flat plain near a small settlement called Poco Velho made up of only several small houses.

Masséna indeed attempted an outflanking manoeuvre on Wellington's right flank in this area, sending three whole infantry divisions with all his cavalry toward the plain opposite Poco Velho. The solitary British 7th Division had not the slightest chance in resisting this force and began to retreat straightaway. As soon as Wellesley spotted the French attack, he immediately sent his elite Light Division led by General Craufurd to aid the retreating British on his right wing. Three French infantry divisions marched forward relatively slowly, but Masséna's cavalry of roughly 4,500 cavaliers posed a grave threat to the inexperienced retreating 7th Division, which had only recently arrived from England. However, at this crucial moment the Light Division proved its worth and, thanks to its intervention, allowed the 7th Division to retreat successfully back to join the main British forces deployed near the village of Fuentes de Oñoro. Craufurd's men managed to complete this heroic action, but only at the price of now finding themselves surrounded by numerous French cavalrymen. The Light Division immediately formed an infantry square (a formation primarily designated for anti-cavalry combat) and continued to retreat slowly in this formation step by step over the same tracks that the 7th Division had taken toward Fuentes de Oñoro.[462]

Marching in a square formation under pressure from enemy cavalry was not an easy task. The French cavalry tirelessly encircled the British and waited for any error that might create a gap in the British lines, a mistake which could immediately be used to the French's advantage. They waited for the opportunity to disrupt the infantry square and massacre the British division one by one. However, the experienced Light Division managed to persevere in the arduous affair and successfully retreated to Fuentes de Oñoro, as the Captain of the 95th Rifles John Kincaid recalled:

> The execution of our movement presented a magnificent military spectacle, as the plain, between us and the right of the army, was by this time in possession of the French cavalry, and, while we were retiring through it with the order and precision of a common field-day, they kept dancing around us, and every instant threatening a charge, without daring to execute it.[463]

Subsequently, the 7th Division and the Light Division created a new defensive line, taking their positions east of the village of Fuentes de Oñoro toward the Almeida Fortress to counter any possible attack by the French, who were attempting the outflanking manoeuvre. Wellington's forces were now positioned in what was in essence a right angle, and the village of Fuentes de Oñoro now formed the corner point of this new position – the original line of Wellesley's troops stretched north of the village, while the new line formed by the 7th and Light Divisions stretched to the east. The French, however, did not attack the newly formed line, and now focused all their might on the village of Fuentes de Oñoro itself, which Masséna began to attack persistently. Wellington's Scottish Highlanders (79th and 71th Regiments) who held the village were gradually pushed back to a church at the very edge of the village where, amongst the graves in the adjacent churchyard, they led man-to-man skirmishes using their last remaining strength against the French Imperial Guard. The whole village was now almost completely under French control, a fact which posed a grave threat to Wellington's centre. [464]

In this critical situation, Wellington quickly rode up to Fuentes de Oñoro and immediately set about ascertaining which regiments still in reserve were ready to engage in battle. The moment Wellesley heard the name of the 88th Regiment (the Connaught Rangers, who had fared so excellently at Busaco) from his aide-de-camp on the list of battle-ready troops, he immediately asked his aide: "Is Wallace with the 88th?"[465]

When he received an affirmative, he ordered the 88th Regiment commanded by Wallace to lead an attack on Fuentes de Oñoro: "Tell him to come down [to the village] and drive these fellows [the French] back, he will do the thing properly."[466] Similarly to Busaco, Wallace did not disappoint Wellington. Thanks to the ferocious attack led by the Connaught

BATTLE OF FUENTES DE OÑORO
3rd–5th May 1811

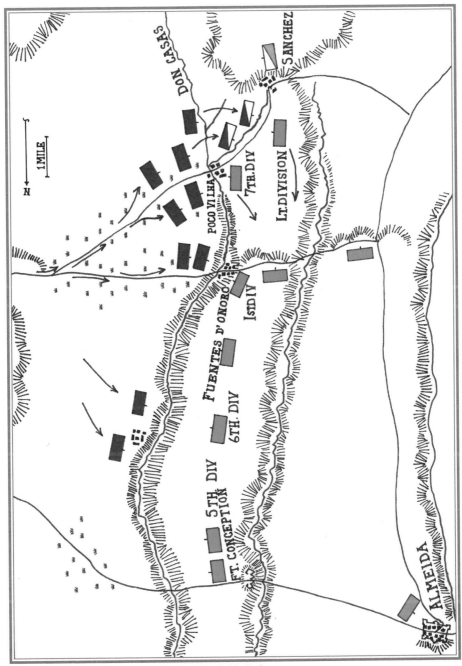

1 MILE

N

DON CASAS

S.ANCHEZ

7TH.DIV

LT.DIVISION

POCO VILHA

1st DIV

FUENTES D'OÑORO

6TH. DIV

5TH DIV

FT. CONCEPTION

ALMEIDA

—— *Map by John Fawkes* ——

Rangers, the British suddenly regained their advantage in the battle for the village. The clashes continued on into the evening, but as night approached the defeated Masséna abandoned his efforts to break through Wellington's centre and retreated from the battlefield. He had lost almost 3,000 men at Fuentes de Oñoro while Wellington, who could now celebrate his next momentous victory, lost 1,800, the majority of which fell during the brutal clashes that took place in the streets of the village.[467]

After Wellington's success at Fuentes de Oñoro, a major in the 95th Rifles serving in Craufurd's division wrote the following home to his parents:

> Lord Wellington is adored by his army, wherever he is, confidence of success is the result. The French own it that, next to Buonaparte, he is the first Captain in Europe. I wish his lordship had Buonaparte to contend with instead of Masséna, we should sooner settle the business.[468]

Nonetheless, Arthur Wellesley, who had always held great respect for Napoleon's military artistry, viewed the matter with a somewhat greater degree of humility. At Fuentes de Oñoro Masséna had greatly endangered his right wing in his attempted outflanking manoeuvre, which was very nearly successful, forcing Wellesley to summon all his prowess to turn the dangerously close battle into a British victory. It was his assumption that if he had stood alone against Napoleon, he may not have had the same results, as he confessed honestly to his brother William: 'the battle of Fuentes... was the most difficult one I was ever concerned in, and against the greatest odds...If Boney had been there, we should have been beaten.'[469]

However, many years before in India, where Wellington's infantrymen frequently found themselves in danger of "partisan" attacks firstly from Tipu's and later Maratas' light horsemen called *Looties*, who tried to do as much damage to Arthur Wellesley's infantry as possible, Wellington stated that: 'a disciplined infantry that keeps its order, and reserves fire has but little to fear from cavalry'[470]

Wellesley's staff officer and good friend Sir Alexander Gordon, who had the opportunity throughout the Battle of Fuentes de Oñoro to meet repeatedly with the French (Gordon negotiated terms with the French in the name of the British Army to ensure that each side could carry its wounded to safety from the battlefield during a short ceasefire), confirmed on the contrary the growing acknowledgment and respect that the French held toward Wellesley, when he noted that Wellington: 're- mains the terror and admiration of the French army... They [the French] said the other day that their Emperor would not disdain to encounter him and that he [Wellington] was superior to the Archduke Charles. [the Austrian commander and victor over Napoleon at Aspern-Essling, whom Napoleon however personally defeated in turn at Wagram].'[471]

Despite his indisputable achievements over the past months, Wellington was faced with the rather sad obligation of writing a person- al letter to an acquaintance from his previous activities in the military, Major-General Cammeron, informing him that his son had succumbed to the injuries he had suffered at Fuentes de Oñoro, where he led one of the British regiments into battle. Such matters are not easily expressed and Wellington endeavoured to write with the greatest of sensitivity:

> You will always regret and lament his loss, I am convinced, but I hope that you will derive some consolation from the reflection that he fell in the per- formance of his Duty at the Head of your brave Regt., loved and respected by all that knew him, in an action in which, if possible, the British Troops surpassed every thing they had ever done before and of which the result was most honourable to his Majesty's Arms.[472]

Unfortunately, it was neither the first nor the last time that Wellington would write such a letter. The first time Arthur Wellesley, as a command- ing officer, took it upon himself to communicate such sad news about the death of an officer serving under him was in 1799 in India after the night attack carried out by Wellesley's 33rd Regiment against Tipu's soldiers in Sultanpettah Tope. During the attack Lieutenant Fitzgerald was killed, and Arthur Wellesley wrote the following lines to Fitzgerald's brother, which – in the author's opinion – are once again very delicately chosen words:

> My Dear Sir, It is with the most unfeigned regret that I sit down to acquaint you of the melancholy event which is the subject of this letter. In an attack which was made upon the enemy's advanced posts on the night of the 5th of April [1799], your brother, Lieutenant Fitzgerald of the 33th Regiment, re- ceived a wound from a rocket which nearly carried away his arm, and another from a bayonet of which he died in the course of that night. I can offer you no

consolation upon this melancholy occasion. To inform you that your brother distinguished himself in the affair in which he lost his life, that in others in which I have seen him engaged during this war, he had conducted himself to my satisfaction, that as an officer I had always, and particularly that I had latterly, reason to be pleased with him, will only add to the grief with which you and his family must naturally be affected. However, whatever may be the effect, it is but justice to the late Mr. Fitzgerald to make known to you and his friends my sentiments for him.[473]

Masséna had suffered another defeat, but his army was still far from being vanquished. However, it was crystal clear to the French Marshal that, at the present moment, Almeida could not be saved. He therefore decided to attempt to deliver the town's garrison to safety. He sent three volunteers to attempt to breach the British lines while carrying exact instructions for the commander of the garrison intended to help save him and his men. Two of the volunteers were shot by British troops, but one managed to slip into the fortress. On the evening of 10th May, the French commander of the fortress had three artillery salvos fired at five-minute intervals, which was a signal confirming he had successfully received Masséna's message and would attempt to flee that same evening under the veil of night. The French proceeded to march out of Almeida and successfully reach the bridge over the nearby Barba de Puerco River without facing any significant enemy troops capable of halting them. On the other side of the bridge, Masséna had set up a special division led by General Reynier that was ordered to wait for the fleeing garrison and help them ultimately flee to safety. Several British units attacked the French near the bridge at the last moment, but more than three quarters of the Almeida garrison (roughly 1,400 men) managed to flee successfully.

The French also enjoyed a fair deal of luck in the matter, as the habitual drinker and wholly unqualified General Erskine was the man responsible that night for defending the bridge. Wellington was forced to tolerate Erskine due to his contacts at the highest levels of command at Horse Guards, who had managed to secure a place for Erskine in the army. Erskine wrote an order to Lieutenant-Colonel Bevan, in which he tasked Bevan's regiment with occupying the bridge. However, Erskine forgot about the order for some time and sent it late in the evening. Lieutenant-Colonel Bevan made a fatal blunder – although he received Erskine's delayed order around midnight, he set out for the bridge only on the following morning, allowing the French to pass over the bridge unmolested the night before. Wellington was naturally infuriated by the whole affair, and therefore decided to make a clear display of it, punishing the officer corps for their mistakes in the same manner that he would with his own men. As Commander-in-Chief he now had no intention of tolerating such behaviour that had so much irritated him as a young officer during the campaign in Flanders, where he had observed the woeful leadership of the officer corps. To Wellington's dismay, General Erskine escaped significant punishment thanks to his political contacts; Lieutenant-Colonel Bevan, however, was to be immediately court marshalled. The Lieutenant--Colonel unfortunately buckled under the pressure of the given situation and took his own life, shooting himself in the head.[474] Bevan's suicide naturally placed the whole situation in a tragic light. Wellington himself was highly frustrated by the whole affair, as is evidenced by a letter he sent on 15th May 1811 to War Minister Lord Liverpool:

> I certainly feel, every day, more and more the difficulty of the situation in which I am placed. I am obliged to be everywhere, and if absent from any operation, something goes wrong. It is to be hoped that the General [Erskine] and other officers of the army will at last acquire that experience which will teach them that success can be attained only by attention to the most minute details, and by tracing every part of every operation from its origin to its conclusion, point by point, and ascertaining that the whole is understood by those who are to execute it.[475]

The day after Wellington wrote these eloquent lines, the situation once again urgently required his presence. On 16th May, Arthur Wellesley received a message that Marshal Soult was planning to attack General Beresford, who had been laying siege to Badajoz since the beginning of April without any significant success. Similarly to Masséna in the north at Almeida, Soult was attempting to free Badajoz from enemy siege. All indicators pointed to another battle soon taking place in the south. For this reason, Wellington hurried from Almeida to Badajoz on horseback using every last bit of his strength, managing to exhaust two horses during the ride. It is likely that he knew his commanding skills could save hundreds if not thousands of his men's lives on the battlefield. He was naturally plagued by the fear that Beresford would be defeated. Despite his best efforts, he arrived too late, as Beresford had already confronted Soult near the village of Albuera on 16th May, the same day that Wellington had learned of the imminent threat of Soult's attack.[476] Beresford's men felt somewhat uneasy without Wellington, as evidenced by a conversation that took place shortly before the Battle of Albuera and which was recorded by one of the battle's participants, John Cooper of the 7th Royal Fusiliers: 'Turning to me Horsefall [another soldier in the Fusiliers] drily said, 'Where's ar Arthur?' Meaning Wellington. I said 'I don't know, I don't see him' He rejoined. 'Aw wish he wor here.' 'So did I.'[477] Captain Kincaid of the 95th Rifles noted in his memoirs the importance that Wellington held for British troops during the Peninsular War in a similar manner: 'We would rather see his long nose in the fight than a reinforcement of ten thousand men any day.'[478]

At Albuera, Marshal Beresford had roughly 35,000 soldiers at his disposal, of which there were 10,000 British, 10,000 Portuguese, and 15,000 Spaniards. Spanish General Venegas had transferred command of his forces to Beresford without question in attempts to limit the potential confusion that could stem from multiple commands, a fact that could have fatal consequences for the allies during the battle. In comparison, Soult's *Armée du Midi* (Army of the South) was made up of roughly 25,000 men, giving the allies a sizeable numerical advantage over the French. Nonetheless, Soult managed to outflank Beresford's wing at the very beginning of battle, which the British commander managed to repel only by incurring heavy losses. Using a surprise cavalry attack, the French had also managed to cut down a large segment of one of Beresford's divisions. Despite all the complications, General Beresford finally secured victory over Soult thanks to the bravery of his troops; his losses, however, amounted to roughly 6,000 men, 4,200 of which were from the ranks of the British, who bore the brunt of the attacks. Nonetheless, Marshal Soult had been defeated, losing between seven and eight thousand men. Wellington received the report of Beresford's victory on 19th May during his quick ride to Albuera.[479] Beresford was certainly not the bragging type, and his dispatch to Wellington, which gave an account of the battle, was written in an apologetic, even defeatist tone in regard to the losses that were incurred. Despite the relatively high number of fatalities and casualties that Beresford suffered even in spite of his large advantage, Arthur Wellesley attempted to comfort the general in his hastily-written reply as best he could: 'You could not be successful in such an action without a large loss, and we must make up our minds to affairs of this kind sometimes, or give up the game.'[480] After receiving news of the victory, Wellington arrived in Albuera on 21st May, as he now had no reason to make haste. Upon arriving, he found Beresford on the verge of collapse as a result of the terrible slaughter which he had witnessed, and thus sent him to Lisbon to recuperate, where it took the General several months to regain his equilibrium. Although Wellesley had not managed to participate in the battle, he did not hesitate to visit his injured soldiers in the field hospital near Albuera after his arrival. "Oh, old 29th, I am sorry to see so many of you here!", said Wellington, to which one injured replied: "Oh, my lord, if you had only been with us, there would not have been so many of us here!"[481]

In the meantime, a significant change had taken place in French command, for as soon as Napoleon learned of the details of Masséna's defeat at Fuentes de Oñoro, his patience with the 'Old Fox' ran out and he immediately replaced him with Auguste Marmont as the head of the so-called *"Armée du Portugal"* (the official name of this French fighting force). Marmont had recently distinguished himself at Wagram, where he could claim the lion's share of the credit for defeating the Austrians. Like Bonaparte, Marmont had begun his military career in the artillery, whereupon he came to Napoleon's aid on his path to power during the Coup of 18th Brumaire (9th November) in 1799.[482] While this change of French command was taking place, the Allied Army continued its siege of Badajoz, albeit now under Wellington's command. However, due to a lack of heavy cannon, Wellesley decided to withdraw his forces and focus his attention on Ciudad Rodrigo, as an army of sixty thousand men belonging to the newly appointed Marshal Marmont was now in dangerous proximity to Badajoz. This army was formed by Masséna and Soult's former men and also included new reinforcements, a fact which presented Wellington with another valid reason to abandon his attempts at taking Badajoz, at least for the time being. Thanks to this, Wellington's men spent most of the autumn of 1811 in a state of relative inactivity, with the exception of one larger-scale skirmish with the French cavalry near the village of El Bodon. More importantly, however, Wellington set out to streamline supply routes for his soldiers over the course of 1811, a matter to which he now turned his full attention.

It was clear to Wellington that, in the event of an offensive aimed at liberating Spain, he would need a well-fed army. However, he would not be able to rely on supplies from Spanish territory, as it was largely controlled by the enemy. Fortunately for Wellington and thanks to his recent achievements, the British Government was now more than willing to provide him with additional finances. Wellington thus drew up a plan that was similar to the campaign in India to keep his men as well-supplied as possible. Concretely, Wellington proclaimed years ago in India that: 'articles of provision are not to be trifled with or left to chance.' and also 'Experience has shown us, that British troops can never depend upon Rajahs [and in this case now upon the Portuguese and Spaniards], or other allies, for their supplies.'[483] Thus, by drawing upon earlier experience, he progressively began to order the much-needed food and other essential supplies for his troops to be sent from all corners of the world to Portuguese harbours and by doing so greatly increased the frequency of supply imports. In addition, the seas and oceans were still safely under the control of the Royal Navy, which guaranteed that the cargo ships had nothing to fear – with the possible exception of pirates. Large amounts of imported goods then travelled from Portuguese harbours down the Douro, Tagus and Mondego Rivers and to the outermost navigable realms of these bodies of water. From these areas, supplies travelled directly to Wellington's troops with the help of a supply chain consisting of hundreds of mules that moved goods constantly to and from established supply stations. Thanks to this complex system, Wellington's men stayed well-equipped in the area of the Portuguese-Spanish border, even during marches over greater distances.[484] Wellington himself wrote about his current system of supplying:

> It is very necessary to attend to all this detail [i.e. the process of transporting provisions to the troops] and to trace a biscuit from Lisbon into the man's mouth on the frontier, and to provide for its removal from place to place by land or by water, or no military operations can be carried on, and the troops must starve.[485]

Many years after the war, Wellington wrote the following about the French, who were accustomed to procuring by ransacking the territory in which their army was located, to Lord Stanhope: 'The French armies were made to take their chance and to live as they could, and their loss of men was immense. It is very singular that in relating Napoleon's campaigns this has never been clearly shown in anything like its full extent.'[486] Napoleon's newly appointed General and Wellington's rival Marshal Marmont himself proclaimed that, thanks to the guerrillas and the insufficient amount of supplies in Spain, he could 'nothing without magazines, which is quite a new era in the modern French military system.'[487]

By the end of 1811, the allies had managed to transport the urgently expected heavy siege cannons (the same cannons that were originally to have been transported to Almeida) to the surrounding area of Ciudad Rodrigo, thus finally allowing Wellington to begin his siege of this fortified city at the beginning of 1812. Shortly before the beginning of the siege, the leader of the Spanish guerrilla band Don Julián Sánchez managed to accomplish something quite remarkable. This ex-soldier and peasant was known by the nickname of 'El Charro', which loosely translates to "a man of Salamanca". Sanchéz's nickname referred to the Spanish city from which he hailed and was evidently meant to emphasize his patriotism. 'El Charro' commanded a cavalry unit called the *"Lanciers of Castilla"* operating at the time on the Spanish-Portuguese border near Ciudad Rodrigo.[488] He had already been providing Wellington with valuable information on the movements of the enemy for some time, and he managed to intercept many French dispatches, which Captain George Scovell of Wellington's staff subsequently decoded. He also fought on Wellington's jeopardized right wing at Fuentes de Oñoro. Here, however, he was naturally unable with his group of partisans to effectively fight against the French cavalry, who were several thousand men strong. He did however pull off a rather extraordinary feat. A report reached 'El Charro's' vigilant ears that the French Governor of Ciudad Rodrigo, General Reynaud, planned to leave the safety of the city walls to look over his herd of cows near the town, a decision that proved to be a grave mistake. As Don Julian was a man of action, he made use of this unique opportunity and ambushed General Reynaud along with his escort, successfully capturing Reynaud and passing on this "rich spoil of war" to Wellington. Thus, the city was stripped of its Governor shortly before the siege, which certainly gave Arthur Wellesley a promising head start.[489]

Ciudad Rodrigo stretches along an elevated area formed by the Greater and Lesser Teson hills. The city's impressive star-shaped fortifications, including its medieval Moorish castle, still stand to this day.

Nonetheless, it should be taken into account that, in the age of gunpowder and artillery, the elevated position of the city – which was advantageous in medieval times – was certainly no longer an insurmountable barrier to the armies of Wellington's time. On 11th January, Wellington's artillery-men dug out batteries for their heavy siege cannons which Wellington now possessed in sufficient numbers in their proper positions and began to bombard Ciudad Rodrigo. Only six days later, two large breaches had been made in the walls, the proportions of which were sufficiently large for Wellington to order an immediate attack on the town.

The larger of the two breaches was located on the northern side of the town, while the second and smaller breach had been opened up to the east around the perimeter of the fortifications. Arthur Wellesley directed General Picton's 3rd Division into the larger of the breaches, while General Craufurd's Light Division was to attempt to penetrate the smaller one. Along with these two primary attacks, an additional plan included sever-al auxiliary escalades led with the help of scaling ladders. The action was launched on 19th January 1812 at roughly seven o'clock in the evening. From the very start, the French put up stiff resistance, including a whole series of nasty surprises they had prepared for their assailants. At the top of the breaches, British divisions faced a menacing obstruction called *chevaux de frise* – wooden logs fixed on all sides with sabre blades. The defenders of the smaller breach also managed to trigger a massive gun-powder explosion under the feet of the attackers of the Light Division. In both attacking divisions, the heaviest losses were naturally incurred by so-called *"Forlorn Hopes"* units*, who were the first to charge the breaches. The Forlorn Hopes were made up of volunteers from various regiments who risked high chances of injury or death for the prospect of financial reward and immediate advancement in rank. For example, a lieutenant who led the Forlorn Hopes into battle was promised the rank of captain if he should survive. Other attacking regiments also suffered heavy losses but continued to pour into battle, as Craufurd and Picton tirelessly drove in more and more regiments of their divisions. Despite the French's ob-stinate resistance, British troops managed to break through the breaches and into the fortress. There they rounded up the remaining defenders on the adjacent square, where the French commander of the fortress finally

---

* The term Forlorn Hope originates from the Dutch "erloren hoop", literally meaning "lost hope."

STORMING OF CIUDAD RODRIGO
19ᵗʰ January 1812

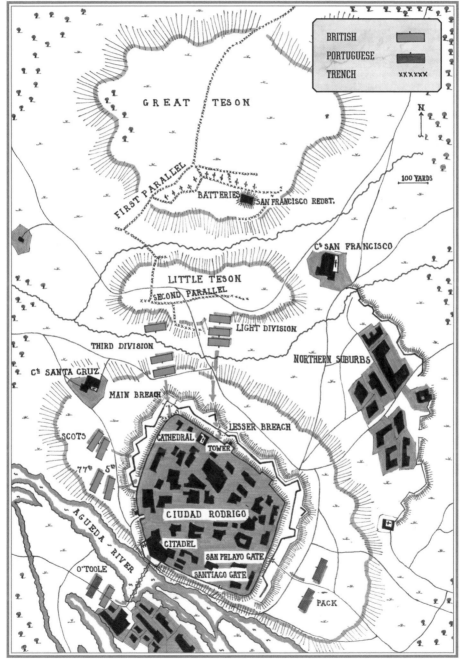

BRITISH

PORTUGUESE

TRENCH   xxxxx

GREAT TESON

N

100 YARDS

FIRST PARALLEL

BATTERIES   SAN FRANCISCO REDBT.

Cᵗ SAN FRANCISCO

LITTLE TESON

SECOND PARALLEL

LIGHT DIVISION

THIRD DIVISION

NORTHERN SUBURBS

Cᵗ SANTA CRUZ

MAIN BREACH

LESSER BREACH

SCOTS

CATHEDRAL

TOWER

77ᵗʰ 5ᵗʰ

CIUDAD RODRIGO

AGUEDA RIVER

CITADEL

SAN PELAYO GATE

O'TOOLE

SANTIAGO GATE

PACK

— *Map by John Fawkes* —

capitulated, handing over his sword to Lieutenant Gurwood,* commander of the Forlorn Hopes that had attacked the smaller breach.[490]

The attackers soon began to behave quite unscrupulously in the streets of Ciudad Rodrigo, as they plundered and looted and roamed around blind drunk. Nonetheless, the worst possible atrocities such as rape and murder occurred only in rare circumstances thanks to the efforts made by British officers, who made all possible attempts to restrain their men. For example, Thomas Picton the Commanding General of the 3rd Division, known for his fiery personality, swore at and threatened his men in the attempt to establish order among their ranks, showering all types of vituperation upon his drunken soldiers and thrashing those whom he came upon mercilessly on the head with the butt of a broken musket. By the next day, the officer corps had managed to re-establish complete order amongst their men.

In the siege of the city, Wellington lost 568 men, while the whole French garrison, made up of roughly 2,000 men, was captured by the British. During the attack on the city, however, Robert Craufurd, who had led his elite Light Division into battle, was seriously injured. At the time of the Battle of Talavera and the retreat behind the Lines of Torres Vedras – a time which was extremely trying for Wellington due to the series of British retreats – Craufurd had been one of the most active "croakers" in the whole British Army and at the time did not spare Wellington his words of criticism.[491] Despite this fact, Craufurd was an honourable man who was not ashamed of his opinion and, above all, had been a capable and brave general. Now he was wholly on Wellington's side and, just before he succumbed to his injuries, he frankly apologized to Wellington for his earlier behaviour: 'he talked to me as they do in a novel.'[492] Wellington recalled of the noble manner of the dying Craufurd. The soldiers of the Light Division had often complained about Craufurd as their direct commander due to his strong hand and pedantic nature. While moving his men, he absurdly insisted that they never break their marching formation, even when faced with various natural hindrances. However, the Light Division did in fact respect him, as its soldiers (and Wellington himself) knew him to be a fearless general who could always be relied upon in the fray. When the soldiers of the Light Division returned from Craufurd's funeral and came upon a marshland,

---

*   John Gurwood would later become the editor of a collection of Wellington's dispatches.

I. Silhouette of Arthur Wesley as a young boy.
It is the only surviving image of Wellington from his childhood.

II. This miniature of eighteen-year-old Arthur Wesley as Lieutenant of the 76ᵗʰ Regiment of Foot, in the ranks of which Wesley served for only a month, is a relatively recent and unique discovery. It is the earliest portrait of the future Duke of Wellington as a young man. The author of the miniature may have been Walter Robertson, and it is assumed to have been created between November and December 1787.

III. Twenty-five-year-old Lieutenant-Colonel Arthur Wesley on a painting by John Hoppner, who was the most prominent portrait painter of his time in Britain (Sir Thomas Lawrence would later take his place). Hoppner, who painted portraits for most of the members of the Wellesley Family, created this work shortly after Arthur's return to Britain from the Campaign in Flanders. Years later, Arthur's oldest brother Richard would claim the painting was the very best of Wellington's portraits.

IV. *Colonel Arthur Wesley when in India*, watercolour on paper by Thomas Hazlehurst.
This unusual and little-known portrait is located in the National Gallery of Ireland.
It may have been created before Wellington's departure to India (or to symbolize this occasion);
the skull in Wellington's hand may be a kind of "memento mori" for soldiers leaving
to the Colonies due to the rather high death rate there.

V. A beautifully crafted miniature depicting General-Major Arthur Wellesley in India.
It was painted by an unknown artist based on an oil painting by Robert Home,
the painter who portrayed Wellington several times in India.

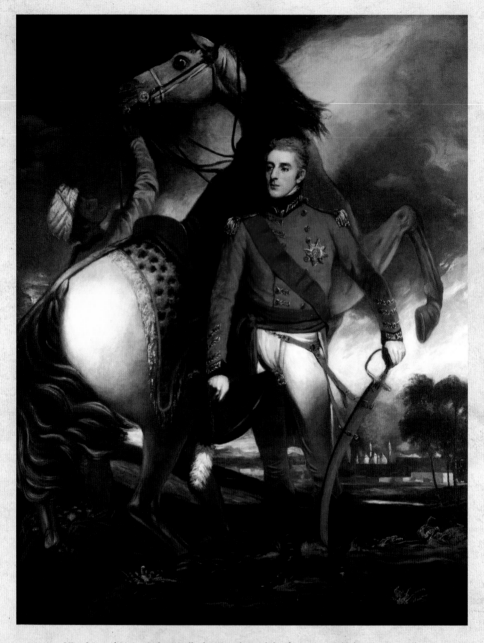

VI. General-Major Arthur Wellesley in India with his favourite Arab charger Diomed,
which he received as a present from his friend Colonel Ashton, who was later fatally shot in a duel.
Diomed was seriously wounded in the Battle of Assaye but, to Arthur's great delight,
survived its injuries and fully recuperated. The painting was made by John Hoppner
after Arthur Wellesley's return from India to Britain and commissioned for the Government House
in Madras. Later, the 7th Duke of Wellington purchased it and today it can be seen at Stratfield Saye House,
the Duke of Wellington's countryside home.

GENERAL the MARQUIS of WELLINGTON, K.B.

MARQUIS of TORRES VEDRAS, MARSHALL GENERAL of the PORTUGUESE ARMIES.

VII. Engraving of Arthur Wellesley as Viscount of Wellington,
based on a painting by Italian artist Domenico Pellegrini.
This painting was made shortly after Wellington's victory at Talavera. Wellington is standing
in the palace in Lisbon with a beautiful view of the harbour and the Belém Tower.

VIII. Highly detailed red chalk drawing of Wellington by famous Spanish painter Francisco Goya made after Wellington's victory at Salamanca in 1812. On Wellington's face, we clearly see the stress of the battle that had ensued shortly prior. According to Goya's grandson, the Spanish master created this drawing just after the Battle of Salamanca; however, the 9th Duke of Wellington has pointed to the improbability of this otherwise generally accepted claim in his work *Wellington Portrayed*.

IX. Oil on Canvas of Arthur Wellesley as the Marquees of Wellington,
made in 1812–1814 by Francisco Goya. It is obviously based on the drawing,
which can be seen on the previous page.

X. An equestrian portrait of Wellington by Francisco Goya, which was likely painted
over an unfinished portrait of the Spanish King Joseph Bonaparte. The portrait was created
in the summer of 1812 shortly after Wellington drove Joseph out of Madrid.
Proof of the fact that the image was somewhat symbolically painted over the likeness of King Joseph
arose from an X-ray analysis carried out in the 20th century.

XI. *The Dispatch*, mixed-method engraving, made by Scottish painter and engraver John Burnet, dedicated to the British Army. On it Arthur Wellesley writes a dispatch that he plans to give to a Spanish guerrilla fighter. Cooperation with the guerrillas was extremely important for Wellington during the Peninsular War. Groups of Spanish and Portuguese guerrillas not only attacked French units and inflicted significant casualties, they also arrested many of their messengers bearing confidential dispatches. They would then hand the messages over to Wellington, who used them to gain invaluable information on enemy plans and movements.

XII. Duke of Wellington by Sir Thomas Lawrence in 1814 after Napoleon's abdication, commissioned by the Prince Regent. Here Wellington is depicted in his field marshal's uniform with many orders and medals. He poses victoriously and raises the Sword of State in his right hand. Saint Paul Cathedral in London is painted in the background.
Today the work is on exhibit as a central piece in the Waterloo Chamber at Windsor Castle.

XIII. *Health and Long Life to the King!*, engraved by William Say after the painting
of Michael William Sharp, private collection. Here the Duke of Wellington, celebrating and dressed
in his military uniform, makes a toast to the King's health with a glass raised high in his right hand.
This evidently depicts the celebration of Napoleon's abdication in 1814 or of Napoleon's final defeat
at Waterloo in 1815. The original painting according to which this quite interesting engraving was created
has unfortunately been lost or destroyed. However, another version of this engraving with
a detail of Wellington's face can be found in the National Portrait Gallery of London.

XIV. The Duke of Wellington on another painting by Sir Thomas Lawrence created in 1817.
This painting is probably the most famous of all portraits of Wellington.
Today it can be admired in Apsley House, Wellington's former home in London.

Peint par Isabey
1817
Gravé par Mécou

Le Duc de Wellington

(Arthur Wellesley, Duc de)

XV. Engraving of the Duke of Wellington by André Joseph Mécou dated 1817,
based on the Duke's portrait by Jean-Baptiste Isabey, the French painter who enjoyed the favour
of Emperor Napoleon as well as King Louis XVIII after the restoration of the House of Bourbon.
In his later life, Isabey was even granted the Legion of Honour by Emperor Napoleon III,
nephew of Napoleon I.

XVI. *An Incident at the Battle of Waterloo in 1815*, painted by Thomas Jones Barker. The Duke of Wellington, atop his charger Copenhagen, gives the order for a frontal attack against Napoleon's army at Waterloo with hat in hand after the French Imperial Guard had been definitively broken by his men.

XVII. *The Triumph of Arthur the Duke of Wellington* by James Ward. This is an original study for a large canvas titled *Allegory of Waterloo* (6.7 × 10m), which has unfortunately been lost. The *Allegory* was commissioned for the Royal Hospital Chelsea, London. According to Ward, it shows: 'The Genius of Wellington on the Car of War, supported by Britannia and attended by the Seven Cardinal Virtues, commanding away the Demons, Anarchy, Rebellion and Discord, with the Horrors of War.'

XVIII. The Duke of Wellington with his favourite charger Copenhagen in a painting by Benjamin John Haydon, looking at the battlefield of Waterloo. At the centre far past the Duke, we see the Lion's Mound, the memorial finished in 1826 by architect Charles Van der Straeten by order of William I, King of the Netherlands.

XIX. and **XX.** Today's view
of the Lion's Mound
at the Waterloo battlefield.

XXI. and **XXII.** Contemporary etchings of "the Lion's Mound". This massive monument, which was built to commemorate the Battle of Waterloo, is made from an incredible amount of soil – roughly 13.7 million cubic feet (390,000 m³). Its construction began in 1820 and was finished six years later. The largest amount of soil was transported from the ridge on which Wellington's allied forces took their positions, causing it for the most part to disappear. In this context, the famous French author Victor Hugo wrote in his timeless novel *Les Misérables* that when Wellington allegedly visited Waterloo after the construction of the Lion's Mound, he angrily blurted out the following words: "They have altered my field of battle!" This is likely to have been fiction created by the author, but it quite succinctly describes how the battlefield had been altered.

XXIII. Cast-iron statuette
of Arthur Wellesley,
1st Duke of Wellington,
Prince of Waterloo
by Simeon Pierre Deveranne.
Dated 1840.

all the soldiers walked straight through the marsh in silence unflinchingly in honour of the fallen general even though the icy water in some areas came all the way up to their chests.

Thanks in part to Craufurd, Ciudad Rodrigo fell within a fortnight. By constant siege of the city, which he carried out in the depths of winter, Wellington took Marmont wholly by surprise, as he had expected the British General to carry out his next offensive in the spring as was customary in wars of the 18ᵗʰ century. The moment the French Marshal learned that Ciudad Rodrigo was being besieged, he set off immediately to aid the beleaguered city; however, a week later the town fell, and Marmont had not yet reached Salamanca, which was still fifty miles away from Ciudad Rodrigo. This spelled a rather poor start for Marmont in the Iberian theatre of war. In addition, a portion of Marmont's forces had been ordered to redeploy under the command of Marshal Suchet to the east in Valencia, which made Marmont's situation considerably more difficult. By conquering Ciudad Rodrigo and Almeida, Wellington gradually gained control over the northern route to Spain. At this moment, it was crucial to try once again to take Badajoz as part of efforts to control the southern route. In mid-March, British troops successfully transported their heavy 24-pound siege cannons from Ciudad Rodrigo to Badajoz and began to dig the first network of trenches (i.e. the first parallel) in which the siege cannons were to be placed.[493]

To Wellington, who still carried in his mind the vivid memories of the failed siege of Badajoz from the year before, it was clear that the city would prove to be much more challenging an obstacle than Ciudad Rodrigo. The city of Badajoz, which today stretches along both banks of the River Guadiana, in Wellington's day stretched along only its southern bank, allowing the Guadiana to serve as a natural defence to the northern part of the town. The bridge over the Guadiana was defended by a *Tête-du-Pont*, and when Badajoz was compared to Ciudad Rodrigo it generally possessed a much more modern and sophisticated system of fortifications. Its walls, surrounded by a deep and impressive moat and lined with countless bastions, were equipped with three independent outlying redoubts intended to make it more difficult for assailants to dig in their siege artillery batteries. The San Cristobal Fortress, which stood on the opposite side of the river, loomed over the north of the town; to the southwest was the Pardaleras Fortress and, finally, to the southeast was the Picurina Fortress. Reminiscent of Ciudad Rodrigo, a portion of the northeast tip of the city walls included a medieval castle. In addition, the area east of the city was partially flooded by a manmade canal linked to the Guadiana River. The Badajoz garrison, led by experienced General Armand Philippon, was made up of 4,000 men, which was double that of the garrison that fought the British at Ciudad Rodrigo.[494]

After consultation with his chief military engineer Colonel Fletcher, Wellington decided to attack Badajoz from the southeast. The combined British-Portuguese force set to its preparation with purpose and ensured that two pontoon bridges were hastily constructed across the Guadiana River. It was first necessary to conquer the latter-mentioned Fortress Picurina, against which Wellington immediately had an artillery battery constructed. As soon as it was finished (25th March 1812), the battery immediately commenced the bombardment of Picurina. The following day, the British stormed the redoubt and captured it by the evening after a short battle.[495] Wellington then had two additional lines of trenches (parallels) created close to Picurina that provided a new and more advantageous position for the British cannons, from which the British soon began to shell the southeast segment of the city walls. After several days of ceaseless efforts on the part of the British artillerymen, by 6th April three breaches had been created in the walls of Badajoz. Wellington was somewhat pressed for time, as Marshal Marmont and his army had withdrawn northward at the order of Napoleon himself. The French were again to attempt to bring Ciudad Rodrigo back under their control. Wellington thus needed to capture Badajoz as quickly as possible in order to march north to face Marmont (if necessary) and defend Ciudad Rodrigo. Although the width of the breaches made thus far were not ideal, Wellington – fully aware of all risks – decided to give the order to attack the formidable walls of Badajoz. He passed command of the primary attack on the fortifications to the 4th Division together with the Light Division.

Wellington's plan also included two sizeable auxiliary attacks by escalade outside the breaches with the help of ladders. The first was to be led by General Picton's 3rd Division directly against the medieval castle located in the northeast of town while the second auxiliary attack, which Wellington planned to execute on the opposite side of the fortifications (i.e. the northwest walls), was to be carried out by General Leith's 5th Division. The attack on the town was launched around 10 o'clock in the evening when Picton's 3rd Division charged the castle with their ladders. Here the British came up against heavy fire and the few men in redcoats who managed to climb up the ladders near the castle to the top of the ramparts were killed within seconds by the defenders. Picton thus decided to call back his troops, and the shaken 3rd Division retreated back to a safe distance from the castle.

In the meantime, the 4th and Light Division launched their attack on the breaches in full force. The first attacking troops from both divisions, which were traditionally made up of the Forlorn Hopes, were also equipped with ladders to ease their climb due to the steepness of the breaches. They also carried grass-bags with them into the attack, which were used to fill in a portion of the moat under the breaches. This was meant to make the breaches more accessible for the following attacking divisions. Similarly to Picton's troops, however, the Forlorn Hopes were cut down on their way to the breaches by heavy French fire while Philippon's men themselves unleashed a hellish attack against their assailants. With deadly speed, the French cast down powder charges and hand-grenades upon the daring British troops that were clambering up the steep rubble of the breaches, mercilessly crushing the first wave of assailants. Nonetheless, more and more men continued to charge fearlessly forward under the command of their officers. However, those who finally managed to survive the deadly fire of the defenders and reach the top of the breaches were greeted by the fearsome *chevaux de frise* obstacles. These in turn were defended by dozens of French muskets including several smaller cannons firing lethal canister shots[496] at close range into the ranks of the attackers, who had miraculously managed to clamber up to the top of the breach. The dreadful defences that the French had prepared for their enemies in the breaches under Philippon's remarkable command were vividly described by a soldier in the ranks of the British troops in the Siege of Badajoz, Lieutenant Robert Blakeney:

> Bags and barrels of gunpowder with short fuses were rolled down, which, bursting at the bottom or along the face of the breaches, destroyed all who advanced. Thousands of live shells, hand-grenades, fireballs and every species of destructive combustible were thrown down the breaches and over the walls into the ditches, which, lighting and exploding at the same instant, rivalled the lighting and thunder of heaven...The roaring of cannon, the

bursting of shells, the rattle of musketry, the awful explosion of mines and the flaring sickly blaze of fireballs seemed not of human invention, but rather as if all the elements of nature had greedily combined in the general havoc, and heaven, earth and hell had united for the destruction alike of devoted Badajoz and of its furious assailants.[497]

Nonetheless, the unyielding British officers continued to regroup their men with a remarkable degree of obstinacy, personally leading their men back into the terrifying havoc of the breaches in the belief that bravery and perseverance would prevail. British soldiers carried out roughly forty such unsuccessful attacks against the breaches over a two-hour period, during which the bodies of their fallen comrades-in-arms continued to pile up below.[498] The commander of the British field hospital Dr James McGrigor,* who at the time was in close proximity to the general staff, recalled Wellington's reaction the moment he learned of the failure of the last British attacks:

> Another officer came up with a still more unfavourable report, that no progress was being made, and that he feared none could be made, for almost all the officers [of the 4th and Light Divisions] were killed, and none left to lead on the men, of whom a great many had fallen. At this moment I cast my eye on the countenance of Lord Wellington, lit up by the glare of the torch held by Lord March [Charles Lennox – the eldest son of the 4th Duke of Richmond],** I shall never forget it to the last moment of my existence... The jaw had fallen, and the face was of unusual length, while the torchlight gave his countenance a lurid aspect, but still, the expression of the face was firm.[499]

At this moment, the 3rd Division under Picton's command (most likely upon Wellington's direct orders) renewed its efforts, as it attacked the castle once again with the use of scaling ladders. As Philippon's men were momentarily engaged in the defence of the breaches, which had hitherto borne the brunt of the attacks, only a handful of French remained to protect the castle. Soon several British companies of the 3rd Division – particularly the Royal Northumberland Fusiliers led by Colonel Ridge,

---

* James McGrigor's extensive record of military service included the following locations: The Low Countries, Egypt, India, the West Indies, and the Iberian Peninsula. He is seen by many as the father of British army medicine.

** Dr. James McGrigor, *Autobiography and Services of Sir James McGrigor*, (London 1861), p. 273.

who were also equipped with ladders – managed to break through the French and successfully scale the walls, fighting their way to the castle. Colonel Ridge, who was the first to scale the ramparts of Badajoz around midnight, was killed by French fire, but the British troops soon seized control of the whole castle area, where they immediately hauled down the French Tricolour flying from its tower. As there was no British flag to be used, the composed Lieutenant MacPherson sent his own redcoat up the flagpole in its place. However, British forces soon found themselves isolated in the castle area as Philippon – who had now learned that the castle was in enemy hands – had all his French reserves sent into the streets surrounding the castle in an attempt to halt the British in the castle complex. However, along with the 3ʳᵈ Division now attacking Badajoz was General Leith's 5ᵗʰ Division, which was leading an assault with ladders (similarly to Picton's men) on the opposite side of the town against the northwest section of the ramparts, which was now only weakly defended. Thanks to this fact, the British quite quickly overcame the weak resistance of the defenders and soon swarmed into the town, where they attacked the rear of Philippon's troops guarding the breaches. It was shortly after midnight when it became clear to the defenders that their assailants had not only broken through into the castle but also into the streets of the town, which could only mean one thing: Badajoz had fallen.

The remaining French garrison then endeavoured to flee for their lives under Philippon's command toward the northern gate, crossing the Guadiana and barricading themselves in the San Cristobal redoubt, the same place where Philippon surrendered to Wellington on the following day. As this battle was a siege of a city rather than a field battle in which large armies stood against one another, the losses that the British incurred at Badajoz were truly appalling. The number of fallen and injured nearly equalled those the British had seen only in their largest field battles at Talavera and Albuera. During the Siege of Badajoz, approximately 4,000 British and 1,000 Portuguese were killed and wounded. The list of casualties included an incredible 62 fallen and 251 injured officers, including six generals.⁵⁰⁰ As for the French, their entire garrison of 4,000 was either killed or captured.

A stark testimony illustrating the harshness of the test the British soldiers were put to during the attack on the breaches at Badajoz was left behind in the memoirs of Sergeant Edward Costello of the 95ᵗʰ Rifles, who personally took part in the first attack against the breaches in the ranks of the Forlorn Hopes:

> For the second time I volunteered on the forlorn hope. After having received a double allowance of grog, we fell in about eight o'clock in the evening, 6th April 1812...Three of the men carrying the ladder with me, were shot dead in a breath, and its weight falling upon me, I fell backward with the grass-bag on my breast. The remainder of the stormers rushed up, regardless of my cries or those of the wounded men around me, for by this time our men were falling fast...Without rifle, sword, or any other weapon [Costello lost both his rifle and sword in his first attempt at entering the town], I succeeded in clambering up a part of the breach, and came near to a chevaux de frise consisting of a piece of heavy timber studded with sword-blades, turning on an axis: but just before reaching it I received a stroke on the breast, whether from a grenade or a stone, or by the butt-end of a musket, I cannot say, but down I rolled senseless... I could not have laid long in this plight, for when my senses had in some measure returned, I perceived our gallant fellows still rushing forward, each seeming to share a fate more deadly than my own. The fire continued in one horrible and incessant peal, as if the mouth of the infernal regions had opened to vomit forth destruction upon all around us... I now, for the first time for many years, uttered something like a prayer. After the horrible and well-known scene of carnage had lasted some time, the fire gradually slackened from the breach, and I heard a cheering which I knew to proceed from within the town, and shortly afterwards a cry of 'Blood and 'ounds! Where's the Light Division? – the town's our own – hurrah!'[501]

During the Siege of Badajoz, British and Portuguese soldiers undoubtedly displayed a tremendous amount of courage; after Badajoz had fallen, however, they ran amok for three days. Partly incited by the horrors they had experienced while laying siege to the town, soldiers rampaged through the streets of the town hellbent on vengeance and retribution. Both British and Portuguese troops took no prisoners and mercilessly slaughtered the injured; they sought their revenge on the local population*, plundering, raping, and drinking all the alcohol they could lay

---

*   It may be noted here that the majority of civilians that had not fled before the siege and remained in the city were mostly French sympathizers – a fact which, however, does not excuse British actions.

their hands upon. The "rampage" that ensued after the British took Ciudad Rodrigo was made up mostly of isolated atrocities committed by only a handful of the most unprincipled men of the individual regiments. However, nearly the whole army took part in the violence that was committed in the streets of Badajoz. The staff of officers managed to re-establish order among the frenzied soldiers only in the afternoon hours of the following day, partially with the aid of a gallows, which Wellington ordered to be built on the main square of the town. What took place during the Siege and following the capture of Badajoz is a stark reminder of just how brutal war can be both for combatants and civilians alike.

Although Wellington was enraged and horrified at the behaviour of his men, he did not have the heart to issue death sentences, especially in the light of what his soldiers suffered during their assault on the ramparts and the bravery that they displayed during the siege.

Ultimately, the gallows merely served a demonstrative purpose.[502] He did not however intend to let his troops off completely for what they had committed and thus many of the disorderly soldiers were sentenced to flogging. As it is always easier to write unflattering things about one's enemy than it is about one's ally, the whole situation was quite bravely described by Lieutenant William Grattan, one of the more upright of the British officers who with all their might attempted to calm the enraged army after taking the town:

> I feel as much pride as any man can feel in having taken a part in actions that must ever shed lustre upon my country, [at the Siege of Badajoz] but no false feeling of delicacy shall ever prevent me from speaking the truth – no matter whether it touches the conduct of one man or ten thousand!... the soldiers became reckless, and drank to such an excess, that no person's life, no matter of what rank, or station, or sex was safe...If they entered a house that had not been emptied of all its furniture or wine, they proceeded to destroy it, or, if it happened to be empty, which was generally the case, they commenced firing at the doors and windows, and not unfrequently at the inmates, or at each other!...The soldiers then fired upon their own comrades, and many men were killed, in endeavouring to carry away some species of plunder, by the hands of those who, but a few hours before, would have risked their own lives to protect those they now so wantonly sported with: then would they turn upon the already too deeply injured females, and tear from them the

trinkets that adorned their necks, fingers, or ears!...many men were flogged, but although the contrary has been said, none were hanged – yet hundreds deserved it.[503]

On the other hand, it should be noted that the British soldiers exhibited noble behaviour in other instances such as after the Battle of Fuentes de Oñoro, a fact which Wellington relayed to Prime Minister Lord Perceval in his request for financial aid for the inhabitants of the aforementioned village whose homes had been almost completely destroyed after the al-most two-day-long battle:

> I am very much obliged to you for your attention to my recommendation in favor of my friends, the Portuguese nation, who really deserve the gen-erosity of the people of England. My soldiers have continued to show them every kindness in their power, as well as to the Spaniards. The village of Fuentes de Oñoro, having been the field of battle the other day, and not having been much improved by this circumstance, they immediately and vol-untarily, subscribed to raise a sum of money to be given to the inhabitants as a compensation for the damage which their properties have sustained in the contest.[504]

It is highly probable that despite all the atrocities that the British sol-diers committed at Badajoz, Wellington did not hand down any death sentences as he himself was so shocked at the horrors of the siege, in which so many good soldiers, including a number of his friends, had died. The commanding general of the 3rd Division Thomas Picton (who was also injured during the attack) recalled how Wellington was wholly overpowered with emotion during a conversation they had shortly after conquering Badajoz.

> This is allowed to be the most brilliant achievement which has taken place in the Peninsula during the War, but it has been most dearly purchased by many valuable Lives: but military reputation is not to be purchased with-out blood, and ambition has nothing to do with Humanity. Yet our Chief [Wellington], when I waited upon him next morning shed as copious a tor-rent of Tears as any woman could have done on the occasion, and appeared most profoundly affected by our loss.[505]

STORMING OF BADAJOZ
6ᵗʰ April 1812

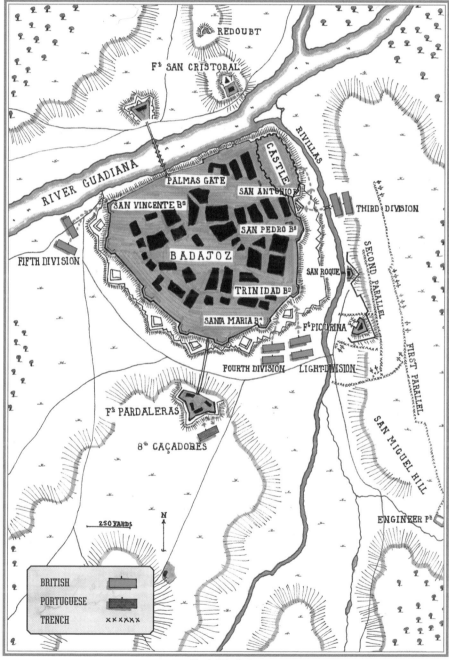

REDOUBT

Fᵗ SAN CRISTOBAL

RIVILLAS

CASTLE

RIVER GUADIANA

PALMAS GATE

SAN ANTONIO

SAN VINCENTE Bᵃ

SAN PEDRO Bᵃ

THIRD DIVISION

FIFTH DIVISION

BADAJOZ

SAN ROQUE

SECOND PARALLEL

TRINIDAD Bᵃ

SANTA MARIA Bᵃ

Fᵗ PICURINA

FIRST PARALLEL

FOURTH DIVISION

LIGHT DIVISION

Fᵗ PARDALERAS

SAN MIGUEL HILL

8ᵗʰ CAÇADORES

ENGINEER Pᵏ

250 YARDS

N

BRITISH	
PORTUGUESE	
TRENCH	×××××

—— *Map by John Fawkes* ——

Later at an advanced age, Wellington verified this event himself in a letter addressed to his good friend Mrs Harriet Arbuthnot:

> I assure you I actually could not help crying. I bit my lips, did everything I could to stop myself for I was ashamed he should see it, but I could not, he so little entered into my feelings that he said. 'Good God, what is the matter?'[506]

The regret that Wellington displayed after Badajoz clearly points to the high value that he placed on the lives of his men and on human life in general; he was strongly aware of its fragility in regard to the horrors that he so often faced. At the same time, this was not the first time Wellington was moved and disgusted by the horrors of war. Here we might recall the Battle of Assaye, where he first found himself overcome with emotion, although not to the same degree as after the Siege of Badajoz. This picture of an empathetic, sensitive Wellington, who 'shed tears as any woman could' is worlds away from the image of the cold and restrained man he is often portrayed to be. While fighting, in which the command of a whole army rested on his shoulders, he would find himself in a sort of "battle trance", allowing him to act with cold-blooded reactions when under enemy fire. After battle, however, he was often seized with regret over his injured and dead comrades. After recovering from these recent horrors, his dispatch to the British Government on conquering Badajoz read as follows:

> The capture of Badajoz affords as strong an instance of the gallantry of our troops as has ever been displayed. But I greatly hope that I shall never again be the instrument of putting them to such a test.[507]

Nonetheless, life is often full of surprises and, even during the unspeakable atrocities that accompanied the Siege of Badajoz, one rather remarkable story of romance, as if from a fairy tale, took place there. After the British entered the streets of the town, Captain Harry Smith (aged 24) – oblivious to the rich spoils and ever-present alcohol surrounding him – quite chivalrously took hold of a terrified Spanish girl, a certain Juana Maria de los Dolores de Leon, and put her under his protection (it should be noted, however, that he was protecting her and her elder sister from his own frenzied comrades-in-arms). Over the course of the next few days, Smith and the rescued girl fell deeply in love, whereupon the British gallant took the young Spanish maiden for his wife a few days later.[508]

While Wellington was conquering Ciudad Rodrigo and Badajoz, a significant change had taken place in Britain that threatened him and the whole British operation on the Iberian Peninsula. On 5th February 1811 the Parliament adopted the Regency Act, which established King George III's son – also named George – as Prince Regent due to King George's inability to carry out his royal obligations due to illness. It was known far and wide throughout Britain that the newly appointed Prince Regent, who was nicknamed 'Prinny' in British society for his extravagant, dissolute and bohemian lifestyle, flauntingly supported the Whigs throughout his life contrary to the favoured stance of his father. If the Whigs gained power in the British Parliament, they would almost certainly attempt to strike a peace deal with Napoleon, a fact which would lead to the irreversible withdrawal of Wellington's forces from the Iberian Peninsula. Nonetheless, the Regency Act was adopted for only one year, as George III had already gone into seclusion several times in the past due to his illness (he evidently suffered from porphyria*), but each time had managed to recover and retake control of government. In February 1812, however, it slowly became clear that George III would not be coming back to his duties anytime soon. Thus, his son's regency was soon prolonged for an indefinite period in the Parliament. The Whigs were now rubbing their hands in expectation, unashamed of their high ambitions and, among other things, hoped for a quick end to the whole war. The Tory Government of Spencer Perceval was shaken to its core and now rightfully felt endangered. To the great surprise of all, however, the Prince Regent did not carry out any profound changes and, quite to the contrary, befriended Perceval shortly after taking up royal office. In addition, he was euphoric about Wellington's success at Ciudad Rodrigo and Badajoz (although bought at a high price) and quite willingly granted Arthur Wellesley the title of Earl. Thanks to these events, Perceval's government and the newly ennobled Earl of Wellington could breathe a sigh of relief – at least for now.

---

* A metabolic disorder negatively affecting the central nervous system – George III is therefore often known for fits of "madness". The story of George III was, for instance, portrayed in the unforgettable British feature film *The Madness of King George* (1994), in which Nigel Hawthorne plays the ailing king while his wife, Queen Charlotte, is portrayed by Helen Mirren. The said film was directed by Nicolas Hytner and adapted from Alan Bennett's play: *The Madness of King George III*.

CHAPTER NINE

The Liberation of Spain: the Story of the "Western Front" of the Napoleonic Wars

The tense political situation had hardly calmed in Britain concerning the Regency Act, which established George Augustus Frederick, the oldest son of the British Monarch King George III, as Prince Regent for an indefinite period, when Arthur Wellesley received another shocking message: Prime Minister Lord Perceval had been assassinated at the beginning of May 1812. The Prime Minister's assassin was the merchant John Bellingham, whose business was on the verge of bankruptcy due to the Continental Blockade declared by Napoleon. Bellingham blamed the British Government for his misfortune and therefore sought his revenge on the Prime Minister. After his crime, the broken man did not resist arrest or attempt to flee from the scene. Lord Perceval thus became the first and hitherto only Prime Minister of Great Britain to be assassinated.

The Prince Regent in common with the majority of his subjects was disgusted by Perceval's assassination; thus, this contemptible act served to deepen the Regent's sympathies toward the Tories. After Perceval's murder, the Prince did not hesitate to name Lord Liverpool, who had so far held the office of Secretary of State for War and the Colonies, to the post of Prime Minister. In the Cabinet of the new government, Lord Castlereagh continued on in his post of Secretary of State for Foreign Affairs, which he had held since the beginning of 1812 when, after almost three years, he returned to government after his scandalous pistol duel with Lord Canning and replaced Wellington's brother Richard Wellesley (who in the meantime, to Wellington's dismay, had managed to discredit himself in the aforementioned scandal with courtesan Sally Dugles) at the Ministry of Foreign Affairs. The position of Minister for War, which was crucial to Wellington, was filled by Lord Bathurst in Liverpool's new administration.[509] Wellington also wanted Lord Canning to take part in government; Canning, however, persistently refused to sit together with the Foreign Minister in one cabinet after what had happened years prior between him and Castlereagh. Wellington remarked disappointedly on this fact by saying: "people's extravagant pretentions and vanity will ruin everything."[510]

At the time that these dramatic events were taking place in Britain, Napoleon found himself fully occupied with preparations for his campaign into Russia, for which he had gathered the largest army hitherto in history, which amounted to approximately 600,000 soldiers. The army contained not only Frenchmen, but other numerous regiments from Bonaparte's satellite states. In addition to the aforementioned Russian violation of the Continental Blockade against trade with Britain (which, for that matter, the Russians never wholly upheld in the first place) together with the collapse of Napoleon's marital aspirations of a union with Alexander's sister Anna Pavlovna, hostilities between Napoleon and Tsar Alexander I continued to escalate. This tension was caused primarily by the Tsar's fear that Bonaparte would attempt to annex the former Polish territory now belonging to Russia to the Warsaw Duchy that Napoleon had created. This would subsequently renew the Polish Kingdom to its previous historical dimensions at Russia's expense. Napoleon's support of Turkey against Russian ambitions in the Balkans was also a thorn in Tsar Alexander's side.[511]

However, it was Emperor Napoleon who decided to strike first. For the Russian campaign, Frenchmen made up only roughly one third of this formidable army. It also included Swiss from the Helvetic Republic and Poles from the Warsaw Duchy led by Marshal Poniatowski, while the

Austrians sent a contingent of 30,000 men to aid the French Emperor, as they were now among the ranks of Napoleon's allies, an alliance which had recently been sealed by Napoleon's marriage to the Austrian Archduchess, Marie Louise. Bonaparte marched towards Moscow on 24th June 1812, also withdrawing a portion of his units from Spain to aid in his Russian campaign.[512] Wellington, who at the time was extremely experienced in the area of military supply provision, held a rather pessimistic outlook for the French Emperor and his men in Russia despite their indisputable advantage and number of soldiers, as it would be crucial to supply them properly in regard to the great distances between strategic points on Russian territory: 'If the Emperor of Russia had any resources and is prudent, and his Russians will really fight, Buonaparte will not succeed.'[513] Wellington wrote on 25th July 1812 to the new Minister for War Lord Bathurst.

Despite this fact, roughly 230,000 Frenchmen remained on the Iberian Peninsula, which still constituted a significant advantage against Wellington's Anglo-Portuguese Army of now less than 65,000 men. Nonetheless, these French forces, who had been divided south of the Pyrenees into five armies, were distributed across all of Spain in an attempt to counter the guerrillas and the scattered remnants of the Spanish Army, which the French had still not managed to quell (for example, the Spanish still held the city of Cádiz). Thanks to the occupation of Ciudad Rodrigo and Badajoz, Wellington's rear was for the moment covered by the open exit route into Portugal, by which he could in a worst-case scenario retreat behind the Lines of Torres Vedras, which were still undergoing improvements over the course of 1812. Once Wellington had both these border cities firmly under his control, he immediately decided to take the initiative and attack the French directly in Spain.

In the proximity to the Spanish-Portuguese border were two strong French armies: Soult's army in the south and Marmont's in the north. As Marmont had already threatened to lay siege to Ciudad Rodrigo during Wellington's siege of Badajoz, Wellington did not take long to issue an order to march north toward Marmont. To be on the safe side, he left 14,000 men under the command of 'Daddy' Hill, who had occupied the ford across the Tagus near the Spanish town of Alcántara and were now tasked with preventing Soult's potential attempt to join up with Marmont. Simultaneously, Wellington devised a plan with the remaining Spanish generals and guerrilla representatives that he managed to contact via his exploring officers and their intermediaries from the ranks of Spanish civilians to heighten their operations across all of Spain during Wellesley's campaign and engage the other French forces as much as possible. These units, or *"los guerrilleros"*, who several years previously had begun merely as poorly organized bands of farmers, gradually began to gain a better reputation in their struggle against the French. During the on-going war, more and more men and women of all social classes continued to join them; thus the ranks of these "irregular units" not only included educated clergymen and former soldiers of the regular Spanish Army, but also noblemen who had often lost their properties during the war. Thanks to this fact, an amazing total of 38,520 *"guerrilleros"* operated in Spain in 1812 and were divided into 22 groups with their own chiefs and territories in which the given troops were deployed.[514] Thus, in terms of the sheer number of fighters and the quality of troop organization from the onset of war, the Spanish guerrilla movement had now evidently reached its peak. Although scattered throughout the kingdom, these roughly 40,000 soldiers were now certainly able to "light a fire" under the French, which was to play a key role in the success of Wellington's subsequent campaign.

Two diversionary actions aimed at preventing Marmont from receiving reinforcements from the other French troops were then carried out directly on the initiative of the Royal Navy. First, several battalions of British marines landing in the north of Spain, establishing contact with the local guerrilla forces there and subsequently carrying out regular attacks on French supply divisions. The second landing of British troops soon followed on the eastern coast of Spain and, although it was less successful than the one to the north, as the British were crushed there at the town of Alicante, it met its purpose in managing to capture the full attention of Marshal Suchet's troops.[515]

After these preparations, Wellington withdrew on 13th July in the command of 50,000 men against Marmont. The French Marshal, who had roughly the same amount of men at his command, retreated from the advancing British toward the famous Spanish university town of Salamanca. Only four days later, Wellington entered the town virtually unchallenged and was welcomed by the jubilant citizens, who like the Portuguese, welcomed the British as liberators. In the streets of the city, Wellington also met in person with the head of his network of spies from the ranks of civilians on the Iberian Peninsula, an old Irishman named

Dr Patrick Curtis, who worked as a professor at the Irish College of the local and renowned university. Reverend Curtis had long been providing Wellington with crucial information on the French with the help of his agents among the peasants and priests scattered throughout the country. Within his Intelligence Department, Wellington had suffered a considerable loss several months earlier. In mid-April 1812, Marmont's patrol had captured Major Colquhoun Grant, an ace among Wellington's exploring officers who had been collecting information for him before his campaign against Marmont. Grant even managed to infiltrate Marmont's camp and carefully note all information on the army there. He subsequently set off with lightning speed back to Wellington and managed to give him a report before the Siege of Badajoz, which stated that he still had some time before Marmont would be able to attack Ciudad de Rodrigo and could therefore continue in his siege of Badajoz. He was to do so with haste, however, as Marmont was on the advance. As soon as Grant passed this report on to his commander, he immediately set off again into action and continued to monitor the movements of Marmont's troops. However, this was a mission from which 'Granto Bueno' would not return. Marmont's dragoons managed to capture him nearby the Portuguese-Spanish border, where he attempted to hide in a tree top with his Spanish guide Leon. When the French caught the two, they found on them detailed and carefully processed notes on the numbers of Marmont's soldiers and cannons, and the movements of his army. The poor Leon was executed mercilessly on the spot as a spy, while Grant escaped certain death for espionage thanks to his British Army officer's uniform, after which he was escorted to Salamanca and thrown into jail.[516] Marmont then invited Grant to dinner in the city, during which he perhaps rather naively attempted to extort information from him on Wellington's plans. Not surprisingly, however, the French Marshal left dinner rather disappointed, as not a single bit of information that could have been of some value to Marmont had slipped from Grant's lips. The following day, Grant – who was closely guarded and had not been treated very kindly hitherto – gave to Marmont his parole, which in his case was a promise according to his deal with Marmont that he would not escape until he was traded for another captured French officer of the same rank. Why did 'Granto Bueno' decide to do so? He most likely did so because he saw his escape as unrealistic at the given moment; at the same time, however, he knew that if he gave his parole, he would not be guarded so unforgivingly and, with a bit of luck, would perhaps be able to continue to send Wellington messages from captivity. Wellington was well aware of the fact that the capture of his best exploring officer and his word of honour not to escape spelled disaster. Despite all odds and with the help of Patrick Curtis, who managed to reach the prisoner under the pretext of providing religious services, he managed to continue to provide information on the enemy during his imprisonment in Salamanca. After Wellington learned of Grant's capture, he told the head of his medical department Dr. James McGrigor, who was related to Grant, that this "James Bond of the Peninsular War" was still sending him valuable information on the French:[517] "I wish he had not given his parole, for I had promised large rewards to the Guerrilla chiefs if they could bring him back [...] what think you of him, at this moment, when a prisoner, sending me information?" McGrigor, who was clearly worried about his brother-in-law, answered with the question: "But I thought, sir, that you had arranged for his exchange?" to which Wellington replied: "So I had, and here is Marmont's answer,"[518] he said and let McGrigor read Marmont's letter, which overflowed with words of politeness, in which the French Marshal solemnly swore that he would naturally exchange Grant immediately for a French officer as was custom. As soon as McGrigor finished reading, however, Wellington handed him a second document, a copy of the French newspaper *Moniteur*. Marmont's dispatch had been printed in the newspaper, in which the Marshal quite clearly bragged of Grant's capture, stating that he 'is a most dangerous fellow of whom I shall not lose sight till he is safe in France'[519]. Curiously enough and certainly only by "remarkable coincidence", Marmont's dispatch in the *Moniteur* carried the same date as the letter in which the French Marshal boldly promised Grant's exchange. In reality, however, it was clear that the French would never voluntarily release this feared exploring officer. Long before Wellington arrived at Salamanca with his army, 'Granto Bueno' was thus handed over to a heavy escort that took him to the city of Bayonne in southeast France where he would be handled by the police agents of Joseph Fouché (the head of Napoleon's police department), where there was no threat that he would be freed by Wellington's feared allies, the hated *"los guerrilleros"*.[520] Therefore, Wellington was forced at least for the time being to come to terms with losing Grant and focus completely on dealing with

Marmont's troops in Salamanca. In order to liberate the city completely, the British still needed to capture three convents in the old section of the town, where Marmont had placed French garrisons, turning them into *de facto* small fortresses. Nonetheless, Wellington's men managed to take the convents, thanks to which the whole town came under British control at the end of June. Wellington and his army subsequently continued south from Salamanca toward Marmont's troops.

Over the course of the coming days, Wellington and Marmont manoeuvred their respective armies, which were led in close proximity of several kilometres to one another. With the exception of isolated clashes, however, neither side dared to attack their opponent with full force in regard to their given positions. Both commanders thus bided their time like two boxers, one waiting for the other to make a false move that would allow for a knockout blow. This was a highly trying time for Wellesley and his men, as the summer temperatures soared, while at night they dropped so low that soldiers were forced to dig up graves in cemeteries in order to try and find enough wood for fires. During this tense situation, when a single mistake could spell complete disaster for either army, Wellington complained of overall exhaustion for perhaps the first time in his life. He slept roughly four hours a day for a whole fortnight and was otherwise constantly on his feet or, to be more exact, in the saddle.[521] Once again, he did his best to personally supervise all operations, and his officer corps, who were well aware of the gravity of the situation, now also requested that he be present along the whole line of the British position.

Wellington described all of this in a letter to his brother William: 'I was never so fagged. My Gallant Officers will kill me... If I detach one of them, he is not satisfied unless I go to him, or send the whole Army, and I am obliged to superintend every operation of the troops.'[522] Later, he also spoke of the officer corps in a similar manner: 'They are really heroes when I am on the spot to direct them, but when I am obliged to quit them they are children.'[523] Thus Wellington caught up on his sleep only at moments when he believed nothing could go wrong, with occasional naps wherever and whenever possible. For instance, during the tiresome manoeuvring around Salamanca, he decided to lie down under a nearby tree. Before he did so, however, he gave the following order to his aide-de-camp, a young FitzRoy Somerset (whom Wellesley did not consider to be an especially talented soldier but appreciated the honesty and carefulness with which he carried out his duties): "Watch the French through your glass, FitzRoy...When they reach that copse near the gap in the hill, wake me."[524]

The two opposing armies often found themselves so close to one another in the hilly terrain south of Salamanca that small skirmishes were inevitable – these mostly took place between light infantry units and dragoons. Wellington himself also became caught up in one of these skirmishes similarly to the Battle of Talavera, when he and his staff clashed with French dragoons close to the Guarena stream. Wellington, for whom riding was not merely a necessity but also a form of entertainment and relaxation, was equipped with the best horses possible and intended to use this to his advantage in the skirmish. He drew his sabre and is quite likely to have exchanged several blows with the enemy himself in this unexpected clash before riding off at full speed toward his lines with a smile upon his face.[525] He was surely aware of the fact that his capture would likely spell catastrophe for the allies but, thanks to the qualities of his horse and his horsemanship, he knew no one was likely to catch up with him. He ultimately rode off quicker than even his own staff could, as Lieutenant James Cooke from the 43rd Infantry Regiment, who was evidently captivated by the whole event, noted in his memoirs:

> The Earl of Wellington was in the thick of it, and escaped with difficulty. His straight sword drawn, he also crossed the ford [i.e. across the Guarena] at full speed, smiling. I did not see his lordship when the charge first took place. When he passed us, he had none of his staff near him, he was quite alone, with a ravine in his rear.[526]

Wellington recalled in retrospect that situations such as these during the Peninsular War were by no means unique in regard to his frequent manoeuvres in the saddle to visit his allies and officers or to analyse enemy positions, during which he often spotted the French light-infantry reconnaissance divisions only "at the eleventh hour": 'Although I had the family eye of a hawk, I have frequently been within an ace of being taken, and have more than once been obliged to take to my 'scrapers'...'[527]

Several days after this small-scale skirmish, both opponents continued on in their seemingly endless manoeuvring. The landscape south of Salamanca where both armies were now situated was dominated by two hills – Arapil Chico and Arapil Grande (i.e. Lesser and Greater Arapil), which situated opposite one another and formed the two strategic points in the given area. During the early hours of 22nd July 1812 both armies formed an almost right-angle position. British forces were spread out toward the north and east of Arapil Chico, which formed the corner point of their position, while Marmont's troops, who faced Wellington's, basically mirrored the British right-angle position; in the French case, however, the corner point of the shift in their line was formed by Arapil Grande. Around noon, Wellington was positioned at a farm in the small village of Los Arapiles situated east of Arapil Chico. It seemed that nothing out of the ordinary would happen that day, and both competing armies and their commanders would continue to try to find a gap in their enemy's position.[528]

At that moment Wellington, who had paused for lunch but could not sit still to eat his meal, walked into the farmyard and directed his telescope at the French in order to survey Marmont's position. Suddenly, he espied the fault in the French position that he had so earnestly hoped for. General Thomières had advanced on the left wing of the French Army too far east, creating a huge gap between his division and the neighbouring division of General Maucune. In addition, Maucune's division, which was made up of the rest of the French left wing, was quite dangerously distant from the French centre. At this moment, Wellington had the unique chance to attempt to destroy Thomières' division and subsequently crush the remainder of the French left wing and finally Marmont's whole army.[529] In retrospect, he recalled the whole event, which preceded the Battle of Salamanca, in the following:

> I got up… and was looking over a wall round the farm-yard…and I saw the movement of the French left through my glass. By God said I, that will do, and I'll attack them directly.[530]

As soon as Wellington saw his chance, he immediately jumped into the saddle and tore off toward the 3rd British Division that was situated on his direct orders far to the east where it was ready to attempt an outflanking manoeuvre on Marmont's left wing, which was now finally possible. A new commander had been put in charge of the 3rd Division – Edward Pakenham, a brother of Wellington's wife Kitty. Contrary to Kitty's oldest brother Thomas, who years before had refused and humiliated Arthur,

Wellington was good friends with Edward Pakenham, whom he frequently addressed as "Ned". Pakenham had replaced Thomas Picton, who suffered a seemingly minor injury at Badajoz that had since worsened to such a degree that he decided to sail back to England in order to recuperate. According to Wellington's plan, Pakenham's 3rd Division was to advance from the east directly against Thomières and attack his flank. Concurrently to Pakenham's attack, Wellington planned to send Lowry Cole's 4th Division and General Leith's 5th Division, which would lead a frontal attack on the French from the north. Wellington left the 6th and 7th Divisions as reserves near the village of Los Arapiles.[531] Thus roughly two thirds of Wellington's whole army prepared to attack the French's excessively outstretched left wing, which was to be attacked from two cardinal directions thanks to Pakenham's outflanking manoeuvre.

Arthur galloped off toward the 3rd Division and issued Edward Pakenham the order to attack: "Ned, d'ye see those fellows on the hill?" he said, pointing to Thomières' division. After receiving an affirmative from Pakenham, he continued: "Throw your division into column, at them! and drive them to the devil.", to which Pakenham replied: "I will my Lord..."[532] Wellington then wished his brother-in-law much luck in battle and both men rather ceremoniously shook hands.[533]

When Pakenham's division suddenly appeared east of Thomières' men, the French were taken utterly by surprise. Thanks to the hilly terrain, they finally spotted the attacking British when they were only roughly five hundred metres away. In addition, Thomières' division was now being attacked by the Portuguese cavalry, with another two British infantry Divisions (4th and 5th) close behind them also advancing toward the French. At the head of Pakenham's troops was the commander of the whole brigade, Lieutenant-Colonel Wallace from the Connaught Rangers Regiment. Wallace's men fired a salvo and, followed by the whole division, immediately rushed the French with fixed bayonets. After suffering heavy losses, the French began to retreat toward their centre, which was located in Arapil Grande.

Perhaps for the first time, Wellington at Salamanca now possessed a sufficiently large cavalry, as over the course of 1811 he was joined by

---

* Le Marchant was instrumental in founding the first British military college, one of the forerunners of the world-renowned Royal Military Academy Sandhurst.

a brigade of heavy dragoons led by Major-General John Le Marchant*and a brigade of heavy cavalry of the King's German Legion, who were predominantly from Hanover. At this moment, Le Marchant's carried out the most effective attack of the whole Peninsular War. The one thousand bare and shining sabres of Le Marchant's dragoons reflected the rays of the afternoon sun, which was fortunately behind the British and blinded their enemy during the attack. In light of the extremely dry summer weather, their horses' hooves drove massive clouds of dust into the air, which also made accurate fire more difficult for the French. Le Marchant could not have asked for better conditions for his cavalry attack, and his heavy dragoons quickly charged at full speed into the already heavily strained and partially disrupted French ranks on the left wing, upon which they quite literally hacked Thomières' retreating divisions to pieces and subsequently split up the majority of Maucune's men who had hurried to aid the desperate Thomières. The destructive power of Le Marchant's dragoons is best evidenced by the fact that, from one of Maucune's brigades, only forty-seven men survived (out of roughly one thousand).[534] Le Marchant's determination and consummate professionalism played a pivotal role in contributing to the allied triumph at Salamanca, yet this battle was to be his last, for as he and his dragoons pressed home their advantage against the French infantry he was shot and killed.

The French left wing was thus completely crushed. The whole slaughter lasted less than forty minutes. Marshal Marmont also happened to be struck by British shrapnel while checking on his men's positions at Arapil Grande. His injuries were serious and thus command had to be passed on to his second-in-command, General Bonnet, who intended to resolve the precarious situation in which the French had found themselves. Wellington's triumphant forces had begun to put pressure on Bonnet's centre from the area of the French left wing. In the ensuing battle, General Bonnet himself also suffered a serious injury, due to which he was forced to pass on command of the French Army several hours later to the third in command: General Clauzel. It was clear to Clauzel that the French left wing had been completely crushed and therefore attempted to attack Wellington's position at Arapil Chico with the last of his reserves, in a desperate attempt to divert Wellesley's attention away from his own beleaguered centre. The British found themselves in grave danger at Arapil Chico, and therefore Wellington ordered his 6th Division, which was prepared and waiting in reserve, to attack Clauzel. Thanks to their attack, Clauzel's attempt at a counterattack at Arapil Chico was quickly repelled, definitively bringing the battle to an end as the men at Clauzel's centre soon began to flee.

The French under Clauzel's command subsequently fled west. Clauzel attempted to rescue the remainder of his army by fleeing across the bridge over the River Tormes, upon which he ordered General Ferey's division, which was now one of the last battle-capable French units on the French right wing, to cover the retreat of the remainder of the French Army toward the said bridge. Ferey was killed while carrying out his task, but his bravely fighting divisions persevered until darkness gradually enveloped the battlefield. Despite the remarkable bravery of Ferey's men, Wellington's triumph could have been even more devastating to the French had Spanish General Carlos d'Espagne not retreated "to safety" with his troops in fear that Wellington had been defeated, as he and his troops had been tasked with guarding the crucial bridge located in the village of Alba de Tormes. Somewhat similarly to the debacle of Masséna's retreat at Almeida, the bridge was thus left unguarded, allowing Clauzel successfully to retreat from battle with his surviving troops.[535]

According to General Edward Pakenham's testimony, Wellington was once again ever-present in directing the battle, but often took dangerous risks while doing so: 'Our Chief was everywhere and sadly exposed himself – in his preservation our little prayers were heard most surely.'[536] These prayers were surely in order, as Wellesley was struck by a bullet in the side while organising the pursuit of the fleeing French Army. Fortunately, just as several times in the past, it was "only" a ricochet and Wellington was again miraculously unharmed.

Lieutenant William recalled Wellington's fearless behaviour at the battle of Salamanca in a manner to similar to that of Ned Pakenham: 'The Duke of Wellington was within fifty yards of the front, when the enemy's lines commenced firing. I though he was exposing himself unnecessarily, the more so, as I heard he had put every division into action that day.'[537]

However, in response to claims that he was taking excessively high risks, Wellington in his defence told the officer corps the following: 'I assure you, it is not the case, but there are situations you know, and Salamanca is one, where a commander in chief must show himself and act in person.'[538] Several months after the Battle of Salamanca, he also told the following to Judge-Advocate Frances Larpent:

> When I come myself, the soldiers think what they have to do the most impor-
> tant, since I am there, and that all will depend on their exertions. Of course,
> these are increased in proportion, and they will do for me what perhaps no
> one else can make them do.[539]

Despite Wellington's desire to have everything under control, he was not able to prevent Clauzel's retreat, a fact which disappointed him despite the great success he had just achieved, as he wrote in a letter addressed to General Graham, his newly appointed second-in-command: "If I had known there was no garrison at Alba [Alba de Tormes], I should have marched there, and probably had the whole."[540] Despite his slight disappointment, he wrote of Marmont's defeat in a letter: "I never saw an Army get such a beating in so short a time."[541] Although the remaining French had managed to escape for their lives during the night, Wellington's victory was a phenomenal one and was his greatest triumph in a field battle to date. Marmont had lost roughly 14,000 men, which meant roughly a fourth of his army, while the allied losses were roughly 5,000 fallen and injured. In the present situation, in which the Portuguese Army was fully trained and scores of reinforcements had arrived from the British Isles, this number of fallen men was a far less serious problem for Wellington than three years ago at Talavera.[542] His brilliantly prepared attack at Salamanca, which brought him fame throughout Europe, also best refutes the myth that Wellesley was a defensive general. Among those who paid tribute to his victory at Salamanca was Wellington's rival and direct participant in the battle, French General Maximilien Sébastien Foy:

> The battle of Salamanca is the most masterly in its management, the most
> considerable in the number of troops engaged, and the most important in
> results of all the victories that the English have gained in these latter days. It
> raises Lord Wellington almost to the level of Marlborough. Hitherto we had
> been aware of his prudence, his eye for choosing a position, and his skill in
> utilizing it. At Salamanca he has shown himself a great and able master of
> manoeuvres. He kept his dispositions concealed for almost the whole day:
> he waited till we were committed to our movement before he developed his

own: he played a safe game: he fought in the oblique order [i.e. the aforementioned, almost right-angle positioning of both armies] – it was a battle in the style of Frederic the Great.*

It is perhaps no surprise that Britain was overcome with enthusiasm after the glorious triumph at Salamanca. All of London arose to cheer for Wellington. The Prince Regent rewarded Arthur Wellesley with the title of Marquess of Wellington together with a reward of 100,000 pounds given to him from state coffers. Contrary to Wellington's previous victories, no one now questioned the sum awarded to him. There were even suggestions in Westminster that the reward was not high enough in the light of the benefits that his victory had for the whole of Europe. One of the best examples of the celebratory statements made in Britain about Wellington's triumph at Salamanca was made by the Prime Minister Lord Liverpool:

> the most decided as well as brilliant victory which has for centuries crowned the British arms, and which, whilst it reflects the highest lustre upon every individual who was engaged in it, redounds so peculiarly to the credit of the Commander, by whose foresight, decision and science those operations were conducted which have led to a result of such incalculable importance.[543]

The citizens of the picturesque university town of Salamanca also expressed a similar euphoria when they made the following declaration, of which the clearly amused Arthur Wellesley did not hesitate to inform his brother William in a letter:

> The people of Salamanca swear my Mother is a Saint, & the daughter of a Saint, to which circumstance I owe all my good fortune!! Pray tell her this The Marhattas discovered that she was a Marhatta![544]

---

*　Oman, *A History of the Peninsular War, vol. V*, pp., pp. 472–473. By Frederic the Great, Foy meant Prussian King Frederick II, who was renowned for his military artistry and the fact that he often led his divisions personally into battle. He distinguished himself in the War of the Austrian Succession (also known as the Silesian Wars) from 1740 to 1748 against the Habsburg Monarchy under the rule of Maria Theresa, during which he stripped the Empress of most of Silesia. He then further distinguished himself in the Seven Years' War in which his greatest achievements included victory over the French at Rossbach in 1759. In the Battle of Kolín in 1757, in which Frederick II was defeated by Austrian Marshal Leopold Daun, by which Daun *de facto* prevented Prague from falling into Prussian hands, the Prussian King spoke the famous sentence to his grenadiers, who continually failed to break through Daun's positions: *"Dogs, do you want to live forever?!"* According to eye witnesses, Frederick II went personally into battle, whereupon the soldiers standing around him were forced to hold him back.

BATTLE OF SALAMANCA
22nd July 1812

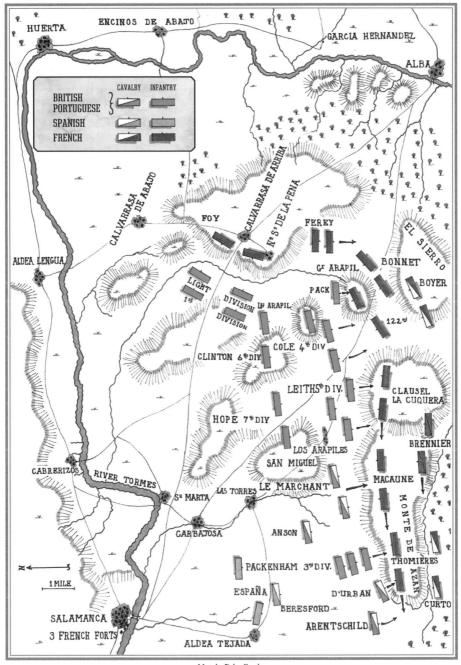

	CAVALRY	INFANTRY
BRITISH PORTUGUESE		
SPANISH		
FRENCH		

HUERTA

ENCINOS DE ABAJO

GARCIA HERNANDEZ

ALBA

CALVARRASA DE ABAJO

CALVARRASA DE ARRIBA

FOY

Nª Sª DE LA PENA

FEREY

EL SIERRO

ALDEA LENGUA

LIGHT 1st

DIVISION

DIVISION

Gª ARAPIL

PACK

BONNET

BOYER

122ª

Iª ARAPIL

CLINTON 6th DIV.

COLE 4th DIV.

LEITHS 5th DIV.

CLAUSEL
LA CUQUERA

HOPE 7th DIV.

BRENNIER

CABRERIZOS

RIVER TORMES

Sª MARTA

LAS TORRES

LOS ARAPILES

SAN MIGUEL

LE MARCHANT

MACAUNE

LE MARCHANT

MONTE DE AZAN

CARBAJOSA

ANSON

N

1 MILE

PACKENHAM 3rd DIV.

THOMIERES

D'URBAN

CURTO

ESPAÑA

BERESFORD

ARENTSCHILD

SALAMANCA
3 FRENCH FORTS

ALDEA TEJADA

— *Map by John Fawkes* —

However, the most important advantage of the victory at Salamanca lay in the fact that Wellington did not have to resort to a strategic retreat back into Portugal. On the contrary, he now had the unique opportunity to continue on in his successful offensive, as the defeat of Marmont's army had opened the path to Madrid, which at the moment was only two hundred kilometres away and surprisingly poorly defended. Wellington did not intend to let this opportunity pass him by and immediately marched toward the Spanish capital. The French Emperor, who was in the middle of his ambitious Russian campaign, was quite alarmed when the news of Marmont's defeat at Salamanca reached him. French Colonel Marcelin Marbot, who had now abandoned the Iberian Peninsula in order to accompany Bonaparte on the march towards Moscow, described Napoleon's reaction:

> Napoleon stayed three days at Mojaisk [in English Mozhaysk, a Russian town located approximately 70 miles from Moscow] to await despatches. One which had come the day before battle [a clash between French and Russian cavalries at Mozhaysk] had done much to cause his indisposition, for it announced the defeat of Marshal Marmont at Salamanca. Marmont was one of Napoleon's mistakes...When he replaced Masséna in 1811 he gave out that he was going to beat Wellington. He was now vanquished and wounded... This catastrophe might have made the Emperor reflect that while he was invading Russia, he was losing Spain.[545]

With the remainder of Marmont's army, which was crushed and incapable of battle, Clauzel retreated quickly to the northwest and thus ceased in any way to be an equal rival to Wellington. In addition, Wellesley's heavy dragoons of the King's German Legion had caught up with the rear guard during Clauzel's retreat at the town of García Hernándéz, where they slaughtered roughly 1,000 Frenchmen while they themselves suffered only minor losses, striking another devastating blow to the French. The other French armies in Spain at the time were not capable of protecting Madrid and Napoleon's brother Joseph Bonaparte, called the 'Intrusive King'[546] by Spanish patriots, was soon forced to hastily abandon the capital in fear of the advancing British.

Wellington triumphantly entered Madrid on 12th August 1812 and the city was immediately alive with exulted cheers and endless celebrations.

The people of Madrid flooded the streets; wine flowed like water along with dancing and singing. Everywhere there could be heard cheers of *"Viva Wellington!"*[547] Wellington, evidently moved, described the exuberant welcome that he was given by the citizens of Madrid in the following:

> I am among a people mad with joy for their deliverance from their oppressors. God send that my good fortune may continue, and that I may be the instrument of securing their independence and happiness.[548]

In addition, one of the most famous artists of the era of Romanticism, Spanish painter Francisco Goya, painted Wellington's portrait in Madrid. The famous portrait painter depicted Arthur Wellesley sitting on his horse and dressed in a dark blue Spanish riding coat. When the work was later subjected to a detailed x-ray analysis in the 20th century, an interesting and also rather curious fact was revealed – Goya had painted Wellington over the original portrait of Joseph Bonaparte, who Arthur Wellesley had driven from the city, a fact that certainly carried symbolic meaning (See Image X).[549] In the author's opinion, the next portrait of Wellington that Goya produced is one of the most impressive of all the existing portraits of Arthur Wellesley. This is thanks to the fact that it was painted just after Wellington had left the fray of Salamanca. Goya spotted the exhausted Wellesley shortly after the battle walking directly down the path to the military camp and used charcoal to sketch Wellington's appearance at the moment.* Wellington's tired face, painted with almost unnaturally wide, sunken eyes and bordered by his drooping hair, which is wet from perspiration and sticking to his forehead, clearly shows the stress of the recent but highly successful battle. Goya's spontaneous sketch made after the battle is also unique in that it was used for the subsequent oil painting, and thus today we can compare the differences between both works of art (See Images VIII and IX).

---

*   Jane Wellesley, *A Journey Through My Family*, p. 190. On the other hand, according to Charles Wellesley, 9th Duke of Wellington, this story about Goya's sketch is probably not true: *'While Wellington was still in Madrid, or in the months following, Goya made a very detailed red chalk drawing, seemingly in preparation for an engraving, which shows Wellington anxious and concerned. Fifty years later Goya's grandson suggested that it had been done on the night following the Battle of Salamanca, and this came to be the accepted view, which, however, almost certainly cannot be true. Goya would not have been so close to the hostilities, and it would have been difficult for him to create such a detailed drawing away from his studio.'* Charles Wellesley, Wellington, 9th Duke of, *Wellington portrayed*, op. cit., p. 38.

In the meantime, General Rowland Hill had managed to reach Madrid with reinforcements, whereupon Wellington marched his 35,000 men north where he continued to pursue Clauzel. Wellington tasked 'Daddy' Hill with the defence of the Spanish capital and left him 30,000 men of the Anglo-Portuguese Army (including his best divisions: the Light and 3rd Divisions) together with 10,000 Spaniards.[550] During his campaign to the north of Spain, Wellington decided to occupy the strategically important town of Burgos, which had a significant French garrison (2,000 men) and a firmly fortified castle on the hill of San Miguel that loomed over the centre of town. The sturdy donjon of the castle surrounded by a double ring of massive ramparts made Burgos Castle a highly troublesome barrier. Wellington's greatest difficulty lay in the fact that he had only three heavy eighteen-pound cannons available to take Burgos and this was agonizingly insufficient to create useable breaches in the walls. Wellington laid siege to Burgos on 19th September, but due to a lack of heavy artillery, decided to carry out several escalades on the castle using only scaling ladders, which had worked for him several times in the past. After great effort the attackers managed to gain control of the outer zone of the ramparts, but failed repeatedly to penetrate the inner defensive wall, no less the donjon itself, and were continually and mercilessly repelled.

The weather also notably worsened at the beginning of October, with harsh autumn rains signalling that winter was on its way. In addition, one of Wellington's favourite intelligence officers and good friend, Major Edward Cocks, was killed during one of the attacks on the castle for which he volunteered. This young man embodied all the traits that Wellington, in all his perfectionism and idealism, so strongly required of his officers and traits which, to his dismay, they often wholly lacked. Cocks was intelligent, brave, persistently optimistic, careful in fulfilling his tasks, and could orient himself excellently in the terrain, thanks to which he often carried out reconnaissance services. Wellington bore the weight of his death quite heavily. A member of his staff, Frederick Ponsonby, remembered his meeting with Arthur Wellesley a day after Cocks' death, in which the disconsolate Wellington could only let out one sentence: "Cocks was killed last night"*. He then proceeded to leave Ponsonby's tent without further comment. Wellington looked so heavy-hearted at Cocks' funeral that no one dared speak to him for the entire course of the service. After roughly

ATTACK ON BURGOS
19ᵗʰ September – 25ᵗʰ October 1812

— *Map by John Fawkes* —

five weeks of almost completely futile siege on Burgos, Wellington aborted the whole mission and withdrew his troops back to Madrid.[551]

The unsuccessful Siege of Burgos is often rightfully dubbed the greatest setback in Arthur Wellesley's whole military career. The failure to conquer the town is most often attributed (e.g. by Holmes and Longford) primarily to Wellington's inability to ensure a sufficient amount of heavy cannons and the fear of carrying out a more concentrated attack on the castle, albeit this time only with ladders, as Wellesley refused to risk another Badajoz. The primary reason that Wellington retreated, however, was the fact that General Hill was now in grave danger in Madrid, as a united army led by Marshal Soult and Joseph Bonaparte, who had managed in a joint effort to gather over 45,000 men, was now advancing towards the Spanish capital. Wellington wrote the following lines to Mr Cook, the aide-de-camp to the War Minister Lord Bathurst:

> I have raised the siege of Burgos and retired, not because there was any pressure upon me, but because I did not think Hill secure, and I knew that if he was obliged to retire, I should be lost.[552]

Why would Wellington have been lost if Hill was defeated? He soon learned that General Clauzel had received reinforcements in the north and prepared a reorganised army of 45,000 men against Wellington's 35,000.

> I ought to have succeeded at Burgos early in October, and then how should I have stood? I might have driven the Army of Portugal [i.e. the name for the French Army that was now retreating from Wellington under the command of General Clauzel], whose reinforcements were not then organised beyond the Ebro, and I might have left there or at Burgos an army of 20 000, English and Portuguese...and from 12,000 to 16,000 Spaniards, against what turned out to be 45,000 French[553]

---

*   Holmes, *Wellington: The Iron Duke*, op. cit. 171. Wellington wrote the following lines concerning Cocks' death to War Minister Lord Bathurst: *"We had the misfortune to lose the Hon. Major Cocks..., who was field officer of the trenches,* (at the Siege of Burgos) *and was killed in the act of rallying the troops who have been driven in. I have frequently had the occasion to draw your Lordship's attention to the conduct of Major Cocks, and in one instance very recently in the attack on the horn-work* (a part of the bastion system of fortifications) *of the castle of Burgos and I consider his loss one of the greatest importance to this Army and His Majesty's service."* See: Wellington, 2nd Duke of (ed.), *Supp. Desp., vol. VII*, p. 441.

,he continued on in the letter to Cook. If Hill was defeated at Madrid by Joseph Bonaparte's army, Wellington would thus find himself trapped in the north between Clauzel and Joseph Bonaparte. His original plan for the whole Burgos campaign also depended to a large degree on Spanish General Francisco Ballesteros, whose task it was to prevent this dangerous unification of Soult and Bonaparte's forces. Ballesteros failed to do so, a fact that absolutely infuriated Wellington. His comment addressed to Ballesteros may have also been influenced by the lasting resentment Wellington held towards the Spanish for Questa's failure at Talavera and the abandonment of the bridge over the River Tormes after the battle of Salamanca by the Spanish garrison, which was ordered to defend it, and was also likely intensified by his momentary rage:

> Had I any reason to expect that it [Ballesteros' role in the campaign] would be well played? Certainly not. I have never yet known the Spaniards do anything, much less do anything well.[554]

This comment is of course rather sharp in the light of the fact that Wellington owed much to the Spanish troops and guerrilla fighters. Despite this fact, as Commander-in-Chief he took full responsibility for the failed attempt at conquering Burgos as he wrote succinctly and clearly to London: 'The Government had nothing to say to the siege. It was entirely my own act.'[555]

After withdrawing from Burgos, Wellington had managed to join General Hill's forces at Madrid before Joseph Bonaparte attacked them; however, Soult, Clauzel, and King Joseph were now approaching Madrid with approximately 90,000 men. Wellington, even with Hill's assistance, was not able to put more than 70,000 soldiers into the field and thus retreated back to Salamanca. There in mid-November, he attempted to face the French in battle as he had done several months before. In the light of the large advantage of Joseph's troops, Wellington assumed a defensive position in the area of Arapil Chico and Arapil Grande, which the massive French Army did not dare to attack after their many previous and agonizing experiences. Joseph seemed satisfied in managing to push Wellington back to Portugal, where Wellesley set up a winter camp in the autumn of 1812 near the village of Freineda near Almeida.[556]

Thus, the British returned to Portugal for the winter, which in the light of their great successes (including the liberation of Madrid) was naturally a disappointment. However, contrary to the British retreat from Spain that took place under Wellesley's command after the Battle of Talavera in 1809, when in the ranks of the British Army there were still numerous "croakers" who refused to believe in the possibility of British victory in the Peninsular War, the British troops now by vast majority had boundless faith in their commander and looked to him with ever-growing admiration after the numerous victories they had won with him. A sergeant in the British regiments of the time recounted in his diary quite vividly what took place in their ranks when Wellington appeared in their camp one rainy day during the retreat toward Freineda in November 1812:

> The spirit of enthusiasm was raised to the highest pitch, by the electric effect of the words 'here he comes', which spread from mouth to mouth with the rapidity of lighting. The noble commander passed our columns in review, as usual unaccompanied by any mark of distinction or splendour, his long horse cloak concealed his under garment, his cocked hat soaked and disfigured with the rain.[557]

The less than ideal mood that persisted in Wellington's army after his failure at Burgos and the forced retreat back to Portugal was soon considerably lifted by continuing reports of Napoleon's crushing defeat in Russia. Napoleon first won a victory on 7th September 1812 at Borodino*, where he finally managed to force Marshal Kutuzov into a large-scale field battle, which became the largest one-day battle of the whole Napoleonic wars in terms of the number of men fighting, which amounted to roughly 130,000 soldiers on each side. Nonetheless, the victory at Borodino ultimately did not greatly profit Napoleon, as he was far from having crushed the Russian Army, which had retreated from Borodino in an organised fashion under Kutuzov's command. Bonaparte had lost roughly 30,000 men in the battle, while Russian losses were approximately 10,000 men higher. Kutuzov, however, still had 90,000 combat-ready soldiers, a force not to be taken lightly. One week later, Napoleon marched triumphantly to Moscow; however, the Russians proceeded to burn the city to the

---

* Although doubt is often cast on Napoleon's victory at Borodino, the author personally considers Borodino to be a victorious battle for Napoleon, as Marshal Kutuzov was forced to abandon the battlefield. However, the strategic consequences of the battle are a wholly different matter. With some exaggeration, we might compare Borodino to Wellington's Battle of Talavera.

RETREAT FROM BURGOS
Autumn 1812

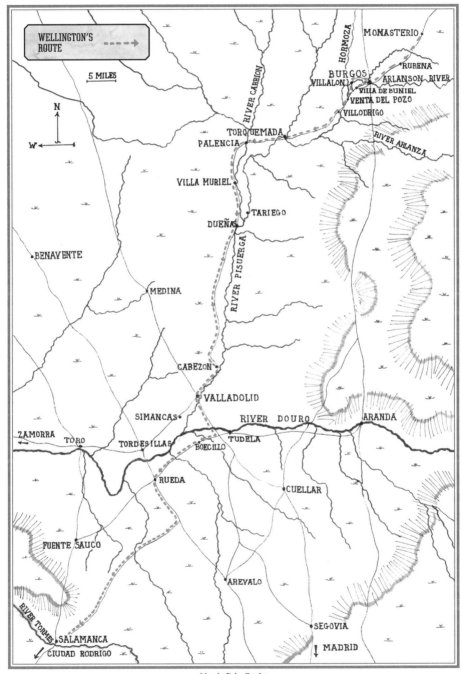

WELLINGTON'S
ROUTE

5 MILES

N

W

MONASTERIO

HORMOZA

RUBENA

BURGOS
VILLALON
ARLANSON RIVER
VILLA DE BUNIEL
VENTA DEL POZO

VILLODRIGO

RIVER CARRION

TORQUEMADA
PALENCIA

RIVER ARLANZA

VILLA MURIEL

TARIEGO

DUEÑAS

RIVER PISUERGA

BENAVENTE

MEDINA

CABEZON

VALLADOLID

SIMANCAS

RIVER DOURO

ARANDA

ZAMORRA

TORO

TORDESILLAS

BOECILLO

TUDELA

RUEDA

CUELLAR

FUENTE SAUCO

AREVALO

RIVER TORMES

SEGOVIA

SALAMANCA

MADRID

CIUDAD RODRIGO

— *Map by John Fawkes* —

ground. The French supply route now completely collapsed as the feared Russian winter was now setting in. Napoleon was left with no choice but to withdraw; during this infamous retreat, which was led through the horrifying conditions of the Russian winter, he lost almost all of his army of over half a million men. Napoleon abandoned the remainder of his decimated army on 8ᵗʰ December and immediately travelled to Paris. A pact of alliance was subsequently signed on 30ᵗʰ December between Russia and Prussia, whose soldiers – who had initially marched with the French Army as Napoleon's allies – now deserted to the Russian camp. Thus emerged the Sixth Anti-Napoleonic Coalition, in which the two aforementioned powers were joined by Sweden and of course Britain, who until then had been the only power fighting against France in the form of Wellington's army on the Iberian Peninsula.[558] It is surely remarkable to note that Wellesley's statement from July 1812 on Napoleon's defeat in Russia had come true, as he claimed that 'Buonaparte will not succeed' in the difficult conditions that awaited him in Russia, i.e. long supply routes, poor roads, and of course the infamous Russian winter. Wellington himself had used scorched earth tactics in Portugal with great success against Marshal Masséna two years earlier and the Russians were evidently well-informed of these events in Portugal. Wellington's victory there may have incited them to use these scorched earth tactics as well, which they perfected by burning down Moscow itself.

After the retreat to the camp in Freineda on the Iberian Peninsula, Wellington continued to take action. In mid-December 1812 he visited Cádiz, which was now fully liberated, as Marshal Soult and his diminished troops failed to renew their siege after withdrawing to aid King Joseph in pushing Wellington back to Portugal. When Wellington rode through the gates of Cádiz, he was welcomed by jubilant cries of "Águila! Águila!" ("Eagle! Eagle!") coming from the mouths of the Spanish, who were curious to catch sight of the famous British general. Unsurprisingly, the Spanish gave Wellesley this name due to the Duke's aquiline nose and his famous endeavours to see over all matters in person with his "eagle eye".[559]

In Cádiz, Wellington negotiated with representatives of the Spanish Government about their planned offensive strategy for 1813 and was wholly satisfied with the outcome of the negotiations. The Spanish Government agreed that all movements of the Spanish armies would be coordinated by Lord Wellington himself during the forthcoming campaign. Wellesley set off from Cádiz to Lisbon, where he discussed strategy for the following year with representatives of the Portuguese Government, whereupon he immediately returned to his camp in Freineda to wait out the coming winter, gather new strength, and thoroughly prepare his offensive.[560] After his return to Freineda, he wrote the following gratified words to a friend:

> I was very well received at Cádiz and Lisbon and throughout the country and I ought to have somebody behind me to remind me that I am 'but a man'*. I believe that I have been upon the whole, the most fortunate and the most favoured of God's creatures and if I don't forget the above mentioned, think I may yet do well...[561]

Throughout the Peninsular War, many men had come and gone in Wellington's general staff and amongst his aides-de-camp. These men, who regularly found themselves in Wellesley's immediate surroundings, in many cases had become friends with Wellesley thanks to the amount of time they spent together. One of the most famous individuals in this circle was the aforementioned FitzRoy Somerset who for many years tended to his commander's most important correspondence (both military and private). FitzRoy had been Wellesley's aide-de-camp in the Peninsular War since 1808 and had made a good impression on Wellington immediately after Wellesley had landed in Portugal during the Battle of Roliça (the first large-scale clash of the Peninsular War in which Wellesley defeated General Loison alias 'Maneta'). At the time, Wellington posed a somewhat mischievous but amused question to the twenty-two-year-old FitzRoy, who had found himself in the fray of battle for the first time: "Well, Lord FitzRoy, how do you feel under fire?" "Better, sir, than I expected."[562] answered the innocent FitzRoy.

Arthur Wellesley and FitzRoy maintained friendly relations for the rest of their lives. Other key members of Arthur's staff included such figures as Sir Alexander Gordon, Charles Gordon Lennox (Lord March) and his younger brother John Lennox – sons of the Duke of Richmond, Lord Burghers (the only son of the Duke of Westmorland), or Lord George Russell (the second-born son of the Duke of Bedford) –

---

*   In Ancient Rome, a slave called an auriga was charged with the responsibility of accompanying Roman generals awarded a triumph through the streets of Rome. During the journey they would whisper to the general the words: *"Memento homo"*. ("Remember you are only a man".).

Russell suffered an injury at Talavera, but returned to the military in 1812 in full health.

As the sons of prominent British peers, Wellington's aides-de-camp were usually considerably younger than Wellesley, who was perhaps somewhat of a "father figure" to them in the light of his growing fame and undeniable charisma. For instance, William, Prince of Orange, a member of the Dutch Royal family who was of a staunchly anti-Napoleon persuasion and who gladly contributed additional aides-de-camp to Wellington's ranks in 1811, celebrated his 20th birthday on 6th December 1812 in Freineda.

There was usually a sociable atmosphere in Wellington's staff and the young aides-de-camp often found mutual amusements. For instance, the aides-de-camp gave William of Orange the nickname 'Slender Billy' for his lanky, almost unnaturally gaunt figure, as George Gleig recalled in his memoirs:

> They had many school-boy tricks, among others, that of giving nick-names, at which nobody took offence. 'Where is Slender Billy?' said Lord FitzRoy Somerset, looking round the table, and apparently missing somebody. 'Here I am FitzRoy', replied the Prince of Orange, 'what do you want?'[563]

In the winter of 1812/1813, one enthusiastic and self-proclaimed "inventor" among the ranks of the officers unintentionally sparked a wave of amusement and commotion in Wellington's camp. The "inventor" requested an audience with Wellington in order to present to the commander a special military exercise for soldiers with their bayonets fixed on their muskets which, once mastered, would allow one British soldier to handle twenty Frenchmen. This inventor was "surprisingly" refused more for the whimsicality of his exercises than their usefulness. Another "inventor" in the field of military innovations came up in a similar manner with an "artificial hill". This invention basically consisted of a massive pole similar to a ship's mast (the "inventor" had served in the Navy) on which Wellington was to be hoisted in order to have a view of the enemy's position from an elevated point. Nonetheless, this innovator was also refused: "Damn me, Sir, I may tumble down and break my neck!" Wellington said, brushing him off: "Oh! My Lord, if that is all, you may send up one of your aides-de-camp." [564] This understandably put an end to the whole discussion.

Wellington naturally had a number of good friends in the army outside of his staff as well, for example General Lowry Cole (Ned Pakenham's brother-in-law), his personal chaplain, the Reverend Samuel Briscall, head military doctor James McGrigor, and many others. However, the moment any of these men failed to obey his orders, Wellington was often unsparing, as he was aware of his immense responsibility. When the latter, head doctor James McGrigor on his own accord changed the route ordered by Wellington to transport the injured toward the Portuguese border after the occupation of Madrid in order to protect them from potential threats by the French, Wellington reprimanded McGrigor with the following words the moment he realised what had happened: "As long as you live, Sir, never do so again, never do anything without my orders."[565]

When Wellington marched with his army during the Peninsular War, he usually had at his disposal one smaller tent in which he slept and a second and considerably larger one which served as his workspace and dining room where he organised dinners with prominent guests and officers. He was not especially choosy when it came to food, and even once proclaimed: 'I don't much care what I eat.'[566] On the contrary, Wellington's good friend and member of his staff, Spanish General Miguel Ricardo de Álava, insisted on being served good meals. Álava once recalled with a fair degree of humour that, during campaigns in which Wellington needed to advance quickly with his army, he was often rather frustrated by the monotonous answers to his questions concerning when Wellington's staff would move and what food would be served: 'I became disgusted with two words: 'daylight' and 'cold meat'.[567] However, it should be mentioned that, in his old age, Wellington claimed his favourite food was properly roasted lamb.

Throughout the course of his military campaigns, Wellington often dined in the company of twelve to sixteen guests and his dinners were generally popular. Participants of these dinners were usually officers from the ranks of his general staff, military doctors, and supply staff. Members of the officer corps from the ranks of the regiments that were camped closest to Wellington's tent were also often invited. Wellington was highly sociable and conversations were held at his table in a wholly informal manner, which brought on a comfortable and relaxed atmosphere, as Ensign George Gleig, who took part in several such dinners during the campaign in the Iberian Peninsula, recalled:

The conversation was, for the most part, both interesting and lively. The Duke himself spoke out on all subjects with an absence of reserve which sometimes surprised his guests. Whether the matters under discussion were foreign or domestic politics, he took his own view of each particular case and stated it broadly. He was rich in anecdotes, most of them taking a ludicrous turn, and without any apparent effort put the company very much at their ease.[568]

A good, dry sense of humour, the telling of various anecdotes, and the ability to entertain his company became typical characteristics of Arthur Wellesley. Wellington liked to laugh, and did so loudly and very often. According to eye-witnesses, his fits of laughter were often likened to 'a man with a whooping-cough'.[569] Around half past eight in the evening, Wellington requested coffee, after which the majority of the company dispersed around nine o'clock. Before turning in, Wellesley would read briefly or see to his correspondence (Wellington's well-known rule, which he often repeated, was: 'to do the business of the day in the day.'[570]), and would aim to retire to bed usually before ten o'clock.

During his campaign, he always had a saddled horse at hand accompanied by two dragoons, allowing him to act as quickly as possible if necessary even in the middle of the night, which was absolutely typical of his nature. One of Wellington's soldiers noted in his memoirs that: 'it has occasionally happened that when his staff awoke in the morning they learnt that their chief had been on horse-back and with picquets of the army hours before.'[571] In most cases, Wellington would sleep until the morning in his field bed, but usually rose relatively early. For example, Judge-Advocate Francis Larpent recalled a dinner that had gone on until late, during which Wellington arranged a meeting concerning several legal issues for the very early morning the next day: 'I dined with Lord Wellington last night, and staid there till near ten. He was all gaiety and spirits, and only said on leaving the room, 'Remember! at four in the morning.'[572] According to Larpent, Wellington always tried to focus on the future during the Peninsular War. However, this does not imply a lack of appreciation for lessons from the past – here, for instance, we might recall his words on the Flanders Campaign: 'I learnt what one ought not to do, and that is always something.' or his assessment of his failure in the attack on Sultanpettah Tope: 'I have come to a determination, when in my power, never to suffer an attack to be made by night upon an enemy who is prepared and strongly posted, and whose posts have not been reconnoitred by daylight.' Wallowing in one's failures and thoughts of what cannot be changed is not ideal for anyone, even in today's seeming age of anxiety. Over the course of time, Wellington gradually became proficient in what today we would call constructive or "positive" thinking. He most likely acquired this trait in India, where he went through a difficult period after failing to be named to the position of Commander-in-Chief for the campaign to Egypt. During this period, Wellington was feeling somewhat "sorry for himself", which only brought about the deterioration of his health. It was, however, a valuable lesson. In this context, Larpent wrote the following about Wellington in 1813: 'I think Lord Wellington has an active, busy mind, always looking to the future...He has too much of everything and everybody always in his way, to think much of the absent.'[573] Wellington later combined his focus on current problems and the careful planning of future campaigns with his ability to skilfully improvise, which he showed, for example, at Assaye, Oporto, and Salamanca. Years later, Wellington himself claimed that one of the main factors that led to his victory over the French marshals was the fact that:

> They planned their campaigns just as you might make a splendid piece of harness. It looks very well, and answers very well, until it gets broken, and then you are done for. Now I make my campaigns of ropes. If anything went wrong, I tied a knot and went on.[574]

Wellington was usually tasked with reading through a remarkable quantity of documents; however, his greatest stress began under normal circumstances at nine in the morning, when the general staff would meet in his tent. Although Arthur Wellesley was not particular about his food, he was fastidious about attire. During the Peninsular War, he preferred to dress austerely but elegantly without unnecessary decorations. He usually wore a blue or black coat which was intentionally cut somewhat higher than was dictated by contemporary fashion trends. He wore white, grey or light-blue riding breeches together with high Hessian leather boots, which were also specially shortened at the tops in contrast to the typical riding boots of the time. Each time it rained, he would cover himself with a large blue or grey cloak and, in colder weather, used a slightly warmer white cloak. He preferred a bicorne hat, which he always wore in the direction from back to front, i.e. lengthways, in contrast to his great-est rival, Napoleon, who always wore his hat sideways. An Indo-Persian type sabre (similar to the type used by some British light dragoons) with a gilded but wholly plain and undecorated handle swung from Arthur Wellesley's hip. The sabre was no ceremonial prop, but a deadly weap-on.* On the inner side of the lid of his travel chest, which contained his clothing, was a water-colour, which Arthur Wellesley had attached dur-ing his operations on the Iberian Peninsula as a reminder of home. The drawing depicted his two small sons: 'Little Arthur' (Arthur Richard) and 'Charley' (Charles). Wellington took care over his ablutions even when campaigning and often shaved twice a day. When he lived at Walmer Castle in Kent in his later life, he had a bathroom installed there, which in those times was still quite a rare amenity.[575] Because of Wellington's pen-chant for elegant attire he was nicknamed 'Beau' by his officers. He caught wind of this moniker in a rather curious manner when a well-known joker from the Coldstream Guards Regiment Dan Mackinnon asked a group of officers if they had seen 'Beau Douro'.[576] Wellington, who was wrapped in his cloak and was napping under a nearby tree (it is well known that Wellington would catch up on his sleep wherever he could – for example before the Battle of Salamanca) slowly got up and chimed in amusedly with Mackinnon: "Well, by ..., I never knew I was a beau before!"[577]

When Captain John Kincaid, who subsequently joined the 95th Rifles, sailed to Portugal, he was eagerly looking forward to laying eyes on Wellington. In place of this 'Beau's' clothing, which Kincaid evidently took no notice of (contrary to many others), he was greatly impressed by Wellesley's charisma and his easily recognizable aquiline nose:

> From the moment that I joined the army [in Portugal], so intense was my desire to get a look at this illustrious chief, that I never should have forgiven the Frenchman that had killed me before I effected it. My curiosity did not remain long ungratified, for, as our post was next the enemy, I found, when any thing was to be done, that it was his also. He was just such a man as I had figured in my mind's eye, and I thought that the stranger would betray a grievous want of penetration who could not select the Duke of Wellington from amid five hundred in the same uniform.[578]

---

* Today we can see this sabre exhibited at *Wellington's Arch* in London.

Kincaid wrote in his memoirs. In moments when his army lingered in its camp, Wellington's greatest pastime was hunting, specifically fox-hunting. In a rather non-traditional fashion, Wellington did not hunt for the pleasure of the kill, but for the pure joy he derived from a gallop on a well-bred horse. Mr Larpent later recalled that Wellesley had bagged perhaps one single fox with his comrades over the course of several months spent in the camp. Nonetheless, Wellington tremendously enjoyed hunting and laughed whole-heartedly when he or any other of his "comrades in arms" missed their target while shooting.[579] The fact that taking a pleasant ride was more important to Wellington that the actual catch is described quite succinctly by Mr Larpent in his memoirs: 'Lord Wellington has a good stud of about eight hunters, he rides hard, and only wants a good gallop, but I understand knows nothing of the sport, though very fond of it in his own way.'[580] During his days of hunting when the army lingered about the camp and "lives were not at stake" while dealing with daily matters, Wellington would see to all matters rather quickly and, if the various generals who had forgotten something in the morning requested another meeting with him, would wave them aside with the words: 'Oh damn them. ...I won't speak to them again when we are hunting.'[581] The playful young man that once was the aide-de-camp to Lord Buckingham in Ireland would awaken in Wellington while hunting.

Wellington did not hesitate to make use of the calmer period during the winter of 1812 to organise a ball in Ciudad Rodrigo in honour of his Division General Lowry Cole, who had recently been promoted by the Prince Regent to the title of knight. The Judge-Advocate Larpent, who had known Wellington at the time only briefly, recalled with admiration and captivation the energy which Wellington possessed the day the ball was to take place and all that he managed to arrange:

> Lord Wellington was the most active man of the party – he prides himself on this, but yet I hear from those about him that he is a little broken down by it. He stayed on business at Frenada [Freineda] until half past three, and then rode full seventeen miles to Rodrigo in two hours to dinner, dressed in all his orders &c., was in high glee, danced, stayed supper, and at half-past three in the morning went back to Frenada by moonlight, and arrived here before daybreak at six, so that by twelve he was ready again for business, and I saw him amongst others upon a Court-martial on my return at two the next day.[582]

During the time spent in the winter camp at Freineda at the turn of 1812 and 1813, both Wellington, who was often occupied with his "hunts", and his whole army were in good spirits. The soldiers were well equipped and those who had not been given accommodation in any of the sheltered areas were now given newly ordered tents from their commander. Wellington's army hitherto had not spent a winter on the Iberian Front in such comfort as they did now. The failure at Burgos had forgotten by the majority of the troops. In addition, after receiving reinforcements, Wellesley now had an army of almost 80,000 Anglo-Portuguese for his proposed spring campaign; the army was supported by another 20,000 Spaniards operating in southwest Spain, which also now fell under his official command. At this juncture it was clear that Wellington had such a fighting force at his disposal as he had never had before. Thanks to this fact, his whole army found itself in a buoyant mood with the arrival of spring. The greatest of expectations could be heard in discussions amongst his soldiers concerning the planned campaign.[583] At the beginning of April, one of Wellington's generals, Sir Frederick Robinson, wrote on the present state of the army, saying that: 'they place such confidence in their Hero (Wellington), that no one questions his conduct. He is their idol, for whom they will offer their lives as freely as they will drink his health.'[584]

Before the campaign, Wellington himself had one especially significant reason to be joyful and optimistic. His best exploring officer, Major Colquhoun Grant, who had been captured roughly a year earlier, had managed to flee from the French. He accomplished his daring escape as soon as he was transported by a military escort to the city of Bayonne in the southwest of France. In this relatively large town, he managed to elude the overly lax French soldiers, who were most likely expecting him rather foolishly to uphold his parole, in the middle of one of Bayonne's squares. Grant, on the contrary, had gradually come to realize that his exchange would never take place. The mere fact that 300 men and six cannons had escorted him to Bayonne gave firm proof that the French were not intending to give him up. Allegedly during his journey to Bayonne, a letter was smuggled to him confirming that he was not to be exchanged under any circumstances. Therefore, he decided to consider his parole to be henceforth invalid, a fact which in retaliation he "neglected to mention" to the French before his escape. The moment he managed to flee from Bayonne, however, he quite surprisingly did not attempt to return to Spain. On the contrary, this was exactly what the French evidently expected of the fleeing prisoner, and therefore placed the most patrols in this direction. Furthermore, it would not have been like 'Granto Bueno' if he hadn't done exactly the opposite of what the French were expecting. The bold Colquhoun Grant therefore plainly set off Paris as an American officer, and this simple guise evidently worked splendidly, as he even managed to travel a part of the way in the company of French General Souham. In Souham's defence, it should be mentioned that America had been at war with Britain since June of 1812, fighting over disputed territories on the border between the USA and Canada. The Americans and French were thus natural allies at the time against the British, and so Grant's choice of a fake American identity was highly cunning to say the least. Once he found himself in the French capital, the "American" immediately contacted a British agent*, who provided him with an American passport and proper uniform. Now Grant's cover was nearly perfect, and he planned to make full use of it. In Paris, he began to mingle amongst the soldiers, politicians and local elite, gathering new information for Wellington and the British Government with an innocent smile on his face.[585] Wellington spoke enthusiastically to Grant's relative Dr McGrigor on the fact:

> Your brother-in-law [Grant] is certainly one of the most extraordinary men I ever met with; even now when in Paris he contrives to send me information of the greatest moment to our government. I am now sending information of his to ministers of the utmost value about the French armies in every quarter, information which will surprise them, and which they cannot by any possibility get in any other way, and, what is more, which I am quite sure is perfectly correct.[586]

Wellington, in good spirits, launched the new campaign by crossing the Spanish border on 22nd May 1813 and marched immediately towards Madrid with his army of 78,000. There were still roughly 200,000

---

* This agent, who created the passport for Grant, was a Mr McPherson, a Scotsman who had lived for many years in Paris. According to James McGrigor, Grant then carried out the following in Paris: "while with Mr McPherson, as an American, and with an American passport, Grant moved freely about Paris, made it a point to be present at all the reviews, and by entering into conversation with various individuals, whom he met out of doors and at Mr McPherson's table, got correct information of the reinforcements sent to all the armies, particularly that of Portugal (i.e. the French army on the Iberian Peninsula). Quoted in McGrigor, *Autobiography*, p. 292.

Frenchmen scattered throughout Spain, but Joseph Bonaparte had only roughly 60,000 men at his disposal at Madrid. In the light of the circumstances, he thus decided as the year before to abandon the city and join his troops with the forces of General Clauzel, who was now operating in the northwest of Spain near the Pyrenees. This time, Wellington was fully determined to prevent the joining of the two armies, and thus drove his men forward at the swiftest possible tempo. Thanks to these fast-paced daily marches, he managed to catch up with Joseph's troops at the town of Vitoria located roughly 220 miles northwest of the Spanish capital before they had a chance to join Clauzel's men.

Once again, Wellington learned of the numbers of the enemy's troops, their intentions, and positions thanks to his Intelligence Department. In addition to Grant's reports from Paris, this time another member of his staff, Captain George Scovell, distinguished himself. As was mentioned previously, this remarkable man had already managed some time before to decipher intercepted French dispatches. Nonetheless, it gradually became clear to the French that Wellington was suspiciously well-informed of their manoeuvres, as a great number of their messengers were disappearing along with their dispatches in the grip of the ubiquitous *guerrilleros*. They thus quickly "put two and two together" and began to alter their codes in order to thwart the enemy codebreakers. With high expectations, the French replaced the originally used and not overly complex code of 50 numbers with a considerably more difficult code of 150 characters called the Army of Portugal Code (according to the name of the French Army on the Iberian Peninsula who was the first to use it).[587] Yet, just as the French code had been perfected, so had George Scovell perfected his skills during the months of deciphering simpler codes. In November 1811, he managed to crack the Army of Portugal code in less than 48 hours as if he had been looking forward to this "somewhat more complex puzzle". At the beginning of 1812, however, the determined French reverted to a much heavier calibre code in the form of the so-called *"Great Paris Cipher"* or simply *"Grand Chiffre"*. In terms of its effectiveness in comparison with the previous ciphers, the introduction of this new code was like being fired upon in battle not with a rusty musket, but with a brand-new twelve-pound cannon. This time, the French had evidently taken offense. *"The Great Paris Cipher"* was based on 1400 numbers, some of which represented whole words, only parts of words, or even had no meaning at all in order to perfectly confuse the decipherer while the addressee simply skipped over them with a decoding book in his hands.[588] However, just as Colquhoun Grant proved that he was Wellington's James Bond, Scovell definitively earned his position in history as the Duke's Alan Turing.

From April 1812 on, Scovell worked intensely on several dispatches written in the *Grand Chiffre*, whereby he discovered that the most commonly used combination of numbers in the encrypted messages was indisputably "210". He then quite logically replaced this combination with the most common French expression "et" (and), which was surely a promising start. In addition, at the beginning of July the *guerrilleros* had managed in the meantime to make a grand catch. The Spanish irregulars intercepted a letter from King Joseph to Marshal Marmont, in which – for absolutely incomprehensible reasons (either Joseph was simply pressed for time or, to speak rather prosaically, simply succumbed to human laziness) – Napoleon's older brother used normal French words here and there among the numbers of the code. Whatever the reason was for Joseph's carelessness, it was without a doubt a wholly fatal error, thanks to which Scovell began piece by piece to decode the cipher with bulldog-like tenacity. For example, a line in Joseph's letter read: *"73. 516. 918 ne negliserai".* The word "neglect" in the first-person future tense gave a clue that 918 stood for "je"("I").[589]

At exactly the same time that Scovell cracked the code, Wellington and Marmont were manoeuvring near Salamanca, each waiting for the other to make a fatal error. In the meantime, Scovell had spent nearly all of his time heroically deciphering the code and was soon able to read the majority of Joseph's letter, which proved to be crucial. The letter revealed that King Joseph would not be able to arrive at Salamanca for a considerable time, and the other French Marshals would not manage to help Marmont at all. Thus, thanks to Scovell, Wellington knew for sure that he would have enough time at Salamanca and could afford to wait longer for Marmont to make an error. Partially due to this fact, Wellington emerged victorious over the French Marshal in the exhausting duel of nerves and measuring of force in manoeuvring skills that ensued, making use of Marmont's error in his overly-extended right wing and ultimately crushing him at Salamanca. Towards the end of 1812, Scovell gave his Commander-in-Chief a slightly belated Christmas present in the form of the completely decoded Great

Parisian Cipher. During the winter of 1812–1813, this allowed Wellington to plan his spring campaign with the complete knowledge of all intercepted French dispatches, which now helped him greatly in catching the isolated army of Joseph Bonaparte near Vitoria.[590]

However, it should also be noted that Joseph Bonaparte made Wellington's whole pursuit considerably easier due to his own greed and folly. From Madrid, his army was now transporting almost all the possible valuables that the French had managed to plunder throughout the whole of Spain: paintings, jewellery, and even expensive furniture. In addition, many French civilians from the ranks of Joseph Bonaparte's royal court, accompanied by Spanish *afrancesados,* marched to safety alongside Joseph's army. The army also included a myriad of wives, mistresses and camp followers of the French soldiers; thanks to this fact, the army was nicknamed "a walking bordello" and was all the slower because of it.[591] The French, whose true commander was the chief of Joseph Bonaparte's general staff, Marshal Jourdan (with whom Wellington had already clashed previously at the Battle of Talavera, where he commanded the army in place of Bonaparte), held a relatively strong position west of Vitoria. They were protected by the River Zadorra from the northwest; from the south they were covered by a system of hills known as the Heights of La Puebla and from the east by the town of Vitoria itself. Wellington, who now had a significant advantage over his opponent for the first time during the whole Peninsular War, did not hesitate to issue the order in the early hours of 21ˢᵗ June 1813 to attack the French immediately. Wellesley led the frontal attack on the French positions against Bonaparte's forces from the west with four massive columns, taking personal command of the two middle columns. North of Wellington's position was Thomas Picton's column, and in the south were troops under the command of Rowland 'Daddy' Hill. All four columns crossed the Zadorra (as the French had left several smaller bridges intact as they evidently were in favour of a battle in the given situation) and subsequently engaged in battle. In addition, Wellington had prepared a rather unpleasant surprise: in order to surround Joseph's right wing, Wellington deployed roughly 20,000 men east of Vitoria led by his second-in command, Sir Thomas Graham, who had arrived to the Iberian Peninsula only the year before and was now preparing to attack the French.

BATTLE OF VITORIA
21ˢᵗ June 1813

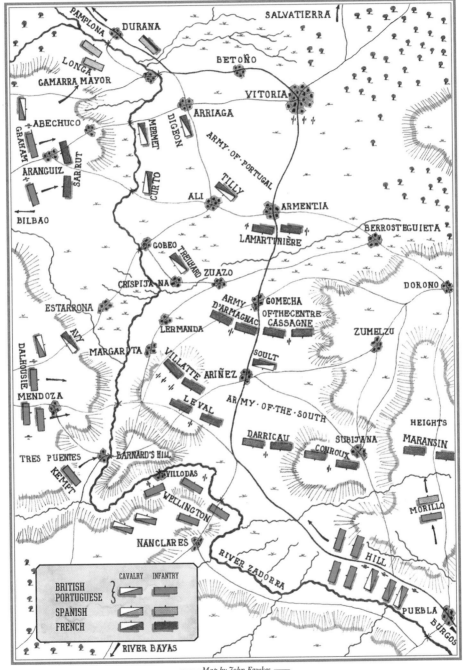

SALVATIERRA

PAMPLONA
DURANA

LONGA
GAMARRA MAYOR

BETOÑO

VITORIA

ARRIAGA

ABECHUCO
GRAHAM
SARRUT
ARANGUIZ

MERNET
DIGEON

ARMY·OF·PORTUGAL

BILBAO

CURTO

ALI
TILLY

ARMENTIA

BERROSTEGUIETA

LAMARTINIÈRE

GOBEO
TREILHARD
ZUAZO

CRISPIJA·NA

DORONO

ESTARRONA

AVY

MARGARITA

ARMY
D'ARMAGNAC
LERMANDA

GOMECHA
OF·THE·CENTRE
CASSAGNE

ZUMELZU

DALHOUSIE

MENDOZA

VILLATTE
ARIÑEZ

LEVAL

SOULT

AR/MY·OF·THE·SOUTH

HEIGHTS
MARANSIN

TRES PUENTES
KEMPT
BARNARD'S HILL

VILLODAS

WELLINGTON

NANCLARES

DARRICAU

SUBIJANA
CONROUX

MORILLO

RIVER ZADORRA

HILL

PUEBLA
BURGOS

	CAVALRY	INFANTRY
BRITISH PORTUGUESE		
SPANISH		
FRENCH		

RIVER BAYAS

— *Map by John Fawkes* —

From a bird's-eye view, Wellington's attack would have looked as if the French were slowly being gripped by a gigantic human palm that gradually and mercilessly closed into a fist. The four columns attacking from the west were the little, ring, middle, and index finger, while Graham's column was the thumb. As soon as Jourdan learned of Graham's advancing men, he immediately ordered a portion of his men away from his centre and towards the east to face Graham before it was too late. Sir Thomas Picton was quick to make use of the weakened French centre and, as it should be noted, likely did so wholly at his own initiative. Picton, who was no stranger to sharp words, led his column on with a cry of: "Come on, ye rascals! Come on, ye fighting villains!"[592] directly at the French centre, which he swiftly struck, a moment that proved to be a breaking point in the battle. In addition, General Graham had also succeeded in the east in spite of significant French resistance. The French opposition completely collapsed around five o'clock in the afternoon, forcing Marshal Jourdan to order a retreat.[593]

Until this point, the allied army had managed to fare phenomenally; now, however, it could not resist the fiendish temptation that lay before it in the form of the priceless valuables that the French had left behind. The army thus began en masse to plunder the French supply train located near Vitoria on the only free path of retreat, which led west to Pamplona and was now teeming with fleeing Frenchmen. There the British pounced upon a copious amount of jewellery, gold, silver, and all various precious works of art looted by the French from every corner of Spain. In addition, the French had recently received soldiers' payments for their whole army in the amount of five million dollars (evidently a portion of the money that Napoleon received for the sale of Louisiana to the Americans); however, Wellington's army coffers only saw a laughable one hundred thousand of these dollars. Perhaps even more despicable was the fact that the British ceased to pursue Joseph's army in favour of plundering. The greed that had put Joseph Bonaparte in these dire straits was now his saving grace, as the majority of the British soldiers proved to be no less greedy than King Joseph himself. The plundering continued in the middle of Vitoria itself and no one managed to reinstate order, as this time many officers joined the common soldiers in looting – in short, they were overtaken by the temptation. To make matters worse, the majority of the British Army became intoxicated to such a degree that Wellington was still unable to organise the army into an orderly pursuit one day later, something that had never happened to him before.*

It is the author's personal opinion that, at this moment, Arthur Wellesley may have had the strongest feelings of indignation and frustration he had ever experienced in his whole life hitherto. As a reaction to the behaviour of his army, he wrote the following brief and unsparing words to Minister for War Lord Bathurst: 'It is quite impossible for me or any other man to command a British army under the existing system. We have in the service the scum of the earth as common soldiers.'[594] These harsh words for the common British soldiers as "scum of the earth" are often found among the first of Wellington's most commonly quoted phrases and is frequently used as proof of his arrogance, pragmatism, and in some cases complete lack of feeling.

The written word cannot be taken back, but the context is essential, and it is evident that Wellington's harsh words carried a tinge of his momentary anger and frustration. Simply speaking, no one is perfect and, after victory at Vitoria the highly rational Wellington demonstrated a textbook example (albeit a human one) of a fit of rage. Namely the claim that it was 'impossible to command a British army' was of course quite exaggerated in the light of what Wellington had achieved at Vitoria.

Wellington attempted to shed light on this offhand statement concerning the common soldiers years later to Lord Stanhope. In a conversation with Stanhope in 1840, he claimed that the main problem lay in the fact that entry into the Regular British Army was based on voluntary enlistment.

> Some of our men enlist from having got bastard children – some from minor offences [i.e. their only choice was the military or prison] – many more for drink [it is my assumption here that Wellington may have also meant isolated cases of drunkenness, which enlisting sergeants used as one of the most

---

* Longford p. 319. Of the various valuables that the British seized at Vitoria, Wellington managed to salvage a series of paintings from the Spanish royal collections: these were works of masters such as Rubens, Correggio, Velasquez, Van Dyck, Titian and many other world-renowned painters. To Wellington's great dismay, some British soldiers used the stolen canvases after battle as tarpaulins to protect their baggage from the rain. After the Napoleonic Wars ended, Wellington intended to return the rescued paintings to Spanish King Ferdinand VII; the King, however, allowed Wellington to keep the paintings as his own expression of gratefulness for everything he had done. Today a portion of the paintings may be admired in the Apsley House – the London house of the Duke of Wellington and another portion in the Stratfield Say House, his residence in the English countryside. See Julius Bryant, *Apsley House: The Wellington Collection* (London 2014), p. 19.

effective "drafting tools"], but you can hardly conceive such a set brought together, and it really is wonderful that we should have made them the fine fellows they are.[595]

Wellington went on to explain to Stanhope that the armies of other countries with an established system of universal and (most importantly) mandatory enlistment were made up of a cross-section of all levels of society. In Britain, on the contrary, men of the lowest levels of society – i.e. the "scum" – enlisted as volunteers, as only a few wished to go to war voluntarily.

Wellington was an ardent royalist and a Tory to the last. In his mind, the Sovereign was to lead the state together with the Parliament. Only aristocrats who had been raised to be responsible from a young age and possessed sufficient education were exclusively to sit in Parliament* – from this perspective, Wellington was clearly arrogant in today's sense of the term. However, the idea that Wellington behaved coldly or heartlessly to his common soldiers or even despised them is arrant nonsense. Only five months after the Battle of Vitoria, he wrote the following of his men: 'the army was never in such health, heart, and condition...and it is probably the most complete machine for its numbers now existing in Europe...'.[596] Some years later, he wrote: 'I could have gone anywhere and done anything with that Army. It was impossible to have a machine more highly mounted and in better order.'[597]

If we were to delve farther into the past, we would also recall how Wellington took care of his regiment as a colonel in India, how he cared for the safety of the injured after the Battle of Assaye, not willing to continue on in the campaign until they were delivered to a safe distance from the front, and finally how he 'shed tears as any woman could' over the dead after the Siege of Badajoz. Wellington later told John Wilson Croker that his success in the role of commander was only thanks to the fact that he began as a lieutenant-colonel, and was thus in close contact with common soldiers at the beginning of his career:

> One must understand the mechanism and power of the individual soldier, then that of a company, a battalion, or brigade, and so on, before one can venture to

---

* During his political career, Wellington was a staunch opponent of extending voting rights (Reform Act).

group divisions and move an army. I believe I owe most of my success to the attention I always paid to the inferior part of tactics as a regimental officer.[598]

In 1844, now as an old man, Wellington went on to say:

> I know of none more important than closely to attend to the comfort of the soldier: let him be well clothed, sheltered and fed. How should he fight, poor fellow! If he has, besides risking his life, to struggle with unnecessary hardships? Also, he must not, if it can be helped, be struck by the balls before he is fairly in action. One ought to look sharp after the young officers and be very indulgent to the soldier.[599]

As chance would have it, only five days after the Battle of Vitoria on the other side of Continental Europe Napoleon also lost his temper (although he was not likely to have known the outcome of Vitoria) during a meeting with Austrian Foreign Minister Klemens von Metternich in Dresden (26th June 1813). Metternich's task was to mediate a potential peace between the French Emperor and the members of the Sixth Anti-Napoleon Coalition. After the Russian catastrophe, Napoleon quickly formed a large but poorly-trained army made up primarily of prematurely enlisted soldiers. Despite this fact, he managed to defeat Russo-Prussian forces at Lützen and Bautzen in quick succession, forcing Russia and Prussia to sign a temporary peace with the French Emperor in June 1813, during which the two states launched peace talks with Napoleon. In attempts to persuade Napoleon that, although he had gathered a new army, his position was now significantly weaker and his new units, made up primarily of inexperienced and prematurely drafted recruits, Metternich told Napoleon that he should consider a peace treaty (albeit an unfavourable one) in their meeting at Dresden:

> "Under normal circumstances armies are created by only a fraction of the population; you have to this day called nearly your whole population to arms... I have seen your soldiers. They are no more than children. And when these infants have been wiped out, what will you have left?"

According to Metternich's own testimony, Napoleon went white in the face after hearing the question. He proceeded to walk to the corner of the room of the Marcolini Palace where the meeting was taking place, then threw his hat on the floor and thundered angrily at Metternich:

"You are not a soldier. You know nothing of what goes on in a soldier's mind. I grew up on the field of battle. A man like me cares little for the lives of a million men."[600]

[And then added:] "If it costs me my throne, I will bury the world under its ruins!"[601]

Napoleon was well-known for being willing to give everything for victory and rarely cared how many soldiers this would cost him; this, on the other hand, was an indisputable part of his phenomenal success and genius as a commander. Wellington, however, always saw to it that casualties remained as low as possible, and was devastated at the number of his losses after the Battle of Assaye and the Siege of Badajoz. Nonetheless, it is true that he commanded a much smaller army in comparison to Napoleon at the beginning of the Peninsular War and could simply not afford such high casualties in the first place.

At Vitoria the French ultimately lost roughly 8,000 men and all their 151 cannons while allied losses under Wellington's command amounted to 5,000 soldiers. The number of French casualties was far from enormous; the great importance of the victory, however, lay in its far-reaching strategic significance. Napoleon was now facing considerable troubles in Central Europe; his main achievement lay in the fact that, for the time being, he managed to hold the Austrians in neutrality despite his argument with Metternich. The report of the British victory at Vitoria was one of the main (if not essential) reasons that the Austrians joined the members of the Sixth Anti-Napoleon Coalition on 12th August 1813.[602] Proof of the great significance of Wellington's victory for the Austrians (and the fact that this pro-war propaganda news managed to spread amongst a wider spectrum of social classes in the Habsburg Monarchy in comparison to Wellington's previous victories) is evidenced in the fact that even the mayor of a small, remote village in the Austrian Empire called Milčice (located near Prague), Jan František Vavák (who although carefully keeping a diary since the beginning of the Napoleonic Wars wrote of the Peninsular War here for the first time), penned the following and rather lengthy note about the

WELLINGTON'S BATTLES AND SIEGES IN THE PENINSULAR WAR 1808-1814

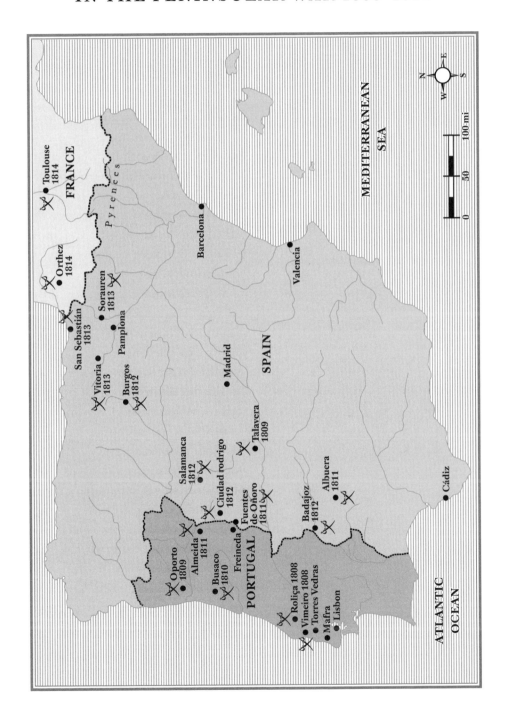

victory in his memoirs, which are perhaps more reminiscent of diaries or village chronicles:

> On the day of St. John the Baptist, in Spain at the town of Vitoria, the Spanish, allied with the English, struck a great and glorious victory over the French, led by Joseph Bonaparte, brother of the French Emperor.[603]

It was now clear that the scales were beginning to tip against Napoleon. Joseph Bonaparte, evidently frightened to death at having escaped capture by only a hare's breath at Vitoria, soon retreated with his whole army back to France and by doing so completely resigning (although not officially) from his hold on the Spanish Crown. Despite several scattered and small-scale French garrisons, the only forces to remain in Spain were the army of Marshal Suchet in Catalonia and Clauzel's troops, who were now preparing to protect the French border in the Pyrenees in the northwest from Wellington's advancing army. All of Napoleon's opponents, of which there were many at the time, were aware of the cardinal importance of the triumph at Vitoria and thus Wellington was showered with congratulations from all over Europe. The famous composer Ludwig van Beethoven composed his work *Wellington's Victory, Op. 91* to celebrate the triumph at Vitoria. The composition was dedicated to the Prince Regent and first performed in Vienna; and whilst highly popular at the time, today it remains one of Beethoven's more neglected creations. When news of Wellington's success reached Britain, it gave rise to unprecedented euphoria: the masses rejoiced and the aristocracy organised countless celebratory banquets in Wellington's honour.[604] Together with other various valuables from Vitoria, Wellesley personally sent Marshal Jourdan's commander's baton to the Prince Regent, upon which he received his own from the Prince Regent in return. Being appointed to the rank of Field Marshal in the British Army, which under normal circumstances did not grant this specific rank, was an unprecedented military honour for Wellington. The Prince Regent proceeded to write the following to Wellington: 'You have sent me, among the trophies of your unrivalled fame, the staff of a French Marshal, and I send in return that of England.'[605] Wellington was now planning to cross the Pyrenees and, after years of battle led often with a significant disadvantage in numbers, attack the French on their home soil with his newly awarded Field Marshal's baton.

CHAPTER TEN

The Victor of Waterloo

fter victory at Vitoria, Arthur Wellesley had two options for advancing into French territory: either march south, attempt to challenge Marshal Suchet, and subsequently cross the Pyrenees from the southeast, or continue north and attack Marshal Soult, who had replaced General Clauzel on Napoleon's orders in the defence of the northwest Spanish-French border. At the end of July 1813 Wellington finally decided to take the northwest route, although in the process the Allied forces had yet to gather in their entirety, a fact that he later admitted could well have proved costly. French numerical superiority of nearly 4:1 came close to triumphing over Anglo-Portuguese forces at the Battle of Roncesvalles (25th July 1813). A tactical retreat during the battle, literally helped by the fog of war enabled the Allied force to live to fight another day. The French in their attempt to relieve Pamplona engaged Wellington's forces at Sorauren in Navarre. The Battle of Sorauren (28th July 1813) witnessed British and Allied forces undergoing a series of bloody onslaughts on the Oricain Ridge, which were valiantly resisted. In typical fashion, Wellington rode audaciously along the ridge, cheering on his troops. Eventually Soult's forces withdrew with a view to returning to France. These engagements, often known as the Battles of the

Pyrenees, underscore the fact that for all France's formidable military strength the tide had turned for it on the Iberian Peninsula.[606]

Despite the fact that Wellington yet again placed himself at the very centre of the fray, as usual emerged unharmed, a fact which he mentioned in a letter to William Wellesley-Pole: 'I escaped as usual unhurt and I begin to believe that the finger of God is upon me.'[607] It is the author's assumption that Wellington developed a deeper personal faith in God during the Peninsular War due in part to the horrors of war and the tragic loss of so many of his friends. His faith in God, the immortality of the soul, and the afterlife – regardless of their nature – naturally served as an irreplaceable comfort in times of conflict. During the Peninsular War, Arthur Wellesley kept his personal chaplain Reverend Samuel Briscall for whose wise counsel and spiritual ministrations Wellington had nothing but praise. Throughout the whole course of the war, Wellington attempted to increase the number of military chaplains, who at that time were relatively scarce in the British Army. Another interesting fact concerning Wellington's attitude toward faith is that his bedroom was adorned with a painting of Pope Pius VII*, although he himself was officially an Anglican.[608]

Before the end of August, Wellington captured the crucial border fortress of San Sebastian and, on 7th October 1813, he crossed the River Bidasoa, entering with his army onto French soil and making him the first commander of all the Anti-Napoleonic powers in history to do so. At the beginning of November, he issued an official declaration to the French people in which he promised absolute safety to the civilian population from his army. This security was of course dependent on the ban of any active help to Bonaparte's soldiers and refraining from any hostile acts against Wellington's forces. In order for Wellesley to prevent potential unrest as effectively as possible, he ordered all the Spanish units in his army to return to Spain. For years, the French had been committing terrifying atrocities in Spain and Wellington rightfully feared that the Spaniards would now attempt to misuse the situation and take their revenge on the French civilian population, a situation that Wellington would not risk at any cost.[609]

---

*   Following on from Napoleon's invasion of the Papal States in 1809, he had been excommunicated by the Roman Catholic Church and in defiance of such an act Napoleon had Pope Pius VII taken prisoner. He was at first held at Savona near Genoa and then transported across the Alps to Fontainebleau Castle in France, where the Supreme Pontiff was kept prisoner until 1814.

By the end of 1813, Wellington had defeated Marshal Soult again in a series of three battles taking place in quick succession: at Nivelle, Nive, and Saint Pierre. Soult's army, which was intended to defend the southern French border and was originally made up of 80,000 men, began to thin precariously in number. Soult now had only 60,000 soldiers at his disposal to defend his country. Due to the approaching winter, Wellington set up a winter camp for his forces near the coastal town of Saint Jean de Lutz, at the mouth of the Nivelle River in the southwest of France, where his guests included figures such as Louis Antoine, Duke of Angoulême, cousin of the legitimate French ruler, Louis XVIII* of the House of Bourbon.

During the autumn and beginning of winter of 1813, Wellington's army was an efficient operation. Perhaps for the first time in his whole military career, Wellington felt comfortable enough to delegate some of his military obligations to others and regularly indulged in restful afternoon walks, which would last for up to two hours along the coast near his camp at Saint Jean de Lutz. The army, primarily the officers' corps, had been transformed into an efficiently operating machine under Wellington's command, a fact which now began to show and drew the attention of Wellington himself. Therefore, in the Battles of Nivelle (River) and Nive, he gave his generals considerable room to command and at the Battle of Saint Pierre, went so far as to give full command of his army to 'Daddy' Hill.[610] To Wellington's relief, Hill fared excellently and received heartfelt thanks from Wellington when he remarked: "My dear Hill, the day's your own!"[611]

In addition, Wellington soon received word of Napoleon's defeat by the Armies of the Sixth Coalition in the four-day Battle of Leipzig (16th–19th October). At Leipzig, an army of 330,000 men made up of forces from Austria, Russia, Prussia and Sweden under the command of Austrian Marshal Karl Philipp, Prince of Schwarzenberg – a member of Czech nobility – stood against Napoleon's 190,000 troops. Another Czech nobleman, Joseph Radetzky von Radetz, was the author of the allied plan of operations at the Battle of Leipzig. Schwarzenberg personally placed von Radetz at the head of his general staff. According to von Radetz's plan

---

* It is often overlooked that King Louis XVIII and virtually the entire French royal family lived in exile in England throughout much of the Napoleonic Wars, where they were in receipt of generous British subsidies.

of operations, the Allies at Leipzig led a coordinated attack on Napoleon from each cardinal direction and, after several days of furious battle, finally scored a definitive victory. After this crucial allied triumph, which was the largest and bloodiest battle in all of the Napoleonic Wars, it became wholly clear that the noose around Napoleon's neck was now beginning to tighten.[612] Thanks to this favourable news from the Eastern Front, Arthur Wellesley and his army immediately ventured forth from their winter camp and, as the weather permitted, marched toward Bayonne. Meanwhile, Napoleon was left with no other choice but to order that 'in the event of the English reaching the château of Marracq [one of his imperial palaces in France located in Bayonne] ... the château and all the buildings belonging to me there be burnt down, so that they may not sleep in my bed...'*

In addition, over the course of January 1814 Wellington's irreplaceable exploring officer Colquhoun Grant returned, bringing to an end one extraordinary personal story that began with Colquhoun's capture, continued with his escape and sensational trip to Paris, and culminated in Grant's sending current and secret reports on the movements of French troops to Wellington's headquarters directly from the heart of the Napoleonic Empire. After a certain time, during which 'Granto Bueno' successfully sent his reports to Wellington under the guise of an American officer in the streets of Paris, the police headed by Joseph Fouché began to have a strong suspicion that there must be a British spy right under their noses in Paris. Ominous clouds soon began to form over Grant's head. It soon became clear to him that if he did not want to be captured once again – which this time might prove fatal – it would be crucial to disappear immediately. He quickly acquired a new American passport in a different name and also changed his appearance as much as possible. He then fled Paris and successfully reached the English Channel, where after various pitfalls he hired two French fishermen for a considerable sum to take him to a British frigate. However, Fouché's men were already hot on his trail and the moment the fishing boat that was hiding Grant left its port on the northern French coast, the French coast guard decided to stop it before allowing it to sail to the open sea and investigate it for

---

* R. M. Johnston, Philip Haythornthwaite (eds.), p. 283. Napoleon bought the Castle of Marracq in 1808. It was here where the capitulation of the rightful Spanish Monarch Ferdinand VII was signed. After this event, Napoleon gave the Spanish throne to his brother Joseph.

potential British spies. Nonetheless, one of the fishermen who was taking Colquhoun Grant to safety made use of the French orders to lower his sail, and swiftly wrapped it around the desperate Major Grant, who had been standing just next to him on deck. The French subsequently searched the boat, but fortunately for Grant, they did not find him wrapped up in the sail. The fishing boat along with Major Grant was thus given permission to continue on in its voyage, upon which the fishermen safely transported 'Granto Bueno' to the deck of a British Royal Navy frigate according to their deal. As soon as Grant found himself safe on British soil, he quickly set about the task of arranging for the release of a captured French major and by doing so "carried out" his own exchange. Without any qualms of conscience, he now considered his parole henceforth as void, where-upon he swiftly and contentedly travelled back to Wellington's army. Arthur Wellesley was understandably overjoyed at Grant's return and quickly promoted this "remarkable man" (in Wellington's own words) to the rank of Lieutenant-Colonel and officially naming him the head of his whole Intelligence Department.[613]

After his phenomenal success with decoding the Great Paris Cipher, Wellington also asked his main decipherer Goerge Scovell to create a system for his own correspondence. On French soil, there was a much greater danger of his letters falling into the "wrong hands". The code that Scovell invented for Wellington was absolutely ingenious in the way that it combined simplicity and maximum efficiency. Scovell came up with a plan in which both the sender and recipient in Wellington's army and headquarters in London would be equipped with identical dictionaries, while the code itself would be based on three simple values: in it was, for example, 52C2. The number 52 meant the page in the dictionary, the letter C represented the third line on that page, and the number two stood for the second word on that line. The code was thus practically indecipherable if one did not discover the necessary dictionary and subsequently find the specific edition.[614]

Before the end of February, Wellington had defeated Soult at Orthez. There, however, he was struck again by an enemy projectile. During the battle, Wellington noticed the Spanish General Álava* jumping about in

---

* Álava held the position of military attaché at the British Army Headquarters and was held in high esteem by Wellington.

a strange manner, swearing and moving up and down as he did so – he had been struck by an enemy bullet directly in the behind. Wellington could not contain his laughter, upon which he himself was also suddenly struck by a projectile. Luckily for him the bullet struck only the sheath of his sabre, a fact which evidently saved his life. However, the intensity of the impact gave Wellington a considerable bruise, leaving him with a limp for several days. Afterwards, Álava – partially in jest and partially with a degree of satisfaction – told Wellington that he had brought the injury upon himself for laughing at Álava's misfortune. After the battle of Orthez, Wellington immediately set off for the nearby field hospital despite his injury to visit the nineteen-year-old John Lennox, the second-born son of the Duke of Richmond and one of Wellington's young aides-de-camp, who had suffered a much more serious wound in the previous battle. Wellington wanted to check in on his state of health in person at all costs. Lennox was fortunately not as serious as it initially seemed, and over time he fully regained his health.[615]

On 10th April, Wellington and his army now arrived at the gates of Toulouse, a city where the Royalists formed a significant majority among its French inhabitants. This was the main reason Wellington decided to seize this city first. Toulouse, however, was defended by Marshal Soult's forces, who managed to fight through Wellington's units, which were deployed around the town, inflicting upon them considerable losses before retreating in an organized fashion. However, despite all efforts and the successful retreat of his men, the French Marshal ultimately failed to prevent Wellington from taking Toulouse on 12th April. As he entered Toulouse's main square, Arthur Wellesley was suddenly met with a bizarre sight – a statue of Napoleon, which had been torn down and shattered as a result of the fall. All of this pointed to the fact that the French Emperor's situation was becoming more and more precarious by the day. Wellington was soon greeted by a delegation of civic worthies who welcomed him and presented Toulouse to the victorious British commander. Toulouse appeared to be *en fête* with the white cockades of the Bourbons much in evidence.

When Wellington was dressing for dinner at the Toulouse Prefecture that evening, Colonel, the Honourable Frederick Cavendish Ponsonby came to him with long-awaited news from Bordeaux, which would either refute or confirm the speculation that abounded in the British Army that a peace deal would be signed with France. This naturally led to a tense atmosphere replete with expectation. In the British camp, the general belief was that a peace agreement would have to be signed, reducing France to its pre-revolution size; Napoleon, however, would be allowed to keep his crown.[616] Nonetheless, Ponsonby brought wholly different news to Wellington: "I have extraordinary news for you." Ponsonby blurted out. "Ay, I thought so. I knew we should have peace, I've long expected it." replied Wellington, unruffled. "No, Napoleon has abdicated." "How abdicated?" "Ay, 'tis time indeed…" "You don't say so, upon my honour! Hurrah!" As John Hobhouse, 1st Baron Broughton, described Wellington's reaction: 'The Commander-in-Chief, still in his shirt sleeves, spun round on his heel snapping his fingers like a schoolboy.'[617]

Over the course of the dinner that Wellington organized that evening in Toulouse, news of Napoleon's abdication was officially confirmed: according to the most recent reports, the Allies had entered Paris on 31st March 1814 and Napoleon, after a short wait and under the pressure of his marshals, abdicated on 6th April. The French throne was then taken by Louis XVIII, brother of Louis XVI, who had been executed in 1793. The triumphant powers were now preparing for the now-former French Emperor Napoleon to be sent into exile to the Mediterranean island of Elba. The terms and conditions of Napoleon's departure had been agreed in the form of the Treaty of Fontainebleau*, an agreement between Napoleon and representatives of the Austrian Empire, Prussia and Russia that was signed on 11th April and ratified two days later. The momentous news of Napoleon's abdication was publicly announced during Wellington's dinner in Toulouse; Wellesley had champagne served and made three toasts to the new French ruler Louis XVIII. General Álava in his capacity as a military attaché and thus an official representative of Spain, then stood up sharply and proposed another toast, this time to the "Liberator of Spain!" This was followed by a wave of unbridled celebration and a series of toasts, most of which were made in Wellington's honour by almost all the guests present. After several minutes of uninterrupted chants of Wellesley's name, congratulations, and glorifying toasts in various languages,[618] Mr Larpent claimed that: 'Lord Wellington bowed, confused, and immediately called for the coffee.'[619]

---

* It is noteworthy that the British had considerable reservations about the terms and conditions of this treaty, not least because they thought them remarkably lenient.

Wellington and all of Europe felt an immense sense of relief, as it now seemed that peace would prevail after years of economic dislocation, military campaigns and exhausting battles. Several days later, Lord Charles Stewart, the step-brother of Minister for War Lord Castlereagh came to see Wellington in person in Toulouse on the orders from the British Government. As the war had now come definitively to an end, Stewart offered Wellington the position of British Ambassador in Paris. Wellington accepted the offer with great pleasure. In addition to this new governmental post, Charles Stewart also informed him that the Prince Regent, together with the Parliament, had decided to grant him the title of Duke of Wellington for his extraordinary service to the British Crown, thus bestowing upon him the highest rank of the English peerage. One month later, Wellesley informed his youngest brother Henry of this fact at the end of a letter mostly analysing the present political situation as if nothing important had taken place: 'I believe I forgot to tell you that I was made a Duke.'[620]

The Duke of Wellington arrived in Paris at the beginning of May 1814. He did not enter the French metropolis as a conqueror, but as a diplomat, and therefore decided to don a pale-blue dress coat and top hat in place of his field marshal's uniform and bicorne hat. However, the Duke did not remain in Paris for long. On 14th June, he fulfilled his last obligation as Commander-in-Chief of British forces when he signed and subsequently presented his declaration, in which he thanked his soldiers for their brave acts during the whole Peninsular War:[621]

1) The Commander of the Forces [Wellington], being upon the point of returning to England, again takes this opportunity of congratulating the army upon the recent events which have restored peace to their country and to the world.

2) The share which the British army has had in producing these events, and the high character with which the army will quit this country, must be equally satisfactory to every individual belonging to it, as they are to the Commander of the Forces, and he trusts that the troops will continue the same good conduct to the last.

3) The Commander of the Forces once more requests the army to accept his thanks.[622]

The text of his thanks certainly does not lack warmth of feeling and once again places Wellington's likening of his common soldiers to the "scum of the earth" in a wholly different light. In later life, Wellington mentioned his soldiers to his friend Croker in the following terms:

> I will venture to say that in our later campaigns and especially when we crossed the Pyrenees there, never was an army in the world in better spirits, better order or better discipline. We had mended in discipline every campaign, until at last I hope we were pretty near perfect.[623]

The Europe-wide significance of the humbling of Napoleon was reflected in innumerable celebrations and gatherings. One of the most significant was the Allied Sovereigns' visit to England that took place over the month of June 1814. A glittering assemblage that included Tsar Alexander I of Russia, King Frederick William III of Prussia, the Prince of Lichtenstein, Prince Leopold of Saxe-Coburg-Saalfield, Prince Klemens von Metternich, Catherine, Grand Duchess of Oldenburg, Prince Michael Andreas Barclay de Tolly, Field Marshal Gebhard Leberecht von Blücher and Count Matvei Platov among others gathered to celebrate the peace and the defeat of France. A gala evening of opera was held at Covent Garden, there was a military review of 14,000 troops in Hyde Park, a day at the races at Ascot, and even a trip to Petworth House. A particular highlight was the visit to Oxford University, where in the presence of the Prince Regent, the Prince of Orange and other prominent British and Continental royalty, politicians and military figures watched as the Tsar of Russia, the King of Prussia and Field Marshal Blücher were awarded honorary degrees - DCL (Doctor of Civil Law) in the famous Sheldonian Theatre followed by a banquet at the Ratcliffe Camera. Throughout the Allied Sovereigns' visit, warm words and honours were exchanged and a magnificent naval review held at Portsmouth prior to the embarkation of many of the august guests and allies for the Continent. George, the Prince of Wales (also known as the Prince Regent) had been in his element, doubly so as 1814 marked 100 years of the Hanoverians' ascension to the British throne Both the British Monarchy and the British Establishment bathed in the reflected glory that was thanks to the service and sacrifice of Wellington and all those who had been instrumental in Napoleon's defeat.[624]

At the end of June, Wellington finally set sail from Calais and landed at the English Channel port of Dover after five long years away. He was welcomed in Dover by an exuberant crowd, and he continued to be greeted with enthusiastic crowds all the way to the doors of Number 4, Hamilton Place, his rented London residence. During the journey, more and more people joined the throng, as each person wished to catch sight of this national hero. Naturally, after five years away campaigning Wellington was eager to be reunited with his family, and first visited his wife Kitty and his two sons, Arthur (aged 7) and Charles (aged 6), and then called upon his mother, Anne Wellesley, the Countess of Mornington. As well as being officially welcomed by Queen Charlotte at Buckingham House on 28th June 1814, a few days later a magnificent ball was thrown in Wellington's honour at Burlington House by White's Club, one of the most exclusive of London's gentleman's clubs, and attended by 1,700 guests. On 7th July a Service of General Thanksgiving for the Allied victory was held at St Paul's Cathedral. Wellington was invited to accompany the Prince Regent there by coach and was given the signal honour of carrying the Sword of State as he processed ahead of the Prince Regent into the Cathedral. Further celebrations followed including a magnificent fête hosted by the Prince Regent in temporary rooms and buildings designed by John Nash in the grounds of Carlton House, to which some 2,000 guests were invited. On 28th July the Duke, this time dressed in his marshal's uniform, accepted official thanks from the House of Lords. Lord Eldon, the Speaker of the House of Lords made a point of mentioning the fact that no man in the history of the existence of the English (and later British) state had ever gone from holding the lowest noble title (Knight) to holding the highest (Duke). In addition, each of his promotions in the ranks of the British aristocracy represented a different and extraordinary triumph. After his return, Wellington was without doubt the most popular man in all of Britain.[625]

After the celebrations and a short period of rest, Arthur Wellesley returned to Paris at the end of August to resume duties as British Ambassador*. En route he visited an old friend, William, Prince of Orange, or 'Slender Billy', as he was known by Wellington's officers during the Peninsular

---

*   Wellington purchased as his official residence Hôtel de Charost in the rue du Faubourg Saint-Honoré from Pauline Borghese, Napoleon's sister. This building remains the Official Residence of the British Ambassador to France to this day.

War. Over the course of several days, Arthur and William mapped out the southern area of today's Netherlands and Belgium, where Wellington also carried out an inspection of border fortresses. During one such trip, Wellington, who was now a seasoned soldier and commander, was highly impressed with a defensive position located roughly fifteen miles south of Brussels in the village of Waterloo.[626] Some might view this visit to Waterloo as serendipitous, yet at the time Wellington had not the slightest clue that this site would soon make an indelible mark on the annals of history.

Wellington's first task, which he was given by the British Government as a diplomat and one which he began to fulfil immediately after returning to Paris, was to put an end to the French slave trade. Although he assured William Wilberforce, a leading Abolitionist, who had been a pivotal political figure in banning the slave trade in Britain in 1807, that he would fulfil the task 'with all the zeal of which I am capable...'[627], he failed repeatedly to meet the request in the position of a mere ambassador, albeit one with an excellent reputation. The final word was held by the newly formed French Parliament, which had been formed by the French Constitution and in which many legislators owed their riches to the slave trade and naturally reluctant to relinquish this cruel yet lucrative livelihood.

In addition to his professional obligations, Wellington was a popular celebrity in Paris in today's sense of the term and could rarely find a free evening when an invitation to a ball or other celebration was not lying on his table. For example, Adèle d'Osmond, Comtesse of Boigne wrote in regard to one of the balls that Wellington attended that no host had 'eyes for anyone else [i.e. but Wellington]'.[628] In the salons and boudoirs of Paris, there were rumours of Wellington's affair with the Italian contralto Giuseppina Grassini, who was Napoleon's former lover and, although no concrete evidence of an affair between her and Wellington exists, she demonstrably enjoyed a great deal of the Duke's affection. During this veritable social whirl, Wellington also met with his former adversaries, specifically Marshals Ney, Soult, and Masséna.[629] It was Marshal Masséna who gave Wellington the best reception and, according to his reputation as a *bon vivant* and being good company, walked directly up to the Duke with a smile on his face. In reference to Wellington's scorched earth tactics and his own impasse at the Lines of Torres Vedras, he said to Wellington:

"My lord, you owe me a dinner – for you made me positively starve." An amused Wellington nonetheless politely and wittily retorted: "You should give it to me, Marshal, for you prevented me from sleeping."[630]

Nonetheless, the calm atmosphere of Paris in the autumn of 1814 was disrupted by growing unrest that slowly spread throughout France. Former exiles from the ranks of the Royalists were now scrambling for power and preferment, whilst many of Bonaparte's veterans were forced to tramp the streets of Paris in search of employment in conditions that appeared increasingly dispiriting, even hopeless. Furthermore, King Louis XVIII and the new French Parliament had not lowered taxes nearly as much as they had promised. Almost all of France appeared to be divided into two irreconcilable camps, Royalists and Bonapartists. Echoing the period before the Revolution of 1789, the situation in 1814 was exacerbated by a miserable harvest and food price inflation, especially of staples such as bread and salt, which caused further hardship and a sense of grievance.

Even the new French King Louis XVIII was not the archetype of the powerful, authoritative monarch who would be able to unify the nation in a period of crisis. The fifty-nine-year-old Louis, who was still without children, had spent the last six years of his life in exile in England. The French monarch was of small stature and increasingly obese, to such an extent that his mobility was somewhat restricted, leading him to rely on a wheelchair. The Prince Regent noted that when he tied the Order of the Garter* around the French monarch's calf during his exile in England, it seemed to him as if he were placing his arms around the waist of an average person.[631] Bonapartists dubbed Louis 'King Pig' and, in the light of the deteriorating economic and social situation, began to call increasingly for Napoleon's return. As well as resenting the new Bourbon ruler and government, the Bonapartists loathed the thought of the increasing influence of the British, embodied by the Duke of Wellington's presence in Paris. Rumours soon spread that Wellington's assassination was being planned.

At the end of October, Wellesley took part in a military parade in the Champ de Mars together with the Duke of Angoulême when a Bonapartist bullet suddenly whizzed past Wellington's head. Whether the bullet was intended for Wellington or Louis XVIII's cousin, the Duke

---

* The Most Noble Order of the Garter today is still a functioning British title of chivalry that was evidently founded in 1348 by English King Edward III. The garter, which is depicted in the Order's main insignia, is worn under the knee of the left leg.

of Angoulême, has never been proven; however, the British Government urged Wellington to leave Paris immediately after hearing of this alarming incident.[632] Wellington, however, refused, claiming that his sudden departure from the French metropolis would look like an act of cowardice. Ultimately, the Duke came to an agreement with the British Government that he would travel to Vienna where the victorious powers had been busy making preparations for the Congress of Vienna and the re-ordering of Europe post-Bonaparte since the beginning of October 1814. Wellington was to replace Lord Castlereagh there, as Castlereagh had been called back urgently to London. Thus, no one could interpret this step as an escape from danger, as it was an evident promotion for Wellington.[633]

During the autumn of 1814, Wellington's wife Kitty, now the Duchess of Wellington, had come to join him in Paris, despite her reluctance to leave her young sons behind. After years of separation, a considerable gulf now existed between the two. In addition, Kitty did not overly enjoy the waves of attention that was now washing over her as the wife of the celebrated commander and newly ennobled Duke. To make matters worse, Wellington was constantly surrounded by a throng of female admirers in Paris. Although no specific love affair has ever been proven, gossip spread around Paris, primarily concerning Wellington's alleged love affair with opera singer Giuseppina Grassini. For Kitty, her time in Paris was rather unnerving and she was clearly relieved when her husband left for the Congress of Vienna, at which time she left for her home back in England.
[634] The Congress of Vienna was essentially a gathering of four great European powers (Austria, Britain, Prussia and Russia), plus Bourbon France. Together these states were represented by Prince Klemens von Metternich (Austria), Viscount Castlereagh (Britain), who was soon replaced by the Duke of Wellington, Count Karl Nesselrode (Russia), Prince Karl Hardenburg (Prussia) and the Duke of Talleyrand (France).[635]

Wellington arrived in Vienna on 1st February 1815 and many of the representatives there rightfully feared that he would be a significantly tougher negotiator than Castlereagh. The first to learn of his unyielding nature was the Russian Tsar Alexander I, who was the first to visit Wellington on the day after the Duke's arrival. The Tsar attempted to gain as much information as possible concerning the situation in Paris and British intentions, but learned nothing from Wellington that was not already public knowledge. The Tsar thus likened him to the experienced

French diplomat Talleyrand. The Prussian ruler, King Frederick William III fared equally poorly, as he forced Wellington to wait in his antechamber before their pre-arranged meeting, as he was not able to tear himself away from his lover. The Duke would have none of this treatment and left, after which he repeatedly refused further invitations from the Prussian ruler, claiming that he was too occupied with work for the upcoming Congress.[636]

Out of all his colleagues at the Congress of Vienna, it is the author's personal assumption that, from a professional and human perspective, Wellington got on best with Talleyrand and Metternich. He knew the former from his time in Paris, where he had apparently made a good impression on Wellington when, together with Louis XVIII, he described the situation to Wellesley frankly and gave him a clear indication that the abolition of the slave trade in the delicate situation in which France now found itself would be near impossible. In September 1814, Wellington wrote the following of Talleyrand: 'I believe both the King and M[onsieur]. de Talleyrand are sincere in what they have said to me and Lord Castlereagh [About abolishing the slave trade]...'[637] Metternich evidently made a favourable impression on Wellington during their first negotiations with other Congress representatives, when, immediately after his arrival, Wellington asked the participants of the conference: "What have you done, gentlemen?" In the dead silence that ensued, it was Metternich who sarcastically but (unfortunately) wholly truthfully answered: "Nothing, absolutely nothing."[638]

Metternich's reply was, however, somewhat exaggerated, and the first solutions slowly became evident over the course of February at least in the most difficult issues concerning the division of Saxony and Poland. Russia, which initially demanded nearly all of Polish territory, ultimately accepted "only" the larger part of the Duchy of Warsaw, which was to be linked via a personal union (in this instance, where two countries have autonomy but the same monarch) embodied by the Russian Tsar. Prussia, which was Russia's greatest ally in the negotiations and had had ambitions to take Saxony since the beginning of the Congress (the King of Saxony had been Napoleon's ally until the Battle of Leipzig), finally agreed in a similar manner to take only a portion of Saxon territory. The Austrians so far had been offered a portion of Galicia that they had lost in 1809. Britain, represented by Wellington, was highly satisfied with this solution, as the country attempted in accordance with tradition to establish a balance between all the great powers on the Continent. However, matters concerning the territories of today's Italy, the Netherlands, Belgium, and Germany had yet to be resolved, matters which were far from insignificant.[639]

Negotiations at the Congress on 7th March 1815 were suddenly disrupted by shocking news of Napoleon's escape from Elba. Napoleon was acutely aware of Bonapartists sympathies in the French military and the relatively favourable domestic political situation in France. On 1st March 1815, Napoleon landed with only 1,100 men in Golfe Juan near the town of Antibes on the Côe D'Azure in South East France, after which he began immediately to march toward Paris. All military units that Louis XVIII gradually sent to face Napoleon either "failed to find" their former Emperor or (in the majority of cases) outwardly joined forces with him. The most infamous incident in this period can be attributed to French Marshal Ney, who solemnly swore to bring Napoleon back to Paris "in an iron cage". Instead, Ney quickly joined forces with his former Emperor. Military units stationed near Paris defected and it soon became clear that the Bourbon Monarch was in an extremely perilous position. On the night of 19th – 20th March, the terrified Louis XVIII voluntarily withdrew from the French capital and crossed the border into what was then the United Kingdom of the Netherlands and based himself in Ghent. On the following evening, the triumphant Napoleon, accompanied by wildly jubilant crowds, once again entered Paris.[640] This marked the beginning of the period now commonly known as 'The Hundred Days'.

In the meantime, Wellington hurriedly left for Pressburg (present-day Bratislava) in the company of Metternich and Talleyrand on 8th March, where Saxon King Frederick Augustus I now resided. The triumvirate of ambassadors was tasked with passing on to the King of Saxony the unpleasant news concerning the decision of the Congress of Vienna to hand over three-fifths of Saxony to Prussia. At the same time, the ambassadors were to attempt to ensure the Saxon monarch's acceptance of these terms as soon as possible. After a weak attempt at resistance, Frederick Augustus soon realized that he had no other choice and, to the ambassadors' delight, soon gave his consent. King Frederick August I of Saxony must have rued the day that he had remained a loyal ally of Napoleon to the bitter end.

Wellington, Metternich and Talleyrand returned to Vienna on 12th March. Just a day later, a special declaration targeting Napoleon was signed, in which Napoleon was, among other things, dubbed an "enemy of humanity".[641] Napoleon himself, who was fully aware of the massive military advantage that the Allies (who were now all working toward a shared cause) could deploy against him, he attempted to portray outwardly that he was a wholly "new person". He repeatedly demanded peace and, evidently in attempts to ingratiate himself with his enemies, abolished the slave trade in France. The matter which Wellington had striven so painstakingly to abolish under the constitutional Bourbon monarchy and which was estimated to take several years was now passed under the rule of this authoritative sovereign within several days. The European powers, however, did not let themselves be fooled by this attempt at populism, for they had come to know Napoleon Bonaparte only too well over the course of the previous decade. The Allied leaders did not respond to Napoleon's correspondence and on 25th March the Seventh Anti-Napoleonic Coalition was formed. This time, however, war was not declared by the Allies against France, but against Napoleon himself.

Within the newly formed Anti-Napoleonic Coalition, the Allies ultimately decided to put five armies in the field. The first two armies, each of which possessed roughly 100,000 men, were deployed at the lower course of the Rhine in the area of today's Belgium and the Netherlands. It was here that Napoleon seemed most likely to strike and, if successful, attempt to force his enemies once again to the negotiating table. The first army was made up of Anglo-Dutch-Hanover units (at the Congress of Vienna, the ruler of the newly formed Kingdom of the Netherlands William I of Orange-Nassau, father of 'Slender Billy', was on the side of the Allies in the oncoming conflict). The second was made up of Prussian forces, and both armies were ordered to be in close cooperation. The third army of 200,000 men and made up of Austrian, Bavarian, and Baden-Wűrttemberg forces was deployed on the upper course of the Rhine. The fourth and equally strong army, formed purely by Russian units, waited as reserves near the town of Wűrzburg. The last of the allied armies, with a strength of 150,000 soldiers, was made up exclusively of Austrian contingents, which the Allies decided to deploy to Northern Italy to prevent a potential advance of Napoleon's former Marshal Joachim Murat, presently the King of Naples, who was married to Napoleon's youngest sister

Caroline and whose neutrality (although Murat vociferously assured the Congress of it) was doubtful to say the least.[642]

The British Government quickly offered Wellington two possibilities for further engagement: he could either continue in the role of British representative at the Congress of Vienna or take command of the newly formed Anglo-Dutch-Hanover Army. Wellington did not hesitate for long and chose the latter. Thus, on 28th March, he travelled from Vienna to Brussels in order to take up the command that had been offered to him.[643] Tsar Alexander I, who was absolutely convinced – much like the majority of the other Congress participants – that Napoleon would either strike first in Flanders in what is present-day Belgium or the Allies would launch their own offensive from there on Paris, he put his right hand on Wellington's shoulder before he departed and said the following in parting in a grave and sombre voice: *"C'est pour vous encore de sauver le monde."* (It's up to you again to save the world).[644]

In view of the gravity of the situation, Wellesley travelled with all possible haste. As an excellent rider, he quickly rode through the territory of today's Germany and reached Brussels on 4th April. By the end of May, his new army, which had gathered just outside of Brussels, had reached a total of more than 90,000 men, and was prepared to leave for the field immediately. They were, however, largely an inexperienced and rag-tag army equipped at the very last minute. Years later, in regard to the quality of the soldiers he had at his disposal at Waterloo, he declared: 'I have got an infamous army, very weak and ill-equipped, and a very inexperienced staff.'[645]

The majority of Wellington's veterans who had been with him during the Peninsular War were gradually sent off to serve in the British colonies around the world after Napoleon's abdication in the spring of 1814. The largest number of these veterans was deployed in North America, where Great Britain had been at war with the United States on the territory of the Canadian-American border over spheres of influence in naval trade and a portion of Canadian territory, the so-called War of 1812, which actually lasted from June 1812 to February 1815. Neither side was able to gain a decisive advantage and thus on 24th December 1814, the British signed the Treaty of Ghent, a peace accord with the Americans. Apart from some cosmetic changes, however, the accord brought little change to the state of affairs prior to the war. As for Wellington's former generals, his brother-in-law and good friend Ned Pakenham was ordered to serve in America and, to Wellington's great regret, fell in the Battle of New Orleans, one of the final engagements of the war. For these reasons, only a third of the ranks of Wellington's "infamous" army were British (i.e. roughly 30,000), of which the majority were fresh recruits from the British Isles who had been only recently transported. The urgency of the situation can be seen in the fact that, for example, 5,000 British troops were withdrawn from Ireland in order to create Wellington's "Flanders Army" more quickly, even though the British Government worried that the withdrawal of these troops from Ireland might lead to an uprising (the army at the time still fulfilled their duty of maintaining public order, i.e. the equivalent of today's police).[646]

Despite this fact, Wellington's army still had many of its familiar faces, who had provided crucial support to Wellesley during the Peninsular War and in many cases were also his good friends and ones he could rely on. In it were men like Sir Thomas Picton who served despite the fact that in 1814 he complained of chronic insomnia and overall nervous exhaustion, claiming that he felt it was high time to retire after years of continual service. Now, however, the highly principled Picton did not hesitate to accept Wellington's offer of command over the 5th British Division in the light of the predicament that the British were in. From the ranks of the former high-ranking officers in the Peninsular War, General Rowland 'Daddy' Hill and long-term member of Wellington's staff Sir Alexander Gordon also offered their services to the Duke. Despite the number of inexperienced recruits, the British forces were still the most reliable part of Wellington's army, thanks in part to the excellent training that the Red Coats were required to undergo.[647]

Six thousand soldiers from the King's German Legion from Hanover formed the next fighting force that Wellington had at his command. Almost all of these men had served under Wellington during the Peninsular War. Another 16,000 men joined the Duke's forces from Hanover over the course of May 1815; the majority of them, however, were freshly conscripted recruits. Subsequently, Frederick William, the Duke of Brunswick* brought almost 7,000 more men to Wellington's

---

*   Known also as Friedrich Wilhelm Braunschweig-Wolfenbüttel, or Friedrich Wilhelm, Herzog von Braunschweig-Lüneburg-Oels.

camp. Frederick William had fought in the Peninsular War since 1810 with a portion of these units, which were now reinforced with new recruits. Thus, Wellesley had several more units of reliable veterans among the 'Black Brunswickers' known also as the 'Black Legion', under the command of Frederick William, nicknamed the 'Black Duke' (who gained his nickname when he dressed his soldiers in black uniforms as a sign of mourning after Napoleon occupied Brunswick).* The remainder of Wellington's forces, which amounted to almost 40,000 men, consisted of units on the territory of today's Belgium and the Netherlands (i.e. the new United Kingdom of the Netherlands established by the Congress of Vienna). Wellington tried to maximize the fighting capability of his army by mixing the most experienced British regiments and contingents of the King's German Legion with other units not yet familiar with battle. He did so by ensuring that in individual regiments and brigades the ratio of veterans to fresh recruits was as balanced as possible. A similar tactic had already been tried and tested when the Duke mixed inexperienced Portuguese units with the more seasoned British soldiers during the Peninsular War. Wellington also requested that, in these critical times, the Portuguese Government send him the Portuguese regiments that had served under him in previous years. The Portuguese, however, refused to send their soldiers to Brussels with the justification that they did not fully trust the Spanish and therefore were certainly not willing to leave Portugal undefended.

The Duke of Wellington subsequently divided his army into three corps: he gave command over the first corps, which consisted of two British and two Dutch divisions, to the twenty-two-year-old Prince of Orange ('Slender Billy') rather reluctantly and for political reasons – units of the United Kingdom of the Netherlands amounted to 40,000 of the total men in his army. Wellington gave command of the second corps, which was identical to the first in its composition, to General Rowland Hill. He took personal command of the remaining corps, which in addition to two British divisions also included the Brunswick contingents.

Wellington's army occupied a position south of Brussels that stretched several miles from the strategic crossroads at the village of Quatre Bras to

---

*   For more on the impressive story of the 'Black Duke' and 'Black Legion', see the Addendum – Wellington, the Austrian Empire and the Kingdom of Bohemia in the Coalition Wars against Napoleon.

the northwest. In order to defeat Napoleon, his army had to work in close cooperation with the Prussian Army of 121,000 men that was located east of Brussels near the town of Ligny. The Prussians were commanded by the experienced and still dynamic seventy-three-year-old Field Marshal Gebhard von Blücher. 'Old Blücher' or 'Marshal Forwards' (a nickname he received thanks to the unyieldingness with which he marched his men forward even in moments in which it seemed that the battle had been lost), as were his two most famous monikers, was a seasoned commander who had a score to settle with Napoleon. Bonaparte had defeated him in the Battles of Jena (1806) and Lützen (1813), during which his horses were killed under him and he himself was lucky to have escaped with his life. Blücher, however, led the Prussian Army, which had forced Napoleon to abdicate to the Allies in 1814 and occupied Paris, a fact which brought Blücher a great deal of satisfaction. It was around this period that this formidable Prussian campaigner met Wellington in Paris for the first-time during the latter's time as British Ambassador to France. According to sources, Wellington and Blücher got along well in Paris and made a mutually favourable impression on one another, a fact which formed a promising basis for their military cooperation.[648]

In a relatively short space of time it is remarkable that Napoleon had managed to put together a fighting force of 300,000 men drawn from across France. However, a portion of these men had been partially disarmed, and a good number of Bonaparte's troops were forced to be deployed in the strongly Royalist region of the Vendée (a coast region in western France) in order to put a timely end to a looming Anti-Napoleon uprising there. Upon Napoleon's orders, additional French garrisons remained at the southern and eastern border of the country in order to stop the potential advance of the remaining Allied armies. Despite these considerable difficulties, Napoleon still possessed a field army near Paris of 124,000 men. Nonetheless, this still meant that Wellington and Blücher had an almost two-fold advantage over the French Emperor. In order to effectively utilize this substantial advantage, it was of grave importance for both men that their armies remained in constant contact with the help of scouts and thus could help one another quickly if attacked. Even so, Wellington was rather taken aback when he learned of the size of Napoleon's new army. By no means did he or Blücher assume that Napoleon would manage in such a short period of time to gather such a formidable fighting force.

Paradoxically, Bonaparte now managed to draft soldiers much more easily than in 1813, when he had to take in younger conscripts, as the newest peace accord led to the release of a large number of French prisoners of war who returned to France and now quite willingly lined up under the flag of their newly returned Emperor. Despite this fact, Napoleon was forced to deal with a problem similar to Wellington. Although he managed once again to reform the old and feared Imperial Guard, his army consisted of too high a number of completely inexperienced recruits. Despite this fact, he (once again similar to Wellington) still possessed many of his former and highly competent generals. Napoleon named Marshal Soult commander of his general staff (surprisingly, the previous commander of Napoleon's general staff Marshal Berthier maintained his loyalty to Louis XVIII after the restoration of the House of Bourbon). He also had men like General Dominique Vandamme (known in the Czech Republic primarily for his defeat at Chlumec and Přestanov* in northern Bohemia by Austrian Marshal Schwarzenberg in 1813 shortly before the Battle of Leipzig, which proved fatal to Napoleon) and, primarily, the 'Bravest of the Brave', Marshal Ney, who had initially claimed he would lock Napoleon in an "iron cage" (although this was likely to have been a purely pragmatic statement made to deceive Louis XVIII).[649]

Napoleon Bonaparte and his field army crossed the border of present-day Belgium on 15th June 1815 at roughly half past three in the morning, beginning a drama that culminated in one of the most famous battles in world history – the Battle of Waterloo. Innumerable books, academic papers, works of non-fiction and historical novels have been written about the events of Waterloo. However, despite the slew of publications on the topic, many scholars disagree about what happened between 15th and 18th June 1815. Nonetheless, this changes nothing of the fact that the events that took place on these days are rightfully among the most dramatic and pivotal moments in history. This fact is quite conveniently summarized in the introduction to the novel *Sharpe's Waterloo*, which deals with this famous battle, by popular British novelist Bernard Cornwell:

> When I began writing this book, I remember trying – ultimately in vain – to insert a plot twist into the story. Despite all efforts, however, I failed. I spent weeks, perhaps months trying to shape the story into an organic part of

---

*   In English commonly known as the Battle of Kulm.

history, but it always ended in failure. In the end, I realized that no story, no plot twist that I could think of could equal the drama that took place during the Waterloo Campaign and in the battle itself. And so I forwent those five or six thousand words that I had pored over for so long and in their place wrote one simple sentence: It was early in the morning (15ᵗʰ June 1815) on the northern border of France.*

After Napoleon Bonaparte crossed the border of the newly-established United Kingdom of the Netherlands early that morning, he evidently hoped that, if he was able to defeat Wellington and Blücher and then quickly take Brussels, the other allies would lose their nerve and agree to peace talks, allowing Napoleon to keep the Imperial Crown. If Napoleon defeated Wellington, he could bet on the fact that the Whigs would come to power the moment that Wellesley was publicly discredited and the boundless trust in his "invincibility" shattered among British Members of Parliament. The Whigs were much more inclined towards allowing Napoleon to rule France in place of Louis XVIII; some Whigs could even be dubbed Bonapartists and held a certain admiration for Napoleon.[650]

Napoleon had three logical options for a direct advance on Brussels after crossing the border. The first would be to march via the town of Tournai, outflanking Wellington's right wing and subsequently cutting off the British supply contingents from his primary army. Then, Napoleon could attack Wellington's right wing from the west and, if he defeated the British Commander and continue on against Blücher's Prussians further east and ultimately defeat them as well. The next alternative was to march in the most direct route possible towards Brussels via the town of Mons, carry out a frontal attack on Wellington, defeat him before Blücher arrived, and finally destroy the Prussians. The third option, which Napoleon ultimately chose, led through Charleroi towards the strategically important crossroads near a village with only a few humble dwellings named Quatre Bras located directly between

---

*   Bernard Cornwell, *Sharpovo Waterloo* (Ostrava 2015), p. 13. (The quoted text has been translated into English from the Czech edition of Bernard Cornwell's novel). In addition to a number of documentary films, Waterloo was also made into a feature film in 1970, in which Wellington is played by Christopher Plummer and Napoleon by Rod Steiger. Despite certain historical inaccuracies, it is the author's opinion that the creators managed to relatively accurately depict the character of both commanders.

Wellington and Blücher's armies. This crossroads was significant for the route that ran through it, which allowed for the fastest link between Wellington and Blücher's armies. As soon as the Allies lost Quatre Bras, it would take each army much longer to come to the other's aid. A commander and strategist of Napoleon's calibre was only too aware of this fact; but Wellington and Blücher, who still had no idea of the direction in which Bonaparte would attack, could not have understood its significance at that given moment. The French Emperor therefore decided to quickly seize the crossroads at Quatre Bras, a task which he entrusted to Marshal Ney, who for this purpose was gradually given approximately 40,000 men. In the meantime, Napoleon prepared to launch a full on attack on the Prussians, who were deployed southeast of Brussels near the village of Ligny. Ney was ordered to hold the crossroads at Quatre Bras from Wellington and prevent him from potentially coming to the aid of Blücher. Once Napoleon defeated Blücher, he would hurry to aid Ney, who would be fighting Wellington at Quatre Bras, and attack Wellington's flank, subsequently crushing him. If everything went according to plan, and the French had fortune on their side, both Allied armies would be destroyed within a day. If by some chance Ney managed to defeat Wellington sooner than Napoleon defeated Blücher (or at least force him to retreat), Marshal Ney would come to Napoleon's aid and attack Blücher's flank. Napoleon's plan thus seemed to be quite simple. But, because there is often great power in simplicity, it can also often be fatal. The crucial factor of Napoleon's whole plan for the upcoming campaign was – "come hell or high water" – to keep both enemy armies divided and destroy them one after the other.[651]

The desultory work of Wellington and Blücher's reconnaissance units and insufficient communication between both Allied armies, which was done via scouts who often made errors, would prove to be a serious handicap for both commanders. In retrospect, Wellington noted sarcastically in regard to the slow movement of information that perhaps the "fattest officer" in the whole army must have been chosen as a scout on the Prussian side. In addition, Wellington currently had none of his own exploring officers on French soil to pass on reliable reports on Napoleon's movements to him. The Duke was also forced to uphold the decree of the Congress of Vienna, which banned him from sending his own spies across the French border due to the fact that war had been declared by the Allies only against Napoleon and not against France.[652] It is questionable whether this "official ban" stopped men such as Lieutenant-Colonel Colquhoun Grant, who at the moment in the position of head of Wellington's Intelligence was located in the field and was at Wellington's disposal. If Grant had crossed the French border despite this ban, of which we have no verifiable information or indications to believe so, he evidently did not provide Wellington with any reliable information in regard to the speed with which Napoleon was advancing. It should also be taken into consideration that in Spain and Portugal, Grant usually had much more time to verify his information thanks to the distances over which the enemy's troops were forced to travel before coming into contact with Wellington, while everything there took place much more quickly and in a smaller space in comparison to the campaign on the Iberian Peninsula. Wellington and Blücher could also partially rely on reports from Paris, where the feared and exceedingly cunning Joseph Fouché, head of French police, had preserved his loyalty to Louis XVIII and the allies, all of course without Napoleon's knowledge. Fouché, who the year before had made efforts to capture Colquhoun Grant, was now ironically sending secret messages along with other royalist Frenchmen. On the other hand, betting everything based on unconfirmed information from a man who had already so many times "changed sides" may have presented a significant risk, as there was a realistic threat that Fouché was only simulating his turn against Napoleon and was ordered by the Emperor to send the Allies disinformation. Therefore, the majority of reports that Wellington and Blücher had received were unreliable and evidently contradictory. The only indisputably certainty continued to be the fact that Napoleon continued to advance with lightning speed.[653]

Wellington finally received the first credible reports of Napoleon's advance in the late hours of the afternoon of 15th June. He immediately declared a state of emergency among the regiments of his army, but information on the direction of French movements hitherto was so ambiguous that Wellington decided it would be best to avoid being too hasty. He thus left his army prepared in their positions in fear that, if he failed to use proper judgement, he might fall into a trap laid by none other than the famous strategist Napoleon Bonaparte. Until then, Wellington only possessed a report of clashes between the British 95th Rifles and French forces near the town of Mons, which was located roughly in the middle of Wellington's forces situated southwest of Brussels, i.e. exactly halfway between Charleroi and Tournai. During this late afternoon, which to Wellington seemed shrouded in uncertainty, he received a dispatch from Prussian Lieutenant-General von Zieten (Wellington's critics claim that he received the dispatch in the morning hours. However, no convincing archive material exists to prove this statement), who informed him of the clash with the French at Charleroi and now called upon him for aid.[654] In the meantime, however, Wellington did not intend to make any rash decisions and concentrate his army in one spot (despite the fact that various critics often hold this fact against him), as he explained to the Prussian liaison officer assigned to his army, Colonel Müffling, who delivered the alarming report from von Zieten:

> If all is as General Zieten supposes, I shall concentrate on my left wing [at Charleroi and Quatre Bras] the Prince of Orange, and shall so be à portée to fight in co-operation with the Prussian army. If, however, a portion of the enemy should advance by Mons, I must then concentrate more to my centre. For this reason I must wait for my advices from Mons before I fix on my rendezvous.[655]

Wellington's intelligence post at Mons was under the command of Major-General Wilhelm von Dörnberg, a seasoned German soldier from Landgraviate of Hesse-Kassel who had been fighting since 1792 in the War of the First Coalition in the ranks of the Prussian Army. Later, during the Napoleonic Wars (and much like many other men, including Wellington), he received his own specific nickname of *'Aufstandsdörnberg'* (Uprising Dörnberg), as he plotted an uprising during the War of the Fifth Coalition in 1809, during which several thousand men attempted to lay siege to Kassel, the capital of the Kingdom of Westphalia created by Napoleon in attempts to capture Napoleon's younger brother Jerôme Bonaparte, who was King of Westphalia. Dörnberg's uprising was dispersed by Jerôme's army while Napoleon defeated the Austrians at Wagram. Dörnberg subsequently fled to Bohemia and in the town of Náchod joined the Black Legion of Frederick William, Duke of Brunswick. With the Black Legion, he made his way to Wellington on the Iberian Peninsula, where he served under his command until the end of 1812, when he left to fight against Napoleon in Russia.* Thus, he was an experienced soldier whom Wellington knew well; it was therefore clearly wise to take his reports seriously. In addition, Dörnberg sent his spies from Mons to the French border with the task of questioning local wayfarers in the attempt to gain credible and vital information for Wellington on Napoleon's advance. However, among these "wayfarers" were also many spies sent cunningly by Napoleon to spread false information and claim that Napoleon was planning to march against Wellington's right wing through Mons, a fact which Dörnberg subsequently reported to Wellington, who could not therefore be sure until the last moment whether Napoleon would attack his centre through Mons.[656]

On the evening of 15th June, Wellington was in Brussels, where he attended the famous ball hosted by Lady Charlotte Lennox, Duchess of Richmond, whose husband, the Duke of Richmond, was now a commander of a small portion of the British reserves. Throughout the Peninsular War, two of his sons were Wellington's aide-de-camps, the oldest of whom was Charles, Lord March and the younger John, whom Wellington travelled to visit after the Battle of Orthez. The Duke and Duchess of Richmond's third son William, who was only fifteen years old, had now also joined Wellington's staff as aide-de-camp to follow on in the family military tradition. The Duchess of Richmond was one of the prominent organizers of social events in the city and, in addition to Wellington, the whole British general staff and the vast majority of highly-ranking officers were present at her ball. Wellington's presence at the ball was important primarily for preventing the spread of panic in the streets of Brussels. The message that his participation in the ball was meant to send to the civilian population was clear: If the British Commander was taking part in entertainment, the situation for the Allies could surely not be so grave. In this case, however, the opposite was true. At roughly one o'clock in the morning, William of Orange's aide-de-camp arrived at the ball with a dispatch from the Major-General of the Dutch Army, Baron Jean Victor de Constant Rebecque. The baron's dispatch was absolutely crucial, as it finally gave Wellington a clear report on the direction of Napoleon's advance across Charleroi and was accompanied by alarming news describing the first clash with the French that

---

*   Gustav Könnecke, *Dörnberg, Wilhelm Caspar Ferdinand, Freiherr von, in: Allgemeine Deutsche Biographie* (ADB). Band 5 (Leipzig 1877), p. 353. Before his journey to Russia, Dörnberg left the Black Legion for a short time and served also for several months in the King's German Legion.

took place south of Brussels, only 40 kilometres away at the crossroads of Quatre Bras, which was highly strategic for further actions.

On 15th June 1815, Wellington left this crossroads unoccupied, but Baron Constant Rebecque thoroughly disobeyed the Duke's orders, according to which he was to gather his soldiers not in Quatre Bras, but farther to the west at Nivelles, which was closer to Wellington's centre at Mons. Nonetheless, Rebecque evidently understood the significance of the position at Quatre Bras and, to be on the safe side, sent 4,000 troops under the command of Colonel Bernhard von Sachsen-Weimar to occupy it. It was only a small army, but it was enough to hold Quatre Bras against Ney's advance forces, a fact which Rebecque now relayed to Wellington in detail in his dispatch, which was written at half past ten in the evening. This was perhaps the first time in Wellington's long military career that the disobedience of his orders subsequently worked in his favour. Wellington then took the Duke of Richmond aside and asked him to prepare a good map of the surroundings in a small cloakroom just off of the ballroom.[657] Wellington then allegedly spoke the following famous words over the unfurled map: "Napoleon has humbugged me, by God! He has gained twenty-four hours march on me."[658]

Nonetheless, this oft-quoted phrase in both academic and non-fiction literature remains problematic – its original author, Captain George Bowles from the Coldstream Guards Regiment, was not present at the scene described and recorded everything "second hand". Regardless of how the situation concerning the map played out, it is certain that Wellington remained at the ball for a time, despite the disturbing news; he did not want to give the impression of leaving in haste due to a looming threat. He left the ball between one and two o'clock in the morning in order to sleep for a few hours.[659] Inevitably, however, a tense atmosphere soon began to prevail at the Duchess of Richmond's ball and came to a head when all officers present were ordered to report to their regiments at three in the morning at the latest. Although the Duke attempted to keep his composure, it is clear from eyewitness reports that he struggled to control his nerves:

> We were told that the troops had orders to march at 3 in the morning, and that every officer must join his regiment by that time, as the French were advancing, you cannot possibly picture to yourself the dismay and consternation that appeared in every face [at the Duchess of Richmond's ball]. Those who had

brothers and sons to be engaged, openly gave way to their grief...We staid at this ball as short a time as we could, but long enough... to see, what was much more extraordinary than all, the Duke's equanimity a little discomposed.[660]

Lady Catherine Arden, who was present at the ball, wrote in a letter to her aunt several days later. Harriet, the Duchess of Hamilton recalled Wellington's behaviour thus: 'Although the Duke affected great gaiety and cheerfulness, it struck me that I had never seen him have such an expression of care and anxiety on his countenance.'[661]

On 16th June, Wellington woke very early, dealt with his necessary correspondence, and around 7 o'clock saddled up and set off for Quatre Bras to oversee the situation. At approximately 10 o'clock, Wellington arrived at Quatre Bras, where roughly 6,000 of his men (which was still desperately few) from the army corps of the Prince of Orange were deployed. Upon his arrival, absolutely nothing seemed to point to the fact that the French might be preparing an imminent concentrated attack.

In the non-fiction work *Waterloo: The history of four days. Three armies and three battles*, author Bernard Cornwell offers a wholly logical explanation for why Ney had not yet attacked: According to Cornwell, Wellington had been saved by his reputation as a master of "reverse slope tactics". Marshal Ney, who had already been defeated several times by Wellington's use of the strategy (the best example of which would be Ney's attack on Busaco), now feared that Wellington's whole army might be hidden beyond the undulating terrain north of Quatre Bras and therefore, similarly to Wellington, awaited more comprehensive intelligence. Advocates of Napoleon naturally blame Marshal Ney for his passivity. In regard to Ney's relative inaction during the previous day (15th June), historian Rory Muir claims that Marshal Ney simply did not have a sufficient number of men deployed at Quatre Bras and subsequently did not receive clear orders from the Emperor.[662] In light of the fact that Ney had not yet attacked, Wellington immediately continued east on from Quatre Bras towards Ligny in order to connect with Marshal Blücher, gain further information concerning his camp, and consult with him on their next move or even perhaps a joint attack on Napoleon's army.

Wellington met with the Prussian Marshal around midday (16th June) at a windmill in the village of Brye near the Prussian camp at Ligny. According to reports, he notified Blücher that he had ordered a significant

WATERLOO CAMPAIGN
15ᵗʰ – 18ᵗʰ June 1815

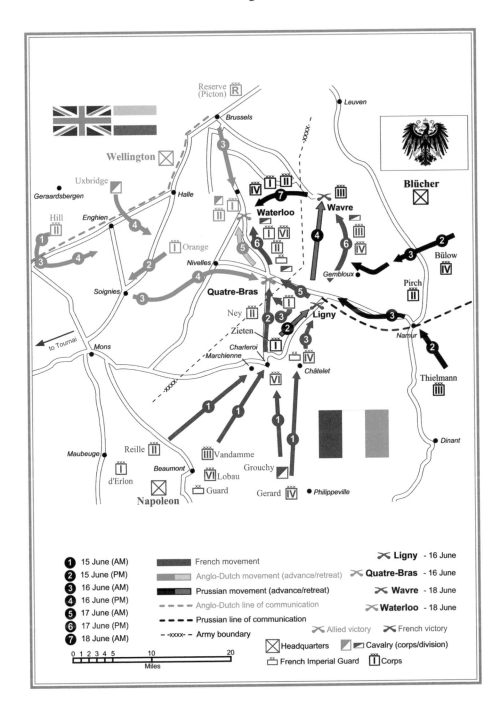

❶ 15 June (AM)	▬ French movement	✕ **Ligny** - 16 June
❷ 15 June (PM)	▬ Anglo-Dutch movement (advance/retreat)	✕ **Quatre-Bras** - 16 June
❸ 16 June (AM)	▬ Prussian movement (advance/retreat)	✕ **Wavre** - 18 June
❹ 16 June (PM)	– – – Anglo-Dutch line of communication	✕ **Waterloo** - 18 June
❺ 17 June (AM)	▬▬ Prussian line of communication	
❻ 17 June (PM)	–xxxx– – Army boundary	✕ Allied victory ✕ French victory
❼ 18 June (AM)		

0 1 2 3 4 5   10   20
Miles

⊠ Headquarters   ◪ Cavalry (corps/division)
⊞ French Imperial Guard   Ⅰ Corps

portion of his army to redeploy to Nivelles and Quatre Bras and that his soldiers should now be in position. This was so that his men could come to the aid of the Prussians as quickly as possible if they were attacked. According to Colonel Müffling, he also told Blücher that he would come to his aid only if he himself were not being attacked by the French.* Nonetheless, Wellington was rather dismayed at the disadvantageous position the Prussians held in the open field near Ligny. During this visit Wellington took aside Sir Henry Hardinge, a British officer assigned to the Prussian Army, and told him: 'If they fight here they will be damnably mauled.'[663] In retrospect, Wellington himself recalled the whole situation in which he attempted to warn the Prussians: 'I said to them [to Marshal Blücher and his staff], everybody knows their own army best, but if I were to fight with mine here, I should expect to be beat.'[664]

Unfortunately for the Allies, Blücher's army was soon attacked by Napoleon at Ligny and defeated in the ensuing battle. Despite the considerable losses that were inflicted to a great degree by Napoleon's artillery on Blücher's unsuitable position at the beginning of battle, the army held its position until the evening. Napoleon suddenly emerged from the south and launched a fierce attack with the force of 60,000 men. Thanks to the element of surprise, he believed that this force would be more than enough to defeat the Prussians and, before the battle, had sent an army corps of 20,000 men under the command of General d'Erlon to assist Ney at Quatre Bras and hold Wellington. In the final phase of the Battle of Ligny, Blücher made a last-minute attempt to turn the battle in the Prussians' favour with a massive cavalry attack that he led personally. However, the whole Prussian cavalry attack ended in failure and during this final counterattack, Blücher's horse fell beneath him. At the very last moment, however, the Prussian Marshal's life was saved by his devoted aide-de-camp Count Nostitz, who delivered him from the battlefield to safety. Nonetheless, the defeated 'Old Blücher' lost 16,000 men along with twenty-one cannons at Ligny, while 8,000 more Prussians took advantage of the situation and deserted.[665] French losses have been

---

*   Compare: Holmes, *Wellington: The Iron Duke*, pp. 229–230. Muir, *Wellington: Waterloo and the Fortunes of Peace*, pp. 43–45. Muir points out the fact that Wellington ordered a significant portion of his army to the west closer to Blücher's position on 15th June at ten o'clock in the evening. Thus, it was before he left for the Duchess of Richmond's ball. He evidently did so because he had not received any reports from Mons and for this reason began to take Napoleon's advance over Charleroi more seriously.

estimated to have been 11,000-12,000. As for Sir Henry Hardinge, who was present throughout the Battle of Ligny, his left hand was shot off and thus he took no further part in the momentous events of the coming days.

Wellington had been unaware of these events and must have heard cannon fire coming from Ligny, which would have alerted him to the onset of battle between Blücher and Napoleon. For the present, Wellington returned to Quatre Bras, where he and a mere 6,000 men were attacked by Ney, who launched his assault around two o'clock in the afternoon with the full force of his 42,000 soldiers.* More and more of Wellington's troops, which he had ordered earlier to report to the area, now arrived at Quatre Bras and began one by one to take part in battle, a fact which, at least for the meantime, remedied the situation. Fortunately, for Wellington, the first to arrive at Quatre Bras was Picton's 5th Infantry Division, which was among the best contingents Wellington had near Brussels. Forces on both sides thus gradually began to balance one another out. Wellesley's right wing, which was supported by the Bossu Wood stretching west of Quatre Bras, was covered by the Scottish Highlanders (92nd Regiment of Foot)** dressed in their traditional kilts immediately after their arrival on the battlefield.

The Brunswick Corps under the command of the 'Black Duke', who arrived at Quatre Bras shortly after Picton, quickly joined the 92nd on the right wing. At the same time, a portion of the Brunswick Regiment was ordered to Wellington's left wing to support the 95th Rifles, which clashed with Ney's men here on one of the adjacent farms.

The fierce battle gradually flared up along the whole length of the position held by Wellington's troops, who continued to swell in number. In addition to Quatre Bras itself, Wellington's forces occupied the area west of the village around the Bossu Wood, whereupon they gradually spread east, taking a position in the neighbouring area of the road leading from Quatre Bras to Ligny (located roughly 6 miles away) where the clash between Blücher and Napoleon was taking place. Due to the fact that fresh units continued to arrive and come to Wellington's aid and were

---

* Military historian Richard Holmes cites this number in his publication *Wellington: The Iron Duke* (p. 230). On the contrary, in his work *Wellington: Waterloo and the Fortunes of Peace 1814–1852*, historian Rory Muir claims that Ney ultimately did not order more than 25,000 soldiers into battle at Quatre Bras.

** The regiment is also known as the 92nd Gordon Highlanders Regiment, named after its founder Colonel George Gordon. In light of the presence of Sir Alexander Gordon in Wellington's staff, the term 92nd Regiment has been used to avoid confusion.

immediately sent one by one to the most critical points of battle, a great degree of chaos prevailed at Quatre Bras. Wellington's forces now largely consisted of infantrymen, the battalions of which were continually forced to withdraw from their two-line firing lines into solidly locked squares in order to withstand repeated attacks from Ney's powerful cavalry. In addition, Wellington's square formations provided the ideal target for Ney's artillery, which inflicted heavy casualties. The fray of battle and the chaotic situation that prevailed at Quatre Bras was summarized succinctly by Edward Macready, an ensign of the Cambridgeshire Regiment:

> The roaring of great guns and musketry, the bursting of shells, and shouts of the combatants raised an infernal game, while the squares and lines, the galloping of horses mounted and riderless, the mingled crowds of wounded and fugitives, the volumes of smoke and flashing of fire...[666]

It may have been around five o'clock in the afternoon when Ney's cavalry under the command of General Piré broke down the Brunswick infantry at the Bossu Wood with the support of the French infantry. However, the Brunswickers along with the 'Black Duke' launched two counter attacks with two of their cavalry regiments of lancers. The 'Black Duke' attempted desperately to reorder his men one last time whilst nonchalantly smoking his pipe throughout the whole course of the furious battle, disregarding enemy fire in order to give the fresh recruits among the "Black Brunswickers" the reassurance they needed for this critical moment. In his efforts, however, he himself was fatally struck by an enemy bullet while his Brunswickers struggled to save their own lives while fleeing in all directions.

Wellington also found himself in imminent danger from Piré's cavalry, who happened to be located nearby with his staff. The advancing French cavalry pursued Wellington all the way to the 92nd Highlanders, which was in square formation and now located past the line of the original positions held by the Brunswickers. When Wellington, who was being pursued by enemy soldiers, stormed towards the front line of the 92nd Regiment's square at full gallop, he called out just a few words to several of his men who now stood facing him: "Lie down 92nd!" [667], upon which he leapt over their heads to safety inside the square. Immediately after his landing in the centre of the square and with the energy so typical

BATTLE OF QUATRE BRAS
16ᵗʰ June 1815

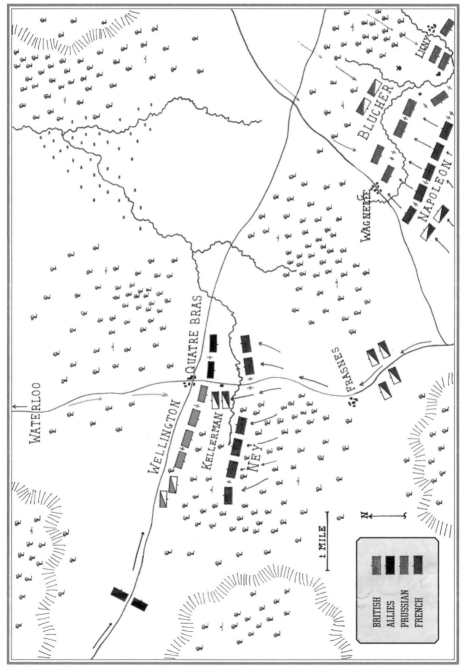

— *Map by John Fawkes* —

for his person, he ordered his men to prepare to fire: "92nd don't fire until I tell you!"[668] According to eyewitness reports, in the following moment that Wellington called out "Fire!", the front lines of the French cavalry were located thirty metres (at most) from the square in which the British Commander had taken shelter. Thus, at such a short distance such withering fire had a devastating effect and forced the French to retreat.

As evening approached, Wellington began to gain a significant advantage over Ney thanks to the troops that continued to arrive, allowing him gradually to take the offensive. His men even managed to take Gemicourt farm located roughly half a mile south of the crossroads at Quatre Bras, near which the French had deployed their artillery that afternoon. In addition, the corps that Napoleon sent to aid Ney did not arrive, as the French Emperor had called d'Erlon back to Ligny due to the Prussians' persistent defence just before he managed to arrive at Quatre Bras. Napoleon wanted d'Erlon to attack the Prussians' wing after his return to Ligny, which would make Napoleon's victory over the Prussians even more crushing. D'Erlon, however, was not at his best that day, and managed to return with his soldiers, who were exhausted from marching "to and fro", back to Ligny around seven o'clock in the evening. Instead of leading a surprise ambush (albeit a late one) on the Prussian wing, he and his corps emerged directly in the area of Napoleon's left wing and caused a short but severe moment of confusion in the Emperor's ranks. Despite the abovementioned facts, Napoleon had managed to deal with the Prussians even without d'Erlon's corps. Marshal Ney, however, finally gave the order to retreat from Quatre Bras that evening and failed to take the crossroads. Nonetheless, he managed to occupy Wellington for the whole day and prevented him from hurrying to Blücher's aid, whom Napoleon had in the meantime managed to defeat. Wellington and Ney both ultimately lost around 4,000 men in the chaotic clash that took place at Quatre Bras.[669]

Marshal Ney, who was often accused of various blunders during Napoleon's campaign in 1815 by the Emperor's supporters, later defended himself candidly in regard to the withdrawal of d'Erlon's corps, which he had evidently relied on in his own plans:

On the 16th [June 1815], I received orders to attack the English in their position at Quatre Bras. We advanced towards the enemy with an enthusiasm difficult to be described... The shock which this intelligence [the report on the withdrawal of d'Erlon's corps back to the Emperor in order to cover his left wing] gave me, confounded me. Having no longer under me more than three divisions, instead of the eight upon which I calculated, I was obliged to renounce the hopes of victory, and, in spite of all my efforts, in spite of the intrepidity and devotion of my troops, my utmost efforts after that could only maintain me in my position till the close of the day...Thus twenty-five or thirty thousand men [d'Erlon's corps] were, I may say, paralized, and were idly paraded during the whole of the battle from the right to the left, and the left to the right, without firing a shot...'[670]

The exhausted Wellington abandoned the battlefield at Quatre Bras around 10 o'clock in the evening. He set off to the village of Genappe several miles north, where he had dinner and slept in the local inn. At three in the morning, he was on his feet again. He jumped onto the saddle of his favourite stallion Copenhagen, which was sold to him in 1813 by Colonel Charles Wood, and rode back to his troops, who were momentarily camped at Quatre Bras.[671] Copenhagen, which was Wellington's favourite stallion during the war and most probably throughout his life, had had a short and relatively lacklustre career (aside from a handful of victories) as a racing horse on the British Isles. Nonetheless, Wellington became very fond of the horse during the last years of the Peninsular War for the stallion's exceptional endurance and intrepid nature, which was a rather rare characteristic among horses.* These were traits that the Duke most highly valued in his horses, as battles dragging on for several days differed greatly from short, speed-based races that required only maximum speed – also a trait which Copenhagen, however, certainly did not lack – along a relatively short distance, after which the horse was immediately allowed to rest.

After his arrival to Quatre Bras, Wellington had a quick breakfast in the company of the 92nd Regiment of Foot, in whose presence he had witnessed the dramatic events of the day before while being pursued by the French cavalry. Subsequently, he sent his aide-de-camp Alexander Gordon to attempt to contact Marshal Blücher. Wellington did not yet know how Blücher's battle played out despite having received a message from him the previous day while the Duke himself was waging his own

---

* *The Sporting Magazine, vol. XXIII*, Published by Rogerson & Tuxford, London 1852, p. 244. According to this magazine, Charles Wood, a colonel in the Light Division, sold Copenhagen to Wellington. Before Wood Copenhagen was in the position of Charles Steward, half-brother of Lord Castlereagh.

fierce battle with Marshal Ney. Gordon, who was escorted by the 10ᵗʰ Hussars Regiment, had found that the site formerly occupied by the Prussians was now suddenly teeming with Frenchmen. Therefore, he skilfully avoided the French troops and continued on north where, roughly two miles on, he managed to catch up with the rearguard of the retreating Prussian troops. There Gordon learned of the Prussian defeat and the direction of their retreat, which was led north toward the town of Wavre. Nonetheless, the most important message that Gordon hurried to report to Wellington was that the Prussians were far from crushed and would in all probability be able to fight again if necessary, the next day. With this important and vital news, Gordon hurried back to Quatre Bras at roughly seven o'clock in the morning (17ᵗʰ June) and relayed it to Wellington. Only two hours later, Wellington also received another dispatch from a Prussian messenger sent by Blücher, which confirmed that which Gordon had reported.[672]

It thus became wholly clear to Wellington at that moment that he would have to abandon his position at Quatre Bras and retreat to a location that would not only offer him the most suitable position for a potential battle with Napoleon's whole army, but one that the shaken but still battle-ready Prussians could also reach in time in order to support Wellington effectively in his battle against Napoleon. This was the scenario that would offer Wellington the greatest chance at triumphing over Napoleon. Therefore, around eleven o'clock in the morning, Wellington issued the order to retreat from north Quatre Bras, where a significant portion of his army was located (at least 35,000 men), closer to Brussels and Wavre, to which the Prussians were now headed. Before ordering this tactical retreat, Wellington said to Colonel Müffling:

> Old Blücher has had a damned good licking and gone back to Wavre, eighteen miles. As he has gone back we must go too. I suppose in England they will say that we have been licked. I can't help it, but as they have gone back we must go too.[673]

Around noon, Wellington's battalions left Quatre Bras. In the afternoon hours of 17ᵗʰ June 1815, his army took up a defensive position at the aforementioned village of Waterloo, which had so impressed Wellington for being by far the most strategically advantageous position as he mapped out the surrounding terrain the year before while accompanied by 'Slender Billy'. By doing so, Wellington once again cut off Napoleon's path to Brussels. Paradoxically, Wellington's momentary position was actually somewhat closer to the village of Mont Saint Jean than Waterloo. Therefore, the ensuing battle could easily have been named the "Battle of Mont Saint Jean", but took its name from Waterloo slightly farther north.[674]

In the meantime, the victorious Napoleon evidently assumed that Blücher had been crushed completely after the Battle of Ligny and was now planning to retreat at least towards the Rhine. The reports that Napoleon had at his disposal from his reconnaissance divisions claimed that the Prussians were retreating through Namur to the east. This, however, was an error – Napoleon's intelligence staff had completely misread the situation. In reality, the Prussian Marshal had only retreated north to Wavre, a fact which Wellington, contrary to Napoleon, was well aware of. At Wavre, he managed to regroup his 50,000 combat-ready men. Also, despite objections from various members of his staff*, 'Old Blücher' un-waveringly insisted once again on taking part in battle. At the beginning of the campaign, Blücher and Wellington made a pact that they would support one another and defeat Napoleon together, and Blücher meant to uphold this promise at all costs. In the author's opinion, this shows that Blücher was well aware of the fact that Wellington was not able to come to his aid in Ligny, as he was being attacked himself by Ney and therefore did not blame Wellington for the events that took place. In ad-dition, if we were to look at a map of the areas surrounding Brussels, we would see that Waterloo and Wavre are located in an almost parallel line, which – as is the author's assumption – confirms the fact that Wellington was relying on Prussian aid in his own plans.

Despite all the optimism stemming from the Prussian defeat at Ligny, Napoleon did have fears of Blücher's return and therefore sent Marshal Emmanuel de Grouchy's army corps of 32,000 men and nearly one hun-dred cannons to keep Blücher out of battle if he attempted to intervene in the events while dealing with Wellington's army himself. However, during the night of 17th–18th June, which Wellington spent in the old Bodenghien inn at Waterloo** where he had set up his headquarters, the Duke received

---

* Primarily General Gneisenau, who skilfully led the subsequent Prussian retreat in place of Blücher, who was battered after falling from his horse.

** The inn still stands today and at present houses a small museum devoted to Wellington.

an urgent dispatch from Blücher, in which the Prussian Marshal assured him that if he were to enter into battle with Napoleon the following day, Blücher and his army would come to his aid. At daybreak, Blücher immediately decided to send the IV Corps commanded by General Bülow* to Wellington's position, followed by an additional corps, after which he would gradually attempt to move the remainder of his army there. For this reason, Wellington did not abandon his position at Waterloo and, on the following day (18ᵗʰ June 1815), offered Napoleon battle.[675]

Over the course of the twenty-two years that Britain spent almost constantly at war with the French, Wellington and Napoleon – dubbed by many historians as the greatest commanders of this whole era – had still yet to face one another. Although both men were of the same age (forty-six), Wellington was, contrary to Napoleon, at the peak of his strength. He maintained a slim, athletic figure and, among other activities, owed his excellent physical condition to daily rides in the saddle for up to several hours. Napoleon Bonaparte, on the contrary, was plagued by his deteriorating health and increasing weight. Nonetheless, Napoleon seemed to feel extremely self-confident before the Battle of Waterloo (or at least presented himself as such before his soldiers). For a number of years, he had regularly referred to Wellington disparagingly as the 'Sepoy General'[676] in reference to his victories in India, which were trivial in the French Emperor's eyes because they were waged against oriental armies. He then attributed Wellesley's achievements in the Peninsular War purely to the ineffectuality of his own marshals, and therefore certainly did not consider Wellington to be a capable commander or worthy opponent.

Contrary to Bonaparte, however, Wellington remained undefeated in the field battle throughout his whole military career as Commander-in-Chief, and had gained a good degree of respect amongst the French marshals. Wellington had had his setbacks in the Peninsular War but had proved himself more than a match for the best that France had pitted against him. The French generals, who had bitter memories of him from the Peninsular War, thoroughly cautioned Napoleon concerning Wellington and his Red Coats immediately before the battle during

---

* Friedrich Wilhelm, Freiherr von Bülow was a seasoned campaigner whose contribution to the battles of Grossbeeren (1813) and Dennewitz (1813) proved decisive. He was a member of the Prussian delegation that took part in the Allied sovereign's visit to England (1814).

a meeting of the French general staff. General Honoré Charles Reille was the first to spark a fit of anger in Napoleon when he said: 'Well posted, as Wellington knows how to post it, and attacked from the front, I consider the English Infantry to be impregnable, owing to its calm tenacity, and its superior aim in firing.'[677] General Maximilien Sébastien Foy continued: 'Wellington never shows his troops [here Foy is evidently referring to the reverse slope tactics], but if he is yonder, I must warn your majesty that the English infantry in close combat is the very devil!'[678]

After the Chief of Napoleon's Staff Marshal Soult, who had also had extensive experience with Arthur Wellesley, piped in with his own words of warning while extolling Wellington in front of Napoleon as an experienced, highly energetic, and excellent commander, Napoleon lost his temper and witheringly silenced Soult with the following words:

> Because you have been beaten by Wellington, you consider him a great general. And now I tell you that Wellington is a bad general, that the English are bad troops, and that this affair is nothing more serious than eating one's breakfast.[679]

In turn, the Duke of Wellington (similarly to many British) referred to Napoleone di Buonaparte, as was the original version of his name denoting his Corsican origin, simply and derisively as 'Boney'. Wellington generally viewed 'Boney' as a war-monger who loved battle and saw war as a simple tool to gain power; he also felt that Napoleon's personal ambitions knew no end. In March 1811, Wellington wrote the following from Portugal to the British Government:

> I can only assure the government that if they don't give Boney employment here [i.e. in Portugal and Spain], or elsewhere on the Continent, he will give them employment at home...[680]

Also contrary to Napoleon, Wellington took no personal pleasure in war and saw it as his duty and a regrettable necessity. Thus, the unambiguous and primary goal of war in Wellington's eyes was peace. He was, however, well aware of the fact that there were few (if any) men that could replace him in a battle against Bonaparte. Wellington despised Napoleon as a person and saw him as a deceitful and wholly unscrupulous opportunist and tyrant who had risen to power thanks to his extremely "strong-elbowed" nature that rose from the chaos and tyranny of the French Revolution. He did strongly believe, however, that such behaviour would sooner or later come back to haunt him. When Wellington's Spanish guerrilla troops intercepted an evidently haughty and contemptuous letter written by Napoleon to his brother Joseph Bonaparte in 1811 during the Peninsular War, Wellington wrote the following words home to William Wellesley-Pole:

> It shows that this tyrant does not treat his relations or even his brothers, better than he does other people, and gives ground for hope that his tyrannical temper will at no distant period deprive him of the advantages which he would derive from the Austrian alliance.[681]

Wellington was in essence correct, as although Napoleon had taken a Habsburg princess for his wife, his alliance with the Austrians only two years later lay in ruins. Despite this, however, Wellington (similarly to the rest of the world) considered Napoleon to be an absolute genius as a military commander and strategist. In this regard, Wellington thus treated him with a considerable degree of respect and reverence.[682] Therefore, Wellington did not hesitate to hang several portraits of Napoleon in his future country home at Stratfield Saye in Hampshire and Apsley House in London to remind himself of the formidable opponent of his life.

For instance, at one of the Parisian soirées that Wellington took part in during his period of office in the role of British ambassador, he was asked by one of the guests present whether in the light of his striking achievements he regretted never coming face to face with Napoleon. Wellington replied to him in all seriousness: "No, and I am very glad I never was. I would at any time rather have heard that a reinforcement of forty thousand men had joined the French army, than that he [Napoleon] had arrived to take the command."[683] Before the Battle of Waterloo, however, Wellington was supremely confident that he could defeat Bonaparte, as he noted to Prussian Colonel Müffling: "Now Bonaparte will see how a general of Sepoys can defend a position."[684]

In the early evening before the Battle of Waterloo, Wellington also had the famous conversation with his second-in-command Henry Paget,

Earl of Uxbridge (the future Marquess of Anglesey), who wished to know the Duke's plans in the event that something might happen to him in battle.

> 'Who will attack the first to-morrow, I or Bonaparte?' 'Bonaparte'. replied Lord Anglesey [Uxbridge]. 'Well', continued the Duke in the same tone. 'Bonaparte has not given me any idea of his projects: and as my plans will depend upon his, how can you expect me to tell you what mine are?' Lord Anglesey bowed: and made no reply. The Duke then said, rising, and at the same time touching him in a friendly way on the shoulder, 'There is one thing certain, Uxbridge, that is, that whatever happens, you and I will do our duty.'[685]

Wellington never acknowledged the position of second-in-command. He himself did not have fond memories of gradually being shifted to such a position (which in his eyes was a "powerless" one) in 1808 after the Battle of Vimeiro by Sir Harry Burrard and Sir Hew Dalrymple. In Wellington's mind, there could simply be only one commander on each side of a battle and commanders were to act according to their own judgement and plans and react swiftly to the developments of battle and movements of the enemy, just as Arthur Wellesley himself had done best at Assaye or Salamanca. In addition, Henry Paget, Earl of Uxbridge had abandoned his wife and children six years earlier and eloped with Wellington's sister-in-law, Lady Charlotte Wellesley, wife of his youngest brother Henry, with whom Arthur had always been on very good terms. Much like Uxbridge's wife, Henry Wellesley was thus left at home to brood with his small children while British society had quite the scandal about which to gossip. In addition, Lady Charlotte divorced Henry Wellesley and married Uxbridge, bringing the whole scandal to a close. It is thus no surprise that Wellington did not take much of a liking to Uxbridge after Charlotte exchanged "one Henry for another".[686] That said, Wellington was not a man to harbour grudges, not least because he had a job of work to do and thus endeavoured to lead by example.

Wellington positioned his army at Waterloo – as he had done successfully several times before – partially on the peak of a relatively steep ridge (it should be mentioned here that, in comparison to Wellington's other positions during the Peninsular War, the ridge at Waterloo was much less steep) and partially on the ridge's reverse side; the Brussels

Road passed through the centre of the ridge. At the foot of the ridge there were three fortified structures that the Duke ordered to be occupied by his best troops. These structures now formed ideal outlying positions. On the right wing was the small Château d'Hougoumont, which in truth was more akin to a farmstead with an adjacent garden lined by a brick wall; in the centre was the La Haye Sainte Farm; on the left wing of Wellington's position was the Papelotte Farm. If Napoleon wished to close in on Wellington's lines on the ridge, he would logically first have to conquer these structures; otherwise, his troops would be in danger of coming under crossfire from the peak of the ridge and the fortified outlying positions simultaneously. The flank of Wellington's left wing was guarded by marshes stretching west from Papelotte; his right wing, however, was in danger of being outflanked through the open landscape in the east. Due to fears of a possible outflanking manoeuvre on his right wing, Wellington sent 15,000 men roughly six miles east of Hougoumont to the area close to the villages of Hal and Tubize. These troops, however, never engaged in battle that day.

On the morning of 18th June 1815, Wellington had an army of 68,000 men and 150 cannons at his disposal on the ridge near Waterloo. Against Wellington, the French Emperor had 72,000 men, whom he used to gradually occupy the hillock that stretched across the relatively shallow valley directly opposite the ridge where Wellington had taken up his position. Despite this fact, Napoleon possessed almost one hundred more artillery pieces than Wellington. On the other hand, however, the Duke's men were naturally covered by the ridge wholly thanks to Wellington's reverse slope tactics.[687] In addition, Napoleon was in the role of attacker and his units would first have to descend the hillock, pass through the valley, and then climb upwards (although not over an exceedingly steep slope) to finally rush into battle against Wellington's prepared troops. Another potentially serious complication for Napoleon's forces was the fact that there had been torrential rain throughout the night of 17th–18th June and thus the ground was likely to be heavy going.

Soldiers on both warring sides attempted to take shelter from the rain where possible; however, on the morning of 18th June most of the men were sodden, stiff and sore. In addition, they knew they were likely to see a fierce battle that day. The experienced soldiers in Wellington's army naturally handled the discomfort and stress somewhat better than the new recruits.

BATTLE OF WATERLOO
18ᵗʰ June 1815 at 11 a.m.

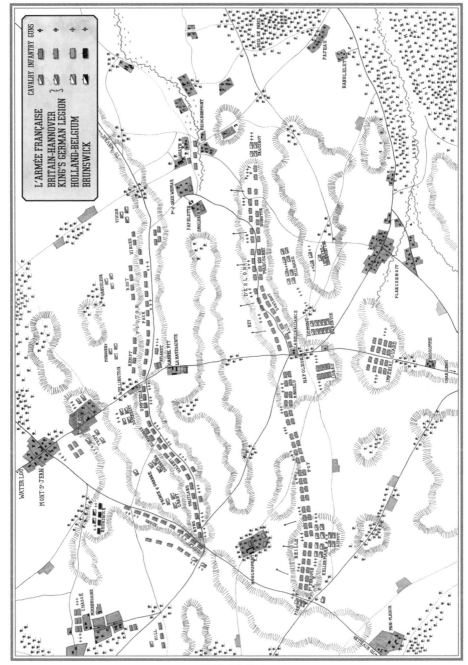

— *Map by John Fawkes* —

One of the myriad of personal stories illustrating the tense atmosphere of that morning was recorded in the memoirs of Thomas Pococke, soldier in the 71ˢᵗ Highland Regiment, who fought in the army corps of General Hill:

> Two hours after day-break...we got half an allowance of liquor, which was the most welcome thing I ever received. I was so stiff and sore from the rain, I could not move with freedom for some time. A little afterwards the weather clearing up, we began to clean our arms and prepare for action. The whole of the opposite heights were covered by the enemy. A young lad, who had joined but a short time before, said to me, while we were cleaning: 'Tom, you are an old soldier, and have escaped often, and have every chance to escape this time also. I am sure I am to fall.' – 'Nonsense, be not gloomy.' – 'I am certain', he said: 'All I ask is, that you will tell my parents, when you get home, that I ask God's pardon for the evil I have done, and the grief I have given them. Be sure to tell I died praying for their blessing and pardon.' I grew dull myself, but gave him all the heart I could. He only shook his head: I could say nothing to alter his belief.[688]

That morning, Wellington put on his white breeches, dark-blue coat and a cloak of the same colour. He then donned his bicorne and fastened his favourite Indo-Persian sabre. Early in the morning he wrote two letters, said a brief prayer, and after seven o'clock left his command station at the Bodenghien inn at Waterloo. He mounted Copenhagen and, in the company of his staff, set off towards his army in order to carry out a final check of individual positions. At this moment, he was spotted by General Picton's aide-de-camp, Captain Rees Howell Gronow:

> We heard the trampling of horses' feet and looking round we perceived a large cavalcade of officers coming at full speed. In a moment we recognized the Duke himself at their head. He was accompanied by the Duke of Richmond and his son, Lord William Lennox. The entire staff of the army was close at hand... FitzRoy Somerset and Delancey were the last that appeared. They all seemed as gay and unconcerned as if they were riding to meet the hounds in some quite English country.[689]

Wellington and his staff set off first to check the garrison deployed on his right wing at Château d'Hougoumont. From there, he galloped over the whole span of his troops' line to the end of the left wing close to the Papelotte Farm. The battle began a short while later.

Napoleon commenced battle at roughly half past eleven with an attack on Wellington's right wing, specifically on Château d'Hougoumont*. The terrain was heavily waterlogged and Napoleon had likely been delaying his attack in hopes that the muddy saturated ground would at least partially dry. By launching a massive attack on Wellington's right wing – aimed ultimately at seizing Hougoumont – the Emperor planned to force the Duke into sending his reserves away from the centre of the Anglo-Dutch position to aid the endangered right wing, significantly weakening Wellington's centre. Napoleon then planned to focus all his artillery power on his opponent's thinned centre and subsequently launch his men's primary attack. Once the Emperor's troops broke down Wellington's forces at the centre of his line, crushing his isolated wings would then be merely a matter of time.

This plan, however, began to go awry almost before it began, as Hougoumont, which was resolutely defended by Wellington's men, refused to fall even after two hours of repeated French attacks. At a certain moment, the French managed to break through the front gate to the complex and subsequently enter, but the allies defending the farmstead carried out a lightning-fast counter attack under the command of their seasoned commander, Lieutenant-Colonel James Macdonell of the Coldstream Guards, whom Wellington greatly trusted. During the counterattack, his troops mercilessly slaughtered all the adversaries that managed to enter the complex. Wellington later noted this as being crucial for the course of the whole battle. The French attack on Hougoumont, which was launched by Napoleon's youngest brother Jérôme Bonaparte and his division headed by General Reille's corps, thus gradually began to collapse. Battle continued to be waged over Hougoumont with varying degrees of intensity until the whole chateau caught fire once Napoleon began bombarding it with his artillery. It was clear to Wellington that he must hold Hougoumont at all costs. As soon as the first attack was repelled, the Duke sent reinforcements down from the ridge to the

---

*   Rory Muir writes that the time the attack began ranges widely from source to source, from ten o'clock in the morning to one in the afternoon, which is the time Marshal Ney cited as the time the battle commenced. General Hill, for example, placed the beginning of battle at ten minutes to twelve. This is an excellent example of how descriptions of battle and all historical events in general can widely differ. See: Muir, *Wellington: Waterloo and the Fortunes of Peace*, p. 64.

farmstead with a message for Macdonell, who had overall command at Hougoumont. The message itself is perhaps the best proof of just how strategic Hougoumont was:

> I see that the fire has communicated itself from the hay stack to the roof of the Château. You must however still keep your men in those parts to which the fire does not reach. Take care that no men are lost by the falling in of the roof or floors. After they will have fallen in, occupy the Ruined Walls inside of the Garden, particularly if it should be possible for the Enemy to pass through the Embers to the Inside of the House.[690]

The whole day long, Hougoumont was bravely guarded by 2,600 of Wellington's men, who defended it against roughly 13,000 attackers, the majority of which ended up dead or injured in its immediate surroundings.*

Despite this failure, Napoleon continued with his original plan. At roughly half past one in the afternoon, his artillery divisions began their massive bombardment of Wellington's centre and, despite the fact that the Duke's men were hidden as far as possible behind the ridge, the number of injured and dead began to grow under the withering artillery fire. Once again, the words of Thomas Pococke of the 71st Highland Regiment can be used, as he recalled this portion of the battle in the following lines;

> A ball struck the ground a little below me, turned me heels-over-head, broke my musket in pieces, and killed a lad at my side. I was stunned and confused, and knew not whether I was wounded or not. I felt a numbness in my arm for sometime. We lay thus about an hour and a half under a dreadful fire, which cost us about 60 men, while we had never fired a shot.[691]

When Thomas came to, he found that the young soldier whom he had spoken to that morning and who was afraid of being struck, now

---

* J. Huw, Davies, p. 237. For the occasion of the 200th anniversary of the Battle of Waterloo, a new memorial was erected at Hougoumont that depicts the re-closing of the gate of the chateau by Macdonell's troops of the Coldstream Guards Regiment during the defence of Hougoumont. British Prince Charles Windsor personally unveiled the memorial. On its pedestal is the inscription 'Closing the gates on war'. On the left wing of the gate, the following quote from the diary of Private Wheeler, who took part in the defence of Hougoumont, has been carved into stone: 'The army never upon any occasion conducted itself better.' On the right wing of the gate, the famous quote by the Duke of Wellington himself has been engraved into the stone: 'Next to a battle lost, the greatest misery is a battle gained'.

unfortunately lie dead next to him – a cannon ball had torn off both his legs during the French bombardment.[692]

After almost two hours of intensive artillery fire, Napoleon sent in General d'Erlon's whole infantry corps (roughly 16,000 men) to attack Wellington's centre. The corps was formed into four massive attack columns, which soon put Wellington's troops in grave danger. The first two of d'Erlon's columns marched in an unusual formation – they were spread out line by line at a length of a whole battalion (roughly 600 men) in attempts to combine the striking force of the column with the firing power of the line. D'Erlon's troops first successfully drove out the defenders from the gardens around La Haye Sainte Farm despite not managing to enter the structure itself. They continued unwaveringly toward the peak of the ridge against Wellington's centre. When they closed in on Wellington's men on the ridge, they began to be decimated by canister fire from the Allies' cannons, which wreaked unimaginable havoc on the French front lines. Thanks to their great number, however, the French seemed unstoppable and continued to march forward in mechanical fashion. They next faced a brigade of Dutch soldiers, who were soon forced to flee as they found themselves outnumbered. Wellington sent Picton's division immediately to this critical point at his centre to fill in the gap left by the Dutch, for whom – honourably speaking – it was extremely difficult to overcome such a disadvantage in number. Picton's men fired a salvo and launched a bayonet attack against d'Erlon's troops in the method they were accustomed to from the Peninsular War. General Sir Thomas Picton, whose luggage including his military uniform had not yet arrived at Waterloo, was dressed in a civilian dress coat and, in place of his military bicorne hat, wore a top hat, a fact which at the given moment must have looked rather comical. Apart from his appearance, however, he boldly drove his men forward, shouting various epithets, when suddenly he was struck directly in the forehead by an enemy projectile. The brave General Picton, who had seen Wellington through nearly the whole Peninsular War, now fell dead.[693]

In the meantime, Wellington was dealing with an attack of several enemy cavalry squadrons, who had massacred a battalion of Hanoverians whom the Prince of Orange had sent to aid the garrison defending La Haye Sainte. Wellington quickly assembled two infantry squares from the two British battalions closest to one another in the line and placed them against the advancing French cavalrymen. A fierce clash surged along the whole length of Wellington's centre, which Napoleon's forces were now attacking ferociously. The fighting took place in the area around La Haye Sainte Farm all the way to the peak of the ridge where Picton's division was still struggling in a merciless man-to-man battle with d'Erlon's corps. At this moment, Henry Paget, Earl of Uxbridge, commander of the Allied Cavalry, ordered a massive attack by Wellington's cavalrymen intended to finally break down d'Erlon's advance. Uxbridge sent in two cavalry brigades (roughly 2,500 cavalrymen, which made up almost the whole allied cavalry). This included the Household Brigade under the command of Lord Edward Somerset (the older brother of the young FitzRoy Somerset) and the Union Brigade led by Sir William Ponsonby, the ranks of which included elite heavy cavalry regiments from Scotland – the legendary "Scots Greys" on their sturdy grey horses. The Scots Greys were later immortalized in the painting *Scotland Forever!* from 1881 by Elizabeth Thompson, Lady Butler* (See Image 87).

Wellington's cavalry, which had gathered for an attack on the reverse side of the ridge, attacked d'Erlon's troops as if from out of nowhere; the slaughter that ensued in d'Erlon's ranks could perhaps only be compared to Le Marchant's attack at Salamanca. D'Erlon's corps was swiftly crushed and rendered incapable of battle, while two of his regiments lost their golden French Imperial Eagle battle standards in the fray. Nonetheless, the British cavalry, exhilarated by their success, became carried away and pursued the French too far, even attacking a portion of Napoleon's artillery batteries and killing several dozen artillerymen. When the cavalry finally came to their senses, however, they were soon confronted with the harsh realities borne out of their impetuosity. Wellington's now battle-weary cavalry had rushed into the flank of Napoleon's cavalry lancers, who proceeded to cut down nearly the entire regiment. Out of two and a half thousand British cavalrymen, barely one thousand riders, now nearly fainting from exhaustion, returned. The exhausted horses that survived were now unable to move and thus Wellington was forced to give up any further hopes of using what was left of his cavalry that day.[694]

---

* Bernard Cornwell states that it is not wholly conclusive whether the final order for the cavalry attack was given by Uxbridge or Wellington himself. However, he does favour the version that Uxbridge gave the order on his own initiative. See Cornwell, *Waterloo: The History of Four Days, Three Armies and Three Battles*, pp. 193–194.

BATTLE OF WATERLOO
18ᵗʰ June 1815 at 4 p.m.

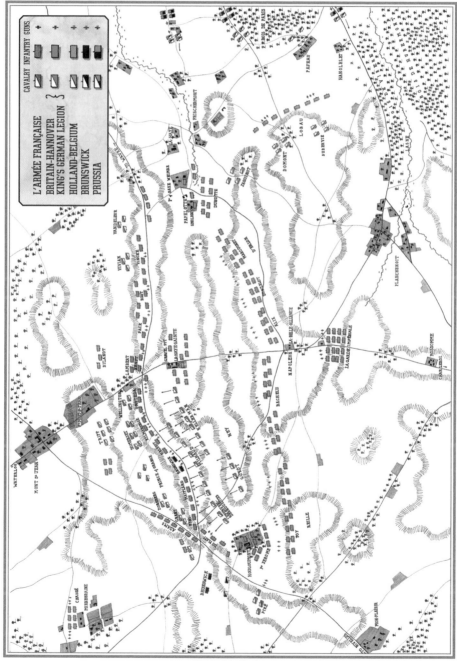

—— *Map by John Fawkes* ——

It was evidently at this moment – which may have been around half past three in the afternoon – that Wellington's aide-de-camp, Sir William Howe De Lancey, was struck by a cannonball (which had likely ricocheted off the ground) right before his eyes:

> When Sir William was riding beside the Duke, a cannon ball struck him on the back, at the right shoulder, and knocked him off his horse to several yard distance. The Duke at first imagined he was killed, for he said afterwards, he had never in all the fighting he had ever been in seen a man rise again after such a wound. Seeing he was alive (for he bounded up again and then sank down), he ran to him and stooping down, took him by the hand[695]

,as the whole event was described in retrospect by De Lancey's wife, Lady Magdalene. At that moment, De Lancey's cousin came to his aid, carrying him off the battlefield to safety as Wellington in the meantime was forced to face another imminent danger: a frontal attack by nearly the whole French cavalry, at the head of which the 'Bravest of the Brave' Marshal Ney now charged forwards.

As soon as Wellington's cavalry was repelled and rendered effectively incapable of battle, Napoleon distanced himself for a moment from the battlefield and left Marshal Ney in command. The French Emperor had likely set off in person to regroup the remainder of d'Erlon's shaken corps or perhaps was afflicted by an issue concerning his health. Another explanation for Napoleon's departure from the battlefield was perhaps his momentary exhaustion and the need to rest at least for a short time. In the meantime, Ney was leading the next infantry attack on Wellington's centre at La Haye Sainte, which, however, the Anglo-Dutch infantry this time repelled with relative ease. What invoked the following frontal attack of the whole French cavalry, which Ney launched against Wellington, remains wholly unclear. The most frequent and also most probable interpretation is that Ney's first attack provoked Wellington to order the Anglo-Dutch troops at his centre to retreat one hundred feet back, which was intended to allow his soldiers to take shelter in the cover beyond the ridge and thus protect them from the intense French artillery fire. Coincidentally, at this relatively "calm" moment of battle, Wellington ordered his myriad of injured men to be carried away from his centre by sending in several vehicles for them to his rear; at the same time, he also sent in several other vehicles carrying new munitions, all of which caused quite a commotion. Evidently, based on these events, Ney came to the conclusion that Wellington was retreating and therefore launched his cavalry attack, in which up to 7,000 French cavalrymen gradually became engaged. Ney led the attack in person; he did so, however, without any significant support from his infantry, a misjudgement that would soon prove fatal. After his return to the battlefield, however, Napoleon also failed to send in his infantry to accompany the cavalry, as he most likely assumed it was too late and opted instead to send the remainder of his cavalry to join Ney.[696]

Wellington ordered his artillery to wait until the last moment to fire into Ney's squadrons. After this, Wellington's artillerymen hurried to conceal themselves in a chain of twenty infantry squares, which Wellington's infantry created at its centre. With these squares, the Duke's infantry continued bravely for several hours to repel continual charges by Ney's cavalry. Disregarding the danger while fully trusting his stallion Copenhagen and his own excellent equestrian skills, the Duke of Wellington galloped from one allied infantry square to another, taking temporary cover in their centres. Throughout the whole course of Ney's attack, he continued to incite his soldiers, as one man in his infantry noted:

> The Duke of Wellington, in riding up to a regiment, which was hard pressed, called to them – 'Soldiers, we must never be beat, what will they say in England?' How this appeal was answered, it is needless to recapitulate.[697]

Soon Wellington asked one of his aides-de-camp what time it was as he was expecting Blücher's arrival. He received the immediate reply that in ten minutes it would be half past four, to which he answered: "The battle is mine, and if the Prussians arrive soon there will be an end of the war."[698]

The massive attack launched by Napoleon's cavalry soon failed, similarly to all his attempts hitherto at breaking Wellington's line. With his 7,000 men, Ney had wholly failed to disrupt even one single infantry square led by Wellington. In addition, around half past four the Prussians began to close in on the battlefield, while Napoleon's primary hope for salvation – Marshal de Grouchy – was still nowhere in sight. Napoleon received the first troublesome report from Grouchy that the Prussians had not retreated to the east where Grouchy had initially and mistakenly pursued them, but to the north towards Wavre around ten that morning. At that time, Napoleon believed that if Grouchy made haste, he would manage to stop the Prussians (if they even dared to attempt to intervene in the battle) and, with some luck, support Bonaparte as well in his fight against Wellington. Grouchy, however, was still far off. Colonel Marcellin Marbot, of the 7th Regiment of Hussars, who personally led Napoleon's right wing, confirms in his memoirs that the French Emperor believed that Grouchy would arrive until the very last:

> One of my squadrons... met with a squadron of Prussian Hussars, from which he captured several men and one officer. I notified the Emperor of this curious capture and sent him the captives. I learned from them that they had marched with a significant portion of the Prussian Army; I thus hurried with a squadron to aid at Saint Lambert [the village on the French Army's right wing]. From there I observed a column marching towards Saint Lambert. I sent an officer at full speed to the Emperor, who replied that I should continue bravely forward and that this army might only be the corps of Marshal Grouchy [...] driving before them a few lost Prussians, to which these captives belong. I soon learned that it was the very opposite...[699]

It now must have become wholly clear to Napoleon that it was not Grouchy approaching, but the Prussian Army. 'Old Blücher', driven by his desire for revenge, now closed in on Napoleon's right wing, driving his men forward with the following words: "Forward, boys!... I have given my word to Wellington and you would not have me break it."[700] Napoleon thus quickly commanded General Lobau's VI Corps (of roughly 10,000 men) to confront the Prussians and hold them for as long as possible. Bonaparte now dearly needed to break through Wellington's centre and finally defeat the Duke's battle-weary army. He could then theoretically turn to the east from where the Prussians were arriving and face the new threat they now represented. Napoleon thus sent in another mighty attack on Wellington's centre, in which he deployed nearly all his remaining battle-ready units. Around six o'clock in the evening after several fierce infantry attacks, the French managed to take La Haye Sainte, from which only 43 defenders escaped alive. However, the French once again failed to break through the centre of the Anglo-Allied line at

BATTLE OF WATERLOO
18ᵗʰ June 1815 at 7 p.m.

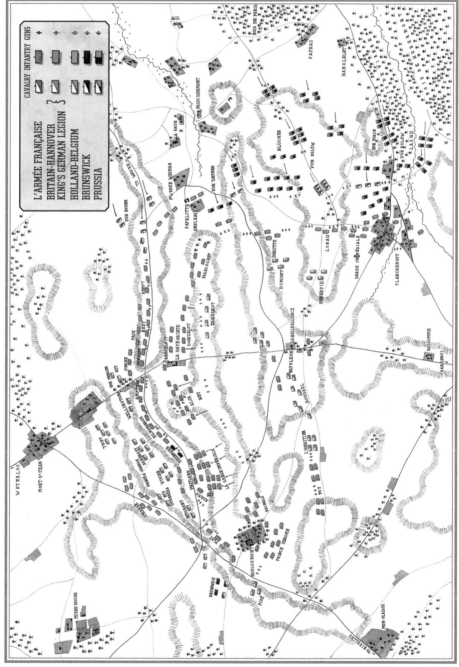

—— *Map by John Fawkes* ——

the peak of the ridge. Nonetheless, Wellington's army had at this point hit "rock bottom". It was suffering heavily from Napoleon's artillery fire as it was forced to face the French cavalry attack on the ridge and could not use its cover at the moment on the other side of the slope.[701] One of the generals whose British infantry brigade had already lost two thirds of its men, sent Wellington an urgent request to allow them to withdraw his units back from the ridge; Wellington, however, knew that the whole battle was at stake and urgently needed all his forces: "Tell him, what he asks is impossible: he and I, and every Englishman on the field, must die on the spot we now occupy."[702]

Wellington continued tirelessly to ride amongst his infantry regiments along the whole length of the allied line, setting an example for his soldiers by giving orders and helping boost morale. To use General Álava's words once again, he was constantly 'exposing himself to every kind of personal danger.'[703] Shortly after the Allies lost La Haye Sainte, an artilleryman who had spotted Napoleon, who was now moving in range of his cannon, suddenly called out to Wellington, who was just riding past: "There's Bonaparte, Sir, I think I can reach him, may I fire?" Officers and especially generals kept their honour and firing intentionally at an enemy commander was highly unethical. Wellington therefore gave the artilleryman the following sharp reply: "No, no, Generals commanding armies have something else to do than to shoot at one another."[704]

Around seven o'clock in the evening, for the second time that day, a dangerous gap opened under pressure from French attacks in Wellington's centre on the peak of the ridge near La Haye Sainte Farm, which was now controlled by the French. It opened as a result of a brave counterattack led by Prince of Orange, with a portion of his corps, which attempted to return the farm building to allied hands. His men, however, were fiercely repelled by the enemy and suffered heavy losses. Therefore, Wellington again personally intervened and led one of his last reserves – the "Black Brunswickers" towards the gap above La Haye Sainte, quickly "patching up" the gap and repelling the ensuing French attack. Wellington now found himself nearly unaccompanied on the battlefield, as the majority of the members of his staff were either dead or injured. Around this time, the young FitzRoy Somerset was also seriously injured in the arm by a bullet fired from somewhere in La Haye

Sainte. Wellington's long-favoured aide-de-camp thus withdrew to the overcrowded field hospital set up in the rear. It was now nearing seven o'clock and, in a final attempt to gain total victory after a score of failures to break Wellington's line, Napoleon sent in his last remaining men – the elite Imperial Guard.

However, Prussian divisions, who were now arriving one after the other on the battlefield, had in the meantime begun to charge towards Napoleon's right wing. On Blücher's orders, Prussian General Zieten led his corps towards Wellington's left wing in order to support his line on the ridge; General Bülow received orders from the Prussian Field Marshal to attack with roughly 30,000 Prussian soldiers somewhat farther to the south directly against Napoleon's right wing over the village of Plancenoit. From there, Bülow gradually drove off Lobau's men, whom the Emperor had placed there to face the Prussians. The moment Napoleon caught sight of this, he immediately opted to use his Imperial Guard, which stood prepared. The Imperial Guard was divided into a Young, Middle, and Old Guard; soldiers were placed in each one according to their merits and abilities. Naturally the Old Guard was the most feared, although the whole of Napoleon's elite unit justifiably commanded respect on all battlefields. Napoleon sent Lobau towards Plancenoit first to aid the Young Guard followed by two battalions of the Old Guard, whose fearless attack gradually drove out the Prussians from the village. It was at this moment that Napoleon sent five battalions of his Middle and Old Guard against Wellington's centre. The Imperial Guard had never before been forced into retreat and rightfully bore the epithet of being "Invincible". At this moment, Napoleon led his "Invincibles" down into the valley, where he passed command onto Marshal Ney. From there, the Imperial Guard set off to face the Anglo-Allied Army.

A fitting description of the men who now climbed the slope against Wellington's soldiers was left behind by British painter Benjamin Haydon, who caught a glimpse of the Imperial Guard after Napoleon's abdication in 1814:

> More dreadful-looking fellows than Napoleon's Guard I had never seen. They had the look of thoroughbred, veteran, disciplined banditti. Depravity, indifference and bloodthirstiness were burnt in their faces, black moustachios,

gigantic caps, a slouching carriage and a ferocious expression were their characteristics. If such fellows had governed the world, what would have become of it?[705]

Nonetheless, Wellington still had fresh reserves from the 1st Regiment of Foot Guards under the command of Major-General Peregrine Maitland, which he had hidden in the wheat that grew just beyond the ridge. When the Imperial Guard had neared the firing range of the Allies' muskets, Wellington – in light of the gravity of the situation – gave the order to fire in person: "Now Maitland! Now is your time! Up Guards! Make ready! Fire!"[706]

Suddenly emerging from the wheat, several mechanical salvos were fired by the men of the Guards, who were soon joined by Colonel John Colborne's 52nd Regiment of Foot stationed nearby. Napoleon's own hitherto-undefeated troops now began to waver. Soon, more and more allied battalions began spontaneously to join Colborne's fight against the Imperial Guard, causing them finally to collapse completely and retreat as all the other attackers before them had done. At this moment, Wellington took off his bicorne hat and aimed it in the direction of the enemy, indicating the order for a final attack by the whole allied line. 'The Duke now ordered the whole line to move forward, nothing could be more beautiful.... the victory was complete, and the enemy fled in every direction...'[707] recalled one officer of the Guards. This moment was described by a French contemporary, historian Louis Antoine Fauvelet de Bourrienne:

> The light troops were close on their front, and the whole line advancing under Wellington, when this body [the Imperial Guard], the élite of the army, and now the only hope to the French, gave way, and mixed in the general confusion and rout, abandoning their cannon and all their material...the irremediable disorder consequent on this decisive repulse, and the confusion in the French rear, where Bulow had fiercely attacked them, did not escape Wellington. 'The hour has come!' He is said to have exclaimed, and closing the telescope, communicated the whole line to advance...[708]

Wellington then marched forward together with his soldiers and continued to incite their efforts. "Go on Colborne! Go on. They won't stand.

Don't give them time to rally."[709] the Duke called to the commander of the 52nd. When Wellington arrived at the 95th Rifles several minutes later after pursuing the retreating Imperial Guard, he was greeted with exuberant cheers. Nonetheless, Wellington planned to finish the matter properly and immediately ordered the 95th to continue its advance: "No cheering, my lads, but forward, to complete your victory."[710] During the final phase of battle, one of the last shots fired by the French artillery struck Lord Uxbridge, who was riding alongside Wellington, in the leg. In the shock that followed, the pale Uxbridge called out to Wellington: "By God, sir, I've lost my leg!" "By God, sir, so you have!"* replied the rather shocked Wellington, who at such a moment could not muster up a better reply. Uxbridge was carried off the battlefield to the village of Waterloo, where the damaged right leg was removed by Dr John Hume, who carried out a procedure known as a flap amputation. Wellington continued forward with his men and when the last few surviving members of his staff attempted to stop him from venturing away from the ridge and risking his life, Wellington said to them resolutely: "Never mind…The battle's gained: My life's of no consequence, now."[711] and continued on in his pursuit. In the meantime, the Prussians had retaken Plancenoit, and the crushed French were now fleeing in all directions – after a whole day of merciless battle, Emperor Napoleon Bonaparte had finally been defeated.[712]

Around nine o'clock in the evening, Wellington met with Field Marshal Blücher at La Belle Alliance, an inn which was located roughly in the middle of Napoleon's original position. Both victorious commanders heartily congratulated one another on their success and agreed that the somewhat more rested Prussians would continue on in pursuing the fleeing French. Arthur Wellesley, Duke of Wellington, who was now exhausted both physically and mentally, used his last remaining strength to gallop back to his command station that had been set up at

---

*   Holmes, *Wellington: The Iron Duke*, op. cit., p. 248. Uxbridge survived the ordeal, and his leg continued to live out a rather odd life of its own – after it was amputated, the limb was put on display in the village of Waterloo as a tourist attraction for visitors that flocked to the site. Today we can still see the "tomb" of his leg and his prosthetic limb in Wellington's Museum at Waterloo (the former Bodenghien inn).During the actual amputation, Uxbridge himself seemed to be in rather high spirits over the imminent victory even despite the prospects of losing his appendage – during the operation he is said to have exclaimed in jest: *"I have had a pretty long run. I have been a beau these forty-seven years and it would not be fair to cut the young men out any longer."*, quoted in: Leo Cooper (ed.), *One Leg: The Life and Letters of Henry William Paget, First Marquess of Angelsey K. G.* (London 1996), p. 150.

the Bodenghien inn at Waterloo. He jumped off Copenhagen and patted him on the back mechanically. The surprised stallion, which must have been just as exhausted as its master, kicked its hoof at Wellington, missing him only be a few inches. Thus, after a whole day of fierce fighting, remarkably the Duke emerged without a single scratch; quite paradoxically, however, Wellington could have been seriously injured or killed by his own horse. However, as he later stated, it seemed once again that: 'The hand of almighty God has been upon me this day.'[713] After the incident with Copenhagen, he entered the inn, where he ate quickly at a table set for an immoderate number of guests, as he would never dine with some of them again. He breathed a deep sigh of relief at each newly-arriving guest at the table who had survived the fearsome battle. After eating, he lay down on a bed of hay on the floor, leaving his own bed to his seriously injured aide-de-camp Lieutenant-Colonel Sir Alexander Gordon, whose state began to worry him increasingly. He then immediately fell asleep.

The first to see Wellington the next day was military doctor John Hume, who arrived in the morning to inform him of the preliminary allied losses, which were horrific. The list of the fallen and injured included General Sir Thomas Picton, killed in battle, Wellington's second-in-command Lord Uxbridge, who lost his leg, and Sir FitzRoy Somerset (who had been Wellington's relative since the year prior after marrying Wellesley's niece), whose injured arm had to be amputated. The Prince of Orange, known as 'Slender Billy', was also injured; William De Lancey was in critical condition (he was to die of his wounds a week later), and Alexander Gordon also later succumbed to his wounds. Many of Wellington's other close friends were not much better off. When Doctor Hume stepped into his room, Arthur Wellesley was still sleeping.[714]

As I [Dr Hume] entered, he sat up, his face covered with the dust and sweat of the previous day, and extended his hand to me, which I took and held in mine, whilst I told him of Gordon's death, and of such of the causalities as had come to my knowledge. He was much affected. I felt the tears dropping fast upon my hand. And looking towards him, saw them chasing one another in furrows over his dusty cheeks. He brushed them away suddenly with his left hand, and said to me in a voice tremulous with emotion, 'Well, thank God, I don't know what it is to lose a battle, but certainly nothing can be more painful than to gain one with the loss of so many of one's friends.*

Once Wellington had regained his composure, he wrote a letter to his brother William Wellesley-Pole:

> You'll see the account of our Desperate Battle and victory over Boney!! It was the most desperate business I ever was in, I never took so much trouble about any Battle, & never was so near being beat. Our loss is immense particularly in that best of all Instruments, British Infantry. I never saw the Infantry behave so well.[715]

Wellington said, commending his men. In return, the British soldiers were proud of their commander: 'indeed the whole army give him [Wellington] the whole credit.'[716] as was summarized by Lord Apsley, son of the Earl of Bathurst. After Waterloo, General Rowland Hill's aide-de-camp Colonel Chatham Horace Churchill complimented Wellington with the following words: 'I believe in the whole army Lord Wellington was the individual who fought the hardest.'[717] Lord Uxbridge later declared that Wellington's 'coolness and decision in action surpassed everything he cd. have conceived.'[718] Sir Hussey Vivian, commander of the 6th Brigade of Lord Uxbridge's Cavalry division, made his praise of Wellington wholly clear: 'Nothing that I can add to the laurels of the Duke of Wellington, but it is to his example as well as to his abilities that we are indebted. Never was courage so conspicuous, never was it so necessary.'[719] The day after the battle, two women cried out in adoration as they spotted the Duke, who passed them on his horse. Despite all the praise and odes sung in his name, Wellington answered sadly and succinctly: "No, no: it has been bought very dearly, I assure you."[720]

---

*   William Pitt-Lennox, *Three Years with the Duke of Wellington in Private Life by an Ex-Aid-De-Camp* (London 1853), pp. 217–218. Here the question arises as to whether Wellington was truly an undefeated general. It is the author's personal assertion that the label is fitting. As a Commander-in-Chief, he was clearly never defeated in a field battle, and it is obvious that he meant this exactly in the words he said to Dr. Hume. On the other hand, Wellington had suffered two defeats as a regimental commander: in Flanders and in India in the skirmish of Sultanpettah Tope. In both cases, however, he was in fact in command of only a small portion of the British Army, as other generals stood above him in command. In India this was General Harris and in Flanders the Duke of York. When Wellington himself was the Commander-in-Chief, he suffered defeat only in the siege on the castle in Burgos. This, however, was not a field battle, but the siege of a fortification.

Several days later, Wellington travelled to Paris, where he was temporarily assigned to the post of Commander of the Army of Occupation, which as a temporary force was intended to reinstate order in France. The corpulent Louis XVIII once again took the throne and the defeated Napoleon now once again awaited exile – this time on the remote volcanic island of Saint Helena in the South Atlantic Ocean. Whilst in Paris, one of the various people Wellington met with was the young Frances, Lady Shelley, who like many others at the time wished to hear the story of the Battle of Waterloo from the victor himself. The still somewhat shaken Wellington told her the following concerning the battle and war in general:

> I hope to God... that I have fought my last battle. It is a bad thing to be always fighting. While in the thick of it, I am much too occupied to feel anything, but it is wretched just after. It is quite impossible to think of glory. Both mind and feelings are exhausted. I am wretched even at the moment of victory, and I always say that next to a battle lost, the greatest misery is a battle gained. Not only do you lose those dear friends with whom you have been living, but you are forced to leave the wounded behind you. To be sure one tries to do the best for them, but how little that is! At such moments every feeling in your breast is deadened. I am now just beginning to retain my natural spirits, but I never wish for any more fighting.[721]

This wish would come true for Arthur Wellesley, as he was never required to fight a military battle again. Apart from local unrest, which culminated in the tumultuous year of 1848, an era of relative peace prevailed after the Congress of Vienna until the Crimean War (1853–1856). In the latter part of the nineteenth century, Britain would again participate in a series of military adventures, many associated with its burgeoning empire, the most bruising being the South Africa War/Boer War. By the time of centenary of the Battle of Waterloo, Britain, much of Continental Europe and indeed the world had become embroiled in the horrors of the cataclysm that was the First World War.

Wellington made his indelible mark on history as a general never to have been defeated in a field battle and – primarily – as the legendary *"conqueror of the world's conqueror"*[722], as Wellington was later dubbed by Russian Tsar Alexander I. After Waterloo, Arthur Wellesley became one of the most celebrated and revered personalities of his time. He found himself flooded with countless gifts, honours and orders of chivalry, and letters of appreciation from the Royal courts throughout Europe*. After his return to Britain, a rich political career awaited him, during which he served twice as Prime Minister of the United Kingdom**. In 1817 Wellington bought a family estate and residence in Hampshire – Stratfield Saye House – which has remained the home of the Dukes of Wellington ever since. From 1828 onwards at Apsley House, Wellington's London residence on the edge of Hyde Park, he hosted the Waterloo Banquet on the day of the anniversary of the Battle of Waterloo, to which he invited veterans of the battle and prominent figures from Britain and throughout the world.

Ship surgeon William Warden was among the first Englishmen to ask Napoleon of what he thought of Wellington's military abilities after the Battle of Waterloo during the voyage of the *HMS Northumberland*, which was now taking Bonaparte into exile on Saint Helena.** The (now former) French Emperor was still clearly so enraged by the definitive defeat that he preferred to give no answer at all. William Warden recorded the whole event in the following words:

> 'The people of England' I said, 'appear to feel an interest in knowing your sentiments respecting the military character of the Duke of Wellington. They have no doubt that you would be just, and perhaps they may indulge the expectation that your justice would produce an eulogium of which the Duke of Wellington might be proud' Silence ensued: I began to think that I might have gone rather too far, for it is most true I had never before addressed him without looking full in his face for a reply, but my eyes dropped at the pause and no reply was made...[723]

Later, however, Napoleon was given "proper room" to criticize Wellington during his exile on Saint Helena, where he would spend the remainder of his days: for example, Bonaparte criticized the Duke for

---

*   Many of these gifts can be admired today in Wellington's Apsley House in London.
**   Firstly from 1828–1830 and briefly as caretaker Prime Minister in 1834 acting for Sir Robert Peel, who was away in Sardinia at the time.
*** Napoleon's deportation to Saint Helena is also linked to the HMS Bellerophon, which first transported him to Plymouth. From this southern English port, however, he continued on aboard the HMS Northumberland, which took him to his exile on Saint Helena.

placing the Sonian Forest* at his rear while holding his position on the ridge at Waterloo. In the event of defeat, Bonaparte claimed the forest would have made Wellington's retreat from the battlefield impossible. Napoleon claimed that if Wellington had been defeated, this fact would have allowed him to massacre Wellesley's whole army to the very last man including the Duke himself, as his soldiers would have had no room to retreat. In accordance with these claims, Napoleon not surprisingly gave primary credit to Blücher's timely arrival at the battlefield as the main reason for his defeat. It is, however, important to consider that Blücher's arrival was wholly planned by the Allies and Wellington was unlikely to have offered the Emperor battle if he had not counted on Blücher's arrival. In regard to the critique concerning the Sonian Forest, which would have blocked the Allies' in their retreat, Wellington's advocates quite logically claim that the forest was not likely to have posed any problem to Wellington's units. This was because the forest was not a low one full of impenetrable shrubs and bushes, but a full-grown forest with tall trees. On the contrary, the forest would have provided ideal cover from the French cavalry, which would not have been able to attack the retreating troops effectively in the forest. While on Saint Helena, Napoleon claimed the following in regard to these previous comments:

> I believe ... that Wellington is a man of great firmness. The glory of such victory [at Waterloo] is a great thing, but in the eye of the historians his military reputation will gain nothing by it.[724]

Personally, I believe that both history and historians have already proved one hundred times over that with this last point, Napoleon could not have been more wrong. Nonetheless, over the course of his exile on Saint Helena, Napoleon was reported by one eye witness to have made a more favourable comment about the Duke of Wellington. This may be seen as the sort of compliment that the ship surgeon Warden was expecting in vain to hear from Napoleon:

---

* It is worth noting that Napoleon had been responsible for ordering the felling of some 22,000 oaks in the Sonian Forest southeast of Brussels in order to supply wood for the construction of the Boulogne flotilla originally intended for the invasion of England in 1801.

On the Abilities of the Duke of Wellington, he [Napoleon] remarked, that it would one day be of bad consequence to the English Nation, who would expect more from their Army than they had capacity for, when not guided by superior knowledge.[725]

In regard to his fall and forced exile, Napoleon said: 'I am assured that it is through him [Wellington] that I am here [on Saint Helena], and I believe it. I centrally gave him a bad quarter of an hour [at Waterloo]...'[726]

It is the author's assertion that, in the minds of most people around the world in the 21st century, the Battle of Waterloo is predominantly perceived as a synonym for absolute defeat and gives the impression of having been an unequivocal affair. In reality, however, it was a highly dramatic, relentless, and bloody battle that ended definitively in the late evening hours of 18th June 1815. The Allies lost roughly 23,000 men; Napoleon lost almost 30,000, which at that time were massive casualties in terms of a single battle. Due to the insufficient technical resources and undeveloped methods of medical care of the time, some of the injured men remained on the battlefield at Waterloo for several days until they were given attention and received the rudimentary medical care available at that time. Nonetheless, for the vast majority of Europe, Waterloo primarily stood as a symbol of victory, emblematic of the great relief that finally brought relative peace and stability throughout Europe after more than two decades of incessant war and suffering. If Waterloo was synonymous with victory and the final defeat of Napoleon, its main hero was Arthur Wellesley, First Duke of Wellington, the Victor of Waterloo.

The Road to the Lion's Mound

W hen painter Benjamin Haydon* finished the painting *Wellington at the Fields of Waterloo* in 1839, he left behind him an absolutely unique work of art much similar to that of Sir Thomas Lawrence.** In Haydon's painting, Arthur Wellesley is depicted as an older man standing pensively on the battlefield of Waterloo. Wellington's only company is his beloved stallion Copenhagen, on whose back he rode that long, fateful June day of 1815, during which the Battle of Waterloo took place. As an evident reference to the battle, which had already taken place many years before, a sabre swings at Wellington's hip while in his left hand, instead of a top hat, he grips his bicorne, which he always wore into battle. Wellington and Copenhagen look on nostalgically at the famous battlefield from roughly the centre of the position

---

*   Haydon was plagued by constant debts, which landed him several times in debtor's prison, and his career was not helped by his impertinent behaviour towards his patrons from within the ranks of the aristocracy and colleagues from the Royal Academy of Arts. He was seen as somewhat of troublemaker and an infant terrible among prominent British artists of the first half of the 19th century.

**   Charles Wellesley, 9th Duke of Wellington, *Wellington Portrayed*, London 2014, pp. 161–162. Haydon also said the following about Wellington: "I studied his fine head intensely... [he found] his conversation powerful, humorous, witty, argumentative, sound, moral." Quoted in: Charles Wellesley, *Wellington Portrayed*, p. 162.

of Napoleon's Army. At his feet in the lower part of the painting, which is subtle at first glance but at the same time wholly evident, are the outlines of a monument symbolizing this final Allied victory over Napoleon, dubbed the Lion's Mound* (See Image XVIII).

This massive monument still represents the main and unmistakably dominant element of the former battlefield to this day. It is an honour to all those who fell at Waterloo. The Lion's Mound is a permanent reminder of the goal of preventing the events surrounding the battle from falling out of memory and disappearing forever in the depths of time. The order to build the Lion's Mound was issued on the occasion of the fifth anniversary of the Battle in 1820 by the king of the newly-founded Kingdom of the Netherlands, William I – father of the Prince of Orange, also known as 'Slender Billy'. The mound was meant to be built roughly on the site where the Prince of Orange was injured by a French bullet, thus approximately between Wellington's centre and right wing. Specific plans for construction were then created by William's royal architect Charles Van der Straeten, and works began in 1823. In regard to the demanding nature of the construction, however, the Lion's Mound was finished later, in 1826, despite great efforts on the part of the builder. This comes as no surprise, as it is a simple yet remarkable work. This breath-taking monument was ultimately made from a 201-foot (62m) high stone pillar, at the peak of which is a massive iron statue of a lion bearing its teeth in the direction of France. Around the stone construction, a 141-foot (43m) high mound of earth was built, measuring 1,706 ft (520m) in diameter. We can thus see roughly the last 60 feet (20m) of the massive pillar, which rises from the top of the mound. The overall weight of the earth that created the mound is an unbelievable 13.7 million cubic feet of soil (390,000 m³).[727] As this massive amount of earth necessary for construction was taken from the surrounding areas, the landscape of Wellington's former battlefield logically underwent a dramatic transformation. The largest amount of soil was transported from the ridge on which Wellington's allied forces took their positions, causing it for the most part to disappear.**

---

* Also known as Butte du Lion.
** Roughly 2,000 labourers and hundreds of horses worked on the project; land was primarily taken from the area stretching from the site of Wellington's centre during the Battle of Waterloo over the La Haye Sainte farm towards his right wing, which stretched west to Hougoumont. See David Buttery, *Waterloo Battlefield Guide*, Kellington 2018, p. 63.

In this context, the famous French author Victor Hugo wrote in his timeless novel *Les Miserables* that when Wellington allegedly visited Waterloo after the construction of the Lion's Mound, he angrily blurted out the following words: 'They have altered my field of battle!'[728]

In regard to the fact that this quote has no other source than Victor Hugo himself, it is in all probability a purely fictitious creation, which has nonetheless written itself into the general consciousness and quite precisely summarized what had become of the battlefield. Today the peak of the Lion's Mound can be climbed using the flight of 226 steps; the peak offers a perfect view of the whole battlefield, as the Lion's Mound was built roughly in the centre of the position that Wellington's Army held at Waterloo (although it is slightly closer to where Wellington's right wing was located). The lion, which is placed on the peak of the stone pillar, is also surely worthy of further attention. The figure of a lion was selected because it embodied the fearsome symbol of both Britain and the House of Orange-Nassau that the new ruler William I hailed from. According to a legend, the sculpture was said to have been created from melted-down French cannons gained by the Allies in battle. In reality (which is always an enemy of myth), however, it was created from nine pieces of iron cast in a factory in Liége. The sculpture is exactly 4.5m high, has the same width, and weighs in at a remarkable 28 tonnes. In its front right paw, the lion clutches a globe, which is meant to symbolize the global significance of the Allied victory at Waterloo, which finally brought long-awaited peace to Europe after decades of unending battle.[729]

When I set off in person to visit the battlefield at Waterloo while completing this book, climbing the 226 steps to the peak of the Lion's Mound during the visit to take in the beautiful view that the site offers, I had to admire Wellington's immense appreciation and understanding of the terrain despite the aforementioned changes to the character of the battlefield caused by the Lion's Mound's construction. As I stood in the wind on the peak of this artificial hill, I couldn't help but recall one of the most famous of all Wellington's quotes, which he spoke in his old age to his friend John Wilson Croker:

All the business of war, and indeed all the business of life, is to endeavour, to find out what you don't know by what you do, that's what I call guessing what was on the other side of the hill.[730]

Wellington, the Austrian Empire and the Kingdom of Bohemia in the Coalition Wars against Napoleon

If Napoleon falls, God will have passed judgment and passed it fairly,
as the measure of sins of this bloodthirsty conqueror is high – too high.

Field Marshal Karl Philipp, Prince of Schwarzenberg,
commander of troops of the Sixth Anti-French Coalition,
in a letter to his wife Marie Anna of Hohenfeld, 3rd April 1814.

A note from the author: As a Czech Historian, I would like to use the context of Wellington's life and his many campaigns to describe the events in the Kingdom of Bohemia (now the Czech Republic), which was in Wellington's time a part of the Habsburg Monarchy and the whole Austrian Empire during the Napoleonic Wars. It is my hope that this chapter will provide readers with a slightly different perspective concerning Wellington's campaign, British foreign policy, and a better understanding of the Napoleonic Wars as such in an international context.

Arthur Wellesley, 1ˢᵗ Duke of Wellington, never set foot on the territory of Bohemia or Moravia. The closest he came to the Czech lands was during the winter and spring of 1815 when he negotiated as a representative of Britain at a peace congress in Vienna. During these negotiations, Wellington, together with Austrian Foreign Minister Metternich and French diplomat Talleyrand, was called upon to visit Bratislava (formerly Pressburg). There, the three men presented the verdict of the Congress to King Frederick Augustus I of Saxony, an erstwhile ally of Napoleon, stripping him of a significant portion of his territory. One noteworthy memento of Wellington remains in Bohemia, however, as part of Metternich's collection at the Kynžvart Chateau [731] in the Karlovy Vary region contains Wellington's waistcoat and a medallion containing a lock of his hair. An equally significant "Czech" reminder of Arthur Wellesley is the correspondence he kept during the successful Campaign of 1815, crowned with the allied victory at Waterloo, with the commander of the Austrian Army on the Upper Rhine, Karl Philipp, Prince of Schwarzenberg, which is deposited in the National Archive in the town of Třeboň (South Bohemia). While Wellington had fought since 1808 in Portugal and Spain, where he successfully opened up the "Western Front" against the French, Field Marshal Schwarzenberg had led the allied troops as Commander-in-Chief in the east since 1813. Due to the importance of cooperation on both fronts in the battle against the French, Schwarzenberg's letters to his wife contain frequent mention of Wellington. In relation to Wellington's clashes with Napoleonic France, the role of Austria and the Kingdom of Bohemia in the war against Napoleon will be examined below in more detail.

During the Napoleonic Wars, Austria was second only to Britain* as the most obstinate adversary of the French. From all seven Coalition Wars led against revolutionary and subsequently Napoleonic France from 1792 to 1815, Austria was absent at the side of its allies only in the War of the Fourth Coalition, which ended in Napoleon's triumph over the Prussians in the Battle of Jena-Auerstedt in 1806 (Great Britain, Russia and Prussia stood against France in the fourth coalition). Simply speaking, the Austrians lacked both the material and human resources at the time to actively engage in the Anti-French Coalition, as the

---

*   Britain was at peace with France during the Napoleonic Wars for only a few months after the Treaty of Amiens in 1802.

country was still reeling from Napoleon's crushing victory at Austerlitz in the winter of 1805.

For the first two years after the outbreak of the French Revolution, the start of which is now traditionally seen as the 14th July 1789, when the Bastille was stormed and captured by revolutionary guards (hence why 14th July is marked as Bastille Day in modern-day France), the events in France, perhaps somewhat surprisingly did not initially garner a great deal of attention in the noble courts of Europe. However, the French Monarch Louis XVI's attempt to escape abroad, where he planned to take command of the French émigrés from the ranks of the aristocracy and clergy against whom the revolution was waged, did gain some military support from fellow European monarchs. Louis intended to lead his troops back into France and restore the *ancien régime* and the divine order of things. However, Louis XVI's plan was thwarted and he was detained in the town of Varennes during his attempt to flee. There, although he was naturally fleeing in disguise, he was recognized by the daughter of the local postmaster* thanks to his image on the French gold coin (called *luis d'or*). The postmaster then alerted the National Guard, who arrested the unfortunate ruler and handed him over to the Revolutionary Guard. It was this event that had an alarming effect on other European rulers, who henceforth began to view the French King as a captive of a "revolutionary" regime. Subsequently, in August 1791 the Declaration of Pillnitz was issued at Pillnitz Castle in Dresden, where the Habsburg Holy Roman Emperor Leopold II and King Frederick William II of Prussia declared solidarity with the French Monarch and called upon other European rulers to do the same. It is important to note that Louis XVI's wife, Marie Antoinette was a younger sister of Leopold II.

For many French deputies in the National Legislative Assembly, the Declaration of Pillnitz by Austria (for the sake of simplicity, the term Austria will be used as a synonym for the Habsburg Monarchy of Leopold II, who was simultaneously the Emperor of the Holy Roman Empire) and Prussia was a provocative and hostile act. In response, a group of radical political faction known as the *Girondins* led by Jacques Pierre Brissot was formed, which began to view war as the only possibility

---

* During the war with Austria in 1793, postmaster Jean-Baptiste Drouet, who arrested Louis XVI, also fell captive and was subsequently imprisoned in Brno at Spilberk Castle. Two years later, he was exchanged for Marie Thérèse of France, daughter of Louis XVI.

of spreading the ideals of the revolution throughout Europe. At the same time, Louis XVI also desired a military solution to his desperate situation and with the help of mediators, continued to correspond in secret with the Habsburg Court. In this correspondence, he called upon his brother-in-law to invade France. However, at the beginning of March 1792, Leopold II died suddenly, and his eldest son succeeded the Imperial throne as Francis II. The French, however, declared the anticipated war against him on 20th April. It should be noted that France at the time was still a constitutional monarchy that, despite all the internal turmoil and pressure on him, was officially led by King Louis XVI, who gladly confirmed the Legislative Assembly's decree to declare war on Austria in the secret hope that Revolutionary France would soon be defeated, allowing him to regain his lost power with the help of Austrian forces.[732] In addition, in an effort to avoid general hostilities with the states of the Holy Roman Empire, the Legislative Assembly declared war on the twenty-four-year-old ruler Francis II in his capacity as the King of Bohemia and Hungary and not as the Emperor of the Holy Roman Empire. This, however, seemed rather comical, as the imperial princes naturally and by vast majority supported their emperor in the upcoming conflict. In addition, the war took on a personal dimension for Francis II, as the emperor's aunt, Marie Antoinette, daughter of Maria Theresa, sat at the side of Louis XVI on the French throne. When Austria entered the war, however, no one could have known that this would spark a Europewide conflict that would end more than twenty years later, on a battlefield near a village called Waterloo entering into the general consciousness under the name of the Napoleonic Wars.

The first battles took place in Flanders, which was a part of the Austrian Netherlands (roughly today's Belgium and Luxembourg), which at the time (similarly to the Kingdom of Bohemia) was part of the lands of the Habsburg Monarchy. In these clashes, the Austrians were joined by the Prussians, who also declared war on France based on a treaty of alliance with Austria. Prussian forces were led into battle by Charles William Ferdinand, Duke of Brunswick, who managed to deepen the diplomatic crisis and terminate the final hope for any peace negotiations by declaring that if the revolutionaries so much as touched a single hair on the head of the royal family, he would burn the French capital to the ground. To everyone's surprise, on 20th September

58. The storming of Ciudad Rodrigo
on 19th January 1812.

59. General Robert Craufurd,
commander of Wellington's famous
Light Division.

60. Picton's British 3rd Division storming the Castle of Badajoz by escalade.

61. General Sir Thomas Picton, who led Wellington's 3rd Division throughout nearly the whole course of the Peninsular War.

62. Marshal August Marmont, who fought against Wellington in 1812 at the Battle of Salamanca. Marmont had recently distinguished himself at Wagram in 1809, where he claimed the lion's share of credit for defeating the Austrians. Like Bonaparte, Marmont had begun his military career in the artillery, whereupon he came to Napoleon's aid on his path to power during the Coup of 18th Brumaire (9th November) in 1799. ▷

△ **63.** George Augustus Frederick, the oldest son of British King George III and Queen Charlotte. He ruled as Prince Regent during the illness of his father and, upon his death, became King George IV in 1820. When he definitively claimed the regency in 1812, this event raised strong concerns in the Tories and Wellington himself. The Prince Regent had hitherto supported the Whigs, who were in favour of a peace treaty with Napoleon. Nonetheless, after taking power, he surprisingly continued to support the war against Napoleonic France.

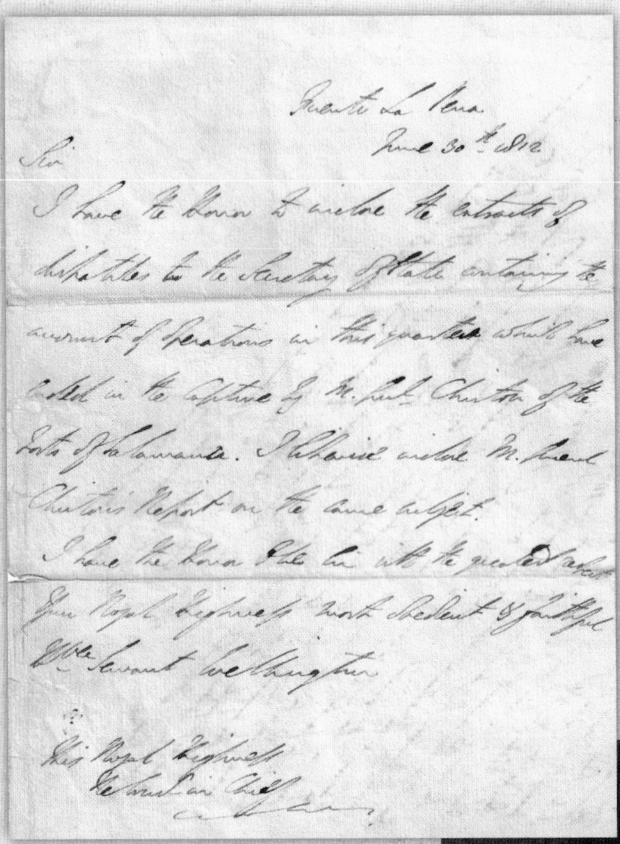

[Handwritten dispatch reproduced, largely illegible]

Puerto La Pera

June 30th 1812

Sir,

I have the honor to enclose the extracts of dispatches to the secretary of state containing the account of operations in this quarter which have ended in the capture by Lt. Genl. Clinton of the Forts of Salamanca. I likewise enclose Mr. General Clinton's Report on the same subject.

I have the honor to be Sir with the greatest respect

Your Royal Highness' most obedient & faithful humble servant Wellington

His Royal Highness
The Commander in Chief

64. Wellington's dispatch informing the British Government about the successful conquering of the fortresses in Salamanca.

65. Sir George Scovell was Wellington's primary decipherer and, alongside Major Grant, played an invaluable role in Wellington's Intelligence Service. Scovell deciphered French dispatches seized by Spanish and Portuguese guerrillas, providing Wellington with crucial intelligence in regard to the great numeric advantage of the French armies on the Iberian Peninsula. Thanks to Scovell, for instance, Wellington knew before the Battle of Salamanca that he had several weeks to outmanoeuvre Marmont before the French Marshall acquired reinforcements.

66. Wellington giving final orders to General Edward Pakenham before the decisive attack
on Marshal Marmont's overextended left wing at Salamanca. Wellington is claimed to have said
"Ned, d'ye see those fellows on the hill?" while pointing to Thomières' division.
After receiving an affirmative from Pakenham, he continued: "Throw your division into column, at them!
And drive them to the devil." to which Pakenham replied: "I will my Lord…".

67. General Sir Edward Pakenham, Wellington's brother-in law, who led Wellington's decisive attack in the Battle of Salamanca. "Ned" Pakenham, as Wellington called him, was one of his most important generals and best friends during the whole Peninsular War. When Pakenham died in January 1815 in the Battle of New Orleans, Wellington was grief-stricken by the news.

68. Major-General John Wallace (later General, Colonel of the 88th Regiment of Foot – Connaught Rangers). Wallace and his 88th Regiment of Foot greatly distinguished themselves at Busaco. Wellington is reported to have said: "Upon my honour, Wallace, I never witnessed a more gallant charge than that just now made by your regiment." In a critical situation at Fuentes de Oñoro in 1811, Wellington sent Wallace to gain back the village of Fuentes, a task which he once again managed excellently. In the Battle of Salamanca in 1812, Wallace's Connaught Rangers were at the head of the decisive attack of Pakenham's 3rd Division on Marmont's extended wing.

69. The attack by Major-General John Le Marchant's Heavy Cavalry at Salamanca. Le Marchant carried out the most effective cavalry attack of the whole Peninsular War. The fact that only 47 men escaped unhurt from the French brigade that faced him speaks for itself. Le Marchant was instrumental in founding the first British military college, one of the forerunners of the world-renowned Royal Military Academy Sandhurst.

70. Young FitzRoy Somerset was Wellington's aide-de-camp in the Peninsular War from 1808, and was also present during the Battle of Waterloo. FitzRoy was a close friend of Wellington and, in 1814, he married Wellington's niece, making the two men relatives. In later life, he was named Lord Raglan and was the Commander-in-Chief of the British forces in the Crimean War (1853–1856).

71. General Galbraith Lowry Cole, who led Wellington's 4th Division in the Peninsular War and had courted Kitty Pakenham, later Wellington's wife, when Wellington was in India. Despite this fact, the relationship between him and Wellington remained cordial.

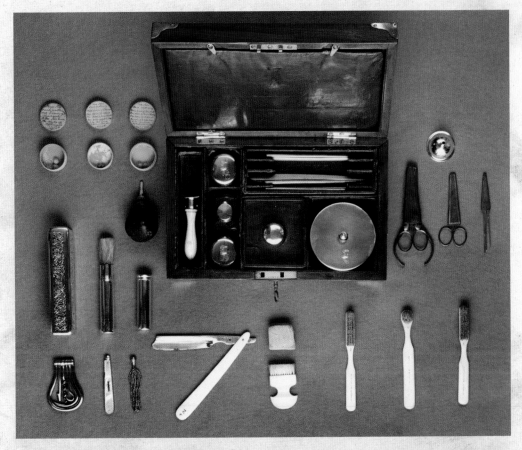

72. Wellington's personal dressing case used during the Peninsular War.

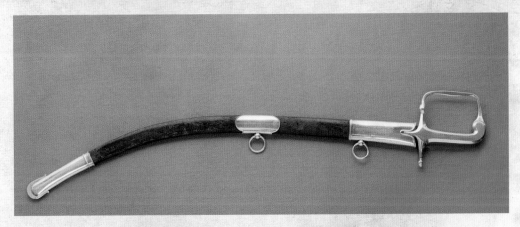

73. The sword carried by the Duke of Wellington in the Battle of Waterloo. It is a special version of a British light cavalry sabre – a wholly deadly and non-ceremonious weapon. Wellington was not fond of excessive decorations, and even his personal sword is austere and elegant, just like his style of dress.

74. British soldiers after their victory in the Battle of Vitoria looting the coaches of the defeated and fleeing French and their allies from amongst the Spanish population, known as *afrancesados*. The coaches were filled with fairy-tale-like riches which the French had gradually pilfered throughout all of Spain and were now trying desperately to preserve. Nonetheless, there was only one narrow road of retreat from Vitoria, which quickly became congested. The rich spoils thus fell easily into British hands.

75. Louis XVIII, the brother of executed French King Louis XVI, was restored to the French throne after the fall of Napoleon. During the Napoleonic Wars, Luis spent many years in exile in England.

76. Italian contralto Giuseppina Grassini. She was – in all probability – the mistress of both Napoleon and later Wellington. All in all, it is an undeniable fact that the Duke spent much time in her company after Napoleon's first abdication in 1814 while holding the function of British ambassador in Paris.

77. Klemens Lothar, Prince Metternich, Foreign Minister and later Chancellor of the Austrian Empire. He was renowned for his remarkable political skills across all of Europe. Metternich's home in the countryside where he spent much of his time was the beautiful Chateau Kynžvart in the Czech Republic, located near the famous spa town of Carlsbad.

78. Negotiations on the organization of Europe after the end of the Napoleonic Wars during the Congress of Vienna, which took place in the capital of the Austrian Empire from November 1814 to June 1815. Wellington stands first left.

Dessiné d'après nature par Mlle de Noireterre 1814 *Volpré f.*

GEORGE LEBRECHT BLUCHER,

PRINCE DE WAGSTAEDT,

Feld-Maréchal au service de S. M. le Roi de Prusse,

Grand-Croix et Chevalier de plusieurs Ordres,

Né le 16 Decembre 1743, à Rostock.

à Paris, chez l'Auteur, rue de Touraine, N.º 5 Faub. S.t Germain.

79. Prussian Field Marshal Gebhart Leberecht von Blücher,
dubbed 'Old Blücher' or 'Marshal Forward'. Blücher's Prussian army cooperated
with Wellington at Waterloo. Wellington is also said to have had
good personal relations with Blücher.

80. Allied officers hurriedly leaving the Duchess of Richmond's ball in Brussels in the morning hours. The Duke of Wellington is sitting in the carriage.

81. French Emperor Napoleon Bonaparte after victory at the Battle of Wagram (1809).

82. Wellington on a painting by Sir Thomas Lawrence, which was commissioned in 1817 by the 1st Earl of Bathurst. The Duke sits on his favourite charger Copenhagen, which he rode into Waterloo. He is dressed in his typical and elegant style, without pompous decoration, with an Indo-Persian sabre at his hip. Catherine, Duchess of Wellington, wrote about the work to Sir Lawrence in the following: 'The Duke … returned quite enchanted with the last Portraid which Lord Bathurst will be so fortunate as to have.'

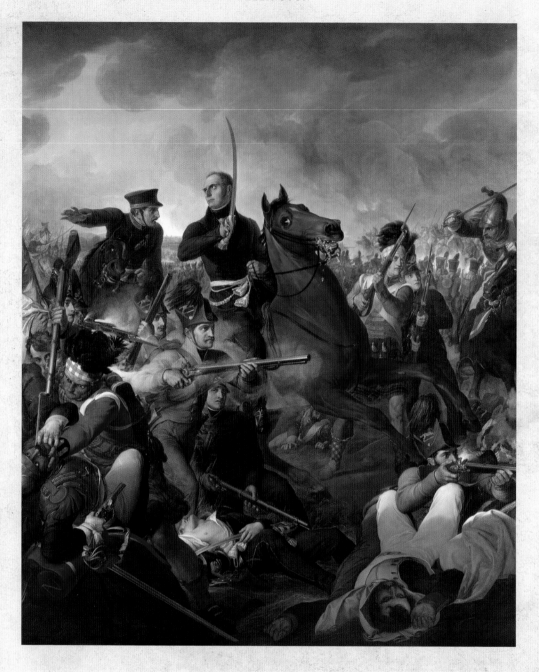

83. The heroic death of the Duke of Brunswick,
better known as the 'Black Duke' at the Battle of Quatre Bras.

84. Lord Henry Paget, Earl of Uxbridge, was commander of Wellington's cavalry at Waterloo and also Wellington's second in command as Commander-in-Chief of the Anglo-Dutch army.

85. Allied Generals before the Battle of Waterloo, from left: the Prince of Orange; the Duke of Brunswick, known as the 'Black Duke'; the Duke of Wellington; General Rowland Hill, General Sir Thomas Picton (sitting); Prussian Marshall Blücher; Henry Paget, Earl of Uxbridge.

86. Counterattack by the Coldstream Guards led by Lieutenant-Colonel Macdonell against the French soldiers who had just broken through the main gate of Château Hougoumont during the Battle of Waterloo. Wellington considered this moment decisive for the whole battle.

87. *Scotland For Ever!* by Lady Elizabeth Butler. The painting captures the attack of the Royal Scots Greys, a British heavy-cavalry regiment in the Battle of Waterloo. The work was produced in 1881 and is one of the most famous paintings connected to the battle.

88. A new memorial at Hougoumont, which was ceremonially unveiled in 2015 for the occasion of the 200th anniversary of the Battle of Waterloo. On its pedestal is the inscription 'Closing the gates on war'. On the left wing of the gate, the following quote from the diary of Private Wheeler, who took part in the defence of Hougoumont, has been carved into stone: 'The army never upon any occasion conducted itself better'. On the right wing of the gate, the famous quote by the Duke of Wellington himself has been engraved into the stone: 'Next to a battle lost, the greatest misery is a battle gained'.

89. Present view of Château Hougoumont.

90. A dried-out but surprisingly well preserved tree with clearly visible bullet holes located just several feet from Hougoumont.

91. Today's view from the top of the Lion's Mound to La Haye Sainte Farm, which lies approximately in the middle of the position that Wellington's forces occupied during the Battle of Waterloo. Behind it, the Papelotte Farm, where Wellington's left wing was located, is also visible.

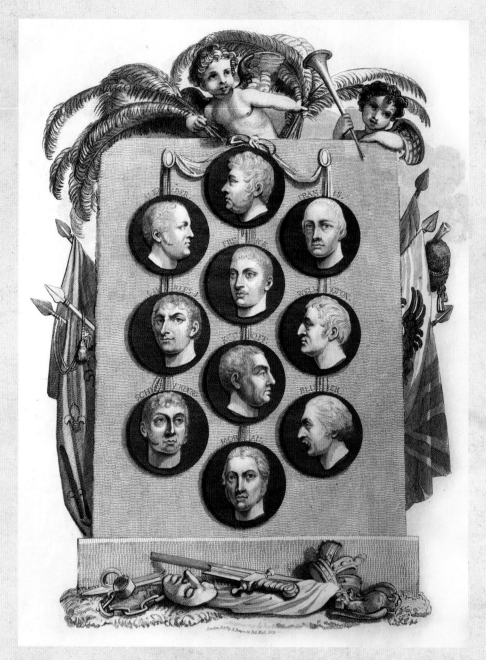

92. Portraits of various Allied Generals and Monarchs
who had a considerable share in Napoleon's final defeat in the Coalition Wars.
From the top left corner: Tsar Alexander I of Russia, probably Prince Regent
(later George IV, King of Britain), Austrian Emperor Francis I, Archduke Charles,
Frederick Wilhelm III of Prussia, Duke of Wellington, Prince Schwarzenberg,
Mikhail Kutuzof, Marshal Blücher, General Moreau.

93. Francis I (and II), also the King of Bohemia and Hungary, was the last Emperor of the Holy Roman Empire as Francis II from 1793 to 1806. In 1804, he declared himself Austrian Emperor as Francis I due to Napoleon's expansion and the weakening influence of the Holy Roman Empire.

94. Archduke Charles, the younger brother of Austrian Emperor Francis I and the first Commander-in-Chief to defeat Napoleon in a field battle during the Battle of Aspern-Essling in 1809. Wellington labelled Archduke Charles the best commander of the Napoleonic Era in a conversation with John Wilson Croker, which surely sheds a new and contradicting light on the widespread claim that he acknowledged Napoleon as the best general.

95. A beautiful painting from one of the best known pre-Raphaelite painters John Everett Millais
called *The Black Brunswicker*. On Millais' masterpiece, we see a Brunswick soldier
of the Black Legion saying farewell to his sweetheart before going to war in 1815.
The Black Legion fought in the ranks of Wellington's allied army at Waterloo.

96. Frederick William, the Duke of Brunswick, dubbed the 'Black Duke'
(he was given this nickname for dressing his soldiers in black uniforms as a sign of mourning
after Napoleon's occupation of Brunswick). After Napoleon conquered Brunswick, the Duke continued
in his struggle against France in Austrian service. The Austrians gave him the opportunity to form a corps
in Northern Bohemia (today the Czech Republic) in the town of Náchod. Despite an Austrian defeat,
from there the Black Duke and his troops fought their way through all of Germany before boarding
British ships that transported them to Portugal to reinforce Wellington's forces.

97. Josef Václav Radecký z Radče (Joseph Vaclav Radetzky von Radetz) was a Czech Nobleman born in 1766 at Chateau Třebnice near Sedlčany, Bohemia. He distinguished himself in the War of the First Coalition in Flanders and later in Italy. Then, as Lieutenant-General, he became chief of the general staff of Prince Schwarzenberg and planned all allied movements in the campaign of 1813. Most importantly, however, he made the plans of operations before the Battle of Leipzig, where Napoleon sustained a crucial defeat. Despite these qualities, von Radetz surprisingly only came to fame later as a field marshal at the age of 82 during his successful suppression of the revolution in Italy in 1848, in which he was given high command.

98. Karl Philipp I, Prince of Schwarzenberg, Austrian Field-Marshall and Commander-in-Chief of the Allied Forces in the Battle of Leipzig 1813, where he led the allies to victory over Napoleon. He then crossed the French border from the east and, after several battles with the French Emperor, he successfully led the Allied Forces to Paris in 1814. In the meantime, Wellington entered France from the West after crossing the Pyrenees and moved to Toulouse, engaging a considerable portion of French forces in the south of France. Napoleon, who was forced to defend France on the fronts, was therefore very soon forced to abdicate.

CHARLES SCHWARZENBERG,

DUC DE KRUMAU,

*Chevalier de la Foison-d'Or, Grand Croix de l'Ordre
Royal de S.t Etienne, Commandeur de l'Ordre Militaire de
Marie-Thérèse, Chambellan, Conseiller intime actuel,
Feld-Maréchal, Ambassadeur de S. M. l'Empereur d'Autriche
près la Cour de France, Grand-Croix de S.t André de Russie*

Né le 15 avril 1771 à Vienne, Autriche.

1792 the Duke of Brunswick was soundly defeated by the revolutionary troops of General Dumouriez at Valmy, marking the definitive over-throw of the monarchy in Paris, allowing France to become a republic. At the beginning of November, the Imperial Army of Albert Casimir, Duke of Teschen received a harsh lesson from Dumouriez-led troops at the Battle of Jemappes, where Casimir's army suffered a crushing de-feat. As is common knowledge, Louis XVI was executed the following year, followed by the execution of his wife, Queen Marie Antoinette. In addition to Austria and Prussia, other powers were gradually joining the ranks of the first Anti-French Coalition. Finally, Great Britain, the United Netherlands (territory of today's Holland, which, contrary to the Austrian Netherlands – today's Belgium – was a sovereign state), Spain, Portugal, and a number of smaller Italian states rallied to the cause. In addition, the Commander-in-Chief of Imperial forces in the Austrian Netherlands, Prince Josias of Saxe-Coburg-Saalfeld, achieved the first significant defeat of Dumouriez and the French at the beginning of March 1793 at Neerwinden in the Austrian Netherlands. The following year, however, the Austrians and their allies were soundly beaten at the Battle of Fleurus by the army of French General Jourdan (who was to become one of Wellington's adversaries, whom he later defeated during the Peninsular War in the Battles of Talavera and Vitoria). This caused the Austrians to lose the whole territory of the Austrian Netherlands.[733] If we were to return to the very beginning of his military career, the young Wellington took part in the clashes in Belgium as a member of the ranks of the British expeditionary forces. As we know, the British under the command of the Duke of York did not lend much support to the Austrians in this campaign.

Over the course of 1795 due to the influence of French military suc-cesses, members of the first Anti-French Coalition began to leave the group. Spain and the United Netherlands also "deserted" to the ene-my's side and even signed a pact with the French. After the Austrians, Prussians and British units were defeated in the Ausrian Netherlands by French armies. Northern Italy became the primary theatre of the War of the First Coalition, where the Austrians fought against the French on the second front together with the Kingdom of Sardinia. In 1796, the twenty-seven-year-old French General Napoleon Bonaparte took command of French forces in Northern Italy. Just after taking command, Bonaparte managed an audacious crossing of the Alps that caught the enemy by surprise and drove a wedge between the allied units of Sardinian King Victor Amadeus III and the Austrians led by General Beaulieu. He then managed to achieve several defeats of the Sardinian units in quick succession, the battles of Montenotte (12th April 1796), Millesimo (13th–14th April 1796) and Mondovi (21st April 1796), ejecting the Kingdom of Sardinia from battle and forcing Victor Amadeus to sign the Treaty of Paris (15th May 1796) with France. Thus, the Austrians found themselves alone in the war against Napoleon on the Northern-Italian battlefield. Napoleon first defeated them 10th May 1796 at Lodi and subsequently seized the strategic Mantua Fortress, gaining control of the whole region. The Austrians managed to reclaim the fortress thanks to a timely intervention by General Wurmser, who quickly brought in large reinforcements. Nonetheless, Napoleon defeated the new Austrian ruler, who was left with no other choice but to withdraw with the rest of his defeated army to Mantua. Due to a lack of food (in a fortress that was already insufficiently stocked), General Wurmser was forced to give up Mantua (which he came to defend, only to find himself trapped) to Bonaparte on 2nd February 1797.[734]

In the meantime, the French Armies under the command of Generals Jourdan and Moreau both headed towards Vienna. They were, however, stopped in the Rhineland and defeated several times by Francis II's brother, Archduke Charles, Duke of Teschen, who was now hastening to reach Northern Italy in the hopes to save Austria at the last moment on the battlefield there. Nonetheless, Archduke Charles was defeated by Napoleon in battle by the bridge over the Tagliamento River (16th March 1797). As a result, Bonaparte pushed the Archduke all the way back to the Brenner Pass. The defeated Austrians were thus forced to sit down with the French at the negotiating table. They signed the Treaty of Campo Formio (18th October 1797), definitively leading to the dissolution of the First Anti-French coalition. Based on this treaty, Emperor Francis II was forced to give up the Austrian Netherlands (Belgium) to France and acknowledge the sovereignty of two Napoleon-led sister republics in Italy – the Cisalpine Republic surrounding Milan and the Ligurian Republic with its centre in Genova. In practice, these republics became *de facto* French protectorates. In order to gain at least partial compensation, the Austrians gained the whole region of Venice.[735]

In 1799, however, Austria did not hesitate to join War of the Second Coalition, which was led on European territory again primarily in Northern Italy. Together with Austrian forces, the Russian Army now stood against the French. The Austrians requested with great expectations that the legendary sixty-nine-year-old Commander Alexander Suvorov be put at the head of the allied Russian-Austrian forces in the upcoming conflict. Suvorov had proved himself on a Europe-wide scale primarily in the wars with the Ottoman Turks in the 1760s and 1770s. At this special request, he was called out of retirement and into battle by Russian Tsar Paul I. The Austrian forces were then to be led by General Michael von Melas under Suvorov's chief command. In addition, General Bonaparte at the time found himself in an unfavourable campaign in Egypt, where he defeated the Mameluks in the Battle of the Pyramids (21st July 1798), but was consequently stopped in his tracks at the Siege of Acre (20th March – 21st May 1799), which he repeatedly failed to conquer, leading to the siege being seen as an Anglo-Ottoman victory.

Almost immediately after launching the allied offensive, Suvorov was victorious in April 1799 over the French Army of General Moreau at the River Adda, allowing the allies to march on without resistance to Milan, where their Commander-in-Chief ordered them to attend a mass of thanksgiving in the beautiful Italian gothic cathedral. Subsequently, the allies successfully captured Turin, where they clashed with the French in the three-day Battle of Trebbia (17th–20th June 1799), where Suvorov overwhelmingly defeated the French once again. French losses at Trebbia amounted to 17,000 men in contrast to only 5,000 fallen allied troops. This all pointed to the fact that Austrian hopes (and the hopes of others) that were placed in Suvorov's commanding prowess were materializing.[736]

In this critical situation for the French, a new commander of French forces, General Barthélemy Joubert, was sent forth against Suvorov. Joubert had already served once in Northern Italy as a brigadier general under Napoleon during Bonaparte's victorious campaign of 1796 and knew the local terrain quite well. Joubert fought the Russo-Austrian forces in the Battle of Novi (15th August 1799). The French general had married shortly before battle, and before he left, he allegedly promised his wife that he would return either as a victor or a corpse, as he would not be able to stand the disgrace of defeat. Nonetheless, the allied forces led by Suvorov triumphed yet again at Novi and Joubert, as he had promised his wife, returned to his homeland in a coffin, having been shot through the heart early on in the battle.[737] All of Northern Italy (the former territory of the Cisalpine and Ligurian Republics) thus found itself in the hands of the allies, who were now planning an invasion of France itself. In order for the Russo-Austrian Army to ensure a rear position, it would first be necessary to conquer Switzerland, where French forces were operating under General Masséna. This French leader proved to be a formidable adversary and was fittingly known under the nickname of 'Old Fox'. Wellington, who defeated Masséna at Busaco and later lured him into the trap of Lines of Torres Vedras in autumn 1809, dubbed Napoleon's soon-to-become marshal the most capable of all the individuals with whom he measured his might during almost six years of operation on the Iberian Peninsula.

Suvorov was tasked with conquering Switzerland only with Russian forces. In the confusing mountainous terrain, he soon found himself surrounded by Masséna's troops. In the end, he managed through a brave manoeuvre to elude Masséna at the last moment by venturing through the St. Gotthard Pass, saving his army from certain capture. This, however, changed nothing about the fact that he suffered heavy losses and did not seize Switzerland. As a result of Suvorov's defeat, Russian Tsar Paul I, who somewhat unjustifiably placed the blame purely on Austria, was strongly discontented by the matter and withdrew from the second coalition at the beginning of 1800. It should also be mentioned that Austrian forces did truly fail in providing supplies to the Russian Army, an obligation which they had promised to fulfil. Subsequently, even a military intervention by the Austrians failed to help Suvorov out of his predicament. Nonetheless, the now solitary Austrians managed to push Masséna, who had since marched out of Switzerland, all the way to Genoa, where they surrounded him together with the British Royal Navy, which laid siege to the city from the sea. Masséna finally capitulated in exchange for the safe exit of his soldiers back to France. [738]

In 1799, however, Napoleon appeared in Paris. In a strong stroke of luck, he had managed to slip past the Royal Navy on a single ship from Egypt. The Royal Navy, under the command of Horatio Nelson, had managed to crush the French flotilla at Abukir Bay, a naval engagement often referred to as the Battle of the Nile (1st–2nd August 1798) and now wholly dominated the Mediterranean. Shortly after his arrival to the French capital, Napoleon took part in the famous military coup that took place according to the date of the French revolutionary calendar on 18th Brumaire (10th November 1799). With a significant contribution from Bonaparte, the coup overthrew the existing French rule of the five-member Directory (which ruled in the country since 1795). The coup resulted in the installation of a three-member Consulate to run France, where many had called for a strong hand to rule in the aftermath of the series of defeats in Italy. In this Consulate, Napoleon was awarded the title of the most powerful First Consul in this ruling "Triumvirate", upon which he hastened to regain his lost French possessions in Italy. Early in 1800, Napoleon led the French Reserve Army across the Alps through the Great St. Bernard Pass, a trans-Alpine crossing that was immortalised in oils by a painting by Jacques-Louis David often known as *Napoleon Crossing the Alps*. Once across the Alps Napoleon soon captured Milan (2nd June 1800), followed a few days later by a battle with the Austrians taking place near Montebello (9th June 1800) in Lombardy with the vanguard of the French forces commanded by General Jean Lannes defeating the Austrians led by Fieldmarshal Peter Ott. Whilst significant, Montebello has come to be seen as the warm up for the main event which was to take place five days later with Napoleon very much at the helm.

The French and Austrians next encountered each other at the Battle of Marengo in Piedmont, with the Austrians under the command of Marshal Michael von Melas. After the first hours of bloody fighting, the battle seemed to have been decided in favour of the Austrians. The French were retreating from the whole span of the battlefield as the elated commander of Austrian forces Melas sent messengers to Vienna with the news of his victory over the feared French leader Bonaparte. Luck, however, was on Napoleon's side, as he was saved from complete disaster in the eleventh hour by the sudden arrival of soldiers under the command of French General Desaix, who paid for his utmost bravery at Marengo with his life. Desaix, however, caught the surprised Austrians completely off guard and thus overturned the seemingly lost battle in the French's favour. Thus, in moments, the Austrians lost the battle and were themselves now forced to retreat. The French victory at Marengo added significantly to Napoleon's standing and helped him further consolidate his political power. In addition, before end of 1800 General Moreau managed to defeat the youngest brother of Francis II, Archduke John Baptist Joseph of Austria at Hohenlinden (3ʳᵈ December 1800), opening a direct path to Vienna, which was only several dozen kilometres away. The Austrians were again forced to negotiate peace. A peace agreement was signed between France and Austria on 7ᵗʰ February, 1801 in Lunéville. Francis II was forced to reaffirm all territorial gains made hitherto by France and in addition had to part with the territory of Imperial princes on the right bank of the Rhine. Francis II was also forced to confirm the foundation of the Helvetic Republic on the territory of Switzerland and the Batavian Republic on the territory of the United Netherlands (Holland), which came under indirect French control as "sister republics".[739]

After agreeing to peace in Lunéville, Britain was practically alone at war against the French – Continental Europe had already been exhausted by practically ten years of unremitting battles and European powers were not interested in another war. Finally, even Britain, which dominated on the sea and in the colonies, signed a peace with the French at the end of March 1802 at Amiens while Napoleon strengthened his position on Continental Europe. However, neither side was yet able to achieve an overall decisive advantage. Both the British and the French saw the Treaty of Amiens as a "time for repose" to gain new energy. In addition, the British ambassadors at peace negotiations labelled Napoleon a man of "unmitigated ambitions", thanks to which – if he remained the leader of France – a lasting peace would clearly be impossible. This would prove to be a prophetic statement in the years to come. As soon as 1803, Britain somewhat unsurprisingly declared a new war against Napoleon. The primary pretext for renewing the military conflict was the dispute over the island of Malta, which the British refused to give up. Similarly, Bonaparte refused to withdraw his French regiments from the Netherlands and Switzerland. After the renewal of hostilities, Napoleon (who in 1802 declared himself lifelong consul and by doing so gained unlimited power over France) had all British civilians on the continent arrested, causing general consternation. The arrests included diplomats, which at the time, in terms of international law, was seen as a flagrant violation. At the beginning of 1803, Napoleon also seized Hanover, which was the inherited territory of British Monarch George III (within the Holy Roman Empire, however, it officially belonged to the administration of Emperor Francis II). In May of the same year, Napoleon Bonaparte had himself nominated as the hereditary Emperor of France (although the official coronation did not take place until 2nd December 1804). In reaction to Bonaparte's decision and his declining power in the Holy Roman Empire, Francis II decided to declare himself Austrian Emperor Francis I on 11th August 1804. From this moment on, the term Austria and Austrians can be used in its proper sense.*

Napoleon's aggressive policy gradually led the Austrian and Russian courts (where Paul I was succeeded by Alexander I) to new and fevered activity. Under the direction of British Prime Minister William Pitt the Younger, the situation in Europe began to lean toward the formation of a third anti-French coalition. In addition to Britain, the ranks of the new alliance in the war against Napoleon came to include Austria, Russia, and Sweden, whose army did not, however, play a significant role. When the Russians and Austrians began to call their men to arms, Napoleon did not hesitate to dissolve his camp at the Northern French town of Boulogne, where his forces were gathered for an invasion of Britain, and marched east toward the new enemy. These events ultimately led to a campaign whose fate would be decided during the famous Battle of the Three Emperors at Austerlitz, close to Brno, i.e. in the territory of the Kingdom of Bohemia.[740] What actually took place in the Czech lands after the French Revolution broke out? What were the reactions of the "third estate" in Bohemia and Moravia to the efforts of the French to "export" the revolution with their flamboyant and provocative slogans of "liberty, equality, and fraternity" to all of Europe?

Czech society as a whole was understandably not nearly as united in its attitude toward the revolution. Representatives of the royal court, the nobility, clergy, bureaucracy, and more affluent burghers were understandably hostile to the French Revolution. In addition, the governing authorities gradually began to develop official state propaganda against the revolution, which they called the "French freedom hoax", and against its representatives. Strong sympathies with the revolution can be observed in the Kingdom of Bohemia logically among the vast majority of the peasantry in the years immediately after 1789. Bohemian and Moravian subjects especially hoped for liberation from *corvée* (unpaid labour), the dissolution of feudalism, and the establishment of general social equality. These ideas were most often spread via narratives of discontented soldiers returning

---

* Skřivan, pp. 145–150. For clarity I use the term 'Austrians' from time to time to refer to the Imperial Army before 1804.

home from the Imperial Habsburg Army, the smuggling in of forbidden brochures propagating revolutionary ideas, but also via official Austrian state propaganda, which often unintentionally popularized the revolution through its criticism. Several French propaganda leaflets that were distributed in the Czech lands in 1796 by Marshal Jourdan's light dragoons have been preserved. These leaflets promise to abolish unpaid labour over the whole Habsburg Monarchy. (Jourdan's men, however, were stopped in the Rhineland by Archduke Charles and his army, as was mentioned above).

Thanks to certain historical connections, Czech peasants may have also seen the French traditionally as liberators. For instance, when (in Czech historiography) the so-called 'Second Winter King' Charles Albert, elector of Bavaria,* occupied Prague with the help of French troops in 1742, he promised to abolish serfdom. In addition, the peasants in many cases were of the opinion that the state under the rule of Leopold II and later Francis II was deviating from Josephine reforms (primarily the abolishment of serfdom and declaration of the freedom of religion, which was put into practice in the Habsburg Monarchy in 1781 based on Joseph II's edicts).[741] Thus, from a modern perspective, bizarre conjectures abounded among the common folk. For example, one anonymous Czech folk chronicler wrote the following: 'That Bonaparte is most likely to be Joseph II's son, and the fact that he was born in Corsica is made up by the lords and princes to deceive the common people.'[742] Generally speaking, however, there is a considerable number of folk chronicles containing the opinion that a new era had arrived with Napoleon in which the common people would be lifted up and general equality would reign. For example, a municipal officer from Čáslav, Josef Opitz, made the following note in 1796:

> The present mood of the Czech country folk is precarious. Everywhere, even in the lowest levels of society, principles that can be seen as a true propensity toward revolution are abound.[743]

According to another chronicler's record, a subject in the region of Pardubice personally walked into a local governing office to speak with the much-disliked officials there, threatening that the subjects, if not treated properly, would be forced to 'become French.'[744] The gravity of the

---

*   Known also as Holy Roman Emperor Charles VII.

situation can also be seen in the following example: After the Austrian armies suffered a series of defeats, Archduke John Baptist Joseph proposed the creation of a militia comprised of the common people by appealing to their national pride. This proposal, however, was denied by his brother and ruler Francis II as being too dangerous, for fear that the militia would turn against the monarchy alongside the French instead of protecting it. The dispute over whether to draw up a militia was eventually solved by the peace treaty signed with the French in February 1797 in Campo Formio, whilst exacting for the Austrians, was not designed to humiliate them.[745]

Once Austria entered into the war again in the ranks of the Second Anti-French Coalition, the Commander-in-Chief of Austrian forces, the Archduke Charles, Duke of Teschen wrote the following in reaction to the revolutionary sentiment among the common folk of the Habsburg Monarchy shortly after the defeat that was the Battle of Marengo:

> I dare say that nine tenths of the country is living in hopes of the French entering the country. Everyone in the countryside says 'let them come, we'll kill our lords and won't have to pay anything'. In the cities, they say 'mainly let them capture Vienna so peace is struck'. This makes the hair on the head stand up in terror.[746]

However, the major turning point in the attitude among citizens of the Czech lands toward French "liberators" came during the War of the Third Coalition. After Napoleon dissolved his camp at Boulonge and renamed the Armée d'Angleterre (Army of England) which was meant to invade Britain, to the Grande Armée, he lead it directly to Vienna in order to destroy his opponent as quickly as possible. At Ulm, Napoleon's armies first forced the Austrian troops under the command of Marshal Mack to capitulate after Napoleon surrounded them with an ingenious manoeuvre. Napoleon's troops then managed to capture Vienna and, as a significant portion of the common folk in the Czech lands hoped, finally "came into the country". However, during the following march to Moravia, which culminated on 2ⁿᵈ December in Napoleon's victory in the Battle of the Three Emperors at Austerlitz where Bonaparte crushed the Russo-Austrian forces of Francis I and Tsar Alexander I, the French in most cases did not behave like liberators importing civil liberty; they acted like any other occupying army. They ransacked, burned villages, and raped women. Nothing was safe in their path. For example, when French units entered the town of Klatovy in the region of Pilsen during their march on Austerlitz, their commander

> requested 15 thousand coins in silver and gold and the same amount in bills... 60 packages of thin cloth and all the silk items from the whole town, 200 horses, 100 oxen, and the general [in reality a colonel] requested for himself 6 gold coins and 30 silver watches, also 80,000 gold coins for the whole region of Klatovy. In addition, he committed atrocious acts of ransacking on the town and shameless behaviour with the female sex. When he had gathered everything, he had the people undressed. One old pensioned oberst [a former Austrian colonel] walked up to the general and knelt down before him, pleading for him to stop the barbarity and cruelty, saying: "I am an old soldier too, and have seen plundering, but such cruelty as this I have never seen..."[747]

After becoming quickly disillusioned, militia divisions began to spring up in a wholly spontaneous manner in various places among the Bohemian peasants (to a much lesser extent similar to the peasant guerrillas in Portugal or Spain) to attack the French. Nonetheless, shortly after the defeat at Austerlitz Francis I had no other choice but to sign another "peace" treaty, this one a particualrly humiliating one, with Napoleon in Pressburg (today's Bratislava). Based on this treaty, the Austrian emperor was forced to give up Venice, Istria, and Dalmatia. In addition, the last remnants of his authority in the Holy Roman Empire were destroyed when Napoleon rewarded the two powerful members of the Holy Roman Empire, Bavaria and Baden-Württemberg, which gladly joined Napoleon in his Austerlitz campaign in the hopes of territorial gains, at the expense of the Austrian Emperor. In July 1806, Napoleon completed his humiliation of the emperor by dissolving the Holy Roman Empire after a thousand years of existence. He founded the Confederation of the Rhine in its place, basically making it another one of France's protectorates.[748] After this fundamental change in the German sphere of power and influence, the Kingdom of Prussia, which had hitherto stood in the background, entered into war against Napoleon alongside Britain and Russia. In the war of the so-called Fourth Coalition, however, the Prussians were crushed within a matter of months to the utter dismay of all the other powers, after which Napoleon marched triumphantly to Berlin. The short process that Napoleon held with the Prussians is described quite succinctly and somewhat humorously by folk chronicler Josef Dusílek, an inhabitant of Eastern Bohemia, over 200 years ago: 'In the Year of Our Lord 1806, the Frenchman marched to Silesia and fought a big war with Prus [meaning Prussia]. He thrashed one prince and captured the other...'[749] By the "thrashed prince", Dusílek was referring to Charles William Ferdinand, Duke of Brunswick (the aforementioned commander of Prussian forces in the War of the First Coalition, who made threats to the French that he would burn down Paris and was then humiliatingly defeated at Valmy), who was killed as the Commander-in-Chief of Prussian forces at Jena. The captured prince most likely refers to Frederick von Hohenlohe, who led the Prussians at Auerstedt. In East-Prussian Friedland, Napoleon subsequently defeated the Russian Tsar's forces and signed a peace treaty with him in Tilsit (July 1807), completing the dissolution of yet another anti-Napoleon coalition.

Austria declared war on France (for the fourth time) in 1809. In addition to the Spanish uprising against French rule, after which Spain fell under French control in 1808, the Austrians were primarily encouraged by the successes of the British Expeditionary Force, which at the time won several important victories under Arthur Wellesley's command over the French in Portugal (at Roliça, Vimeiro, and Oporto). According to the allies' plan, Austria was to attack the French in the east. By entering into the War of the Fifth Coalition, in which it was the only larger power to join Britain as an ally, the Austrians lured Napoleon out of Spain as he hurried to face the new Austrian threat in person. Due to this fact, Wellington was "only" up against Napoleon's marshals during the Peninsular War. He ultimately measured his might against Bonaparte himself in the Battle of Waterloo. What events would have ensued if Austria had not entered the war in 1809, leaving Wellington to confront Napoleon in 1809 must be the subject of conjecture and speculation. In addition, the atmosphere among the people of the Habsburg Monarchy at the time was largely anti-French, which proved to be a fundamental change from the era before Austerlitz. In the light of the lack of combat-capable troops due to the losses incurred in the three previous Coalition Wars and thanks to the change in the common people's sentiment toward the French and the ideals of the revolution, a militia made up of the ranks of the common folk could be created for the first time in the history of the Habsburg Monarchy. The Imperial edict to create it was issued during preparations for war on 9th June 1808. The militia system was based on the principle of arming reserves taken from the ranks of the common citizenry. These reserves existed in parallel to the army. They were trained regularly to use weapons and, in the event of a military conflict, they would be called up to defend the country. Men from the age of 18 to 45, were required to serve in the ranks of the militia, with the exception of the nobility, clergy, and the main administrators of aristocratic estates.[750] By creating a militia, the first step was made toward establishing mandatory military service in the territory of the Habsburg Monarchy. In reaction to the creation of the militia, František Vavák, a mayor of the village of Milčice known as "a great appraiser of the Holy Writ"* and a staunch opponent of revolutionary and Napoleonic France in Czech circles since the beginning of the conflict, composed the famous song *The Good Czechs March into Battle*. The song contains the following lines:

> Hark, Czechs, hear the voice, the times have come once more. As in years before, we shall know now. Burghers and peasants, we shall be soldiers again... In order for the battle to be good, we must train. We shall exercise and observe the course of battle. This is the primary thing an army should know... Our kind King Francis, yearning for peace, let him take pleasure in our success, achieved by the Czechs, as we gladly dispel the enemy.[751]

Because many did not share Vavák's zealous patriotism and despite various advantages offered by the government (these were usually financial benefits or relief from unpaid labour), there was still an insufficient number of volunteers for the regular army. Therefore, the state decided to begin a massive war propaganda campaign. The primary goal of the Habsburg Monarchy was to appeal to patriotism throughout the Habsburg Monarchy – in the Czech lands this meant appealing to being Czech.

---

* In Czech "Písmák" – a term used for a person knowledgeable of the Bible and basic religious literature but otherwise of peasant rank and lacking any systematic education – today we might call this individual "self-taught". Those with the distinction may have been chroniclers, authors of memoirs; in some cases, they wrote spiritual poetry and other literary works.

In this new strategy to attract recruits into the Austrian military and the effort to portray the looming war with France as a national liberation war, government pamphlets were issued, calling upon inhabitants of the Kingdom of Bohemia to take up arms for the glory of the Czech nation while referring to the honour and bravery of the Přemyslid rulers, who often fought in the Middle Ages side by side with Holy Roman Emperors as allies. The pamphlets also logically included mention of the bravery of the Hussites and reference to the invincible commander Jan Žižka. Furthermore, the offices of the monarchy cooperated with well-known Czech patriot newspapers of Václav Matěj Kramerius, who wrote articles for the monarchy that appealed to the age-old bravery of the Czechs and their patriotism.[752] Thanks to this, the Napoleonic Wars played a strong role in the shift of the Czech National Revival from its first phase, which was characterized by the interest of only a handful of scholars in the country and its culture and represented in the Czech environment most often by Josef Dobrovský, to the second revival phase, sometimes called the "campaigning" phase, in which a group of patriots actively strove to spread Czech culture and national consciousness. Josef Jungmann is most commonly cited as the representative of this phase.[753]

The next common tool of national propaganda used by the Habsburg Monarchy to promote the war was the theatre. In a Czech translation by Václav Thám, the Austrian authorities ordered the theatrical play *Czechs are true patriots, or: Life for Francis, Charles, and the homeland* * to be performed. The author of the play was Chief of Austrian Police in Prague Filip Heimbacher. The name of the play itself and the identity of the author perhaps need no further commentary. The official state-run war propaganda culminated after the Archduke Charles, Duke of Teschen scored a sensational victory at the very beginning of the War of the Fourth Coalition in May 1809 over Napoleon at Aspern-Essling. During this surprising victory, which brought Archduke Charles a sudden wave of justified fame around Europe as the first man to defeat Napoleon on the field of battle, a relatively large number of militia regiments from Bohemia were fighting on the Austrian side. Some 20 regiments, i.e. 8,000 men, were recruited from the Czech lands, which was certainly not an

---

*   Referring to Francis I and Archduke Charles, Duke of Teschen, the younger brother of Francis I.

insignificant number. In the euphoria after this triumph, a pamphlet was issued in reaction and entitled *The valour of the glorious Czech nation according to national history presented to our ardent defenders*, which sought faithfully to name all Czech military successes from the victory of Samo's Empire over the Franks and the victorious battles fought by the Czech kings of the medieval dynasty of Přemyslids, the House of Luxembourg, and Hussites to Albrecht of Wallenstein's triumphs during the Thirty Years' War. Nonetheless, Austrian troops suffered a defeat by Napoleon at Wagram on 5th–6th July 1809, which practically erased all of the memory of the success of the Battle of Aspern-Essling. However, the fact that the victory of Archduke Charles broke the cult of Napoleon's invincibility should not be underestimated.[754] Napoleon's victory at Wagram was not nearly as decisive as the one for instance against the War of the Third Coalition at Austerlitz. Archduke Charles managed to retreat in a wholly organized fashion with his army from Wagram thanks to his excellent manoeuvring tactics (a fact which even Napoleon later acknowledged) and took an advantageous defensive position at the city of Znaim (Znojmo in Czech) in the southeast of today's Czech Republic. Although at the time he was striving for peace within Austrian foreign policy, at Znaim he led another balanced two-day battle (10th–11th July) with the French Emperor, which in the general consciousness today still remains somewhat overshadowed of the Battle of Aspern-Essling and Wagram. Therefore, the accepted cliché that Napoleon definitively defeated Austria in 1809 at Wagram is often cited. This, however, is not completely true. The French Emperor, who at the time was also gripped by a feverish illness, evidently decided to agree to a peace treaty out of fear that the Archduke Charles would retreat again in an orderly fashion from Znaim farther west to the Bohemian-Moravian Highlands, where he would have a new and advantageous defensive position from which to conduct further resistance. He did this despite his evident initial plans to wipe the "incorrigible" Austrians from the map of Europe for good, just as he had done three years earlier with the Holy Roman Empire.[755] As the Austrian ambassador in Paris at the time, Count Metternich informed Austrian Emperor Francis I even before the start of the War of the Fifth Coalition of the plan to "divide" Austria, as was done for example to Poland several times throughout history:

It is not France who has been at war since the Treaty of Lunéville (1801) ... It is Napoleon, and he does so with French supplies... In Bohemia they should be warned that, judging by what has recently become public in France, they should be transformed into a similarly dependent state as Bavaria is now. In Austria, they should know that the name of one French Marshal has already been chosen, who will rule there with the title of Archduke; in Hungary, they should also not harbour any hopes of remaining whole.[756]

Austria had thus been defeated, but not destroyed. Thanks to determined resistance and despite Metternich's terrifying prognosis for the Austrians in the event of a defeat, Austria for the meantime kept its independence. In addition, by entering the war it provided Wellington the time to build the Lines of Torres Vedras. All in all, as a consequence of the defeat at the Battle of Wagram and the following armistice after fierce fighting at Znaim, where another 5,000 Austrians and at least 3,000 French soldiers fell, Austria was forced to sign another humiliating peace treaty on 14th October 1809 with the French at the Schönbrunn Palace in Vienna after several long months of negotiations.[757] According to the treaty, Austria was forced to transfer Salzburg and Innviertel in Upper Austria. Western Carinthia, Carniola, and a portion of today's Croatia reaching all the way to Dubrovnik (the so-called Illyrian Provinces) to become a direct part of the French Empire. The last of the extensive territorial losses included the surrender of Western Galicia to the Duchy of Warsaw, which became another of Napoleon's protectorates on the territory of Poland, and the surrender of Eastern Galicia to Russia. To put this "list" into numbers, the Austrians lost approximately 100,000 km^2 of territory and 3.5 million inhabitants. The Austrian emperor's army was not allowed to surpass 150,000 men. At the time, the French had over 300,000 men deployed against Wellington and the Spanish on the Iberian Peninsula alone; in total, Napoleon possessed more than one million soldiers. The final blow that struck Austria was in the form of war reparations dictated by Napoleon to the sum of 85 million francs.[758]

Although Austria had been defeated, a strong Austrian-Czech thread leading from Northeast Bohemia all the way to Wellington endured even after 1809 in the fight against Napoleon. On 25th February 1809, a secret treaty was signed in Vienna between the Austrian court and Frederick

William, Duke of Brunswick during preparations for a War of the Fifth Coalition with Napoleon. For the purposes of the upcoming war under Austrian patronage, the treaty called for the creation of a voluntary brigade of roughly 2,000 men, half of which would comprise cavalry and the other half infantry. The Duke of Brunswick himself was to take command of this newly formed regiment. The treaty designated Northeast Bohemia (specifically Náchod, Nové Město nad Metují, and Broumov), today a part of the Czech Republic, as the location for the formation of the Duke's troops.[759]

Thus, Frederick William, Duke of Brunswick-Wolfenbüttel (henceforth referred to as the Duke of Brunswick) arrived in Bohemian territory. He was a fascinating character, who had genuine reasons to fight against Napoleon. Frederick William was born as the fourth son of Charles William Ferdinand, Duke of Brunswick, and no one initially assumed that he would inherit his father's duchy. As many younger sons of the nobility without a claim to inheritance, the young Frederick looked to prove his worth in the army. He served as a captain in the ranks of the Prussian Army, which was led by his father – a Prussian Field-Marshal – alongside the Austrians against the French during the War of the First Coalition in 1792 into the Austrian Netherlands, where he experienced the defeat of Prussian troops at Valmy*. He fought again in the Prussian Army under the command of his father against Napoleon in 1806 in the Battle of Auerstedt, which proved fateful to the Prussians. In the few weeks after the battle, his father, as Commander-in-Chief, succumbed to the wounds he sustained from canister shot during the fighting. To reiterate the words of the Czech chronicler Dusílek mentioned above, it was Frederick William's father that Napoleon "thrashed". After the death of Charles William Ferdinand of Brunswick, Frederick William legally became Duke of Brunswick, as his oldest brother had died without descendants and his other brothers suffered from mental illnesses that barred them from governing, whereupon his father officially named him his successor before taking his last breath.[760] After Napoleon dissolved the Holy Roman Empire and signed the treaty in Tilsit with Russia, he seized the duchy from Frederick William, Duke of Brunswick, incorporating it in the newly formed Kingdom of Westphalia, with the city

---

* Charles William Ferdinand was offered the position of Commander-in-Chief of the British Army after the removal of the Duke of York. However, he refused this offer. See chapter three.

of Kassel as its capital. On its throne, Napoleon placed his youngest brother, Jérôme Bonaparte, who began to call himself Hieronymus I of Westphalia.

Frederick William certainly had enough compelling reasons to wish for revenge against Napoleon, and his hatred of the French Emperor seemed to have no bounds. Therefore, as a sign of grief over what Bonaparte had done to his family and homeland, the Duke of Brunswick had his newly formed army at Náchod in Bohemia dressed in specially tailored black uniforms. He chose the skull and crossbones as the symbol for his regiment.

Thanks to the black uniforms that the Brunswick unit wore, Frederick William was from then on called *'Der Schwarze Herzog'* ('The Black Duke' – for a likeness of the Black Duke, See Image 96) and his soldiers, *'Die Schwarze Legion'* ('The Black Legion'), *'Die Schwarze Schar'* ('Black Corps') or sometimes simply *'Die Schwarzen'* ('The Blacks'). In Northern Bohemia where the Legion was created, members were also often called *'Todtenköpfe'* ('Death's-heads') for the skulls that the soldiers had placed in the centre of their firmly fitting shako hats.* Soldiers of the Brunswick unit were recruited primarily from the ranks of soldiers of the Prussian army**, who made up the majority of the Black Legion. These were Frederick William's subjects, who had fled from Brunswick along with their Duke, and other discontented individuals from the territory of the dissolved Holy Roman Empire who did not agree with Bonaparte's arrangement in the area of today's Germany.

Despite this fact, the Black Legion initially suffered from a lack of recruits, and drafting went slower than expected. In the light of the fact that the regiment was created on the territory of Northeast Bohemia and

---

* Otto von Pivka, *Brunswick Troops 1809–1815* (Oxford 1985), pp. 7–8. Compare to: Karel Sáček, *Čeští dobrovolníci ve sboru vévody brunšvického* in: *Třetí koaliční válka 1805*, Akcent (Třebíč 2004) p. 73. According to the contract for the creation of the corps of volunteers signed with Austria, the Black Duke's corps was officially named "Herzoglich Braunschweigisches Corps" (The Duke's Brunswicker Corps).

** After Prussia's defeat by Napoleon in 1806, Prussia's army was not allowed according to the peace treaty to surpass 42,000 men including 1,791 officers (before 1806 it had 235,000 soldiers and 6,500 officers). Many former Prussian soldiers thus lost their jobs and found themselves in financial trouble. In addition, those who remained in their function were generally rather hostile towards Napoleon. For example, the commander of the garrison in Kladsko, Count von Götzen, wrote to the Prussian King that *'The best Prussian officers and men are leaving to join the Duke of Brunswick'*. See, Karel Sáček: *Smrtihlavové zrození v Čechách roku 1809* online article in: https://www.primaplana.cz/news/smrtihlavove-zrozeni-v-cechach-roku-1809-1-cerni-legionari-vevody-brunsvickeho-a-jejich-puvod/

that most of the population of the Czech lands had a negative attitude towards Napoleon after 1805, several dozen volunteers who joined the 'Death's Heads' in order to face the French Emperor's forces on the battlefield were from today's Czech Republic. The Brunswick unit became combat-ready at the end of April 1809, when the numbers in its ranks reached roughly 600 men.[761] The Black Duke did not hesitate to march from Náchod and through Trutnov directly against Zittau in Saxony. The Duke attacked the territory of the King of Saxony, as at the time he was Napoleon's ally in the war with Austria. The Duke managed to seize Zittau after several clashes but was subsequently forced to retreat back into Bohemia. There several skirmishes took place between the Black Corps and Saxon troops. In the meantime, Archduke Charles won a victory over Napoleon at Aspern-Essling. Thus, it was decided that the Black Corps should be assigned to Austrian General Am Ende's regiment, which ultimately consisted of 10,000 men. Under Am Ende's command, the Black Corps marched into Saxony again, where the Austro-Brunswick troops successfully seized Dresden. Before the end of June, Frederick William and Am Ende managed briefly to capture Leipzig, the siege of which was initiated by the Black Duke. Two days later, however, the troops were forced to abandon the city and retreat from the advancing French forces of General Junot, who were supported by regiments from the Kingdom of Westphalia led into battle personally by Jérôme Bonaparte. After this failure, Am Ende was replaced by General Kienmayer as Commander-in-Chief. Under the new commander, the Austro-Brunswick forces first defeated Junot at Berneck and Gefrees and Jérôme Bonaparte at Plauen, from where they pushed him farther and farther west. At the same time, however, Kienmayer and the Duke of Brunswick received the first news of the Archduke Charles' defeat at Wagram and the consequent armistice that was agreed upon in Znaim, which later led to the Treaty of Schönbrunn. Despite their recent victories, they were thus forced to return to Austrian territory and terminate all military actions.[762]

The enraged Black Duke, however, felt no personal obligation to the Treaty of Schönbrunn that was signed between Austria and France in 1809, as peace with Napoleon would have spelled the final catastrophe for his duchy. He decided to continue the fight against Napoleon at all costs, in any place and with all means possible. He finally devised an ambitious plan in which he intended to break through with his regiment into the north across all of today's Germany, finally reaching the North Sea. There he would board British vessels that would subsequently take him and his men to the only place where a war was still being waged against the French, to Wellington's Army on the Iberian Peninsula.

The majority of the Duke's men agreed with this audacious yet madcap scheme, as it might seem to some, to fight their way through all of Germany. Naturally, however, there were also – to use Wellington's words – several "croakers" who refused to go with the Black Duke. Frederick William convinced some to join him on this brave undertaking by offering them an advancement in rank; he was, however, forced to part with others. Nonetheless, at the beginning of the campaign to the North Sea he possessed roughly 2,100 men willing to follow him (roughly 600 soldiers from this number were cavalrymen). The regiment possessed four field cannons. Based on written sources, there is proof that at least forty nine 'Death's Heads' in the Black Legion came from today's Czech Republic. Among them was even one officer: the nineteen-year-old son of a local postmaster, Ignác Sperling, who was born in Náchod and became a member of the Black Legion soon after its foundation. Young Ignác was even a neighbour to the Black Duke in Náchod, as he lived in the U Slunce Inn where Frederick William took up lodging during his visit to the town. The man with the most typical Czech name on the list of Czechs in the Black Duke's Legion – although from the completely opposite part of the social spectrum than Sperling – was the notorious gambler Antonín Čejchan from Újezdec. It is not difficult to guess that Čejchan had not been faring well in his "profession" and he joined the 'Death's Heads', who happened to be drafting soldiers in the area, in order to escape paying his debts or perhaps some other greater punishment imposed upon him by his angry creditors. Such people formed the core of soldiers that made up the Black Legion, and therefore Archduke Charles quite fittingly called them 'men without a homeland'. From the beginning, the Duke of Brunswick primarily suffered from a lack of recruits in the ranks of his artillerymen. We know that from the total of forty nine Czechs, he was happy to take on twelve Czech artillerymen despite the fact that they spoke Czech exclusively at the beginning of the campaign and evidently only knew a few "small words" of German. Nonetheless, it was more important for the Black Duke that they knew how to handle their cannons properly, an opportunity that was to arise very soon.*

Frederick William and his men successfully reached Zwickau on 24th July 1808 and two days later managed successfully (and, more importantly, without being noticed) to enter the town of Halle, which was located in the territory of the Kingdom of Westphalia (today Halle is a part of Saxony-Anhalt), where the Duke emptied the town's coffers and tore down Jérôme Bonaparte's standard that had flown above the town. He then continued north. Jérôme Bonaparte was quickly informed of the event, and whilst initially astonished by such audacity immediately ordered his most reliable commander General Reubell to call upon his troops and crush the Black Duke for his arrogance. It was the Black Legion, however, who yet again struck first, confronting the isolated 5th Westphalia Infantry Regiment with the strength of 3,000 men in the town of Halberstadt. Although the Westphalia Regiment had an advantage in numbers, the Black Duke attacked. After the Black Legion managed to destroy one of the town gates with cannon fire, the Duke's men, including the cavalry, charged into the streets of Halberstadt, screaming: *"Sieg oder Todt!"* ("Victory or death!"), mercilessly slaying their enemies. In addition, the Black Legion managed to capture the commander of the Westphalian forces along with the regimental Colours, forcing the whole Westphalian regiment to capitulate shortly afterwards. During the battle for the town, the Black Duke lost 400 men while his adversary counted 600 fallen and 2,080 taken prisoner. To the Black Duke's grief, one of

---

*   Karel Sáček, *Čeští dobrovolníci ve sboru vévody brunšvického*, pp. 72–77. Historian Karel Sáček has carried out a considerable body of research into the origin of the members of the Black Legion and has been studying the topic since 2002. Sáček points to the fact that of the approximate 2,000 men in the ranks of the Black Legion, we have more detailed sources for the year 1809 on only 340 specific men. From this number, however, Sáček claims that there were no records for 84 of these men that would make it possible to trace their place of origin. This thus leaves us with 256 men, from which various sources attest that 48 were from Bohemia, i.e. roughly one fifth of the troops. Among the 112 officers, all of whom (contrary to the men in ranks) are documented in greater detail, we know of one single Czech officer, Ignác Sperling. The famous 19th century Czech author Alois Jirásek chose Sperling as the main hero of his story dedicated to the Black Legion, in which he claims that, in addition to Sperling, *'a score of Czechs'* joined the Duke of Brunswick in battle. Another Czech author from the 19th century, Václav Řezníček, claims that *'many Czechs'* joined the Black Legion. In his work *Válečné dějiny československé* (Military History of Czechoslovakia) from 1937, military historian František Kurfust claims that in Bohemia there was *'enough fighting blood'* and there were *'hundreds of capable men'* for the Black Legion. These claims are unfortunately quite general and the author does not list specific sources of information; however, if we take into consideration that roughly one fifth of the soldiers for which there is more detailed information came from today's Czech Republic and we analogically count one fifth of the 2,000 soldiers of the Duke of Brunswick (excluding officers), theoretically hundreds of Czechs could easily have served. This, however, is pure speculation.

the men that fell during the daring attack on the town was his only Czech officer and recent neighbour from Náchod, nineteen-year-old Ignác Sperling.

After victory at Halberstadt, Frederick William continued on with his remaining troops north in order to rendezvous with the ships of the British Royal Navy. During his advance, the Black Legion (which was significantly more mobile and compact than its pursuers due to its relatively small number of soldiers) managed repeatedly to elude Reubell's troops. Frederick William even marched into his former capital of Brunswick. The Black Duke briefly liberated the town, which was, however, only of a demonstrative character as it was clear to all that there was no hope that the Black Duke could hold the town for long. Frederick William thus quickly left Brunswick and marched on to the port of Elsfleth (several dozen kilometres below Bremen) on the confluence of the rivers Hunte and Weser, which after mutual agreement with the British was selected as the site where he planned to embark with his Black Legion.

Reubell's men almost thwarted the Black Duke and his forces at Ölper, where a battle ensued on 1st August 1809. Nonetheless, Frederick William ultimately managed to flee to Hanover, where he skilfully confused his pursuer by dividing his troops into two independent groups. Soon after, the Black Legion managed to cross the Weser, landing on its western shore where the town of Elsfleth is located. The Duke's men successfully managed to blow up the bridge they had crossed just moments before their pursuers were upon them. On 8th August 1809, approximately 1,600 Black Legion boarded the promised British naval vessels in Elsfleth without incident. They first sailed via Heligoland (an archipelago in the North Sea that had capitulated to the British in 1807) and then onto the Isle of Wight off Southern England, where after a brief rest and reorganization they set for Portugal. There, on 8th October 1810, they joined Wellington's forces. If we take into consideration that – similar to poor Sperling – some Czech soldiers from the ranks of the Black Legion may have fallen during their journey to rendezvous with the British ships, we may assume that roughly forty men from today's Czech Republic may have joined Wellington as a part of the Black Legion. Truly, what the Black Duke and his Black Legion had achieved was a remarkable martial feat, one that inspired others to defy Napoleon and his occupying forces across the Continent of Europe.

As for poor General Reubell, who had failed to stop the Black Duke and now anticipated the prospect of disgrace and punishment, he took the initiative and fled (along with his American wife) from the wrath of the Bonaparte family to America.[763] The Black Legion, known to the British also as the "Black Brunschwickers" or the "Brunschwick-Öels Jagers" (Brunschwick-Oels Hunters. "Öels" in the name referred to the small Oleśnica Voivodship in the territory that is modern-day Poland, which was also a part of Frederick William's property), was first ordered to join the brigade led by Wellington's brother-in-law Ned Pakenham. Soon, however, the brigade was incorporated into the troops of the famous Light Division of General Craufurd, the ranks of which took part in pursuing the dejected units of French Marshal Masséna during their retreat from the Lines of Torres Vedras back to Spain. Craufurd himself joined the battle in the various skirmishes that took place during this pursuit. The first great battle of the Brunswick unit under Wellington's command then took place at Fuentes de Oñoro in 1811. Before this battle, which Wellington won, the majority of the Black Legion had been transferred to the newly formed 7th Division of General Houston. If we recall the clash at Fuentes de Oñoro, it was the same 7th Division that prevented French Marshal Masséna from surrounding Wellington's right wing, ultimately becoming surrounded by the enemy themselves. However, thanks to good discipline and the arrival of reinforcements sent to them by Wellington in the nick of time, the division managed to fight its way through and connect safely to the centre of the British forces. The Black Legion was subsequently present during the hellish situation the British went through during the Siege of Badajoz in 1812. Nonetheless, the 7th Division, along with the Brunswick unit, was one of the few that did not take part in any of the attacks on the city's massive walls. During Wellington's triumph at Salamanca, the Black Legion also played a rather insignificant role. However, at the Battle of Vitoria they were in the centre of the action, as they and the 7th Division stormed the gap that an attack by General Picton's 3rd Division had created in the French lines. The Black Legion actively participated in other victorious battles fought by Wellington on French soil. The unit took place in its final battle under Wellington's command at Orthez in February 1814. Once Napoleon abdicated at the beginning of April of that year, the Black Legion was released from British service and the Black Duke could now return to the homeland that had been returned to him. Nonetheless, after Napoleon's escape from Elba, the Duke of Brunswick set off without hesitation once again into battle against his "old-new" deadly enemy, recruiting roughly 7,000 soldiers (the core of which was naturally formed by veterans of the original Black Legion). He marched to Belgium where, under the allied armies that had remobilized against Napoleon in 1815, he was assigned to the units of his old commander, the Duke of Wellington. Three days before the fated clash at Waterloo, the Black Duke fell during a counter-attack of his troops on the French positions of Marshal Ney during the fierce Battle of Quatre Bras.* The Brunswick contingent subsequently took part in the Battle of Waterloo without Frederick William, where they fought bravely and certainly defended the honour of the Black Duke.[764] The monumental equestrian statue by Ernst Julius Hähnel in the main square of Brunswick serves as a permanent reminder of Frederick William and his martial valour.

Let us now shift from the tale of the Black Legion back to the position of Austria in the period of the Treaty of Schönbrunn. In the aftermath of the unsuccessful war in 1809, Austria, similar to almost all of Continental Europe, found itself in France's (i.e. Napoleon Bonaparte's) vice-like grip. However, one of the most adept and soon to be one of the most influential politicians of his age, Klemens Lothar Metternich, who had hitherto been the Austrian ambassador in Paris, appeared at the centre of the Austrian political scene. He was nominated by Emperor Francis I to the post of Foreign Minister, replacing Johann Graf Stadion. Over the course of the peace 'negotiations' with the victorious French in 1809, Metternich wrote to the Emperor Francis I the following eloquent missive:

> Be the conditions of peace what they will (i.e. the Treaty of Schönbrunn), the result will always lead to our having to find our safety solely by clinging to the triumphant French system. Once the final convention is signed, we will have no choice but to limit ourselves to flattery, cajolery, appeal, and adulation. Only in this way shall we ensure our existence until the time of liberation and reprisal.[765]

---

* The Battle of Quatre Bras and the circumstances surrounding the death of the Black Duke have already been described in detail in the previous chapter.

After his next victory, the forty-year-old Napoleon planned to divorce and remarry, as he still had no child with his current wife Joséphine de Beauharnais. In an effort to ensure that the French Empire had a successor, and at the same time legitimize the Bonaparte dynasty in the eyes of European powers, he planned to marry a bride that had the blood of a venerable royal family. Two female candidates were chosen and busily courted by the French Emperor: Russian Grand Duchess Anna Pavlovna, the sister of Alexander I of the House of Romanov and Archduchess Marie Louise, daughter of Austrian Emperor Francis I of the Habsburg-Lorraine Dynasty. Napoleon ultimately chose the Austrian Archduchess Marie Louise, who somewhat paradoxically happened to be the grand-niece of Marie Antoinette, executed by French Revolutionaries. It is true that Metternich significantly influenced Napoleon's decision with his policy of "appeal and adulation" while the Russian Court took a rather negative stance on a marriage with Anna Pavlovna.

Because Napoleon was certainly not known for his patience, he married the Austrian archduchess (albeit by proxy) without delay at the Augustinian Church in Vienna on 11th March 1810. The French Emperor was represented by Archduke Charles, who hitherto was the only one to have defeated Napoleon on a field of battle. The act was thus a gesture on the part of Napoleon of his acknowledgment of the Archduke. Several days later, Napoleon's newlywed wife Marie Louise travelled to France where the whole wedding ceremony – this time with Napoleon in the role of groom – was repeated, firstly with a civil ceremony, then with a religious ceremony, the latter of which took place in the Salon Carr chapel in the Louvre. Maria Carolina of Austria, grandmother to the French Emperor's new wife and at the same time his staunch adversary, who was now fated to become his grandmother-in-law as well, noted the following about the marriage: 'The final thing that all of my misery lacked was to become grandmother to the devil.'[766] Naturally, just as in the case of Marie Carolina, the marriage was not met with much joy on the territory of the Austrian Empire. It was however generally seen to be politically expedient and as a necessary concession. Charles Joseph de Ligne, Field Marshal of the Austrian Army described Austria's desperate situation succinctly but rather coarsely in the following note: 'It will be better for one archduchess to be fucked than the whole of the Monarchy.'[767] Czech patriot Václav Hanka stated the following in a song to glorify the Austrian Emperor and Bohemian ruler Francis I in connection with the wedding:

> Rejoice, nation, rejoice still… praise and esteem your King [Francis I]. He has renounced his own child [Maria Louise], he has renounced his own blood so that your gallant, mighty lion* might not fall into the guileful net.[768].

However, one man on the Austrian side was secretly rejoicing – the newly appointed Foreign Minister Metternich, who saw the whole marriage as time that Austria could use to internally consolidate the country without a member of the Bonaparte family being placed on the throne, as was the case for instance in Spain (Joseph Bonaparte), the Kingdom of Westphalia (Jérôme Bonaparte), or the Netherlands (Louis Bonaparte). As one of Metternich's close colleagues noted: 'Von Metternich is flush with joy.'[769] At the time, Austria truly needed a period of rest and recuperation, as it was forced on 15th March 1811 to declare bankruptcy due to the debts incurred from its costly wars and subsequent reparations. Only five days later, Marie Louise bore Napoleon (who took the lion's share of responsibility for leading Austria to destitution) his much-longed-for heir, François Bonaparte, later nicknamed 'L'Aiglon' ('the Eaglet') in Paris.[770]

At the time, Karl Philipp, Prince of Schwarzenberg, who had replaced the recently promoted Klemens von Metternich as the newly appointed Austrian ambassador to France, was helping to further improve relations following the wedding between Marie Louise and Napoleon in Paris in the name of Francis I and the Foreign Minister Metternich. In addition to being a diplomat, the Prince of Schwarzenberg was primarily a soldier. This significantly influenced the Austrian Emperor's decision to nominate him to this key diplomatic function, as the Austrian court assumed that Napoleon would be more willing to listen to a soldier who had gone through the hell of battle than a "parlour politician". In addition to this fact, the Prince of Schwarzenberg's carrier had also brought him experience in the Russian court. At that moment, Napoleon could not have guessed that the Prince of Schwarzenberg would soon lead the allied troops against him as the Commander-in-Chief of the Armies of the Sixth Anti-French Coalition and play a decisive role in – to use Metternich's

---

*   The lion is a symbol of the Czech lands in the Czech Coat of Arms.

words – the Austrian 'time of liberation and retribution'. Let us now take a more detailed look at the career hitherto of this remarkable soldier and diplomat, who was a member of Bohemia nobility thanks to his residence at the Orlík Estate (called *inkolat* in the Czech lands).[771]

Karl Philipp I was born in 1771 in the Schwarzenberg Palace in Vienna as the second-born son of Johann Nepomuk Anton of Schwarzenberg and Marie Eleonore, Countess of Öttingen-Wallerstein. His father strove to ensure that Karl began a successful military career from very early on. When the Habsburg Empire entered into war with its age-old enemy Turkey in 1789, it was thus no surprise that the seventeen-year-old Karl Philipp (whom Johann Nepomuk had helped gain the rank of cavalry lieutenant in the Habsburg Army) left for the Balkans to gain his first military experience there in battle against the Turks. Soon after reaching the front, he distinguished himself in battles near Šabac (a town in modern-day Serbia), earning a promotion to the rank of captain. During the course of the Turkish campaign, the Commander-in-Chief of the Austrian troops and evidently one of the greatest leaders in the history of the Habsburg Imperial Army General Ernst Gideon von Laudon wrote a commendatory report on the young Schwarzenberg addressed to the Emperor Joseph II, praising him for his: 'courage, observation skills, and relentless activity.'[772] Together with Laudon's army, Karl Philipp then took part in the Siege of Belgrade in 1789, during which he became seriously ill (most likely with dysentery) and was plagued by a perpetual high fever, causing him to return to his homeland to recuperate. Belgrade later fell and came under Habsburg control, after which Schwarzenberg was promoted to the rank of major following his recovery.[773]

When war broke out with revolutionary France, Karl Philipp, who now served in Latour's cavalry regiment, left with the Imperial soldiers of Prince Josias of Saxe-Coburg-Saalfeld for the Austrian Netherlands. There he took active part in the successful Austrian Battle of Jemappes (1792) and Neerwinden (1793). At the beginning of 1794, his military services to the Emperor led to a promotion to rank of colonel, after which he became commander of the Moravian Zezschwitz Regiment of cuirassiers (heavy cavalry). He and his regiment, along with other Austrian cavalry units, were assigned to the allied British Army of Prince Frederick, Duke of York. In these ranks, on 26th April 1794, he took part in the famous cavalry attack led by the allied Anglo-Austrian cavalry under the command of Lieutenant-General Rudolf von Otto against the left wing of the French Army led by General Chapuis in the Battle of Beaumont*. Chapuis himself was taken captive at the very beginning of the crushing attack. In a matter of minutes during the subsequent massacre, up to 2,000 French soldiers fell, causing the whole demoralized French Army to retreat.[774] For his participation in this attack, which was one of only a few victories of the First Anti-French Coalition in the Austrian Netherlands, Karl Philipp was awarded the Military Order of Maria Theresa by Emperor Francis II. Subsequently, when the First-Coalition allies lost the Austrian Netherlands primarily due to defeat at Fleurus in June 1794, Schwarzenberg fought with his regiment under Archduke Charles of Teschen in the Rhineland, where he helped to defeat Marshal Jourdan at Amberg, gaining him another promotion to the rank of major-general. He then marched with Archduke Charles to Italy, where he witnessed Napoleon's military prowess first hand in battle on the River Tagliamento, in which Bonaparte convincingly defeated the Austrian army in which Schwarzenberg served. After the Austrians subsequently signed a peace treaty with the French, Karl Philipp used the time during which his services were not immediately needed as a soldier to marry. As a wife, he took Maria Anna, Countess of Hohenfeld and Princess of Esterhazy. The wedding ceremony took place in Vienna at the end of January 1799.[775]

However, he did not enjoy a long period of marital bliss, as a year later during the War of the Second Coalition he commanded the right wing of the Austrian Army of Archduke John Baptist Joseph in the Battle of Hohenlinden as a Lieutenant-Field-Marshal (an Austrian rank to which he had once again been promoted). Despite suffering defeat there, he managed skilfully to cover the retreating Austrian troops from the triumphant French and by doing so prevented the Austrian Army from becoming surrounded, a situation that would have proved catastrophic and led to the destruction of the entire army. When Austria signed the peace treaty with France at Lunéville, which for Karl Philipp Schwarzenberg spelled the end of the War of the Second Coalition and another period of peace, he decided to begin a career as a diplomat. His first task in the role of Austrian ambassador was to visit St. Petersburg. He set off for the city

---

* Sometimes called the Battle of Coteau, or in France the Battle of Troisvilles.

in 1801 in order to congratulate the newly ascended Tsar Alexander I in the name of the Habsburg Monarchy and ascertain his position on the current international situation.[776] In the same year, he returned to Bohemia, where he planned to take over a family inheritance based on the final will of his great grandfather Ferdinand Wilhelm Eusebius, who in his will in 1703 declared that in the future the House of Schwarzenberg was to be divided into two independent branches. This was to be in place for an event in which two brothers would be born in one generation and both would be fully able to take on the family titles and assets. This situation became a reality in the form of Karl Philipp and his older brother Joseph II, who became the ruling Prince of Schwarzenberg in 1789 when Johann Nepomuk, father of both brothers, died. At first, due to the fact that Karl Philipp was not of age and subsequently his absence in the wars with France, proceedings on the division of the House were postponed. Now, however, this division could officially take place. This happened on 13th December 1801 as Joseph II and Karl Philipp signed an agreement. The House was thus divided into a so-called "primogeniture" (i.e. the older branch under the rule of Joseph II) and a secundogeniture (the younger branch ruled by Karl Philipp). Joseph II continued to rule the majority of the existing Schwarzenberg dominion (the Duchy of Český Krumlov, the Třeboň Estate, Vimperk, Chýnov, properties in Prague ...), while the younger Karl Philipp obtained the Orlík Estate, upon which the secundogeniture was named the "Orlík Secundogeniture". Because the most prominent building of the Orlík Estate, the Orlík Castle, burned down shortly before the arrival of the secundogeniture's founder, Karl Philipp immediately commenced reconstruction of the castle, which gave it the appearance it still bears today, with some later remodelling and modifications undertaken between 1849–1860.*

However, Karl Philipp was not able to enjoy this state of peace for long, as he received orders after the War of the Third Coalition broke out in 1805 to join the Austrian Army of Karl Freiherr (Baron) Mack von Leiberich. Marshal Mack did not heed the appeal made to him by Prince Schwarzenberg and scores of other officers, who recommended

---

* Martin Gaži (ed.), *Schwarzenbergové v české a středoevropské kulturní historii* (České Budějovice 2013), pp. 26–35. Both branches of the family reunited in 1965 with Karel VII Schwarzenberg (born 1937), originally only the heir to the secundogeniture, as he was adopted in 1962 by member of the primogeniture Henry Schwarzenberg (1903–1965), upon which he named Karel VII Schwarzenberg his successor.

that he immediately retreat, as the Austrian Army was in danger of being surrounded at Ulm. By ignoring their request, his army soon found itself in the infamous "cauldron", surrounded on all sides by Napoleon's troops. Present at the Battle of Ulm as the official commander (although in fact Marshal Mack was commanding) was the relative of the Austrian Emperor Francis I, forty-two-year-old Archduke Ferdinand (son of the Emperor's cousin). His capture would have caused yet another disgrace to the Habsburg court. Young Ferdinand thus agreed with Karl Philipp's courageous plan to attempt to break through French lines with eighteen hundred cavalrymen. In the middle of the night on 14th October 1805 (three days before the whole of Mack's army was captured), the group, led by Karl Philipp and Johann Kollowrat-Krakowsky, headed for French lines. Despite constant pursuit and several skirmishes with the cavalry of French Marshal Murat, they were finally able to reach safety on 22nd October in Cheb, Bohemia.[777] Whilst some Austrian honour was salvaged by this audacious escape through French lines, the Battle of Ulm was a devastating defeat that enabled Napoleon to go on to conquer Vienna within a month. Subsequently, Schwarzenberg hurriedly left for the Russo-Austrian Army's camp near Austerlitz, where he recommended Emperor Francis (similarly to Mack at Ulm) to withdraw for the time being and wait for the arrival of further reinforcements. Specifically, these were to be troops of Archduke Charles, Duke of Teschen from Italy and the remainder of the Russian troops. Nonetheless, as we know today, the Russo-Austrian forces led the fateful Battle of Austerlitz (2nd December 1805), otherwise known as the Battle of the Three Emperors, in which the allies were crushed. Schwarzenberg – evidently due to his opposing opinion of the suitability of the clash – was not given any command and acted only in the role of aide to one of the Austrian generals. After the next peace treaty (Peace of Pressburg), for which Austria paid dearly, Schwarzenberg continued to devote himself to his diplomatic career. At the time the War of the Fifth Coalition with the French broke out in 1809, Karl Philipp was ambassador at the Russian Court. This meant he was absent during the Austrian victory over Napoleon at Aspern-Essling. Nonetheless, he took part in the next, somewhat less glorious battle for the Austrians at Wagram, where (just as several times before) he skilfully covered the retreating Austrian troops. Later, Karl Philipp was named ambassador to Paris in 1809, and Napoleon took an earnest liking to him for his methods and direct nature. Napoleon regularly invited him to hunt and provided him with audiences that he lectured to on military matters, world trade, and even his own plans for the future. The moment Napoleon began to prepare his fateful Russian campaign, he insisted that Schwarzenberg be nominated for the rank of field marshal. He went on to request that Karl Philipp be put at the head of an auxiliary corps of 30,000 men, which Austria was forced to provide to Napoleon for his Russian campaign.[778] This "honour", which Schwarzenberg was given for his commanding abilities by such a military genius as Napoleon, was on one hand a high distinction, but on the other placed Schwarzenberg (similarly to the forced negotiations with Napoleon in the role of Austrian ambassador) in an invidious position. Prussia, however, was also forced to provide Napoleon a contingent of a similar number of men. Other allies of the French Emperor (Confederation of the Rhine, the Duchy of Warsaw etc.) were also forced to contribute what they could in the form of auxiliary military corps. By doing so, Napoleon mobilized an army of roughly 600,000 men in the beginning of June 1812. This massive army, the size of which was unprecedented in history, went on to attack the Russians.

Schwarzenberg and his regiment, who took their position on the left wing of Napoleon's forces, first defeated the Russian Army at the Battle of Gorodechno in the vicinity of the villages of Gorodechno and Poddubno (in modern-day Belarus) on 12th August 1812. However, based on encoded correspondence with Metternich and Emperor Francis I, he subsequently avoided any other clashes. During October, he definitively ceased his advance at Volin (in what is now Ukraine) and allowed the Russian soldiers operating near there to pass to the north without ever leaving his encampment. In the meantime, Napoleon and the Grande Armée entered Moscow on 14th September 1812, a week after the Battle of Borodino, a battle that some historians and scholars have seen as a Pyrrhic victory. Even the occupation of Moscow was short lived, as two-thirds of the city was destroyed by a fire deliberately started by the Russians, leaving the French without much of the supplies that they so desperately needed. Therefore, Napoleon was forced on 19th October 1812 to give orders for the now infamous retreat, which took place under horrific conditions during the Russian winter. Barely 50,000 of Bonaparte's soldiers returned home.[779]

During the Russian campaign, Prince Schwarzenberg wrote an interesting letter to his eldest son Bedřich,[780] who like his father had also chosen a military career, this letter perhaps best describes the marshal's attitudes on life:

> Continue for now, my son, in using your precious young years to educate yourself and exercise yourself in the virtues that cultivate a man, for as a soldier you will need them, primarily if you do not want to blame yourself for seeming that your origin conceals a lack of merits. Belonging to a higher social class, endowed upon a man by chance on the day of his birth, is a heavy debt, the payment of which must be considered from the very moment that person reaches a full realization of himself. Dear Bedřich, learn to listen and speak the truth always and honestly. Be silent, however, if your speech would not only be useless but could also do harm... Obedience is the cement of the state, without which the building would crumble at the slightest tremor. Learn patience, be upstanding, and loyal to death, be of a cheerful and clear mind, humble in luck, protect your brothers well, rejoice in their happiness, honour the law and obey them exactly, be steadfast in carrying out your duties. Only then will you sleep soundly at night. Be charitable, fear vices constantly and never death.[781]

Prussia was the first to challenge Napoleon after his catastrophic failure, when General Ludwig Yorck von Wartenburg, commander of Prussian forces signed the Convention of Tauroggen, an armistice with Russia on the state's own accord on 30th December 1812; this in turn paved the way for the Treaty of Kalisz (1813) that saw Prussia and Russia ally themselves against Napoleon. The Russians attempted to persuade Schwarzenberg to do the same, but in January 1813 – with the words that 'an Austrian soldier is not accustomed to acting gratuitously; he carries out the orders of his Emperor' – he only negotiated an armistice for an undefined period in the name of Francis I. After this, he set off for Paris in the role of ambassador to emphasize to Napoleon that Austria was willing to play the mediator for a general peace between hostile powers. Because Napoleon wanted nothing to do with peace, Karl Philipp returned to his country, where he was appointed Commander-in-chief of 120,000 men of a so-called "army of observation", which began to form on Bohemian territory. In the meantime, Metternich was leading intense negotiations with the Prussian and Russian courts while the Austrians were considering entry into the War of the Sixth Coalition. In addition to Russia and Prussia, the Coalition was joined by Britain, Portugal, Spain (these states had already long been at war with Napoleon as Wellington had led joint forces against the French on the Iberian Peninsula), and Sweden. Napoleon hastily formed a large but poorly trained army made up primarily of conscripted and inexperienced recruits. Despite this fact, he managed in rather quick succession to defeat the Russo-Prussian forces at Lŭtzen and Buatzen, forcing the allies to sign a temporary peace treaty with the French Emperor in June 1813, during which they began to hold peace negotiations with Napoleon. Because still-neutral Austria held the role of mediator during talks on the details of the peace treaty as Schwarzenberg had proposed to Napoleon in the past, crucial negotiations took place on the territory of the Habsburg Monarchy during the so-called Congress of Prague, which met on 12ᵗʰ July 1813 in what is now the capital of the Czech Republic.

In Napoleon's name, however, the French representatives repeatedly refused all allied propositions, which simply speaking requested a return to the state of affairs of 1805 (i.e. before Prussia was humiliated and the Holy Roman Empire was dissolved), declaring them unacceptable.[782] In addition, at the beginning of July the first messages of Wellington's crushing victory over French forces in Spain began to arrive, a fact that was also known to Karl Philipp Schwarzenberg, who described the whole event to his wife on 7ᵗʰ July 1813 in the following manner:

> My dear... Wellington crushed three French Corps led by Reille, Clauzel, and the Spanish King [Joseph Bonaparte] at Vitoria on 21ˢᵗ June [1813]. All the belongings of the Spanish King, meaning all cannons and chattels, have fallen into the hands of the victor. The defeated have been pushed off the road to Bayonne and were forced to retreat from Pamplona. And how will Suchet [commander of the last combat-capable French army in Spain] extricate himself from the situation? It could have been assumed that due to its numbers the greatly reduced "Spanish" army [meaning French units in Spain] would suffer a defeat, but no one expected that it would happen in this way. Wellington has deserved a fine wreath of laurels.[783]

In his memoirs, which he kept with surprising diligence from the end of the 1780s until his death in 1816, the aforementioned "patriot" and mayor of Milčice František Vavák also made an extensive entry on the Battle of Vitoria despite not mentioning Wellington or the Peninsular War even once in his work hitherto. Nonetheless, from the Battle of Vitoria onwards, Vavák began to write relatively often about Wellington's campaign on the western front, as we will see below. This is proof once again of the far-reaching strategic significance of Wellington's victory.

Thanks to the news of Wellington's decisive victory and the French refusal of the allies' proposals, the Austrian Emperor entered the war against his son-in-law Napoleon. On 10th August 1813, Austria expanded the ranks of the Sixth Anti-French Coalition, leading to the dissolution of the Congress of Prague and termination of the temporary cease-fire. During the next few days, a so-called "Bohemian" allied army was formed in the Czech lands and comprised 120,000 Austrians (originally Schwarzenberg's "army of observation"), 80,000 Russians, and 45,000 Prussian soldiers. They were supported by three additional armies: The "Silesian" army located near Wrocław and Świdnica, the "Northern" army located near Berlin, and the reserve "Polish" army, deployed near Warsaw. The "Silesian" army led by Prussian Marshal Blücher (Wellington's future co-belligerent at Waterloo) was made up of Prusso-Russian units and reached a total of 105,000 men. The "Northern" army was made up of 125,000 Swedish soldiers under the command of former French Marshal Bernadotte, who now as the Swedish aspirant to the throne had joined the allies. His loyalty, however, was naturally deemed suspect. A reserve army of 60,000 troops was primarily made up of Russian units of General Bennigsen. It should be noted that the names of the allied armies were not according to their "national" makeup, but rather according to the area where they were formed and where they operated, although the "Bohemian" army was genuinely made up of a significant number of re-cruits from the Czech lands. Against the allies stood Napoleon, with an army of 180,000 men at Dresden, Marshal Ney with an army of 130,000 on the Bobrava River, and General Oudinot with another 80,000 Frenchmen southwest of Berlin.[784]

After much arguing between the allies' royal courts and the relent-less efforts of the Russian Tsar to gain the position, Karl Philipp, Prince of Schwarzenberg was nominated Commander-in-Chief of the allied forces. He simultaneously took command of the "Bohemian" army, thus giving him the force of more than a quarter of a million soldiers with roughly eight hundred cannons. As Chief of the general staff, he chose Lieutenant-General Joseph Radetzky von Radetz, a Czech nobleman, experienced soldier, and most importantly a highly skilled military strategist. Despite these qualities, von Radetz surprisingly only came to fame later as a field marshal at the age of 82 during his successful suppression of the revolution in Italy in 1848, in which he was given high command.[785] Nonetheless, Schwarzenberg's chief of staff proved to be a key figure in the upcoming campaign, as he was the author of all the operational plans of the allied armies. Joseph Radetzky (born Josef Václav) was born in 1766 at Chateau Třebnice near Sedlčany, Bohemia and was orphaned soon after. His grandfather and subsequently his uncle cared for his upbringing and decided that he would have a career in the military. Radetz was accepted into the Habsburg Army after several attempts, as he was initially refused for being "physical weak". Still not yet eighteen years of age, he managed to gain the position of so-called *"cadet ex propriis"* (i.e. at his own expense) with Caramelli's cuirassier cavalry regiment. Similar to the Prince of Schwarzenberg, he took part in clashes with the Turks from 1788 to 1791 and the Wars of the First Coalition in the Austrian Netherlands. In 1796, he fought with the French in Italy, distinguishing himself as an adjutant by saving the Commander-in-Chief of the Imperial Army General Beaulieu from capture. During the following retreat of Austrian forces from the Italian battlefield, he was assigned to the military corps of Karl Philipp, Prince of Schwarzenberg, where he held the rank of colonel. There is proof that these two soldiers first established cooperation while covering the Austrian retreat. In the War of the Third Coalition, Radetz served as major-general again on the Italian battlefield under Archduke Charles, Duke of Teschen, where only more minor battles took place. Radetz did not take part in the Battle of Austerlitz. Proof of Radetz's exceptional abilities can be seen in his nomination by the Emperor to the court military counsel and the Quartermaster-General of military staff after the Austrian defeat in 1809. After this, Radetz continued with much needed military reforms in the spirit of the general modernization of the Austrian Army that had been launched by Archduke Charles in 1805 and were now expected to pay off in the new war with Napoleon.[786]

In 1813 Schwarzenberg and Radetz, two exceptionally capable men (who also belonged to Bohemian nobility under the Austrian Empire), now stood against the French Emperor in positions of the two highest military functions of the allied armies. In his camp, the Prince of Schwarzenberg also had all three monarchs whose forces made up the massive "Bohemian" army: Austrian Emperor Francis I, Russian Tsar Alexander I, and Prussian King Frederick William III. Contrary to Radetz, the monarchs made life difficult for Karl Philipp, as it often took great effort to convince the crowned heads to heed the plan of operations created by the Chief of the general staff. Radetz placed emphasis on cooperation between the allied armies (i.e. Bohemian, Silesian, Northern, and Polish) and hoped to manoeuvre Napoleon into a decisive battle where all the allied armies would strike in unison:

> No army shall in any way allow itself to be pitted against a greater power, thus marring the aim of joint operations. A primary attack should be lead with certainty, expelling Napoleon from his base on the Elbe and surrounding him as closely as possible. Every single defeat should be prevented, finally and utterly destroying him in a decisive battle...[787]

,wrote Radetz in his plan of operations. After a series of smaller clashes in Northern Bohemia, Napoleon himself came to Bohemian territory, spending several hours in the Pachtů Hunting Lodge in Jablonné v Podještědí. Schwarzenberg's "Bohemian" army continued on to Dresden during August 1813, where it was defeated by Napoleon (it should be mentioned that disagreements in the allied camp made this somewhat easier for the French Emperor), but was still far from being wholly destroyed thanks to a timely retreat. Subsequently, almost all of the French army corps was completely destroyed as they pursued the retreating allies under the command of General Vandamme into Bohemia. There, Schwarzenberg and Radetz managed to surround him and crushed the French in the two-day Battle of Chlumec (29th–30th August 1813) and Přestanov, (known as Battle of Kulm in English) during which even Vandamme himself was taken captive. After several more battles took place, Napoleon retreated with his army to Leipzig. Less than 200,000 of Bonaparte's men now stood against more than 300,000 allies, to which more and more reinforcements continued to arrive.[788] Everything seemed to point to the decisive battle that Schwarzenberg and Radetzky had hoped for. The General Military Plan issued by the Commander-in-Chief and planned by Radetzky stated the following about the allied force on 13th October 1813:

> Reports coming from the enemy coincide in the fact that he is concentrating all his corps en masse between Leipzig, Grimma, Wurzen, and Altenburg... Our goal must be to contain the enemy in this position and advance upon him with the allied forces. The advantages of our current position allow us to think of how to destroy the enemy army.[789]

Karl Philipp also had a leaflet handed out among the troops with the following emotive declaration, which invoked jubilation in the army:

> The most important time in this holy battle has come, the decisive hour has struck, prepare for battle! ... The bond linking mighty nations to a great goal on the battlefield will more firmly and closely link together Russians, Prussians, and Austrians! Fight for one cause, fight for the freedom of Europe, for the freedom of your affairs, and for the immortality of your name! One for all and all for one! With this noble and manly call, begin your holy war! Remain faithful to it in this decisive hour and victory shall not pass you by![790]

Around 8 o'clock on the morning on 16th October 1813, Schwarzenberg launched his attack on Napoleon's position at the village of Wachau south of Leipzig, sparking the Battle of Leipzig (16th–19th October 1813), the largest engagement of the whole 19th century, which is often rightfully dubbed the "Battle of the Nations". Napoleon's units successfully repelled the first allied attack and in turn took the offensive. For a short time, it seemed that the French had the upper hand and would break through the allied lines at Wachau. However, around four o'clock in the afternoon, reinforcements called in by Schwarzenberg arrived and thanks to them the allies were able to hold their positions. The first day of battle was inconclusive. On the second day, dark clouds materialized over Leipzig, quickly leading to torrential rain. The exhausted armies, who were continuously joined by new contingents (of which there were much greater numbers joining the allies), were attempting to gain the energy for a final attack. Apart from several small skirmishes, there was hardly any fighting. The decision came on the following day – 18th October. The allied armies attacked Napoleon simultaneously from three cardinal directions: The "Bohemian" and "Polish" army from the south, the "Northern" army from the east, and Blücher's "Silesian" army from the north. In the situation he found himself in, Napoleon was not able to handle this concentrated pressure. To make matters even worse for Bonaparte, nearly all his Saxon troops defected from the French camp to the side of the Allies. Despite his brave and superbly skilful defence, Napoleon gave up his attempts to reverse the battle in his favour and break through the circle of allied units that closed in around Leipzig. Around four o'clock in the afternoon, he ordered a general retreat to the west, which was the only escape route that was left possible at the given moment. The French proceeded to retreat while taking part in brutal urban clashes that now played out in the streets of Leipzig throughout the night of 18th to 19th October. During their retreat, the bridge over the River Elster, which wound west of the city, became their only possible escape route from the otherwise wholly encircled city. Napoleon's troops held the bridge, but French military engineers prematurely detonated explosions, partially destroying the bridge, around one o'clock in the afternoon. This led to state of sheer panic in the retreating French ranks. Several thousand Frenchmen, who were still fighting frantically in Leipzig, were thus inevitably cut off and captured, and several thousand more drowned in the Elster as they attempted to save their lives by swimming across a river swollen by heavy autumn rains. In addition to the other victims it claimed, the famous Polish Marshal Józef Poniatowski, who led troops of the Duchy of Warsaw alongside Napoleon and was defending the French retreat, also drowned in the Elster's current.[791] The battle was finally complete and on 19th October 1813, Napoleon left Leipzig defeated. If we remember the fact that exactly one year prior marked the date of his orders to retreat from Moscow due to a lack of supplies, 19th October was surely not one of Napoleon's favourite dates.

Losses on both sides took on massive proportions. Roughly 38,000 Frenchmen were killed on the battlefield and another 36,000 were captured. Allied losses were around 50,000 men, setting the total number of human lives ultimately lost at the Battle of the Nations at almost 90,000.[792] Nonetheless, the allies under Schwarzenberg's command immediately began to pursue Napoleon. On the way, they were confronted with grisly scenes as they happened upon more and more injured, dying and dead French soldiers. In the meantime, Wellington had managed to cross the River Bidasoa on the "Western Front" and by doing so entered onto French territory. Napoleon, who had retreated from his pursuers behind the Rhine on the "Eastern Front", now found himself in a truly precarious situation. In November 1813, Prince Schwarzenberg wrote the following words to his wife Anna on Wellington's advance and the course of the pursuit:

> The road looked awful. At every 50 paces lay a dead horse, and at every hundred lay one or more corpses; all the homes are full of the dead and dying. I have never seen anything more horrifying. People are dying of hunger and exhaustion as the heavens fearfully punish the vain wrong-doers. On 7th and 8th October Wellington pushed the enemy to the River Bidasoa and now stands on French soil.[793]

The mayor of Milčice František Vavák wrote the following on Wellington's entrance into French territory in his village chronicle:

> Lord Wellington... has set foot on French soil ... Once the Spanish rid themselves of the French, all of Bonaparte's falsehoods, trickery and tyranny came to light. Anyone who served him or his brother Joseph or deserted his country was pronounced disreputable; they established new laws and confirmed the Catholic religion as the only one for the country and the future king.[794]

He also wrote: 'It is said that the English have been welcomed there [in France], as the French have no will to fight them and are, on the contrary, making known their dissatisfaction with their government.'[795]

Under Schwarzenberg's command, the allies crossed the Rhine with an army of 350,000 men in December 1813. With barely 100,000 combat-capable men, Napoleon could do nothing to stop them. Meanwhile, those who had hitherto supported him were now abandoning him one by one. The Netherlands and all the German states quickly shifted to the side of the Sixth Anti-French Coalition, causing both the Confederation of the Rhine and the Kingdom of Westphalia to collapse as a result. Switzerland proclaimed neutrality while the remaining Austrian forces

under the command of Marshal Johann von Hiller, who was supported by the British expeditionary force and units of the King of Naples
Joachim Murat (another of Napoleon's former marshals and his brother-
in-law, who had now defected to the allies as Marshal Bernadotte had
done), pushed from Italy the French troops of Italian Viceroy Eugène
de Beauharnais – the son of Napoleon's former wife from her first marriage, Empress Joséphine – who was the only one to keep, his loyalty to
Bonaparte.[796]

The Prince of Schwarzenberg, who now carried the burden of leading
the invasion of France on the Eastern Front, pointed out in a letter to
his wife, written shortly after crossing the Rhine (4th January 1814), the
importance of a coordinated advancement of all fronts and cooperation
with Wellington's advance in the west:

> My task is something great and if I am supported, peace may and must be
> won; if I will, however, not be accompanied in my steps by the Northern
> Army [Bernadotte], Wellington and the Italian Army [Hiller and Murat],
> I may stumble heavily, but I shall now how to endure it, for my conscience
> acquits me of all indictment; thusly and not otherwise must I act if I am to
> deserve the trust and blessing of Providence.[797]

At the beginning of February 1814, the allies offered to negotiate with
Napoleon in Châtillon, but he typically refused all conditions of peace,
under which the representatives of the Sixth Coalition additionally required a return of French borders to their state in 1792 in exchange for
leaving Bonaparte on the French throne. Instead, Napoleon defeated
Blücher's "Silesian" army at Champaubert. It was characteristic of the
whole allied advance on French soil for Blücher to hasten forward into danger with his "Silesian" army (one of his nicknames was rightfully
'Marshal Forwards!'), while Schwarzenberg marched more slowly, ensuring escape and supply routes, a fact that he was often criticized for
by the Russian Tsar and Prussian King. For this reason, Schwarzenberg
often felt disheartened by the monarchs' interventions in his work as
Commander-in-Chief.[798] He also therefore envied the freedom afforded
to Wellington by the British Government and King: 'Oh how enviable
of Wellington, who hardly says what he has done and never says, even
to his Government, what he plans to do,'[799] wrote Karl Philipp to his

wife during the campaign. In these words, he may have been referring to the construction of the Lines of Torres Vedras, which Wellington skilfully hid not only from the French, but also from the British ministers. Nonetheless, Wellington was clearly inclined towards a cautious allied advance on the Eastern Front, as he wrote to Lord Bathurst, the Secretary of State for War and the Colonies: 'The allies must not expect battles of Leipzig every day, and that which experience shows them is, that they ought, above all things, to avoid any great military disaster.'[800]

Although Napoleon once again proved his genius as a commander and dealt a blow both to Blücher and Schwarzenberg in a series of defeats – out of a dozen battles that took place, Bonaparte came out as the victor in nine of them; that said, he was not able to stop the cautiously advancing allied forces. In addition, Wellington had taken Bordeaux in the west and pushed the French, led by Marshal Soult all the way to Toulouse. Once Schwarzenberg defeated Napoleon on 21st March 1814 at Arcis-sur-Aube, Napoleon attempted to lure him away from Paris by marching on the Rhine, by which he threatened allied supply routes. Schwarzenberg, who was being sent vital intelligence by Napoleon's former minister Talleyrand, nonetheless decided to march directly on Paris. In this pursuit of Napoleon, which in many ways was reminiscent of a game of chess, the move definitively spelled checkmate. On 30th March, the Allies dispersed French Marshals Marmont and Mortier near Paris, negotiated the capitulation of the French capital, and marched victoriously the next day through the streets of the city. The French marshals soon convinced Napoleon to abdicate on 6th April 1814, after which the Allies signed a peace treaty with France on 31st May in Paris. The vacant French throne was occupied by Louis XVIII of the House of Bourbon (the brother of executed Louis XVI) and Napoleon was sent into exile on the Island of Elba in the Mediterranean.[801]

Unfortunately, the news of Napoleon's abdication had reached Wellington's forces in Southern France too late, and therefore on 10th April he attacked Marshal Soult at Toulouse, as noted by František Vavák in his memoires:

> The conquering of Paris, repudiating Bonaparte, and bringing a halt to the bloodshed and the news about the peace wasn't reported quickly enough from Paris, neither to the French nor the English, who stood against one

another. English Lord Wellington attacked Marshal Dalmát [Marshal Soult, who was named by Napoleon Duke of Dalmatia]... on 10th April at the city of Toulouse, defeated him and took the city of Toulouse, during which several thousand people fell and where many brave heroes died.[802]

As soon as the report of a truce reached Wellington, he set off immediately for Paris, where an impassioned debate was taking place on the specific terms of peace. It was fitting that Wellington joined the peace celebrations and ongoing negotiations. František Vavák left behind one interesting anecdote relating to Wellington's arrival to Paris and meeting with representatives of the Allies and French royalists around the newly established court of King Louis XVIII:

> When English Commander-in-Chief Wellington entered the Royal palace [in Paris], he was asked by the French lords what he would like to take home. And he answered: 'Russian grenadiers!', a now-famous reply.[803]

Although Vavák's story seems improbable when considering Wellington's character, it is interesting to note that a massive and extremely valuable Russian vase made solely from malachite is still on display in the Great Hall at Wellington's home in England at Stratfield Saye House. Wellington, however, received this vase in 1826 from Russian Tsar Nicholas I, which refutes any connection with Vavák's anecdote that Wellington may have taken something home with him from Paris.

The new alignment of European power was now to be decided at the Congress of Vienna. In time, Wellington arrived to represent British interests in the role of ambassador, leading him to meet in person with Metternich and Schwarzenberg. When news of Napoleon's escape from Elba reached Vienna on 7th March 1815, Wellington, Blücher and Schwarzenberg set off once again for battle. Wellington and Blücher took command of the armies in Belgium, while Schwarzenberg led the renewed allied forces in the Rhine. At that moment, evidently under the weight of his own conscience, Murat, King of Naples and former deserter, supported his ex-emperor. He was, however, defeated while still in Italy at the beginning of May by the Austrian forces of General Bianchi at Tolentino.[804] Wellington heartily congratulated Schwarzenberg as Commander-in-Chief of the Austrian forces on his victory and hoped that

Napoleon would be as easily disposed of as Murat. Blücher now planned to advance on Bonaparte with Schwarzenberg's support:

> My dear Prince, yesterday I received a letter from your lordship dated the 13th [of May] and I would like to congratulate you wholeheartedly on the successes of your military operations in Italy which are, as I hope, a good precursor of what we want and must achieve in our campaign in France. I am also glad that our opinions regarding our future military operations are so perfectly in agreement[805]

,Wellington wrote in a letter to Schwarzenberg. Nonetheless, the French Emperor managed to gather a surprisingly large army in the atmosphere of dissatisfaction that reigned after Bourbon rule was renewed in France. With this army, Napoleon defeated Blücher at Ligny and then quickly attacked Wellington at Waterloo on 18th June 1815. In the subsequent merciless day-long battle, Wellington definitively defeated Napoleon with the help of Blücher's units, who arrived in the evening after consolidating from their previous defeat. Napoleon was subsequently forced to leave to a harsher exile on Saint Helena, a small island in the South Atlantic Ocean. The countless words of congratulation, which were sent to the victor of Waterloo and former General on the Western Anti-Napoleon Front by prominent individuals from all of Europe, also included a letter from Field Marshal Schwarzenberg, the victor at Leipzig and former general, who had lead the Eastern Front against Napoleon since 1813:

> Accept, my dear Duke [i.e. Wellington], my most sincere congratulations on the wonderful victory that you have recently so gloriously achieved. Every soldier not present in the battle [of Waterloo] may rightfully regret that he was not present at such a memorable occasion. Believe me, however, my Lord, and I say this with my whole heart, that there is not a soul that deserves such glory as you... Please, my dear Duke, do accept this affirmation of my highest respect to you and my loyal friendship. Schwarzenberg[806]

Wellington, who thanks to the battle was still somewhat shaken after losing many of his good friends at Waterloo and countless times finding himself in danger of losing his own life, as he was constantly moving about the whole breadth of the battlefield aligning his troops, answered with the following words:

> My dear Prince, thank you for your letter from the 21st [of June], that I received this evening. Our battle on the 18th [of June] was one of the most important and, as you yourself know, was absolute. God has hitherto been well-disposed to me and I shall not want to ever fight again, for I am crushed by the loss of my long-time friends and acquaintances. My partner in war and ally [Marshall Blücher] is enjoying good health, although he is still somewhat plagued by the results of his fall from his horse, which they killed under him in the battle [of Ligny]. With highest regards, Wellington.[807]

After Waterloo, Wellington met with Schwarzenberg in Paris, where both men took part for a time in the renewal of the Bourbon Monarchy under the rule of Louis XVIII. They cared mostly for military matters, as Schwarzenberg wrote home to his wife at the beginning of August 1815:

> The ministers of Louis XVIII make up a ministerial council by which all matters will be handled. In order to prevent isolated negotiations with the French cabinet, which lead to misunderstandings among the allies themselves, four ministers of the great courts of Austria, Russia, England, and Prussia create a conference, in which I and Wellington sit on military matters.[808]

Prince Karl Philipp Schwarzenberg died in 1820 after his gradually deteriorating health was complicated by a sudden stroke. At that time, a very diverse political career was still in store for Wellington, during which he twice rose to the height of being British Prime Minister.

ACKNOWLEDGMENTS

First and foremost I would like to thank my parents, who have been a great inspiration to me, for the invaluable support they have given me in my life hitherto and during the writing of this book. I would also like to extend a wholehearted word of thanks to Mark Thomas Jones, who led me to the idea of publishing this book in English and subsequently aided me with his countless consultations and advice, tirelessly reading my text and ultimately devoting an immense amount of his free time to this book. Thank you so much for everything Mark! Another great word of thanks clearly goes to Skyland Vaclav Kobylak, who translated the whole work into English. Cooperation with Sky was excellent throughout the course of translation, as he continually showed great patience and understanding in places where I simply "had to" add an interesting new finding or quote to the already "finished" and translated text. In addition, he provided his extremely valuable feedback on the book's content throughout the course of translation. Furthermore, I would like to thank Professor Martin Kovář, under whose professional instruction at university I first began more seriously to study the figure of Arthur Wellesley, 1st Duke of Wellington. For his expressed support, a word of thanks should also be given to the excellent author Bernard Cornwell, in whose phenomenal novels from the period of the Napoleonic Wars on the soldier Richard Sharpe I first read about the Duke of Wellington at the age of thirteen. I would also like greatly to thank Professor Charles Esdaile from the University of Liverpool, who read the seventh chapter and addendum of the book in detail, provided me with his immensely valuable opinions, and most importantly was kind enough to correct several factual errors. I am also indebted to Czech historian Karel Sáček for pointing out the possibility that Czech soldiers may have fought under Wellington's command in the ranks of the Black Legion and providing advice in this area. I am also grateful to Czech journalist Věra Drápelová, who advised me on the best way to seek out information on the issues surrounding Wellington's birth. I would also like to extend my great thanks to Mr Karel Schwarzenberg, whose predecessor Charles I Philipp of Schwarzenberg I mention abundantly in connection with Wellington in the final supplementary chapter, for his support and encouragement of my writing and helping to launch the Czech-language edition. I am also indebted to David Dušek, who after reading a chapter of Wellington gave me the opportunity to edit a collection of texts devoted to his grandfather Zdeněk Urbánek, and to Jana Dušková – both of whom supported me from the very start and gave me the courage to continue writing, for which I am sincerely grateful. Great thanks also go to former Defence Attaché at the British Embassy in Prague, Gp Capt Michael Longstaff, who became a patron of the Czech edition and to his family for their attendance at the book launch in Prague. I would also like to acknowledge the staff members of the museums in Santarém and Sobral de Monte Agraço, Portugal, who provided me with valuable information and materials. Similar thanks go to the staff of the archive at Stratfield Saye House, Wellington Estate. A large word of thanks for their excellent cooperation goes to the following two individuals, without whose endeavours this book would never have been published: graphic designer Marek Jodas and Paula Charles from YPS. I also owe great thanks to John Armytage, who provided his excellent maps of Wellington's campaigns, and to Eliza Pakenham, who willingly lent the portrait of her ancestor and Wellington's good friend, Hon. General Edward 'Ned' Pakenham to be used in the book. In conclusion, I would like to thank wholeheartedly all of the following friends who supported me, listened untiringly to my deliberations, and continuously came to my aid with their advice, opinions, and feedback on the text throughout the course of writing this book: Thank you Štefánia Ebenová, Vojtěch Hrdlička, David Smrček, Petr Talacko, Max Weiss, and David Zavoral.

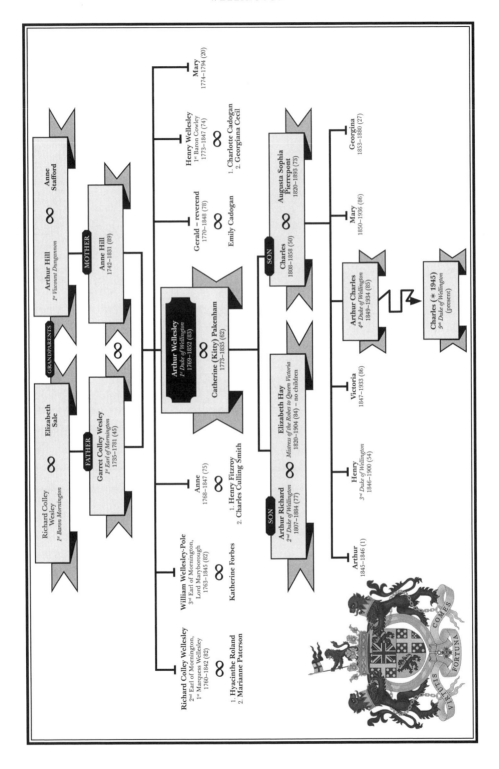

A CHRONOLOGY OF KEY EVENTS

in Wellington's life from his birth up
until the Battle of Waterloo (1769 – 1815)

1769	circa 1st March – 29th April	Birth of the Hon. Arthur Wesley (Dublin, Trim, Dangan Castle?). However, Wellington himself always celebrated his birthday on 1st of May.
1781		Death of Garret Wesley, 1st Earl of Mornington, father of Arthur Wellesley (A. W.). Enters Eton College. Britain loses Colonies in America.
1784		Leaves Eton with his studies unfinished.
1785		Studies with a private tutor, lawyer Mr. Goubert in Brussels.
1786	January	Enters Royal Academy of Equitation at Angers, France. Its director Marcel de Pignerolle is the first person who recognises some potential in A. W.
	December	Finishes Royal Academy of Equitation at Angers and returns to England.
1787		Receives his first promotions in the army: Ensign and later Lieutenant.
1788		Leaves England for Ireland. Appointed Aide-de-Camp to the Lord Lieutenant of Ireland.
1789	14th July	The French Revolution begins.
1790		Elected as MP for Trim in the Irish Parliament.
1791		Promoted to Captain.

1792		Starts openly courting Catherine 'Kitty' Packenham, daughter of Edward Pakenham, Lord Longford. Asks for Kitty's hand. Is refused.
1792	April	France declares war on Austria, Prussia enters the war against France as Austria's ally.
1793	21st January	Execution of French Monarch Louis XVI.
1793	February	Britain at war with France.
1793	30th September	Becomes Lieutenant-Colonel of 33rd Regiment of Foot.
1794		Asks a second time for Kitty's hand – refused by new Lord Longford, Thomas Pakenham. A. W. leaves for war with France as a commander of 33rd Regiment of Foot to Flanders/Austrian Netherlands. Serves under the command of the Duke of York.
1794	15th September	A. W.'s first battle at Boxtel. He successfully covers the British retreat with his 33rd.
1795		Returns to England.
1796	3rd May	Appointed Colonel.
1796	June	Leaves for Calcutta, India, as commander of the 33rd Regiment of Foot.
1798		A. W.'s brothers Richard and Henry arrive to India. Richard becomes Governor General and changes the family name from Wesley to Wellesley.

1799 3rd February — Britain declares war on the King of Mysore, Tipu Sultan. A. W. serves under General Harris. Manages supplies and commands the auxiliary force of the Nizam of Hyderabad.

1799 5th April — A. W.'s unsuccessful night attack on the Sultanpettah Tope.

4th May — Seringapatam (capital of Mysore) is conquered by the British. A. W. is appointed Governor of Seringapatam.

1800 — Pursues rebel Dhoondiah Waugh and his army.

1802 — Becomes Major-General.

1803 August — The beginning of the Second Anglo-Maratha War.

1803 23rd September — Battle of Assaye.

29th November — Battle of Argaon (Argaum).

15th December — Fall of Gawilghur fortress.

30th December — Marathas capitulate.

1804 28th August — Made a Knight of Order of the Bath.

1805 10th March — Sails from India to England. Stops at the island of Saint Helena en route.

10th September — Returns to England. Meeting with Admiral Nelson.

21st October — Nelson's Victory at Trafalgar over the Franco-Spanish fleet.

2nd December — Battle of Austerlitz – Napoleon defeats Austria and Russia – the end of the Third Anti-French Coalition.

1806 1st April — Elected as an MP for Rye in the British Parliament.

10th April — Marriage with Kitty Pakenham at Pakenham Hall (today Tullynally Castle), Ireland.

	12th July	Napoleon establishes the Confederation of the Rhine.
	21st November	Napoleon conquers Berlin and initiates the Continental blockade on Britain.
1807	3th February	Arthur Richard, A. W.'s son and heir is born.
1807	3th April	A. W. is appointed Chief Secretary for Ireland
	16th August – 5th September	Siege of Copenhagen.
	29th August	Battle of Køge.
	5th September	Copenhagen capitulates after three days of bombardment.
	30th November	General Junot captures Lisbon.
1808	16th January	Birth of A. W.'s second son Charles.
	25th April	Promoted to Lieutenant-General.
	2nd May	*Dos de Mayo Uprising* erupts in Madrid against the French occupation of Spain.
	1st August	A. W. disembarks in Mondego Bay nearby the village of Figueira da Foz, Portugal.
	17th August	Battle of Roliça.
	21st August	Battle of Vimeiro.
	30th August	Convention of Cintra is signed at the Palace of Queluz.
	November	Represents himself at Court of Inquiry at Royal Chelsea Hospital for involvement in signing the Convention of Cintra – found not guilty.
1809	February	General Beresford starts to train the Portuguese Army.
	7th March	A. W. writes *Memorandum on Defence of Portugal*, which gains him an appointment as the Commander-in-Chief of the British forces on the Iberian Peninsula.
	22nd April	A. W. lands in Lisbon with British Expeditionary Force.

	12th May	Crosses the Douro River – liberates Oporto.

12th May — Crosses the Douro River – liberates Oporto.

22nd-23rd May — Archduke Charles, Duke of Teschen becomes the first to defeat Napoleon on the field of battle at Aspern-Essling.

5th- 6th July — Battle of Wagram, Napoleon defeats Archduke Charles.

27th-28th July — Battle of Talavera.

4th September — Ennobled as Viscount Wellington of Talavera.

21st September — Duel at Putney Heat between Lord Castlereagh and Lord Canning.

14th October — Treaty of Schönbrunn, Austria leaves the Fifth Anti-French Coalition.

20th October — A. W. gives orders for building the Lines of Torres Vedras.

1810 5th April — Memoirs of William of Schaumburg-Lippe (*Mémoire de la Campagne de Portugal de 1762*) are delivered to A. W.

27th September — Battle of Busaco.

8th October — A. W. withdraws behind the Lines of Torres Vedras.

14th October — French Marshal Masséna moves to the Lines of Torres Vedras.

14th November — Masséna retreats from the Lines of Torres Vedras.

1811 5th February — The Regency Act adopted by the British Parliament.

April — Masséna reaches Salamanca, Spain. Loses almost 25,000 men during the retreat.

3rd-5th May — Battle of Fuentes de Oñoro.

11th May — Assassination of British Prime Minister Lord Percival by bankrupted businessman John Bellingham.

16th May — Battle of Albuera.

1812 7th-20th January — Siege of Ciudad Rodrigo.

28th February — Ennobled as the Earl of Wellington.

	16th March – 6th April	Siege of Badajoz.
	April	A. W.'s best intelligence (exploring) officer Major Grant is captured by the French.
	24th June	Napoleon marches to Russia with an army of approximately 600,000 men.
	Mid-July	George Scovell partly decodes the *Great Paris Cipher* – the secret code which the French used for their despatches.
	22nd July	Battle of Salamanca.
	12th August	Enters Madrid.
	19th September – 21st October	Siege of Burgos.
	3rd October	Ennobled as the Marquess of Wellington.
	October–November	Withdraws back to Portugal, sets up winter camp in Freineda.
	December	Scovell fully decodes the *Great Paris Cipher.* Subsequently, A. W. is able to read all intercepted French despatches.
1813	4th March	Becomes a Knight of the Garter.
	21st June	Battle of Vitoria, afterwards named Field-Marshal.
	25th July	Battle of Roncesvalles.
	28th July	Battle of Sorauren.
	8th September	Capture of the San Sebastian fortress.
	7th October	Crosses the River Bidasoa, entering into France with his army.
	16th–19th October	Battle of Leipzig – Prince Schwarzenberg as Commander-in-Chief of Allied forces on the eastern front defeats Napoleon.
	10th November	Battle of Nivelle (River).
	9th–13th December	Battle of Nive.
1814	27th February	Battle of Orthez.
	31st March	Allied Forces under Prince Schwarzenberg's command enter Paris.

	6th April	Napoleon abdicates.
	10th April	Battle of Toulouse.
	4th May	A. W. arrives in Paris to join the victorious Allied commanders and monarchs.
	11th May	Ennobled as the Duke of Wellington.
	21st June	A. W. publishes his final order before demobilizing the army – gives thanks to his army for their service in the whole Peninsular War.
	23rd June	Sails to England.
	7th July	Service of General Thanksgiving for the Allied Victory is held at St Paul's Cathedral, London.
	28th July	A. W. accepts official thanks from the House of Lords.
	July–August	Appointed British Ambassador to France, leaves for Paris.
	October	Attempted assassination of A. W. or Louis XVIII's cousin, the Duke of Angoulême, who stood next to A. W., during the military parade in the Champ de Mars, Paris.
	24th December	Peace Treaty of Ghent between Britain and USA is signed.
1815	8th January	Battle of New Orleans, death of General Edward 'Ned' Pakenham, A. W.'s relative, good friend and capable general.
	1st February	A. W. arrives at the Congress of Vienna as the British Ambassador replacing Lord Castlereagh.
	1st March	Napoleon lands in Southern France with 1,100 men.
	7th March	News gets out about Napoleon's escape from Elba and his successful landing in France reaches the Congress of Vienna.
	25th March	The Seventh and final Anti-Napoleonic Coalition is formed.
	28th March	A. W. travels from Vienna to Brussels in order to take up the command of the hastily established Anglo-Dutch Army.

4th April	Arrives to Brussels, taking command of the Anglo-Dutch Army.
May	7,000 men of the Black Legion under the command of Frederick William, Duke of Brunswick (dubbed the Black Duke) join A. W.'s allied army.
15th June	Napoleon crosses the border of the Kingdom of Netherlands (modern day Belgium) and marches towards Brussels.
15th-16th June	A. W. attends the Duchess of Richmond's Ball in Brussels. Receives conflicting news about the route of Napoleon's advance throughout the day.
16th June	A. W. gives orders to concentrate the army near Quatre Bras. Meets Prussian Marshall Blǔcher at a windmill in the village of Brye, Battles of Quatre Bras and Ligny.
18th June	Battle of Waterloo.
15th October	Napoleon goes into exile on the island of Saint Helena after having been transported aboard *HMS Northumberland*.
1820	William I, King of Netherlands orders that a huge memorial be constructed for the occasion of the 5th anniversary of the Battle of Waterloo on the former battlefield.
1826	Architect Charles Van der Straeten finishes the construction of the Lion's Mound: the magnificent memorial on the Waterloo Battlefield, which commemorates one of the most momentous battles of human history.

LIST OF COALITION WARS (1792–1815)

1) War of the First Coalition,
20th April 1792 – 18th October 1797
Prussia, Holy Roman Empire (Habsburg Monarchy) Britain, Portugal, Spain, Netherlands (Dutch Republic), Naples, Sardinia and several other Italian states

France, Spain (French ally since 1795), Batavian Republic (since 1795, former Netherlands) and sister republics in Italy

2) War of the Second Coalition,
29th November 1798 – 25th March 1802
Britain (officially the United Kingdom since 1801), Holy Roman Empire, Russia, Portugal, Naples, Ottoman Empire, Grand Duchy of Tuscany, Order of Saint John/Knights Hospitaller (engaged during Napoleon's siege of Malta)

France, Spain, Denmark, sister republics in Italy, Batavian Republic.

3) War of the Third Coalition,
18th May 1803 – 18th July 1806
Britain, Russia, Holy Roman Empire (as Austrian Empire since 1804), Sweden, Naples, Sicily

France, Spain, French satellite states in Italy, Batavian Republic, Bavaria, Württemberg

4) War of the Fourth Coalition,
9th October 1806 – 9th July 1807
Britain, Prussia, Russia, Sweden, Sicily, Saxony (switches sides in December 1806)

France, Spain, Confederation of the Rhine, Saxony (joins Napoleon in December 1806), satellite states in Italy, Kingdom of Holland, Switzerland.

5) War of the Fifth Coalition,
10th April – 14th October 1809
Britain, Austrian Empire, Kingdoms of Sicily and Sardinia, Portugal
and Spain (guerrillas and troops loyal to King Ferdinand VII)

⚔

France (Napoleon Bonaparte), Spain (Joseph Bonaparte), Kingdom
of Holland (Louis Bonaparte), Kingdom of Westphalia (Jérôme
Bonaparte), Confederation of the Rhine, Duchy of Warsaw (Poland),
French satellite states in Italy

6) War of the Sixth Coalition,
3rd March 1813 – 30th May 1814
Britain, Austrian Empire, Prussia, Russia, Portugal and Spain
(guerrillas and troops loyal to King Ferdinand VII), states of the
former Confederation of the Rhine (many states join after Prince
Schwarzenberg's victory at the Battle of Leipzig on 16th-19th October
1813), Sicily, Sardinia, Denmark (joins in January 1814)

⚔

France (Napoleon), Spain (Joseph Bonaparte), Kingdom of Holland
(Louis Bonaparte), Kingdom of Westphalia (Jérôme Bonaparte),
Confederation of the Rhine (divided, many states leave Napoleon
one by one), Duchy of Warsaw (Poland – Marshal Józef Antoni
Poniatowski), Kingdom of Italy (Eugène de Beauharnais, Viceroy of
Kingdom of Italy), Denmark-Norway

7) War of the Seventh Coalition ('Hundred Days')
20th March – 8th July 1815
Britain, Prussia, Austrian Empire, Russia, Kingdom of Netherlands,
Hannover, Nassau, Brunswick (and many other former states
of the Confederation of the Rhine), Denmark, Sweden, Portugal,
Spain, Sardinia, Sicily, Tuscany, Switzerland, France – royalists loyal
to King Louis XVIII /
This time war is declared against Napoleon, not France as a whole

⚔

French Empire (Napoleon), Kingdom of Naples
(Joachim Murat – Napoleon's brother-in-law)

BIBLIOGRAPHIC NOTE

Here I would like to briefly present the current state of research into the study of Arthur Wellesley, 1st Duke of Wellington together with a basic overview of primary and secondary sources, which I hope will provide easier orientation for all those who have a deeper interest in this topic. The most important primary source for anyone interested in Arthur Wellesley, 1st Duke of Wellington and invaluable to all researchers is Wellington's correspondence, which – fortunately for scholars – is today still largely preserved. The editor of the first collection of Wellington's correspondence of a primarily military character was Colonel John Gurwood, who still as a Lieutenant in Wellington's Army on the Iberian Peninsula led the so-called *Forlorn Hopes* to the breach at the Siege of Ciudad Rodrigo in the 1811. Gurwood's thirteen-volume edition was first published in 1834–1839 in two successive and partly combined editions under the title *The Dispatches of Field Marshal Duke of Wellington during his various campaigns in India, Denmark, Portugal, Spain, the Low Countries, and France: From 1799 to 1818* (in the second edition, titled *A New Edition*, the first nine volumes were printed again and expanded to include new letters written by Wellington; the last four volumes are combined for both editions).

The next and evidently more valuable source are the fifteen volumes of Wellington's correspondence, *Supplementary Despatches, Correspondence and Memoranda of Field Marshall Arthur, Duke of Wellington* published from 1858 to 1872 on the initiative of Arthur Richard Wellesley, 2nd Duke of Wellington. In addition to the official military dispatches, this edition includes many letters and documents of a private character, which significantly heightens its scholarly value. The immense amount of Wellington's preserved correspondence (each of the volumes of Dispatches and Supplementary Despatches is roughly 700 pages long) offers an almost inexhaustible body of research material; however, due to its sheer size, it is (at least initially) a rather "tough nut to crack" in terms of orientation. Nonetheless, the present scholar's work has been made considerably easier in comparison to previous generations thanks to the internet, where both aforementioned editions are digitalized and freely accessible (both editions can be found for instance at www.archive.org or on Google Books). Contrary to their predecessors, who relied exclusively on an index, each scholar today can find necessary letters regarding the questions they are trying to answer by entering key words into the digitalized files.

Another fundamental and nearly inexhaustible primary source for study of Wellington's person are the individual memoirs, private diaries, and published collections of correspondence written by the soldiers who served under Wellington during his rich military career. The primary importance of this source clearly lies in the evaluation of Arthur Wellesley from an "external" point of view. There are countless numbers of this type of correspondence, while more are being discovered and published in new editions. Therefore, due to limitations of space, from the many scores of sources I have listed only those used for the purposes of this book which I consider to be the most interesting and well-known. From the period of Wellington's operations in India, I would highlight the memoirs of Colonel Biddulph, *The Nineteenth and Their Times* (London 1899) and Captain George Elers's *Memoirs of George Elers* (New York 1903). Of the extensive collections of sources on the Peninsular War, I would primarily cite the memoirs of Captain John Kincaid, who served with the legendary 95th Rifles: *Adventures in the Rifle Brigade, in the Peninsula, France, and the Netherlands, from 1809 to 1815* (London 1830) and of Private Edward Costelello from the same regiment: *The Adventures of a Soldier* (London 1852). Other especially interesting sources of information on Wellington's person from the times of the Peninsular War unquestionably include the correspondence of Major Edward Charles Cocks, *Intelligence Officer in the Peninsula: Letters and Diaries of the Major the Hon. Edward Charles Cocks* (New York 1986) and the diaries of military lawyer Francis Seymour Larpent, *The Private Journal of F.S. Larpent: Attached to the Head-quarters of Lord Wellington During the Peninsular War, from 1812 to its Close* (London 1853). Cocks' aforementioned memoirs are especially interesting in mapping the everyday duties of Wellington's intelligence officers. Generally speaking, the operation and organization of the Intelligence Service on the Peninsula casts new light upon Wellington's organizational skills and primarily on the excellent work done with intelligence while planning his campaigns. Other excellent primary sources on Wellington's Intelligence certainly include the work of the head of Wellington's Medical Department Dr James McGrigor, *The Autobiography and Services of Sir James McGrigor* (London 1861). Because

McGrigor was brother-in-law to the best of Wellington's intelligence officers Major Colquhoun Grant, he recorded in this work the twists of fate of his relative in considerable detail.

A highly useful source of information on the Peninsular War thanks in general to its complexity is the collection of letters and documents edited by Professor Ian Fletcher, *Voices from the Peninsula: Eyewitness Accounts by Soldiers of Wellington's Army 1808–1814* (London 2001). For a British perspective on Wellington in the Battle of Waterloo, I would recommend for instance the memoirs of Sergeant Major Cotton, *A Voice from Waterloo* (London 1849) and of Wellington's aide-de-camp Pitt-Lennox, *Three Years with the Duke of Wellington in Private Life by an Ex-Aide-De-Camp* (London 1853). For a reconstruction of Wellington's behaviour during his most famous battle, a very helpful source was the collection of relatively recently collected primary sources published for the 200th anniversary of the Battle of Waterloo edited by Martin Beardsley: *Waterloo Voices 1815: The Battle at First Hand* (Stroud 2015). Among the memoirs, diaries and editions of correspondence of British statesmen and Wellington's other contemporaries, which are also naturally very significant sources and again can be found in huge quantities, I would primarily recommend three volumes of the edition of documents by John W. Croker, *The Croker Papers Vol. I, II, III* (London 1885) and documented conversations (in the form of memoirs) with Arthur Wellesley by Earl Stanhope, *Notes of Conversations with the Duke of Wellington* (New York 1888). A very important source from the non-military environment – primarily for a summary of Wellington at the Battle of Waterloo – is without a doubt the diary of Lady Shelley, *The Diary of Frances Lady Shelley Vol. I, II* (New York 1912). For the seventh chapter devoted to the Lines of Torres Vedras, the seventh volume of correspondence of the Prince Regent (later George IV) edited by Professor Aspinal, *The Correspondence of George, Prince of Wales Vol. VII: 1810–1811* (New York 1971) was absolutely crucial. In it I stumbled upon two letters written by Lords Moira and Northumberland, which are mentioned in Chapter 7 and were quite fundamental for my whole book. Similarly important sources for this key chapter were the memoirs of Count William of Schaumburg-Lippe, *Mémoire de la Campagne de Portugal de 1762, in: Shriften und Briefe II,* (Frankfurt am Main 1977) edited by German historian Vittorio Klostermann. In the Czech and Central European context, the edition of sources by Josef Hanechs, the personal archivist of the House of Schwarzenberg at the turn of the 19th and 20th centuries, *Osvobozenecká válka 1813–1815 v dokumentech rodinného archivu schwarzenberské sekundogenitury* (State Regional Archive Třeboň 1986) (*War for Liberation 1813–1815 in documents of the family archive of the House of Schwarzenberg's secundogeniture*), was also an interesting addition to the topic, as it contains documents archived in the Czech town of Třeboň, where we can find Wellington's correspondence with Field Marshal Karl I Philipp, Prince of Schwarzenberg. Another interesting source from the Czech environment is the private correspondence of Field-Marshal Schwarzenberg, which was edited by another prominent archivist of Czech origin, Jan Bedřich Novák: *Polní maršál Karel, kníže ze Schwarzenberka, historický portrét podle rodinné korespondence* (Praha 1913) (*Field Marshal Karl Philipp, Prince of Schwarzenberg, a historical portrait based on family correspondence*). Extremely interesting primary sources from the Czech Republic were without doubt the memoirs of Jan František Vavák, the mayor of a small Czech village near Prague called Milčice. Especially important for the study of the Napoleonic era were the sixth and seventh volumes of these works, which were edited several years ago by *Carolinum* of the Charles University in Prague: *Paměti Františka Jana Vaváka, souseda a rychtáře milčického z let 1770–1816 Kniha VI–VII (1810–1816)*, Carolinum (Praha 2009) (*Memoirs of František Jan Vavák, neighbour and Mayor of Milčice from years 1770–1816, vol. VI–VII (1810–1816)*. In these memoirs, we find much interesting information on Vavák's perspective of how the common folk of his village perceived the situation in the Habsburg Monarchy during the Napoleonic Wars and many other fascinating facts. Wellington's name appears here several times (a fact which is rather noteworthy). In typical style, the first record on Wellington is of his great victory at Vitoria (21st June, 1813), which was crucial for the Austrian Empire's entrance into the War of the Sixth Coalition.

In regard to other primary sources, the French point of view as Wellington's opponents is naturally also extremely interesting. Here, for instance, very important sources were found in Marbot's *The Memoirs of Baron de Marbot, Late Lieutenant-general in the French Army in Two Volumes* (London 1903), as Marbot served in the Peninsula and Russia, and also fought in the Battles of Aspern-Essling and Wagram. For Napoleon's opinion on Wellington, good sources of information in my opinion include the publication by William Warden, *Letters Written on Board of*

HMS Northumberland and at Saint Helena (London 1816) – memoirs of the ship's surgeon, who was on board the boat that escorted Napoleon to St. Helena from Plymouth, Henry Meynell's *Conversation with Napoleon at St. Helena* (London 1911), and finally quite a new edition of Napoleon's correspondence edited by R. M. Johnston and Philip Haythornthwaite, *In the Words of Napoleon* (London 2002).

In the field of academic literature, we can also find countless publications on such a distinguished figure as the 1st Duke of Wellington, many of which were written during the Duke's lifetime and again make it fairly difficult for the reader to orient him or herself in their content. In terms of academic literature, I would first and foremost recommend the relatively recently published two-part and evidently most detailed biography to date: *Wellington: The Path to Victory, 1769–1814* (vol. I, New Haven and London 2013), and *Wellington, Waterloo and the Fortunes of Peace 1814–1852* (vol. II, New Haven and London 2015) written by Rory Muir, Professor at Yale and Adelaide Universities. Another publication from the scores of biographies on Arthur Wellesley's person that must be mentioned here is the two-part biography of the Duke of Wellington by Elizabeth Longford, written in the early 1970s, which is still among the most authoritative works to have been written on the topic of the Duke of Wellington's life: *Wellington: The Years of the Sword* (vol. I. London 1970) and *Wellington: Pillar of State* (vol II. London 1972). In my opinion, this work stands out from other biographies in the captivating style in which it was written. For the purposes of this book, I have used only the first volume focusing on Wellesley's military career. In terms of biographies, I would also like to cite the work of well-known military historian Richard Holmes, *Wellington: The Iron Duke* (London 2007), which in my opinion is a suitable book for those who plan to read something on Wellington but do not want to delve into such great detail. Together with this publication, Professor Holmes is also the creator of a three-part television documentary for the BBC of the same name, which I consider to be one of the best in terms of educational television programmes about Wellington. In regard to older biographies, I should not neglect to mention the work of Philip Guedalla, *The Duke*, which was written at the beginning of the 1930s. The traditional "Victorian Biographies" are also another important source, including works such as George Robert Gleig's *The Life of Arthur, Duke of Wellington* (London 1871). Additionally, we might mention the work of Sir Herbert Maxwell, *The Life of Wellington and Restoration of the Martial Power of Great Britain* (London 1883) and also William Hamilton Maxwell's *Life of Field-Marshal His Grace the Duke of Wellington, vol. I, II* (London 1839).

In the context of Wellington's operations in the Peninsular War, anyone with interest in the Duke's military career should not overlook the exhaustive seven-volume work by Sir Charles Oman, *A History of the Peninsular War* (in my work I have used only the first five volumes) from the beginning of the 20th century. In terms of newer literature focusing on the Peninsular War, one of the highest-quality publications has been written by University of Liverpool Professor Charles Esdaile, *The Peninsular War: A New History* (London 2002). In my opinion, Esdaile's work primarily offers an excellent Spanish context. As traditional works on general British military history are concerned, I have also made use of the monumental work by John Fortescue, *A History of the British Army* (in my work I cite volumes IV–VI dealing primarily with the Peninsular War). Another valuable piece of literature bordering between a primary source and academic writing is the second volume of the work by James Grant, whose father served under the Duke of Wellington over the course of the whole Peninsular War, entitled *British Battles on Land and Sea, vol. I, II* (London 1886). In regard to works devoted to the British Army and military history in the Napoleonic Wars, I would again highlight works by Richard Holmes: *Redcoat: The British Solider in the Age of Horse and Musket* (London 2002) and Rory Muir's, *Tactics and the Experience of Battle in the Age of Napoleon* (New Haven and London, 1998).

In terms of studies focusing on individual aspects of Wellington's military career, I would like to mention the work by Mark Thompson, *Wellington's Engineers: Military Engineering in the Peninsular War 1808–1814* (Barnsley 2015), which helped me greatly in my work on the chapter about the Lines of Torres Vedras. In addition to the aforementioned literature, I utilized the work of the excellent novelist Bernard Cornwell, *Waterloo: The History of Four Days, Three Armies and Three Battles* (London 2014) in my description of Wellington's historical role at the Battle of Waterloo. A highly valuable study on the Battle of Waterloo and beyond it is the work by Andrew Roberts, *Wellington and Napoleon* (London, 2003). From the perspective of Wellington's personal and family life, another excellent source of information is the work by Jane Wellesley, *A Journey*

Through My Family: The Wellington Story (London, 2009). The work of Joan Wilson, *A Soldier's wife, Wellington's Marriage* (London 1987), is another extremely useful publication on Wellington's discordant marriage. An excellent narrative work on Wellington's iconography was recently published by Charles Wellesley, 9th Duke of Wellington titled *Wellington portrayed* (London 2014).

On the topic of Wellington's Intelligence, very informative works have emerged over the last couple of decades. I consider one of the most interesting of these books to be Mark Urban's *The Man Who Broke Napoleon's Codes, The Story of George Scovell* (London 2001), which maps the life path of Wellington's main decoder and excellently illustrates the vital importance and value of information on the movement of superior French troops on the Iberian Peninsula. In this area, the work by Terry Crowdy, *The Enemy Within: A History of Spies, Spymasters and Espionage* (Oxford 2006) is a highly valuable work from a general standpoint, and the seventh chapter is especially valuable in terms of Wellington's Intelligence.

I would certainly not like to omit the excellent anthology created by Portuguese historians published bilingually in Portuguese and English by Rui Brás (ed.), *Guerra peninsular / The Peninsular War 1807–1814* (Torres Vedras 2010). In regard to Czech works with a Central European context, the best source on the Napoleonic Wars in my opinion is the anthology of texts written by Czech historians and edited by Ivan Šedivý, *Napoleonské války a české země* (Praha 2001) (*The Napoleonic Wars and the Czech Lands*), which maps from many angles the situation in the Habsburg Monarchy during the whole Napoleonic period. In addition, the work of Jiří Kacetl *Znojmo/Znaim 1809* (Znojmo 2019) is an interesting although rather brief monograph dealing with the War of the Fifth Coalition, in which Britain and Austria were *de facto* the only great powers fighting against France. In this work, Kacetl refutes the myth that Napoleon decided the fate of the whole war in Central Europe with his victory at Wagram, which he demonstrates by presenting the story of another ferocious battle that took place on the territory of today's Czech Republic at Znaim several days after Wagram. It was followed by a peace treaty that was extremely severe on Austria; however, if the Battle of Znaim had never taken place, Austria was likely to have perished, only to remain in individual protectorates under the government of those loyal to Napoleon. The final and highly interesting contribution from the Czech historical community is

Karel Sáček's article *Čeští dobrovolníci ve sboru vévody brunšvického* in: *Třetí koaliční válka 1805*, Akcent (Třebíč 2004) (*Czech Volunteers in the Duke of Brunswick's Corps in the War of the Third Coalition 1805*). Many German historians have also written excellent work on the topic of the Black Legion of the Duke of Brunswick. Nonetheless, Karel Sáček, who has devoted himself to the topic for fifteen years, has exhaustingly documented Czech participation in the Black Legion using contemporary sources and has drawn the conclusion that the corps contained 49 members from today's Czech Republic (according to place of birth – there is proof that twelve of these men spoke Czech exclusively). In the light of the fact that the Black Legion fought its way from Northern Bohemia across Germany to the Northern Sea and the British fleet there, which transported it to Wellington's forces in Portugal, we can easily claim that approximately 30 Czechs (counting certain losses on their way across Germany) served under the Duke of Wellington in the ranks of the Black Legion.

In the 21st century, the quantity of online sources and possibilities for research is rapidly increasing, a fact which we should not neglect, as many high-quality articles can be found in this new "deluge" of sources. The very best online article that I encountered was the work of Christopher Bell from The Waterloo Association, entitled *The Birth of Arthur Wesley*. In this excellent article, Christopher Bell summarizes in great detail (and in my opinion better than in all biographies printed hitherto) the issues surrounding Wellington's birth. The article is available at: *https://www.waterlooassociation.org.uk/2019/03/29/the-birth-of-arthur-wesley/*.

I would also recommend two online articles that excellently and succinctly summarize the issue of Wellington's Intelligence by Chuck Hudson:

Spying for the Crown: Part 3: Military Intelligence During the Peninsula Campaign and Spying for the Crown, available at: https://historicinterpreter.wordpress.com/2015/08/25/spying-for-the-crown-part-4-civilian-spies-for-wellington/

Spying for the Crown: Part 4: Civilian Spies for Wellington https://historic-interpreter.wordpress.com/2015/08/11/spying-for-the-crown-part-3-military-intelligence-during-the-peninsula-campaign/#more-403.

I know that I am not alone in finding Wellington's life and career fascinating, and trust others will continue in the quest to elucidate his story and legacy.

BIBLIOGRAPHY

Primary Sources:

The Sporting Magazine, vol. XXIII, Published by Rogerson & Tuxford, London 1852.

The United Service Journal and Naval and Military Magazine, Part I, Henry Colburn, London 1829.

ARBUTHNOT, Harriete, *The Journal of Mrs. Arbuthnot, 1820–1832, vol. I*, Macmillan London 1950.

ASPINALL, Arthur (ed.), *The Correspondence of George Prince of Wales 1770–1812, vol. VII: 1810–1811*, Cassel and Company Ltd., London 1971.

BAYLY, Richard, *Diary of Colonel Bayly, 12ᵗʰ Regiment, 1796–1830*, Army and Navy Cooperative Society, London 1896.

BARRINGTON, Sir Jonah, *Personal Sketches of His Own Times in Two Volumes, vol. I.*, Townsend Young LL.D., London 1871.

BEARDSLEY, Martin (ed.), *Waterloo Voices 1815: The Battle at First Hand*, Amberley Publishing, Stroud, 2015.

BERRY, Mary, *Extracts from the Journals and Correspondence of Miss Berry, vol. III*, Longmans, Green and Co., London 1886.

BIDDULPH, John, *The Nineteenth and Their Times,* John Murray, London 1899.

BOOTH, John, *The Battle of Waterloo Containing a Series of Accounts*, Military Library Whitehall, London 1816.

BOWRING, John, *Autobiography of Sir John Bowring*, Henry S. King. And Co., London 1877.

BRETT-JAMES, Anthony (ed.), *Wellington at War, 1794–1815: A Selection of His Wartime Letters*, Macmillan, London 1961.

BROUGHTON, John, *Recollection of a Long Life, vol. I*, John Murray, London 1911.

BUCKLEY, Roger (ed.), *Napoleonic War Journal of Captain Thomas Henry Browne*, Bodley Head for the Army Records Society, London 1987.

BUNSEN, Frances, *A Memoir of Baron Bunsen, vol. II*, Longmans, Green & Co., London 1868.

BURGHCLERE, baroness of, Winifred, *A Great Man's Friendship; Letters of the Duke of Wellington to Mary, Marchioness of Salisbury, 1850–1852*, Payson, New York 1927.

BYRON, George, Gordon, *Childe Harold's Pilgrimage A Romaunt: and the Other Poems*, T. Davison, Whitefriars 1812.

COLEBROOKE, Sir. T. E., *The Life of Honourable Sir Mountstuart Elphinstone*, John Murray, London 1884.

COOKE, James, *A True Soldier Gentleman: The Memoirs of Lt. John Cooke 1791–1813*, Shinglepicker, Swanage 2000.

COOPER, S. John, *Rough Notes of Seven Campaigns*, Spellmount, London 1996.

COSTELLO, Edward, *The Adventures of a Soldier*, Colburn and Co., London 1852.

COTTON, E., Sergeant-major, *A Voice from Waterloo*, B. L. Green, London 1849.

CROKER, John, Wilson, *The Croker Papers, 3 vols.,* John Murray, London 1884–1885.

DAVIES, George, *The Completeness of the Late Duke of Wellington as a National Character*, Joseph Masters, London 1854.

DE BOIGNE, Comtesse, Louise-Eléonore, *Memoires of the Comtesse de Boigne, vol. I*, C. Scribner's Sons, London 1907.

DE BOURRIENNE, Louis Antoine Fauvelet, *Memoirs of Napoleon Bonaparte, vol. IV*, Richard Bentley, London 1836.

DUMOURIEZ, Charles, *An Account of Portugal, as it Appeared in 1766 to Dumouriez*, C. Low, London 1797.

EDWARDS, Edward (ed.), *Some Unpublished Letters to Sir Thomas Picton, vol. XII*, Historical Society of West Wales, 1927.

ELERS, George, *Memoirs of George Elers*, D. Appelton, New York 1903.

ELLESMERE, Earl of, Francis, *Personal Reminiscences of the Duke of Wellington by Francis, First Earl of Ellesmere*, John Murray, London 1903.

ERNSTBERGER, Anton, *Böhmens Freiwilliger Kriegseinsatz gegen Napoleon 1809*, München 1936.

FLETCHER, Ian (ed.), *Voices from the Peninsula: Eyewitness Accounts by Soldiers of Wellington's Army 1808–1814*, Greenhill Books, London 2001.

FRASER, Sir William, *Words on Wellington*, John, C., Nimmo, London 1889.

GLOVER, Gareth, *Waterloo in 100 Objects*, History Press, Stroud 2015.

GLOVER, Gareth (ed.), *Wellington's Voice*, Frontline Books, London 2012.

GRANVILLE, Castilia (ed.), *G. Leveson Gower, First Lord Granville, Correspondence, vol. II*, John Murray, London 1916.

GRATTAN, William, *Adventures of the Connaungt Rangers from 1808–1814, 2 vols.*, Henry Colburn, London 1847.

GREVILLE, Charles, *The Greville Memoirs, vol. IV*, Longmans, Green and Co., London, New York and Bombay 1896.

GURWOOD, John*, The Dispatches of Field Marshal Duke of Wellington, in 13 vols.*, London 1834–1839, John Murray London 1834–1839.

GURWOOD, *Dispatches, A New Edition,* (In vols. 8; vols. 9–13 are combined with the first edition), London 1837–1839).

HANESCH, Josef (ed.), *Osvobozenecká válka 1813–1815 v dokumentech rodinného archivu schwarzenberské sekundogenitury*, Státní oblastní archiv Třeboň 1986.

HANGER, George, *To All Sportsmen*, J. J. Stockdale, London 1814.

HANSARD, T.C. (ed.), *The Parliamentary Debates from the Year 1803 to Present Time*, Hansard Printer, London 1812.

HAYES, Edward (ed.), *The Ballads of Ireland*, A. Fullarton and Company, London, Edinburgh and Dublin 1855.

HIBBERT, Christopher (ed.), *The Recollections of Rifleman Harris,* Cassel and Windrush Press Book, London 2006.

HICKEY, William, *Memoirs of William Hickey, vol. IV*, Hurst and Blackett Ltd., London 1925.

HOWARD, Donald (ed.), *The French Campaign in Portugal 1810–1811: An Account by Jean Jacques Pelet*, University of Minnesota Press, Minneapolis 1973.

HOWELL, John (ed.), *Journal of a Soldier of the 71th*, Printed by Balfour and Clarke Edinburgh 1819.

HOUSSAYE, Henry, *1815: Waterloo*, Adam and Charles Black, London 1900.

HUGO, Victor, *Les Misérables, vol. I*, London, Edinburgh, Paris, Thomas Nelson and Sons, Melbourne and New York Ltd., 1874.

CHAMBERS, Robert, Chambers William (eds.), *Chamber's Journal, vol. XXXVIII*, London 1863.

CHURCHILL, Winston Spencer, *Never Give in! The Best of Winston Churchill's Speeches*, Pimlico, London 2004.

JOHNSTON, R. M., Haythornthwaite, Philip, (eds.), *In the Words of Napoleon*, Greenhill Books London 2002.

JONES, Rice, *An Engineer Officer under Wellington*, Trotman, London 1986.

KINCAID, John, *Adventures in the Rifle Brigade, in the Peninsula, France, and the Netherlands, from 1809 to 1815*, T. and W. Boone, Strand, London 1830.

KINCAID, John, *Random Shots from a Rifleman*, T. and W. Boone, London 1847.

LARPENT, F. Seymour, *The Private Journal of F.S. Larpent: Attached to the Head-quarters of Lord Wellington During the Peninsular War, from 1812 to it's Close*, Richard Bentley, London 1854.

LOW, Edward (ed.), *With Napoleon at Waterloo and Other Unpublished Documents of the Waterloo and Peninsular Campaigns*, Francis Griffiths, London 1911.

LUSHINGTON, S. R., *The Life and Services of Lord General Harris,* John W. Parker, London 1845.

MÁCHAL, Jan (ed.), *Hankovy písně a prostonárodní srbská múza do Čech převedená*, Česká akademie císaře Františka Josefa, Praha 1918.

MALMESBURY, James, *Letters of First Earl of Malmesbury: 1745–1820, vol. II*, Richard Bentley, London 1870.

MARBOT, Jean-Baptiste-Antoine-Marcelin, baron de, *The memoirs of Baron de Marbot, late lieutenant-general in the French army, 2 vols.*, Longmans, Green and Co., New York and Bombay 1903.

MARBOT, Jean-Baptiste-Antoine-Marcelin, baron de, *Berezina, Lipsko, Waterloo: Paměti*, Karel Stan. Sokol, Praha 1909.

MAXWELL, W. H., *Peninsular Sketches by Actors on the Scene, vol. II*, Henry Colburn, London, 1845.

MCGRIGOR, Dr James, *Autobiography and Services of Sir James McGrigor*, Longman and Green, London 1861.

MEYNELL, Henry, *Conversation with Napoleon at St. Helena*, Hupreys, London 1911.

NAPIER, George, *Passages in the Early Military Life*, John Murray, London 1884.

NOVÁK, Bedřich Jan, *Polní maršál Karel, kníže ze Schwarzenberka, historický portrét podle rodinné korespondence*, Zvláštní otisk Českého časopisu historického, Tiskem AL. Wiesnera – Nákladem vlastním, Praha 1913.

ÖSTERREICH-TESCHEN, Erzherzog von, Karl, *Strategie erläutert durch die Darstellung des Feldzugs 1796 Teil I*, Wien 1814.

PAGE, Julia (ed.), *Intelligence Officer in the Peninsula: Letters and Diaries of the Major the Hon. Edward Charles Cocks*, Spellmount, New York 1986.

PITT-LENNOX, William, *Three Years with the Duke of Wellington in Private Life by an Ex-Aid-De-Camp*, Saunders and Otley, London 1853.

RAYMOND, John (ed.), *The Reminiscences and Recollection of Captain Gronow*, Bodley Head, London 1964.

SCHAUMANN, August, *On the Road with Wellington*, Heinemann, London 1924.

SCHAUMBURG-LIPPE, Graf zu, Wilhelm, *Mémoire de la Campagne de Portugal de 1762, in: Schriften und Briefe II,* Frankfurt am Main 1977.

SHELLEY, Frances, *The Diary of Frances Lady Shelley, vol. I*, C. Scribner's Sons, New York 1912.

SIDNEY, Edwin, *The Life of Lord Hill*, John Murray, London 1845.

SIMMONS, George, *A British Rifleman: The Journals and Correspondence of Major George Simons, Rifle Brigade, During the Peninsular War and Campaign of Waterloo*, A. and C. Black, Soho Square, London 1899.

SPEHR, Luis, *Friedrich Wilhelm, Herzog von Braunschweig-Lüneburg-Oels*, Drud von Gebrüder Meyer, Braunschweig 1848.

STANHOPE, 5th Earl of, Philip Henry, *Notes of Conversations with the Duke of Wellington*, Green and Co., New York 1888.

STANHOPE, 5th earl of, Phillip Henry, *The Life of Right Honourable William Pitt, vol. I*, John Murray, London 1861.

TIMBS, John, *Wellingtoniana: Maxims and Characteristics of the Duke of Wellington*, Ingram, Cooke, and Co., London 1852.

TRENCH, Mellisa, *The Remains of the Late Mrs. Richard Trench*, Parker and Son and Bourn, London 1862.

VAVÁK, František, *Paměti Frnatiška Jana Vaváka, souseda a ryhtáře milčického z let 1770–1816, Kniha VI-VII (1810–1816)*, Nakladatelství Karolinum, Praha 2009.

VIBART, H. M., *The Military History of the Madras Engineers and Pioneers, vol. I*, W. H. Aleen and Company, London 1881.

VIVIAN, Claude, (ed.), *Richard Hussey Vivian, A Memoir*, Isbister and Company Ltd., London 1897.

WARDEN, William, *Letters Written on Board of HMS Northumberland and at Saint Helena*, R. Ackermann, London 1816.

WARRE, William, *Letters from the Peninsula 1808–1812*, Spellmount, Staplehurst 1999.

WEBSTER, Charles (ed.), *Some Letters of Duke of Wellington to his Brother William Wellesley-Pole*, Offices of the Royal Historical Society, London 1948.

WELLINGTON, 2th Duke of (ed.), Arthur Richard Wellesley, *Supplementary Despatches, Correspondence and Memoranda of Field Marshall Arthur, Duke of Wellington*, in 15 vols. John Murray, London 1858–1872.

WELLINGTON, 7th Duke of (ed.), Gerald Wellesley, *A Selection of the Private Correspondence of the First Duke of Wellington*, Dropmore Press, London 1952.

WELLINGTON, 7th Duke of (ed.), Gerald Wellesley, *The Conversations of the First Duke of Wellington*, The Saint Nicolas Press, Cambridge 1956.

Secondary sources:

ABERCROMBY, James, Baron Dunfermline, *Lieutenant-General Sir Ralph Abercromby, K.B., 1793–1801*, Edmonston and Douglas, Edinburgh 1861.

ALDINGTON, Richard, *Wellington*, William Heinemann Ltd. London, Toronto 1946.

ARTETA, Antonio Ubieto, Campistol, Juan Reglá, Zamora, José María Jover, Serrano, Carlos Seco, *Dějiny Španělska*, Nakladatelství Lidové Noviny, Praha 1995.

BAUGH, Daniel, *The Global Seven Years War*, Routledge, London and New York 2014.

BĚLINA, Pavel, *Napoleonské války: Předěl v dějinách mezinárodních vztahů a vojenského umění, in: Napoleonské války a české země*, NLN, Praha 2001.

BĚLINA, Pavel, Hlavačka, Milan, Tinková, Daniela, *Velké Dějiny zemí Koruny české, IX-a,* Paseka, Praha-Litomyšl 2013.

BLAKE, Nicholas, Lawrence, Richard, *The Illustrated Companion to Nelson's Navy*, Stackpolebooks, London 2005.

BLAND, Caroline, Maierhoffer, Waltraud, Rosch, Gertrude, (eds.), *Women Against Napoleon,* Campus Verlag/The Chicago University Press, Frankfurt, New York 2007.

BORGES, Augusto, CHAVES, Luís (eds.), *Museo do Exército em Portugal: História, Cultira e Memórias, Portuguese Army Museums: History, Culture and Memories*, Book – Edicoes Especiais, Lisbon 2016.

BRADSHAW, John, *Sir Thomas Munro and the British Settlement of Madras Presidency*, Clarendon Press, Oxford 1894.

BRÁS, Rui (ed.), *Guerra peninsular/The Peninsular War 1807–1814*, Camara Municipal de Torres Vedras, Torres Vedras 2010.

BRUCE, Robert (ed.), *Bojové techniky období Napoleonských válek*, Deus, Praha 2008.

BRYANT, Julius, *Apsley House: The Wellington Collection*, English Heritage, London 2014.

BUTTERY, David, *Waterloo Battlefield Guide*, Pen and Sword, Kellington 2018.

CARRINGTON, C. E., Jackson, H. J., *A History of England*, Cambridge University Press, Cambridge 1949.

COOPER, Leo, (ed.), *One Leg: The Life and Letters of Henry William Paget, First Marquess of Angelsey K. G.*, Leo Cooper, London 1996.

CORNWELL, Bernard, *Sharpovo Waterloo*, Oldag, Ostrava 2015.

CORNWELL, Bernard, *Waterloo: The History of Four Days, Three Armies and Three Battles*, William Collins, London 2014.

CORRIGAN, Gordon, *Wellington: A Military Life*, Hambledon, London and New York 2001.

CRAWLEY, W. J., Chetwode (Senior Grand Deacon), *Notes on Irish Freemansory, No. VI*, Margate 1902.

CROWDY, Terry, *The Enemy Within: A History of Spies, Spymasters and Espionage*, Osprey, Oxford 2006.

DANLEY, Mark, SPEELMAN, Patrick (eds.), *The Seven Year's War: Global Views*, Brill, 2012.

DAVIES, J. Hew, *Wellington Wars: The Making of Military Genius*, Yale University Press, New Haven and London 2015.

DELAFORCE, Patrick, *Wellington: The Beau, The Life and Loves of the Duke of Wellington*, Pen and Sword, Barnsley 2004.

DOSTÁL, Tomáš, *Rakousko-francouzská válka 1809*, Historický obzor, č .16/2005

ESDAILE, Charles, *The French Wars 1792–1815,* Routledge, London 2001.

ESDAILE, Charles, *The Peninsular War: A New History*, Allen Lane The Penguin Press, London 2002.

ESDAILE, Charles, *The Spanish Army in the Peninsular War,* Manchester University Press, Manchester and New York 1988.

FARLANE, Charles, *The Great Battles of the British Army*, George Routledge and Co., London 1853.

FERGUSON, Niall, *Britské impérium, cesta k modernímu světu*, Prostor, Praha 2007.

FOORD, Edward, *Napoleon's Russian campaign of 1812,* Little, Brown and Co. Boston 1915.

FORTESCUE, Sir John, *A History of the British Army*, in 13 vols, Macmillan, London 1899–1930.

GAŽI, Martin (ed.), *Schwarzenbergové v české a středoevropské kulturní historii*, Tomáš Halama, Národní památkový ústav. Územní památková správa v Českých Budějovicích, České Budějovice 2013.

GLEIG, George, Robert, *The Life of Arthur, Duke of Wellington*, Longmans and Green, London 1871.

GRANT, James, *British Battles on Land and Sea, vol. II*, Cassel and Co. London 1886.

GUEDALLA, Philip, *The Duke*, Wordsworth Military Library, London 1997.

HAFFNER, Sebastian, *Churchill*, Votobia, Olomouc 1996.

HANESCH, Josef, *Karel I. Filip, kníže Schwarzenberg: polní maršál*, Veduta, České Budějovice 2003.

HAVEL, Petr, ROMAŇÁK, Andrej, *Maršál Radecký*, Paseka, Praha-Litomyšl 2000.

HAYTHORNTHWAITE, Philip, *British Riflemen 1797–1815*, Osprey, Oxford 2002.

HERRE, Franz, *Metternich*, Themis, Praha 1996.

HERRE, Franz, *Radecký: Nejoblíbenější polní maršálek rakouské armády a jeho pohnutá doba*, Books, Praha 1997.

HIBBERT, Christopher, *Wellington: A Personal History*, Harper and Colins, London 1998.

HOLMES, Richard, *Wellington: The Iron Duke*, Harper and Perenial, London 2007.

HOLMES, Richard, Redcoat: *The British Solider in the Age of Horse and Musket*, Harper Press, London 2002.

HOWARD, Michael (ed.), *Wellingtonian Studies*, Gale and Polden Ltd., Aldershot 1959.

JOHNSON, Paul, *Napoleon*, Barister and Principal, Praha 2015.

JŮN, Libor, *Napoleonské války*, Triton, Praha 2005.

JŮN, Libor, *České země a dobrovolnické sbory habsburské armády v období koaličních a napoleonských válek, in: Napoleonské války a české země*, NLN, Praha 2001.

KACETL, Jiří, *Znaim/Znojmo 1809*, Herbert a Theodor s.r.o., Znojmo 2019.

KEEGAN, John, *Historie válečnictví*, Beta-Dobrovský, Praha–Plzeň 2003.

KIERAN, L. Brian, *Corunna 1809: Sir John Moore's Battle to Victory and Successful Evacuation*, AuthorHuouse Ltd., Milton Keynes 2011.

KLÍMA, Jan, *Dějiny Portugalska*, Nakladatelství Lidové Noviny, Praha 1996.

KÖNNECKE, Gustav, *Dörnberg, Wilhelm Caspar Ferdinand, Freiherr von,* in: *Allgemeine Deutsche Biographie* (ADB). Band 5, Duncker & Humblot, Leipzig 1877.

KRYŠTŮFEK, Jan, *Boj monarchické Evropy* s *revolucí francouzskou, Díl II.*, J.M. Kryštůfek, Praha 1888.

LAWFORD, James, *Wellington's Peninsular Army*, Osprey, Oxford 2010.

LEGGIERE, Michael, *The Fall of Napoleon: Volume I, The Allied Invasion of France, 1813–1814*, Cambridge University Press, Cambridge, New York 2007.

LONGFORD, Elizabeth, *The Years of the Sword*, The Literary Guild, London 1970.

MAXWELL, Sir Herbert, *The Life of Wellington and Restoration of the Martial Power of Great Britain, vol. I*, S. Low and Marston, London 1899.

MAXWELL, Sir Herbert, *The Life of Wellington: New Edition, Revisited, Condensed and Completed, H. M. Society*, London 1883.

MAXWELL, William Hamilton, *Life of Field-Marshal His Grace the Duke of Wellington, vol. I*, A. H. Baily and Co., London 1839.

MILLAR, Simon, *Assaye 1803: Wellington's First and Bloodiest Victory*, Osprey Publishing, Oxford 2006.

MUDIE, James *An Historical and Critical Account of a Grand Series of National Medals,* Henry Colburn and Co., London 1820.

MUIR, Rory, *Britain and the Defeat of Napoleon 1807–1815*, Yale University Press, New Haven and London 1996.

MUIR, Rory, *Tactics and the Experience of Battle in the Age of Napoleon*, Yale University Press, New Haven and London, 1998.

MUIR, Rory, *Wellington: The Path to Victory, 1769–1814*, Yale University Press, New Haven and London 2013.

MUIR, Rory, Wellington, *Waterloo and the Fortunes od Peace 1814–1852*, Yale University Press, New Haven and London 2015.

MULTHOFF, Robert (ed.), *Friedrich Wilhelm, Herzog von Braunschweig-Lüneburg-Oels.*, in: *Neue Deutsche Biographie (NDB). Band V*, Duncker & Humblot, Berlin 1961.

NABOKOV, Vladimir, *The Real Life of Sebastian Knight,* New York 2008, p. 52.

NAPIER, Sir William Francis Patrick*, History of the War in the Peninsula and in the South of France: from the Year 1807 to the Year 1814,* (in 6 vols. London), T. and W. Boone, London 1828–1840.

OMAN, Sir Charles, *A History of the Peninsular War, in 7 vols.*, Oxford 1902–1930, Clarendon Press, Oxford 1902–1914.

PERNES, Jiří (ed.), *Pod císařským praporem, historie habsburské armády*, Elka Press, Praha 2003.

PIVKA VON, Otto, *Brunswick Troops 1809–1815*, Osprey, Oxford 1985.

PORTER, Whitworth, *History of the Corps of Royal Engineers*, Longman and Green, London 1889.

PRICE, Munro, *The Perilous Crown: France Between Revolutions: 1814–1848*, Macmillan, Basingstoke and Oxford 2010.

ROBERTS, Andrew, *Napoleon and Wellington*, Phoenix, London 2003.

SÁČEK, Karel, *Čeští dobrovolníci ve sboru vévody brunšvického* in: *Třetí kaoliční válka 1805*, Akcent, Třebíč 2004.

SHAW, Matthew, *The Duke of Wellington*, The British Library, London 2005.

SKŘIVAN, Aleš, *Evropská politika 1648–1914*, Nakladatelství Aleš Skřivan, Praha 1999.

SMITH, Thomas, *Historical Recollections of Hyde Park,* John Smith, London 1836.

SNAPE, F. Michael, *The Royal Army Chaplains' Department 1796–1953: Clergy Under Fire,* The Boydell Press, Woodbridge 2008.

STELLNER, František, *Sedmiletá válka v Evropě*, Libri, Praha 2007.

STOCQUELER, Joachim Hayward, *The Life of Field Marshal the Duke of Wellington: In two volumes, vol. I,* London 1852.

ŠAŠINKA, Zdeněk, *Bitva u Znojma: k otázce péče o raněné a pohřbívání v období napoleonských válek* in: Historický obzor, 21(1/2), Praha 2010.

ŠEDIVÝ, Ivan (ed.), *Napoleonské války a* české *země,* Nakladatelství Lidové Noviny, Praha 2001.

TARABA, Luboš, *Vídeňský kongres: salony, kuloáry, budoáry*, Baset, Praha 2002.

THACKERAY, William Makepeace, *The Memoirs of Barry Lyndon*, Oxford University Press, London, New York and Toronto 1847.

THOMPSON, Mark, *Wellington's Engineers: Military Engineering in the Peninsular War 1808–1814,* Pen and Sword Books, Barnsley 2015.

URBAN, Mark, *Generálové: Deset britských velitelů, kteří ovlivnili svět*, Naše Vojsko, Praha 2011.

URBAN, Mark, *The Man Who Broke Napoleon's Codes, The Story of George Scovell*, Faber and Faber Ltd., London 2001.

WELLESLEY, Jane, *A Journey Through My Family: The Wellington Story*, Phoenix, London 2009.

WELLINGTON, 9th Duke of, Charles Wellesley, *Wellington portrayed*, Unicorn Press Ltd. London 2014.

WELLER, Jack, *On Wellington, The Duke and his Art of War*, Greenhill Books, London 1998.

WILSON, Joan, *A Soldier's wife, Wellington's Marriage*, Weidenfeld and Nicolson, London 1987.

Online sources:

BELL, Christopher, *The Birth of Arthur Wesley,* online article in: https://www.waterlooassociation.org.uk/2019/03/29/the-birth-of-arthur-wesley/

BERESINER, Yasha, *Wellington: Soldier, Politician and Initiated Freemason*, online article in: http://www.freemasons-freemasonry.com/beresiner13.html

HUDSON, Chuck, *Spying for the Crown: Part 3 – Military Intelligence During the Peninsula Campaign,* online article in: https://historicinterpreter.wordpress.com/2015/08/11/spying-for-the-crown-part-3-military-intelligence-during-the-peninsula-campaign/#more-403

HUDSON, Chuck, *Spying for the Crown – Part 4: Civilian Spies for Wellington*, online article in: https://historicinterpreter.wordpress.com/2015/08/25/spying-for-the-crown-part-4-civilian-spies-for-wellington/

SÁČEK, Karel: *Smrtihlavové zrození v Čechách roku 1809* online article in: https://www.primaplana.cz/news/smrtihlavove-zrozeni-v-cechach-roku-1809-1-cerni-legionari-vevody-brunsvickeho-a-jejich-puvod/

TROWBRIDGE, Ben, *History's Unparalleled Alliance: the Anglo-Portuguese Treaty of Windsor, 9th May 1386, online article in: https://history.blog.gov.uk/2016/05/09/historys-unparalleled-alliance-the-anglo-portuguese-treaty-of-windsor-9th-may-1386/*

The Capture of Grant, online article in: http://www.nationalarchives.gov.uk/spies/spies/grant/gr1.htm

The Great Paris Cipher, online article in: http://www.nationalarchives.gov.uk/spies/ciphers/scovell/sc1.htm

The Art of Deciphering, online article in: http://www.nationalarchives.gov.uk/spies/ciphers/scovell/sc2.htm

https://www.zamek-kynzvart.eu/en

USEFUL WEBSITES THAT SHED FURTHER LIGHT ON ARTHUR WELLESLEY, 1ST DUKE OF WELLINGTON, HIS LIFE, CAMPAIGNS AND REPUTATION

Apsley House
www.english-heritage.org.uk/visit/places/apsley-house/history/
BBC Radio 4 – Great Lives – The Duke of Wellington
www.bbc.co.uk/programmes/b0076s3l
Catholic Herald - Wellington – the Iron Irishman
https://catholicherald.co.uk/commentandblogs/2015/06/18/wellington-the-iron-irishman/
History Hit – Why Did the Duke of Wellington Consider his Victory at Assaye his Finest Achievement?
www.historyhit.com/1803-wellingtons-first-great-victory-assaye/
Mémorial Waterloo 1815
www.waterloo1815.be/en/
National Portrait Gallery
www.npg.org.uk/collections/search/person/mp04752/arthur-wellesley-1st-duke-of-wellington
Project Hougoumont
http://projecthougoumont.com
Stratfield Saye House
www.wellingtonestates.co.uk/stratfield-saye-house
Walmer Castle
https://www.english-heritage.org.uk/visit/places/walmer-castle-and-gardens/
The Napoleonic Association
www.napoleonicassociation.org
The National Army Museum
www.nam.ac.uk/explore/old-nosey-duke-wellington
The Society for Army Historical Research
www.sahr.org.uk
The Waterloo Association
www.waterlooassociation.org.uk
The Wellington Paper Database
www.southampton.ac.uk/archives/cataloguedatabases/well/index.page

The Wellington Society of Madrid
    https://wellsoc.org/
Wellington and the Battle of Waterloo
    www.futurelearn.com/courses/wellington-and-waterloo
All of Wellington's main battles in one place
    https://www.britishbattles.com/
Online commentary of Rory Muir's biography of Wellington
    https://www.lifeofwellington.co.uk/explore-the-commentary/
Interpretation Centre of the Lines of Torres Vedras | Sobral de Monte Agraço
    https://www.cilt.pt/en/lines-of-torres-vedras
Exploring the Lines of Torres Vedras – The Wellington Trail
    https://www.rhlt.pt/en/wellington-en/

NOTES

1   Both quotes in: John Wilson Croker, *The Croker Papers, vol. I*, (London 1884),
    p. 338.
2   Rui Brás (ed.), *Guerra peninsular/The Peninsular War 1807–1814* (Torres Vedras
    2010), op. cit., p. 17.
3   Frances Shelley, *The Diary of Frances Lady Shelley, vol. I* (New York 1912),
    p. 102.
4   John Gurwood, *The Dispatches of Field Marshal Duke of Wellington, vol. XII*
    (13 vols., London 1834–1839) p. 510. The original letter can be found in the
    Třeboň Archive: 1. arch., oktáv., Sing–II–72–6.
5   Winifred Burghclere, baronnes of, *A Great Man's Friendship; Letters of the Duke of
    Wellington to Mary, Marchioness of Salisbury, 1850–1852* (New York 1927), p. 108.
6   Vladimir Nabokov, *The Real Life of Sebastian Knight* (New York 2008), p. 52.
7   Gareth Glover, *Waterloo in 100 Objects* (Stroud 2015), pp. 35–36. Compare to:
    Philip Guedalla, *The Duke* (London 1997), p. 208.
8   Elizabeth Longford, *Wellington: The Years of the Sword* (London 1970),
    p. 279.
9   John Booth, *The Battle of Waterloo Containing a Series of Accounts, A Night Edition*
    (London 1816), p. 83.
10 Longford, p. 5.
11 Matthew Shaw, *The Duke of Wellington* (London 2005), p. 6.
12 Jane Wellesley, *Wellington: A Journey Through My Family* (London 2009),
    pp. 15–16.
13 Longford, pp. 6–7.
14 Jane Wellesley, p. 16.
15 Rory Muir, *Wellington: The Path to Victory 1769–1814* (New Haven and London
    2013), p. 6.
16 Andrew Roberts, *Napoleon and Wellington* (London 2003), p. 3.
17 Ibid, p. 7.
18 Muir, *Wellington: The Path to Victory*, p. 5.
19 Longford, p. 12.
20 Longford, p. 15.
21 George Robert Gleig, *The Life of Arthur, Duke of Wellington* (London 1871), p. 4.
22 Christopher Hibbert, *Wellington: A Personal History* (London 1997), p. 5.
23 John Timbs, *Wellingtoniana, Maxims and Characteristics of the Duke of Wellington*
    (London 1852), p. 6.
24 Longford, op. cit., p. 15.
25 Longford, op. cit., p. 16.
26 Sebastian Haffner, *Churchill* (Olomouc 1996), p. 14.
27 Longford, p. 18.
28 Jane Wellesley, op. cit., p. 31.
29 Gleig, p. 6.
30 Sir Herbert Maxwell, *The Life of Wellington and Restoration of the Martial Power of
    Great Britain, vol. I* (London 1899), p. 4.
31 Richard Holmes, *Wellington: The Iron Duke* (London 2007), pp. 19–20.
32 John Bowring, *Autobiography of Sir John Bowring* (London 1877), p. 105.
33 Roberts, p. 8.
34 Longford, p. 20.
35 Hibbert, *Wellington*, p. 7.

36   Sir Herbert Maxwell, *Life of Wellington, vol. I* (London 1899) p. 5.
37   Gleig, p. 4.
38   Longford, op. cit., p. 21.
39   Jane Wellesley, op. cit., p. 38.
40   Muir, *Wellington: The Path to Victory*, op. cit., p. 11.
41   Ibid, p. 27.
42   Muir, *Wellington: The Path to Victory*, pp. 10–11.
43   Philip Guedalla, *The Duke* (London 1997), p. 28.
44   Muir, *Wellington: The Path to Victory*, p. 21.
45   Holmes, *Wellington: The Iron Duke*, pp. 23–24.
46   W. J. Chetwode Crawley (Senior Grand Deacon), *Notes on Irish Freemansory, No. VI* (Margate 1902), p. 24. We can see in this source (p. 25.) also the image of the original manuscript of Wellington's letter to Mr. Carleton, dated London, August 13, 1836.
47   Sir Jonah Barrington, *Personal Sketches of His Own Times in Two Volumes, vol. I.* (London 1871) p. 176.
48   Longford, p. 26.
49   William Makepeace Thackeray, *The Memoirs of Barry Lyndon* (London, New York and Toronto 1847), p. 58.
50   Guedalla, p. 49.
51   Muir, *Wellington: The Path to Victory*, p. 19.
52   Gleig, p. 9.
53   Muir, *Wellington: The Path to Victory*, pp. 15–16.
54   Ibid, op. cit., p. 18.
55   Mellisa Trench, *The Remains of the late Mrs. Richard Trench* (London 1862), p. 361.
56   Gareth Glover, (ed.), *Wellington's Voice* (London 2011), p. 3.
57   Muir, *Wellington: The Path to Victory*, p. 18.
58   Longford, pp. 27–28.
59   Jane Wellesley, p. 41.
60   Muir, *Wellington: The Path to Victory*, pp. 27–28.
61   Holmes, *Wellington: The Iron Duke*, pp. 27–28.
62   Muir, *Wellington: The Path to Victory*, pp. 23–25.
63   Longford, op. cit., p. 34.
64   Holmes, *Wellington: The Iron Duke,* p. 28.
65   Joan Wilson, *A Soldier's Wife, Wellington's Marriage* (London 1987), op. cit., p. 14.   Holmes, *Wellington: The Iron Duke*, p. 28.
66   Holmes, *Wellington: The Iron Duke*, p. 12.
67   Ibid, op. cit., p. 12.
68   Niall Ferguson, *Britské impérium, cesta k modernímu světu* (Praha 2007), pp. 66–67.
69   Holmes, *Wellington: The Iron Duke*, p. 13.
70   Richard Holmes, *Redcoat: The British Solider in the Age of Horse and Musket* (London 2002), p. 138.
71   Ibid, p. 139.
72   Michael Howard (ed.), *Wellingtonian Studies* (Aldershot 1959), op. cit., p. 78.
73   Holmes, *Wellington: The Iron Duke*, p. 18.
74   Sir John Fortescue, *A History of the British Army, vol. IV– part I*, (In 13 volumes) (London 1899–1930), pp. 296–297.
75   Michael Howard (ed.), *Wellingtonian Studies*, op. cit., p. 79.

76 Robert Bruce (ed.), *Bojové techniky období Napoleonských válek* (Praha 2008), p. 7.
77 Holmes, *Redcoat*, p. 12.
78 James Lawford, *Wellington's Peninsular Army* (Oxford 2010), pp. 8–9.
79 George Hanger, *To All Sportsmen* (London 1814), p. 205.
80 Holmes, *Wellington: The Iron Duke*, p. 14.
81 Rory Muir, *Tactics and the Experience of Battle in the Age of Napoleon* (New Haven and London, 1998), pp. 68–69.
82 Lawford, pp. 6–7.
83 Ibid, p. 8.
84 Muir, *Tactics and the Experience of Battle*, pp. 105–106.
85 Ibid, p. 106.
86 Holmes, *Wellington: The Iron Duke*, pp. 15–16.
87 Ibid, p. 16.
88 Libor Jůn, *Napoleonské války* (Praha 2005), pp. 19–20.
89 Rory Muir, *Britain and the Defeat of Napoleon 1807–1815* (New Haven and London 1996), p. 1.
90 John Keegan, *Historie válečnictví* (Praha–Plzeň 2003), pp. 287–289.
91 Mark Urban, *Generálové: Deset britských velitelů, kteří ovlivnili svět* (Praha 2011), pp. 114–115.
92 Muir, *Wellington: The Path to Victory*, pp. 31–33.
93 Ibid, op. cit., p. 33.
94 William Hamilton Maxwell, *Life of Field-Marshal His Grace the Duke of Wellington, vol. I* (London 1839), pp. 17–18.
95 Guedalla, op. cit., p. 42.
96 Longford, p. 39.
97 Arthur Richard Wellesley, 2nd Duke of Wellington (ed.), *Supplementary despatches and memoranda of Field Marshal Arthur, duke of Wellington, K. G., Ed. by his son, the Duke of Wellington, vol. XIII* (15 vols. London 1858–1872), pp. 1–2.
98 Longford, op. cit., p. 37.
99 Ibid, op. cit., p. 38.
100 Philip Henry Stanhope, 5th Earl Stanhope, *Notes of Conversations with the Duke of Wellington* (New York 1888), p. 23.
101 Ibid, p. 182.
102 Holmes, *Wellington: The Iron Duke*, p. 31.
103 Gleig, p. 12.
104 Muir, *Wellington: The Path to Victory*, op. cit. p. 35.
105 Ibid, pp. 34–35.
106 Joachim Hayward Stocqueler, *The Life of Field Marshal the Duke of Wellington: In two volumes, vol. I* (London 1852), p. 5.
107 Holmes, *Wellington: The Iron Duke*, p. 32.
108 Fortescue, *A History of the British Army, vol. IV–Part I*, pp. 320–321.
109 Stanhope, 5th Earl Stanhope, *Notes of Conversations with the Duke of Wellington*, p. 182.
110 Michael Howard (ed.), *Wellingtonian Studies*, op. cit., p. 80.
111 Guedalla, pp. 49–51.
112 Muir, *Wellington: The Path to Victory*, p. 39.
113 Charles Wellesley, Wellington, 9th Duke of, *Wellington portrayed* (London 2014), op. cit., p. 25.
114 Muir, *Wellington: The Path to Victory*, op. cit., p. 39.
115 Ibid, pp. 40–41.

116 Hibbert, *Wellington*, p. 17.
117 Guedalla, pp. 54–55.
118 Roberts, p. 4.
119 George Elers, *Memoirs of George Elers* (New York 1903), p. 55.
120 Muir, *Wellington: The Path to Victory*, p. 57.
121 Holmes, *Wellington: The Iron Duke*, p. 44.
122 Muir, *Wellington: The Path to Victory*, op. cit., p. 47.
123 Ibid, op. cit., p. 47.
124 Wellington, 2nd Duke of ed., *Supp. Desp., vol. I*, pp. 19–24.
125 Muir, *Wellington: The Path to Victory*, op. cit., p. 53.
126 William Hickey, *Memoirs of William Hickey, vol. IV* (London 1925), p. 79.
127 Ibid, pp. 190–191.
128 Longford, p. 46.
129 Hickey, *Memoires, vol. IV*, for all quotes of Mr Hickey concerning the incident with Mr Blunt, pp. 171–172.
130 Muir, *Wellington: The Path to Victory*, op. cit., p. 54.
131 Holmes, *Wellington: The Iron Duke*, p. 45.
132 James Grant, *British Battles on Land and Sea, vol. II* (London 1886), p. 269.
133 Muir, *Wellington: The Path to Victory*, p. 72.
134 Grant, p. 272.
135 Holmes, W*ellington: The Iron Duke*, p. 47.
136 Grant, p. 276.
137 H. M. Vibart, *The Military History of the Madras Engineers and Pioneers, vol. I* (London 1881), p. 295.
138 Muir, *Wellington: The Path to Victory*, pp. 75–77.
139 Fortescue, *A History of the British Army, vol. IV – Part II*, p. 732.
140 Ibid, p. 735.
141 Holmes, *Wellington: The Iron Duke*, p. 54.
142 Fortescue, *A History of the British Army, vol. IV – part II*, pp. 735–736.
143 Muir, *Wellington: The Path to Victory*, p. 81.
144 Ibid, pp. 81–82.
145 S. R. Lushington, *The Life and Services of Lord General Harris* (London 1845), p. 218.
146 Fortescue, *A History of the British Army, vol. IV – part II.*, p. 736.
147 Lushington, p. 218.
148 Muir, *Wellington: The Path to Victory*, p. 83.
149 Wellington, 2nd Duke of (ed.), *Supp. Desp., vol. I*, p. 209.
150 Fortescue, *A History of the British Army, vol. IV – Part II*, pp. 739–740.
151 Grant, p. 274.
152 Holmes, *Wellington: The Iron Duke*, pp. 59–60.
153 John Wilson Croker, *The Croker Papers, vol. II* (London 1885), pp. 102–103.
154 Longford, p. 68.
155 Ibid, p. 68.
156 Muir, *Wellington: The Path to Victory*, op. cit., p. 92.
157 Wellington, 2nd Duke of (ed.), *Supp. Desp., vol. I*, pp. 245–246.
158 Gurwood, *Dispatches*, vol. I, p. 48.
159 J. Huw Davies, *Wellington's Wars: The Making of Military Genius* (New Haven and London 2015), pp. 36–37.

160 Gurwood, *Dispatches, vol. I, A New Edition* (8 vols.; vols. 9–13 are combined with the first edition, London 1837–1839), p. 200, p. 205.
161 Muir, *Wellington: The Path to Victory*, op. cit., p. 95.
162 Jack Weller, *On Wellington, The Duke and his Art of War* (London 1998), pp. 36–39.
163 Holmes, *Wellington: The Iron Duke*, p. 85.
164 Wellington, 2nd Duke of (ed.), *Supp. Desp., vol. I*, p. 247.
165 Gurwood, *Dispatches, vol. I* (London 1834), pp. 521–522.
166 Longford, p. 74.
167 Wellington, 2nd Duke of (ed.), *Supp. Desp., vol. II*, p. 356.
168 Gurwood, *Dispatches, vol. I* (London 1834), p. 82.
169 Michael Howard (ed.), *Wellingtonian Studies*, p. 21.
170 Wellington, 2nd Duke of (ed.), *Supp. Desp., vol. II*, p. 355.
171 Longford, pp. 76–77.
172 James Abercromby, Baron Dunfermline, *Lieutenant-General Sir Ralph Abercromby, K.B., 1793–1801* (Edinburgh 1861). pp, 297–298.
173 Elers, p. 124.
174 Ibid, pp. 120–121.
175 Nicholas Blake, Richard Lawrence, *The Illustrated Companion to Nelson's Navy* (London 2005), p. 104.
176 Wellington, 2nd Duke of (ed.), *Supp. Desp., vol. II*, p. 501.
177 Michael Howard (ed.), *Wellingtonian Studies*, p. 14.
178 Elers, p. 144.
179 Muir, *Wellington: The Path to Victory*, pp. 102–103.
180 Wellington, 2nd Duke of (ed.), *Supp. Desp., vol. II*, p. 443.
181 Muir, *Wellington: The Path to Victory*, p. 107.
182 Holmes, *Wellington: The Iron Duke*, p. 69–70.
183 Muir, *Wellington: The Path to Victory* op. cit., p. 121.
184 Ibid, op. cit., p. 121.
185 Ibid, pp. 135–136.
186 John Bradshaw, *Sir Thomas Munro and the British Settlement of Madras Presidency* (Oxford 1894), pp. 125–126.
187 Fortescue, *A History of the British Army*, vol. V, p. 25.
188 Croker, *The Croker Papers, vol. I* (London 1885), p. 354.
189 Fortescue, *A History of the British Army*, vol. V, pp. 27–29.
190 Muir, *Wellington: The Path to Victory*, p. 139.
191 Wellington, 2nd Duke of (ed.), *Supp. Desp., vol. IV*, pp. 186–187.
192 Simon Millar, *Assaye 1803: Wellington's First and Bloodiest Victory* (Oxford 2006), p. 72.
193 John Biddulph, *The Nineteenth and Their Times* (London 1899), p. 142.
194 Biddulph, p. 143.
195 Muir, *Wellington: The Path to Victory*, p. 140.
196 Wellington, 2nd Duke of (ed.), *Supp. Desp., vol. IV*, p. 186.
197 Sir. T. E. Colebrooke, *The Life of Honourable Sir Mountstuart Elphinstone* (London 1884), pp. 71–72.
198 Bradshaw, p. 122.
199 Millar, p. 82.
200 Gurwood, *The Dispatches, vol. II, A New Edition* (London 1837), p. 354.
201 Bradshaw, p. 127.
202 Gerald Wellesley, Wellington, 7th Duke of (ed.), *The Conversations of the First Duke of Wellington* (Cambridge 1956), p. 20.

203 Muir, *Wellington: The Path to Victory*, op. cit., p. 140.
204 Gurwood, *The Dispatches, vol. II, A New Edition* (London 1837), p. 350.
205 Ibid, p. 387.
206 Ibid, p. 436.
207 Gurwood, *The Dispatches, vol. III* (London 1835), p. 330.
208 Ibid, p. 267, p. 263.
209 Muir, *Wellington: The Path to Victory*, op. cit., p. 164.
210 Holmes, *Wellington: The Iron Duke*, pp. 82–88.
211 Longford, op. cit., p. 98.
212 Gurwood, *The Dispatches, vol. II* (London 1835), p. 345.
213 Aleš Skřivan, *Evropská politika 1648–1914* (Praha 1999), pp. 148–149.
214 Longford, p. 110.
215 Croker, *The Croker Papers, vol. II* (London 1885), p. 233.
216 Guedalla, pp. 122–123.
217 Croker, *The Croker Papers, vol. II* (London 1885), p. 234.
218 Winston Churchill, *Never Give in! The Best of Winston Churchill's Speeches* (London 2004), pp. 216–218.
219 Longford, p. 118.
220 Stanhope, 5th earl of, *The Life of Right Honourable William Pitt, vol. IV* (London 1861), p. 346.
221 Ibid, p. 375.
222 Gleig, p. 48.
223 Muir, *Wellington: The Path to Victory*, p. 169.
224 C. E. Carrington, H. J. Jackson, *A History of England* (Cambridge 1949), p. 583.
225 Wellington, 2nd Duke of (ed.), *Supp. Desp., vol. V* (London 1860), p. 69.
226 Guedalla, p. 125.
227 Wilson, op. cit., p. 45.
228 Ibid, op. cit., p. 47.
229 Ibid, p. 49.
230 Patrick Delaforce, *Wellington The Beau: The Life and Loves of the Duke of Wellington* (Barnsley 2004), op. cit., pp. 26–27.
231 Muir, *Wellington: The Path to Victory*, op. cit., pp. 163–164.
232 Gerald Wellesley, Wellington, 7th Duke of (ed.), *A Selection from the Private Correspondence of the First Duke of Wellington* (London 1952), pp. 7–8.
233 Ibid, pp. 9–10.
234 Ibid, pp. 9–10.
235 Longford, op. cit., p. 118.
236 Delaforce, pp. 23–30.
237 Muir, *Wellington: The Path to Victory*, p. 181.
238 Michael Howard (ed.), *Wellingtonian Studies*, op. cit., p. 18.
239 Delaforce, pp. 30–31.
240 Shaw, p. 38.
241 Longford, pp. 123–131.
242 Ibid, p. 129.
243 Ibid, op. cit., p. 127.
244 Wellington, 7th Duke of, *A Selection from the Private Correspondence*, p. 11.
245 Ibid, p. 13.
246 Ibid, pp. 12–13.
247 Jůn, pp. 96–110.

248 Fortescue, *A History of the British Army, vol. V*, pp. 71–72.
249 W. H. Maxwell, *Life of Field-Marshal His Grace the Duke of Wellington, vol. I*, op. cit., p. 228.
250 Muir, *Wellington: The Path to Victory*, op. cit., p. 214.
251 Ibid, op. cit., p. 215.
252 Ibid, op. cit., p. 215.
253 Wellington, 2nd Duke of (ed.), *Supp. Desp., vol. VI.*, pp. 13–14.
254 Ibid, p. 13.
255 Muir, *Wellington: The Path to Victory*, p. 219.
256 Castilia Granville (ed.), *Lord Granville Leeveson Gower Private Correspondence, vol. II* (London 1916), pp. 284–285.
257 Longford, p. 136.
258 Wellington, 2nd Duke of (ed.), *Supp. Desp., vol. V.*, p. 139.
259 Guedalla, p. 148.
260 Brás (ed.), op. cit., p. 133.
261 Antonio Ubieto Arteta, Juan Reglá Campistol, José María Jover Zamora, Carlos Seco Serrano, *Dějiny Španělska* (Praha 1995) pp. 384–388.
262 Guedalla, pp. 151–152.
263 Terry Crowdy, *The Enemy Within: A History of Spies, Spymasters and Espionage* (Oxford 2006), op. cit., p. 154.
264 Ibid, pp. 155–157.
265 Croker, *The Croker Papers, vol. I* (London 1885), p. 13.
266 Pavel Bělina, *Napoleonské války: Předěl v dějinách mezinárodních vztahů a vojenského umění*, in: *Napoleonské války a české země* (Praha 2001), p. 27.
267 Bruce, pp. 18–19.
268 Muir, *Tactics and the Experience of Battle*, p. 71.
269 Ibid, p. 72.
270 Guedalla, pp. 160–164.
271 Muir, *Wellington: The Path to Victory*, op. cit. p. 239.
272 Gurwood, *The Dispatches, vol. IV* (London 1835), p. 46.
273 Brás (ed.) op. cit., p. 136.
274 Longford, p. 146.
275 Ibid, p. 147.
276 Wellington, 2nd Duke of ed., *Supp. Desp., vol. VI*, p. 95.
277 Sir Charles Oman, *A History of the Peninsular War, vol. I* (7 vols., Oxford 1902–1930), p. 236.
278 Philip Haythornthwaite, *British Riflemen 1797–1815* (Oxford 2002), pp. 12–16.
279 Ibid, op. cit., p. 15.
280 Ibid, op. cit., p. 27.
281 Oman, *A History of the Peninsular War, vol. I*, pp. 235–237.
282 Brás (ed.), op. cit., p. 140.
283 Sir William Francis Patrick Napier, *History of the War in the Peninsula and in the South of France: from the Year 1807 to the Year 1814, vol. I* (6 vols. London 1828) p. 209. Compare to: Holmes, *Wellington The Iron Duke*, pp. 113–114.
284 Oman, *A History of the Peninsular War, vol. I*, p. 253.
285 Ibid, p. 254.
286 Haythornthwaite, *British Riflemen*, op. cit, p. 31.
287 Oman, *A History of the Peninsular War, vol. I*, pp. 254–255.
288 Christopher Hibbert (ed.), *The Recollections of Rifleman Harris* (London 2006), pp. 58–59.

289 Muir, *Wellington: The Path to Victory*, op. cit., p. 254.
290 Napier, *History of the War in the Peninsula vol. I*, pp. 215–216.
291 Ian Fletcher, *Voices from the Peninsula: Eyewitness Accounts by Soldiers of Wellington's Army 1808–1814* (London 2001), p. 24.
292 Oman, *A History of the Peninsular War, vol. I*, pp. 261–262.
293 Fortescue, *A History of the British Army, vol. VI*, p. 231.
294 Oman, *A History of the Peninsular War, vol. I*, p. 265.
295 Longford, pp. 157–158.
296 Muir, *Wellington: The Path to Victory*, op. cit., p. 268.
297 R. M. Johnston, Philip Haythornthwaite (eds.), *In the Words of Napoleon* (London 2002), p. 210.
298 Brás, (ed.), op. cit., p. 150.
299 George Gordon Byron, *Childe Harold's Pilgrimage, A Romaunt: and the Other Poems* (Whitefriars 1812), p. 21.
300 Muir, *Wellington: The Path to Victory*, op. cit., p. 260.
301 Ibid, op. cit., p. 260.
302 Gurwood, *The Dispatches, vol. IV* (London 1835), p. 193.
303 Hibbert, *Wellington*, pp. 77–81.
304 Brian L. Kieran, *Corunna 1809: Sir John Moore's Battle to Victory and Successful Evacuation* (Milton Keynes 2011), p. 51.
305 Grant, pp. 382–386.
306 Gurwood, *The Dispatches, vol. IV, A New Edition* (London 1837), pp. 261–236.
307 Longford, p. 173.
308 Julia Page (ed.), *Intelligence Officer in the Peninsula: Letters and Diaries of the Major the Hon. Edward Charles Cocks* (New York 1986), p. 24.
309 Longford, p. 179.
310 Grant, pp. 387–388.
311 Gordon Corrigan, *Wellington: A Military Life* (London and New York 2001), pp. 135–136.
312 Grant, p. 388.
313 Longford, pp. 180–181.
314 Grant, p. 388.
315 Fletcher, p. 42.
316 Guedalla, p. 248.
317 Longford, pp. 185–186.
318 Jan Klíma, *Dějiny Portugalska* (Praha 1996), pp. 99–101.
319 Brás (ed.), op. cit., pp. 123–125.
320 Ibid, p. 103.
321 Ibid, p. 105.
322 Holmes, *Wellington: The Iron Duke*, pp. 134–135.
323 Guedalla, p. 184.
324 Holmes, *Wellington: The Iron Duke*, p. 135.
325 Oman, *A History of the Peninsular War, vol. II*, pp. 508–512.
326 Holmes, *Wellington: The Iron Duke*, op. cit. p. 136.
327 Ibid, pp. 135–136.
328 Ibid, op. cit., p. 139.
329 Grant, pp. 390–396.
330 Page (ed.), p. 37.
331 Gurwood, *The Dispatches, vol. IV, A New Edition* (London 1837), p. 566.
332 Muir, *Wellington: The Path to Victory*, p. 339.

333 Ibid, p. 320.

334 Longford, pp. 198–202.

335 George Davies, *The Completeness of the Late Duke of Wellington as a National Character* (London 1854), p. 97.

336 Wellington, 2nd Duke of (ed.), *Supp. Desp., vol. VI* (London 1860), p. 431.

337 Muir, *Wellington: The Path to Victory*, op. cit., p. 343.

338 Longford, op. cit., p. 199.

339 Roberts, p. 72.

340 Longford, op. cit., p. 205.

341 Ibid p. 213.

342 Jiří Pernes (ed.), *Pod císařským praporem: Historie Habsburské armády*, pp. 216–217.

343 Croker, *The Croker Papers, vol. I* (London 1884), p. 338.

344 Erzherzog Karl, Erzherzog von Österreich-Teschen, *Strategie erläutert durch die Darstellung des Feldzugs 1796, Teil I* (Wien 1814), p. 3.

345 Pernes, op. cit, p. 235.

346 Libor Jůn, *České země a dobrovolnické sbory habsburské armády v období koaličních a napoleonských válek*, in: *Napoleonské války a české země* (Praha 2001), p. 123.

347 Muir, *Wellington: The Path to Victory*, op. cit., p. 342.

348 Ibid, op. cit., p. 319.

349 Gurwood, *The Dispatches, vol. IV, A New Edition* (London 1837), p. 377.

350 Muir, *Wellington: The Path to Victory*, pp. 348–349.

351 Richard Aldington, *Wellington* (London, Toronto 1946), p. 142.

352 Wellington, 2nd Duke of (ed.), *Supp. Desp., vol. VI*, p. 421.

353 Longford, p. 207.

354 Ibid, op. cit, p. 207.

355 Gurwood, *The Dispatches, vol. IV* (London 1835), p. 317.

356 Brás (ed.), op. cit., p. 136.

357 Gurwood, *The Dispatches, vol. IV* (London 1835), p. 317.

358 Crowdy, p. 151.

359 Charles Esdaile, *The Peninsular War: A New History* (London 2002), pp. 254–255

360 Crowdy, p. 152.

361 Ibid, pp. 153–154.

362 Gleig, p. 162.

363 Dr James McGrigor, *The Autobiography and Services of Sir James McGrigor* (London 1861), p. 283.

364 Both Wellington's quotes on Colquhoun Grant in: McGrigor, p. 289.

365 Jean Marcellin Marbot, *The Memoirs of Baron de Marbot, Late Lieutenant-General in the French Army in Two Volumes, vol. II* (London 1903), p. 445.

366 Chuck Hudson, *Spying for the Crown: Part 3 – Military Intelligence During the Peninsula Campaign*, online article in: https://historicinterpreter.wordpress.com/2015/08/11/spying-for-the-crown-part-3-military-intelligence-during-the-peninsula-campaign/#more-403

367 Page (ed.), pp. 46–47.

368 Ch. Hudson, *Spying for the Crown: Part 3 – Military Intelligence During the Peninsula Campaign*, online article in: https://historicinterpreter.wordpress.com/2015/08/11/spying-for-the-crown-part-3-military-intelligence-during-the-peninsula-campaign/#more-403

369 Mark Urban, *The Man Who Broke Napoleon's Codes, The Story of George Scovell* (London 2001) pp. 95–96. For more details about the French ciphers see: http://www.nationalarchives.gov.uk/spies/ciphers/scovell/sc1.htm

370 Ibid, p. 114.

371 Holmes, *Wellington: The Iron Duke*, p. 145.

372 Gurwood, *The Dispatches, vol. V* (London 1837), p. 163.

373 Muir, *Wellington: The Path to Victory*, pp. 355–356.

374 Edwin Sidney, *The Life of Lord Hill* (London 1845), pp. 116–118.

375 William Warre, *Letters from the Peninsula 1808–1812* (Staplehurst 1999), pp. 45–47.

376 Michael Howard (ed.), *Wellingtonian Studies*, p. 81.

377 Esdaile, *The Peninsular War*, pp. 313–315.

378 Muir, *Wellington: The Path to Victory*, op. cit., p. 357.

379 Charles Webster (ed.), *Some Letters of Duke of Wellington to his Brother William Wellesley-Pole* (London 1948), pp. 31–32.

380 Muir, *Wellington: The Path to Victory*, op. cit. p. 352.

381 Rice Jones, *An Engineer Officer under Wellington* (London 1986), pp. 45–46.

382 Mark Thompson, *Wellington's Engineers: Military Engineering in the Peninsular War 1808–1814* (Barnsley 2015), pp. 49–50.

383 Brás (ed.), pp. 42–45.

384 Ibid, pp. 94–97.

385 Longford, p. 238.

386 Whitworth Porter, *History of the Corps of Royal Engineers* (London 1889), p. 260.

387 Wellington, 2nd Duke of (ed.), *Supp. Desp., vol. VI*, p. 582.

388 Longford, pp. 217–218.

389 Gurwood, *The Dispatches, vol. VI* (London 1836), p. 21.

390 Edward Edwards, (ed.), *Some Unpublished Letters to Sir Thomas Picton, vol. XII* (Historical Society of West Wales 1927), p. 141.

391 Muir, *Wellington: The Path to Victory*, op. cit., p. 360.

392 Guedalla, p. 198.

393 Oman, *A History of the Peninsular War, vol. III*, pp. 182–187.

394 Muir, *Wellington: The Path to Victory*, p. 382.

395 Oman, *A History of the Peninsular War, vol. III*, pp. 348–349.

396 Gurwood, *The Dispatches, vol. VI* (London 1839), p. 428.

397 Oman, *A History of the Peninsular War, vol. III*, p. 353.

398 Longford, pp. 222–224.

399 Charles Esdaile, *The Peninsular War*, pp. 324–325.

400 William Grattan, *Adventures of the Connaught Rangers from 1808–1814, vol. I* (London 1847), p. 51.

401 Edward Haeys, (ed.), *The Ballads of Ireland* (London, Edinburgh and Dublin 1855), p. 271.

402 Grattan, *Adventures of the Connaught Rangers, vol I*, p. 121.

403 August Schaumann, *On the Road with Wellington* (London 1924), p. 249.

404 George Napier, *Passages in the Early Military Life* (London 1884), p. 142.

405 Augusto Borges, Luís Chaves, (eds.), *Museo do Exército em Portugal: História, Cultira e Memórias/Portuguese Army Museums: History, Culture and Memories* (Lisbon 2016), p. 68.

406 Marbot, *The Memoires, vol. II*, p. 426.

407 Muir, *Wellington: The Path to Victory*, pp. 389–390.

408 Schaumann, p. 249.

409 Ibid, p. 249.

410 Gurwood, *The Dispatches, vol. VI* (London 1836), pp. 448–449.

411 Wellington, 2nd Duke of (ed.), *Supp. Desp., vol. VI*, pp. 606–607.

412 Marbot, *The Memoirs, vol. I* (London 1903), p. 106.

413 Muir, *Wellington: The Path to Victory*, op. cit., pp. 396–397.

414 Shaw, p. 56.

415 Donald Howard, (ed.), *The French Campaign in Portugal 1810–1811: An Account by Jean Jacques Pelet* (Minneapolis 1973), pp. 232–242.

416 Gurwood, *The Dispatches, vol. VI* (London 1836), p. 456, and p. 502.

417 Michael Howard (ed.), *Wellingtonian Studies*, p. 21.

418 Esdaile, *The Peninsular War*, p. 333.

419 T. C. Hansard (ed.), *The Parliamentary Debates from the Year 1803 to Present Time* (London 1812), p. 767.

420 Thompson, p. 46.

421 Guedalla, p. 59.

422 František Stellner, *Sedmiletá válka v Evropě* (Praha 2007), p. 133.

423 Ibid, p. 206.

424 Mark Danley, Patrick Speelman (eds.), *The Seven Year's War: Global Views* (Leiden and Boston, 2012), pp. 438–439.

425 Stellner, pp. 279–280.

426 Ibid, p. 298.

427 Daniel Baugh, *The Global Seven Years War* (London and New York 2014), pp. 590–598.

428 Danley, Speelman (eds.), p. 447.

429 Wilhelm, Schaumburg–Lippe, Graf zu, *Mémoire de la Campagne de Portugal de 1762, in: Shriften und Briefe II* (Frankfurt am Main 1977), p. 47.

430 Stellner, p. 298.

431 Wilhelm Schaumburg–Lippe, Graf zu, pp. 47–48.

432 Charles Dumouriez, *An Account of Portugal, as it Appeared in 1766 to Dumouriez* (London 1797), p. 247, p. 254.

433 Stellner, p. 298.

434 Danley, Speelman (eds.), p. 457.

435 Ibid, p. 457.

436 Wellington, 2nd Duke of (ed.), *Supp. Desp., vol. XIII*, pp. 396–397.

437 Gurwood, *The Dispatches, vol. IV, A New Edition* (London 1837), p. 261.

438 Ibid, p. 262.

439 Ibid, p. 261.

440 Arthur Aspinall (ed.), *The Correspondence of George Prince of Wales, vol. VII: 1810–1811* (London 1971), p. 12.

441 Ibid, p. 16.

442 Croker, *The Croker Papers*, vol. I, p. 354.

443 Gurwood, *The Dispatches, vol. VI* (London 1836), p. 481.

444 Ibid, p. 504.

445 Ibid, pp. 504–505

446 Brás (ed.), op. cit., p. 17.

447 Oman, *A History of the Peninsular War, vol. III*, p. 421.

448 Interview (conducted by the author on the 9th May 2018.) with the curator of the Museo Diocesiano in Santarém (the museum is located in the area of the former town hall).

449 Wellington, 2nd Duke of (ed.), *Supp. Desp., vol. VII*, p. 76.

450 Muir, *Wellington: The Path to Victory*, op. cit., p. 408.

451 John Howell (ed.), *Journal of a Soldier of the 71th*, (Edinburgh 1819), pp. 122–123.
452 Schaumann, p. 288.
453 Wellington, 2nd Duke of (ed.), *Supp. Desp., vol. VII*, p. 82.
454 Gurwood, *The Dispatches, vol. VII* (London 1837), p. 442.
455 Ibid, p. 434.
456 Wellington, 2nd Duke of (ed.), *Supp. Desp., vol. VII*, p. 102.
457 Gurwood, *The Dispatches, vol. VII*, (London 1837), p. 511.
458 Muir, *Wellington: The Path to Victory*, op. cit., p. 431.
459 Corrigan, pp. 186–187.
460 Muir, *Wellington: The Path to Victory*, p. 418.
461 Oman, *A History of the Peninsular War, vol. IV*, pp. 305–314.
462 Oman, *A History of the Peninsular War, vol. III*, pp. 322–329.
463 John Kincaid, *Adventures in the Rifle Brigade, in the Peninsula, France, and the Netherlands, from 1809 to 1815* (London 1830), p. 75.
464 Sir William Napier, *History of the War in the Peninsula, vol. III*, pp. 511–517.
465 Grant, p. 404.
466 Ibid, p. 404.
467 Oman, *A History of the Peninsular War, vol. IV*, pp. 334–344.
468 George Simmons, *A British Rifleman: The Journals and Correspondence of major George Simmons, Rifle Brigade, During the Peninsular War and Campaign of Waterloo* (London 1899), p. 183.
469 Wellington, 2nd Duke of (ed.), *Supp. Desp., vol. VII*, p. 177.
470 Michael Howard (ed). *Wellingtonian Studies*, op. cit., p. 38.
471 Muir, *Wellington: The Path to Victory*, op. cit., p. 424.
472 Gurwood, *The Dispatches, vol. VII* (London 1837), pp. 544–545.
473 Wellington, 2nd Duke of (ed.), *Supp. Desp., vol. I*, p. 210.
474 Sir William Napier, *History of the War in the Peninsula, vol. III*, pp. 520–522.
475 Gurwood, *The Dispatches, vol. VII* (London 1837), pp. 552–553.
476 Muir, *Wellington: The Path to Victory*, p. 429.
477 John S. Cooper, *Rough Notes of Seven Campaigns* (London 1996), p. 63.
478 Kincaid, *Adventures in the Rifle brigade* (London 1830), p. 72.
479 Corrigan, pp. 180–181.
480 Gurwood, *The Dispatches, vol. VII* (London 1837), p. 558.
481 W. H. Maxwell, *Peninsular Sketches by Actors on the Scene, vol. II.* (London 1845) p. 331.
482 Paul Johnson, *Napoleon* (Praha 2015), p. 27.
483 Gurwood, *Dispatches, vol. II* (London 1835), p. 390.
484 Muir, *Wellington: The Path to Victory*, pp. 437–439.
485 Gurwood, *The Dispatches, vol. VII* (London 1837), p. 394.
486 Stanhope, *Notes of Conversations with the Duke of Wellington*, p. 86.
487 Michael Howard (ed.), *Wellingtonian Studies*, op. cit., p. 29.
488 Esdaile, *Peninsular war*, p. 292.
489 Ch. Hudson, *Spying for the Crown – Part 4: Civilian Spies for Wellington*, online article in: https://historicinterpreter.wordpress.com/2015/08/25/spying-for-the-crown-part-4-civilian-spies-for-wellington/
490 Sir William Napier, *History of the War in the Peninsula, vol. IV*, pp. 375–378.
491 Holmes, *Wellington: The Iron Duke*, pp. 155–156.
492 Ibid, op. cit., p. 156.
493 Ibid, pp. 156–158.
494 Edward Costello, *The Adventures of the Solider* (London 1852), pp. 108–109.

495 Oman, *A History of the Peninsular War, vol. V*, pp. 239–241.

496 Muir, *Wellington: The Path to Victory*, pp. 451–453.

497 Fletcher, (ed.), pp. 130–131.

498 Holmes, *Wellington: The Iron Duke*, p. 159.

499 Muir, *Wellington: The Path to Victory*, pp. 454–457.

500 Ibid, pp. 454–457.

501 Costello, pp. 114–117.

502 Corrigan, pp. 202–203.

503 Grattan, *Adventures of the Connaungt Rangers, vol. II*, (London 1847), pp. 7–8.

504 Gurwood, *The Dispatches, vol. VII* (London 1837), pp. 571–572.

505 Muir, *Wellington: The path to Victory*, op. cit., p. 457.

506 Michael Howard (ed.), *Wellingtonian Studies*, p. 16.

507 Longford, op. cit., p. 273.

508 Ibid, p. 274.

509 Muir, *Wellington: The Path to Victory*, pp. 458–459.

510 Longford, op. cit., p. 281

511 Esdaile, *The French Wars 1792–1815* (London 2001), pp. 61–62.

512 Johnson, pp. 130–131.

513 Gurwood, *The Dispatches, vol. IX, A New Edition* (London 1838), p. 313.

514 Esdaile, *The Spanish Army in the Peninsular War* (Manchester and New York 1988), p. 161.

515 Muir, *Wellington: The Path to Victory*, pp. 459–463.

516 Gleig, pp. 164–165. or McGrigor, pp. 284–285. For more on Grant's capture see also *The Capture of Grant*, online article in: http://www.nationalarchives.gov.uk/spies/spies/grant/gr1.htm

517 McGrigor, pp. 286–288.

518 Gleig, pp. 163–164.

519 Ibid, p. 164.

520 McGrigor, p. 291.

521 Holmes, *Wellington: The Iron Duke*, pp. 163–164.

522 Muir, *Wellington: The Path to Victory*, op. cit., p. 465.

523 Longford, op. cit., p. 328.

524 Ibid, op. cit., p. 282.

525 Muir, *Wellington: The Path to Victory*, pp. 465–466.

526 James Cooke, *A True Soldier Gentleman: The Memoirs of Lt. John Cooke 1791 – 1813* (Swanage 2000), p. 138.

527 Longford, op. cit., p. 262.

528 Oman, *A History of the Peninsular War, vol. V*, pp. 410–415.

529 Muir, *Wellington: The Path to Victory*, pp. 468–469.

530 Charles Greville, *The Greville Memoirs, vol. IV* (London, New York and Bombay 1896), p. 40.

531 Longford, op. cit., p. 285.

532 Ibid, op. cit., p. 436.

533 Francis Ellesmere, *Personal Reminiscences of the Duke of Wellington by Francis, First Earl of Ellesmere* (London 1903), p. 159.

534 Muir, *Wellington: The Path to Victory*, pp. 470–471.

535 Holmes, *Wellington: The Iron Duke*, pp. 167–168.

536 Longford, op. cit., p. 288.

537 *The United Service Journal and Naval and Military Magazine, Part I*, (Henry Colburn, London 1829), p. 294.

538 Muir, *Wellington: The Path to Victory*, op. cit., p. 473.
539 Francis Seymour Larpent, *The Private Journal of F. S. Larpent: Attached to the Head-quarters of Lord Wellington During the Peninsular War, from 1812 to its Close* (London 1854), p. 227.
540 Gurwood, *The Dispatches, vol. IX* (London 1837), p. 310.
541 Muir, *Wellington: The Path to Victory*, op. cit., p. 477.
542 Oman, *A History of the Peninsular War, vol. V*, pp. 469–471.
543 Wellington, 2nd Duke of (ed.), *Supp. Desp., vol. VII*, pp. 401–402.
544 Longford, op. cit., p. 289.
545 Marbot, *The Memoirs, vol. II*, p. 548.
546 Longford, p. 289.
547 Ibid, pp. 288–290.
548 Wellington, 2nd Duke of (ed.), *Supp. Desp., vol. VII*, p. 384.
549 Julius Bryant, *Apsley House: The Wellington Collection* (London 2014), p. 36.
550 Wellington, 2nd Duke of (ed.), *Supp. Desp., vol. VII*, p. 477.
551 Holmes, *Wellington: The Iron Duke*, pp. 170–172.
552 Wellington, 2nd Duke of (ed.), *Supp. Desp., vol. VII*, p. 478.
553 Ibid, p. 477.
554 Ibid, p. 478.
555 Holmes, *Wellington: The Iron Duke*, op. cit., p. 173.
556 Longford, pp. 297–301.
557 Holmes, *Wellington: The Iron Duke*, op. cit., p. 172.
558 Edward Foord, *Napoleon's Russian campaign of 1812* (Boston 1915), pp. 385–389.
559 Longford, p. 302.
560 Esdaile, *Peninsular War*, p. 424.
561 Longford, op. cit., p. 302.
562 Holmes, *Wellington: The Iron Duke*, op. cit., p. 180.
563 Ibid, op. cit., p. 190.
564 Longford, op. cit. p. 295.
565 McGrigor, p. 302.
566 Gleig, p. 494.
567 Michael Howard (ed.), *Wellingtonian studies*, op. cit., p. 14.
568 Gleig, pp. 161–162.
569 Michael Howard (ed.), *Wellingtonian studies*, p. 13.
570 Ibid, op. cit., p. 22.
571 Roger Buckley (ed.), *Napoleonic War Journal of Captain Thomas Henry Browne* (London 1987), p. 201.
572 Larpent, p. 296.
573 Ibid, p. 227.
574 Longford, op. cit, p. 442.
575 Michael Howard (ed.), *Wellingtonian studies*, p. 14.
576 Holmes, *Wellington: The Iron Duke*, pp. 177–178.
577 Kincaid, *Random Shots from a Rifleman* (London 1847), p. 198.
578 Kincaid, *Adventures in the Rifle Brigade*, p. 14.
579 Holmes, *Wellington: The Iron Duke*, pp. 182–183.
580 Larpent, p. 49.
581 Ibid, p. 96.
582 Ibid, p. 72.

583 Esdaile, *Peninsular War*, pp. 443–445.

584 Anthony Brett-James, *Wellington at War, 1794–1815: A Selection of His Wartime Letters* (London 1961), p. 241.

585 McGrigor, pp. 292–293.

586 Ibid, p. 293.

587 *The Great Paris Cipher*, online article in: http://www.nationalarchives.gov.uk/ spies/ciphers/scovell/sc1.htm

588 Urban, *The Man Who Broke Napoleon's Codes*, pp. 127–129.

589 Ch. Hudson, op. cit., online article in: https://historicinterpreter.wordpress. com/2015/08/11/spying-for-the-crown-part-3-military-intelligence-during-the-peninsula-campaign/

590 Urban, *The Man Who Broke Napoleon's Codes*, pp. 194–206. and pp. 241–256.

591 Holmes, *Wellington: The Iron Duke*, p. 185.

592 Ibid, op. cit., p. 186.

593 Esdaile, *Peninsular War*, pp. 445–454.

594 Gurwood, *The Dispatches, vol. X* (London 1838), pp. 495–496.

595 Stanhope, *Notes of Conversations with the duke of Wellington*, p. 18.

596 Gurwood, *The Dispatches, vol. XI* (London 1838), p. 306.

597 Michael Howard (ed.), *Wellingtonian Studies*, op. cit., p. 81.

598 Croker, *The Croker Papers, vol. I* (London 1885), p. 337.

599 Frances Bunsen, *A Memoirs of Baron Bunsen, vol. II* (London 1868), p. 74.

600 Both quotes on the meeting between Napoleon and Metternich in Dresden: Jan Kryštůfek, *Boj monarchické Evropy s revolucí francouzskou, Díl II.* (Praha 1888), p. 364.

601 R. M. Johnston, Philip Haythornthwaite (eds.), p. 270.

602 Skřivan, p. 163.

603 František Jan Vavák, *Paměti Františka Jana Vaváka, souseda a rychtáře milčického z let 1770–1816 Kniha VI–VII (1810–1816)* (Praha 2009), p. 197.

604 Longford, pp. 323–324.

605 Gurwood, *The Dispatches, vol. X* (London 1838), p. 532.

606 Aldington, pp. 187–190.

607 Longford, op. cit., p. 330.

608 F. Michael Snape, *The Royal Army Chaplains' Department, 1796–1953: Clergy Under Fire* (Woodbridge 2008), pp. 41–47.

609 Longford, pp. 330–337.

610 Holmes, *Wellington: The Iron Duke*, pp. 189–191.

611 Longford, op. cit., p. 388.

612 Skřivan, p. 163.

613 McGrigor, pp. 293–296.

614 *The Art of Deciphering*, online article in: http://www.nationalarchives.gov.uk/ spies/ciphers/scovell/sc2.htm

615 Michael Howard (ed.), *Wellingtonian Studies*, p. 17.

616 Holmes, *Wellington: The Iron Duke*, pp. 192–194.

617 John Broughton, *Recollection of a Long Life, vol. I* (London 1911), p. 190.

618 Longford, pp. 344–345.

619 Larpent, p. 487.

620 Wellington, 2nd Duke of (ed.), *Supp. Desp., vol. IX.* (London 1862), p. 100.

621 Holmes, *Wellington: The Iron Duke*, pp. 197–199.

622 Gurwood, *The Dispatches, vol. XII* (London 1838), p. 62.

623 Croker, *The Croker Papers, vol. I.*, p. 353.

624 James Mudie, *An Historical and Critical Account of a Grand Series of National Medals* (London 1820), pp 123–124. See also Thomas Smith, *Historical Recollections of Hyde Park* (London 1836), pp. 73–75.

625 Muir, *Wellington: Waterloo and the Fortunes of Peace 1814 – 1852* (New Haven and London 2015), pp. 9–11.

626 Ibid, pp. 12–14.

627 Gurwood, John, *The Dispatches, vol. XII* (London 1838), p. 114.

628 Louise-Eléonore, Comtesse De Boigne, *Memoires of Comtesse de Boigne, vol. I,* (London 1907), p. 301.

629 Holmes, *Wellington: The Iron Duke*, pp. 204–205.

630 Castilia Granville (ed.), *G. Leveson Gower, First Lord Granville, Correspondence, vol. II* (London 1916), p. 516.

631 Munro Price, *The Perilous Crown: France Between Revolutions: 1814–1848* (Basingstoke and Oxford 2010), pp. 9–10.

632 Longford, p. 378.

633 Bernard Cornwell, *Waterloo: The History of Four Days, Three Armies and Three Battles* (London 2014) p. 21.

634 Longford, pp. 374–375., p. 404.

635 Skřivan, p. 165.

636 Luboš Taraba, *Vídeňský kongres: salony, kuloáry, budoáry* (Praha 2002), pp. 214–215.

637 Gurwood, *The Dispatches, vol. XII* (London 1838), p. 95.

638 John Raymond (ed.), *The Reminiscences and Recollection of Captain Gronow* (London 1964), p. 374.

639 Taraba, pp. 216–222.

640 Muir, *Britain and the Defeat of Napoleon*, pp. 344–347.

641 Taraba, pp. 246–247.

642 Muir, *Britain and the Defeat of Napoleon*, pp. 347–349.

643 Holmes, *Wellington: The Iron Duke*, p. 208.

644 Sir William Fraser, *Words on Wellington* (London 1889), p. 40.

645 Martin Beardsley (ed.), *Waterloo Voices 1815: The Battle at First Hand* (Stroud 2015), p. 27.

646 Muir, *Britain and the Defeat of Napoleon*, pp. 353–354.

647 Holmes, *Wellington: The Iron Duke*, pp. 209–211.

648 Cornwell, *Waterloo: The History*, pp. 28–32.

649 Muir, *Britain and the Defeat of Napoleon*, pp. 356–358.

650 Cornwell, *Waterloo: The History*, p. 26.

651 Holmes, *Wellington: The Iron Duke*, pp. 222–226.

652 Cornwell, *Waterloo: The History*, pp. 41–51.

653 Crowdy, pp. 156–157.

654 Muir, Rory, *Wellington: Waterloo and the Fortunes of Peace*, pp. 40–41.

655 Wellington, 2nd Duke of (ed.), *Supp. Desp., vol. X.*, p. 509.

656 Crowdy, p. 157.

657 Muir, Wellington: *Waterloo and the Fortunes of Peace*, pp. 40–43.

658 James Malmesbury, *Letters of First Earl of Malmesbury: 1745–1820, vol. II* (London 1870), pp. 445–446.

659 Holmes, *Wellington: The Iron Duke*, p. 228.

660 Muir *Wellington: Waterloo and the Fortunes of Peace*, op. cit., pp. 41–42.

661 Holmes, *Wellington: The Iron Duke*, op. cit., p. 227.
662 Cornwell, *Waterloo: The History*, p. 81., Compare to: Muir, *Wellington: Waterloo and the Fortunes of Peace*, pp. 50–52.
663 Stanhope, *Notes of Conversations with the Duke of Wellington*, p. 109.
664 Ibid, p. 109.
665 Muir, *Wellington: Waterloo and the Fortunes of Peace*, p. 53.
666 Cornwell, *Waterloo: The History*, op. cit., p. 91.
667 Holmes, *Wellington: The Iron Duke*, p. 231.
668 Muir, W*ellington: Waterloo and the Fortunes of Peace*, op. cit., p. 49.
669 Holmes, *Wellington: The Iron Duke*, p. 232.
670 Beardsley (ed.), pp. 45–46.
671 Holmes, *Wellington: The Iron Duke*, p. 233.
672 Muir, *Wellington: Waterloo and the Fortunes of Peace*, pp. 53–54.
673 Holmes, *Wellington: The Iron Duke*, op. cit., p. 233.
674 Ibid, p. 234.
675 Muir, *Wellington: Waterloo and the Fortunes of Peace*, p. 57.
676 Roberts, p. 16.
677 Henry Houssaye, *1815: Waterloo* (London 1900), p. 178.
678 Charles Farlane, *The Great Battles of the British Army* (London 1853), p. 412.
679 Houssaye, p. 178.
680 Wellington, 2nd Duke of (ed.), *Supp. Desp., vol. VII.*, p. 94.
681 Muir, *Wellington: The Path to Victory*, op. cit., p. 431.
682 Cornwell, *Waterloo: The History*, p. 10.
683 Mary Berry, *Extracts from the Journals and Correspondence of Miss Berry, vol. III* (London 1886), p. 16.
684 Edward Low (ed.), *With Napoleon at Waterloo and Other Unpublished Documents of the Waterloo and Peninsular Campaigns* (London 1911), p. 125.
685 Fraser, p. 3.
686 Longford, pp. 172–137, p. 235.
687 Holmes, *Wellington: The Iron Duke*, pp. 234–236.
688 Howell (ed.), pp. 216–217.
689 Holmes, *Wellington: The Iron Duke*, op. cit., p. 238.
690 Ibid, p. 240.
691 Howell (ed.), pp. 218–219.
692 Ibid, p. 219.
693 J. Huw, Davies, p. 237.
694 Ibid, pp. 237–238.
695 Beardsley (ed.), p. 124.
696 J. Huw Davies, pp. 238–239.
697 Beardsley (ed.), p. 120.
698 Robert Chambers, William Chambers (eds.), *Chamber's Journal, vol. XXXVIII* (London 1863), p. 185.
699 Jean Marcellin Marbot, *Berezina, Lipsko, Waterloo: Paměti* (Praha 1909), pp. 409–410.
700 Holmes, *Wellington: The Iron Duke*, op. cit., p. 247.
701 Ibid, pp. 244–245.
702 Ibid, op. cit. p. 246.
703 Beardsley (ed.), p. 152.
704 Longford, op. cit., p. 472.
705 Cornwell, *Waterloo: The History*, op. cit. p. 53.

706 Edward Cotton, Sergeant-Major, *A Voice from Waterloo* (London 1849), p. 113.
707 Beardsley, (ed.), p. 159.
708 Louis Antoine Fauvelet de Bourrienne, *Memoirs of Napoleon Bonaparte, vol. IV* (London 1836), p. 166.
709 Holmes, *Wellington: The Iron Duke*, op. cit., p. 249.
710 Kincaid, *Adventures in the Rifle Brigade*, p. 46.
711 Holmes, *Wellington: The Iron Duke*, op. cit., p. 249.
712 J. Huw Davies, pp. 239–245.
713 Holmes, *Wellington: The Iron Duke*, op. cit., p. 250.
714 Ibid, pp. 249–250.
715 Muir, *Wellington: Waterloo and the Fortunes of Peace*, op. cit., p. 80.
716 Ibid, op. cit., p. 81.
717 Ibid, op. cit., p. 81.
718 Ibid, op. cit., p. 81.
719 Claude Vivian (ed.), *Richard Hussey Vivian, A Memoir* (London 1897), p. 327.
720 Michael Howard (ed.), *Wellingtonian Studies*, op. cit., p. 16.
721 Shelley, p. 102.
722 Cornwell, *Waterloo: The History*, p. 10.
723 William Warden, *Letters Written on Board of HMS Northumberland and at Saint Helena* (London 1816), pp. 196–197.
724 De Bourrienne, *Memoirs, vol. IV*, p. 373.
725 Henry Meynell, *Conversation with Napoleon at St. Helena* (London 1911), p. 45.
726 R. M. Johnston, Philip Haythornthwaite (eds.), p. 334.
727 Glower, pp. 300–301.
728 Victor Hugo, *Les Misérables, vol. I* (London, Edinburgh, Paris, Melbourne and New York 1874), p. 320.
729 David Buttery, *Waterloo Battlefield Guide*, Kellington 2018, pp. 63–64.
730 Croker, *The Croker Papers, vol. III* (London 1885), pp. 276–277.
731 For the collection at Kynžvart Chateau see: https://www.zamek-kynzvart.eu/en
732 Skřivan, pp. 133–135.
733 Jůn, pp. 19–25.
734 Petr Havel, Andrej Romaňák, *Maršál Radecký* (Praha-Litomyšl 2000), pp. 43–46.
735 Esdaile, *The French Wars 1792–1815*, pp. 12–13.
736 Jůn, p. 56.
737 Havel, Romaňák, p. 50.
738 Esdaile, *The French Wars 1792–1815*, pp. 21–23.
739 Jiří Pernes (ed.), *Pod císařským praporem, historie habsburské armády* (Praha 2003), p. 211.
740 Muir, *Britain and the Defeat of Napoleon*, p. 5.
741 Ivan Šedivý (ed.), *Napoleonské války a české země* (Praha 2001), pp. 45–51.
742 Ibid, op. cit., p. 56.
743 Ibid., op. cit., p. 50.
744 Ibid, p. 50.
745 Jůn, p. 34.
746 Šedivý, op. cit., p. 52.
747 Pavel Bělina, Milan Hlavačka, Daniela Tinková, *Velké Dějiny zemí Koruny české, XI. a* (Praha-Litomyšl 2013), op. cit., p. 103.
748 Ibid, p. 102.
749 Šedivý (ed.). op. cit., p. 47.

750 Bělina, Hlavačka, Tinková, p. 112.
751 Anton Ernstberger, *Böhmens Freiwilliger Kriegseinsatz gegen Napoleon 1809* (München 1936), pp. 65–68.
752 Šedivý (ed.), pp. 57–61.
753 Ibid, p. 57.
754 Ibid, p. 58.
755 Jiří Kacetl, *Znaim/Znojmo 1809* (Znojmo 2019), pp.1–24.
756 Ibid, op. cit., p. 1.
757 Ibid, pp. 24–25.
758 Franz Herre, *Metternich* (Praha 1996), p. 89.
759 Luis Spehr, *Friedrich Wilhelm, Herzog von Braunschweig-Lüneburg-Oels* (Braunschweig 1848), p. 78.
760 Robert Multhoff (ed.), *Friedrich Wilhelm, Herzog von Braunschweig-Lüneburg-Oels.*, in: *Neue Deutsche Biographie (NDB). Band V* (Berlin 1961), p. 502.
761 Šedivý (ed.), p. 131.
762 Pivka, pp. 8–13.
763 Ibid, pp. 12–14.
764 Ibid, pp. 14–24.
765 Tomáš Dostál, *Rakousko-francouzská válka 1809*, Historický obzor, č .16/2005, op. cit. p. 232.
766 Caroline Bland, Waltraud Maierhoffer, Gertrude Rosch (eds.), *Women Against Napoleon* (Frankfurt, New York 2007), p. 58
767 Bělina, Hlavačka, Tinková, op. cit., p. 119.
768 Jan Máchal (ed.), *Hankovy písně a prostonárodní srbská múza do Čech převedená* (Praha 1918), p. 27.
769 Herre, *Metternich*, p. 97.
770 Bělina, Hlavačka, Tinková, pp. 118–127.
771 Jan Bedřich Novák (ed.), *Polní maršál Karel, kníže ze Schwarzenberka, historický portrét podle rodinné korespondence* (Praha 1913), pp. 13–14.
772 Josef Hanesch, *Karel I. Filip, kníže Schwarzenberg: polní maršál* (České Budějovice 2003), op. cit., p. 24.
773 Pernes (ed.), p. 236.
774 Fortescue, *A History of the British Army, vol. IV*, pp. 240–243.
775 Novák (ed.), p. 12.
776 Hanesch, *Karel I. Filip, kníže Schwarzenberg*, pp. 29–30.
777 Novák (ed.), p. 13.
778 Hanesch, *Karel I. Filip, kníže Schwarzenberg*, pp. 41–51.
779 Novák (ed.), p. 14.
780 Bedřich is Czech for Frederick.
781 Hanesch, *Karel I. Filip, kníže Schwarzenberg*, op. cit., p. 54.
782 Jůn, pp. 147–150.
783 Hanesch (ed.), *Osvobozenecká válka 1813–1815 v dokumentech rodinného archivu schwarzenberské sekundogenitury* (Regional State Archives in Třeboň 1986), p. 42.
784 Michael Leggiere, *The Fall of Napoleon: vol. I, The Allied Invasion of France, 1813–1814* (Cambridge, New York 2007), p. 128.
785 Havel, Romaňák, pp. 66–67.
786 Jiří Pernes, pp. 260–261.
787 Franz Herre, *Radecký: Nejoblíbenější polní maršálek rakouské armády a jeho pohnutá doba* (Praha 1997) op. cit., p. 74.
788 Esdaile, *The French Wars 1792–1815*, pp. 69–71.

789 Franz Herre, *Radecký: Nejoblíbenější polní maršálek rakouské armády*, op. cit., p. 82.

790 Šedivý, (ed.), p. 149.

791 Pernes (ed.), pp. 231–232.

792 Esdaile, *The French Wars 1792–1815*, pp. 70–72.

793 Hanesch, (ed.), *Osvobozenecká válka 1813–1815*, p. 59.

794 Vavák, p. 260.

795 Ibid, p. 239.

796 Bělina, Hlavačka, Tinková, pp. 146–151.

797 Hanesch, (ed.), *Osvobozenecká válka 1813–1815*, p. 76.

798 Hanesch, *Karel I. Filip, kníže Schwarzenberg*, p. 72.

799 Novák, (ed.), p. 56.

800 Muir, *Wellington: The Path to Victory*, op. cit., p. 569.

801 Jůn, pp. 152–158.

802 Vavák, p. 293.

803 Ibid, p. 315.

804 Hanesch (ed.), *Osvobozenecká válka 1813–1815*, p. 23.

805 Gurwood, *The Dispatches, vol. XII* (London 1838), p. 414. The original is archived in the Regional State Archives Třeboň: 1. arch., kvart. Sign–II7–2–3.

806 Wellington, 2nd Duke of (ed.), *Supp. Desp., vol. X.*, p. 552.

807 Gurwood, *The Dispatches, vol. XII* (London 1838), p. 510. The original is archived in the Regional State Archives Třeboň: 1. arch, oktáv., Sing–II–72–6.

808 Novák (ed.), p. 80.

INDEX

XVIII JUNI MDCCCXV

Wellington

The Road
to the Lion's Mound
1769–1815

—•◦◦◯◦◦•—

DANIEL RES

TRANSLATED BY SKYLAND VACLAV KOBYLAK

Front jacket | The Duke of Wellington by Thomas Lawrence,
© Mark Fiennes Archive | Bridgeman Images
Typographic design | Marek Jodas
Maps© John Armytage (John Fawkes), Marek Jodas, Marketa Jodasova
First published in the Czech language in 2018
This fully revised and updated edition in English
was published 24th May 2020
By Amerigo, s.r.o. – Citadelle
Podebradska 56, 19800, Praha 9, Czech Republic
Printed by Typos, tiskarske zavody, s.r.o.

ISBN 978-80-907311-2-7